OUR COMMON GROUND

JOHN D. LESHY

Our
Common
Ground

A HISTORY OF AMERICA'S PUBLIC LANDS

Yale UNIVERSITY PRESS   NEW HAVEN AND LONDON

Published with assistance from the foundation established in memory of Calvin Chapin of the Class of 1788, Yale College.

Yale University Press books may be purchased in quantity for educational, business, or promotional use. For information, please e-mail sales.press@yale.edu (U.S. office) or sales@yaleup.co.uk (U.K. office).

Set in Scala type by IDS Infotech Ltd., Chandigarh, India.
Printed in the United States of America.

ISBN 978-0-300-23578-4 (hardcover : alk. paper)
Library of Congress Control Number: 2021932803

A catalogue record for this book is available from the British Library.

This paper meets the requirements of ANSI/NISO Z39.48-1992 (Permanence of Paper).

10 9 8 7 6 5 4 3 2 1

To Peggy Karp and Alec Leshy

CONTENTS

PREFACE

This is a political history of the more than 600 million acres of land that the American people now collectively own and manage through their national government. Nearly all of it is administered by four agencies. The least known of these, the Bureau of Land Management, looks after the most, about 256 million acres. The other three are the U.S. Forest Service (193 million acres), the U.S. Fish & Wildlife Service (91 million), and the best known, the National Park Service (78 million). This book does not deal with the much smaller amounts of land managed by the military or by niche agencies like the Bureau of Reclamation and the Tennessee Valley Authority.

Two things about these lands stand out. One is simply how extensive they are, covering about 30 percent of the nation's land surface. This is especially noteworthy considering that American culture has long extolled private property and regarded government—particularly the national government—with considerable wariness. The second is that even though some of these lands have been subject to mining, logging, and other industrial activities, and a significant portion are grazed by domesticated livestock, today most primarily serve values of recreation, inspiration, environmental conservation, science, and the preservation of cultural heritage.

This book aims to explain how this came about. All of the public lands share a political history, one that is deeply rooted in the history of the nation and the events that have shaped our culture and the structure and operation of our government. There is a huge literature on the public lands, but nearly all of it tends to focus on particular categories, such as national parks or national forests, or on particular historical episodes or eras, or on particular activities, such as logging or mining. This volume, by contrast, considers the entire history of these lands as a single American institution.

I have had the great fortune to spend much of my professional career on matters involving public lands. For a dozen years I served in the U.S. Department of the Interior (in two different administrations) and on the staff of the Natural Resources Committee in the U.S. House of Representatives. I have taught and written on public land issues for decades in legal academia. I have litigated and advocated on public land questions for nonprofit groups. All of these experiences have deeply informed my approach here.

The narrative proceeds chronologically in eight parts, from the American Revolution down to the modern era. Within those parts, chapters are divided by subject matter. Although every tract of public land has a political story behind it, the focus here is on the more important decisions, mostly made by Congress and officials in the executive branch, plus some from the courts, that have produced today's public lands.

This book does not give much attention to the actions and decisions by which the U.S. government first acquired these and other lands from foreign governments and from Native Americans. Nor does it deal in detail with Congress's decisions to transfer ownership of many lands to states and private interests.

After the nation secured its independence from Great Britain, an often repeated sequence of events led to Native Americans losing title to nearly all of their lands. It usually began when indigenous peoples were dispossessed through chicanery, duress, and sometimes violence by an evolving cast of characters—speculators, squatters, miners, and other developers—often backed by the U.S. military. The government then acquired formal title to the lands from Native nations through arrangements that, while providing Natives some compensation, would never make up for the injustices that were perpetrated or the enormity of their losses.

Almost without exception, it was not until years—often, many years—after this conquest, dispossession, and title acquisition that a powerful political movement emerged that led the United States to retain title to significant amounts of public lands, and eventually to manage them for broad protective purposes. This is not to deny, of course, that key participants in these political decisions, like most people of the time, held racist beliefs. It also does not excuse the fact that federal agencies Congress vested with responsibility to manage these lands sometimes did not act with honor in dealing with Indians who sought to use them for traditional spiritual and other purposes. A growing literature addresses these events and injustices in considerable detail.

Many of the pivotal events addressed in this book took place between 1890 and World War II. Indeed, except for the special case of Alaska, the overall amount and location of the public lands, and the government agencies charged with managing them, have not fundamentally changed since 1945. Native Americans, women, and persons of color did not play prominent roles in the decisions the United States made in this era because they were largely excluded from the political system at the relevant times. Besides racial restrictions on voting that persisted through the first two-thirds of the twentieth century, the Nineteenth Amendment giving women the right to vote was not ratified until 1920, and Congress did not give Native Americans citizenship and the right to vote until 1924.

Although Native Americans, women, and people of color were largely excluded from participating in many of the key decisions that produced America's heritage of public lands, the future promises to be much different. This is part of the beauty of this national institution. Because these lands are in public hands, they remain subject to the will of the people—as defined more broadly today than ever before—which means they can play a part in redressing some of the injustices of the past.

Because of this, making the public lands story accessible in a single volume has never been more important. As discussed in the last part of the book, public land policy remains a subject of lively debate. Political rhetoric has taken on a more partisan cast than at any time since the Civil War. Recent Republican Party platforms have contained a plank advocating that the United States relinquish ownership of significant amounts of public land, and the Trump administration moved to transfer as much control of public lands as possible to fossil fuel and other development interests. The polarization has spawned exaggerated or misleading claims about the history of the public lands. Some who advocate stripping the United States of control of significant amounts of public land offer narratives about how "elites" in the national government control the public lands and have put a "stranglehold" on local communities, and how an "angry West," in a "sagebrush rebellion," aims to "get our lands back."

The truth is quite different. As shown in the following chapters, the national government has rarely made decisions regarding public lands without carefully considering local sentiment. The movement that developed after the Civil War to hold large tracts of land in national ownership had significant grassroots support. Public land policy debates almost never broke neatly along regional lines. Although the public lands are still somewhat concentrated in the West and Alaska, significant tracts of public land are found throughout the nation, making this a national story, not a regional one. Indeed, in the twentieth century, state governments outside the West acquired significant tracts from private owners and donated them to the national government so that they could be conserved. The United States also acquired a considerable amount of the public lands from private owners in consensual transactions.

The nation has never adopted a grand design for its public lands. Instead, decisions have been made incrementally and for reasons that evolved over time. Since the Civil War, the more notable reasons to hold lands in national ownership have included safeguarding resources such as scenery and wildlife for inspiration and recreation, preserving cultural and ecological resources for scientific study, stimulating tourism-related economic activity, protecting watersheds and water supplies for users downstream, restoring and holding timber supplies for future use, and strengthening government control over the private exploitation of natural resources. Increasingly, public lands have come to be regarded as an effective way to protect ecosystems, following principles developed through the emerging science of conservation biology.

For more than a century, the arc of public land history has bent decisively toward the national government conserving more and more lands for conservation, public education, and inspiration. The Trump administration made efforts to alter that trajectory by reducing protections for and encouraging industrial activity on many millions of acres of public land, but the Biden administration has started out doing the opposite. Some of the dozens of executive orders President Biden issued on his first days in office were aimed at public lands. The most notable revisited his predecessor's drastic downsizing of two large national monuments in Utah and called for a comprehensive review of fossil fuel leasing policy on public land. He also named Deb Haaland, a member of Congress from New Mexico, to be Interior secretary—the first Native American to hold a cabinet post in U.S. history.

Haaland's appointment is a signal event in the evolving relationship between Native Americans and public lands. This book explores in some detail how, beginning in the 1960s with the flowering of the modern Indian sovereignty movement, Indian nations began demanding, and winning, greater consideration of their values, interests, and traditions in how public lands are managed. In some places they have been given a formal role in management and in some places recovered title to ancestral lands. Using public lands to help redress some past injustices would have been much more difficult to realize had they been transferred out of national ownership, and they will likely provide other opportunities for healing societal wounds in the years ahead.

The Biden administration has also taken many steps to make climate change and biodiversity loss a central focus of national policy, which the book's final chapter describes as primary challenges facing America's public lands. While the president has considerable power to take action, it is Congress that holds ultimate authority over U.S. policy on such matters. The history of public lands can help inform how actors in our political system will grapple with these issues.

These same challenges face the world's community of nations. Here too the history of public lands can be relevant. The United States has been a leader in protecting large landscapes and biodiversity, establishing the world's first national park, pioneering efforts to protect wildlife habitat and natural values through designations such as "wilderness," and protecting cultural and spiritual qualities especially valued by indigenous populations. Bringing more attention to how its public land policy has evolved to put such protections in place may provide useful lessons for other nations.

Over many changes in administrations, public lands have played a consensus-building, unifying role in American life. Indeed, political decisions about public lands offer some of the best examples of long-term thinking the American political system has ever produced. Public land grants early on helped establish a tradition of public education and build an infrastructure that knit the nation together. The U.S. Forest Service and the National Park Service helped pioneer models of effective government. With recreational visits skyrocketing in recent decades, the public lands have offered millions of people life-changing encounters with nature, and public-lands-related tourism has become the economic anchor of many communities. Public land policy has also begun, admittedly tardily, to better reflect the diversity of our society and to acknowledge past injustices. In an age of skepticism about our political process, decision making about public lands demonstrates our ability as a people to work together and find genuine common ground.

I have many to thank for helping me bring this project to completion. I am especially indebted to Bruce Babbitt, the late Cecil Andrus, and George Miller for giving me splendid opportunities to work on these issues in the federal service, and to Hansjörg Wyss and Molly McUsic and the staff of the Wyss Foundation, who have likewise allowed me to engage in many of these issues at the ground level. I have learned much from many colleagues in the academy and co-workers at the public-lands-related posts I have been fortunate enough to hold over the years.

Several people read parts or drafts of the manuscript and provided helpful suggestions, beginning with my partner, Peggy Karp, and including Bill deBuys, Charles Wilkinson, Lori Potter, Don Barry, Rob Fischman, Kip Keller, and anonymous reviewers. Donald Lamm nurtured this project in many ways, including reviewing drafts.

The Hastings College of the Law at the University of California has been a most accommodating venue for this project, thanks to its leadership and support staff, in particular Hilary Hardcastle and other staff members in its law library. I have benefited from able work by many student research assistants over the years at Hastings and during my visiting-professor stints at Harvard Law School, including Peter Harman, Rebecca Kim, Ethan Pawson, Jency Butler, Ellis Raskin, Darcy Vaughan, Caitlin Coleman, Leo Delgado, Jemel Amin Derbali, and Shahiedah Shabazz.

Finally, no work on public lands should fail to acknowledge the contributions of all those in and out of government who help safeguard America's public lands for future generations, especially the thousands of unsung civil servants who have made it possible for millions of people every year to have meaningful encounters with public lands.

OUR COMMON GROUND

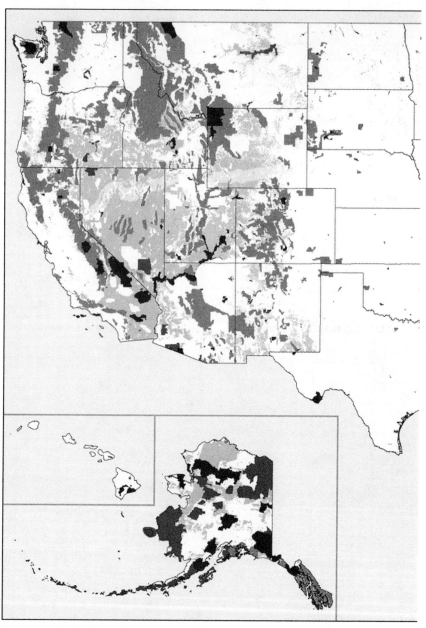

America's public lands as of 2020, by managing agency (Map by Kara Clauser, Center for Biological Diversity, and Bill Nelson)

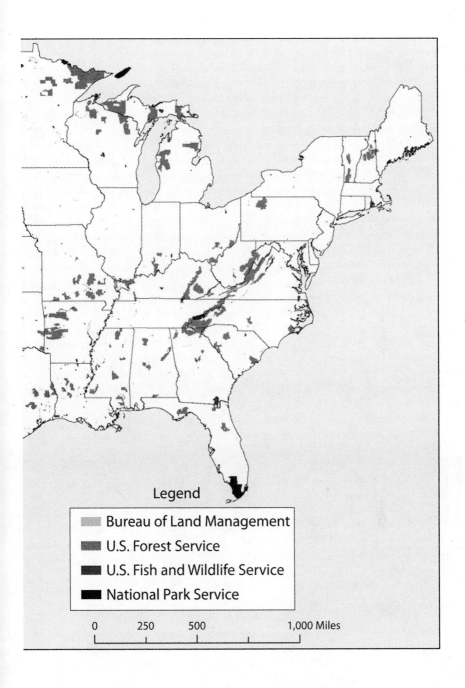

Legend

Bureau of Land Management

U.S. Forest Service

U.S. Fish and Wildlife Service

National Park Service

0   250   500   1,000 Miles

PART ONE PUBLIC LANDS IN THE FORMATIVE ERA, 1776–1789

CHAPTER ONE

The Nation's Founding and the Public Lands

IT WOULD BE AN EXAGGERATION TO CALL Philip Schuyler, a wealthy third-generation Dutch American, the political father of the nation's public lands, but he is as good a candidate as may be found. A general in the Continental Army early in the Revolutionary War, Schuyler was representing New York in the Continental Congress in the fall of 1779 when he became involved in discussions about how vigorously New York and some other former colonies should defend their claims to the so-called western lands across the Appalachian Mountains.

The origin of these claims takes a little explaining. Before the Revolutionary War, the territorial reach of each of the American colonies was determined by the arrangements they had made with the English Crown. Unfortunately, sometimes the Crown's representatives approached the delineation of the colonies' boundaries with a mixture of ignorance, indifference, and carelessness. Virginia's charter from 1609, for example, characterized the colony as extending "from the seacoast up into the land from sea to sea, west and northwest." Charters issued to other colonies likewise had vague and sometimes overlapping boundaries.[1]

All told, seven of the thirteen former colonies—Massachusetts, Connecticut, New York, Virginia, North Carolina, South Carolina, and Georgia—had some basis for claiming western lands. The western boundaries of

Philip Schuyler, 1733–1804 (Courtesy of
the Library of Congress, LC-USZ62-45170)

the other six—New Hampshire, Rhode Island, Pennsylvania, New Jersey,
Maryland, and Delaware—were fixed in their colonial charters.

For a long time, the matter was of little consequence. The British established limits on the American colonies' western claims in 1763 by recognizing
Spanish claims to land across the Mississippi River, and again in 1764 by giving
the territory north of the Great Lakes to the Quebec colony. Moreover, looking
to reduce conflicts with Native Americans, a royal proclamation issued in
October 1763 prohibited settlers from the American colonies from crossing the
Appalachian crest.

These limits on the American colonists' ambitions to claim and settle the
western lands became a significant source of conflict between Britain and the
colonies. Land was, after all, then a primary source of wealth. Some leading
citizens in the colonies were deeply engaged in land speculation. Claims to
western lands were a potential source of economic and political power for those
colonial governments possessing them.

In 1774 the colonies formed the Continental Congress, which sought
to assert the rights of colonists against the British government. Tensions
continued to mount, and clashes at Concord and Lexington, Massachusetts,
in 1775 led the Second Continental Congress to approve the Declaration
of Independence in early July 1776. The Declaration's litany of complaints

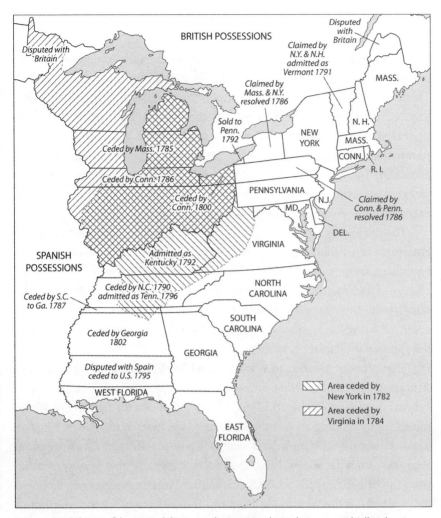

Western land claims of the original thirteen colonies (Map by Karl Musser and Bill Nelson)

included Crown policies that sought to rein in colonial aspirations regarding the western lands.[2]

Although the Declaration gave the former colonies common cause in resisting what they saw as British infringements, their unity was fragile. Claims to western lands by the seven former colonies that had them—most of which were already larger in area and population than the other six—became a prominent source of tension. Led by Maryland, the disadvantaged six feared, reasonably enough, that the others would use the western lands to become even richer and more dominant. Private speculators in the western lands who were influential citizens of states like Maryland, concerned about being shut out of the West, stoked the conflict.

All of this greatly complicated the task of the new Americans as they worked to establish a governing structure for their coalition of former colonies. The Second Continental Congress formed a committee to prepare the charter that became known as the Articles of Confederation. The committee's draft, presented eight days after independence was declared, would have vested the new national Congress of the Confederation with authority to settle questions about the boundaries of former colonies and the control of western lands. That proposal met with considerable resistance from Virginia and others unwilling to cede this responsibility to the national government.

The dispute escalated into a fractious struggle that threatened the entire enterprise of establishing the new nation. After much discussion, but little forward progress, the Continental Congress in November 1777 sent the former colonies a revised draft of the Articles that papered over the dispute with ambiguity about how the western land claims would be resolved. The Congress asked for this revised draft to be ratified by the following spring, and it required the approval of all thirteen former colonies.

That strategy seemed to work for a while. Virginia approved the draft Articles in December. Nine other former colonies followed suit between February and early April 1778. Then Virginia's governor, Patrick Henry, stirred things up by sending an expeditionary force westward under George Rogers Clark to secure Virginia's land claims from the British. Clark captured Kaskaskia (in what is now Illinois) and Vincennes (in what is now Indiana) from the British in 1778–79. After this military success, Virginia underscored its ambitions in the West by establishing "Illinois County" as part of Virginia, declaring void the claims of non-Virginia land companies and authorizing the opening of an office to beginning selling land in the region.

THE WESTERN LANDS AS "COMMON PROPERTY" WON WITH THE "BLOOD AND TREASURE" OF ALL THE FORMER COLONIES

Each of the four former colonies that had not yet voted to ratify the Articles had fixed western boundaries, and they balked because, as the Frenchman Alexis de Tocqueville observed in his classic *Democracy in America* some decades later, they "saw with a jealous eye the immense future open to their neighbors."[3] New Jersey and Delaware eventually voted to ratify the Articles in November 1778 and February 1779, respectively, but qualified their approval by demanding that the dispute over the western lands be resolved. Maryland refused to go that far. In December 1778 it announced it would not ratify the Articles. Insisting that the western lands were being "wrested from the common enemy by blood and treasure of" every single former colony, it called on the Continental Congress to take control of that "common property."[4]

Maryland's holdout meant that the new United States operated without a formal legal charter for two more years. While the unratified Articles served as the de facto governing structure, disagreement continued to fester, and the future of the new nation hung in the balance.

In the early part of the Revolutionary War, while the nascent nation was in a desperate struggle simply to survive, the dispute could be put to one side. But as prospects for military victory brightened, making the Americans' ambition to join the world's community of nations more realistic, the disagreement could no longer be ignored. For one thing, the fledgling national government had been busily giving away land it did not own. Not long after declaring independence, the Second Continental Congress agreed to provide grants of land to members of the Continental Army who served throughout the war, and also offered fifty acres of land to every soldier who deserted from the enemy. There was also growing concern about how to pay other large debts the former colonies were accumulating to prosecute the war. The most obvious available asset was land. Former colonies without western land claims, like New Jersey, feared they would be left, as its legislature put it, to "sink under an enormous debt."[5]

As the dispute dragged on, some supporters of Maryland's position sought to raise the stakes. They argued that once the Revolutionary War was won, the new national government should take title to all nonprivatized land anywhere within the boundaries of any of the former colonies. This potential land grab was a much bigger threat to those with western land claims than to the smaller former colonies that lacked them.

The stalemate threatened to unwind the coalition just as it was prosecuting the war toward a successful conclusion. Looking back some years later, James Madison observed that the dispute over western-land claims caused "much discussion and heart-burning and proved the most obstinate of the impediments" to ratifying the Articles, and Chief Justice John Marshall of the U.S. Supreme Court wrote that the western-land question had been so "momentous" that it "threatened to shake the American confederacy to its foundation."[6] Its resolution was a pivotal episode in establishing the first government of the United States.

SCHUYLER'S COMPROMISE

As the 1770s drew to a close, it became clear that the western lands were likely to be settled by colonists and others of European extraction, with or without government sanction. Some in the former colonies with claims to western lands began to think it was, in fact, better to have the national government control the settlement process than to continue the stalemate. Thomas Jefferson of Virginia and John Jay of New York, among others, began to speak openly of possibly giving up at least some of their states' claims to western lands. But there was also strong opposition to the national government unilaterally fixing western boundaries and setting the terms by which states would cede their claims to land west of those boundaries.

At this point, Philip Schuyler gambled that the struggle for independence had strengthened the quarrelsome former colonies' commitment to a common enterprise sufficiently to open the way to a fair compromise. He and his New York colleague Robert Livingston proposed to give the former colonies with unsettled western boundaries the option of fixing those boundaries and retaining control over unsettled land within their borders once they were set, if they agreed to cede lands west of those boundaries to the United States. In late January 1780, Schuyler recommended this solution to the New York Assembly and proposed as part of it that New York fix its western boundary at a line extending from Pennsylvania's northwest corner north to Lake Ontario. The State Assembly agreed and quickly approved legislation to carry it out, which it called "an act to facilitate the confederation and perpetual union among the United States of America."[7]

Schuyler's gamble worked. The stalemate began to give way. In September 1780, the Second Continental Congress endorsed a committee report recommending that the landed states make "a liberal surrender of a portion of their territorial claims" to foster "confidence" in the national government and help support the military and the nation's "reputation abroad." Otherwise, the report warned, the "stability of the general confederacy" would be threatened.[8] A few weeks later, Connecticut followed New York by agreeing to cede most of its western-land claims to the national government.

THE WESTERN LANDS TO BE "DISPOSED OF FOR THE COMMON BENEFIT OF ALL THE UNITED STATES"

On October 10, 1780, the same day that Connecticut acted, the Continental Congress adopted another resolution calling on all states with western-land claims to follow New York's lead. To allay concerns that the national government might perpetually maintain colonies under federal control on the ceded lands, the resolution provided that the lands would be "disposed of for the common benefit of all the United States" and be "settled and formed into" new states, with the "same rights of sovereignty, freedom and independence, as the other states." This process would, the resolution provided, go forward "at such times and under such regulations as shall hereafter be agreed on by the United States in Congress assembled."9

This was a sensible, politically adroit solution. The national government would take title to the ceded western lands, and its Congress would decide how to use them as an instrument of national policy to secure and develop the nation, with the specific objective of encouraging their settlement by people loyal to the new nation who would organize and seek to join the union of states.

This decision had lasting significance. It meant that the new nation would not, as its territorial reach expanded, permanently administer a colonial empire, as Britain and other imperial powers had done. Instead, the United States would grow organically, by admitting new states to the union alongside the existing states. As for the lands themselves, the general expectation was that some would be used to honor the new nation's earlier commitment to its soldiers, some would be sold to raise funds to help pay war debts, and the future of the rest of them would be up to the Congress.

The proposal found general acceptance. Maryland ended its holdout in early 1781, on assurances that the former colonies with western-land claims would cooperate. Its ratification allowed the Articles of Confederation to take formal effect—which in turn allowed the former colonies finally to become full-fledged states in the federal union—just months before the rebel forces prevailed at Yorktown in October 1781.

After the British surrender, all the states with western-land claims eventually implemented the deal that Schuyler had helped engineer. The process was, however, far from tidy, and it took more than twenty years to complete. Virginia ceded most of its large claims in 1781 but attached a series of conditions. Among other things, it kept what is now Kentucky until that state was admitted to the Union in 1792, and a portion of what is now Ohio, in order to deliver on its promise to give land grants to Virginia soldiers. Connecticut made its cessions in two stages; the second one, involving the so-called Western Reserve of four million acres in what is now northeastern Ohio, was not completed until 1800. North Carolina first moved to cede its claims in 1784, but complications prevented its completion until 1790. South Carolina's cession was not completed until August 1787.

Georgia, the youngest and least populous of the thirteen original states, was the last one to fall in line, and its path was the most colorful. Its legislature purported to sell some forty million acres, about two-thirds of the area of present-day Alabama and Mississippi, to private speculators for around a penny an acre. The sale was eventually rescinded and much of the land recovered, but it took until 1802 for Georgia to complete its cession of western-land claims to the United States.

The formal documents by which these lands were ceded to the nation reinforced the terms of the 1780 congressional resolution. They provided that the lands being ceded to the nation would, as Virginia's cession put it, be "considered as a common fund for the use and benefit of the United States"—that is, of the nation—rather than just for the use and benefit of the states to be carved out of these ceded lands. To underscore this crucial point, Virginia's cession went on to provide that the ceded lands "shall be faithfully and bona fide disposed of for that purpose, and for no other use or purpose whatsoever."[10] Cessions by other states contained similar language.

Through this process, the U.S. government gained title to nearly a quarter billion acres of land between the Alleghenies and the Mississippi, north of Florida and south of Canada. This almost equaled the total acreage of the thirteen original states, once the western boundaries of those colonies ceding their western claims were set.

That vast amount of territory formed the nation's first public lands. Historians have long noted how these lands were a "bond of union," as Benjamin Hibbard put it nearly a century ago, "at a time when the life of the new nation depended upon a harmonious relation of its parts." It was the first and far from the last time the public lands would help unify the country and build a bright future for succeeding generations of Americans; what Thomas LeDuc described as an "enormous initial birthright" would remain, in Daniel Feller's phrase, a "potent agent of nationalization."[11]

Although the cession of the western claims gave the nation a large stock of land, some members of the founding generation were thinking even bigger thoughts about what might lie ahead. Thomas Hutchins, who became the first and only geographer general of the United States in 1781, prepared a crude estimate in 1784 of the habitable area of the entire continent as it stretched to the Pacific, adding: "If we want it, I warrant it will soon be ours."[12]

As Hutchins assumed, the pattern was already firmly set. Over time the U.S. government acquired title to vast amounts of land stretching across the entire continent. It would administer those lands for the common benefit of all

Americans, overseeing their settlement and the admission of new states. It would also eventually come to keep a considerable amount of territory in national ownership, which would become the bulk of today's public lands.

AN ASIDE: TO "DISPOSE OF" DOES NOT MEAN TO "DIVEST OWNERSHIP OF"

Most of the pertinent documents of the founding era called for the new national government to "dispose of" these public lands for the common benefit of all the states in the United States. Those words appear, for example, in two of the important land ordinances the Congress of the Confederation soon adopted, as well as in the U.S. Constitution, drafted in 1787.

In modern times, some who seek to wrest ownership of public lands away from the national government have equated "dispose of" with "relinquish ownership of," arguing that the language reflected the founders' understanding that the U.S. government would not own these lands permanently. But "dispose of" did not then (or now) mean only "relinquish ownership." Among its several meanings in the third edition of Samuel Johnson's famous *Dictionary of the English Language,* published in 1786, were to "regulate," "place in any condition," and "apply to any purpose." Neither the states that ceded their western-land claims nor the states without claims ever demanded that the national government relinquish ownership of the entirety of these vast landholdings.[13]

If the architects of the U.S. government had intended "dispose of" to require relinquishing ownership, they would have had to confront some knotty questions. Relinquish to whom—to states only, or to private interests as well? In any particular proportion? Would there be a deadline for completing the task? If so, when? By the time new states were carved out of the western lands and admitted to the Union, or sometime later? Would the national government be permitted to retain ownership of any lands to serve national purposes? If so, what might those purposes be, how much land might be retained, and under what conditions?

The nation's founders never tried to answer those questions; indeed, there is no evidence they ever considered requiring the United States to relinquish ownership of all the western lands or to dedicate them to particular purposes. Instead, they chose to leave the future "disposal" of these lands (to what "purpose" they would be "applied," to use one of Johnson's definitions) up to the new nation and its political process.

Nor is there any evidence that the founders considered giving new states ownership of all the public lands within their borders upon their admission to the union. The reasons were obvious enough. As Maryland and its allies had successfully argued, all of the existing states had contributed "blood and treasure" to wrest these lands from the British. (Indeed, soldiers who died in the Revolutionary War made up a larger percentage of the population than did troops in any future conflict other than the Civil War, and the conflict lasted longer than any American war until Vietnam.)[14] Yielding control of all of them to new states as they were admitted could, by reducing the influence of the existing states on the process of settling the frontier, jeopardize the claims or investments in the western lands held by people in the existing states. Even worse, it could fray the ties that bound settlements in the West to the new nation.

LEAVING CONGRESS IN CHARGE OF THE
NATION'S PUBLIC LANDS

While the resolution left the U.S. government in control of vast tracts of land, that government was not a monarchy. Instead, it was to be controlled by its voting citizens, which at the time tended to be Anglo men of means. The Congress of the Confederation they elected would determine the national interest and mediate differences that might emerge among the states regarding how the western lands could best be used to facilitate westward expansion and develop a nation.

Settling the future of these national public lands would require an ongoing discussion, and the founders did not foreclose the possibility that the nation might decide to keep some of those lands to serve national purposes, before or even after new states were admitted to the union.

In 1782, when the western-land claims were finally on their way to resolution, an influential series of essays on the new American society was published by an aristocratic Frenchman who had immigrated to North America in 1755. His American name was J. Hector St. John de Crèvecoeur, and his collected essays were called *Letters from an American Farmer*. In one of his most famous passages, he wrote how, in America, "individuals of all nations are melted into a new race of men, whose labors and posterity will one day cause great changes in the world." The American, he wrote, leaves behind "all his ancient prejudices and manners, receives new ones from the new mode of life he has embraced, the new government he obeys, and the new rank he holds." He "acts upon new principles; he must therefore entertain new ideas, and form new opinions." The new nation's riches of land, Crèvecoeur noted, allowed common people to carve out a living "without any part being claimed, either by a despotic prince, a rich abbot, or a mighty lord." Eventually, the new thinking that Crèvecoeur celebrated would lead the United States to decide to hold a significant amount of land in common ownership, open to all.[15]

As for Philip Schuyler, he was soon asked by the Continental Congress to inform the Indians who had fought alongside the British that their lands would be appropriated.[16] In 1789, he became one of New York's first two senators in the new U.S. Congress. Defeated for reelection in 1791 by Aaron Burr, he was once again elected to the U.S. Senate in 1797, but ill health forced his resignation within a year. He died in November 1804, a few months after Burr, by then Thomas Jefferson's vice president, had killed Schuyler's son-in-law, Alexander Hamilton, in a duel. Ironically, Burr soon became embroiled in a scandal involving western lands that finished his political career.

CHAPTER TWO

Public Lands and the Ordinances of 1784, 1785, and 1787

SERIOUS SHORTCOMINGS IN the Articles of Confederation, many of them structural, began to emerge not long after the signing of the Treaty of Paris in September 1783 brought the Revolutionary War to a close. State legislatures selected the members of the single house of the Congress of the Confederation. Decisions on most important matters required the approval of the delegations of nine of the thirteen states. There was no separate executive branch or judiciary. Congress had no fixed venue, meeting at times in Philadelphia, Princeton, Annapolis, Trenton, and New York City.[1]

The Articles said almost nothing regarding the public lands—the more than a quarter billion acres west of the Appalachian crest that the United States was now on a path to own. That awkward silence regarding what was by far the nation's biggest tangible asset was the result of the Articles having been drafted and sent to the states for ratification in 1776, which was years before the landed states agreed to cede their western-land claims to the nation.

Once peace was at hand, practically everyone recognized that restless new Americans would move west and, as Thomas Jefferson had warned in a private letter written shortly after the colonies had declared their independence, "settle the lands in spite of everybody."[2] This meant the national government needed to establish a system for prescribing how these lands would be, as the Continental Congress had resolved in 1780, "disposed of for the common benefit of all the United States."[3]

And so, undeterred by the silence of the Articles, the Congress of the Confederation adopted three laws, or ordinances, between 1784 and 1787 that established the nation's first policies toward its public lands. As the Supreme Court justice Joseph Story later wrote in his authoritative *Commentaries on the Constitution*, "the importance, and even justice," of the national government exercising authority over the western public lands, including the "additional security" it provided for the fragile union, was sufficient to overcome the "serious doubts" whether the Articles of Confederation gave Congress such authority.[4]

THE LAND ORDINANCE OF 1784

Although many of the features of this first ordinance did not long survive, the way it proposed to handle public lands in connection with the admission of new states proved durable. It compressed the language of the October 1780 resolution of the Second Continental Congress—which called for admitting new states with the "same rights of sovereignty, freedom and independence, as the other states"—to provide simply that new states would be admitted "on an equal footing with" the original states.[5]

At the same time, the 1784 ordinance made clear that "equal footing" did not give new states the same authority over all lands within their borders that the thirteen original states possessed. To the contrary, it provided that "in no case" shall new states "interfere with the primary disposal of the soil [within their borders] by the United States in Congress assembled; nor with the ordinances and regulations which Congress may find necessary for securing the title in such soil to the bona fide purchasers." It also, for good measure, prohibited new states from taxing "lands" that are the "property of the United States."

The ordinance of 1784 thus struck a sensible balance between the interests of the existing states and the ones to be admitted to the union in the future. Its promise of "equal footing" sought to assure settlers migrating to the West that if they could organize governments and persuade Congress to admit them into the Union, they would have the same political rights as those in the existing states. At the same time, it sought to protect the interests of the existing states, whose "blood and treasure" had secured these lands for the nation, by providing that statehood would not automatically give new states title to and complete authority over public lands within their borders. Instead, after statehood, just as before, the national political process would decide how these lands would be "disposed of for the common benefit of all the United States."

36	31	32	33	34	35	36	31
1	6	5	4	3	2	1	6
12	7	8	9	10	11	12	7
13	18	17	16	15	14	13	18
24	19	20	21	22	23	24	19
25	30	29	28	27	26	25	30
36	31	32	33	34	35	36	31
1	6	5	4	3	2	1	6

Rectangular survey system illustrating the numbering of
one-mile-square sections in thirty-six-section townships
(Diagram by Bill Nelson)

THE LAND ORDINANCE OF 1785

Several provisions of a land ordinance passed the following year had lasting
effects. One established the rectangular survey system, by which the public
lands would be divided into six-mile-square townships, each containing 23,040
acres, an area more than one and a half times the size of Manhattan Island.[6]
Each township would in turn be divided into thirty-six sections of 640 acres, or
one square mile, each. Each section was assigned a number, and the numbering
system was uniform across townships.

This rectangular grid encouraged generations of Americans to look at
land as, in Andro Linklater's words, a "commodity defined by numbers."[7] Its
rigid uniformity did not readily accommodate irregular natural features of the
landscape, like watercourses and slopes, important to farmer-settlers. Also, in
more recent times, it has not readily accommodated the felt need to manage
landscapes for ecological purposes, such as protecting wildlife habitats and
migration corridors.

The underlying notion was that a survey would be completed before
lands were sold or title was transferred by other means, thus making land

transactions transparent and efficient. This plan worked far better in theory than in practice. The difficulties of making on-the-ground surveys significantly slowed the government's ability to transfer ownership. In the meantime, the eagerness of many to settle the western country made common the practice of "squatting," or occupying unsurveyed public land without legal sanction. Nevertheless, for decades Congress resisted creating a mechanism to allow squatters to gain legal title to the lands they occupied, for fear that it would foment conflict with Native Americans, outstrip institution building, and undermine loyalty to the union.

The most farsighted social policy of the Land Ordinance of 1785 was its reservation of section 16 in every township "for the maintenance of public schools" on the frontier. The expectation was that revenue derived from these lands would support public education. This notion of using government land to promote education was not unknown in Europe and in some of the New England colonies, but many of the original states had not embraced the concept of government-supported public schools. Congress's implementation of this model spurred the development of universal public education in the United States. As the U.S. Supreme Court once put it, this feature in the 1785 ordinance helped unify the nation by planting "in the heart of every community" the promotion of "good government and the happiness of mankind."[8]

The ordinance also "reserved for the United States" four scattered 640-acre sections in every township "for future sale." This idea that the national government ought to reserve some public land as a conservative hedge against an uncertain future eventually helped justify more permanent reservations of land in national ownership.

Another notable feature of the ordinance of 1785 was its treatment of minerals. Although deposits of metallic minerals like gold were rare along the eastern seaboard of the new United States, the ordinance reserved to the nation "one third part of all gold, silver, lead and copper mines, to be sold, or otherwise disposed of, as Congress shall hereafter direct." This idea was borrowed from royal charters granting lands to early American colonies, and ultimately rested on common law the English courts had developed more than two centuries earlier. The Crown's reserved share was called, unsurprisingly, a "royalty," a term that has survived. This part of the 1785 ordinance did not endure, and national policy regarding minerals found on the public lands has remained subject to lively debate right down to the present.

THE NORTHWEST ORDINANCE OF 1787: A ROAD
MAP TO STATEHOOD

In 1787, the new nation found itself in an increasingly precarious position. The revolutionary fervor that had produced victory over the British on the field of battle had dissipated. The Congress of the Confederation was finding it harder to exercise authority of any kind, including over the western public lands. As George Washington wrote to James Madison late in 1786, the nation was "fast verging to anarchy and confusion." This made it "entirely conceivable," in the words of the historian Jack Rakove, that Britain and Spain would dominate the interior of the continent, leaving the thirteen original states "clinging to the ocean, deprived of the resources of the west." To prevent that result, the Congress of the Confederation in early 1787 began taking steps to chart a more definitive course for the western public lands, concentrating on the area north of the Ohio River then known as the Northwest Territory.[9]

The effort succeeded. In New York on July 13, the Congress of the Confederation gave final approval to what became known as the Northwest Ordinance.[10] It reaffirmed and amplified the policy of decolonization and statehood contained in the 1780 resolution of the Continental Congress. It contemplated that three, four, or five states would ultimately be formed out of the Northwest Territory, and it delineated specific stages on the journey to statehood.

It also reaffirmed the balance between the interests of new states and existing states struck in the ordinance of 1784. Most important, it kept the national government in firm control of the nation's public lands, repeating the requirement of the 1784 ordinance that new states carved out of this territory "shall never interfere with the primary disposal of the soil by the United States," or tax the public lands. With that understanding, the ordinance continued to call for the admission of the new states "on an equal footing with the original States, in all respects whatever."

The ordinance of 1787 contained a number of other features that proved influential in subsequent national lawmaking. It promoted the free flow of goods and people by making the "navigable waters" in the region "common highways, and forever free" from "any tax, impost or duty." It called for each new state to have a republican form of government, and included several other ideas that would soon appear in the Bill of Rights affixed to the U.S. Constitution.

The ordinance prohibited slavery in the Northwest Territory and in new states to be created out of it. Southerners acquiesced in the prohibition, expecting that the national government would permit slavery when it organized a territory south of the Ohio River. (Their expectation was fulfilled when, three years later, the first Congress established under the new Constitution organized the southwest territory along the lines of the 1787 ordinance but left out the slavery prohibition.) There was little controversy about this, because the slavery issue was not then as divisive as it became in later decades. Indeed, slavery still existed in parts of the North at that point. (Both Philip Schuyler and Alexander Hamilton held slaves.)[11] Many expected that the practice would gradually end, because it was regarded as marginally profitable at best as well as cruel and inhumane.[12]

This expectation was, of course, dashed by subsequent events. The development of the cotton gin around 1800 gave slavery a new economic life. Gradually, a movement to abolish the heinous practice gained sufficient strength to create a deep political divide. As the nation acquired vast amounts of land farther west, the status of slavery in that territory, and in new states that might be carved from it, led some slavery defenders (including some justices of the U.S. Supreme Court) to call into question the national government's authority over public lands and the admission of new states.

SUMMING UP THE THREE ORDINANCES

The Ordinances of 1784, 1785, and 1787 left the national government firmly in control of policy regarding public lands. They codified the founders' consensus understanding that the nation's highest priority was to maintain national unity as the process of settlement advanced and new states were formed and admitted into the union.

Most political leaders of this era doubtless thought it unlikely the national government would retain ownership of many of its public lands. But none of these ordinances prohibited the United States from choosing to retain ownership of some lands within the boundaries of new states. It might have many reasons for doing so, including military or economic considerations, or simply hedging against uncertainty. It had, after all, a huge supply.

Like the earlier struggle between those states with and without western-land claims during the Revolutionary War, the challenge of forming policies for the western public lands after the war tested the young nation's commitment to national unity. Historians have generally viewed these three ordinances as the most notable exceptions to the dysfunction that characterized the national government under the Articles of Confederation in the 1780s. Their enactment gave the nation a boost of self-confidence at a time when it was badly needed.

In that fateful summer of 1787, a number of the nation's leaders— including some members of the Congress of the Confederation that produced the Northwest Ordinance—assembled in Philadelphia to design a new national governing structure to replace the Articles of Confederation. That gathering, which became known as the Constitutional Convention, produced the U.S. Constitution. But the core public land policies embodied in these three ordinances endured and helped keep the nation functioning while its new government was finding its footing.

CHAPTER THREE

The U.S. Constitution and the Public Lands

THE CHALLENGE FACING THE Constitutional Convention that met in Philadelphia from May 27 to September 17, 1787, was to design a workable national government to replace the one set up by the flawed Articles of Confederation. The nation's public lands were a small and almost entirely uncontroversial part of its agenda. This might seem surprising, because these lands would, once the cessions of the western-land claims were completed, make up nearly half the real estate in the country. Moreover, the "Western territory" was a "mine of vast wealth," a "rich and fertile country," as James Madison later wrote in the *Federalist Papers*—those campaign tracts that he, Alexander Hamilton, and John Jay prepared in late 1787 and early 1788 to persuade New Yorkers to ratify the Constitution.[1]

There is, however, no mystery why the public lands did not engage much attention at the Constitutional Convention. The framers' primary task regarding them was simply to provide an explicit constitutional underpinning for the national government to carry on what it was already doing. In contrast to most parts of the governing system, a new framework did not need to be devised for the public lands.

The Congress of the Confederation had adopted the ordinances of 1784, 1785, and 1787 "without the least color of constitutional authority," as Madison put it in Federalist 38. But the case for national action had been compelling. Settlement of the western lands was already under way and could not be ignored. Congress had to formulate a policy for those lands, Madison wrote, because the "public interest, the necessity of the case, imposed upon them the task of overleaping" the limits of the Articles of Confederation.[2]

Public opinion was firmly supportive of what Congress had done. "No blame has been whispered; no alarm has been sounded" on the matter, Madison wrote, because a consensus already supported the idea that the national legislature should exercise unfettered authority over public land policy. The new Constitution simply needed to leave no doubt that, in Madison words, the national government had "regular powers commensurate to its objects."[3]

THE PROPERTY CLAUSE

Article IV, section 3, clause 2 of the Constitution, which has come to be known as the Property Clause, came to the convention floor relatively late in the proceedings. It addressed national authority over property simply and directly.

> The Congress shall have Power to dispose of and make all needful
> Rules and Regulations respecting the Territory or other Property
> belonging to the United States; and nothing in this Constitution shall
> be so construed as to Prejudice any Claims of the United States, or of
> any particular State.

The first part of this clause neatly filled the vacuum the Articles of Confederation had left on the subject. It generated almost no reported discussion, according to James Madison's handwritten notes, which constitute the principal surviving contemporaneous record because the framers decided not to keep an official transcription of their discussions.

The second part, which did generate some comment, requires a brief explanation. The "claims" it mentions referred to the fact that when the Constitution was being framed, not all the states with western-land claims had completed the process of ceding them to the United States. The disclaimer of effect on such "claims" was included on a motion by Gouverneur Morris, an influential New Yorker who had moved to Philadelphia and represented Pennsylvania at the convention, where he became a principal architect of the Constitution.[4] The Supreme Court justice Joseph Story later described this second part as having been "adopted from abundant caution, to quiet public jealousies upon the subject," which at the time were still being asserted "by some of the States to some parts of the Western Territory." "Happily," Story wrote nearly forty years after all the western lands had been ceded, "these sources of alarm and irritation have long since dried up."[5]

In Federalist 7, Alexander Hamilton put the importance of resolving disputes regarding the vast western territory at the top of his list of reasons to have a robust central government, ahead of the need to address war debts, to reduce trade barriers, and to discourage discriminatory tax policies among the states. History, he darkly observed, taught that "territorial disputes" were perhaps responsible for "the greatest proportion of wars that have desolated the earth." Hamilton lauded the Congress of the Confederation for its "prudent policy" designed to quell the controversy over some states' western-land claims by prevailing on them "to make cessions to the United States for the benefit of the whole." The "vast tract of unsettled territory" within the nation's boundaries created "an ample theater for hostile pretensions," he warned, so that if the Constitution were not ratified, disputes over control of the western lands could be revived that "might not easily be susceptible of a pacific adjustment." In Federalist 43, Madison echoed Hamilton, calling the Property Clause "a power of very great importance."[6]

Besides wanting to confirm the national government's broad authority over territory within its borders as they then existed, the framers of the Constitution knew that the United States might, in the future, acquire territory currently under the control of foreign governments. Indeed, many in the founding generation had ambitions for territorial expansion. They had no desire to constrain the national government's authority to take advantage of such opportunities; from their perspective, the broader and more flexible Congress's authority over public lands, the better.

ADMITTING NEW STATES

The constitutional provision addressing admission of new states, Article IV, section 3, clause 1, also bears on the power of the national government over public lands. It must be read against what came before. Article XI of the Articles of Confederation would have automatically admitted Canada to the union were it to apply, and added that "no other colony shall be admitted" unless agreed to by nine of the original thirteen former colonies. The ordinances of 1784 and 1787 had provided that new states were not to interfere with U.S. decisions regarding public lands within their borders, and the latter ordinance had also laid out, in some detail, the process of admitting new states.

Compared with these earlier enactments, the Constitution aimed for simplicity. The framers left the admission of new states almost entirely to the national political process. Thus, whereas the ordinance of 1787 provided that Congress "shall" admit new states that met specified criteria, the Constitution provides that Congress "may" admit new states, with one sensible limitation. It forbade Congress from admitting a state "formed or erected" out of the territory of another state, or "formed" by combining two states or parts thereof, without the consent of each of the affected states.[7]

The framers considered a proposal that would have admitted new states "on the same terms with the original States," language that echoed the "equal footing" language in the 1784 and 1787 ordinances. But they stripped out those words on the motion of Gouverneur Morris, who argued that it was prudent to leave it open to Congress to give new states somewhat less authority than existing states possessed. James Madison opposed Morris's motion, arguing that the "Western States neither would nor ought to submit to a Union which degraded them from an equal rank with the other States." But Morris prevailed, with only two states voting against his motion.[8]

Other provisions in the Constitution required equality or uniformity among the states on specific issues. The most important of these gave each state, new as well as old, equal representation in the U.S. Senate, the upper house of Congress. But none of those provisions called for or even hinted at a notion that all states should be treated the same regarding public lands. By accepting Morris's motion, the framers confirmed that it was completely up to Congress to decide how to treat new states regarding public lands.

As it turned out, Congress would include an "equal footing" clause in almost every "enabling act" that authorized the admission of a new state. But almost without exception, those enabling acts also included language, like that found in the 1784 and 1787 ordinances, making clear that new states were not to interfere with U.S. policy regarding public lands lying within their borders.

In preserving the national government's broad authority over public lands as new states were admitted, the framers made it very difficult for new states to argue that they had a claim to public lands within their borders simply by virtue of their admission to the union. Difficult but, as it turned out, not impossible. Four decades later, a few members of Congress advanced just such an argument, and some years after that, a singular opinion of the U.S. Supreme Court seemed to look kindly on the idea. It was, however, so contrary to general understanding and long-standing practice that almost nothing came of it.[9]

THE ENCLAVE CLAUSE

Whereas the Property and Admission Clauses were simple and straightforward, another part of the Constitution that might have some relevance to public lands—the second part of the Enclave Clause—is a distinct oddity. The Enclave

Clause also came to the floor relatively late, in early September, more than three months after the convention began. It reads in its entirety:

> Congress shall have power to exercise exclusive Legislation in all Cases whatsoever over such District (not exceeding ten Miles square) as may, by Cession of particular States, and the Acceptance of Congress, become the Seat of the Government of the United States, and to exercise like Authority over all Places purchased by the Consent of the Legislature of the State in which the Same shall be, for the Erection of Forts, Magazines, Arsenals, dock-Yards, and other needful Buildings.

The clause had been stitched together from two proposals made by James Madison. The first empowered the national government to "exercise exclusively Legislative authority at the seat of the General Government" and an area around it. The reason for this was obvious to the framers. In 1783, unpaid soldiers had laid siege to the Congress of the Confederation, then meeting in Philadelphia, and when the Commonwealth of Pennsylvania failed to protect the assembly, Congress had to retreat in ignominy to Princeton, New Jersey, to continue its deliberations. This gave rise to the idea that the "Seat of the Government of the United States"—what is now known as the District of Columbia—should be located outside the boundaries of any state. As Joseph Story later wrote in his *Commentaries on the Constitution,* had the framers ignored the lesson of this episode, it "would have been as humiliating to their intelligence, as it would have been offensive to their honor."[10]

The second part of the Enclave Clause was very far from the framers' best work, raising many more questions than it answered. It started out as a separate proposal by Madison to give Congress "exclusive" authority over "places" the national government might "purchase" in states to construct "Forts, Magazines, Arsenals, dock-Yards, and other needful Buildings." Madison may have intended it to apply only to the existing thirteen states, where the national government owned almost no land. That interpretation would make it congruent with the first part of the clause, because the seat of the new national government would also be carved out of land in the existing states—as it turned out, through cessions from Maryland and, initially, Virginia. The requirement that purchases of such "places" be made with the "consent" of the pertinent state legislatures was added on the floor of the convention, in response to a concern expressed by one delegate that Congress might coerce a state "by buying up its territory" and forcing it "into an undue obedience to the General Government."[11]

Even if the clause were to apply to states beyond the original thirteen, it contained no guidance regarding public lands that the United States already owned inside those states. Those lands were and would remain subject to Congress's broad Property Clause power. That being the case, there was little point to the requirement added on the convention floor that the United States secure state consent if it wanted to acquire *other* lands in that state and exercise exclusive authority over them. The second part's peculiar language also does not prevent the national government from purchasing lands inside a state *without* the state's consent, so long as Congress chooses not to exercise "exclusive" authority over them. And its peculiar language raises other questions. Does it apply only to defense installations like forts and arsenals, or does its reference to "other needful Buildings" have more general application? Could the language be stretched to apply to raw land?

In Federalist 43, Madison wisely avoided all these questions. Writing to persuade readers that the Constitution was well considered, well drafted, and worthy of ratification, he was understandably reluctant to delve into such perplexing issues. Instead, he blandly described the objective of this second part as being to ensure that "places on which the security of the entire Union may depend" and which were established by the general government with public money "should be exempt from the authority of the particular State" where they are found. The requirement that the pertinent state must consent to the national government's purchase, Madison said, eliminated any possible objection to it.[12]

Perhaps the most curious thing about this second part of the Enclave Clause is that almost none of the questions it raises have ever been authoritatively answered. The U.S. Supreme Court has never applied it to restrict the authority of Congress over public lands in any consequential way. The clause has, therefore, played no meaningful role in public land policy. Instead, it has remained a constitutional oddity that few—especially those who justly celebrate the overall genius of the Constitution—are eager to discuss.

From time to time, this second part of the Enclave Clause has been invoked by those who oppose the national government owning significant amounts of land. They argue that the framers meant to give states a veto over public land policy. That argument has never found traction in the courts or, indeed, anywhere else, an unsurprising result considering the language of the Enclave Clause and its history, especially in relation to the more straightforward Property Clause.[13]

THE CONSTITUTION AND PUBLIC LANDS: SUMMING UP

While the second part of the Enclave Clause was a particularly inferior example of constitutional drafting, the Property Clause and the clause authorizing the admission of new states were the opposite. Speaking in broad terms, they left the nation's future policy regarding its public lands up to the national political process. In so doing, they exemplified what the historian Joseph Ellis has praised as the Constitution's core strength—namely, that its design was "less to resolve arguments than to make argument itself the solution"; not to offer specific guidance on many issues but "instead to provide a political arena in which arguments about those contested issues could continue in a deliberative fashion."[14]

None of these constitutional provisions attracted much discussion either in the Constitutional Convention or in the ratifying conventions held in the states. This lack of attention underscored how a strong national consensus had already developed on the wisdom of giving Congress broad authority over public lands. All states, both the original thirteen and those admitted later, would be fully represented in the process by which this authority would be exercised.

The Constitution also placed no limits on the power of the nation to enlarge its territorial reach by acquisition. The most logical direction for significant growth was to the west, so it became customary to refer to national expansion as directional. The lands and resources of America's western frontier held what Henry Nash Smith described as a kind of "magnetic attraction" for empire builders, statesmen, and ordinary people alike.[15]

Although the phrase "manifest destiny" was not coined until the 1840s, the idea that the new nation was destined to spread over the entire continent was hardly new. Following the cessions of western lands by the former colonies, the United States over the next few decades acquired clear title to a much larger land area from foreign governments and Indian tribes. The Constitution's creation of a workable national government, and the broad authority it gave Congress over public lands, enabled those lands to become a principal mechanism for the nation's advance.

PART TWO THE PUBLIC LANDS AND NATION
BUILDING, 1790–1861

CHAPTER FOUR

Admitting New States and Acquiring New Territory

IN THE 1780S, THE COUNTRY'S FOUNDERS contemplated that the new nation would grant some public lands to new states as it admitted them to the union while retaining other public lands within their borders to serve national objectives. In the Constitution, they left these matters almost entirely up to the congressional political process.

Congress admitted Vermont and Kentucky as the fourteenth and fifteenth states in 1791 and 1792. It regarded lands not already privately owned within their borders as having been ceded directly to them by the states of New York and New Hampshire, in the case of Vermont, and by the state of Virginia, in the case of Kentucky—without passing through U.S. ownership. In those states, therefore, the nation asserted no claim to own public lands.[1]

The admission of Tennessee in 1796 as the sixteenth state was much more complicated. In 1790, Congress organized the Southwest Territory in the region south of the Ohio River that included what became Tennessee. Following the model outlined in the Northwest Ordinance of 1787, Congress provided that any new states admitted from the territory should "never interfere with the primary disposal of the soil by the United States." That same year, North Carolina ceded to the nation its claims to lands in what would become Tennessee, but it continued to make grants of land there. When Congress accepted the North Carolina cession in 1790, it provided that the ceded lands "shall be considered as a common fund for the use and benefit of" the entire nation. The congressional act admitting Tennessee to the Union in 1796 on an "equal footing" with the original states made no specific reference to public lands.

In early 1799, Tennessee's leaders, who included Andrew Jackson, its first member of the U.S. House of Representatives, began to press a claim that Tennessee owned all the public lands within its borders. They pointed out that the United States had not, in the act of admission, explicitly reserved those lands for its own use. Congress vigorously contested the state's position and set in motion a process to sell some of those lands. Years of wrangling followed. In 1806, Tennessee, North Carolina, and the United States reached a compromise that recognized U.S. control of public lands in the western part of the state, but left unresolved other issues that would not be settled until 1846, a half century after statehood.[2]

Tennessee's brash claim to own all the public land within its borders helped persuade Congress that it should more clearly address public lands in subsequent statehood-enabling acts, beginning with the admission of the seventeenth state, Ohio, in 1803. That act's chief architect was one of the most influential figures in early public land policy, Treasury secretary Albert Gallatin. Born into a wealthy Swiss family but orphaned before he turned ten, Gallatin immigrated to the United States in 1780 at the age of nineteen. In the 1790s, he briefly represented Pennsylvania in the U.S. Senate and then served three terms in the House of Representatives. President Thomas Jefferson named him secretary of the Treasury in 1801, and he served until 1814, one of the longest-serving cabinet secretaries in U.S. history. There, he had supervisory responsibility for public lands.[3]

Gallatin's proposal was to give Ohio one section of public land in each thirty-six-section township—a little less than 3 percent of the state's land area—for public education, as recommended in the ordinance of 1785. It also required that the new state's constitution and government "not be repugnant" to the Northwest Ordinance, which provided that new states "shall never interfere with" the national government's disposition of public lands it retained within the new state's borders. To make public land more attractive for buyers and thereby hasten the Treasury's retirement of Revolutionary War debt, Gallatin proposed to exempt every tract of public land that the United States sold in Ohio from all state and local taxation for ten years from the date of sale.[4]

Some proponents of Ohio statehood, led by Arthur St. Clair, the territorial governor, were not satisfied. While making no claim that Ohio should be entitled to all the public lands within its borders, they asked for more public lands

Albert Gallatin, 1761–1849 (Courtesy of the Library of Congress,
LC-USZ62-110017)

and related benefits. Their acquisitiveness met resistance in the nation's capital.
Secretary of State James Madison removed St. Clair for his "intemperance,"
sending the message that until statehood was achieved, a territory remained
subject to the full authority of the national government. After some modest
tinkering with Gallatin's terms, but leaving his basic framework intact,
Congress admitted Ohio to the union.[5]

The nation's resistance to Ohio's request for more public land was perfectly
understandable, and reflected a political dynamic that could be observed in
nearly all subsequent congressional decisions regarding statehood. Senators
and representatives were selected by voters in the existing states, many of
whom believed that because it was the "blood and treasure" of existing states
that had secured these lands, it was entirely appropriate for the national government to use them to advance such national purposes as promoting education
and building infrastructure. It was not surprising, then, that the United States
would generally specify, in statehood legislation, that it retained ownership and
full control of the public lands not granted to the new state. On the other hand,
Congress recognized that giving a new state title to some public lands could

have benefits, including cementing bonds of loyalty to the nation (although loyalty concerns declined after the Civil War).

In the end, each statehood decision stood on its own. Because Texas and Hawaii had been independent countries before being annexed, the United States asserted no claim to lands within their borders. But those were exceptions. Everywhere else, the United States owned substantial amounts of public lands and generally followed the Ohio model, which included giving the new state a significant amount of public lands at statehood. The sixteen states other than Texas admitted between 1803 (Ohio) and early 1861 (Kansas) were each awarded, at statehood, between 700,000 and 5.5 million acres of public land for schools, plus substantial additional acres for other purposes. The ungranted public lands, usually a much larger amount, remained under U.S. ownership and control. (Sometimes Congress later made some of these retained lands available to states for various purposes.) Statehood decisions after the Civil War generally followed the same pattern, although Alaska, admitted in 1959, was granted a far greater proportion of public lands than any other.[6]

EXPANDING THE NATION'S TERRITORIAL REACH

On July 4, 1803, twenty-seven years after the Declaration of Independence and just a year after Georgia completed the former colonies' last cessions of western-land claims to the nation, President Thomas Jefferson announced the purchase of the Louisiana Territory. The seller was Emperor Napoleon of France, whose ambitions in North America had been thwarted by a slave revolt in present-day Haiti and who needed money because a war with Great Britain was looming.

The single largest acquisition of land in U.S. history, the Louisiana Purchase doubled the land area of the United States. Coming at a time when two out of every three Americans lived within fifty miles of the Atlantic Ocean, it expanded the nation far to the west across a broad front. Ultimately, once Indian title was resolved, it tripled the acreage of U.S.-owned public lands.

The Constitution did not expressly authorize the nation to acquire lands from foreign governments. It did, however, give the president power to make treaties (which is how the Louisiana Purchase was done) with the concurrence of two-thirds of the U.S. Senate. Also, both houses of Congress would need to vote to provide the funds to cover the purchase price of $15 million (several hundred billion in current dollars). Nevertheless, Jefferson privately harbored doubts whether the deal was constitutional, going so far as to draft in secret a constitutional amendment to overcome a problem he was practically alone in perceiving. When he was told in August 1803 that Napoleon was having second thoughts about the sale, however, Jefferson promptly sent the treaty to the Senate for ratification. Besides forever shaping his presidential legacy, the Louisiana Purchase launched a tradition of enterprising executive leadership on matters relating to public lands that would have lasting influence.[7]

There were objections. Senator William Plumer of New Hampshire predicted the "vast wilderness world" being acquired will "prove worse than useless to us," and a Federalist newspaper grumbled that the government was going to spend money it did not have "for land of which we already have too much."[8]

But most Americans were not disturbed by the idea of the national government acquiring millions of acres. They were content to let the political process decide how these lands would be "disposed of" to carry out national objectives. Ultimately, Congress decided to make much of the purchased land available to settlers, new states, and others. Eventually, however, a considerable amount of the purchased land was held in U.S. ownership, to serve a wide variety of purposes that evolved over time. Most notably, before seven decades had elapsed, Congress would, at a place called Yellowstone, establish the world's first national park.

Over the half century following the Louisiana Purchase, the United States acquired the remainder of the land that would eventually make up the contiguous forty-eight states. A treaty with England in 1818 fixed the nation's northern boundary in Minnesota and the Dakota Territory. A treaty with Spain in 1819 settled boundary questions between the two nations and resulted in Florida coming into the union. A treaty with England in 1842 settled Maine's boundary with the Canadian provinces of New Brunswick and Lower Canada (later called Quebec), and adjusted Minnesota's boundary with the Canadian provinces of Alberta and Manitoba.

As Congress was considering annexing Texas in 1845, a political commentator, John L. O'Sullivan, coined the phrase that captured the entire era, in an essay published in a Democratic Party paper. "The American claim," he wrote, "is by the right of our *manifest destiny* to overspread and to possess the whole of the continent which Providence has given us for the development of the great experiment of liberty and federative self-government entrusted to us."[9]

Within three years of O'Sullivan's pronouncement, the United States, under the leadership of President James K. Polk, acquired not only Texas (including parts of what are now New Mexico, Colorado, Kansas, and Wyoming), but also the Oregon Territory (including what are now Oregon,

Territory of the Original Thirteen States

State cessions to the United States

North Carolina cession to the United States, 1790
United States cession to Tennessee, 1806 and 1846

Area considered part of the Original Thirteen States

Territory of the Republic of Texas

United States purchase from Texas, 1850

State of Texas (present area)

Other Acquisitions of the United States

Louisiana Purchase from France, 1803

Treaties with Great Britain, 1783 and 1817

Treaty with Spain (cession of Florida and adjustment of claims), 1819

Oregon Compromise with Great Britain, 1846

Cession from Mexico, 1848

Gadsden Purchase with Mexico, 1853

ALASKA

Purchased from Russia, 1867

Territorial expansion of the United States (Map by Bill Nelson)

Washington, and parts of Idaho, Montana, and Wyoming) and the Southwest (including what are now California, Nevada, Utah, and parts of Arizona, New Mexico, Colorado, and Wyoming). The so-called Gadsden Purchase in 1853 brought 30 million acres below the Gila River, in what is now Arizona and New Mexico, into U.S. ownership.

Because Texas was an independent republic after it broke away from Mexico in 1836, the terms of its annexation and admission to statehood in 1845 allowed it to retain ownership of most of the public lands that were already under its jurisdiction. Five years later, as one part of the complicated Compromise of 1850, engineered by Henry Clay, the national government agreed to pay off $10 million in debt the Lone Star State had incurred during its period of independence. In return, the United States acquired ownership of 73 million acres of land that eventually became the eastern part of New Mexico, the Oklahoma Panhandle, southwestern Kansas, and parts of Colorado and Wyoming.

All told, in the eight years between 1845 and 1853, the lands subject to the jurisdiction of the United States grew by nearly 800 million acres. Of these, the U.S. government eventually took ownership of more than 600 million acres. The remainder included—besides lands owned by the State of Texas—lands held in trust for Native Americans and lands that had been granted by prior sovereigns before the United States took control of them.

How the United States came to acquire lands from Native Americans, and to resolve claims to lands under grants from prior sovereigns, are distinct and complicated stories only very briefly summarized here. An important feature common to both was that the national government generally had exclusive control of the process, which had the effect of strengthening national authority vis-à-vis the states.

INDIAN LANDS

The European invasion of the Americas led to the deaths of large numbers of Native Americans, many because they lacked immunity to diseases the invaders brought.[10] Those who survived were not easily shunted aside, which some-times led to bloody clashes between them and the invaders. Yet almost from the beginning, the Europeans generally acknowledged that the Native Americans had sovereignty over, and a legal right to, the lands they possessed—what came to be known as aboriginal or Indian title. This led to a common practice of formally acquiring Indian title to lands through agreements in which Indians ceded their rights to land in return for money or other benefits, including assurances they would not be disturbed if they moved elsewhere.[11]

Once the United States secured its independence from Britain, the national government followed the same course of dealing, after a relatively brief period under the Articles of Confederation during which it took Indian land without making any effort to pay compensation. The Northwest Ordinance of 1787 called for treating Indians with the "utmost good faith," meaning that "their lands and property shall never be taken from them without their consent" or except through "just and lawful wars" authorized by Congress. The U.S. Supreme Court issued three landmark decisions between 1823 and 1832 (known as the "Marshall trilogy" because Chief Justice John Marshall spoke for the unanimous court in each) that confirmed foundational principles. These were that Indian tribes were "domestic dependent nations" with inherent sovereignty and a direct relationship with the national government, not the states, and that they retained title to their traditional lands until title was extinguished by proper means.[12]

The process by which the United States acquired Indian lands for Euro-American settlement was seldom orderly and often difficult, with a dark side. To try to minimize conflicts with Indians, the national government usually did not formally open public lands to entry and eventual ownership by non-Indians until Indian title had been acquired. But the government had only a limited capacity to control the movement of impatient settlers and exploiters who, in the words of one historian, "pushed aside" native peoples they considered to be racially inferior and using land "inefficiently by capitalist standards."[13] A gold rush in Georgia in 1828, for example, was instrumental in pushing Cherokees off their land, and eventually the United States forcibly removed them to an Indian territory in what is now the state of Oklahoma. Despite the optimistic words of the Northwest Ordinance, the failure of the United States to prevent the forcible dispossession of Indians by miners, settlers, loggers, livestock operators, and others was all too common for many decades during the nineteenth century.

When the United States did intervene to keep order, its efforts were usually more harshly visited on Indians. In 1783, George Washington foresaw what would happen, coldly predicting that the "gradual extension" of Euro-American settlements westward "will as certainly cause the Savage as the Wolf to retire."[14] Moreover, the U.S. government did many other things that were not justified by principles of law or fair dealing. Abraham Lincoln's first secretary of the interior put the matter bluntly in his *Annual Report* of 1862. When the "consent of the Indians" to yield their territory to advancing settlement had "been obtained in the form of treaties," he wrote, "it is well known that they have yielded to a necessity which they could not resist."[15] Still, as Felix Cohen, the first great scholar of U.S. law governing Indian affairs, wrote in 1947, "the historic fact is that practically all of the real estate acquired by the United States since 1776 was purchased" from its original Indian owners. Indeed, Cohen noted, after paying Napoleon $15 million for the Louisiana Territory, the U.S. government eventually paid tribes more than twenty times that amount to acquire Indian title to most of those lands, with the Indians reserving some for themselves by agreement with the United States. While many transactions were not fair and honorable, they did operate to give the United States clear title.[16]

Once that was done, the government proceeded to relinquish ownership of most of these lands to settlers, states, railroads, and many other entities. Generally speaking, the United States did not begin to reserve significant amounts of land in public ownership until years or sometimes many decades after Indian title to those lands had been acquired. Chapter 60 describes how, after World War II, Congress established a process by which Indians could be compensated monetarily for past losses of land in cases when the United States had not followed a course of "fair and honorable dealings," and how the United States has in some particular situations restored ancestral lands to tribes.[17]

RESOLVING LAND CLAIMS DERIVED FROM PRIOR NON-INDIAN SOVEREIGNS

A good many of the lands the United States acquired by cession from the original colonies were subject to competing claims of ownership that were grounded in conveyances allegedly made earlier by those colonies or their English predecessors. Indeed, according to an inventory conducted in 1791 by Secretary of State Jefferson, some 21 million acres were encumbered with such claims. In the treaty ending the Revolutionary War, the United States agreed to respect valid land grants that Britain or its colonies had made when they controlled these lands. This established a model that the nation would uniformly follow thereafter, in the Louisiana Purchase and other transactions by which it acquired lands from foreign governments.[18]

While the general principle was simple—the United States would respect legitimate property rights that grew out of valid transactions made by prior governments before acquisition by the United States—its application posed enormous challenges. There were many thousands of such claims, and they sometimes conflicted with one another. Each had to be scrutinized to determine whether it had been made and maintained in accordance with the applicable law of the prior sovereign, before the U.S. acquisition. Adding even more complexity, this sometimes turned on the validity of earlier transactions between the preceding sovereign and Native Americans.

To adjudicate such claims, Congress usually established a special legal process before a tribunal or commission, with appeal available to federal courts. The task was formidable. Documentation was sometimes incomplete or nonexistent. Language and translation issues were common. Boundaries were often imprecisely expressed. Surveys that purportedly fixed boundaries on the ground were sometimes unavailable or untrustworthy. Dishonesty plagued the process—forged documents and surveys were common, bribery a constant concern. One claim investigator wrote of being immersed in the "very mire and filth of corruption."[19]

It took generations to complete this job. The U.S. Supreme Court rendered decisions in more than one hundred such cases before the Civil War, and many more thereafter. Claimants to large tracts sometimes prevailed because of their persistence and their superior legal representation. But not always, as a German-Swiss immigrant named Johann Sutter could painfully attest. His claims to a vast expanse of California, pursuant to grants he received from Mexico in the early 1840s—including the site of the discovery in 1848 that triggered the California gold rush—were eventually rejected by the courts.

Some lawyers did well in the process. Prominent nineteenth-century lawyer-politicians like U.S. senators Daniel Webster and Thomas Hart Benton represented claimants while serving in national office, something that modern ethical standards would likely not permit. A San Francisco law firm representing interests asserting claims to the scenic Point Reyes peninsula north of the city that were grounded in grants from Mexico in the 1840s not only prevailed but eventually ended up owning much of the land.[20]

Although the process to get there had many flaws, once Indian title had been resolved, and valid claims from previous sovereigns had been identified, the United States emerged with clear ownership to the lands that remained: hundreds of millions of acres from the crest of the Appalachian Mountains out to the Pacific coast.

CHAPTER FIVE

Exploration, Science, and the Appreciation of Nature

THOMAS JEFFERSON'S INFLUENCE on public lands went far beyond engineering the Louisiana Purchase. Deeply curious about science and nature, he once wrote that politics was his "duty" while science was his "passion." He meticulously described the natural resources of his state in the only book he ever published, and he regarded it as self-evident, as he wrote to James Madison in 1789, that "the Earth belongs in *usufruct* to the living generation." This term, derived from Roman law, acknowledged a right to use and derive profit from property only so long as it was not depleted or damaged. Its hint of an obligation to future generations anticipated modern notions of stewardship and sustainability that have profoundly influenced public land policy.[1]

The land acquired in the Louisiana Purchase—what the Massachusetts congressman Fisher Ames saw as a "great waste, a wilderness unpeopled with any beings except wolves and wandering Indians"—was deeply attractive to Jefferson, for many reasons. Although he never ventured west of Virginia's Shenandoah Valley, his personal library at Monticello reportedly contained one of the world's most extensive collections of maps and books dealing with the western lands.[2]

Jefferson had contemplated an expedition to explore the West months before the opportunity to acquire the Louisiana Territory arose. Once the purchase was put in motion, he wasted no time in commissioning his personal secretary, Meriwether Lewis, to lead, with William Clark, the famous Corps of

Discovery on its fabled twenty-eight-month journey through the newly acquired territory and beyond, to the Pacific.

A few weeks after the expedition left St. Louis in mid-May 1804, Jefferson welcomed Alexander von Humboldt for a weeklong visit to Washington, D.C. A Prussian aristocrat and pioneering naturalist, Humboldt, then thirty-five, had just finished a five-year exploration of South America. That experience led him to write groundbreaking works about nature and how human activity could affect it. Thousands of copies of the English translation of his best-known work, *Cosmos: A Sketch of the Physical Description of the Universe,* published in two volumes in 1845 and 1847, were sold in the United States and England. By the time he died, in 1859 at age eighty-nine, Humboldt was the era's most famous scientist, and his work would come to have a significant influence on America's policy toward public lands.[3]

The Lewis and Clark expedition was a huge success at every level, an epic journey that has captured public attention ever since. Like the mission to land humans on the moon, it stirred pride in the national government that sponsored it. An edited version of Lewis and Clark's journals, which carefully catalogued and described what they encountered, was widely read when published in 1814.

James Madison, who succeeded Jefferson in the presidency, nurtured a similar respect for the natural world. In 1818, not long after he left office, Madison delivered a widely noted speech in which he warned against making "all the productive powers" of the land "subservient to the use of man," and condemned the tendency toward "excessive destruction of timber."[4]

All of this contributed to what Andrea Wulf has called a "distinctly American glorification of the wilderness" that imbued "the American landscape with patriotism."[5] Eventually, these sentiments were channeled into a powerful movement to hold some of that landscape permanently and relatively undeveloped in national ownership.

It was, then, most fitting that Lewis and Clark named three rivers that flow together to become the Missouri River in what is now the state of Montana after three of the most influential figures in America's early public land policy— Jefferson, Madison, and their Treasury secretary, Albert Gallatin.

"THE GREAT RECONNAISSANCE"

Some of the exploration and information gathering after Lewis and Clark was done by famed mountain men like Jedediah Smith and representatives of private commercial interests, like fur trappers and traders. But as the historian William Goetzmann noted, they "often called upon the central government or its representatives to aid them in their march to the West." Indeed, by far the most systematic exploration of the western lands was carried out by the government, in what Goetzmann called the "Great Reconnaissance." The reports that flowed from these ventures described, with wonderment, magnificent landscapes and exotic flora and fauna, along with warnings of how hostile the conditions were to settlement.[6]

There were many such government expeditions. One to the southwest launched in 1806 and led by Thomas Freeman, a cartographer, and Peter Custis, a botanist, was halted in southern Oklahoma by the Spanish Army.[7] Another, begun around the same time under the leadership of Lieutenant Zebulon Pike, and sent to explore the prairies and the Rockies in what are now Colorado and New Mexico, had more success. Still another set out in 1820 to explore the Great Plains and locate the source of the Platte River, and it was the first to include artists as well as scientists. Under the command of Major Stephen Long, its widely disseminated report concluded that the area was "almost wholly unfit for cultivation" and famously labeled it the "Great American Desert" on one of its maps.

In the 1830s, Captain Benjamin Bonneville, technically on leave from the U.S. Army but operating under its detailed instructions, directed explorations of a considerable amount of the Rocky Mountain West. One led by Joseph Walker went from the Great Salt Lake to California. Working from Bonneville's journals, Washington Irving published a book called *The Rocky Mountains* in 1837. It gave many Americans their first look at what became known as the Great Basin in the intermountain west, the vast expanse between the eastern Rockies and the Sierra Nevada range in California. Irving concluded that the "desolate" region "must ever remain an irreclaimable wilderness."[8]

John C. Frémont's report of his three western expeditions with the Army Corps of Topographical Engineers between 1842 and 1845—written with his wife, Jessie, a writer, activist, and daughter of the prominent Missouri senator Thomas Hart Benton—was also given wide circulation. The report did not soft-pedal the harshness of the conditions sometimes encountered, but also used adjectives like "grand," "magnificent," and "romantic" to describe what they had seen. Francis Parkman's *The Oregon Trail* and Edwin Bryant's *What I Saw in California,* best sellers published in 1846, also helped introduce Americans to scenic western landscapes.[9]

One of the most memorable pre–Civil War explorations came in 1858 when Lieutenant Joseph Christmas Ives led a military exploration of the canyons, Indian villages, and prehistoric ruins in the lower Colorado River region, including the Grand Canyon. Ives is most remembered today for his bleak, comically wrongheaded assessment of the region's prospects. Calling the stunning scenery "altogether valueless," where there is "nothing to do but leave," he predicted that his expedition would be not only the first, but also "doubtless . . . the last, party of whites to visit this profitless locality. It seems intended by nature that the Colorado River, along the greater portion of its lonely and majestic way, shall be forever unvisited and undisturbed."[10]

Today, many of the magnificent landscapes described in these explorers' reports are preserved in public ownership for all to enjoy. Within a century of Ives's encounter, Grand Canyon National Park hosted one million visitors in a single year; in another half century, the figure was more than six million.

THE SMITHSONIAN INSTITUTION NURTURES INTEREST IN ARCHAEOLOGY AND ETHNOLOGY

Up to the mid-1840s, government science was mostly the province of the military. At that point, an English chemist, James Smithson—who never set foot in the United States but bridled at the lack of respect he was accorded in England because he was born out of wedlock—left the U.S. government a tidy sum to create an establishment "for the increase and diffusion of knowledge among men." A Vermont congressman, George Perkins Marsh, co-authored legislation to establish the Smithsonian Institution in 1846, and soon became a member of its governing board of regents. Under the leadership of the prominent scientist Joseph Henry, the Smithsonian helped make Washington, D.C., a center of the nation's scientific world in the latter half of the nineteenth century.[11]

The Smithsonian's first publication, *Ancient Monuments of the Mississippi Valley* (1848), was a systematic survey of large mysterious mounds erected by Native American cultures in the Midwest. Henry worked with Marsh to edit the work, and it was well received, stimulating much interest in both archeology and ethnology. The peripatetic Albert Gallatin had promoted interest in ethnology with his publication of two highly regarded studies of Indian languages and tribal culture in 1826 and 1836, in which he concluded that natives of North and South America had common ancestors who had migrated from Asia. In 1842, six years before his death at the age of eighty-eight, Gallatin cofounded the American Ethnological Society. Although it took several more decades, these activities came to have considerable influence on public land policy.[12]

GROWING INTEREST IN SCENIC LANDSCAPES

Although some, like Ives, saw no value in scenic landscapes, from the nation's founding there were those who did. Thomas Jefferson, for one, keenly appreciated the inspirational qualities of natural wonders. In 1774, he had purchased from King George III a parcel of land in Virginia containing a geological formation called the Natural Bridge, a ninety-foot span more than two hundred feet above a tributary of the James River. Jefferson, who called it one of the "most sublime of Nature's works," built a cabin there to use as a retreat. The idea of the sublime would come to signify, in the words of one historian, Roderick Nash, a "new feeling about wild places" that found in them "exultation, awe, and delight" rather than "dread and loathing." A few years later, Jefferson described the view of the Potomac River from what is known as Jefferson Rock in West Virginia, now part of Harpers Ferry National Historical Park, as "one of the most stupendous scenes in Nature," one "worth a voyage across the Atlantic."[13]

Pride in the nation's landscapes, aptly called "scenic nationalism" by another historian, Anne Farrar Hyde, took root in American culture. The longtime New York political leader, wide-ranging intellectual, and amateur naturalist DeWitt Clinton captured the idea in an address to the American Academy of the Arts in 1816. In the United States, Clinton said, "Nature has conducted her operations on a magnificent scale," which produced a "correspondent impression in the imagination—to elevate all the faculties of the mind, and to exalt all the feelings of the heart." Within a few years, Clinton was calling for preservation of the state's northern forests. This attitude eventually had great impact on public land policy.[14]

In 1819, Able Crawford and his son Ethan cut a trail to the top of Mount Washington in the White Mountains of New Hampshire, inviting visitors to climb the mountain simply, as Dyan Zaslowsky and T. H. Watkins later put it, "for the pleasure of being there." The Crawford Path, now part of the Appalachian Trail, is said to be the oldest continuously used recreational footpath in North America. Within a few years, shelters for adventurers began to be erected in Catskill Mountains of New York, north and west of New York City.[15]

Also helping nurture "scenic nationalism" were luminous, popular depictions of natural landscapes by artists such as Thomas Cole, who founded what became known as the Hudson River school of painting. Before photography became widely available, these detailed paintings played an important role in introducing faraway scenes of the natural world to much of the population. Following Cole's death in 1848, his students and followers, including the painters Asher Durand and Frederic Church, continued to celebrate the sublime in nature. The sense of national identity this helped create was a distraction from the growing divide over slavery and the harsh effects of an industrializing economy.[16]

Travel for the pleasure of enjoying natural scenery developed slowly. It required a population with means and leisure time, adequate infrastructure and modes of transportation, and reasonably secure conditions, none of which were very abundant before the Civil War. People in some of the nation's fast-growing urban areas sought solace in the restorative powers of nature by developing urban cemeteries as places for contemplation and recreation. The first was Mount Auburn in Cambridge, Massachusetts, in 1831, soon followed by others in Philadelphia and Brooklyn.

With the rapid growth of New York City, sentiment began to build, promoted by the well-known romantic poet and journalist William Cullen Bryant, for a major park on Manhattan Island. A few years after the city government acquired the land in the early 1850s, what became Central Park was designed and built by Frederick Law Olmsted in partnership with Calvert Vaux. Olmsted, who would become America's greatest landscape architect, was then just in his thirties. He had already produced (and first published in a fledgling newspaper that became the *New York Times*) the most searching inquiry into the slavery system in the South after two long journeys through the region. Olmsted grasped how public parks promoted the mingling of people of all classes, and Central Park almost instantly became enormously popular; Olmsted called it a "democratic development of the highest significance." His advocacy for making nature, even if tamed, available to city dwellers soon helped nourish the idea that the national government should protect large tracts of lands in public ownership for public enjoyment.[17]

The most celebrated of the nation's natural attractions before the Civil War, and one of the first to become a destination resort for tourists, was Niagara Falls in western New York. As cataracts go, Niagara's magnificence owed as much to its volume as to its height. One-fifth of the world's freshwater that is not frozen in ice is found in the Great Lakes, and most of the water in the four upper lakes flowed over Niagara Falls, day after day, with little seasonal variation—until, shortly before the turn of the twentieth century, a good deal of that water began to be routed around the falls to generate electricity.

Early visitors found the cascade mostly frightening, but soon after 1800, two entrepreneurial brothers, Peter and August Porter, saw its commercial-tourism potential and bought up as much land as they could. Soon, all the land on both sides of the river was in private hands. Railroad construction and the completion of the Erie Canal in the mid-1820s improved access from popu-lation centers, and Niagara Falls became a booming commercial resort. Developers built structures to enable tourists to experience the falls from all angles, as well as an assortment of hotels, mansions, taverns, and shops.

It did not take long for this visual blight to garner criticism, especially from European visitors. After he visited the falls in 1831, Alexis de Tocqueville urged a friend to "hasten" to see the place, because "if you delay, your Niagara will have been spoiled." By 1850, as commercialism was taking its toll, what had been America's "best claim to scenic superiority" over Europe had, according to the historian Alfred Runte, lost "credibility as a cultural legacy." Frederic Church's monumental painting of the falls, completed in 1857, was a tightly focused view that eliminated the visual blight; when it was displayed in New York City, it was viewed by 100,000 people in two weeks. After the Civil War, a movement arose to restore a more welcoming scenic experience for visitors to the falls. Spearheaded by Frederick Law Olmsted, it illuminated not only evolving American attitudes toward scenic landscapes but also the role of government in preserving them for public enjoyment.[18]

EARLY SUGGESTIONS OF A GOVERNMENTAL ROLE IN
NATURE PRESERVATION

In the 1820s, a young Pennsylvanian, George Catlin, then in the process of abandoning his law career, began painting Indians. His first portrait to gain fame was of the Seneca chief Red Jacket pointing to Niagara Falls in the back-ground. Catlin soon went west and spent eight years visiting nearly fifty tribes. His several hundred paintings of Indians and Indian culture and his descrip-tions of Indian life became nationally known. William Goetzmann called him the "greatest of the American explorer-naturalists," a "naturalist who loved nature—the perfect embodiment of the romantic as scientist." Catlin predicted the destruction of the Native peoples and the vast herds of bison that roamed the plains, and dedicated his career to painting what he observed before it fell into what he called the "desolating hands of cultivating man."[19]

In an article published in a New York newspaper in 1833, Catlin advocated preserving for "her [America's] refined citizens and the world, in future ages," the natural and cultural trappings of the plains region in a "nation's Park, containing man and beast, in all the wild and freshness of their nature's beauty." While Catlin immodestly added that he would "ask no other monument to [his] memory" than to have the reputation of being "the founder of such an institu-tion," a leading historian of America's national parks concluded that Catlin's proposal had no direct effect on the emergence of the national-park idea three decades later. But influence in such matters is often indirect, and no less important for it. An early champion of protecting California's Yosemite Valley, James Mason Hutchings, was motivated to immigrate to the United States from England in 1844 after seeing an exhibit of Catlin's western paintings.[20]

Others eventually advocated bold measures along those lines. In *Wild Northern Scenes; or Sporting Adventures with the Rifle and the Rod* (1857), Samuel Hammond called for setting aside five million acres in the Adirondacks as a "forest forever." Around that time, transcendentalists such as Ralph Waldo Emerson and Henry David Thoreau were gaining much public attention with essays celebrating encounters with wild nature as a source of spiritual renewal and universal truths. Thoreau first pronounced his famous dictum "in Wildness is the preservation of the world" in a speech in 1851. Echoing others who had emphasized the difference between American democracy and European monarchy, Thoreau suggested, in an article published in the *Atlantic Monthly* in August 1858, that Americans, having "renounced" the authority of the kings of England, should establish "national preserves . . . for inspiration and our own true recreation." His vision of a "national commons" made him, in Lewis Mumford's words, the first prominent American to call for "publicly preserving the wild places of the continent for our own enjoyment, lest, in the ruthless quest of possessions," humans should "lose a greater part of what was worth possessing."[21]

Thoreau, who died during the Civil War, never traveled west of the Mississippi. But many of the explorers, scientists, and artists who had firsthand experience of western landscapes regarded them through Thoreau-like lenses. The New York–based artist Albert Bierstadt made several trips to the West beginning in 1859, and his huge paintings of western landscapes gained wide popularity, helped by his entrepreneurial flair. This patriotic boosterism was in sharp contrast with sensibilities on the other side of the Atlantic. The English writer and painter John Ruskin, then widely considered the leading judge of artistic taste in Europe, rejected invitations to visit America because, as he noted in 1871, he could not live, even briefly, "in a country so miserable as to possess no castles."[22]

For all this budding interest in preserving natural landscapes, neither scenery nor science possessed sufficient political appeal to affect public land policy in any significant way before the Civil War. The perceived need to expand settlement across the continent and stoke economic growth was too strong, and the nation's intensifying struggle over slavery had come to dominate American politics. That would change as the nation recovered from the devastation wrought by that conflict.

CHAPTER SIX

Divesting Public Lands to Build a Nation

THE FIRST CONGRESS THAT ASSEMBLED under the new Constitution in 1789 established four so-called cabinet departments in the executive branch—the Departments of War, State, and Treasury, and the Office of the Attorney General. One of the Treasury secretary's duties was to "execute such services relative to the sale of the lands belonging to the United States, as may be by law required." The next year, Secretary Alexander Hamilton suggested forming a distinct land bureau for that purpose, but Congress moved slowly. It was not until 1796 and 1812 that it established, respectively, the Office of the Surveyor General and the General Land Office, both under the Treasury secretary. On Capitol Hill, the House of Representatives created a standing committee on public lands in 1805; the Senate followed suit in 1816.[1]

Public land policy before the Civil War primarily focused on divestiture in service of goals on which there was broad consensus—advancing settlement by Euro-Americans and keeping the nation unified through the admission of new states. While that meant relinquishing ownership of significant amounts of public land, Congress did not simply let a free market operate. Instead, it used the divestment process to serve a number of national policy objectives, which required grappling with many details. These included how much land (if any) to transfer to states, military veterans, farmers, speculators, or others; whether to do it by gift, auction, or negotiated sale; whether payment should be in cash or on credit; whether land should be sold in small lots, farm-sized parcels, or large tracts; whether sales should have strings attached; whether revenues from sales should be shared with the states and, if so, with which states and in what proportion. Given the myriad questions involved, it was not surprising that Henry Clay of Kentucky, a dominant figure in national politics from 1810 until his death in 1852, said that of all the matters that came before Congress in this era, none was "of greater magnitude than that of the public lands."[2]

Before the Civil War, the national government took on relatively few other responsibilities. Its military was mostly occupied with securing the nation's shores and territorial frontiers and dealing with Indian uprisings. The national government also operated post offices, customhouses, and lighthouses, but its single biggest responsibility could fairly be said to be dealing with the public lands.

The responsibilities of the General Land Office—which required the skills of a politician, manager, revenue collector, auditor, and adjudicator—attracted the prominent and the ambitious. The GLO's first commissioner, Edward Tiffin, had been elected the state of Ohio's first governor and then to the U.S. Senate. His successor was Josiah Meigs, a Yale graduate, lawyer, and former president of the University of Georgia. He was succeeded by John McLean, formerly a justice on the Ohio Supreme Court, who would go on to serve on the U.S. Supreme Court from 1829 until 1861. Abraham Lincoln of Illinois made a serious but unsuccessful bid to become GLO commissioner when he was denied reelection in 1848 after a single term in the House of Representatives.

Besides being a significant force in the economy, land speculation was, from the time of George Washington, a national pastime. Given the widely scattered population and primitive means of transportation and communication, even an ample bureaucracy would have been challenged to keep up with the nation's vast public domain. But Congress's frugality meant that the GLO had a lean staff. Moreover, some of the public land laws that Congress enacted were ill designed, and the machinery for enforcing them was cumbersome. Congress was not entirely oblivious of the possibility of corruption; in 1836, it forbade GLO officials from engaging personally in public land transactions. But there were few systems or tools to check abuses.[3]

In *Democracy in America*, Alexis de Tocqueville described the U.S. government that he observed on his sojourn through the United States in 1831 as a kind of "invisible machine." After elections chose leaders, he wrote, the country might "be said to govern itself, so feeble and so restricted is the share left to the administrators." All this meant the national government superintended its vast public landholdings with a light touch in this era.[4]

Despite the many obstacles, the process of divesting title to millions of acres was not always a free-for-all and did serve to fulfill Congress's broad objectives. Along the way, principles and precedents were established, congressional restrictions were sometimes notably enforced, and experience was gained that proved useful for future policy initiatives.

AN OVERVIEW OF EARLY DIVESTITURE POLICY

Public land policy making in the nation's first few decades has sometimes been characterized as a struggle between Jeffersonians and Hamiltonians, with the former favoring freely giving public lands to farmer-settlers in order to build grassroots democracy, and the latter supporting the sale of public lands to the highest bidder, to raise revenue to pay down the national debt and finance governmental operations. That characterization vastly oversimplifies what actually happened.

At the very beginning, Congress paid lip service to the Hamiltonian idea, directing in 1790 that proceeds from the sale of "lands in the western territory, now belonging, or that may hereafter belong, to the United States" should be used "solely" for paying the nation's debts.[5] But the 1790 Congress could not bind future ones, and later Congresses used the proceeds of land sales to serve many other purposes.

Even more often, Congress simply gave lands away rather than selling them. Almost half the acreage transferred out of U.S. ownership up to about 1830 was by means other than sales. Public lands were given to states and many other entities. Former soldiers were given rights (which they could sell) to more than sixty million acres of public land. Tariffs on imports and exports, not land sales revenues, were the U.S. Treasury's primary source of funds in the nation's first few decades.[6]

GRADUATION, DISTRIBUTION, AND CESSION

In his third annual message to Congress, in December 1827, President John Quincy Adams expressed satisfaction with the nation's public land policies. By that point, some 140 million acres, or about half the total, had been surveyed, and nearly 20 million acres had been sold. He reminded Congress that those lands remaining in U.S. ownership were still the "common property of the union," and he expressed concern that yielding to calls for faster divestment could produce slapdash settlement that could undermine national unity.

Those pressing for more rapid divestment, mostly politicians in newer states, advocated what came to be known by the misleading label "graduation," which referred to gradually reducing over time the selling price of lands that remained in public ownership. At the same time, politicians in older states grew concerned that as settlement proceeded westward, the opportunity was slipping away for them to derive value from public lands that their "blood and treasure" had helped the nation acquire. The policy they supported came to be known as "distribution," which could take various forms; for example, giving older states rights to public lands that they could sell, or giving them a direct cut of the revenue from sales of public lands. Congress from time to time incorporated elements of both "graduation" and "distribution" into public land policies.[7]

In the late 1820s, a handful of members of Congress championed a third position—that the U.S. Constitution should be interpreted to give all states after the original thirteen the right to all the public lands within their borders. It was labeled "cession," since it called on the United States to "cede" title to all public lands to new states. Because some opponents of public lands in modern times have sought to revive this idea, cession's fate is worth brief scrutiny.

Proponents of cession offered a grab bag of arguments, some half-baked and some not baked at all, in support of their position. While a handful of state legislatures in newer states such as Illinois—once they were safely admitted into the union—lent "cession" some support, it was dismissed by the nation's political establishment, including James Madison, Henry Clay, John C. Calhoun, Albert Gallatin, and John Quincy Adams. Senator John Holmes of Maine noted that those in western territories seeking statehood did not call for cession, because "they well knew that it would be a great argument against their admission to the Union." Southerners were equally dismissive, one calling the claim "preposterous."[8]

The hostile reaction was predictable. Older states derived no direct benefit when lands they had helped the United States acquire were given to newer states. Even those urging faster divestment of public lands rejected cession, believing it did their cause more harm than good. Their agenda—which included more grants of public lands for various purposes, lower prices on public land offered for sale, more relief for debtors who had purchased public land on credit, and the enactment of laws giving squatters the right to purchase public lands—was premised on the fact that the national government, and not the states, held lawful title to these lands.

The views of cession held by two political titans of the era were of particular note. One was President Andrew Jackson. He was a complex character: a leader of the effort to drive Indians from their homelands, he nonetheless adopted an Indian orphan; an unrepentant slaveholder, he was also a staunch defender of the union. This last attitude led him to reject arguments put forth by John Calhoun and South Carolina in the 1832 crisis over "nullification," the claim that states could decide whether to follow national laws. Jackson was steadfastly opposed to cession, even though it bore a passing resemblance to the argument that he and some of his fellow Tennesseans had put forward in the years after Tennessee was admitted to the union.[9]

The Missouri senator Thomas Hart Benton was also a complicated figure. Born in 1782 in North Carolina, he moved with his mother to rural Tennessee after his father died, and later became a lawyer, serving a term in the Tennessee legislature. In March 1813, he was involved in an altercation in Nashville with Andrew Jackson, who was shot and seriously wounded. Not long after, Benton moved to Missouri, where he became one of the new state's first U.S. senators, and eventually the first senator in American history to serve thirty consecutive years. Notwithstanding his near-deadly encounter with Jackson, they eventually became "the closest and warmest of personal and political friends," according to Benton's biographer, the future president Theodore Roosevelt. A firm believer in manifest destiny, Benton wanted to put public lands in the hands of settlers as fast as possible. But he also believed that a primary aim of public land policy was to keep the country unified and that cession, on the contrary, would foment sectional conflict "most destructive to the harmony of the States."[10]

The coup de grace to cession was delivered in early 1830 in the course of the Webster-Hayne debate in the U.S. Senate, one of the most famous in the history of Congress. Although the dispute is remembered mostly as a discussion of the rights of states in relation to the nation, both Daniel Webster of Massachusetts and Robert Hayne of South Carolina took the occasion to cast cold water on cession. Hayne warned its advocates that their argument would "never be recognized by the Federal Government" and would only create "a prejudice against the claims of the new States," since those states would be "constantly looking up to Congress for favors and gratuities." In the face of such widespread opposition, the case for "cession" quickly sank, as the leading historian of public land policy of that era put it, "like a stone." Its fate was another demonstration of public lands operating as an agent of national unity rather than division.[11]

SQUATTERS AND PREEMPTION

One of the biggest challenges in the administration of public lands before the Civil War was how to deal with squatters, people who occupied public lands without waiting for surveys to be completed or sales to be made. As the practice mushroomed, squatters began to petition Congress for the right to obtain title, by purchase or otherwise, to those lands. The idea came to be known as preemption, because giving squatters the right to acquire the land they occupied would preempt the operation of other laws authorizing the transfer of ownership of public lands.[12]

Preemption was controversial. Jefferson opposed the idea, even though he ardently supported measures to get land in the hands of settlers, because he was concerned that it would reward scofflaws and trigger conflicts with Indians. For a time, Congress agreed. In 1807 it enacted, and Jefferson signed, a so-called ouster law making it unlawful for any person to "take possession of, or make a settlement on" any public land without the permission of the national government. This law also authorized the president to "employ such military force as he may judge necessary and proper" to enforce its provisions.[13]

From time to time, efforts were made to enforce the ouster law. In 1815, for example, President James Madison issued a proclamation warning "uninformed or evil-disposed persons" who have "unlawfully taken possession of or made any settlement on the public lands" to cease or face ejection by the army and prosecution for trespass. In 1821, U.S. attorney general William Wirt approved using the ouster law against settlers who harvested timber on public lands in Illinois, even though no federal law at the time specifically prohibited that activity. Because the United States was authorized to "hold these lands for the common good," Wirt opined, it "must have all the legal means of protecting" them.[14]

Overall, however, Congress never committed the resources that would have been needed to stem the tide of extralegal settlement on the vast public domain, and gradually it began to embrace the idea of preemption. At first it enacted limited preemption laws that applied only to existing squatters in a particular locale. Then the specter of squatter-Indian conflicts was reduced with implementation of the Indian Removal Act of 1830, which accelerated the process of settling Indians in Indian Territory, established by Congress in what is now Oklahoma.[15]

That same year, over the protest of the General Land Office, Congress granted a preferential right of purchase to all those currently occupying public lands anywhere. Then, in 1841, Congress broadened it to apply to future squatters as well. These laws had some limitations. They applied only to small tracts of already-surveyed public land to which Indian title had been "extinguished," which were not "in any reservation" previously made by Congress or by the president, and which contained no "known salines or mines." They also required the settler to erect a dwelling on the land and to "inhabit and improve" it.[16]

By rewarding squatters with title, preemption laws fostered misrepresentation and other forms of graft and contributed to an aura of corruption and maladministration in public land policy. The government's experience with squatting illustrated a common problem in the nation's first century; namely, that the legal structure Congress put in place for public lands repeatedly lagged behind reality on the ground, forcing it to play catch-up again and again.[17]

Eventually, Congress developed more effective ways to deal with that challenge, primarily by giving the executive branch—which could have a constant presence on the ground at a time when Congress was in session only for limited periods—authority to protect a broader public interest in public lands. Congress repealed the Preemption Act as part of a reform package in 1891 that also gave the president sweeping authority to reserve public lands from all divestiture laws, authority that would lead to a system of national forests that today encompasses nearly 200 million acres of public land.

PUBLIC LANDS PROVIDE A CONSTITUTIONAL RATIONALE FOR U.S. SUPPORT FOR "INTERNAL IMPROVEMENTS"

No serious constitutional objections were ever voiced about the national government's use of grants of public lands to promote public education in new states, even though the U.S. Constitution does not give Congress any explicit authority over education. The Land Ordinance of 1785 had reserved one section of public land in every township to maintain public schools, and it was generally accepted that the Constitution's Property Clause provided Congress all the authority it needed to continue that policy.

There was, by contrast, much debate about how far the Constitution allowed Congress to extend national authority into other areas of American life—for example, whether it had the constitutional power to charter a national bank. Another point of contention was whether Congress had the power to undertake so-called internal improvements—public works such as wagon roads, canals, and railroads.

Treasury secretary Gallatin believed strongly that the national government should promote the construction of such infrastructure. To justify a federal role, he pushed proposals that followed the "land grants for public education" model. The act that Gallatin crafted to authorize Ohio's admission to the union in 1803 applied 10 percent of the net revenue from sales of public land within the new state to construct a system of public roads to connect it with states on the Atlantic seaboard. It was a politically deft idea because as it expanded national authority, it produced revenue to build infrastructure to cement the bonds of union, and it made more public lands available for settlement.

In 1806, Gallatin persuaded Congress to apply revenues from the sale of public lands to construct a road from Cumberland, Maryland, through what was then Virginia (now West Virginia), to a community on the Ohio River called Wheeling. Jefferson signed the measure, regarding the public land connection as sufficient to justify the extension of national authority inside his home state. In 1808, Gallatin published a report on "public roads and canals" in which he argued that only the national government had the means and will to carry out large transportation projects.

For decades, other prominent politicians hedged or waffled on the issue, but those who sought to limit national authority were fighting a losing battle. The Erie Canal, which the State of New York built between 1821 and 1825, proved to be such a commercial success that it spawned a spate of proposals for similar projects. Using public lands to justify federal support for such projects eventually eroded political resistance, and Gallatin's view prevailed. In his *Commentaries on the Constitution,* Justice Joseph Story succinctly summarized the consensus view, writing that the public lands "may be properly devoted to any objects, which are for the common benefit of the Union."[18]

Congress added a new wrinkle in 1827 in legislation promoting the construction of a canal linking the Wabash River to Lake Erie. Working from the rectangular survey established in the 1785 Land Ordinance, it granted the State of Indiana title to alternate 640-acre sections of public land in a ten-mile-wide band, creating a checkerboard pattern of ownership. The proposed canal would bisect this band. The rationale for the checkerboard was that when the United States sold the alternating sections it retained ownership of, it could capture some of the value that the canal's proximity would add to all the lands along its route.[19]

Within a few more years, railroad technology became the transportation means of choice, moving goods and people far faster and more efficiently than roads or canals. In 1829, with only 20 miles of working railroad track in the nation, Andrew Jackson traveled from his home in Tennessee to his inauguration in the nation's capital in a horse-drawn carriage. When he retired from office in 1837, there were nearly 3,000 miles of railroads, and he returned to Tennessee in a steam train.[20]

The advent of railroads helped change the terms of the political debate over internal improvements. The master strategist Henry Clay steered legislation through Congress in 1841 that included a grant of 500,000 acres of public land to every state admitted to the Union since 1800, to finance such public works. Some politicians from states where slavery remained lawful were uncomfortable with this assertion of national authority, but John Calhoun, a fierce defender of slavery, supported a public land subsidy for a southern railway in 1846.[21]

In 1850, when more than 9,000 miles of railroads had been built, Congress took the checkerboard idea to a new level. It enacted legislation giving the states of Illinois, Mississippi, and Alabama nearly three million acres of public land, scattered in even-numbered sections across a twelve-mile-wide corridor along the route of the proposed Illinois Central Railroad from northwestern Illinois to Mobile, Alabama. The rail line also went through Kentucky and Tennessee, but those states received no public lands because the United States held none within their borders. The railroad was promptly completed anyway, raising a question about how necessary gifts of public land were to the line's construction.[22]

The Illinois Central grant legislation, promoted by Illinois senator Stephen A. Douglas, added another wrinkle. It doubled the sale price of public land that the United States retained in the checkerboard. This provision allowed Douglas to argue that the grant was financially prudent, since it purported to capture for the U.S. treasury more of the value added by the railroad.

This plan did not always work out as intended. Some of the public land in the twelve-mile corridor had already been claimed by or sold or granted to others, and thus could no longer produce revenue for the federal treasury. Already claimed, sold, or granted lands in the corridor likewise could not be given to the states, but Douglas's bill would "compensate" them for this "loss" by giving them the right to select, as "indemnity," equivalent acres of public land outside the twelve-mile corridor. This "indemnity" concept became common in many future grants of public land to states and railroads.

To retain as much land in public ownership as possible while the public lands along the route were being surveyed and the railroad was being constructed, the General Land Office began, in 1850, a practice of withdrawing all public lands along the grant corridor from sale or entry under preemption and other divestment laws. As railroad land grants became ever more generous over the next two decades, these large-scale withdrawals—often made as soon as land grant legislation was introduced in Congress, and done without its explicit sanction—helped change public opinion about the wisdom of the grants, because the withdrawals put vast amounts of public lands off-limits to entry by ordinary people, often for decades.[23]

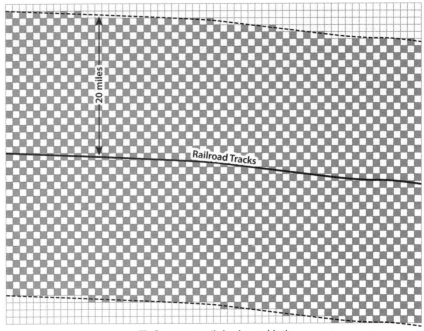

20 miles

Railroad Tracks

■ One square mile land grant block

Checkerboard pattern of land grants for railroads. The extent of the grants out from the rail line varied somewhat from grant to grant. (Diagram by Bill Nelson)

It took time for those downsides to become widely appreciated. In the near term, Douglas's legislation led to a spate of similar proposals. In the decade before the Civil War broke out, Congress gave well over 30 million acres to states, mostly in the nation's midsection, for these purposes. In 1897, Commissioner Binger Hermann of the General Land Office looked back on the Illinois Central land grant as the moment when a "rising tide" of congressional "generosity" became an "overrunning flood" of public land grants in "princely munificence" that rapidly swept "onward to the Pacific."[24]

THE SWAMPLAND ACTS

Around the same time, a loose coalition of a dozen or so states mounted a successful campaign to persuade Congress to give them title to so-called swamplands that the United States owned within their borders. Even though the preemption laws had already made large amounts of public land that was suitable for cultivation and development readily available to prospective settlers, the notion of making even more land available, while at the same time helping reduce the amount of boggy, insect-ridden, impassable swamplands, proved too alluring for Congress to resist.

Several such statutes were enacted, the most important of which was the General Swamp Land Act. Congress enacted it the same week in September 1850 when it approved the Illinois Central Railroad land grant, the Oregon Donation Act (an important forerunner of the Homestead Act), and the act admitting California as the thirty-first state.[25] The swampland acts were badly drawn up and indifferently administered.

The General Swamp Land Act, for example, simply directed the executive branch to compile lists and maps of public lands "wet and unfit for cultivation," to transmit the lists to state governors, and to convey title to lands that states claimed from the lists. Politically powerful interests wasted no time in working with indifferent or corrupt officials to wrest title to millions of acres of public land from the United States. Some so-called swamplands made their way onto lists for conveyance even though field notes by U.S. surveyors described them as "too mountainous and hilly for cultivation." The historian Paul Gates recounted a story of how the State of Mississippi gained title to thousands of acres after an agent "judged as swampland all tracts over which a boat could pass" and then hitched a canoe to a work animal and drove it across the landscape. Plagued by such shenanigans, the swamplands grant program soon became widely known for fraud.[26]

When the General Swamp Land Act was being debated in Congress, its sponsors suggested that perhaps 5 or 6 million acres of public land would qualify for transfer. In fact, states eventually selected more than 80 million acres of public land under the swampland acts and were awarded title to nearly 65 million acres, an area larger than Wyoming or Oregon. Florida got more than 20 million acres, well over half the entire state. Louisiana received nearly 10 million, Arkansas nearly 8 million, Michigan nearly 6 million, Minnesota nearly 5 million, and Indiana, Mississippi, Illinois, Missouri, Wisconsin, and California more than 1 million acres each.

A good many of these lands, being well suited for agriculture or other development, might have eventually passed out of U.S. ownership anyway under preemption or other laws. Still, the swampland acts constituted the largest single program of grants of public lands to states in the nation's history, other than statehood grants for public schools and the special case of Alaska. Supervision tightened in the 1880s, ending most divestment, although the General Swamp Land Act was not formally repealed until 1976.[27]

As for genuine swamplands, in the mid-nineteenth century only a few people—primarily, those who hunted and fished for subsistence or pleasure—grasped the possibility that draining them had costs. That all changed in modern times as the ecological value of what are now called wetlands has come to be more widely appreciated, with some scientists calling them "biological supermarkets." In the 1972 Clean Water Act, Congress required that a federal permit be obtained in order to drain or develop any privately owned wetlands anywhere in the nation. In 1986, President Ronald Reagan signed into law the Emergency Wetlands Resources Act, which extolled the "integral role" that wetlands play in maintaining the quality of American life, and in 1989, President George H.W. Bush made "no net loss" of wetlands a major policy initiative. Over the past several decades, the U.S. government has spent many millions of dollars acquiring, protecting, and restoring wetlands—including, ironically, some lands the U.S. earlier gave the states— with some becoming national wildlife refuges and other protected areas of public lands.[28]

The abuses of the swampland acts, as well as similar if less flagrant abuses under other programs granting public lands to states, eventually made Congress less willing to hand over vast tracts of public lands to them with little oversight. This growing skepticism had a significant impact on public land policy in the decades after the Civil War.

ESTABLISHMENT OF THE DEPARTMENT OF THE INTERIOR

In 1849, Congress took an important step to bring more visibility and order to the nation's administration of public lands. For several decades, it had refused to establish a separate cabinet department to handle public lands and related domestic affairs, rebuffing proposals by Presidents James Madison (in 1816) and John Quincy Adams (in 1825) to establish a "home" or "interior" depart-ment. But the idea would not disappear, and over time it gained influential supporters such as Daniel Webster and Henry Clay.

As James K. Polk's eventful presidency was winding down, his Treasury secretary, Robert J. Walker, pushed the idea forward once again. Over his nearly four years in office, Walker had experienced firsthand the shortcomings of the nation's capacity to administer its public lands. In his annual report to Congress in late 1848, he noted how the "rapid increase" in the nation's "area, business and population" was making enormous demands on the General Land Office, and occupying much of his own time, and yet such matters had "no necessary connection with" the commercial and financial matters that were the principal business of the Treasury Department. In the same vein, he pointed out that the duties of the commissioner of Indian affairs in the War Department "do not necessarily appertain to war, but to peace, and to our domestic relations with those tribes."[29]

Although by then the struggle over slavery was dividing the nation and Congress ever more sharply along regional lines, Walker's proposal to create a new Department of the Interior did not. Walker had represented Mississippi in the Senate for nine years before becoming Treasury secretary. Prominent senators including Daniel Webster of Massachusetts and Jefferson Davis of Mississippi supported it, Davis reminding his colleagues that notable southerners such as James Madison had supported the idea in the past.

Still, John Calhoun, slavery defender from South Carolina, remained concerned by what he saw as the implications of the new department's national reach. Finding "something ominous" in the expression "the Secretary of the Interior," he called the proposal "monstrous" and "one of the greatest steps that has ever been made in my time to absorb all the remaining powers of the States." Nevertheless, on March 3, 1849, the final day of the Thirtieth Congress, the Senate approved Walker's idea by a 31–25 margin, and President Polk signed it into law on his last day in office.[30]

The Department of the Interior was only the fifth cabinet department in the national government, and the first formed after the original four were created sixty years earlier. At its core were the General Land Office, extracted from the Department of the Treasury, and the Indian Affairs Bureau, extracted from the Department of War, where it had been located since its creation in 1824.

Interior's establishment was a milestone in public land policy. It reflected the new reality that the U.S. government administered a vastly enlarged, truly continental land base, and that national policy toward Native Americans was evolving away from its historic focus on conflict and security. The department's existence helped broaden the focus of public land policy beyond divestment and custodial concerns. In the future, it would assemble useful information, provide longer-term thinking, and offer many recommendations for reforming the nation's public land laws and policies to keep pace with evolving public opinion.

CHAPTER SEVEN

Reservations and Acquisitions of Public Lands

ALTHOUGH THE PRIMARY THRUST OF public land policy before the Civil War was to transfer ownership of public land to promote national objectives, early on the U.S. government sometimes decided to put some public lands off-limits to divestiture laws and hold them indefinitely in public ownership. As this happened, a shorthand terminology developed that would be used ever after.[1]

Lands acquired from state cessions, foreign governments, and Indian tribes came to be known as the "public domain." When the U.S. government acted to keep ownership of those lands, it did so by what came to be known as "reservations" or, sometimes, "withdrawals." There was, as the U.S. Supreme Court observed in a decision in 1915, "no distinction in principle between" a "reservation" and a "withdrawal," for both put public lands beyond the reach of laws that could transfer ownership.[2]

The terminology reflected the general understanding in public land policy before the Civil War that the "public domain" was available for divestment unless and until lands were "reserved" or "withdrawn." Lands that the United States later came to own by donation or purchase, which would simply be known as "acquired" lands, were not considered part of the "public domain" and were not subject to divestment laws unless Congress specifically directed it.

The practices of "reserving" the public domain and acquiring other lands developed slowly. Reservations and acquisitions made before the Civil War were much smaller than ones made later, but they show how, practically from the nation's beginning, Congress found it appropriate to hold some lands in public ownership in order to serve specific objectives. Those objectives changed as the nation's territory and population increased and its economy and culture evolved. The precedents that were created before the Civil War laid the foundation for making many more reservations beginning late in the nineteenth century, and many more acquisitions beginning early in the twentieth century.

Sometimes decisions to reserve public lands were made by Congress. Other times they were made by the president or other officials in the executive branch, often with little or no guidance from Congress. Even though the Property Clause of the Constitution gave Congress, not the executive, authority over public lands, from very early on Congress showed no interest in contesting the executive's practice of reserving specific tracts of public lands from divestment laws, even when it had not formally authorized such actions.

To the contrary, its laws often recognized and confirmed such executive reservations. In 1807, for example, Congress enacted a law maintaining reservations of public lands in the Michigan Territory that the president had earlier "set aside" for unspecified "public uses." As this showed, reservations by the executive were, in effect, part of a continuing conversation between the executive and Congress about whether specific tracts of public land would be subject to the primary policy favoring divestment.[3]

RESERVING PUBLIC LANDS CONTAINING SALT

Before the Civil War, public lands believed to contain sources of salt were often reserved in public ownership. Salt had been highly prized for millennia in part because of its use in food preservation and preparation. In the Revolutionary War, the British sought to intercept colonial salt shipments in order to interfere with the rebel army's food supplies. On the frontier, paths created by bison wandering from salt lick to salt lick helped settlers locate salt sources and guided the course of human occupation.[4]

The primary reason for such reservations was simply to discourage the establishment of private monopolies. The worry was not imaginary. In what is now Kentucky, where there were no U.S. public lands, concern had grown in the 1780s over monopolistic pricing by private owners of salt sources. The government might have tried to combat monopolistic practices by regulation, such as by requiring private owners of salt deposits to make the commodity available to the general public at reasonable prices. But it was more defensible, politically and legally, for the government to make salt widely available to the public through its ownership of the source.[5]

The practice established a powerful precedent. Ever after, protecting the citizenry from private monopolies remained a powerful theme in public land policy, and was applied to other valuable resources found on public lands, including precious minerals, sites that could readily be dammed to store water and generate electricity, and unique landscapes prized for their scenery and ecological value.[6]

As early as the 1790s, Congress enacted laws that reserved from sale all 640-acre sections of public lands containing salt springs in the western territories. In the Ohio Enabling Act, Congress granted reserved sections containing salt springs to the new state but, doubting Ohio's will to safeguard them, authorized it to lease such lands for a maximum of ten years and forbade their sale.[7]

The policy of routinely reserving public lands believed to contain salt sources continued for several decades, extending, before the Civil War, across the territory of what became nearly a dozen states. Its value was demonstrated when salt produced from publicly reserved sources in Illinois helped break the monopoly of salt producers operating on private lands in Kentucky. Eventually, as salt sources were discovered in abundance and the threat of monopoly subsided, the reservations were rescinded, and the withdrawn lands made available for divestment.[8]

RESERVATIONS FOR INDIANS, THE MILITARY, AND TIMBER PRESERVES

Beginning in the 1830s, Congress set aside vast tracts of land west of the Mississippi as "Indian country," to which many Indians were moved from the path of settlement by non-Indians. Around midcentury, as Euro-American settlement overran parts of Indian country and reached all the way to and along the Pacific coast, U.S. policy shifted toward creating separate reservations of land for Native peoples at various locations around the country.[9]

Many early reservations of public land were for military and defense needs. Congress often vested the executive with broad discretion to make such reservations and to give them priority. In 1812, for example, Congress authorized the reservation of public lands in the Missouri Territory to support local schools, but only those public lands that the president "may not think proper to reserve for military purposes."[10]

After threats posed by pirates on the Barbary Coast of northern and western Africa persuaded Congress to establish a permanent navy in 1794, it began taking steps to protect sources of wood suitable for shipbuilding. That undertaking eventually resulted in a significant program of holding forests in U.S.

ownership. The government already owned some of this land, and other tracts were purchased from private owners. As one historian, Samuel Trask Dana, put it, the program was the "first federal experiment in reservation, timber culture, and forest management" and "paved the way for" today's national forest system.[11]

In 1817 Congress directed the executive to identify "vacant and unappropriated lands of the United States" that contained "live oak and red cedar timbers," and to reserve them from sale in amounts "necessary to furnish for the navy a sufficient supply." Eventually a quarter million acres of public land in the states of Georgia, Florida, Alabama, Mississippi, and Louisiana were reserved. The program also included a reforestation component. In his last annual message to Congress, in 1828, President John Quincy Adams lauded the steps that had been taken "for the preservation of the live oak timber growing on the lands of the United States, and for its reproduction," in order to meet shipbuilding needs in "future and distant days" for commercial as well as military use.[12]

In 1831, Congress expanded and put considerably more teeth in the effort. The measure, which Andrew Jackson signed into law, not only prohibited taking timber from any U.S.-owned lands reserved or purchased to supply the navy with timber, but also penalized the removal of *any* timber from *any* U.S. lands for transfer or export elsewhere, whether or not the timber was useful for the navy, and whether or not the public lands had been formally reserved from sale. Underscoring Congress's seriousness of purpose, the law made violators subject to incarceration for up to a year, and to fines not *less* than triple the value of the trees destroyed or removed. Any ship carrying such timber could be seized and sold. One-half of all penalties and forfeitures were to be paid to informers, and the other half to the navy pension fund.[13]

The 1831 law remained on the books for several decades. It was not easy to detect and prosecute violators, especially because it was lawful for squatters to settle on forested public lands that had been surveyed, to cut down the trees in the interest of farming, and to gain title under the preemption laws. But the government did go after violators from time to time. In the 1840s, it brought more than two dozen lawsuits against thieves of timber from public lands, and in 1850 the U.S. Supreme Court upheld the law's application to unreserved as well as reserved public lands.[14]

The advent of ironclad warships in the Civil War led to the gradual repeal of the forest reservations on public lands in the southeastern part of the nation, although a few survived into the twentieth century.

THE HOT SPRINGS RESERVATION IN ARKANSAS

Hot Springs in the Arkansas Territory yielded mineralized water thought to have medicinal properties at a reliable temperature of 143 degrees. In 1820, the territorial legislature asked Congress to reserve public lands containing the springs and adjoining mountains. Twelve years later, Congress finally acted on the request, enacting legislation that reserved four square miles of public land surrounding the springs for the "future disposal of the United States," and provided that the lands "not be entered, located or appropriated for any other purpose whatever." This reservation contained a glimmer of the idea of a national park. In 1836, proponents of Arkansas statehood sought to have the reserved land transferred to the new state, but Congress turned them down.[15]

It took nearly a century and many additional steps for Hot Springs to become a national park. After the General Land Office proved ineffectual in preventing people from claiming land in the reservation under various divestment laws, Congress in 1870 established a legal process for adjudicating the claims. Some of the land within the reservation was eventually privatized and developed, but in 1877 the courts confirmed U.S. control of the public lands that remained, and finally, in 1921, Congress made it the nation's eighteenth national park. Three decades after that, a young Bill Clinton spent his childhood years in the residential neighborhood surrounded by the park.[16]

THE U.S. SUPREME COURT UPHOLDS PUBLIC LAND RESERVATIONS

In 1839, the U.S. Supreme Court addressed the legality of reserving public lands from divestment. A squatter sought title to a tract of public land near the mouth of the Chicago River in Illinois under preemption legislation that Congress had enacted in 1830. The land in question had been reserved by a series of executive actions dating back nearly to 1800 that implemented acts of Congress authorizing defense fortifications, a lighthouse, and Indian trading posts. By its own terms, the preemption act of 1830 did not apply to public lands that had been "reserved for the use of the United States," reserved from sale "by order of the President," or already "appropriated, for any purpose, whatsoever." Finding the executive actions fully consistent with this statutory landscape, the Court rejected the squatter's claim.

This case, *Wilcox v. Jackson,* was just the first of what became a long line of court decisions upholding reservations of public land from divestment. Over the next century, the executive's increasingly vigorous exercise of the power to reserve public lands from divestment laws became a major theme in public

land policy. It played a primary role in the United States maintaining ownership and control of hundreds of millions of acres of public land.[17]

ACQUISITIONS

While the United States owned an immense amount of land, it was not always
in the right places to meet particular needs, making further acquisitions necessary. This imbalance was especially prevalent in the original thirteen states,
where national landholdings were sparse.

Although the U.S. Constitution contained no explicit grant of power to the
national government to take title to private property needed for public purposes,
several of its provisions assumed or implied the existence of that power. Most
notably, the Takings Clause of the Fifth Amendment, ratified as part of the Bill
of Rights in 1791, obliged the national government to provide "just compensation" whenever "private property" was "taken" for "public use."

The Constitution's peculiar Enclave Clause, which spoke of the need for
securing state consent if Congress wanted to purchase and exercise "exclusive"
legislative authority over certain "places," was generally regarded as placing no
limits on the ability of the United States to acquire lands needed for national
purposes. Supreme Court justice Joseph Story put it this way in his authoritative 1833 treatise on the Constitution: "Surely it will not be pretended" that
a state's permission was needed for such acquisitions, he wrote, because
Congress had the constitutional authority to override state law if necessary
when acquiring land within states for "any public purposes indispensable for
the Union, either military or civil," so long as it paid for it.[18]

Congress began authorizing the acquisition of private property for particular public purposes almost as soon as the Constitution was ratified. In 1789,
for example, it launched a program to maintain and repair lighthouses and
other aids to navigation in harbors and ports throughout the country, and specified that federal support would terminate if the pertinent state had not, within
one year, ceded title and jurisdiction over the site to the United States. Other
times, Congress did not require state consent, as in 1790 when it simply authorized the president to purchase a parcel of land along the Hudson River in New
York where the fort at West Point was located.

The federal lighthouse program evolved into a major undertaking; by 1850,
the national government owned and operated more than three hundred lighthouses, including several on the Great Lakes. Some were located on land that
was already public, including land that had been owned or acquired by states
and conveyed to the nation. In at least one instance—its 1797 acquisition of ten

acres on Baker's Island near Salem, Massachusetts—the U.S. government exercised authority to take title to private land (paying just compensation) not only without the consent of the owner, but also without seeking the consent of the state.[19]

Congress took the same approach in 1799 in authorizing the executive to purchase timberlands for "future uses of the Navy." The executive implemented this authority almost immediately, purchasing two islands along the Georgia coast with two thousand acres containing valuable live oak. Not long afterward, the United States purchased cutover lands from private parties in order to reforest them, in what might be regarded as the earliest environmental restoration program undertaken by the national government. Similarly, in 1828, Congress authorized the purchase of lands in Florida that the president deemed necessary and proper to supply the navy with timber.[20]

These programs excited no controversy, political or legal. Purchasing land for lighthouses and military use could easily be justified as an exercise of Congress's constitutional powers over national defense and interstate and foreign commerce. Moreover, states usually welcomed the U.S. government's presence, which often gave local economies a welcome boost.

After many decades of practice, it was largely a formality when, in 1875, the U.S. Supreme Court confirmed the government's authority to acquire land inside states to meet national objectives. In the twentieth century, acquiring land for resource protection and environmental restoration became an important component of U.S. public land policy. (In a merger of old and new purposes for acquisitions, one of the islands the government purchased off the Georgia coast in 1799 for naval timber eventually became part of a national wildlife refuge.) Today a little more than 10 percent of the nation's public lands were "acquired" rather than having been reserved from the public domain.[21]

RESERVING AND DEVELOPING MINERAL LANDS

Metal mining has long held a special place in human history. A lust for gold drove the Spanish conquistadors to enter North America after plundering the Aztec and Inca kingdoms in Central and South America. The Royal Charter of Virginia in 1606 directed the colonists to "dig, mine, and search for all Manner of Mines of Gold, Silver, and Copper," reserving to the Crown one-fifth of the gold and silver, and one-fifteenth of the copper.[22] Before the middle of the nineteenth century, however, gold and other metallic minerals were not often encountered in U.S. territory. There were exceptions—iron ore was mined and smelted on a small scale in some of the original thirteen states and evolved into a major industry in the foothills of New York's Adirondack Mountains. Copper was mined in the Lake Superior region that the United States controlled after the Revolutionary War. A gold rush that began in Georgia in 1828 led the national government to remove Cherokee Indians to west of the Mississippi.

The nation's first mineral policy, announced in the Land Ordinance of 1785, reserved for the United States a one-third interest in "all gold, silver, lead and copper mines" on public lands that were "sold or otherwise disposed of." In 1796, Congress required federal surveyors of public land to note the "true situations of," among other things, "all mines" about which they gained "knowledge." Four years later, it authorized the president to collect information on lands containing mines, including the status of Indian title, in case the government might "deem it expedient to work" them.[23]

Beginning around 1800, Congress abandoned the approach of the 1785 Land Ordinance. Rather than reserving a one-third interest in minerals produced, it enacted an array of statutes that simply reserved in U.S. ownership public lands believed to contain minerals. Some of these reservations were of public lands with "known" mines or "lead mines," some were of lands thought to contain specific minerals, and some were of "mineral lands" without elaboration.

Lead was a mineral of particular interest. Dense, malleable, and with a low melting point, it could readily be made into bullets. American soldiers in the Revolutionary War had sometimes suffered shortages of lead, and the U.S. remained dependent on imports until the 1820s. Therefore, as with salt, public lands thought to contain sources of lead were commonly reserved from divestment. Lead was more complicated than salt to mine and process, however, and so Congress decided to enlist the private sector in the task, without relinquishing ownership.[24]

Since at least the seventeenth century, Indians had mined lead deposits in what is now southwestern Wisconsin, east of the Mississippi River, in an area that the United States acquired through the cession of western-land claims of some of the original states. West of the Mississippi, an area southwest of St. Louis had been mined for lead under the Spanish and then the French. After the Louisiana Purchase, several hundred people moved to the area, and new mines were opened. Apprised of these events, Treasury secretary Gallatin, with the support of President Jefferson, wrote the chair of the new House Committee on Public Lands in late 1806 to advocate that the national government take control of the exploitation of lead deposits on public lands.[25]

In March 1807, Congress agreed by enacting two laws. One reserved "for the future disposal of the United States" the "several lead mines" in what was then the Indiana Territory—essentially, the entire area north of the Ohio River to Canada between the state of Ohio and the Mississippi River—along with as many sections of land contiguous to such mines as the president deemed necessary. It also authorized the president to "lease any lead mine which has been or may hereafter be discovered" in the region for a maximum of five years, and provided that any future grant of public land that contained a lead deposit that had been already "discovered" would be "considered fraudulent and void."[26]

The other law was the so-called ouster legislation discussed in connection with preemption in chapter 6. It had a broader reach. Applying to all public lands, including those acquired in the Louisiana Purchase where the Missouri lead mines were found, it made any unauthorized occupancy of public lands a trespass and subjected the trespasser to fine and removal. Persons already occupying public land could remain, as tenants of the United States, but if the occupied lands included "either a lead mine or salt spring," the occupant could not exploit those resources until a lease was obtained from the president, for a term not exceeding three years, "on any such conditions as he shall think proper."[27]

The leasing program that Congress established in these laws allowed the United States to control the development of lead for military and other strategic purposes and to capture some of the profits as it was extracted and sold. The program also allowed mineral prospectors to deal with a single landowner rather than many.

Unfortunately, since this was several years before the General Land Office was created, the national government did not have administrative capacity in place to administer such a program. It was not until four years after the GLO was established in 1812 that it sought to enforce the leasing law. It had only limited success. In Missouri, many of the miners claimed to have established ownership under Spanish law when Spain had sovereignty over the area. (Such claims were not a problem in the Indiana Territory.)

In 1821, when Missouri was admitted to the union, President James Monroe put the leasing program under the administration of the War Department. Missouri senator Thomas Hart Benton attacked the reservation and leasing program and proposed that the United States simply relinquish ownership of reserved mineral lands. In a characteristically bombastic speech on the Senate floor in February 1823, he offered a comparison to the Old World that critics of public landholdings have repeated ever since, accusing the government of seeking to exclude people from a large amount of public land, just as monarchs and nobles had done on the "forest lands" on the Continent. Benton's attack did not go unanswered, for in a rare breach of senatorial courtesy, the other senator from Missouri, David Barton, accused him of misleading the public and attempting to poison the attitude of Missourians toward the national government.

Undeterred by Benton's attack, a new army superintendent, Martin Thomas, took charge in late 1824 and set about strengthening governmental authority over mineral production from the reserved lands. He insisted that producers sign leases, prosecuted violators, and greatly expanded the reservations of public lands thought to contain lead, by some accounts quadrupling them to more than 600,000 acres by 1828.

It was not long, however, before the Missouri mines entered a decline. They were outproduced by more profitable mines on public lands east of the Mississippi River in what came to be known as the Galena district, named after the principal ore of lead. Some of those public lands were in the state of Illinois, admitted in 1818, and some were in the Wisconsin Territory. The U.S. leasing program was more successful there, in part because those mines were not developed until after the United States had acquired ownership of the region and were thus not subject to claims of grants from prior sovereigns. By 1827, the Galena district accounted for most of the nation's output of lead.[28]

At that point, Superintendent Thomas decided the challenges of dealing with those in Missouri claiming entitlements under Spanish law were too great, and he recommended that the reserved public lands in Missouri be sold. Senator Barton finally agreed as well, and Senator Benton's legislation authorizing the president to sell both the "reserved lead mines" and contiguous lands still owned by the United States was signed into law by Andrew Jackson in 1829. Mining continued in Missouri after the divestiture; indeed, George Hearst got his start by mining there in the late 1840s before moving to California and greater fortune and fame.[29]

THE LEAD LEASING PROGRAM PRODUCES A LANDMARK SUPREME COURT DECISION

Throughout the 1830s, lead production from the leased public lands in the Galena district in Illinois boomed, eventually yielding, according to one estimate, nearly 100 million pounds. To simplify administration, the government took its royalty in the form of a share of the lead processed by smelters, rather than collecting it from individual miners. In the late 1830s, the United States sued the Gratiot brothers, scions of the wealthy Choteau family, based in St. Louis, for failing to provide the six pounds of "clear, pure lead" it owed for every hundred pounds it smelted from lead ore obtained from the public lands in Illinois.

The brothers hired Senator Benton to defend them. He took a hard line, arguing that the Constitution did not give the national government authority to retain ownership of public lands indefinitely. In effect, he interpreted the Property Clause as giving Congress authority to "make all needful rules and regulations respecting" only the *divestment of ownership* of public lands. The U.S. attorney general, Henry Gilpin, countered that the clause's "unusually broad" language contained no such limit. The "whole management of the public domain rests upon these few words," Gilpin maintained, and has allowed Congress to keep "timber and salt-springs" for "public use" and to permanently secure the "spots on which many of our fortifications and public buildings are placed." This consistent practice, involving "repeated instances, for nearly sixty years," fully supported the U.S. decision to retain and lease the public lands.[30]

The Supreme Court ruled unanimously in favor of the United States. The Property Clause, it said, gave Congress the same power over public lands that it has "over any other property belonging to the United States; and this power is vested in Congress without limitation." It rejected Benton's argument that the clause's use of the words "to dispose of" meant that "they vest in Congress the power only to sell, and not to lease such lands," and concluded that the lands' "disposal must be left to the discretion of Congress." It also tersely rejected Benton's assertion that the rights of the State of Illinois were involved, because Illinois "surely cannot claim a right to the public lands within her limits."[31]

The *Gratiot* decision was an unequivocal repudiation of arguments that the Constitution gives states a claim to own public lands within their borders and that Congress has only temporary, custodial authority over public lands. Although the Court ignored *Gratiot* in slavery-inspired decisions in 1845 and 1857, since the Civil War it has never called into question its conclusion that Congress's authority over public lands is practically unlimited.

CHAPTER EIGHT

Public Land Policy in Confusion in the Period Before the Civil War

IN JANUARY 1848, JAMES MARSHALL, a carpenter and former soldier, found gold flakes in a channel that his work crew had dug along the South Fork of the American River in California in order to convey water to power a sawmill he was building in partnership with Johann Sutter. The discovery set in motion changes that rippled across America, with considerable consequences for public lands.[1]

It was far from clear who owned the land at the discovery site. The recent U.S. military victory over Mexico gave it control of California, but a formal peace treaty had not been signed or ratified. Sutter claimed he had been given ownership by grants from the Mexican government in 1841 and 1845. Moreover, Indian title to the area had not been resolved.

In early February, unaware of Marshall's discovery, America's envoy in Mexico, Nicholas Trist, ignored a directive summoning him to Washington and remained in Mexico City to complete negotiation of the peace terms. The Treaty of Guadalupe Hidalgo was then sent to Washington, and the U.S. Senate, unaware of Marshall's discovery, ratified it on March 10 after a vigorous debate. Mexico gave its approval in May, and the treaty was proclaimed to be in effect on July 4, 1848. At that point, the California gold fields, along with nearly all the remainder of the territory south and west of the Louisiana Purchase, belonged to the United States—subject to resolving Indian title and claims like Sutter's.

Marshall's find, by far the largest discovery of precious metal made up to that point in U.S. history, triggered an unprecedented outbreak of mining fever. The storied gold rush swelled California's population fivefold in a single year, to 100,000; within four more years, that figure had tripled, to 300,000. Prospectors fanned out by the thousands across public lands in what John McPhee described as a "sunburst pattern—to Idaho, to Arizona, to Nevada, New Mexico, Montana, Wyoming, Utah, Colorado—finding zinc, lead, copper, silver, and gold."[2]

There was one hitch—the miners had no credible legal claim to own the minerals they were extracting or the lands they were occupying. The unresolved claims of Native Americans and those who, like Sutter, claimed to have valid grants from prior sovereigns were only part of the problem. Long-standing U.S. policy excluded mineral lands from preemption and other laws authorizing the divestment of public lands, and Congress had not supplied any legal authority to govern mineral extraction on those lands. To the contrary, Congress's ouster law of 1807 made unauthorized occupation of public lands a criminal trespass, and as recently as 1845 the Supreme Court had made clear that the United States could, like any landowner, enjoin unauthorized mining activity on public lands. Although Congress had ended the lead-leasing program in the Midwest in 1846 and authorized the sale of those public lands, that legislation was limited to that specific region. In short, the gold rush miners and their counterparts elsewhere around the West were subject to ejectment, fines, and even indictment.[3]

They were hardly troubled by their outlaw status. After all, thousands of settlers and squatters had occupied public lands in the nation's first few decades without any legal authorization, and eventually, in a series of laws culminating in the Preemption Act of 1841, Congress had permitted them to purchase the lands under certain conditions. This history offered miners some confidence of eventually getting similar treatment, especially because few in the nation's capital wanted to dampen the gold fever. In the meantime, to handle inevitable disputes, many mining camps organized informal quasi-governments and developed regulations to govern the locating, maintaining, and adjudicating of mining claims on public land.

In the summer of 1848, Colonel Richard Barnes Mason, the military governor of California, based in Monterey, toured the Sierra gold fields with his assistant, Lieutenant William Tecumseh Sherman, the future Civil War general. Mason's report of August 17, 1848, to his superiors recounted his "serious reflection" about how the government could extract a fee for the "privilege" of

mining its gold. But having lost many of the men under his command to deser-
tion when news of Marshall's discovery hit Monterey, he allowed prudence to
prevail. After "considering the large extent of country, the character of the
people engaged, and the small scattered force at my command," Mason wrote,
"I resolved not to interfere, but permit all to work freely, unless boils and crimes
should call for interference." He clearly understood the consequences of inaction. The United States was, he wrote, "entitled to rents for this land, and
immediate steps should be devised to collect them, for the longer it is delayed
the more difficult it will become." To this day Congress has never authorized
the collection of rents or royalties from mines extracting precious metals from
any public lands.[4]

PUBLIC LAND POLICY IN THE 1850S

The first important step that Congress took in response to the economic and
population boom triggered by the gold rush was to admit California to the
union. This was done hastily, before it was ever formally organized as a U.S.
territory. The act of admission was part of the famous five-part Compromise of
1850, engineered by Henry Clay and Stephen A. Douglas. It ordered the new
state to "pass no law and do no act whereby the title of the United States to, and
right to dispose of, the [public lands] shall be impaired or questioned," but it did
not resolve how much public land to give the new state. Three years later,
Congress decided to give California two sections of public lands in every township for its common schools, double the amount given to states admitted
earlier.[5]

Another part of the Compromise of 1850 was the infamous Fugitive Slave
Act, which gave southerners the protection of federal law when they ventured
outside slave states to take possession of runaway slaves. Ardent states'-rights
advocates demanded its enactment even though it was, in the historian Eric
Foner's words, "the most robust expansion of federal authority over the states,
and individual Americans, of the ante-bellum era." The Fugitive Slave Act
prompted Harriet Beecher Stowe to write *Uncle Tom's Cabin*, and the 200,000
copies sold in 1852, its first year in print, fueled the abolition movement.[6]

The turmoil over slavery helped forestall significant congressional action
throughout the 1850s on almost all subjects, including mineral policy on public
lands. On that question, the biggest issue concerned how much return the U.S.
Treasury should receive from the riches these lands were yielding. President
Millard Fillmore told Congress in 1850 that he was "at first inclined to favor
the system of leasing, as it seemed to promise the largest revenue to the

government and to afford the best security against monopolies." But because of the government's less-than-satisfactory experiences with selling public lands on credit and leasing lead mines, he recommended instead that public mineral lands be divided into small parcels and sold, with restrictions to prevent monopolies.[7]

Thomas Hart Benton led the opposition to Fillmore's proposal. Benton's son-in-law, Senator John Frémont of California, proposed legislation to establish a federal licensing scheme and require miners to pay a nominal monthly rental. It failed in the House after passing the Senate. Thereafter, distracted by the widening cleavage over slavery, Congress did nothing. The frenzied mineral rushes had captured the public imagination, and the industry anchored on public lands was now producing much of the world's gold.[8]

With the miners operating free from government interference, California Indians—whose numbers had declined by two-thirds under many decades of Spanish and Mexican rule—paid the price. The new Interior Department made an effort to resolve Indian title, negotiating eighteen treaties with more than one hundred bands of California Indians that would have set aside several million acres for them, but the California legislature protested, and the U.S. Senate never ratified them. After that, the Native Americans were basically pushed out of the way, or worse—by some estimates, thousands of Indians were killed in California, many without provocation, in the decades after the gold discovery. By the time the U.S. government began asserting some authority over mining activity on public lands in the late 1860s, most of the few surviving Native Americans had been moved to reservations of public land created by executive order or had disappeared into the general population.[9]

The mineral rushes across the West had other important consequences for public lands. To supply meat to the growing population, cattle and sheep were introduced to many thousands of acres of public lands across the intermountain West, although no law explicitly authorized it. Public lands were purchased for town sites under an obscure 1844 law that gave preemption rights to settlements that sprang up on public lands. All of this activity spurred Congress to organize territorial governments across the region, but California remained the only state in the western half of the nation until Oregon was admitted in 1859.[10]

While all this was happening, the mining industry was rapidly evolving from a treasure hunt into a sophisticated industrial enterprise. The first wave of the gold rush rapidly exhausted the so-called placer deposits that individual miners could comb from streambed gravel. By the mid-1850s, mining enterprises in California's northern Sierra began investing heavily in hydraulic mining, building miles of flumes to deliver water under high pressure through nozzles to erode entire mountainsides into gravel that was then sifted to expose gold.

Then, in the late 1850s, a remarkably pure vein of silver called the Comstock Lode was found buried deep in rock on public lands in what was then part of the Utah Territory, a dozen miles northeast of Lake Tahoe. Major capital investment was required to solve the engineering challenges involved in bringing its riches to the surface, and its development accelerated mining's conversion into a heavily capitalized enterprise using wage laborers. That did not, however, deter the industry's captains from deploying the romantic image of the solitary prospector-miner effectively to help fend off government regulation of their activities on public land.

Throughout the 1850s, just about everyone except Native Americans and the U.S. Treasury seemed to be benefiting from mining on public lands. No other government in the world, lamented Interior secretary Caleb Smith in his *Annual Report* for 1861, "has ever refused to avail itself of the opportunity of deriving a revenue from the privilege of mining such lands," which were "the property of the whole people," making it "obviously just and proper" to require the mining enterprises to "pay a reasonable amount."[11]

The western mineral rushes also accelerated interest in building railroads westward to the Pacific. There was a consensus that grants of public lands should be made for that purpose, but selecting routes for transcontinental railroads required grappling with sectional divisions over slavery. Southerners favored routes running from Memphis or more southerly cities to southern California. Thomas Hart Benton promoted a "great central national highway" beginning in St. Louis. Stephen A. Douglas suggested building several different lines, but Congress remained paralyzed until the southern states seceded from the union.

Gridlock over slavery also prevented enactment of legislation that would make public land available for free to farmer-settlers. So-called homestead acts had first been introduced in the House in 1845 by future president Andrew Johnson of Tennessee, and in the Senate in 1849 by Stephen A. Douglas of Illinois. Slavery supporters fought the idea because they knew it would be difficult to extend slavery into areas dominated by small farms, which over time could give abolitionists the political power to outlaw the heinous practice. At their behest, President Buchanan vetoed a homestead bill that Congress sent him in 1860.

PUBLIC LAND POLICY ON THE EVE OF
THE CIVIL WAR: SUMMING UP

If the increasingly bitter national division over slavery were put to one side, by 1860 the nation's public land policies could be regarded as successful from just about every perspective except that of Native Americans. Public lands had helped confirm and strengthen national authority through a vast territorial expansion. They had fostered settlement west of the Appalachians by millions of Americans. They had facilitated the admission of more than a dozen new states. They had promoted the establishment of systems of public education and had helped build a transportation network and related public works that were knitting the country together and promoting economic development. Along the way, the public lands were changing public perceptions of the national government's proper role.

Since the nation's founding, the United States had relinquished title to more than 400 million acres of land. This was, however, more than offset by huge acquisitions from foreign governments and by the resolution of Indian claims over much of the eastern half of the nation. As a result, in 1860, the nation owned nearly one billion acres of land, though some of it was still subject to resolving Indian title and claims derived from other prior sovereigns. Plainly, public land policy would remain vitally important to the nation's future.

SLAVE INTERESTS CHALLENGE CONGRESS'S
CONSTITUTIONAL POWER OVER PUBLIC LANDS

It was inevitable that the nation's deepening divide over slavery would come to be deeply implicated in policy deliberations over public lands. Defenders of slavery had long understood that the more authority the national government could exercise, the bigger the threat it posed to their interests. Congressman John Randolph of Virginia put it simply in 1824, in opposing a bill authorizing federal surveys for roads and canals: "If Congress possesses the power" to do this, he told his colleagues, it can "emancipate every slave in the United States."[12]

Slavery supporters fought every effort to restrict slavery in territories and in new states as they were admitted to the union, fearing that eventually the delicate political balance between free and slave states would tip against them, permitting the practice eventually to be outlawed everywhere. Yet Congress had outlawed slavery in some U.S. territory beginning with the Northwest Ordinance of 1787, and it possessed what seemed to be complete authority over the terms of admitting new states. As the abolition movement gained political strength and polarization over slavery grew, slavery advocates sought to persuade the U.S. Supreme Court to read some limits into the Constitution on Congress's power in these regards. In 1845 and 1857, the Court obliged by handing down two decisions that purported to greatly restrict Congress's constitutional authority over public lands and, with it, Congress's ability to limit where slavery might be practiced.

The first of these decisions, *Pollard v. Hagan,* seemingly had nothing to do with slavery. It raised the narrow, obscure question of whether newly admitted states owned lands submerged under navigable waters within their borders. Three years earlier, the Court had acknowledged that the thirteen original states owned those submerged lands because their colonial charters had incorporated English common law on the subject. It was far from clear, however, whether that rule should extend to newly admitted states. Their sovereignty derived not from colonial charters but from acts of Congress.[13]

The Court's muddled majority opinion in the case was written by Justice John McKinley at a time when issues of territorial expansion and the status of slavery in the territories, and in the new states admitted from them, were being hotly debated in the presidential campaign of 1844. Newly admitted states owned the submerged lands, McKinley wrote, but his opinion contained pronouncements that went far beyond that narrow issue. Every new state, McKinley wrote, could exercise the same governmental powers as the original states "except so far as they are, *temporarily,* deprived of control over the public lands" (emphasis added). He thus seemingly called into question the Court's five-year-old unanimous decision in *Gratiot* upholding Congress's broad authority over public lands. McKinley, a slaveholder who, as a U.S. senator from Alabama nearly two decades before, had been among the handful advocating "cession" of all public lands to new states, simply ignored *Gratiot.*[14]

The second decision came in the infamous *Dred Scott* case. Dred Scott, born a slave, had lived for years in Illinois and the free territory of Wisconsin, where Congress had outlawed slavery in 1789 by reenacting the Northwest Ordinance of 1787. Scott petitioned for his freedom when his master took him back to Missouri, where Congress had permitted slavery in the famous Missouri Compromise of 1820.

Chief Justice Roger Brooke Taney's opinion rejecting Scott's claim is mostly remembered for its assertion that at the time the U.S. Constitution was framed and adopted, not just slaves but the entire "unfortunate race" of African Americans had "been regarded as beings of an inferior order, and altogether unfit to associate with the white race, either in social or political relations, and so far unfit that they had no rights which the white man was bound to respect."[15]

But Taney went further and sought to engineer a radical shift in constitutional understanding about the breadth of Congress's authority under the Property Clause. Properly understood, he wrote, that clause applied only to those lands over which the United States had jurisdiction *in 1787*. That meant it could have "no influence upon a territory afterwards acquired from a foreign Government," which included lands from Florida to the Pacific coast.

By such reasoning, Taney did more than strike down the congressional prohibition on slavery in the northern part of the western territory, enacted in 1789 and extended in 1820. He also called into question the very source and extent of Congress's authority over the hundreds of millions of acres of land the United States had acquired since 1787. In one fell swoop, he cast into doubt the legitimacy of many hundreds of public land laws that Congress had enacted by using the authority of the Property Clause, and countless land transactions that had been made in reliance on those laws.

Chief Justice Taney's objective was clear. He aimed to foreclose the possibility that Congress might use its constitutional authority over public lands and the admission of new states to engineer a gradual, peaceable end to slavery. Amending the Constitution to override his decision was out of the question, because there were enough slave states to thwart any such effort, which required the approval of three-quarters of the states. In short, by reading into the Constitution the idea that African Americans could have no rights, and that the Property Clause had no application to territory that the nation had acquired since the Constitution was adopted, Taney's decision made the Civil War practically inevitable.

The most notorious decision in Supreme Court history, *Dred Scott* has earned almost universal condemnation from historians and constitutional scholars. Akhil Reed Amar, a Yale law professor, succinctly summarized the verdict: it "did violence to the Constitution's text, structure, enactment history, and early implementation."[16]

Dred Scott fully deserves its infamy. It ushered in human carnage on American soil never seen before or since, creating, in a phrase coined by Frederick Law Olmsted, a "republic of suffering." Like hundreds of thousands of Americans whose lives were ended prematurely, and like Taney himself— who died in late 1864 on the same day that his home state of Maryland abolished slavery—*Dred Scott*'s view of the Property Clause did not survive the Civil War. Indeed, since 1857 the U.S. Supreme Court has almost never even mentioned Taney's interpretation of the Property Clause. Even before the war, Taney's view that Congress had no power to deal with slavery in the territories had been demolished in meticulous detail by Abraham Lincoln in his famous speech in February 1860 at the Cooper Union in New York City, which by many accounts was his launching pad to the presidency that fall.[17]

CHAPTER NINE

New Divestment Policies Sow Seeds of a Backlash

THE DEPARTURE OF SOUTHERN secessionists from Congress broke a logjam that for more than a decade had stymied significant legislation regarding public lands. On May 20, 1862, President Lincoln signed into law the Homestead Act; on June 2, a major change in the Preemption Act; on July 1, the Pacific Railroad Act; and on July 2, the so-called Morrill Land-Grant College Act. These laws resulted in privatizing hundreds of million acres of public land. They also accelerated westward expansion, laid the basis for admitting more than a dozen new states to the union, and set in motion currents of change that eventually persuaded Congress to alter the primary thrust of the nation's public land policy.[1]

The Homestead Act, embodying the Jeffersonian vision of an "agrarian utopia of hardy and virtuous yeomen," allowed agricultural settlers to gain title to 160 acres of surveyed public lands for free if, over five years, they could make a living by farming the land. It included a so-called commutation feature that allowed homesteaders to gain title sooner by paying the government $1.25 an acre. The Preemption Act amendment for the first time allowed squatters to occupy public lands before they were surveyed, and eventually purchase them.[2]

The Pacific Railroad Act led to construction of the first transcontinental railroad line. It was just the first in a series of railroad land-grant statutes enacted over the next nine years that altogether allowed railroad enterprises to take title to many tens of millions of acres of public land. The laws were the ultimate victory for advocates of using public lands to foster "internal improvements."

The Morrill Act, named after Vermont congressman Justin Morrill, was the last important "distribution" law, disseminating revenues from public lands sales directly to all states, old and new, on the basis of population. Designed to promote the "liberal and practical education of the industrial classes," it supported what became known as land-grant colleges, many of which evolved into major universities such as Cornell, M.I.T., Michigan State, Penn State, Purdue, and the University of California, Berkeley. James Buchanan had vetoed an earlier version of the law in 1859. Robert Gordon, an economic historian, called it "one of the most fundamental interventions by the federal government in the process of economic growth."[3]

THE LEGACY OF THE CIVIL WAR

The Civil War transformed the nation in ways that would profoundly affect public land policy. It expanded the authority of the national government and demonstrated its capacity to meet enormous challenges. It fundamentally changed the relationship between the states and the national government so that, ever after, the operative verb after "the United States" was usually the singular "is" rather than the plural "are."[4]

The war also prompted many Americans to seek ways to ameliorate and transcend its horrors and bitter divisions—to "bind up the nation's wounds," in Lincoln's timeless phrase. For decades afterward, state and national governments were led by men who had been deeply engaged in and affected by the war. All presidents from Lincoln to McKinley fit that description, with the exception of Grover Cleveland (who, as permitted under the Conscription Act of 1863, paid a substitute to fight in his stead). So did many other politicians, from both sides of the conflict, who would come to play influential roles in public land policy.

Economic factors were also at work. Just before war broke out, the value of industrial products exceeded the value of agricultural products for the first time in the nation's history, and the first oil well was drilled. After the conflict ended, large-scale railroad, mining, and timber enterprises, most nurtured by public land policies, came to dominate many parts of the economy.

PUBLIC LAND LAWS FACE NEW CHALLENGES

By 1876, the nation's centennial year, the General Land Office had surveyed most of the more humid parts of the plains, facilitating divestment of the public lands there. In the meantime, primarily as a result of the gold rush,

Euro-American settlement leapfrogged to the Pacific coast. In the vast land-scape between those regions, Congress, spurred by mineral rushes, organized new territories in the Dakotas and Nevada in 1861; Arizona, New Mexico, and Idaho in 1863; and Montana in 1864.

Much of the remaining hundreds of million acres found in that 1,400-mile-wide stretch from the western Great Plains to the Sierra Nevada and Cascade Mountains near the West Coast possessed a different character from the central part of the country: more rugged, higher elevation, generally more arid, and somewhat more forested. These public lands were, as Wallace Stegner put it, "a fact, a problem, a challenge, and a threat."5

Here the laws that Congress had enacted to transfer public lands to settlers did not work as well, so settlement proceeded much more slowly and haphaz-ardly. Mineral rushes that followed the gold rush in California sprinkled mining-related communities around the intermountain West, while agricul-tural settlement was concentrated along streams and on valley floors where crops could be grown through irrigation. While irrigated acres in the West quintupled to one million between 1870 and 1880, they occupied but a tiny slice of the total land area.

Congress was very slow to adjust the divestiture laws to take account of these different conditions, and the uncertain application of ill-fitting laws shaped a major part of the public lands story over the next few decades. The intersection of all these forces—war-wrought changes in the political culture, industrializa-tion, economic concentration, geography, awkward laws—gradually changed public opinion and ultimately led the national government to hold on to owner-ship of ever increasing amounts of public land.

A CLOSER LOOK AT RAILROAD LAND GRANTS

In one sense, the Pacific Railroad Act of 1862 merely extended westward the decades-old congressional practice of granting public lands to support trans-portation infrastructure. The grants were made in the now familiar checker-board pattern, interspersed with lands still held by the United States in a band extending many miles on either side of the rail line. The amount of land involved was, however, on an entirely new scale, and the 1862 legislation was the first in which land grants were made directly to the railroads instead of to the states as intermediaries.

The act granted the builders of the first transcontinental line ten square miles of public land for every mile of track laid. Two years later, Congress doubled that amount. At the same time, it approved a grant making an even larger amount of public land available to the Northern Pacific Railway. Over the seven years after that, it made generous grants to several other lines.[6]

If the lands in the primary grant area had already been claimed or appropriated under other divestment laws, Congress typically gave the railroad the right to select other public lands in a secondary band extending farther out from the roadbed, as indemnity for the previously spoken-for public lands in the primary grant area. This meant that railroad land grants could extend as much as *forty miles* on either side of the tracks.

All told, the railroads were given nearly 100 million acres of public land—twenty times the area of Massachusetts. The largest single grant, bestowed on the Northern Pacific in 1864, was about the size of New England. A few states, notably Texas, did something similar. Beginning in 1854, the Lone Star State granted railroads about one-fifth of the vast amount of land it retained upon being admitted to the union in 1845.[7]

Not every member of Congress was enthusiastic about such generosity. Representative William Holman (D-Ind.), a lawyer who had served as a state legislator and judge, emerged as its most vocal critic. As early as 1864, he voiced an objection to such "stupendous" grants. In 1870, he persuaded his colleagues in the House to adopt a resolution calling for an end to "the policy of granting subsidies in public lands to railroad and other corporations." Holman's career in the House extended across five decades, from 1859 to 1897 (interrupted three times for a total of eight years), making him the longest-serving House member in history up to that time. Throughout, he remained a champion of the homesteader and an opponent of freewheeling large enterprises that tended to concentrate wealth in the hands of a few. In the 1880s, as settlement came up hard against rugged, arid terrain, Holman played a pivotal role in the movement to keep more public lands in national ownership.[8]

Public revulsion at the scale of the largesse, and the odor of corruption it exuded, led Congress to rather abruptly end the practice in 1871. A year later, the so-called Crédit Mobilier scandal, named after the company established by principal owners of the first transcontinental railroad, erupted when the *New York Sun* broke the story that company stock had been liberally distributed to influential public officials. It deepened public hostility toward railroad land grants. One transcontinental, the Great Northern, was completed from St. Paul to Seattle in 1893 without the benefit of any grants of public land. Its construction contributed to public disaffection by suggesting that the lavish gifts of public lands to other railroads were an unnecessary extravagance.[9]

William Holman, 1822–1897 (Brady-
Handy Collection, Prints & Photographs
Division, Library of Congress,
LC-BH826-1409)

Nationwide, railroad mileage grew from 9,000 in 1850 to 123,000 in 1895, tripled between 1860 and 1880, and doubled between 1870 and 1876. The journey from St. Louis to San Francisco was reduced from many weeks to a few days upon the completion of the first transcontinental railroad, at Promontory Point, Utah, in 1869, heralding, in Ron Chernow's phrase, "a new geographic unity in American life."[10]

It also hastened the subjugation and dispossession of Native Americans and their confinement to reservations. The Pacific Railroad Act directed the executive branch to "extinguish as rapidly as may be, the Indian titles to" all affected public lands; the Northern Pacific grant two years later added the qualifier "as may be consistent with public policy and the welfare of the said Indians." Charles Francis Adams, Jr., the grandson and great-grandson of U.S. presidents, did not exaggerate much when, as president of the Union Pacific, he wrote in 1885 that the transcontinental railroads "have settled the Indian question."[11]

Expectations that boom times would follow railroad construction often proved false, feeding public antipathy to the land grants. For years, sometimes many years, railroad land grants substantially reduced the supply of free public land available to farmer-settlers and speculators. This happened because of the practice of withdrawing all the public lands within many miles of the rail line from occupation—overall, more than 100 million acres—until the lands were surveyed and the railroads took title to the lands they had been given. Sometimes these withdrawals were called for in the grant legislation, but even when they were not, the Interior Department made the withdrawals and the Supreme Court upheld them.[12]

The process of transferring the granted lands to the railroads was very slow. By 1893, for example, only about 10 percent of the grants of public land authorized by the 1862 act to the Central Pacific in Utah and Nevada had been transferred to the company. Although the General Land Office bore some responsibility for the lag, railroads were typically in no hurry to take title and did not press Congress to give the GLO sufficient support to complete the task. Increasing public protest did lead Interior secretary Lamar to revoke withdrawals of public land in the secondary, "indemnity" band in 1887, restoring more than 21 million acres to entry under divestment laws.[13]

A considerable number of companies receiving land grants failed to follow through and construct railroads. Although most grants contained a deadline for completing construction, the Supreme Court interpreted the granting legislation as passing title to the recipient upon its enactment. The result was that the defaulting railroad kept title until and unless Congress enacted new legislation mandating that the grant be forfeited. Beginning in the 1880s, Congress began enacting the necessary legislation for forfeitures, and eventually, some 35 million acres were recovered.[14]

The supposition underlying the checkerboard grants was that the railroads would eventually sell the vast acreages they were granted along the route to settlers and others. A few grants required such sales and dictated their terms. Because the national government would likewise eventually make the interspersed lands it retained available for sale and settlement under divestment laws, the expectation was that the checkerboard ownership pattern would gradually disappear.

In the middle of the country, this usually worked out more or less as planned, but farther west it did not. One reason was that railroads and their lawyers found ways—helped by sloppy legislative drafting and friendly courts—to keep title. Countless disputes over land between railroads and settlers taxed the attention of the GLO and the courts. In one noteworthy decision, a majority of the U.S. Supreme Court held that the builder of the first transcontinental railway had met the terms of its grant, and put the land it was granted beyond the reach of preemption claims, simply by issuing bonds and mortgaging the granted lands as security, without making any effort to transfer granted land to settlers or others.[15]

By such devices, railroads held on to their granted lands or sold them in large chunks to timber or ranching enterprises, some controlled by railroad insiders. This was especially true in more mountainous and arid parts of the West. Such maneuvers allowed the concentration of land ownership created by the initial grants to persist. (Even today, corporate successors to the transcontinental railroads are counted among the largest private landowners in the nation.) At the same time, the United States often found itself still owning the alternating sections of land, because divestment under the Homestead Act and similar laws was often next to impossible in arid, rugged areas.

As a result, the checkerboard pattern of land ownership has remained in place on some parts of the western landscape to this day. It can create thorny issues of access rights and pose challenges to those attempting to manage large landscapes for wildlife, watershed, and other conservation values. As Jack Ward Thomas, the salty former chief of the U.S. Forest Service, once put it, "The [SOB] that invented checkerboard[ed land grants] ought to be sitting in hell on coals roasting. For a very long time. Let's face it: ecological systems don't come in squares." To overcome these problems, substantial efforts have been made in modern times to consolidate ownership through land exchanges and strategic purchases made with public and philanthropic funds.[16]

CHAPTER TEN

More Giveaways Sow More Seeds of Discontent

CONGRESS GIVES FREE REIN TO MINERS

While Congress was bestowing huge grants of public lands on the western railroads, it was also furnishing the legal basis for extracting minerals found on the public lands. It started with coal, authorizing the president to sell public lands believed to contain coal in a series of laws enacted between 1864 and 1873. Railroads were the largest beneficiary, because coal was replacing wood as their primary fuel source.[1]

Then, starting in 1866, Congress finally provided legal footing for those who had since 1848 been extracting gold and other minerals from public lands. The Mining Law of 1872, which combined and modified laws that Congress had enacted in 1866 and 1870, has proved amazingly durable—indeed, it remains in effect, albeit somewhat modified and reduced in scope.

How it came about was characteristic of the era. By the end of the Civil War, with the national debt mushrooming, the idea of ending the miners' free ride on public land was gaining support. George Washington Julian (R-Ind.), chairman of the House Public Lands Committee, proposed putting public lands with the potential for mineral development up for auction. Julian, who had been an ardent supporter of homesteading since serving a single term in the House (1849–51), returned to Congress in 1861 and served as chair of the House Public Lands Committee from 1863 to 1871. There he joined his fellow Hoosier William Holman in criticizing the railroad land grants. Julian's

William Stewart, 1827–1909 (Brady-Handy Collection, Prints &
Photographs Division, Library of Congress, LC-BH83-1893)

proposal to auction off mineral lands finally persuaded the mining industry
that it needed to drive legislation through Congress to legalize its activities and,
hopefully, preserve its free ride.[2]

The industry's principal spokesperson was "Silver Senator" William
Stewart (R-Nev.). Born in upstate New York in 1827, he entered Yale in 1848 but
left after three semesters to seek his fortune in California. Arriving via Panama
in the spring of 1850 and settling in the northern Sierra foothills, he began a
meteoric rise. Mining while studying law on the side, he was admitted to the
bar in 1852 and promptly became the local district attorney. He also chaired a
committee of local miners that developed rules to govern claim staking and
mining, an experience that later informed his drafting the national mining law.
In 1854, he was briefly the acting attorney general of California.

In the fall of 1859, Stewart moved to Nevada, joining thousands lured by the
recent discovery of the Comstock Lode. He put himself in the thick of litigation
over rights to the Comstock, disputes so hard-fought that, according to one estimate, one-fifth of the mine's $45 million output was spent in litigation. There
was considerable irony in this. Some of the mining camps had adopted rules

forbidding lawyers from representing disputants, and an 1848 guidebook to California's gold regions warned against "lawyers and licentiousness ... the whole horrid train of civilized vices and diseases." It was particularly ironic that these enormous sums were spent litigating over rights to extract a mineral deposit that was actually owned by an uninvolved third party—the United States.[3]

The Comstock Lode's riches prompted Congress in 1861 to organize the Nevada Territory, carving it out of the much larger Utah Territory (established in 1850). President Lincoln named Orion Clemens to be secretary of the territory, and he persuaded his younger brother Samuel, soon to gain fame as Mark Twain, to join him in the trek west. In 1864, seeking to secure additional votes in the Senate for an antislavery constitutional amendment, Congress admitted Nevada as the thirty-sixth state, and William Stewart was chosen by the Nevada legislature to be one of the new state's first senators.

Not yet forty, the tall, bearded, long-haired Stewart was already a millionaire, the richest man in the Senate. Mark Twain's biographer described him as "possessed by augustitude," and Wallace Stegner called him a figure "to delight a caricaturist and depress a patriot." Twain briefly served on Senator Stewart's staff in Washington, memorializing the experience (without identifying Stewart by name) in a political satire published in *Galaxy* magazine in 1868 that is still funny today.[4]

In 1866, Stewart drafted and steered through the Senate a bill that would not only legalize the miners' activity on public lands but also give them title to the land as well as the minerals. When it went over to the House, it was assigned to Congressman Julian's Public Lands Committee, where it was buried. At that point, Stewart showed his parliamentary skill by appending his mining bill to one authorizing rights-of-way across public lands for ditches and canal owners that had already passed the House. There it had gone through the new Committee on Mines and Mining, established a few months earlier. When it went back to the House with Stewart's measure attached, it was assigned back to the Committee on Mines, not the Public Lands Committee. Julian could not muster enough votes on the House floor to refer the bill to his committee, leaving him to fume as the House approved the Senate bill and sent it to President Grant for his signature. Julian's bitterness was still palpable nearly two decades later when he wrote in his autobiography how this "clumsy and next to incomprehensible bill," which was "for the benefit of lawyers" rather than miners, became law "by legislative methods as indefensible as the measure itself."[5]

The 1866 law addressed only one category of minerals—so-called lode or quartz deposits found in veins of ore locked in rock, like the Comstock Lode.

Because only larger mining enterprises had the capital to mine such deposits, protecting them was, unsurprisingly, Stewart's top priority. In 1870, Congress enacted a mining law that extended, with a few variations, the provisions of the 1866 law to placer deposits found among loose gravels typically near the surface, which were the most common target of smaller enterprises or individual miners. Two years after that, the two were fine-tuned and merged into a single law that President Grant approved on May 10, 1872.

The Mining Law, sometimes called the miner's "Magna Carta," declared that "all valuable mineral deposits in lands belonging to the United States," whether surveyed or not, were "free and open to exploration and purchase." It went on to lay out an unruly combination of minute specificity on some matters, great silence on others, and profound ambiguities on still others. For example, because it did not define "mineral" and was not limited to unreserved public lands, it literally applied to common minerals, like clay, found in places like the U.S. Capitol grounds. Its central device was an individual mining claim that could be located on public lands only after the "discovery" of a "valuable mineral deposit," but the law defined neither of those key terms. Claims generally could not exceed 20 acres in size (although placer claims of up to 160 acres could be filed by groups of miners), yet it contained no express limit on the number of claims a single entity could locate. Claims could also be located for "tunnel sites" and "millsites," each with somewhat different requirements.

Finally, Stewart included a peculiar legal doctrine called the "apex law," a so-called extralateral rights provision that he was credited with inventing when he was a lawyer in California. It permits the holder of a mining claim, under certain ill-defined circumstances, to follow and mine the discovered deposit of ore outside the boundaries of the claim, regardless of whether that land was claimed by others. It was, as one historian put it, a "recipe for legal hell."[6]

For all these reasons, Stewart's Mining Law was a lawyer's paradise. Over the next several decades, the U.S. Supreme Court was called on to decide many dozens of disputes involving it. Stewart continued to participate in mining ventures and the litigation associated with them while serving in the Senate, giving rise to the suspicion he deliberately "salted" his legislation with opportunities for personal gain through litigation, much as scoundrels salted worthless rock with traces of precious minerals to swindle unsuspecting investors.

Despite these complications, the mining industry was generally pleased with Stewart's handiwork, for he had delivered what it most wanted: namely, the right to freely access and extract minerals from public lands without paying anything—no rent, no royalty, no fee of any kind—to the owner, the United States. If a mining enterprise wanted ownership of the public land embraced within the claim, it needed to pay only $2.50 or $5.00 per acre, depending on the type of claim. But ownership was not required, because the law allowed a claimant to mine freely without it.

Much of Stewart's handiwork, including this generally free ride, has not changed since 1872. Congressman John Saylor (R-Pa.), a staunch advocate of protecting public lands while serving in the House from 1949 to 1973, was hardly alone in suspecting that a chief reason for its durability was "the gold it showers on law offices throughout the West."[7]

The Mining Law undergirded the settlement and privatization of much public land in gritty industrial areas such as Butte, Anaconda, and the Silver Valley in Montana, as well as numerous other places reborn many decades later as ski resorts and playgrounds for the wealthy—Aspen and Telluride, Colorado; Sun Valley, Idaho; and Park City, Utah. Eventually, as Congress closed other legal pathways to obtain title to public lands, the Mining Law became a favored way to wrest ownership from the United States, often for purposes that had nothing to do with mining. For many decades, the national government tolerated such abuses, not looking closely at whether the vaguely expressed requirements of the industry's Magna Carta were met.

All told, the Mining Law resulted in the privatization of more than three million acres of public land, an area about the size of Connecticut. One of its legacies is that a number of today's national parks, forests, wildernesses, and other conservation areas—reserved and protected so that their natural qualities can be enjoyed by future as well as present generations—are dotted, buckshot style, with privately owned inholdings. Many millions of public and philanthropic dollars have been spent to reacquire such lands for public ownership.

Stewart came to symbolize the corrupt nexus of politics, business speculation, and showy wealth that characterized the Gilded Age. In 1874, not long after he completed building a 19,000-square-foot mansion known as "Stewart's Castle" on DuPont Circle in Washington, D.C., he decided not to stand for reelection, because he had become deeply enmeshed in a scandal for helping peddle stock in the worthless Emma Mine in Utah to British investors in return for a share of the profits. He was never formally charged with a crime, and twelve years later, the Nevada legislature obligingly returned him to the Senate, where he served until 1905.[8]

RIGHTS TO WATER AND RIGHTS-OF-WAY ON PUBLIC LANDS

The legislation of 1866 on which Stewart grafted his original mining law dealt with two other important questions of public land policy—water and rights-of-way for canals and highways—in ways that would have lasting effects. One part of the bill allowed water-conveyance facilities like ditches and canals to be built on public lands if they were needed to fulfill rights to use water that were "protected and acknowledged by the local customs, laws, and the decisions of courts." This law was the first time Congress addressed the question of water resources found on public lands. While its wording left many questions unanswered, it began a general practice of Congress deferring to state law regarding water rights, a policy that, with some important exceptions, continues today.9

The legislation also contained a single cryptic sentence that came to be known as RS 2477: "The right of way for the construction of highways over public lands, not reserved for public uses, is hereby granted." RS 2477 was practically unique among public land laws because it required no formalities of any kind. Congress repealed it in 1976 but made the repeal "subject to valid existing rights." Because no documentation had ever been required, determining just which "rights" were "valid" and "existing" in 1976 has in recent decades become a mighty engine of litigation. Taking advantage of Congress's failure to legislate a deadline for claiming valid existing rights, the State of Utah has asserted the right to build many thousands of miles of RS 2477 rights-of-way across public lands within its borders, with the undisguised purpose of thwarting U.S. efforts to put some limits on where vehicles can travel.10

The Mining Law and RS 2477 are, along with the railroad land grants, particularly notable examples of how long-ago enactments have fundamentally shaped public lands and continue to affect them today.

THE "HUGE BARBECUE," THE "GILDED AGE," AND HENRY GEORGE

In his prize-winning intellectual history of the United States published in 1928, Vernon Parrington described the post–Civil War era as a kind of "huge barbecue," during which Congress bestowed lands and other gifts on politically influential citizens and enterprises. The description was apt. Many public land laws enacted in the first decades after the Civil War led to large businesses acquiring control of, and in many cases title to, vast amounts of public land, allowing them to wield much power over the lives of ordinary Americans. "All the important persons, leading bankers and promoters and business men, received invitations" to the barbecue, Parrington wrote, and it was "a splendid feast."11

For a growing number of Americans, the railroads were regarded as, in Ron Chernow's words, a "festering source of corruption" and a symbol of the "bucca-neering tactics of big business" characteristic of the era. Their influence on public land policy and American life was enormous; by the end of the 1880s, they employed more than 700,000 workers in a nation of some 60 million people.[12]

The era, dubbed the Gilded Age by Mark Twain and Charles Dudley Warner in their book of that name published in 1873, was one of the low points of public morality in the United States. Twain was, as the historian Ben Tarnoff put it, "disgusted by the postwar free-for-all," the "sleaze and rapacity of new industrial order, how capitalism perverted people's sense of right and wrong and perverted the mechanisms of democracy." Reaction to the Gilded Age's excesses eventu-ally gave rise to a backlash that profoundly changed public land policy.[13]

In 1871, the same year that Congress approved the last railroad land grant, a thirty-two-year-old, largely self-trained political economist named Henry George published a short book titled *Our Land and Land Policy*. From a Philadelphia family of modest circumstances, the second of ten children, George went to sea at age fifteen. A few years later, after circumnavigating the globe, he settled in San Francisco, where he became a journalist and pamphle-teer. He observed the coming of the transcontinental railroad to the city, and one of his first essays, "What the Railroad Will Bring Us," published in the *Overland Monthly* in 1868, worried that it would increase income inequality.

His musings on land policy climaxed in his most notable book, *Progress and Poverty*, self-published in 1879. It was a sensation, selling more than three million copies, one for every seventeen Americans, making him by some accounts the third most famous person of the age after Thomas Edison and Mark Twain. One contemporary compared his influence on political economy to Darwin's on science.[14]

The essence of George's argument was that the concentration of land ownership in a relatively few private hands had increased the divide between rich and poor. The American people had not appreciated those effects, he argued, because the nation's vast public landholdings—the "enormous common" that had characterized much of the nation's existence—had "formed our national character and colored our national thought." His time in the American West had taught him that most of the remaining public lands were not fit for agriculture, and he feared they would fall into a few hands. "We are giving away our lands in immense bodies, permitting, even encouraging, a comparatively few individuals to monopolize the land," with the result that in a few years, "the public domain will all be gone." Over time, he warned, the "evil effects" of "making the land of a whole people the exclusive property of some" will become obvious.[15]

The solution George advocated was to regard land and associated natural resources as societal property to be shared by all. He did not make the retention of public lands in national ownership a centerpiece of his campaign; instead, he advocated that the government levy a "single tax" on the value of land held in private hands. His enormous impact was, according to Lewis Mumford, in calling attention to "the political importance of the land," which stirred up the "torpid political and economic thought of his day." Wallace Stegner wrote that by offering his "millions of readers an analysis of economic facts," his warnings about the concentration of land ownership would "breed something close to a revolution," launching a political movement that eventually achieved fundamental change in public land policy. Influential figures in that movement such as John Muir could, according to Stephen Fox, a historian, "trace their political awakening" to George, making him the "strongest single political influence on conservation" in the movement's early years.[16]

George's philosophy was reflected in the platforms of the nation's two major political parties. From 1868 until the turn of the century, their most common refrain was, as the Democratic Party platform put it in 1868, for the public lands to be distributed "as widely as possible among the people" and "to none but actual occupants." The Democratic platform in 1872 opposed "all further grants of lands to railroads or other corporations" and called for holding the public domain "sacred to actual settlers." The Republican platform in 1876 similarly opposed "further grants of the public lands to corporations and monopolies" and demanded that "the national domain be devoted to free homes for the people."

Such sentiments helped clear the way for the idea that where the arid, rugged western terrain made homesteading impossible, public lands should be held in public ownership and used for broad public purposes. Congressman William Holman was a key proponent of the most significant step in that direction, which was taken on March 3, 1891, twenty years to the day after Congress approved the last (and one of the largest) railroad land grants, to the Texas and Pacific Railroad.[17]

CHAPTER ELEVEN

Protecting Public Lands for Inspiration

YOSEMITE AND YELLOWSTONE

THE GROWING INTEREST IN SCIENCE and the scenic wonders of the West did not leave a mark on public land policy until 1864, when a war-weary Congress took a remarkable step. It called for the permanent preservation in public ownership, for the public's "use, resort and recreation," of some thirty thousand acres of public land in California in a region called Yosemite. It was, in the historian Simon Schama's words, a kind of "redemption for the national agony" wrought by that terrible conflict. Eight years later, as the nation was struggling with Reconstruction, Congress did something similar with an area of public land fifty times larger, known as Yellowstone, in the Wyoming Territory. These actions marked the beginning of a profound change in the direction of public land policy.[1]

YOSEMITE

The 1864 legislation protected the stunningly beautiful Yosemite Valley and what was known as the "Mariposa Big Tree Grove" of giant sequoias some twelve miles to the south. Located in the Sierra Nevada mountain range a hundred miles east of San Francisco, the area had come to national attention only in the previous few years, primarily through the work of the publicist James Mason Hutchings and a handful of artists, photographers, and writers. Few non-Indians had seen the area firsthand; fewer than 150 people were known to have visited Yosemite in 1864.[2]

The first documented visit to the valley was made in 1851 by a volunteer California state militia known as the Mariposa Battalion. It was pursuing a band of Ahwahneechee Miwok Indians who were thought to have raided gold rush settlements to the west. The United States had acquired the land from Mexico only three years before in the Treaty of Guadalupe Hidalgo and had yet to resolve Indian title. The militia's campaign was but one small element in a dark chapter in U.S.-Indian relations as, building on decades of exploitation by the Spanish and Mexicans, California Indians were subjugated, pushed aside, or exterminated.[3]

Notwithstanding the dreary character of its mission, a battalion member named Dr. Lafayette Houghton Bunnell wrote later how the "grandeur" of the beautiful valley filled his "whole being" with a "peculiar exalted sensation," leaving him "in tears with emotion." While Bunnell was overwhelmed by the valley's sculpted rock walls and waterfalls—what John Muir later called its "strikingly perfect" grand design—most gold rush participants tended to view nature and Native Americans merely as obstacles on the path to material riches.[4]

The Mariposa Battalion removed hundreds of Indians to a small reservation near Fresno. Some made their way back to their seasonal ancestral homelands in the Sierra, including Yosemite Valley, where they remained for many decades with almost no official recognition. (Although non-Indians would not realize it until many decades later, the Indians had left their mark on Yosemite Valley, employing fire to keep forests open and maintain food sources during their seasonal occupation.)[5]

The Mariposa Big Tree Grove was one of a small number of stands of giant sequoias in the Sierra Nevada. The remarkable trees gained national attention when, in the early 1850s, in a grove north of Yosemite, entrepreneurial vandals stripped more than sixty tons of bark up one-third of the 330-foot height of a tree dubbed the "Mother of the Forest" and shipped it around Cape Horn to New York, where it was reconstructed and exhibited for profit. The butchery aroused protests from establishment figures such as Oliver Wendell Holmes and *Harper's Weekly*. The tree's size so strained credulity that when the bark display was shipped to London to be exhibited in 1856, it was widely thought to be fraudulent.[6]

Yosemite's pioneering publicist, James Mason Hutchings, had joined the gold rush shortly after emigrating from England. His first visit to Yosemite, in 1855, spurred him to reinvent himself as a journalist-entrepreneur. *Hutchings' Illustrated California Magazine*, which he launched in 1856, published some of the first images of Yosemite, drawn by the artist Thomas A. Ayres; some of them were reproduced in prominent national magazines.[7]

A handful of well-known visitors also publicized its wonders. In 1859, Horace Greeley published an account of his visit to Yosemite that summer in his *New York Tribune*—its circulation at the time, exceeding 300,000, was by far the largest in the country—and later in a book. Greeley called the valley the "greatest marvel of the continent" and advocated its protection, along with the Big Tree Grove. In December 1860–January 1861, Thomas Starr King, a Unitarian minister, author, and noted orator who a few months before had moved to San Francisco from Boston, published an eight-part account of his visit to the valley in the *Boston Evening Transcript*. King began using Yosemite's inspirational qualities in speeches and articles that gained wide circulation, urging people to "build Yosemites in the soul." He also worked references to Yosemite into his many orations in support of the Union's cause in the Civil War, advocacy so effective that Lincoln later credited him with keeping California in the Union.[8]

The relatively new technology of photography and its cousin, stereography—which positioned two photographs side by side in a viewing device to create the illusion of depth, providing a "you are there" experience—were crucial to bringing Yosemite's beauty to the nation's attention. The photographer Carlton Watkins designed a very large camera specifically to capture Yosemite's immense features. Thirty of his large photographs and a hundred of his stereoscope views of Yosemite were displayed in a New York gallery in 1862, following an exhibition of photographs of Civil War battlefield dead by the famed studio of Matthew Brady. They provided, in the words of the historian Hans Huth, a dramatic "contrast between the destruction of war and the healing potential of Yosemite's landscape."[9]

As the region's fame grew, so did threats, for the lands remained subject to privatization under the Preemption Act, as well as vandalism. Hutchings—who was devoted to Yosemite but also saw an opportunity to profit while sharing it with others—recognized this, and in early 1864 he filed a claim under the act to acquire title to 160 acres on the valley floor.

The effort to safeguard Yosemite Valley and the Big Tree Grove in public ownership began very soon after that. On February 20, a businessman named Israel Ward Raymond wrote California Senator John Conness, asking him to sponsor legislation to grant the lands to the State of California, but with a federal mandate to preserve them in public ownership while making them accessible to the general public.

This mixed federal-state approach was probably influenced by a number of considerations. The national government was consumed by the Civil War, which left it with no attention or money to spare. Its General Land Office was oriented toward surveys and transactions, not management. California, far removed from both the theater of war and the seat of the national government, had been a state for nearly fourteen years. Federal policy had long been to give states tracts of public land on the condition they be devoted to national objectives—like public education or public works. By contrast, it was still relatively unusual for the United States to retain public land inside states indefinitely for reasons other than those of indisputably national concern like defense.

Raymond's letter also recommended that the legislation require the state to establish a commission to govern the area, and suggested possible commissioners, most notably Frederick Law Olmsted. Since his pioneering work on New York's Central Park, the multitalented Olmsted had served more than two years as the first leader of the U.S. Sanitary Commission, a precursor of the Red Cross, which tended to sick and wounded Union soldiers. Burned out from this work, he left the commission after the Battle of Gettysburg in the summer of 1863 and moved to California, hired by New York businessmen to manage the Mariposa Estate, a large property derived from a Mexican land grant they had recently acquired in the Sierra foothills west of Yosemite.[10]

The recipient of Raymond's letter, Senator John Conness, then forty-three years old, had immigrated to the United States from County Galway, Ireland, at the age of fifteen. He made pianofortes in New York before joining the gold rush. After mining for two years, he opened a store in the Sierra foothills, selling mining supplies. The state legislature elected him to the U.S. Senate in 1863 as a Democrat, but influenced by Lincoln, he soon became a Union Republican. The Yosemite legislation was the crowning achievement of his abbreviated Senate career. A pallbearer at Lincoln's funeral, he became a strong advocate for civil rights and for Chinese immigration. After the latter stance cost him his Senate seat in 1868, he relocated to Boston, a center of Irish American life, where he lived another four decades.

In early March 1864, Conness asked the General Land Office to prepare appropriate legislation, and before the end of the month he introduced the bill. Using the language of Raymond's letter nearly verbatim, it called for protection of the "Cleft" or "Gorge" known as "the Yo-Semite valley, with its branches and spurs, in estimated length fifteen miles, and in average width one mile back from the main edge of the precipice, on each side of the valley," as well as up to

2,560 acres at the Mariposa Big Tree Grove. The total area, around 30,000 acres, was nearly fifty times the size of New York's Central Park.[11]

The legislation provided that these lands would be given to the State of California on the "express conditions" that, first, they "be held for public use, resort, and recreation," and, second, that they "be inalienable for all time." Its enactment was the first official recognition by the U.S. government that inspirational scenery and outdoor recreation had national significance, and that parcels of public land possessing those values should be permanently ("for all time") preserved in public ownership. It was, in the words of the historian Robin Winks, "a statement about national unity, continental status, and hopes for an optimistic future in the midst of a devastating civil war."[12]

The bill was swiftly reported out of the Senate Committee on Public Lands without amendment. On the Senate floor in mid-May, Conness told his colleagues there was a pressing need to preserve these wonders for "public view" and "the benefit of mankind," citing the vandalism of a giant sequoia tree in the early 1850s and the filing of preemption claims aimed at privatizing some of the land. He sought to disarm potential opponents by arguing that no federal money would be required to maintain the area, and that the state could be trusted to safeguard it because the effort was supported by California "gentlemen of fortune, of taste, and of refinement."[13]

No one spoke in opposition, and that same day the bill passed the Senate on a voice vote. The House concurred six weeks later with little discussion, and the bill was signed into law by President Lincoln before the end of June. California's governor, Frederick Low, soon named Olmsted, who would spend much of the remainder of his career promoting the restorative powers of nature for mental health, chair of the Yosemite Commission.

The Yosemite legislation had passed none too soon. Hutchings and another claimant continued to pursue their Preemption Act claims. The state's Yosemite Commission eventually proposed to give them leases, but they refused, so the commission sued to oust them in 1867. While the litigation dragged on, the state legislature proposed to grant them title to 320 acres in the valley if Congress would agree, but a bill to do that failed in the Senate. When the California Supreme Court ruled against Hutchings, he appealed to the U.S. Supreme Court.

In 1872, the Court unanimously ruled against Hutchings in an opinion written by a recent Lincoln appointee to the Court, Stephen J. Field, a forty-niner and former chief justice of the California Supreme Court. Persons like Hutchings who settle on public lands, Field wrote, do not acquire "such a vested interest in the premises" as to "deprive Congress of the power to reserve such lands from sale" in order to devote them to any of "the numerous public purposes for which property is used by the government." This was the correct approach, Field wrote, because it "preserves a wise control in the government over the public lands, and prevents a general spoliation of them under the pretence of intended settlement and pre-emption." The Court's decision ended the immediate threat. The California legislature eventually paid Hutchings for investments he had made on the land.[14]

Hutchings v. Low was Justice Field's third opinion for the Court over a five-year period that addressed the breadth of U.S. authority over public lands. In an 1867 case, *Grisar v. McDowell,* he observed that "from an early period in the history of the government it has been the practice of the President to order, from time to time, as the exigencies of the public service required, parcels of land belonging to the United States to be reserved from sale and set apart for public uses." That practice, Field noted, had been recognized "in numerous acts" of Congress and was not to be questioned. In 1869, Field wrote for the Court in *Gibson v. Chouteau* that the Property Clause vests Congress with a power over public lands that is "subject to no limitations," giving it the "absolute right" to decide their future, and states cannot "interfere with this right or embarrass its exercise."[15]

None of these three decisions mentioned the Court's slavery-era opinions in *Pollard v. Hagan* (1845) and *Dred Scott v. Sandford* (1857), which purported to limit the reach of Congress's power over public lands. The underlying message was clear. The loose statements in the *Pollard* majority opinion and the aberrational holding in *Dred Scott* had no place in the post–Civil War world. The Court would, instead, defer to the political branches on public lands matters, just as it had done in its unanimous 1840 decision in *Gratiot.*

THE PATH FROM YOSEMITE TO YELLOWSTONE

The Yosemite legislation helped produce a cascade of publicity about natural attractions found on the nation's public lands. In 1865, Samuel Bowles, the nationally known editor of the *Springfield Republican,* in Massachusetts, then widely regarded as one of the best newspapers in the nation, took the first of two months-long journeys through the American West. To mark the pending completion of the transcontinental railroad, he intended to show "how magnificent" was the country's "domain" and to illustrate its possibilities for patriotism and healing as the nation sought to recover from the Civil War. His traveling companions included Schuyler Colfax, Speaker of the U.S. House of

Representatives and a future vice president under Grant. In August, they met in the Yosemite Valley with Frederick Law Olmsted, who predicted with uncanny accuracy that within a century it would be visited by millions of people.[16]

Bowles helped inaugurate what one historian called a "new type of tourism"—not so much a "pleasure trip" as a "voyage of discovery" that "offered the chance to see and know America, to celebrate a united nation, to be an American." There followed, in Wallace Stegner's words, an "extraordinary rush of journalists and editors and artists who after the end of the war began interpreting the opening West, its natives, flora, fauna, scenery, resources, and opportunities, for eastern readers." The International Exposition of 1867, in Paris, included 28 photographs and 300 stereoscopic views of Yosemite by Carleton Watkins. The first guidebook to Yosemite, published in 1868, included twenty photographs by Eadweard J. Muybridge. The California state geologist and Yosemite Commission member Josiah Whitney, who came from a prominent family that had supplied Yale with three presidents, published a kind of travel guide called *The Yosemite Book* in 1869. Popular magazines such as *Leslie's Illustrated Newspaper, Harper's Weekly, Scribner's Monthly,* and the *Century* helped feed a growing pride in American landscapes.[17]

John Muir came to Yosemite in 1868. Born in Scotland, he immigrated to the United States at the age of eleven with his family in 1849, settling in Wisconsin. After taking courses at the University of Wisconsin, he followed his brother to Canada, avoiding conscription in the Civil War. Afterward he lived in Indiana, where a freak industrial accident temporarily cost him his sight and changed the course of his life. He soon took off on a thousand-mile walk through the war-ravaged South and visited Cuba before embarking for California. Upon arriving, he set out for the Yosemite region, where for a time he herded sheep and worked for James Mason Hutchings.[18]

In 1871, he published his first piece, in the *New York Tribune,* on the glacial origins of Yosemite Valley. Like Lincoln, he had been thoroughly schooled in the King James Bible (he reportedly could recite long passages from memory), which gave his writings an appeal few could match. "Scientist and mystic in one," in Grant McConnell's phrase, Muir was an admirer of Alexander von Humboldt and Henry David Thoreau; his copies of their books were thoroughly marked up—in his copy of *The Maine Woods,* the passage calling for "national preserves" was underlined. He got to know Henry George in San Francisco in the 1870s and led the Transcendentalist philosopher Ralph Waldo Emerson around Yosemite in 1871, Emerson remarking that the valley was the "only place that comes up to the brag about it, and exceeds it."[19]

Public sentiment for preserving some of America's scenic wonders was further nurtured by *Picturesque America* (1872–74), a two-volume set of 950 engravings based on landscape paintings. In that era, the notion of the "picturesque" had come to occupy a middle ground between the "beautiful" and the "sublime." The engravings were accompanied by essays written by William Cullen Bryant. Besides Yellowstone and Yosemite, *Picturesque America* included scenes from the Rocky Mountains, the Cañons of the Colorado, Mammoth Cave, the California coast and the Sierra, the Delaware Water Gap, the Maine coast, and a number of other places that would eventually be protected in public ownership.[20]

A tourism industry began to develop, nurtured by the railroads and the publication of numerous guidebooks. During the 1870s, the number of people taking the rail journey to the West Coast tripled, to 100,000 a year. In his celebrated book *Roughing It*, published in 1872, Mark Twain contrasted his traveling west by horse-drawn coach in the early 1860s with the ease of train travel, noting that "nothing helps scenery like ham and eggs."[21]

At Congress's direction, systematic surveys of the western public lands had resumed after the war. Some were administered through the War Department, some through the Interior Department, and some sponsored by the National Academy of Sciences, which Congress had chartered in 1863. What would become the most famous of these, John Wesley Powell's exploration in 1869–71 of the last big blank spot on the western map, the canyon country of the Green and Colorado Rivers, initially had only modest government support.

These government surveys helped turn the West, and particularly its public lands, into what Anne Farrar Hyde called a "workshop for the study of earth's creation." One example was a public spat between Josiah Whitney and John Muir over whether Muir was correct in contending that the Yosemite Valley had been carved by glaciers. Although Whitney, who called Muir an "ignoramus" and a "mere sheepherder," never abandoned his belief that the valley had been created by a cataclysmic sinking of its floor, modern geologists universally agree with Muir. Another example was a wave of interest in paleontology following prewar discoveries of bones of prehistoric creatures on a government expedition in South Dakota.[22]

Through all these means, public lands were inspiring and, by opening windows into earth's history, educating many Americans. In the process, they fostered public appreciation of the value of science and of the constructive role that the national government, and land the government owned, could play in furthering it.

YELLOWSTONE: THE WORLD'S FIRST NATIONAL PARK

The framework employed at Yosemite in 1864—combining a national preservation mandate with state ownership and management—proved to be transitional rather than enduring. In 1872, Congress took a different tack, establishing the country's (and the world's) first national park, on a large tract of scenic public lands that contained geysers and other manifestations of geothermal activity at a place called Yellowstone. It was mostly in the Wyoming Territory, with small portions intruding into the Montana and Idaho Territories. As at Yosemite, Congress acted to protect Yellowstone long before it began attracting many non-Indian visitors; only three hundred visited in 1872, according to one historian.[23]

The remote, high-altitude region had come to public notice through occasional reports of explorers and trappers over the decades before the war. By treaties signed in 1868, the Crow and Shoshone tribes had ceded to the United States their claims to nearly all of the land in the region while preserving their right to hunt on "unoccupied lands of the United States so long as game may be found thereon, and so long as peace subsists among the whites and Indians on the borders of the hunting districts." A band of Shoshone known as Sheepeaters seasonally occupied the Yellowstone region, but did not figure in the park establishment.[24]

Samuel Bowles's party visited Yellowstone on its second western excursion, in 1868, and he described it in a book published the following year. In August 1870, the nineteen-person Washburn-Langford-Doane expedition mounted the first systematic, documented exploration of Yellowstone country. The idea of preserving the region as a "national park" was reportedly hatched on this expedition in response to speculation by one of the party that great profit might be made by acquiring ownership of some of its most scenic public lands under the Preemption Act, much as James Mason Hutchings was then trying to do in Yosemite. In fact, however, the idea of creating a public park at Yellowstone had been mentioned a few years earlier, and Josiah Whitney had used the term "National public park" in referring to Yosemite in 1868.[25]

The Northern Pacific Railroad played a significant role in the Yellowstone legislation. It was then led by Jay Cooke, an Ohioan who became a Philadelphia banker, capitalist, promoter, and a principal financial architect of the Union cause in the Civil War. Seeing a profit-making opportunity by bringing tourists and adventure seekers to Yellowstone, he began making the case to officials in Washington for reserving the area permanently in public ownership.

As at Yosemite, art and photography played a key role in the campaign. Nathaniel Langford, whom Cooke had hired to publicize the area, published an article titled "The Wonders of the Yellowstone" in *Scribner's Monthly Magazine* in May 1871, describing in detail its geothermal features, mountains, canyons, and waterfalls, and predicting that "thousands of tourists" would be attracted to the area once the railroad was completed.[26] Working from Langford's descriptions, the artist Thomas Moran, an immigrant from England associated with the Hudson River school of artists, prepared woodcuts to illustrate the article.

At this point, Ferdinand Hayden became involved in the effort. A surgeon during the Civil War, he ended up as chief medical officer of the Army of the Shenandoah, commanded by General Philip Sheridan. Afterward, he led surveys in the West and was appointed director of the U.S. Geological and Geographical Survey of the Territories in 1867, around the same time that Sheridan was appointed commander of the army in the Missouri River region. (Hayden, Sheridan, and Lieutenant Gustavus Cheyney Doane were much criticized later for their harsh attitudes toward Indians, and Doane was implicated in a massacre of around two hundred innocent Indians, mostly women and children, on Montana's Marias River in 1870.) After hearing Langford lecture on Yellowstone in Washington, D.C., Hayden worked his political connections, including ties to the Speaker of the House, James Blaine, to persuade Congress to fund an exploration of the region that he would lead.[27]

Hayden's expedition to Yellowstone in the summer of 1871 included Thomas Moran and William Henry Jackson, then in the early stages of a long career photographing the American West. Upon the expedition's return, Moran's watercolors and Jackson's photographs were displayed in the U.S. Capitol, and copies of Langford's *Scribner's Monthly* article were given to every member of Congress. In October 1871, a young Henry James published an article in the *Nation* magazine criticizing the "horribly vulgar" commerce that had "pushed and elbowed to within the very spray of" Niagara Falls, and offered the observation that protecting the Yellowstone region might "help confirm the national possession of the Yo Semite [*sic*], and may in time lead us to rescue Niagara from its present degrading surroundings."[28]

It did not take long for Congress to act. The bill to create a public park at Yellowstone was introduced shortly before Christmas 1871, and the Senate approved it a little more than a month later. On the Senate floor, Samuel Pomeroy of Kansas invoked the sacred, calling on the national government to "consecrate" what he predicted would be a "great place of national resort," and to do so promptly, "before individual preemptions or homestead claims attach." Only Senator Cornelius Cole (R-Calif.) was openly skeptical, arguing that the "geysers will remain no matter where the ownership of the land may be," and calling the entire Rocky Mountain region "all one great park," most of which "never can be anything else."[29]

The bill reached the House floor one month later. There, one of its chief sponsors, Henry L. Dawes (R-Mass.), who had been an influential supporter of the Yosemite legislation, described Yellowstone as "containing the most sublime scenery in the United States except the Yosemite valley." No one spoke against the bill on the House floor, and President Grant signed the bill into law on March 1, 1872.[30]

A month later, Thomas Moran completed his gigantic eight-by-fourteen-foot painting of the Grand Canyon of the Yellowstone. The U.S. government promptly purchased it for $10,000 and installed it in the Senate lobby in the Capitol. In 1873, Moran accompanied another expedition that John Wesley Powell led into the Grand Canyon region, and later that year produced a painting of the Grand Canyon of the Colorado River that was nearly as large as the Yellowstone painting. Congress bought it for the same price and installed it alongside. Gracing the heart of the nation's government for nearly eighty years, the Moran paintings, now housed in the National Museum of American Art, were a constant reminder to politicians of the magnificence that could be found on the public lands.[31]

As at Yosemite, the political fuel propelling designation of Yellowstone as a national park was a blend. Some wanted to demonstrate pride in a national scenic wonder, and some, like Cooke's Northern Pacific Railroad, saw an opportunity to profit from tourism. Because the United States owned all the land, now that Indian title had been resolved, protecting it carried little cost and, as Congressman Dawes told the House, "treads upon no rights of the settler." No one in Congress commented on Native American use of the area, and in fact, Indians continued to use the area for hunting, gathering, and other traditional purposes for some time after the park was created.[32]

The park's size was remarkable given the eastern frame of reference of most members of Congress. At more than 2.2 million acres, it was two-thirds the size of Connecticut. Each of its four borders, drawn in straight lines, exceeded the distance between Baltimore and Washington, D.C. Its boundaries were intended to capture all of the region's geothermal surface features, but within a dozen years, serious efforts were being made to expand them.

The legislation reserved the lands from "settlement, occupancy, or sale" under the public land laws and set them apart "as a public park or pleasuring-ground for the benefit and enjoyment of the people." That language, or something very close to it, became standard in future national park legislation. As at

Yosemite, Congress's most important objective was to secure permanent public ownership of, and access to, the land. In creating the nation's first national park, Congress wrote on a blank slate, and it had no well worked-out ideas about exactly how such an area should be managed.[33]

At Yosemite, Congress had simply commanded California to hold it "for public use, resort, and recreation," leaving most details to the state commission it had created to manage the area. At Yellowstone, Congress provided more management direction, authorizing the Interior secretary to publish rules and regulations to "provide for the preservation, from injury or spoliation, of all timber, mineral deposits, natural curiosities, or wonders within said park, and their retention in their natural condition."

The legislation also allowed the secretary to grant leases of "small parcels of ground" within the park for up to ten years for the purpose of erecting buildings "for the accommodation of visitors." (The Yosemite legislation had authorized leases of similar duration but without limitation of purpose.) This showed how, from very early on, Congress contemplated a role for the private sector in managing reserved public lands. In the future, that public-private partnership model would be applied to many more lands retained in public ownership, such as those containing timber, minerals, or hydropower sites that might be exploited. By retaining ownership of the land, Congress sought to ensure that the government maintained a large measure of control over where and how private enterprise was to operate. At Yellowstone, the secretary's actions regarding the private sector would soon cause controversy.

The Yellowstone legislation, like the Yosemite legislation, provided that the government agency managing the area (the state commission at Yosemite, and the Interior secretary at Yellowstone) could expend revenues derived from the leases in managing the park, including building roads to facilitate visitation. These were early examples of "revolving funds," which bypassed the ordinary government funding process. Revolving funds were later used in other public land management statutes, with mixed results, because they incentivized revenue-generating activities even when these might collide with preservation mandates.

CHAPTER TWELVE

Pillaging Public Lands for Wood, Grass, and Minerals

AS THE NATION RECOVERED FROM the devastation wrought by the Civil War, and Euro-American influence spread across the continent, many of the resources of the lands that remained in public ownership were plundered to fuel an industrializing economy. Some profited handsomely, but many, including Native Americans confined to reservations or otherwise shunted aside, did not. As this happened, a movement arose to put limits on largely unchecked exploitation. By the century's last decade, it would be powerful enough to persuade Congress to act.

WOOD

Timber in forests across the nation was in demand for construction, fuel, and other purposes to meet the needs of a growing and urbanizing population.[1] As more of the abundant eastern forests fell to the ax, efforts to curb the worst practices and to preserve some forests began to gain traction in states such as Pennsylvania, Michigan, and New York.

In the middle of the country, where most land cleared of timber could support crops, the homestead and preemption laws allowed forested public lands to be privatized without too much difficulty, even by timber enterprises, if the General Land Office did not pay close attention. The laws of 1817 and 1831 that generally prohibited the commercial harvesting and export of timber from public lands were still on the books, and the executive branch occasionally tried to enforce them. But it could not make much headway without funding and political support from Congress.

For years after the Civil War ended, the annual reports by the commissioner of the General Land Office regularly warned of the need to control commercial timber harvesting on public lands. Sometimes the GLO would allow commercial timber operators that were stealing timber from public lands to keep it if they paid market value for it. The Interior secretary defended this policy but admitted that it was "not free from embarrassment," because no law empowered the department to sell timber.[2]

The historian Jenks Cameron described the decades after the Civil War as an "era of magnificent plundering," in which vast amounts of lumber were "looted" from public lands and "forests of literally imperial vastness passed out of public into private ownership." Divestiture laws aimed at creating a "great number of small holdings, each occupied by a sturdy pioneer home maker," had, Cameron dryly observed, "fallen considerably short of that objective" as ownership became concentrated in a relatively small number of enterprises.[3]

In the rugged, arid lands of the West, railroads needed huge amounts of timber for fuel, ties, trestles, and many other purposes. By some estimates, railroads consumed 20–25 percent of the timber harvested in the nation in the last couple of decades of the nineteenth century. When generous grants of public lands to railroads proved insufficient to meet this enormous demand, some governmental officials took a flexible view of the pertinent legal strictures. A law that Congress enacted in 1875 authorized the Interior secretary to give railroads a two-hundred-foot-wide right-of-way across public lands and allow them to cut timber "from the public lands adjacent to" the rail line. In 1883, Interior secretary Henry Teller, a former and future senator from Colorado, construed the statute as giving a railroad the right to harvest timber from public lands *fifty miles* from its tracks.[4]

The western mining industry also needed vast quantities of wood, far in excess of what it could obtain from twenty-acre claims. Although no law authorized its harvesting timber on unclaimed public lands, the industry did it anyway. In the 1870s, the popular writer Dan DeQuille called Nevada's fabled Comstock Lode "the tomb of the forests of the Sierras," because of the huge amount of timber (by one estimate, nearly one billion board feet over thirty years) that was removed from the public lands on those nearby mountains to be "buried in the mines, nevermore to be resurrected." (The ore's depth and the weak ground led to the development of what was called square set timbering.)

Rossiter Raymond, the U.S. commissioner of mining statistics, described the "wanton destruction of timber" as "one of the worst abuses attendant upon the settlement of the mining regions," leading to "denuded hillsides" and "dismal wastes upon the mountain slopes."[5]

Eventually, Congress was persuaded to take steps to curb the wholesale harvesting of timber, but for a long time it made only token gestures in the direction of forest conservation. One was the Timber Culture Act, enacted in 1873, which authorized grants of up to 160 acres of public land to anyone who would "plant, protect, and keep in a healthy, growing condition" 40 acres of trees for ten years.[6]

GRASS

By the 1870s, most of the remaining public lands were concentrated in the interior West.[7] Precipitation was usually insufficient to support farming without irrigation, and most of the lands were too rugged, and water was too scarce, to permit irrigation on a large scale. Small parcels of arable land along watercourses that could be irrigated without significant capital investment were being privatized under settlement laws. The GLO commissioner's *Annual Report* for 1875 advised that in the more arid regions, except for public lands of that character, title "cannot be honestly acquired" under the homestead laws. The vast majority also lacked valuable minerals or large stands of commercially accessible timber.[8]

In the first two decades after the Civil War, most of these lands were overrun by tens of millions of domesticated animals. As was the case initially with mining and timber harvesting, no law sanctioned the conversion of this territory into rangelands. The homestead and preemption laws contemplated crop farming in small plots, not livestock foraging over vast acreages. This legal vacuum did not deter grazers. Like miners and loggers, they simply took control of public lands without worrying about legal niceties.[9]

California, with its mild climate and abundance of available public lands, was a paradise for sheepherders; the number of sheep in the state more than tripled in a decade, to nearly 7 million in 1876. Numerous observers reported how the immense herds, along with the fires that herders set to increase forage production, ravaged the landscape. John Muir, who briefly herded sheep after arriving in the Sierra in the late 1860s, famously described the animals under his charge as "hooved locusts."[10]

In the middle of the continent, the slaughter of the bison and the dispossession of Native Americans allowed a cattle industry to develop on a vast scale, mostly to supply the burgeoning cities of the East and Midwest. Eventually, as mineral discoveries and railroad construction attracted more people to the Rocky Mountains, the cattle industry expanded to the west and intermingled with livestock, mostly sheep, being herded north from New Mexico and east from California. According to one estimate, cattle numbers in the seventeen western states and territories nearly tripled, from less than 8 million to nearly 22 million, between 1870 and 1886.

During this era, large operators—many financed by some of the nation's richest people as well as aristocrats from England and elsewhere—dominated the western livestock industry. In 1880, Cheyenne, Wyoming, claimed eight millionaires among its three thousand residents. Most operators had little interest in stewarding or gaining ownership of the public land they were using, even if public land laws had permitted it.[11]

The U.S. Supreme Court eventually addressed the grazers' legal status on public land in an 1890 decision, *Buford v. Houtz*. Its facts provide a glimpse of how arid grasslands in the intermountain West had been exploited in the previous two decades. The Promontory Stock-Ranch Company—established by George Crocker, one of California's "Big Four" promoters of the first transcontinental railroad, along with his son—acquired title to 350,000 acres of land in the northern part of the Utah Territory from the Central Pacific Railway in an insider deal. The company ran some 20,000 cattle on its land, as well as on several hundred thousand acres of checkerboarded public land. It sued to stop nomadic sheep operators from driving some 200,000 sheep across its private land in order to reach the interspersed public lands.[12]

Although the cowboy has long symbolized the western livestock industry, sheep—often tended by itinerant herdsmen for absentee corporate owners—outnumbered cattle in many parts of the interior West until after World War II. Unlike cattle, sheep require constant herding, but eat a wider variety of vegetation and need less water. Cattle operators tended to view sheep as "inferior animals raised by inferior men," in the historian Richard White's words, because the herders were often Basque, Hispanic, or Mormon.[13]

The Court's unanimous decision in *Buford v. Houtz* began by characterizing the grazers' legal position as comparable to that of miners on public lands before enactment of the Mining Law. That is, they had an "implied license" to use the native grasses of "open and unenclosed" public lands where the U.S. government "has known of this use, has never forbidden it, nor taken any steps to arrest it." The Court painted a bland picture of the consequences of the government's passivity, noting that the livestock of all comers could feed on the "nutritious grasses" found on the public and interspersed private lands "as a public common."

The Court refused to stop the sheepherders from crossing Promontory's private land because to do so would give Promontory a monopoly on the adjacent public lands. In a later case with similar facts, a lower court went further, holding that the private landowner could not recover damages even though the defendant's sheep had, on their journey to the public lands, stripped 90 percent of the grass from its land. The only option for private landowners in the checkerboard was a prohibitively expensive one, of fencing each of their 640-acre sections.[14] In some places, as the Court noted in *Buford,* homesteaders competed with both cattle and sheep owners for the use of public lands. Control over water was often a deciding factor, leading to races to acquire title to parcels of public land that contained water sources and to establish water rights under state or territorial laws. Ownership of the engine, the water, could provide effective control of the rest of the vehicle, the rangelands, which were owned by the government.[15]

During those years of livestock inundation, Congress was not completely mute. In 1877 it enacted the Desert Land Act, which authorized persons who intended to "reclaim a tract of desert land" by irrigation—that is, by "conducting water upon the same"—to enter up to 640 acres of public land, whether surveyed or not, in all of the states and territories in the arid West except Colorado. The act defined "desert land" as that which "will not, without irrigation, produce some agricultural crop," but it excluded "timber lands and mineral lands." After "satisfactory proof" was submitted that the land had been "reclaimed"—that is, had produced crops—the United States would convey title to the land for $1.25 an acre. Congress assumed that private enterprise or state and local governments would build the projects needed to furnish the water; the U.S. government simply made the land available.[16]

Over 33 million acres of public land would eventually be entered under this law, but less than a third of it was transferred out of U.S. ownership, and not many of those acres were ever actually irrigated. The works needed to capture and deliver water to arid land were generally not affordable by private entrepreneurs or state and local governments. The understaffed and underfunded General Land Office did what it could to enforce the law, but much of the land acquired under the Desert Land Act ended up being grazed by livestock. In Oregon in the 1880s, for example, the GLO uncovered what Commissioner William Sparks described as the "most unblushing frauds," where public lands claimed under the Desert Land Act were immediately adjacent to lands being claimed under the Swampland Act.[17]

The Desert Land Act of 1877 said nothing about the vastly larger amount of arid public land that could not feasibly be irrigated and was being used primarily for livestock grazing. For these lands, President Rutherford B. Hayes suggested in 1877, Congress should consider a leasing system to legalize the grazing and bring in some revenue. A few months later, John Wesley Powell, by then an official in the Interior Department, issued his *Report on the Lands of the Arid Regions of the United States,* which made recommendations for reforming public land policy.

Powell had studied at Oberlin College in Ohio and what became Wheaton College in Illinois, but never earned a degree. He taught school and then enlisted in the U.S. Army at the beginning of the Civil War, lost most of his right arm at the Battle of Shiloh, recovered, and went back to the front lines and participated in the siege of Vicksburg and the Atlanta campaign. He then became a professor of geology at Illinois Wesleyan, and in 1869–71 led celebrated explorations of the canyon country of the Green and Colorado Rivers in the intermountain West. Upon his return, he moved to Washington, D.C., where for the next nearly three decades he was a significant presence in public land policy, helping found and lead several scientific institutions, including the U.S. Geological Survey. He was, as William deBuys has noted, a "self-taught polymath" who "combined the life of mind with a life of action."[18]

Following publication of Powell's report, Congress created a Public Land Commission, with Powell as one of its members. Its report, submitted in separate parts between February 1880 and January 1881, heavily reflected his views. It recommended that public lands deemed chiefly valuable for grazing be offered for sale in four-square-mile tracts (2,560 acres).[19]

The idea was dead on arrival in Congress, killed by the concerted efforts of varied interests. It was opposed by big operators, some of whom were using vastly larger amounts of public land and who were, in the words of Ernest Staples Osgood, the leading historian of the rangeland industry in this era, "more willing to take their chances on the open range" than to bid for ownership of part of it. It was also opposed by many smaller livestock operators, who raised the specter of a "land grab" that could create "vast monopolies" on public rangeland. The commission had anticipated this reaction, noting the "deep-seated" belief of most people in the region that any system permitting the "aggregation of very large tracts of land" in a single entity is "unjust." Finally, the idea was opposed by advocates of farmer-settlers. Although much of the public land in the arid West was unsuitable for dry farming, many opposed being denied, as Osgood put it, the opportunity "to fail as well as to succeed on a quarter-section of free land." These tangled forces operated for several more decades to limit congressional action regarding livestock grazing on a goodly proportion of public lands.[20]

Around this time, a new factor, barbed wire—what some called the "devil's rope"—was coming into play. Patents on barbed wire dated to the late 1860s, but it was not until techniques for mass manufacture were developed a decade later that the industry took off—production rose from 300 tons in 1875 to 125,000 tons in 1890. By allowing vast tracts of public land to be fenced, barbed wire gave an advantage to well-capitalized livestock enterprises. In Colorado, the Arkansas Cattle Company had fenced almost a million acres by 1884. In Wyoming, fencing helped the Swan Land and Cattle Company graze 100,000 cattle on more than 3 million acres, an area fifty miles wide by one hundred miles long.[21]

By 1885, the fencing of public lands by large livestock enterprises had provoked so many complaints from homestead advocates and smaller ranching enterprises that Congress prohibited the practice. The aptly named Unlawful Inclosures Act simply forbade "all inclosures of any public lands" constructed by anyone without "claim or color of title made or acquired in good faith." President Cleveland issued a proclamation the next year ordering all offending fences to be removed, and his Interior secretary, a Mississippian named Lucius Quintus Cincinnatus Lamar, who later served on the U.S. Supreme Court, threatened to prosecute violators. Despite these brave words, the task was immense, resistance was stout, and progress was slow.[22]

The livestock invasion of public land wrought permanent changes in rangeland ecosystems in a few brief years. Albert Potter, a prominent livestock grazer in Arizona between 1880 and 1900, and later a senior official in the U.S. Forest Service, described the effect this way: "Vegetation was cropped by hungry animals before it had opportunity to reproduce; valuable forage plants gave way to worthless weeds and the productive capacity of the lands rapidly diminished." Philip Foss's assessment was even more dire: "Overgrazing caused millions of acres of grassland to become desert." Although the "chief sufferer," the historian Louise Peffer wrote, was "the range itself," Albert Potter thought "no class of men deplored this state of affairs more deeply than did the stockmen themselves," who were "victims of circumstance and governmental inaction with no course open to them other than the one they followed."[23]

Still, the adverse ecological effects of abusing grasslands tended to be less dramatic than that of razing forests; as the historian William Voigt put it, the contrast was comparable to that between a drought and a flood. Thus, the movement that was forming to curb abuses of public land resources focused much more on protecting forests and water supplies than on controlling overgrazing.[24]

The most intense phase of the livestock invasion of the western public rangelands was remarkably brief. It extended from the completion of the first transcontinental railroad in 1869 to a punishing drought in 1885, which was followed by a harsh winter in 1885–86 in the southern Great Plains and by the even more severe winter of 1886–87 in the northern regions. Large cattle operations did not feed their animals in the winter, and illegal fences contributed to a massive cattle die-off in those grim winters by preventing them from finding refuge.

The result was what the historian Donald Worster called one of the greatest losses of animal life in the history of pastoralism. In Wyoming, the number of cattle plummeted from 1.5 million in 1885 to 900,000 in 1886 to 300,000 in the mid-1890s. Future president Theodore Roosevelt, who not long before had predicted that a severe winter could cause a massive die-off of cattle, saw his brief ranching career in the Dakota Badlands end at a substantial loss, although he did not sell his ranch until a dozen years later. In 1887, Wyoming's Swan Land and Cattle Company declared bankruptcy; a local lawyer named Willis Van Devanter—who would come to have a significant influence on public land policy, first in the Interior Department and later as a U.S. Supreme Court justice—acted as its receiver.[25]

It was the end of what Louise Peffer called the "high period of the reign of the cattle barons." But it was hardly an end to the public-land-dependent livestock industry. Its character, however, began to change, as a Forest Service study later put it, "from an adventure to a business." For one thing, foreign investment declined, in part because of business losses but also because Congress passed the Alien Property Act in 1887. It responded to increasing criticism of public lands being dominated by "foreign nobility and gentry," in the words of a House Committee on Public Lands report the previous year, by restricting land ownership in the western territories (but not states) to American citizens or to enterprises mostly owned by citizens.[26]

The industry consolidated as it shrank; the Wyoming Stockgrowers Association had 416 members in 1886 and only 68 in 1890. More cattle ranchers began to grow hay to feed their animals through the winter. Some operators accelerated efforts to acquire title to significant amounts of public land by hiring agents to enter public lands ostensibly as homesteaders, pay

$1.25 per acre, obtain title under the "commutation" provision of the Homestead Act, and immediately transfer ownership to them. According to Osgood, such manipulations of the public land laws peaked during the last half of the 1880s.[27]

From a national perspective, the downsizing of the public-lands-dependent livestock industry in the late 1880s was scarcely felt. Although that industry continued to use most of the public land in the arid regions, even at its peak, the number of livestock it put on the public commons was but a small fraction of the nation's total supply. In 1880, for example, Illinois was home to a half million more cattle than could be found in all the western states combined, minus California. Over the decade that followed, the number of cattle in the nation as a whole increased by one-third despite the huge losses in the West. In fact, the production of meat from cattle grazed on public land has never been more than a small portion of the national total.[28]

All the turmoil around grazing livestock on public lands in the second half of the 1880s contributed to a growing movement to hold more lands permanently in public ownership, and to regulate activities on them to protect the larger public interest. Beginning in the 1890s, grazing on tens of millions of acres of public land in the upper reaches of many western watersheds, where grasslands and forested lands were usually interspersed, would be brought under control through the establishment of so-called forest reserves. The government did not begin to control grazing on mostly hotter, drier, less forested, lower-elevation public lands outside the forest reserves until the 1930s.

MINERALS

Mineral exploration and development flourished on public lands around the West in the decades after the Civil War. As the industry applied the engineering techniques it had developed to exploit the Comstock Lode in Nevada and moved far beyond pick-and-shovel mining, it produced a great deal of industrial pollution. The permissive terms of Senator Stewart's Mining Law helped the industry escape accountability for it, with one significant exception.

That exception involved a method that came to be called "hydraulic mining," which was used primarily on public lands in the northern Sierra in California. Developed in the 1850s, it involved spraying water under high pressure to blast mountains into silty runoff, to which copious quantities of mercury were applied to bind with gold particles and facilitate their recovery. Soon more than a million pounds a year of the toxic metal were being deployed, much of which traveled with sediments that washed downstream.

Its scale nearly defied belief. By 1880, one hydraulic mining company was moving 12 million units of rock and earth to get one unit of gold, or 375 tons for every ounce. Over the years, an estimated 41 *billion* cubic feet of debris were washed into the rivers of the Central Valley in northern California, destroying tens of thousands of acres of rich agricultural bottomlands and causing devastating floods. A contemporary observer found it "impossible to conceive of anything more desolate, more utterly forbidding, than a region which has been subjected to this hydraulic mining treatment."[29]

The industry's political power prevented Congress or the California state legislature from doing anything about it. The political paralysis finally led suffering downstream interests to file suit in both federal and state courts, alleging that hydraulic mining violated the common law doctrine prohibiting "nuisances"—that is, unreasonable interferences with another's property or with the rights of the general public. The industry's lawyers served up numerous defenses. The Mining Law of 1872, they argued, gave miners property rights in public lands that insulated them from common law regulation. The downstream destruction was simply an inevitable and necessary part of the mining. They also maintained, shamelessly, that the mercury-laden sediments actually enriched the soil downstream. Finally, they argued that shutting down the industry would cause widespread economic suffering.[30]

In separate decisions handed down within months of each other in 1884, a federal court of appeals and the California Supreme Court rejected all these arguments and effectively halted the practice. (Almost a century later, the California Supreme Court called its hydraulic mining decision in 1884 "epochal," marking California's "transition from a mining economy to one predominantly commercial and agricultural.")[31]

Today, the staggering impact of hydraulic mining can be glimpsed at the California's Malakoff Diggins State Historic Park. Its establishment in 1965 was an ironic validation of an argument advanced a century earlier by industry publicists—that hydraulic mining operations could be marketed as tourist attractions because they allowed visitors to observe "the mountain removing to the sea." A more insidious result is the millions of pounds of mercury-laced sediments that are still working their way downstream through the Sacramento River system into San Francisco Bay, accompanied by posted warnings not to eat fish caught in those waters.[32]

Protests against environmental degradation caused by mining were occasionally heard elsewhere in the West, but the mining industry's economic and political power allowed it to continue to escape meaningful governmental regulation of its operations on the nation's public lands for many more decades. Compared with timber harvesting and livestock grazing, mining, especially of precious metals, usually had a bigger economic impact. It was also concentrated in fewer areas, although its effects, especially on water quality, were often visited on much larger areas. For those reasons, the mining industry's activities were not a big factor in the growing movement to reserve public lands permanently in public ownership.

Some contemporary observers deplored the destruction occasioned by mining. Isabella Bird, an English writer and naturalist who traveled extensively through the Rocky Mountains in 1873, wrote how mining "destroys and devastates, turning the earth inside out, making it hideous, blighting every green thing, as it usually blights man's heart and soul." In an 1883 article in the *Atlantic Monthly*, the noted author Helen Hunt Jackson contrasted the mining she observed along O-Be-Joyful Creek above Crested Butte, Colorado, with the "field of purple asters" on the opposite slope. The miners, she lamented, "do not see the asters."[33]

Congress did not begin to take steps to control the pollution produced by hard-rock mines and processing facilities until the late twentieth century, after the environmental and human health effects had become more widely appreciated. The Mining Law's legacy includes many thousands of abandoned mine sites on public lands, as well as dozens of areas of public and formerly public land that have been designated as so-called Superfund sites, prioritized for remediation under the Comprehensive Environmental Response, Compensation, and Liability Act, which Congress adopted in 1980. Estimates of the total cost of remediation, most of which will be borne by the federal and state governments, run into tens of billions of dollars; some sites will require water treatment in perpetuity. Meanwhile, the hard-rock mining industry continues to extract minerals from public lands royalty- and rent-free, thanks to the Mining Law of 1872.[34]

CHAPTER THIRTEEN

Efforts Launched to Protect Public Forest Land

PROTECTING WOODLANDS BECAME a dominant theme of the backlash against the wholesale exploitation of public lands. America's forests had long been celebrated as a "national treasure," as a prominent Lutheran minister named Nicholas Collin put it in 1789, that deserved the "solicitous care of the patriotic philosopher and politician." Before the Civil War, other high-profile figures such as James Fenimore Cooper, John James Audubon, and William Cullen Bryant had advocated forest conservation.[1]

The idea was given a powerful push in 1864 with the publication of a book titled *Man and Nature, or, Physical Geography as Modified by Human Action*. It was written by a remarkable Vermonter, George Perkins Marsh, who, as a three-term member of Congress in the 1840s, had helped found and guide the Smithsonian Institution. Marsh was, according to his biographer, the "broadest scholar of his day." Multilingual, he had written a pathbreaking book on the origins and development of the English language, practiced law, and served as a diplomat in Constantinople before being appointed ambassador to Italy by President Lincoln in 1861. He remained in that post until his death twenty-one years later, the longest-serving chief of mission in U.S. history.[2]

Marsh's book went through four printings in seven years before he revised and republished it twice under the title *The Earth as Modified by Human Action* (1874, 1884). Inspired by the work of Alexander von Humboldt—an entire section of his library was dedicated to the Prussian, whom he called the "great apostle"—Marsh drew upon his observations in Vermont and the Mediterranean to describe how forest destruction affected watersheds. Previously, disasters like floods and landslides had generally been viewed as isolated acts of God, like earthquakes or volcanic eruptions. Marsh, by contrast, treated humankind as "an active geological agent," as Lewis Mumford put it, whose actions could bring desolation. Like Charles Darwin, who only five years before had published *On the Origin of Species,* Marsh helped propel scientific study away from merely describing and classifying the natural world toward exploring relationships between species and their environments.[3]

Marsh's political experience made his scholarship, in William Cronon's words, "never merely academic but always pointed toward the wider world of affairs," and he sounded an alarm. "The earth is fast become an unfit home for its noblest inhabitant," he wrote. In one of his most famous passages, he noted that humans were "breaking up the floor and wainscoting and doors and window frames of our dwelling, for fuel," which seems eerily prescient given the modern scientific consensus about the dire effects of the buildup of greenhouse gases in the atmosphere.[4]

Using a term that Thomas Jefferson had employed a half century earlier, Marsh lamented that humans had "forgotten that the earth was given to [them] for *usufruct* alone, not for consumption, still less for profligate waste." "The world cannot afford to wait," he wrote, "till the slow and sure progress of exact science has taught it a better economy." Unless humans took prompt steps to change their improvident ways, the earth could be reduced "to such a condition of impoverished productiveness, of shattered surface, of climatic excess, as to threaten the depravation, barbarism, and perhaps even extinction of the species."[5]

Marsh's years in public life had given him a keen appreciation of the political obstacles in the path of reform, and he warned that the threats he described "demand new triumphs of mind over matter." In a section titled "Royal Forests and Game Laws," he drew attention to the European tradition of the nobility controlling forests and hunting for their own purposes, and severely punishing commoners for logging or poaching. While such measures helped preserve forests and wildlife, he observed, they came at a high political price, for they led the general public to associate stewardship with "the abuses of feudalism," and blinded them "to the still greater . . . mischiefs" that destruction of forests would visit on mankind. Although he did not specifically advocate that the national government hold forested lands in public ownership, in his 1874 revision he noted that "public property is not sufficiently respected in the United States," and that it "is desirable that some large and easily accessible region of

American soil should remain as far as possible in its primitive condition, at once a museum for the instruction of the students, a garden for the recreation of the lovers of nature, and an asylum where indigenous trees . . . plants . . . [and] beasts may dwell and perpetuate their kind."[6]

Marsh's influence grew with each new edition. His marriage of scientific inquiry and public policy made his book, in Andrea Wulf's description, the "first work of natural history fundamentally to influence American politics," and led Mumford to call him "the fountainhead of the conservation movement."[7]

CONGRESS BEGINS DEBATING PUBLIC LAND FOREST POLICY

In 1872, Congressman Richard Haldeman (D-Pa.) sponsored a bill that would have required all future recipients of public land grants to keep at least 10 percent of the land in "timber trees" in perpetuity, or else the land would be forfeited back to the United States. Citing *Man and Nature,* Haldeman told his colleagues that the "wholesale destruction of forests now going on in this country" had to stop, because the "character" of "the American people is largely dependent upon the amount and proper distribution of her future forests." Other supporters argued that the bill would help protect watersheds, reduce flood risk, support irrigation of arid regions, and even, by supporting more birds, reduce populations of destructive insects. The House rejected Haldeman's proposal, but only by a narrow margin after a vigorous debate.[8]

In February 1876, John Muir published his first call for the government to take steps to preserve the nation's forests, which he called, characteristically, "God's first Temples." Later that year, Congressman Greenbury Lafayette Fort (R-Ill.), a Union Army veteran, introduced a bill entitled "For the Preservation of the Forests of the National Domain." It would have reserved from public entry and sale "all public timber-lands adjacent to the sources" of all the nation's rivers, in order to prevent them from becoming "scant of water." It called for a three-person commission—the chief of the Army Corps of Engineers, the commissioner of agriculture, and the head of the Smithsonian Institution—to submit recommendations to Congress on how best to manage these lands. Fort's proposal never made it out of committee, but it was the first bill calling for the establishment of what came to be known as "forest reserves." Over the next decade and a half, at least one such bill was introduced in every Congress.[9]

In 1875, a group of citizens organized the American Forestry Association to promote forest science and advocate for forestry conservation. In 1876, Congress established a special office in the Department of Agriculture to examine the condition of the nation's forests. Franklin Hough, whose 1873 paper "On the Duty of Governments in the Preservation of Forests" had gained considerable attention, was assigned to the task. His 650-page *Report on Forestry*, completed in 1877, contained what one economic historian called the "first good estimates of U.S. timber consumption" and documented timber thefts, or "depredations," on public lands. Congress had 25,000 copies of Hough's report distributed, and he became the first chief of the Agriculture Department's Division of Forestry. More information about the state of the nation's forests came in an 1880 report titled *Forests of North America*, prepared by the Harvard professor Charles Sargent for the Tenth U.S. Census. It drew particular attention to the rapid harvesting of remaining stands of white pine in the Great Lakes states.[10]

Over in the Interior Department's General Land Office, Commissioner James Alexander Williamson was devoting considerable attention to the forestry question. A lawyer from Iowa twice wounded in the Civil War, for which he earned the Medal of Honor, Williamson had been appointed by President Grant in 1876 and had stayed on when Rutherford Hayes became president. In his *Annual Report* for 1877, Williamson cited Marsh's teachings in concluding that deforestation on the public lands was having "disastrous" effects.[11]

Hayes's Interior secretary, Carl Schurz, an immigrant from Germany who had led an eventful life as a journalist, diplomat, Civil War general, and U.S. senator from Missouri, devoted nearly two dozen paragraphs to the matter in his first *Annual Report*. Expressing "alarm" at the "rapidity with which this country is being stripped of its forests," he called for permanent retention of all forested public lands in public ownership, except those that could be made fit for farming, and for selling timber for harvest under close governmental supervision. The Congress that enacts "effective laws for the preservation of our forests," he concluded, "will be ranked by future generations in this country among its greatest benefactors." In his annual message to Congress later that year, Hayes called for prompt enactment of Schurz's recommendations.[12]

In 1878, Senator Preston B. Plumb (R-Kans.) introduced legislation to carry out Schurz's recommendation. When his bill languished in committee, Schurz and Williamson sought to force action by vigorously enforcing the 1817 and 1831 laws that prohibited commercial logging on public lands. Their move backfired, because Congress enacted two laws that had the opposite effect.

The first, the Timber and Stone Act of 1878, authorized the Interior Department to sell, in 160-acre parcels for $2.50 per acre, unreserved public lands that were "valuable chiefly for" timber or stone and "unfit for cultivation."

The act, which applied only to timber-rich California, Oregon, and the Washington Territory (plus Nevada), fell prey to evasion and manipulation. One lumber company reportedly offered $50 to any crew member of any ship stopping at any port in the redwood region of northern California who would go ashore, lay claim to 160 acres under the act, and immediately deed the land to the company. In several regrettable decisions, the U.S. Supreme Court made it very difficult to nullify sales of public land obtained through such manipulations. One such decision held that sales could not be set aside without "clear, unequivocal and convincing" proof of a specific prior agreement among co-conspirators to evade the law, a demand impossible to satisfy if, as was usually the case, the conspirators had scattered.[13]

The second law, the Free Timber Act, licensed residents of Colorado, Nevada, and the territories of the intermountain West to harvest timber from public mineral lands, with the United States retaining title to the land. It took a small step toward conservation by authorizing the Interior secretary to regulate the harvest "for the protection of the undergrowth, and for other purposes," and by excluding railroads from its operation.[14]

President Hayes reluctantly signed these bills into law, but his next message to Congress again called the "rapid destruction of our forests" an "evil fraught with the gravest consequences," one that made "preservation of the timber on the public lands" a "matter of urgent public necessity." In his next three annual reports, Schurz harshly criticized the Timber and Stone Act, and once again echoed Marsh in warning that stripping mountainsides of timber could have devastating effects.[15]

In the debates over forest policy in the 1870s, one question that captured some attention was whether indiscriminate deforestation could alter the climate. Some argued that the relative lack of precipitation in more arid, less forested western regions was the result of the absence of forests, rather than the other way around, and advocated planting forests in order to enhance rainfall. But information about the relationship between forests and precipitation was, as George Perkins Marsh wrote, "vague and contradictory." A consensus of experts, reporting in an 1879 article in the *Nation* magazine, found no evidence that precipitation was affected by "the presence or absence of forests."[16]

In any event, attacking the plunder of publicly owned forests for private profit was more influential politically than concerns about deforestation's possible effects on climate. Although the Supreme Court had put obstacles in the way of holding abusers of public land laws accountable, it occasionally expressed frustration at Congress's failure to devise effective ways to tackle the problem. A unanimous decision in 1882 noted that it had "long been a matter of complaint" that "depredations" visited upon the "immense forest lands of the government" are "rapidly destroying the finest forests in the world." The "liberality" of laws like the Free Timber Act, it lamented, "has been used to screen the lawless depredator who destroys and sells for profit."[17]

The experts writing in the *Nation* made another powerful argument for forest preservation—that forests "play the most important part in retaining and distributing" precipitation that does fall, so that as an area "becomes cleared of its forests its springs disappear and its rivers flow more irregularly," exacerbating floods and droughts. Westerners could readily see how forests retained winter snows where, as John Wesley Powell underscored in his 1878 report on arid lands, they served as "reservoirs which hold the water for the growing seasons." (Modern hydrologists generally agree that, as William deBuys put it, "broken, low-density forest stands produce optimum water yield: Their trees provide shade and windbreak, and their openness allows snow to accumulate on the ground and build into well-packed drifts.")[18]

PROPOSALS TO PROTECT PUBLICLY OWNED
FORESTS IN CALIFORNIA

Interior secretary Schurz and GLO commissioner Williamson made special efforts to protect some of California's magnificent forests. The campaign, though unsuccessful in the short run, marked the emergence of John Muir as the nation's most forceful advocate for using public land ownership as a tool for nature preservation.

Congress's Yosemite legislation in 1864, by protecting the Big Tree Grove as well as the Yosemite Valley, had brought more attention to the magnificent giant sequoias. By the mid-1870s, it was known that several dozen small groves of these trees, totaling some 35,000 acres, were sprinkled along the western slopes of the southern Sierra Nevada at elevations between 4,500 and 7,000 feet. Title to some was already in private hands, usually acquired through the manipulation of public land laws. But some groves remained in U.S. ownership, protected primarily by their relative inaccessibility.

The trees' immensity made them difficult to harvest and handle. As Muir noted, they had to be "blasted into manageable dimensions with gunpowder," which destroyed much of what was useful. Moreover, their wood was brittle and poorly suited for construction, useful mainly for firewood, fence posts, shingles, and shakes. None of these drawbacks seemed to deter loggers: dozens of the giant trees were cut down in mostly mindless destruction. A young editor of the *Visalia Delta* newspaper in California's Central Valley, George W. Stewart, began writing editorials calling for the preservation of those stands that remained.[19]

Another stately tree species found in California, the coastal redwood, is a taller (reaching nearly four hundred feet), slenderer (around half the diameter), and somewhat shorter-lived relative of the giant sequoia. But unlike its cousin, the coastal redwood made superb lumber—straight, light, strong, mostly knot-free and rot-proof—as Muir once put it, "as timber the redwood is too good to live." It was also much more abundant, found on more than one million acres along the northern, much wetter half of the California coast. Because of its commercial value, the public lands where it was found were big targets for privatization, and timber enterprises wasted no time in acquiring large tracts by manipulating the Timber and Stone Act.[20]

In 1879, excoriating the wanton "waste and destruction" of both species of giant trees, Schurz urged Congress to authorize the president to put at least 46,000 acres in both the coastal range and in the southern Sierra off-limits to divestment in order to preserve these "grandest of primeval forests." Freshman congressman George Converse (D-Ohio), who chaired the House public lands committee, promptly introduced a bill to "set apart" the lands as—mimicking the language of the Yellowstone legislation—"public parks or pleasure-grounds for the benefit and enjoyment of the people," under the stewardship of the Interior secretary. Converse's bill passed the House on a voice vote in January 1880 but died in the Senate. Schurz kept pushing for protective legislation until he left office in March 1881. Later that year, Senator John F. Miller (R-Calif.) introduced a bill to set apart about 1.5 million acres of scenic, mostly forested public lands in the southern Sierra as a "public park." Miller's bill, like Converse's, followed the Yellowstone rather than the Yosemite model, most likely because of growing dissatisfaction with state administration of Yosemite. Although these bills did not become law, they did lay down markers for future action.[21]

CHAPTER FOURTEEN

Moving Beyond "Paper Parks"

AS PUBLIC SUPPORT GREW FOR reserving more lands in national owner-ship, the Interior Department grappled with how to implement Congress's direction to make the 2 million acres of public land at Yellowstone available as a "pleasuring-ground" for people's "enjoyment" while holding park resources "in their natural condition." There was no template for this. For one thing, there was no consensus on what was "natural." Within a few years of the park's establishment, Yellowstone's waters were being stocked with non-native fish, charismatic species like bison and elk were being fed in the winter, and efforts had begun to exterminate predators such as wolves.[1]

For the first several years, with the nearest railroad line still many miles away, Yellowstone's remoteness was its chief protection. As the number of visi-tors began to grow, and neither a cultural ethic nor specific rules were available to guide visitors' conduct, reports soon began to emerge that some of the geysers and other "curiosities" were being defaced, and that elk, deer, and other game were being slaughtered. But the government could do little without personnel or legal machinery in place to provide meaningful protection.

An even bigger threat soon emerged. In 1883, the same year that the Northern Pacific began operating trains from Minneapolis to Seattle, it completed a branch line from the main-line town of Livingston, Montana, south to Cinnabar, a few miles north of Gardiner, the gateway settlement at Yellowstone's northern entrance. Mining interests, real estate speculators, and

Livingston business interests started pushing to extend this spur line into and through the park's northeast quadrant, seeking either to shrink the park's boundaries or to secure a right-of-way through it. Jay Cooke, who had made a new start after going bankrupt in the Panic of 1873, supported building the railroad to mines located just outside the park's northeast boundary in the hardscrabble mining camp Cooke City, named after him. It would run through the Lamar Valley, one of the park's most scenic and wildlife-rich areas.

The debates that began in the 1880s over how the government should balance preserving natural wonders found on public lands with accommodating visitors and developing the lands for profit have been replayed countless times, right down to the present. Private enterprises, especially railroads, played a complicated role in the matter. Among the first promoters of western tourism, they often supported keeping scenic attractions in public ownership. But a dogged focus on bottom-line profit sometimes led them, as at Yellowstone, to support measures that threatened the very values that made these places attractive.[2]

CIVIL WAR ADVERSARIES JOIN FORCES TO "SAVE" YELLOWSTONE

Two unlikely allies emerged as leaders of the campaign to rescue Yellowstone from these threats—General Philip Sheridan and Senator George Vest (D-Mo.). Sheridan had been a leading figure in the Union Army, and Vest had been a member of the Confederate Congress. They aligned in a campaign to protect one of the most splendid examples of America's common ground, in order to help heal the wounds of war, rebuild national pride, and inspire its citizens.

Sheridan took on the cause of Yellowstone protection as a personal crusade. After graduating from West Point, he served in California and Oregon, and during the Civil War he rose quickly through the ranks. A major general in 1863 at the age of thirty-two, by the end of the war he was outranked only by Ulysses S. Grant, William Tecumseh Sherman, and George Meade. In 1867, he became head of the army in the West, the so-called Department of the Missouri. There he so vigorously discharged his principal responsibility of subjugating and pacifying Native American populations on the Plains that massacres of innocent Indians by subordinates stained his reputation. Sheridan authorized military escorts for the Washburn and Hayden expeditions in 1870–71, and visited Yellowstone three times before his death in 1888 at age fifty-seven. In the early 1880s, he proposed extending the park's eastern and southern boundaries to nearly double its size, and suggested that the military take control of park administration to protect its natural wonders.[3]

George Vest was a Kentuckian and lawyer who moved to Missouri in 1853. He served almost the entire Civil War in the Confederate Congress—three years in its House and the last few months in its Senate. Returning to Missouri after the war, he was elected to the U.S. Senate in 1879. A visit to the Yellowstone region in the summer of 1882 inspired him to become the park's leading congressional champion. When the nation has "a hundred million or a hundred and fifty million people," he told his Senate colleagues in 1883, Yellowstone will be "a great breathing place for the national lungs."[4]

One of the issues confounding the Interior Department was how to define an appropriate role for private enterprise. In early 1883, an assistant Interior secretary struck a sweetheart deal with some politically connected businessmen, including a Northern Pacific executive, that gave their Yellowstone National Park Improvement Company exclusive rights to 4,400 acres of parkland for ten years at a rental of $2 per acre, along with a monopoly on hotels, stage transportation, and telegraph lines within the park. Senator Vest and others criticized the deal as inconsistent with the 1872 legislation establishing the park, which had authorized Interior to lease "small parcels of ground" for "the erection of buildings for the accommodation of visitors." Vest told his colleagues that the park furnished a "great purpose in our national life," namely, to check America's "materialistic tendencies." He invoked precedents from Europe, though he astutely took care to distinguish America from monarchical England: "England has her royal parks, and why should not America have a republican park, free to the people," a place with "great curiosities that exist nowhere else"?[5]

Vest and his allies succeeded in amending the Interior Department appropriation bill in 1883 to prohibit Interior from leasing "any ground within one-quarter of a mile of any of the geysers or of the Yellowstone Falls," or from leasing more than ten acres to any one person or corporation, or granting any "exclusive privileges" within the park except on the leased ground. It also authorized the secretary of war, at the request of the Interior secretary, to detail troops "to prevent trespassers or intruders from entering the park" for any purpose prohibited by law, including "destroying the game or objects of curiosity therein." Though helpful, the measure failed to give the government the legal machinery needed to punish poachers and vandals; it could only eject wrongdoers from the park.[6]

Four months after signing this legislation, Chester A. Arthur—an avid fly fisherman who succeeded James Garfield when the latter died from an

President Chester A. Arthur (*seated, center*) and his party at Yellowstone, 1883, including General Philip Sheridan (*seated, second from left*), Robert Todd Lincoln (*seated, second from right*), and (*seated, at right*) Senator George Vest (Courtesy of the Library of Congress, LC-USZ62-137259)

assassin's bullet in 1881—became the first president to visit Yellowstone, guided by Sheridan and Senator Vest. According to the historian George Black, Sheridan by this time had become increasingly angered by the "mindless destruction" of Yellowstone's wonders by vandals, the "wanton slaughter" of its game, and the Interior Department's inadequate management. (His vigorous defense of the park might have been an indirect gesture of atonement, because Sheridan was also coming to believe the army might have been too harsh toward the Indians.) The well-publicized trip helped focus attention on the park and the threats it faced.[7]

In 1884, Vest introduced a comprehensive bill to give the Interior Department the authority to prosecute those who despoiled park resources and, following Sheridan's suggestion, to enlarge the park by nearly 1.3 million acres on its southern and eastern flanks. Vest invoked scenic wonders familiar to some of his eastern colleagues, warning against a "materialistic" attitude that would "think that the Natural Bridge in Virginia should be macadamized" or that the "water-power of Niagara should be used for a mill." He also formally inquired of Sheridan whether a railroad might be built to provide access to the

Cooke City mines without passing through the park. A study by one of Sheridan's engineers concluded it was "entirely feasible."[8]

Vest's legislation was strongly supported by his colleague, the future president Benjamin Harrison (R-Ind.), and it passed the Senate in 1884. But the House refused to go along without adding unacceptable conditions. This established a pattern that was repeated no fewer than six times over the next nine years. Each time Vest persuaded the Senate to approve legislation giving the executive branch authority to punish violators of park rules, the House bowed to the demands of mining and real estate speculators by amending Vest's bill to grant a railroad right-of-way through the park. Vest and his supporters refused to accede to the House amendment, and so the legislative deadlock continued. The matter was not put to rest until the mid-1890s.[9]

MILITARY ADMINISTRATION OF YELLOWSTONE

In the summer of 1886, proponents of the railroad persuaded the House to cut off all funding to the park except for road construction. The Senate objected, but the House refused to budge, and so the appropriations bill signed into law in August 1886 zeroed out funds for park administration. Almost immediately, Interior secretary Lamar invoked the authority that Congress had provided in 1883 for the military to patrol the park. General Sheridan promptly assigned the task to a troop of the U.S. Calvary, and for the next thirty years, the army looked after Yellowstone.[10]

Military control did not work wonders, but it did furnish a visible and disciplined governmental presence somewhat removed from politics. The Interior Department had allowed mining with the permission of the superintendent, and hunting, trapping, and fishing to procure food for visitors and residents. After the army took control, it prohibited mining, hunting, and trapping, as well as fishing except with hook and line, and livestock grazing around "various points of interest within the Park frequented by visitors." The military also developed creative ways to deal with the fact that it could only eject violators from the park, such as by walking offenders to one park boundary while depositing their livestock or other property outside another boundary many miles away.[11]

The arrangement between the local military commander, who was acting park superintendent, and the Interior secretary, who still had overall responsibility for park administration, including leases and permits, occasionally proved complicated. At one point, an entrepreneur proposed to build an elevator alongside the famous Yellowstone Falls, from its top to its bottom.

Captain F. A. Boutelle, the acting superintendent, initially recommended approval, but had a change of heart after Interior secretary John Noble issued the necessary lease, pleading with Noble to cancel it because the contraption would "destroy the wild view," which was "one of the grandest in the Park." Eventually, Noble agreed.[12]

Although the overall number of visitors remained small, they were increasing substantially. By the late 1880s, more than 5,000 people were touring the park each summer. (In 2015, visitors exceeded 4 million for the first time.) Congress did not resolve the railroad, boundary, and law enforcement issues for several more years, and did not restore the park to full civilian control until 1916.

The lengthy tussles over how to manage Yellowstone held several lessons for future public land policy. One was that a landscape's capacity to inspire usually proved to be the most powerful argument for its preservation. Nearly every member of Congress who visited the park—and quite a few did over the years—became a strong advocate for protecting it. This capacity to inspire crossed party lines and healed historic divisions. The park's most vocal defenders included Republicans and Democrats, and members of Congress who were on opposite sides in the Civil War, such as Wilkinson Call (D-Fla.), a former general in the Confederate Army; Augustus Garland (D-Ark.), who, like Vest, had served in both Houses of the Confederate Congress; and Union Army veterans John Logan (R-Ill.), a former major general, and Joseph Keifer (R-Ohio), who had been wounded in the war.

Another lesson was that although private enterprise had a role to play in accommodating visitors, it needed to be carefully controlled. Still another was how much political power was contained in the democratic notion that access to the park's splendors should not be reserved to the privileged but be freely open to all.

Also significant for the future was the engagement of Congressman William Holman, who would soon emerge as a key architect of the law that led to creating a system of national forests. In the summer of 1885, he led a subcommittee of the House Appropriations Committee on a firsthand assessment of Yellowstone as part of a three-and-a-half-month tour of the West to examine public land and Indian policy. Its 1886 report touted the park's "display of wonderful sources of nature, the ever varying beauty of the rugged landscape, and the sublimity of the scenery," and recommended that it "should so far as possible be spared the vandalism of improvement."[13]

YOSEMITE FARES POORLY UNDER STATE MANAGEMENT

As debates over how to manage Yellowstone intensified, California's administration of the Yosemite grant was facing significant challenges. The California
legislature had started out strong, enacting legislation in 1866 to formally
accept the grant and the conditions laid down by Congress and to give the
Yosemite Commission "full power" to administer what it called "the trust" that
Congress had bestowed on it.[14]

But the state's reluctance to provide funds to manage Yosemite left the
commission in the uncomfortable position of having to rely on revenues
produced by leases that Congress had authorized in the 1864 act. Illustrating
the downside of such a funding mechanism, it leased a substantial amount of
the granted land for activities such as timber harvesting. It also engaged
contractors to build roads and trails and authorized them to charge tolls to cover
their costs. In 1880, after allegations of mismanagement and corruption
emerged, the state brought a lawsuit that eventually resulted in the commission being dissolved and a new one appointed. That change improved matters
for a time, but starting in the mid-1880s, a new controversy erupted when, to
raise more revenue, the commissioners proposed cultivating hay on 90 percent
of the valley floor. The criticism helped feed growing congressional skepticism
about how well states were generally doing in administering grants of public
lands.[15]

That was how matters stood when, in the summer of 1889, John Muir took
a camping trip in the Yosemite region with Robert Underwood Johnson, editor
of a popular and influential national monthly magazine. When they descended
into the valley, Johnson reported later, they were appalled at the sight of
hayfields and acres of tree stumps, large piles of refuse, a ramshackle hotel, a
saloon, and a pig sty, and dismayed to learn of plans to project colored lights on
the waterfalls. The experience led them to launch a campaign to create a
national park around the state-administered park at Yosemite, and ultimately to
have the state cede its Yosemite grant back to the United States.[16]

CHAPTER FIFTEEN

Wildlife Protection Enters the Policy Universe

HUMANS HAVE AFFECTED WILDLIFE since they came to what is now the United States as the last ice age was ending, many thousands of years ago. Most scientists now believe that along with a changing climate, the earliest inhabitants played a large role in the extinction of large animal species such as mastodons, mammoths, giant ground sloths, and saber-toothed cats around eight thousand years ago. Ever since, and at a much accelerated pace in the last couple of centuries, overharvesting and human-caused habitat destruction, introduction of alien species, and pollution have made many more species extinct or vulnerable to extinction.[1]

The groundwork for legislation to protect wildlife on public land was laid in the years leading up to the Civil War. John James Audubon (1785–1851) was an influential advocate for wildlife, developing one of the first techniques for banding birds in order to track migrations and becoming, in the words of Nathaniel Reed and Dennis Drabelle, a "tireless critic of the prevalent notion that wildlife populations were endlessly abundant." The publication of Darwin's *Origin of Species* in 1859 was also important, for it connected humans with other forms of life and helped professionalize the field of wildlife biology.[2]

In Europe, the aristocracy's pursuit of fish and game for sport had often meant harsh punishments for commoners who intruded on their privilege. In America, sport hunters and anglers were among the earliest campaigners for protecting wild animals and their habitats (as well as for taking game only by "fair means"), which often put them at odds with less well-off market and subsistence hunters. William Elliott's landmark monograph *Carolina Sports by Land and Water* in 1846 astutely identified these class-based conflicts as a political problem for the wildlife conservation movement. The public's "deep disgust at the tyranny of the English game laws" had, he warned, associated wildlife conservation "in the popular mind with ideas of aristocracy—peculiar privileges to the rich—and oppression towards the poor."[3]

Henry William Herbert, a prominent contemporary of Audubon and Elliot who wrote under the pen name Frank Forester, identified another challenge to effective political action, namely, the "want of union among themselves of genuine sportsmen." This proved easier to address. By the end of the 1850s, according to the historian John F. Reiger, sport hunters and anglers were "easily the largest, most influential, and best-organized" advocates for better laws to protect wildlife and other features of the natural world.[4]

The earliest wildlife laws were enacted by states, initially simply to set fishing and hunting seasons and control amounts and, sometimes, methods of "take." But gradually appreciation grew that if wildlife populations were to thrive, habitat needed to be preserved. In 1837, Nathaniel Hawthorne speculated in his *Sketchbooks* about how migratory species of fish might be affected by the Edwards Dam, which he observed being built across the Kennebec River in Maine's capital city of Augusta. (The removal of this structure in 1999 was a landmark in the modern campaign to restore American rivers.) Fishery declines sometimes attracted the attention of state governments. George Perkins Marsh prepared a pathbreaking report in 1857 for the Vermont legislature that identified other causes of declining fisheries besides dams, including overfishing, particularly in spawning season, and pollution from sawmills and other industries. Marsh presciently warned that protecting migratory fish could require action by the national government, because most rivers crossed state lines.[5]

THE BEGINNINGS OF FEDERAL WILDLIFE LAW

Until the late 1860s, no federal laws addressed wildlife, on or off public lands. But a diverse group of advocates for wildlife protection was beginning to make its presence felt. Besides sport hunters and anglers largely drawn from the more comfortable classes, it included scientific collectors and naturalists, some who simply loved nature, and some concerned with animal welfare, such as the American Society for the Prevention of Cruelty to Animals, organized in New York in 1866. These disparate groups did not always see eye to eye, for lumbering could improve habitat for some species prized by sportsmen, such as white-tailed deer, ruffed grouse, and wild turkey, and some anglers preferred introduced species to native fish stocks. But there was enough overlap in their interests for them often to work together for wildlife protection in what Wallace Stegner once described as "an unlikely combination of bleeding hearts and gunners."[6]

As sport hunters and anglers broadened their focus to include the protection of habitat, it was inevitable that they would eventually devote attention to public lands. It was there that the Property Clause gave Congress unquestioned authority, and it was there, particularly in the western parts of the nation, that the best habitat was usually found. Moreover, many of their guidebooks rated places for hunting and angling according to their scenic attributes and romantic grandeur, which public lands had in abundance.[7]

Congress enacted the first federal wildlife law in 1868, the year after the United States purchased Alaska from Russia. It called on the Treasury secretary to take steps to regulate the taking of fur-bearing animals throughout Alaska. In 1869, Congress declared Alaska's Pribilof Islands, where northern fur seals were being heavily hunted for their skins, a "special reservation for government purposes," and required government permission to go there. That action marked the first reservation of public lands in the nation's history specifically to protect wildlife. In 1870, Congress gave Native Alaskans the right to harvest seals on the islands for traditional purposes, and authorized the Treasury secretary to regulate seal harvests as "necessary for the[ir] preservation" and to lease rights to harvest seals to a private company for an annual rental of $50,000 plus a duty of $2 per skin. Over the next two decades, this program produced almost as much revenue for the treasury as the government had paid Russia for the entire Alaska territory.[8]

RAPID DESTRUCTION OF WELL-KNOWN
SPECIES SPARKS PUBLIC CONCERN

Millions of colorful, raucous Carolina parakeets were once found from Florida to New York and as far west as Colorado, but Audubon had noted their decline as early as the 1830s. After the Civil War, the birds' numbers plummeted, mostly because of deforestation and harvesting for plumage. The passenger pigeon had a similar fate. In the early nineteenth century, it ranged across much of the eastern half of the country in vast flocks that obscured the sun and created a din that could rival a locomotive. In 1831, Audubon described a forty-mile-wide gathering of the birds that he had observed in Kentucky. By the middle of the nineteenth century, however, the population had begun a steep decline, the result of deforestation, disease, and being slaughtered in enormous numbers, mostly for food. The fate of the Carolina parakeet and the passenger pigeon helped awaken Americans to the impact that human activity could have on wildlife, reinforcing Audubon's argument that wildlife populations were finite and sending ripples of concern through the political system. Both species became extinct early in the twentieth century.[9]

The wildlife slaughter that likely had the biggest impact on public land policy in this era was of the bison—the largest mammal in North America, with males weighing as much as a ton. Modern scholarship has suggested that bison may have been in decline since the Spanish reintroduced the horse to North America in the late sixteenth century. In the early nineteenth century, according to some estimates, some 25–30 million bison could be found on the grasslands in the West. From that point forward, the decline accelerated as improvements in firearms made hunting more efficient and as industrialized tanning technology made hides more valuable.[10]

By the mid-1850s, the remaining bison herds were concentrated on the Great Plains, much of it still public land. The completion of the first transcontinental railroad in 1869 bisected the remaining population, and by the end of the 1870s, only a few hundred were left south of the rail line. To the north, the herds were increasingly displaced by the massive numbers of domestic livestock being introduced into Wyoming and Montana. By this time, bison destruction had become closely linked with the goal of subjugating Plains Indians by starving them into submission.[11]

In 1873, with more members of the public recoiling from the scale and cruelty of the bison slaughter, Congress seriously entertained curbing it. Congressman Greenbury Fort, who would soon introduce the first forest reserve bill, proposed to make it unlawful for any non-Indian to kill or wound any female bison of any age, or any male not used for food, in any U.S. territory. Fort's bill attracted many supporters, including Congressman William Holman, but was opposed by those who argued that the Plains Indians would not be pacified so long as bison roamed the plains. Fort's bill made it to the president's desk at the very end of the Forty-Third Congress in 1874, but Grant pocket vetoed it.

Fort tried again in the next Congress, securing House approval of his bill by a wide margin in February 1876. But Sitting Bull's defeat of George Armstrong Custer at the Battle of Little Bighorn a few months later doomed the effort. In the mid-1880s, Theodore Roosevelt recounted how someone who had traveled a thousand miles across the northern plains told him of being "never out of sight of a dead buffalo and never in sight of a live one." Soon only a handful of small herds remained, one of which was in Yellowstone National Park.[12]

Declining fish stocks were another growing concern. In 1865, Robert Barnwell Roosevelt, a well-known sportsman (and Theodore's uncle), published a book on fishing in which he lamented that the streams around New York were "absolutely depopulated." Six years later, concern had grown to the point that Roosevelt, by then serving a term in Congress, secured enactment of legislation to establish the U.S. Commission on Fish and Fisheries. Finding that both coastal and river food fish were "rapidly diminishing in number, to the public injury," the legislation directed the commission to investigate and report on the causes of, and remedies for, the decline.[13]

Spencer Baird, a naturalist-scientist, was named to head the commission. Its report in 1873 foresaw the need for Congress to intervene to protect fishery resources on interstate rivers. Baird served on the commission for seventeen years, advocating limits on harvest and promoting research, including establishing in 1882 what became the famous research station at Woods Hole, Massachusetts. The commission's record was not without blemish—it sometimes promoted the introduction of non-native species, with calamitous results—but Congress's continuing support for it demonstrated the growing political power of advocates for wildlife conservation. Renamed the Bureau of Fisheries and folded into the Department of Commerce and Labor in 1903, it was the predecessor of today's U.S. Fish & Wildlife Service (in the Department of the Interior) and NOAA Fisheries (in the Department of Commerce).[14]

SPORT HUNTERS AND ANGLERS POLITICALLY ENGAGE

New journalistic outlets played a major role in fueling a movement, led by sport hunting and sportfishing advocates, to stem the decline of wildlife populations. The first issue of the monthly newspaper *American Sportsman* appeared in late 1871. It was followed by *Forest and Stream* (1873), *Field and Stream* (1874), and *American Angler* (1881). Each developed a national audience, in part by tapping into nostalgia for earlier days when fish and game seemed unlimited. *Forest and Stream*, a weekly based in New York, was the most influential. Founded by Charles Hallock, it was devoted, according to its prolix subtitle, to "Field and Aquatic Sports, Practical Natural History, Fish Culture, The Protection of Game, Preservation of Forests, and the Inculcation in Men and Women of a Healthy Interest in Outdoor Recreation and Study."

George Bird Grinnell, originally Hallock's business partner, bought him out and became editor in chief in 1880. Grinnell (1849–1938) was a naturalist, anthropologist, historian, and journalist who for a half century was an influential participant in public land policy making. As a boy growing up in a rural area near the Hudson River in what is now Washington Heights in northern Manhattan, he developed a love for nature from his neighbor Lucy Audubon, the widow of John James Audubon. Educated at Yale, Grinnell accompanied the noted paleontologist Othniel Marsh on a fossil-collecting expedition to the West in 1870. He was a naturalist on Custer's expedition in 1874 to investigate the Black Hills, and on the Ludlow expedition through Yellowstone in 1875. (Other commitments caused him to decline appointment to Custer's ill-fated 1876 expedition.) Grinnell later wrote or co-authored books on several Plains Indian tribes and on the American bison.[15]

A keen political strategist, Grinnell worked tirelessly, behind the scenes as well as in print, to advance the cause of conserving wildlife and wildlife habitat. Like William Elliott and George Perkins Marsh, Grinnell was sensitive to the potential for conflict between democratic egalitarianism and the idea of protecting game for sport hunters and anglers, who were mostly drawn from the urban elite. Mimicking their European counterparts, wealthy sportsmen had created numerous private game enclaves, such as the 12,000-acre Blooming Grove preserve in eastern Pennsylvania, established in 1871, and later a similar one in the Adirondacks that eventually grew to control nearly 180,000 acres, mostly by leasing. Their rural neighbors mostly viewed such private preserves as maneuvers by the urban upper classes to deprive them of both sport and subsistence opportunities. Their disdain hardened after the Johnstown flood of 1889, in which the collapse of a dam built by a private hunting and fishing preserve frequented by Pittsburgh's elite killed more than two thousand people.[16]

Grinnell devoted considerable efforts to overcoming the "elitist" tag. In an 1881 editorial, he argued that persons of modest means "should be interested in game preservation even more than he whose fortune is ample." His argument was made easier by the continuing decline of the use of wild game as a subsistence food source. Drawing liberally on the teachings of George Perkins Marsh, the next year he launched an editorial campaign calling for the "proper and sensible management of woodlands," because, as he succinctly put it, "no woods, no game; no woods, no water; and no water, no fish." It advocated for protecting habitat on lands already in public ownership, as well as for governmental acquisition of prime, privately owned habitat in order to make it accessible to all. A Republican, Grinnell never let partisan considerations deflect him; he not only voted for Grover Cleveland, a Democrat, but also put his name on the tallest peak in what would become Glacier National Park.[17]

Through the efforts of Grinnell and others, the protection of wildlife and wildlife habitat began to gain prominence in campaigns for reserving public lands. One of the first places this happened was at Yellowstone. In 1883, Arnold Hague of the U.S. Geological Survey cited the need to protect habitat for wide-ranging big game as a rationale for expanding the park's boundaries. "Enlarge the park," he wrote, "and you make the whole area a game country." The next year, noting the continuing decline of wild game in the region, Hague took the argument a step further, suggesting that a "natural zoological reservation, suffi-ciently large to allow all wild animals to run free without molestation," could produce a surplus that would migrate outside the park's boundaries and provide "ample sport" for hunters. Grinnell followed up with a spate of edito-rials and letters to the editor advocating the expansion of Yellowstone so that "the large game of the West" could be "seen by generations yet unborn," adding, "It is for the Nation to say whether these splendid species shall be so preserved in this, their last refuge."[18]

In 1885, *Forest and Stream* published Grinnell's review of *Hunting Trips of a Ranchman* by twenty-seven-year-old Theodore Roosevelt. The book recounted some of Roosevelt's experiences while operating a ranch in North Dakota. Grinnell owned a ranch in Wyoming and, like Roosevelt, would soon suffer financial losses in the harsh winter of 1886–87. Grinnell's review was generally favorable, but he criticized Roosevelt's assertion of several of what Grinnell called "hunting myths," which Grinnell ascribed to the "author's limited expe-rience." After the review was published, a bruised Roosevelt sought out Grinnell and forged a lasting friendship. In December 1887, the two of them founded the Boone and Crockett Club in New York. With a limited, blue-ribbon member-ship, it became a leading advocate for wildlife and habitat conservation, including reserving public lands for such purposes.[19]

Roosevelt was not only an ardent hunter, but also a serious birder who had published ornithological studies. He remained an avid collector throughout his life, an era when no bright line was drawn between scientific collecting and recreational hunting. Many influential politicians of the era counted them-selves sport hunting and sportfishing enthusiasts. Grover Cleveland, who succeeded Chester A. Arthur as president in 1885, wrote a book about the joys of bird hunting and freshwater fishing. His successor, Benjamin Harrison, was fond of duck hunting. The support of these high-ranking figures helped wild-life concerns play a larger role in public land policy making.

INDIAN DISPOSSESSION ACCELERATES

The destruction of the bison illustrated a connection between declines in wild-life (and related exploitations of natural resources) and increasing dispossession of Indians from their ancestral homelands in the western part of the country. After the Civil War, the national government's push to acquire Indian lands became relentless, spurred by those who desired the lands in order to build railroads and to exploit their grasses, minerals, and timber. Seeking to minimize conflicts and bloodshed, the United States tried to adhere to its long-standing policy of not formally opening public lands to divestment and exploitation by non-Indians until Indian title had been resolved. But as before, events on the ground often outran the government's capacity to control the advance of prospectors and other exploiters. Even on those occasions when the government intervened to keep order, its efforts were usually more harshly visited on Indians than on non-Indians. Although the United States made efforts to compensate Indians for their losses, these actions sometimes came after, even long after, dispossession had occurred.

After the Civil War, the government accelerated its program to reduce Indian landholdings and move Indians to reservations set aside for them on public lands. Congress ended the practice of making treaties with tribes in 1871, when the Senate yielded to the demand of the House of Representatives that it be given a role. Thereafter, Congress as a whole, along with the executive branch, made key decisions without giving the tribes a formal role in the process. As a result, many western tribes were located on reservations on public lands mostly established by executive order. The primary purposes of shrinking tribal landholdings were, as Daniel and Amy Cordalis have written, "to open the rest of the [public] land for non-Indian settlement, and to assimilate the Indians into the 'civilized' non-Indian world by imposing on them Christianity, private property, and agriculture."[20] Indian dispossession was almost never done to advance protection and conservation of the natural resources of the public lands; instead, it was done to make those resources available for non-Indian exploitation through building railroads, mining, logging, and settlement by homesteaders and others.

By the 1870s, Indian title had been cleared from more than a billion acres of public land, leaving tribes collectively with a little more than 150 million acres. By the middle of the 1880s, according to the historian Stuart Banner, Indians "retained virtually no land that was not part of a reservation" that the United States had set aside for them. As Banner put it, "It had taken whites 250 years to purchase the eastern half of the United States, but they needed less than 40 years for the western half." Further cessions would drop this number to a little more than 100 million acres by 1890 and to 78 million acres by 1900. Meanwhile, the number of Indians continued to decline, from an estimated 400,000 in 1850 to fewer than 250,000 in 1890, when the U.S. population reached 63 million. The common expectation of policy makers during this era was that those Indians who did not die off would simply be absorbed into the general population.[21]

CHAPTER SIXTEEN

The Campaign for Forest Reservations Gains Momentum

IN HIS ANNUAL MESSAGE TO Congress in December 1882, President Chester A. Arthur urged enactment of legislation to "secure the preservation of the valuable forests still remaining on the public domain," especially in the arid West. He called the destruction of forests "wasteful," because their value in "regulating and sustaining the flow of springs and streams" was "now well understood." He sounded the same Marsh-like theme in his message the following year.[1]

Reservation bills were introduced in Congress throughout the 1880s. Some would have simply reserved all public forested lands, while others would have given the president some discretion in the matter. Some focused broadly on safeguarding water supplies and reducing the risk of erosion and flooding, while others sought to preserve trees in order to sustain wood supplies. Some would have created "parks" rather than "forest reserves"— distinctions between the two labels did not begin to emerge for another decade or two.

Some bills proposed to reserve specific geographic areas. Senator George F. Edmunds (R-Vt.) introduced a bill in 1884 to establish a "forest reserve" on nearly 4 million acres of public land in the upper reaches of the Missouri and Columbia Rivers in the western part of the Montana Territory. Edmunds explained that his bill was not intended to protect "curiosities like the Yellowstone Park," but rather to safeguard "great headwaters" by putting the area entirely off-limits to settlement and timber harvesting. His bill passed the Senate but did not make it to the House floor.[2]

Earlier that year, the Senate, in a change freighted with symbolism, added "and Forestry" to the name of its Committee on Agriculture. It was done at the behest of Senator Omar Conger (R-Mich.), who pointed out that the "destruction of timber and timber lands" was attracting worldwide attention. As the campaign to protect public forests gained strength, it remained thoroughly bipartisan, and so the election in November 1884 of the first Democratic president since the Civil War, Grover Cleveland, did not slow its momentum. His first Interior secretary, Lucius Lamar, repeated the call of his Republican predecessors to preserve public forests, noting that a good government "should use some care for the future." Senator Edmunds reintroduced his bill to reserve the Missouri and Columbia River headwaters in 1885 and 1887 but could not push it across the finish line.[3]

RESERVATIONS OF PUBLIC LANDS BY THE EXECUTIVE

Meanwhile, officials in the executive branch were continuing their long-standing practice of reserving particular areas of public lands from the operation of laws that could lead to the loss of U.S. ownership, even where Congress had not provided explicit authority to do so. As before, Congress continued to refrain from disturbing those executive actions. Also as before, the U.S. Supreme Court generally rejected challenges to these executive actions—most notably, in no fewer than seven decisions handed down between 1866 and 1887 involving reservations of public lands along the Des Moines River in Iowa.[4]

As the public's appetite for public land reservations increased, the executive began reserving more lands to protect their scenic and other natural values. In 1883, for example, President Arthur reserved 84,000 acres of public lands, including Mount Whitney, the highest point in the lower forty-eight states, in California's southern Sierra Nevada. Although his executive order called it a "military reservation," the army never stationed anyone there. (In 1906, it became part of what was then known as the Sierra Forest Reservation.)[5]

Another noteworthy executive reservation involved Crater Lake in Oregon. Located in a punch-bowl-shaped caldera formed nearly eight thousand years ago when a Cascade Range volcano exploded, Crater Lake has no significant inflow or outflow, its water level being maintained by precipitation. Six miles wide, with depths reaching two thousand feet, it is the nation's deepest lake. In 1885, William Gladstone Steel, a Portland outdoorsman who as a Kansas farm boy had read about it in a newspaper fifteen years earlier, camped on its shore. With his fellow campers, including Clarence Dutton of the U.S. Geological Survey and the University of California geologist Joseph LeConte, he hatched a plan for protecting the lake and the surrounding lands.

Steel eventually persuaded more than one hundred Oregon leaders, including Governor Z. F. Moody and Congressman Binger Hermann, to sign a petition calling on the U.S. government to reserve the land. The Oregon legislature chimed in with its own petition, urging that the area be established as a "public park or pleasure ground for the benefit of the people of the United States." In early 1886, Oregon senator Joseph Dolph introduced a bill to make the area a public park. A few days later, after meeting with Steel, Interior secretary Lamar sent President Cleveland a brief handwritten note recommending the reservation of more than 230,000 acres of public land in the area. A few days after that, Cleveland scrawled his approval at the bottom, and the reservation was made. Cleveland's rationale—maintaining U.S. ownership while Congress considered legislation to permanently protect the area—proved to be a useful precedent for similar executive actions in the future.[6]

Opposition by livestock operators, timber interests, and speculators stymied congressional action on Crater Lake for well over a decade, despite an outpouring of support for it in periodicals across the country, which compared its scenic beauty to that of Yosemite, Yellowstone, and Niagara Falls. Through all this, Cleveland's executive reservation remained in place. Never put to a judicial test, it kept the public lands free from the legal claims of miners, timber companies, squatters, and speculators, and paved the way for the eventual enactment, in 1902, of legislation making Crater Lake a national park.

The episode illustrated some important truths about the politics of protecting tracts of public lands. The executive, with a national constituency and an uncomplicated decision-making process, was usually able to take action much more quickly than Congress. The executive was also freer than Congress to act in the face of opposition, especially if it had the support of some politicians in the affected area. Political partisanship rarely played a role; at Crater Lake, the Democrat Cleveland followed the recommendation of the Republicans Moody, Hermann, and Dolph. Finally, when the executive did take action, the opposition usually found it difficult to persuade Congress or a future administration to overturn it.

Another example of vigorous executive action was provided by William Sparks, a lawyer from Illinois who became commissioner of the General Land Office in 1885, appointed by President Cleveland. The reform-minded Sparks, who had served in Congress from 1875 to 1883 before declining to seek a fifth term, was not one to mince words. He expressed outrage at "widespread, persistent, public land robbery" and condemned the plunder of public timberlands as "universal, flagrant and limitless." He also took action. After a General Land Office inspector reported that questionable Timber and Stone Act claims had been made on forested lands in California's southern Sierra Nevada, some of which contained giant sequoia groves, Sparks issued an order halting all actions that could lead to privatizing more than 400,000 acres of public lands, pending a thorough investigation. Even though this and many of his other actions had some local support, Sparks's hard-edged rhetoric eventually led to his forced resignation. But many of his withdrawals were affirmed by his successors, never disturbed by the courts, and ultimately saved much public land that is now protected from privatization and exploitation.[7]

Where local support did not exist, it was more difficult for the executive to take protective action, especially if the public lands were known to have resources of immense value in the marketplace. A prime example was public lands containing California's coastal redwoods, *Sequoia sempervirens*. When Interior secretary Carl Schurz asked Congress in the late 1870s to give him explicit authority to reserve some public lands containing redwood forests, timber interests were strongly opposed. They wanted to continue their schemes to acquire the lands under laws like the Timber and Stone Act for a few dollars an acre, when a single tree was worth many times that.

When Congress did not act, and Schurz was replaced in early 1881, the GLO proceeded to privatize some of the "choicest tracts of valuable redwood lands" in Northern California, as GLO commissioner Sparks put it when he described the episode in some detail in his *Annual Report* of 1886. This legislative and executive inaction ultimately proved costly. Years later, to meet the growing public demand to protect the shrinking numbers of ancient redwood forests, the State of California, private philanthropy, and eventually the U.S. government spent vast sums to buy remnants from private owners and restore them to public ownership.[8]

LESSONS FROM THE ADIRONDACKS

In the 1880s, New York, then home to about one in ten Americans, took a number of steps to protect scenic lands in the Adirondack Mountains. Much of the land had been privatized in the eighteenth century in a complex series of transactions involving the British Crown, Indians, and wealthy speculators. In the first few decades after the Revolutionary War, the state sold off large chunks of the land it still owned to logging companies. A considerable amount of the forest in the southern Adirondacks was logged in the 1850s and 1860s.

Some of the cutover land came back into public ownership when logging companies defaulted on their property taxes, but much of it remained in private hands. The area came within easy reach of New York City and other eastern population centers when a railroad reached it in 1871, the year twelve-year-old Theodore Roosevelt first tramped around the area, and it became a magnet for those seeking outdoor recreation and solitude. Urban plutocrats built lavish retreats called "Great Camps" on private lands bordering lakes in the region.[9]

In 1869, Samuel Bowles, influenced by his tour of the west, advocated protecting 1.6 million acres in the Adirondacks. Three years later, a young lawyer from Albany, Verplanck Colvin, called for the area to be made a "park for New York, as is the Yosemite for California." The New York legislature, concerned about protecting a principal water source for the Erie Canal and the Hudson River, created a commission to study Colvin's proposal. It recommended that the state establish a public park of 834,000 acres in the Hudson River watershed, of which the state then owned only a fraction.

A national economic depression triggered by the Panic of 1873 stalled legislative action for the next several years, but Colvin and others kept pressing the case. In 1883, the state took a first step by agreeing to stop selling land that it still owned in the Adirondacks. Two years later, the legislature established the Adirondack Forest Preserve on nearly 700,000 acres of state-owned land scattered across the region, mandating that the lands "be forever kept as wild forest lands." The same law created a somewhat smaller forest reserve in the Catskill Mountains, to the south, and established a state commission to manage state-owned forests in both ranges, with the apparent expectation that some logging could occur.[10]

New York's actions did not escape the notice of those deliberating public land policy in the nation's capital. Advocates for expanding Yellowstone National Park, for example, emphasized that the United States already owned the land proposed to be added to the park, and contrasted this situation with the difficulty and expense that New York was incurring in repurchasing land for the Adirondack Forest Preserve.[11]

LESSONS FROM NIAGARA FALLS

Around the same time, a campaign began to rescue the visitor experience at Niagara Falls from tawdry commercialization. It was based on the premise that public ownership of outstanding natural features was insufficient if the use of surrounding private land seriously interfered with the public's ability to fully experience those features. The book *Picturesque America* (1872, 1874) made this point effectively by describing Niagara Falls as a "superb diamond set in lead": the "stone is perfect, but the setting lamentably vile and destitute of beauty," marred by all sorts of inappropriate development in pursuit of short-term profit.[12]

Frederick Law Olmsted took up the challenge of fixing the problem. In 1880, he co-authored a report calling on the State of New York and the Province of Ontario to acquire the land in the immediate vicinity of the falls and restore it to as natural an appearance as possible. The report was accompanied by a petition signed by such luminaries as Vice President William Wheeler, eight U.S. Supreme Court justices, the secretary of war, eight senators, and two governors. Members of Congress and others were quick to spell out the implications of Niagara's degraded conditions for the nation's public lands. Advocating for the protection of Yellowstone on the floor of the Senate, George Vest argued that allowing the construction of hotels at strategic vista points in Yellowstone would make it "worse than Niagara is today."[13] George Bird Grinnell issued a similar warning.

The campaign that Olmsted led, called "Free Niagara," sought to create a Niagara Falls "reservation" to provide the general public with free access to a congenial view of the falls. In 1883, with the strong support of New York governor Grover Cleveland, the state legislature authorized the acquisition of the private property needed, and two years later it provided the funds to move forward. Eventually, all of the land on the American side that the falls were visible from became public property, and the reservation was formally dedicated with the words "from this hour Niagara is free." Always attentive to detail, Olmsted followed up in 1887 with a prescient report cautioning that scenic viewing areas should not be designed to accommodate carriages, because that kind of infrastructure interfered with the goal of allowing visitors to experience the falls "in an absorbed and contemplative way."[14]

LESSONS FROM CANADA

Around the same time that Olmsted's campaign was succeeding, Ontario enacted counterpart legislation, the Queen Victoria Niagara Falls Parks Act. Its park adjoining the New York reservation was dedicated on the queen's birthday in May 1888.

Canada also furnished parallels to the U.S. experience in the West. It had subsidized the building of its transcontinental railroad by making grants of public land (as in the United States, a process not free from scandal) to the Canadian Pacific Railway, which became one of the most powerful corporations in the country. Canada had established its first national protected area of public land in Alberta west of Calgary in 1885, when Prime Minister John A. Macdonald established the 7,000-acre Banff Hot Springs Reserve. In 1886, he protected a larger area, called Yoho, in the same region. In 1887, with the support of the Canadian Pacific, the Parliament of Canada enacted the Rocky Mountains Park Act, expanding the protected area to more than 166,000 acres and designating it a national park. Over time, Canada established other protected areas of public lands in the same region, just as the United States was doing south of the border. In 1932, the two nations designated the Waterton-Glacier International Peace Park along their shared border.[15]

THE SUPREME COURT EXHUMES AND REBURIES THE CONSTITUTION'S ENCLAVE CLAUSE

In 1885, the U.S. Supreme Court handed down a decision in *Fort Leavenworth Railroad v. Lowe* that swept away a potential constitutional obstacle in the path of the budding movement to reserve more public lands. The opinion for the unanimous court, written by Justice Stephen J. Field, was the most complete consideration the Court has ever given to the Constitution's obscure Enclave Clause, which spoke of Congress exercising "exclusive legislation" over certain places that the United States purchases inside a state with its consent.[16]

Field's opinion acknowledged that the clause's peculiar language might be taken as suggesting that states must consent to all acquisitions of property by the general government within their borders. He noted that "this view has not generally prevailed" since the Constitution was adopted, and that "if any doubt has ever existed" about U.S. authority, it "has not had sufficient strength to create any effective dissent from the general opinion." He also pointed out that the United States had, from time to time, "reserved certain portions" of its "immense domain" in order to use them to serve national objectives, and that such actions had never been regarded as raising Enclave Clause questions.

In effect, *Fort Leavenworth* exhumed the Enclave Clause from its obscure grave and, finding it had nothing important to say about public land policy making, reburied it. Ever since, as before, the clause has played no significant role in matters involving public lands. The Constitution's Property Clause, which gives Congress practically unrestricted authority to act, has remained the bedrock constitutional authority regarding public lands.[17]

CHAPTER SEVENTEEN

Congress Closes In on Major Reforms

THE FIFTIETH CONGRESS, WHICH took office in 1887, included "Silver Senator" William Stewart, returned to office by the Nevada legislature after he left the Senate in 1875 under a cloud of scandal. Stewart, who had spent the intervening years pursuing mining ventures and practicing law, soon squared off with John Wesley Powell in a celebrated struggle that had public land policy at its core.[1]

The arid western lands had been beset by a combination of multiyear droughts and devastating winters. It was clearer than ever that the Desert Land Act of 1877, which depended on state and private investment in irrigation works, was not fulfilling its goal of promoting crop farming in the region. Stewart and Henry Teller of Colorado, who had rejoined the Senate two years earlier after a stint as Interior secretary, became leaders of an "irrigation caucus"—an informal group of western members of Congress who advocated direct federal investment in irrigation projects. In February 1888, they persuaded the Senate to support a systematic investigation of the irrigation potential of western public lands.

Powell quickly saw in it an opportunity to advance his idea of how settlement should proceed in the region, so he worked with Stewart and others to craft a joint resolution, approved by both houses on March 20, calling on the Interior secretary to undertake what came to be known as the Irrigation Survey. A few months later, Congress enacted an appropriations bill that included

$100,000 for assessing "the extent to which the arid region of the United States can be redeemed by irrigation" and to select sites for "reservoirs and other hydraulic works."[2]

Had Congress said only that, no ruckus might have ensued. But a significant amendment had been added to the bill in the House by George Symes (R-Colo.) and William Breckinridge (D-Ky.). It provided that all the public lands designated or selected for reservoirs and other irrigation facilities, and "all the lands made susceptible of irrigation" by such facilities, were to be "from this time henceforth hereby reserved from sale" and put off-limits "to entry, settlement or occupation until further provided by law." That sweeping language would, if it became law, immediately close vast amounts of public land in the arid regions to entry or occupation until Congress provided otherwise. (Congressman William Holman criticized the amendment because he thought it restricted opportunities for homesteading and would ultimately lead to more governmental subsidies for powerful interests.)[3]

When the appropriations bill moved to the Senate, Teller immediately saw the political problem that the Symes amendment created, complaining to his colleagues that the House "could not have understood" what it was doing in withdrawing practically "all of what we call the arid lands." To keep the survey moving forward, Stewart intervened to craft an awkward compromise. It retained the language of the Symes-Breckinridge amendment, but gave the president authority "at any time in his discretion by proclamation" to open any or all of the "lands reserved by this provision to settlement under the homestead laws." As so amended, President Cleveland signed it into law on October 2, 1888.[4]

A few weeks later, Benjamin Harrison was elected president even though Cleveland, in his bid for a second term, had won the popular vote by a slim margin. In his last annual message to Congress before yielding to Harrison, Cleveland praised the Irrigation Survey, specifically mentioning its wisdom in suspending all public land entries until the survey was complete, because they could "create rights antagonistic to the common interest." "No harm can follow this cautionary conduct," he added, because "the public good presents no demand for hasty dispossession of national ownership and control" of these lands. Despite his soothing words, speculators, developers, and prospective settlers would not be pleased at being denied, even temporarily, the opportunity to enter and gain title to public lands.[5]

Powell, ever the capable, disciplined civil servant, immediately set his small staff to work on the Irrigation Survey. Understanding the magnitude of the task, he persuaded Congress to give him another $350,000 in March 1889. By midyear, his staff had identified dozens of reservoir sites and several million acres of land suitable for irrigation, but serious political trouble loomed. Despite the Symes-Breckinridge amendment, thousands of claims were filed under divestiture laws like the Preemption Act and the Homestead Act throughout the arid region.

In August, the GLO directed all local land offices to cancel all claims filed after October 2, 1888, when the bill containing the Symes-Breckinridge amendment became law. Although this did no more than confirm what Congress had already done, it made the effect of the amendment more concrete, and provoked outcry. The chair of the House Committee on Irrigation, William Vandever (R-Calif.), later claimed that the protests were fueled more by speculators than by bona fide settlers, but no bright line separated the two. In the meantime, Powell's staff continued the survey. The controversy intensified as 1889 drew to a close.[6]

President Harrison had a tool in hand that might have quieted the protests—the language that Senator Stewart had added to the Symes amendment, giving the president authority, "at any time in his discretion," to open "any portion or all" of the lands to settlement "under the homestead laws." But Powell wanted to complete his survey before restoring any public lands to any kind of entry, in order to put into practice his long-held vision of orderly development of an irrigation economy in the arid region, and he persuaded Harrison to back him.

As protests mounted, the Department of Justice was asked to examine the matter. In late May 1890, the acting attorney general, future president William Howard Taft, confirmed that the 1888 legislation had indeed effected an immediate withdrawal of all public land "upon any part of the arid regions which might possibly come within the operation of" the Irrigation Survey. Although acknowledging that the law had a "far-reaching effect," Taft said he could not "deprive the words of the act of their ordinary and necessary meaning." Taft's opinion did not pacify Senator Stewart.[7]

CONGRESS CONSIDERS GENERIC FOREST RESERVATION AUTHORITY

Meanwhile, the larger campaign to curb abuses and redirect public land policy had been steadily gaining steam. In the mid-1880s, the House and the Senate each twice approved bills making major reforms of the public land laws, including tightening the Homestead Act and repealing the Timber Culture Act,

Preemption Act, and Desert Land Act. The bills had somewhat different features, and the two houses could not reconcile the differences. As is often the case with major legislative reforms, the disagreement was not so much over what the new policy should be, but over the transition to the new regime, such as how to handle certain contested preemption claims.[8]

The idea of reserving public forested lands, which had been the subject of numerous bills since 1876, became a component of the broader campaign to reform public land policy. In 1886, Bernhard Fernow, born and educated in Prussia, became the head of the new Division of Forestry, which Congress established in the Department of Agriculture. He soon added his voice to the growing chorus calling for reserving public forest lands in U.S. ownership. The next year, at the Interior Department, a General Land Office lawyer, Edward A. Bowers, prepared a detailed report titled "Plan for the Management and Disposition of the Public Timber Lands."[9]

In early 1888, Senator Eugene Hale (R-Me.) introduced a bill that was based substantially on Fernow's and Bowers's ideas. It would withdraw all public forestlands from divestment laws, establish a program for classifying them, and authorize the president to designate some as "permanent forest reserves." These reserves would be managed by a bureau in the Interior Department, with the president having discretion to use the military to patrol them. Hale's bill was referred to the Senate Committee on Agriculture and Forestry, but further action was blocked by Senator Preston Plumb, the chair of the Public Lands Committee. Plumb's objection was not to the substance of Hale's bill. Indeed, as a first-term senator ten years earlier, Plumb had sponsored legislation to reserve all forested public lands in national ownership. Now, he argued that his committee should have exclusive jurisdiction over Hale's bill. This jurisdictional tussle between committees in Congress foreshadowed conflicts between the Agriculture and Interior Departments in the executive branch that would play out for decades to come.[10]

In the House of Representatives, the chair of the Public Lands Committee, William Holman, introduced a major public land reform bill in 1887. It listed as its purposes "to secure to actual settlers the public lands adapted to agriculture" and "to protect the forests on the public domain." Holman, then in his twelfth term, was known for his mastery of legislative rules, his close attention to detail, and his fiscal conservatism. Like the bills that had passed both houses in the two previous Congresses, Holman's bill would have repealed some divestment laws, tightened others (such as the fraud-plagued commutation provision of the Homestead Act), and authorized the United States to auction timber from public lands classified as "chiefly valuable" for lumbering while retaining ownership of the lands themselves.[11]

The most significant feature of Holman's bill was its section 8. It gave the president discretion to "set apart and reserve, in any State or Territory," public lands that are "wholly or in part covered with timber or undergrowth, whether of commercial value or not, as public reservations, on which the trees and undergrowth shall be protected from waste or injury, under the charge of the Secretary of the Interior."

Holman's bill received extensive consideration on the floor of the House in late March and again in late June 1888. When Congressman John McShane (D-Neb.) moved to strike section 8, Holman vigorously defended it. The "whole country is aroused to the importance of preserving" public lands not fit for "agricultural purposes or for the establishment of homes," Holman told his colleagues, so they "ought to go to the benefit of the whole people rather than to any favored classes." After McShane's motion was rejected on voice vote, the House approved Holman's reform bill with section 8 intact in late June 1888.[12]

In the Senate, Holman's bill never emerged from committee, and the Fiftieth Congress adjourned on March 3, 1889, without enacting any significant public land reform legislation. Despite this setback, it was plain, as the 1880s drew to a close, that bipartisan support existed for making major changes in public land policy.

DISPARATE STRANDS COME TOGETHER IN A POWERFUL MOVEMENT

Congress had mostly tinkered on the margins of public land policy ever since its great burst of activity between 1862 and 1872 had produced landmarks such as the Homestead Act, the transcontinental railroad land grants, the Yosemite and Yellowstone legislation, and the Mining Law. Over the next fifteen years, laws that addressed public lands issues piecemeal did not work well in practice, even though most public lands had by then been cleared of Indian title.

The Desert Land Act of 1877 and the Timber and Stone Act of 1878, both of which aimed to privatize more public lands, had mostly failed to achieve their objectives and had proved at least as susceptible to manipulation and abuse as earlier laws. The Unlawful Inclosures Act of 1885 had not quieted the concerns of homestead advocates and others about the dominance of large corporate livestock interests on public lands to which they had no legal claim.

Although Congress had halted generous grants of public lands to railroads in 1871, their exercise of monopoly power fueled protests, especially among agricultural interests that depended on them for shipping products to market. The protests found expression in the Granger movement, which began in the 1870s, and later in the Populist Party. It also led Congress in 1887 to enact general legislation requiring railroad companies to forfeit grants of public lands where they had failed to construct rail lines. That same year, Congress brought railroad practices under federal regulation through a pioneering regulatory agency, the Interstate Commerce Commission, established in the executive branch.[13]

These changes reflected a growing sense that public land policy was simply not working for the benefit of ordinary Americans. While public opinion still favored using public lands to people the landscape with yeoman farmers, it was clear to ardent supporters of homesteading like William Holman that the arid, rugged West could never be thickly settled with small family farms. Henry George's warning that the large proportion of public lands not suitable for agriculture was likely to fall into a few hands reverberated with a populace that was increasingly alienated from the Gilded Age's corruption-tinged celebration of wealth.

Keeping a significant portion of the public lands in national ownership emerged as an attractive option because it could serve several objectives. Reserving lands in headwaters areas could help safeguard water supplies for use downstream. Curbing unregulated overgrazing could forestall further desertification of arid lands while providing more stability for livestock operators. The works of artists, photographers, and charismatic evangelists like John Muir had given a growing number of Americans a sense of the magnificent scenery that could be found on the nation's remaining public lands. Improvements in transportation fed a flourishing public taste for scenic excursions, creating a fledgling tourist industry. Those concerned about disappearing wildlife and habitats were also beginning to wield influence, especially among opinion leaders.

More Americans, inspired by the teachings of Marsh and others, saw public landscapes through the lens of science. One manifestation of this was a growing interest in protecting archeological sites on public lands. As Indian numbers and conflicts with non-Indians diminished, Euro-Americans slowly began to develop a deeper appreciation of Indian culture, making it, in the words of Anne Farrar Hyde, "something to preserve rather than to destroy." In the Southwest, Indians had successfully adapted to the region's aridity for millennia, and evidence of ancient occupation was all over the landscape, much of it on public lands that had been cleared of Indian title. It was becoming apparent that, without governmental action, many sites and relics would be destroyed or plundered—either way, they would be lost to science as well as to their cultural heirs.[14]

In 1888, Congressman William Holman introduced a bill to safeguard archaeological sites on public lands near Santa Fe, New Mexico, and to instruct the director of the Geological Survey to identify other ones for Congress to protect "from injury and spoliation." While his bill failed to advance, the General Land Office began in 1889 to withdraw specific sites from divestment laws, despite lacking specific authority to do so. That same year, Massachusetts senator George Hoar, responding to a petition by several prominent Bostonians, amended an appropriation bill to authorize the president to "reserve from settlement and sale" public land in the Arizona Territory containing a prominent ruin called Casa Grande. Known to Europeans for nearly two centuries, the large, multistoried ancient structure had suffered considerable damage from vandalism and erosion, made even worse when adjacent land began to be irrigated and cultivated. Hoar's amendment, which also appropriated $2,000 to protect the structure, soon became law.[15]

All told, disparate impulses were converging to persuade a growing number of Americans that their public lands could and should be something more than an instrument of national expansion through agricultural settlement. Holding a significant portion of these lands for broad public objectives could help recover a sense of national pride and unity shattered by the Civil War, allowing the public lands to reprise the role they had played during the nation's formative period, of helping to stitch a nation together.

As the last decade of the nineteenth century dawned, proposals to facilitate keeping significant amounts of lands in public ownership were combined with proposals to reform, repeal, and otherwise address the inadequacies and abuses of programs designed to privatize public land. Like water behind an obstruction, this current of reform was searching for a way through the congressional process. It soon found one.

PART FOUR THE GREAT TRANSITION, PHASE ONE, 1890–1901

CHAPTER EIGHTEEN

Congress Guts Powell's Irrigation Survey and Establishes New National Parks

DURING THE FIFTY-FIRST CONGRESS, which was in session from March 4, 1889, to March 3, 1891, six new states were welcomed into the union—Montana, North and South Dakota, and Washington in November 1889, and Idaho and Wyoming in July 1890. Only two others, Nebraska in 1867 and Colorado in 1876, had been admitted since the end of the Civil War. The new states' twelve new senators, all Republicans, gave the western part of the country considerably more political power than before. Their influence would be further enhanced because from that point forward, members from the West would almost always form a solid majority on the committees in both the House and the Senate that were primarily responsible for public lands.[1]

In that Fifty-First Congress, the Republicans took control of the House by the narrow margin of 164–159 and maintained their slim 39–37 majority in the Senate. It was the first time in sixteen years that both houses were controlled by the president's party. Lewis Payson, a Republican lawyer from Illinois in his fifth and final term (he was defeated in 1890), replaced William Holman as chair of the Public Lands Committee.

This Congress did little on public lands in its first session, but that changed dramatically in the second session, beginning in March 1890. As the year began, John Wesley Powell was working to preserve as well as advance the work of his Irrigation Survey. By June, the survey had identified two hundred reservoir sites and about thirty million acres of public land that might be irrigated from them.

The General Land Office then began to take steps to open the potentially irrigable lands to entry under laws like the Homestead Act, but progress was slow.[2]

Senator Stewart, whose relationship with Powell had frayed during their joint western tour the previous summer, wanted faster action, and he lined up allies in Congress. The showdown was not long in coming. In July, Powell testified before a hostile Senate Appropriations Committee. Though not a member of the committee, Stewart participated in the hearing and complained to Powell that he had "the whole country reserved" from settlement. Powell fought back, pointing out that Congress had approved the Symes-Breckinridge amendment, which made the sweeping reservation that was causing the trouble, and that he, Powell, had never advocated it. But Stewart, too canny to let Powell off so easily, asked him whether he would support simply repealing the reservation. Powell's reply had a candor that proved fatal: "No, sir," he said; the reservation was "wise."[3]

Powell also refused to consider having President Harrison restore some public lands to the operation of the homestead law while the survey proceeded. Had it been a classroom exercise, it would have been easy to defend Powell's insistence that public lands remain off-limits to the homestead law while all the facts were being collected. But this was the rough-and-tumble world of politics, and his stubbornness cost him dearly.

Powell and the administration were not without allies. In the House, both the current (Payson) and former (Holman) chairs of the Public Lands Committee opposed reopening the public lands to the hodgepodge of divestment laws before Congress could reform them.[4]

But Stewart and his allies were not to be denied. The Sundry Civil Appropriations Act, signed into law on August 30, 1890, included a rider that not only repealed the Symes-Breckinridge amendment but also gave effect to entries under the homestead law and similar statutes that had been made since it became law, excepting only those on reservoir sites that the survey had already identified. For good measure, Congress also gutted Powell's budget. The effect was what William deBuys described as a kind of "national repudiation" that greatly curtailed Powell's influence.[5]

This congressional rebuff owed more to Stewart and his allies reacting to Powell's stubbornness than to anything else. Specifically, it did not derail or even slow the political movement to reserve more public lands from divestment. Within six months, this same Congress would give the president broad and unilateral authority to establish what came to be known as forest reserves on public land.

As the movement for establishing forest reserves was gaining strength, Powell complained that reserves could impede rather than benefit the development of an irrigation-based economy, and he was harshly criticized by forest reserve advocates like Bernhard Fernow. On the other hand, Powell published an article in April 1890 in the *Century* magazine in which he described the "beauty and grandeur" of the arid region's "living forests" as "unexcelled," and noted that there "is universal sentiment in the West" that "measures should be taken by the General Government for the protection of the forests." (Powell had also endorsed establishing a national park at the Grand Canyon and had encouraged Arnold Hague at the U.S. Geological Survey to write about protecting the greater Yellowstone region.)[6] In the end, far from derailing the movement, the Irrigation Survey debacle may fairly be said to have helped prepare the way for well over 150 million acres of public land to be put in forest reserves over the next two decades.

CONGRESS PROTECTS LARGE TRACTS OF SCENIC PUBLIC LAND IN CALIFORNIA

At almost exactly the same time that it was gutting Powell's Irrigation Survey, Congress was approving two pieces of legislation that protected three areas of public land totaling more than a million acres in California's southern Sierra Nevada. By far the largest of these surrounded the 30,000 acres of Yosemite lands that Congress had given to California in 1864. The other two areas, considerably smaller and located dozens of miles to the south, encompassed giant sequoia groves.[7]

The campaign to secure these laws enlisted a coalition of diverse interests at both the grassroots and the national levels, a strategy followed many times in the decades to come. It began in January 1890 when, shortly after he returned to New York City from his California sojourn with John Muir, Robert Underwood Johnson of the *Century* magazine published an editorial calling for a large national park in the Yosemite region. In mid-March, Congressman William Vandever introduced a bill to "establish the Yosemite National Park" on some 128,000 acres of public land surrounding the 1864 grant to the state. For the next six months, the bill sat in Payson's Public Lands Committee.[8]

It had been known for some time that the very largest giant sequoias were located in groves considerably south of Yosemite. In 1880, General Land Office commissioner Williamson had withdrawn more than 2,000 acres of public land that included the so-called General Grant Grove, the largest tree having been named for the Civil War hero in 1867. In 1885, GLO commissioner Sparks had withdrawn 400,000 acres containing more giant sequoia groves some miles farther south, including the world's biggest tree (later named for General William T. Sherman), while his staff investigated whether a fraudulent land grab might be happening.

Upon taking office in 1889, the Harrison administration's new GLO commissioner began rescinding some of these withdrawals. Advocates for protecting the sequoia groves, such as the Fresno County journalist George Stewart, protested loudly. Both Interior secretary Noble and Congressman Vandever responded favorably to the complaints. Noble reinstated the withdrawals, and Vandever introduced legislation to establish a "public park, or pleasure ground" on some 23,000 acres. The bill was promptly reported out of the Public Lands Committee, with Chairman Payson emphasizing the need to "preserve these immense trees for future generations." Eventually, the bill was amended to add other sequoia groves, bringing the total area to nearly 50,000 acres. Vandever's bill, which did not give the area a name, sailed through both houses, and President Harrison signed it into law on September 25.[9]

Payson's committee then took up the Yosemite bill that Vandever had introduced six months earlier, and quickly reported out a substitute bill that expanded the area to be protected eightfold, to more than a million acres. The new boundaries generally conformed to recommendations that John Muir had made a month earlier in the *Century* magazine, and also included more sequoia groves near lands that Congress had just protected in the September 25 legislation. Both the House and Senate approved this second measure on September 30, and President Harrison signed it into law the next day, October 1, 1890.[10]

How this substitute bill came to be put together and enacted, with very little discussion, has never been satisfactorily explained. Some have suggested that the Southern Pacific Railroad was the catalyst, because its lawyer-lobbyist Daniel Zumwalt was apparently involved in moving the bill through Congress. Southern Pacific operated a spur line to Raymond, north of Fresno, which was a jumping-off point for stagecoaches to Yosemite, and also had extensive forest and agricultural landholdings in California. While its motivations can only be guessed at, it may have wanted to safeguard uplands that produced water supplies useful for irrigating its extensive Central Valley landholdings, to derive revenue from tourism that the region's splendid resources were already beginning to attract, and to protect its own commercial forestlands from competition.[11]

Details in both pieces of legislation strongly resembled the Yellowstone National Park legislation that Congress had approved nearly two decades earlier. But they also showed that a standard practice for naming public land reservations had not yet emerged, because one created an unnamed "public park" around some sequoia groves, and the other created "reserved forest lands" around the Yosemite Valley. In his annual report for 1890, Interior secretary Noble christened the reservation around Yosemite Valley "The Yosemite National Park," and the reservations to the south "Sequoia National Park" and "General Grant National Park." Although Congress eventually acquiesced in Noble's names, this was the first and last time that an executive branch official appended the "national park" label to an area of public land without Congress's advance approval. Ever since, Congress has claimed exclusive authority to create "national parks," and the executive has not contested it.[12]

As 1890 drew to a close, President Harrison directed the War Department to patrol the new California parks, as it had been doing at Yellowstone since 1886. At the same time, the U.S. Seventh Cavalry was providing a tragic coda to the U.S. government's long effort to move American Indians off most of the lands they had traditionally occupied. On December 29, 1890, near Wounded Knee, South Dakota, it massacred nearly three hundred Lakota Indians, mostly women and children, as part of a campaign to suppress the Ghost Dance, a spiritual movement that had gained adherents in many Indian communities and sought to revive and restore Indian traditions and ultimately recover their homelands. The massacre at Wounded Knee spelled the end of most such efforts for decades. It underscored how railroad, lumber, mining, and livestock interests, as well as ordinary settlers, had secured unrestricted access to public lands cleared of Indian title. But it also came at a time when the idea of holding some areas of public land permanently in public ownership was gaining considerable favor.[13]

The army remained in the California parks for the next quarter century. The soldiers were generally enthusiastic about fulfilling what they regarded as a patriotic responsibility; in an magazine article in 1899, Lieutenant John Lockwood expressed appreciation for the opportunity to help protect the wonders of nature that Congress's "wise decision" had preserved "in perpetuity" for "our common country." An African American infantry regiment known as the Buffalo Soldiers was stationed there for several years, and in 1903 one of its men, Captain Charles Young, served as acting military superintendent of Sequoia and General Grant Parks.[14]

As much as 5 percent of the land inside the boundaries of these new California parks was subject to claims filed earlier by miners, speculators, and settlers, which caused headaches for the military authorities. The claims were eventually addressed through boundary adjustments. One of the military superintendents expressed more sympathy for a few dozen Indians who were still residing inside park boundaries, acknowledging they had a "moral right" to the land superior to that of other claimants. Reflecting the spirit of the times, the boundary adjustment legislation was mute on the Indian presence.[15]

CONGRESS ESTABLISHES NEW NATIONAL PARKS IN THE EAST

As it was taking steps to preserve scenic natural landscapes in California, Congress was elsewhere expanding the purposes of national land ownership to include other parts of the nation's heritage. On August 19, 1890, President Harrison, who had served in the Union Army, signed legislation establishing the nation's first national military park at Chickamauga and Chattanooga along the Georgia-Tennessee border. The symbolism was obvious: Confederates had won the battle of Chickamauga, and the Union Army later prevailed at Chattanooga. Eleven days later, Harrison signed legislation establishing the Antietam National Battlefield site in Maryland.

These actions came more than a quarter century after Lee's surrender at Appomattox ended a war in which more than 3 million Americans took up arms against each other, and 2 percent of the nation's population died as a result. Congress soon took similar action for other battlefields, including Shiloh in 1894, Gettysburg in 1895, and Vicksburg in 1899. Most of these battlefield parks, all put under the supervision of the War Department, were sizable— Chickamauga covered nearly eight thousand acres; Shiloh, six thousand.[16]

Nearly all of these lands were privately owned, requiring Congress to provide both authority and funds to acquire them. A noteworthy feature of the Chickamauga legislation was its authorizing the Interior secretary to strike agreements with local landowners that allowed them to retain ownership if they would agree to preserve their lands in accordance with secretarial regulations. This was the seed of an idea that would ripen into what are today called "conservation easements," a mechanism in property law whereby a landowner makes a legally binding commitment, usually for some financial benefit, to limit development on its land to serve a public objective.

The authorizing legislation called these areas "national parks" or "national military parks," and characterized their purpose as "preserving and suitably marking" the battlefield lands so that armies "may have the history" of their battles "preserved on the ground where they fought." The battlefield parks, which were managed by the War Department until the 1930s, soon attracted many thousands of visitors annually, far more than were then coming to the few national parks in the West.[17]

Some years later, John Lacey, who had served in the Union Army throughout the Civil War and went on to serve eight terms in Congress, described the purpose of these parks as to "commemorate the full and complete reconciliation that has come upon the participants in our Civil War," allowing the survivors to meet "on this scene as friends rejoicing in a Union cemented by so much of sorrow and strife." Not everyone shared this view. Frederick Douglass argued that death "has no power to change moral qualities," and that one should "never forget the difference between those who fought for liberty and those who fought for slavery."[18]

But this was an era when, after Reconstruction ended in 1877, Jim Crow racial segregation was gradually being imposed throughout the South and would be upheld by the Supreme Court in its infamous *Plessy v. Ferguson* decision in 1896. That the temper of the times was running against Douglass was also shown in 1897 when Congress specified, in appropriating funds for Gettysburg National Park, that the field of battle should be marked with tablets giving historic facts "compiled without censure and without praise."[19]

Earlier efforts to preserve historic areas—in New York and at Mount Vernon and Monticello in Virginia in the middle of the nineteenth century—had not involved public ownership of the properties. The battlefield parks were the leading edge of a broader movement that called for public ownership of significant features of the nation's heritage. Within a few years, Lacey championed generic legislation, the Antiquities Act, that would help protect in national ownership many lands important to the nation's history.

A month after signing the legislation establishing the first national military park, President Harrison signed into law a bill creating a "public park or pleasure ground for the benefit and enjoyment of the people"—cribbing language from the Yellowstone legislation—along a tributary of the Potomac that bisected the District of Columbia, the seat of the national government. The land in what became Rock Creek Park was mostly privately owned, and Congress established a commission to select up to two thousand acres of land for acquisition. In contrast to its tightfistedness in funding the big western parks, Congress appropriated up to $1.2 million for Rock Creek, the nation's first urban national park. Eventually, several more followed.[20]

CHAPTER NINETEEN

Congress Gives the President Broad Authority to Reserve Public Lands

EARLY IN 1890, PRESIDENT HARRISON asked Congress to enact legislation to prevent the "rapid and needless destruction of our great forest areas," and forwarded the recommendation by the American Association for the Advancement of Science to establish reservations of public lands in the higher reaches of watersheds in order to preserve favorable hydrologic conditions.[1] In February, House Public Lands Committee chair Lewis Payson introduced a bill to repeal the Timber Culture Act of 1873, a measure that he criticized as facilitating "land grabbing." Payson's bill did not address the matter of reserving public lands, probably because of the controversy then beginning to stir about the reservation made by the Symes-Breckinridge amendment to the Irrigation Survey legislation Congress had earlier enacted.[2]

Shortly before the House approved Payson's bill in late March, William Holman reminded his colleagues of the need to take other steps, such as those that had "been under consideration for some years past," to protect the remaining forests on public lands. Congressman Mark Dunnell (R-Minn.) agreed, drawing attention to a recent American Forestry Association petition calling for the reservation of all public lands containing forests.[3]

Payson's bill then went to the Senate Committee on Public Lands. There, a number of other reforms of public land laws were added, drawing from ideas that had been discussed for years. Still more reforms were added on the Senate floor. In late September, by a vote of 41–3, the Senate approved the measure. By then it consisted of nineteen separate provisions, but still did not address reservations of public lands.[4]

As was customary, a six-person conference committee (two Republicans and one Democrat from each chamber) was convened to reconcile the very different House and Senate versions. Its members included Payson, Holman, and Senator Preston B. Plumb, chair of the Senate Public Lands Committee. Before the conference committee made its report, elections were held in November 1890. The Democrats picked up 86 seats, which meant they would control the House in the Fifty-Second Congress, which would convene late the following year, while the Republicans retained control of the Senate. On February 28, 1891, three days before the end of the outgoing Fifty-First Congress, the conference committee sent its recommended bill to the House and the Senate.

Most of its twenty-four sections were drawn from the Senate-passed bill. Some, like a repeal of the preemption act, reflected opposition to giving away public land to anyone other than genuine farmer-settlers, a stance that Holman and Payson and many other members of Congress had supported. But the twenty-fourth section had not appeared in either bill. It authorized the president to "set apart and reserve, in any State or Territory having public land bearing forests, in any part of the public lands wholly or in part covered with timber or undergrowth, whether of commercial value or not, as public reservations."[5]

The deliberations of the conference committee were not recorded, so how and why it decided to include section 24 has never been conclusively established. Later, several claimed credit for it, illustrating the maxim, attributed to the Roman senator and historian Tacitus, that while failure is an orphan, success has many parents.[6]

The most likely explanation is the most straightforward—it was inserted at the suggestion of William Holman. Adlai Stevenson, who had served with Holman in Congress and was later elected vice president under Grover Cleveland in 1892, once wrote (borrowing from Shakespeare) that it sometimes seemed as though Holman could "look into the seeds of time and tell which grain will grow and which will not." That was an apt description of section 24, because the seed it planted would, within two decades, grow into a national forest system of well over 150 million acres.[7]

Section 24 closely follows the wording of section 8 of Holman's public land reform bill that the House had approved in 1888. Like many who had championed using public lands first and foremost to people the landscape with small farms, Holman had come to recognize that this outcome simply was not possible on vast tracts of public land in the more arid and rugged regions of the West. The realization was a turning point in America's public land policy. The question became, if these lands were not suitable for small farms, how should they be deployed to advance the national interest, the common good? For Holman and, ultimately, Congress, the next logical step was to give the president broad power to reserve these lands, removing them from the operation of divestment laws and the abuses that plagued them.

Whoever transposed section 8 of Holman's 1888 bill into section 24 of the 1891 bill deleted the last few lines of the former. This was a shrewd decision, because it eliminated two features that could have been red flags for some members of Congress. The first deletion removed a clause giving the president authority to deploy the military to protect the reserves. Even though the army was already involved in policing Yellowstone National Park and would shortly do the same in the brand-new California parks, providing the president with blanket authority to deploy troops surely would have invited opposition. Senator George Vest, for example, though an ardent defender of Yellowstone, opposed its occupation by the military.

The second deletion removed language from the 1888 bill that called for "trees and undergrowth" found on the reserves to be "protected from waste or injury." Its removal meant section 24 provided no congressional guidance for how these reserves should be administered. Silence on this point allowed the bill to attract support from members of Congress who likely held differing views on, for example, the extent to which livestock grazing, mining, or logging would be permitted on the reserves. For the conferees, and ultimately the Fifty-First Congress, the most pressing task was to give the president the authority to prevent entry or claims on public lands that could lead to the loss of U.S. ownership. Taking that first step would give Congress time to deliberate over the details of how such reservations should be managed. As it turned out, because opinions differed and the politics were complex, those deliberations extended over the next six years, showing just how politically wise was the decision to streamline section 24.

Neither the new section nor any other part of the conference bill prompted discussion on the Senate floor, where it was quickly approved by a voice vote. Discussion on the House floor that same day, February 28, probed more deeply. Congressman Payson told his colleagues that parts of the bill had been "debated and discussed during the last six or eight years almost *ad infinitum*" and had "passed the House on more than one occasion." He drew specific attention to the fact that section 24 had been added to the bill in conference. He

Thomas McRae, 1851–1929 (Bain Collection, Prints & Photographs Division, Library of Congress, LC-B2-5813-3)

emphasized how it served the interests of the irrigation lobby because it was aimed at preserving watersheds, including reservoir sites and land "tributary" to them, thus protecting "the water supply in that country."[8]

Thomas McRae (D-Ark.), who had served as a courier for the Confederate Army when barely in his teens and who would become chair of the House Public Lands Committee in the next Congress, expressed concern that section 24 gave the president an "extraordinary and dangerous power," because it could apply to public land "fit for agricultural purposes," and thus invite a repeat of the Irrigation Survey debacle. Significantly, however, McRae did not object to it becoming law, confident that if the president abused the power he was given, Congress could reverse him.

As the debate was drawing to a close, Congressman Roswell Flower (D-N.Y.) not only strongly defended section 24 but also advocated extending the principle of public ownership of watershed lands to other parts of the nation. People in the East, he pointed out, "suffer" because their uplands have been "denuded of its timber," causing floods and erosion and rendering water supplies uncertain. (It took two more decades, but in 1911 Congress agreed with Flower by enacting the Weeks Act, authorizing the national government to acquire lands to protect watersheds throughout the nation.)

After that vigorous debate, the bill came back to the House floor briefly on March 2, when it was approved without further comment. That day, as the bill was on its way to the White House, a last-minute complication arose. President Harrison threatened to veto the entire bill, now called the General Revision Act of 1891, because it included an obscure provision sponsored by Senator Wilbur Sanders (R-Mont.) that gave persons accused of illegally cutting timber on certain public lands some new defenses. The president had become convinced Sanders's measure was so loosely worded that it effectively immunized plunderers of public forests from punishment.

To head off the veto in a way that avoided having to rewrite the bill, Senator Plumb quickly drafted and put forward a *separate* bill to fix the problem that Harrison perceived. (The fix simply gave the Interior secretary specific authority to prescribe regulations governing timber cutting on those public lands affected by Sanders's proposal.) In urging enactment of that separate bill, Senator Plumb told his colleagues that he thought the president's concern about Sanders's measure was grossly exaggerated, and he drew particular attention to section 24, which, as Plumb put it, gave the president broad authority to "set apart forest reservations, and thereby gives him a control which he has not now over the forests of the United States." Nevertheless, Plumb said, the president's veto threat on the eve of the adjournment of the Fifty-First Congress created a "very considerable" emergency that had to be addressed, because it threatened to bring down the entire bill, which was of "great consequence to the whole public-land system of the United States and its administration."[9]

Plumb's last-ditch strategy worked. His bill amending Sanders's provision to meet President Harrison's objection was quickly approved by both houses that same day, and on March 3, Harrison signed into law both it and the big reform package, the General Revision Act, that included section 24.

Because section 24 was added to the bill by the conference committee, a number of historians have considered its pedigree suspect—calling it a "fluke" that was "consummated in half-hidden haste" or that "slipped through Congress without question and without debate," was "little-noticed," "poorly understood," or was enacted "entirely by accident," passing "almost unnoticed" or even "unintentionally."[10] Such characterizations make a good story. They also feed into a narrative that over time has found considerable acceptance, especially in the West; namely, that presidents used (and abused) their section 24 authority to grab public lands for the nation over the objection of states and local communities. Even more, because section 24 is perhaps the single most important law that has produced today's public lands, these characterizations have fueled a general impression that this important American institution has not been the product of well-considered political judgments reflecting prevailing public opinion.

But section 24 was not a fluke. Its core idea had been around for years and had been approved by the House in the previous Congress. It was hardly unusual for Congress to enact an important measure as part of a multipart package rather than a stand-alone bill. Even adding such a measure late in a complex reform bill's journey through Congress was hardly without precedent. The addition was not hidden. Its significance was discussed on the floor of the House and specifically mentioned by Senator Plumb on the Senate floor. Any member in either the House or the Senate could have moved to strike it as being out of regular order, but no one did.

It was also not uncommon for Congress to give the executive broad power to reserve public lands from divestment laws for particular reasons, or to acquiesce in presidential reservations made without express sanction, an executive practice since the founding era. Moreover, the idea of giving the executive explicit and broad power to reserve forested public lands had steadily gained adherents from both Republicans and Democrats since the 1870s. Even though William Holman once described the Fifty-First Congress as the "most disagreeable" he had ever known, the General Revision Act that included section 24 provoked no disagreement along either party or sectional lines. Two of the six members of the conference committee were from South Dakota, a state with a substantial amount of public land. Five other recently admitted western states also had a great deal of public land within their borders.[11]

By expressly conferring on the president such broad power to reserve public lands from divestment, Congress did somewhat alter the political dynamic. When Congress considers legislation that applies to a specific tract of public land, it typically gives substantial deference to the view of its members who represent that area. The president, representing all the people in the nation, tends to give somewhat less deference to local views. Even though Congress can always reverse the president's action, it is usually considerably easier to stop legislation from being enacted than it is to enact it. The effect of section 24 on the balance of power between the executive and legislative branches was demonstrated many times in the next couple of decades.

There is little doubt that members of Congress, especially Holman, understood the political dynamics involved. When, in the summer of 1890, Congress debated repealing the Symes-Breckinridge amendment, which had reserved most western public lands pending completion of the Irrigation Survey, Senator

Stewart had tried to blame the executive, not Congress, for the uproar. But Holman emphasized that Congress was responsible for it, and at the same time drew attention to his reform bill that the House had passed in 1888, which included the provision on which section 24 was based. The repeal of the Symes-Breckinridge amendment in late August 1890 thus helped clear the way for Congress to give the president authority to make reservations on an area-by-area basis, for this made the president, not Congress, politically responsible for the reservation decisions.[12]

CHAPTER TWENTY

The First Forest Reserves

THE MOST CONVINCING EVIDENCE that the enactment of section 24 was not a quirk, and that the reservation movement enjoyed wide public support in the West as well as elsewhere, was furnished by its implementation. Over the next three years, mostly in response to requests from local communities, Presidents Harrison and Cleveland established seventeen reserves encompassing approximately 18 million acres of public lands in five states (California, Colorado, Oregon, Washington, and Wyoming) and three territories (Alaska, Arizona, and New Mexico).[1]

Section 24 did not use the word "forest," and it authorized public lands to be reserved even if they contained only "undergrowth" or trees without "commercial value." And from the very beginning, section 24 was used to reserve large areas of grasslands, shrublands, and even deserts with relatively little vegetation. Even if it had been thought desirable to reserve only lands covered with trees (which it was not), it would have been impossible to do so because of the wide variation in vegetative coverings over large landscapes. Nevertheless, the lands reserved under section 24 came to be known as "forest reserves."

The legislation was not four weeks old when President Harrison used it to proclaim a "public forest reservation" on 1 million acres of public land in Wyoming abutting the eastern and southern boundaries of Yellowstone National Park. Five months later, Harrison added more than 200,000 acres to this first reserve. The reserve included the headwaters of the Yellowstone River, rich wildlife habitat, timber stands, grasslands, and abundant scenery. It was not surprising that Harrison started there; he had been a champion of Yellowstone while representing Indiana in the U.S. Senate from 1881 to 1887.

The day after Harrison signed the first proclamation, Thomas Carter of Montana became the twenty-sixth commissioner of the General Land Office, and the first one from a state west of Iowa. Carter, who had been Montana's first House member on its admission to the union in 1889, had voted in favor of the bill containing section 24. Since he was narrowly defeated for reelection in 1890, it became law on his last day of serving in the House.

It was an important moment for the GLO. For eight decades it had been mostly concerned with overseeing the transfer of public lands out of U.S. ownership. Now it had to grapple with a different challenge, namely, managing large tracts of land that the United States was keeping, a challenge made more difficult because section 24 gave it no guidance on how the lands were to be managed. It was also an important moment for the politically ambitious Carter, whom the Montana legislature later twice elected to the U.S. Senate.

On May 15, 1891, Carter directed his staff to undertake a systematic inventory of candidates for forest reserves, looking, he emphasized, to "reserve all public lands in mountainous and other regions" where timber or undergrowth "is the means provided by nature to absorb and check" water flows for the use of "communities and settlements" downstream. Besides examining the terrain, resources, and ownership patterns, the process that Carter put in place called for personally interviewing local officials and residents and advertising the GLO's recommendations in local and state or territorial newspapers and inviting comment on them. Although that kind of systematic consultation with affected interests would become routine in modern times, in that era it was an innovation.[2]

Initially, Carter encouraged his staff to recommend "early action" if it thought a particular tract of public land was at risk of being "despoiled" while the review was in process. This highlighted a problem that quickly emerged. In the months that it could take to investigate an area, consult with stakeholders, and decide whether to establish a forest reserve, speculators had ample time to enter the area and make homestead, mining, or other claims on public lands, claims that could ripen into ownership. In July, therefore, the Interior Department decided that *all* public lands being considered for forest reserves should be temporarily withdrawn from the operation of laws that could result in privatization. Although these temporary freezes lacked the explicit sanction of Congress, they provoked no outcry from the irrigation lobby or homestead advocates, most likely because, in general, they applied to uplands that lacked irrigation potential.

In October 1891, President Harrison established what was later labeled the White River Plateau Timber Land Reserve on more than a million acres of public land in Colorado. Today it attracts more visitors than any other national forest. The next year, he established three others in Colorado, including the Pikes Peak Timber Land Reserve. In 1893, following a visit to that reserve, Katharine Lee Bates was inspired to write the stirring words to "America the Beautiful." All told, before leaving office in March 1893, Harrison created fifteen forest reserves, covering more than 13 million acres. One was at the Grand Canyon in the Arizona Territory—not surprising, since in the 1880s then-senator Harrison had sponsored bills to make it a national park.

Most of Harrison's forest reserves were, as the House Public Lands Committee noted in an 1893 report, the result of petitions submitted by local groups "interested in the preservation of forest conditions" in their surroundings. A Senate committee report in 1892 quoted a memorial from the Colorado State Forestry Association, signed by several state officials, the chambers of commerce of Denver and Colorado Springs, and five hundred leading citizens, recommending the reservation of "all public lands along the crests of the mountain ranges and spurs in this state" and approximately six miles on either side.[3]

Petitioners had various motivations. At the time, as has been the case ever since, a higher percentage of westerners lived in urban areas than in any other region in the nation, and many favored curbing the willy-nilly divestment process that had long characterized U.S. public land policy. Some feared what might happen if large private enterprises came to own these areas. Some, like Portland's Water Commission in advocating for what became the Bull Run Timberland Reserve in Oregon in June 1892, were concerned that erosion and flooding could follow if the watersheds from which they drew their municipal water were skinned of vegetation. Some were concerned about preserving dam sites and protecting water supplies for irrigation. Some were concerned about fire and believed that public ownership would reduce that risk. Some wanted to preserve scenery for inspiration and areas of scientific interest for study, and to safeguard public access for hunting, fishing, and other forms of recreation.[4]

Harrison's largest single reservation was the 4-million-acre Sierra Forest Reserve in California. It included nearly all the lands that Commissioner Carter had temporarily withdrawn in late 1891 in response to requests from many of the same local interests that had supported Congress's establishment of the three national parks in the region the year before. The GLO described the bene-fits of the Sierra reserve as "beyond estimate," because not only would water supply sources be "guarded and preserved," but the "scenic features will attract tourists from all over the world." The boundaries were drawn to exclude lower-elevation lands and private land where feasible, leaving as opponents mostly herders who grazed, by some estimates, a half million sheep in the Kings and Kern River canyons.[5]

Harrison's proclamation in December 1892 reserving Afognak Island in Alaska, the second-largest island in the Kodiak Archipelago, southwest of Anchorage, showed the flexibility of section 24. It reserved not only the island but also "its adjacent bays and rocks and territorial waters," finding that the "public good would be promoted" if the "salmon and other fish and sea animals," as well as wildlife, timber, and other vegetation onshore, were protected and preserved "unimpaired." (The proclamation's call for preserving nature "unimpaired" anticipated by more than two decades language that Congress used in the establishing the national park system.) The proclamation noted that the U.S. commissioner of fish and fisheries had "selected" the island and the waters around it as a "reserve for the purpose of establishing fish culture stations," and in Interior Department records, it was called the Afognak Forest and Fish Culture Reserve. (Today it is part of the Chugach National Forest.)[6]

The breadth and depth of support for Harrison's reserves drowned out oppo-sition from speculators and other advocates of divestment. While there were occasional grumblings from a member of Congress or a western newspaper, nearly all of the criticism concerned where reserve boundaries were drawn.[7]

Nationally, the reception was enthusiastic. The *New York Times* editorial-ized in early 1893 that the value of the reserves "can hardly be overestimated," with benefits "both local and national—in securing the sources of water supply and thus insuring irrigation and bountiful crops, and in preserving unimpaired the glories and beauties of natural scenery."[8]

PRESIDENT CLEVELAND'S EARLY FOREST RESERVES

In the presidential election of 1892, Grover Cleveland denied Harrison a second term, becoming the only American president to serve nonconsecutive terms in office. In that election, James B. Weaver, the nominee of the Populist Party, whose platform was to the left of the two major parties in seeking to limit the influence of large corporations and financial interests, carried Colorado, Idaho, Kansas, Nevada, and North Dakota, making it the first third party since the Civil War to win electoral votes.

The Democrats gained control of the Senate by a 42–38 margin, and though they lost some seats in the House, they remained firmly in control there too. Immediately on reclaiming the office, Cleveland found himself dealing with severe economic troubles that came to be known as the Panic of 1893 and plunged the nation into an economic depression lasting for his entire term of office. Still, in September of that year he used section 24 to create two new "public reservations" on public lands in Oregon. His GLO commissioner, Silas W. Lamoreaux, explained that both were "favored by the people directly affected."[9]

A 19,000-acre reservation was made in response to a petition by the town of Ashland to protect the watershed above it. A vastly larger one, embracing 4.5 million acres along more than two hundred miles of the Cascade Range, was the result of a campaign that had begun well before section 24 was enacted. In 1889, an Oregon state legislator and former chief justice of the state's supreme court, John Waldo, introduced a resolution calling on Congress to set aside the entire Cascade Range in Oregon in order to keep it "free and open forever as a public reserve, park and resort." Livestock operators who grazed sheep in the Cascades blocked Waldo's resolution, but over the next few years the idea gained the support of the governor, other state and local officials, and influential citizens.

Cleveland's Cascade Range Forest Reserve was the largest of its kind at that time. Its establishment by a Democratic president with the support of Oregon's Republican congressman, Binger Hermann, underscored the bipartisan character of the forest reserve movement. Thereafter, when sheep and mining interests sought to dismantle it, assiduous advocacy by Waldo helped preserve it intact.[10]

In his *Annual Report* of 1893, Cleveland's secretary of agriculture, J. Sterling Morton—who two decades earlier had led a movement to designate Arbor Day a holiday for celebrating tree planting—recommended that the president proceed to reserve all of the "remaining timber lands on the public domain." Cleveland decided instead to wait until Congress provided more guidance on how the reserves should be managed. He did not expect the wait to last four years.[11]

CONGRESS STRUGGLES WITH FOREST RESERVE LEGISLATION

In hindsight, it was understandable that Congress found the task challenging. There were many issues to resolve. One was whether the General Land Office, the army, or some new agency should manage the reserves. Other questions included whether and under what conditions logging, mining, grazing, water projects, and other such activities should be permitted on them.

There were also questions regarding what to do with inholdings of private or state land within the reserves' outer boundaries. The GLO had tried, with varying degrees of success, to draw reserve boundaries in a way that would minimize inholdings. Harrison's Pikes Peak Timber Land Reserve in Colorado, for example, excluded the Cripple Creek and Cheyenne mining districts. But the sheer size of many reserves made it almost inevitable that they would contain inholdings or claims that could ripen into inholdings. Adjusting reserve boundaries might resolve some inholding issues, but section 24 did not expressly authorize making such adjustments once the reserves were established.

Finally, there was the question of how to deal with claims looking to gain title that had been made before the lands were withdrawn from operation of the divestment laws. There was opposition to allowing such claims to go forward no matter how dubious they might be, but claimants naturally objected to their being disallowed. Resolving this kind of transitional issue had thwarted enactment of public land law reform bills in the past.

Soon after section 24 became law, bills to address all these matters began to be introduced in Congress—there would be more than two dozen over the next few years. The two most significant were sponsored by Senator Algernon S. Paddock (R-Neb.) and Representative Thomas McRae. Both were introduced in 1892, while Harrison was still president. McRae, chair of the House Public Land Committee, emerged as the principal architect of the legislation that finally emerged from Congress in June 1897.[12]

During its long gestation, McRae's 1892 bill underwent some modification, but from the beginning his general approach was, as a House committee report on his bill explained, that the forest reserves would not be "parks set aside for nonuse, except to satisfy pleasure and curiosity."[13] Instead, the Interior secretary would be authorized to sell timber of commercial value from the reserves under certain restrictions. Indeed, McRae's original bill would have given the secretary authority to sell timber from public lands outside as well as inside the reserves. It also would have allowed the executive to restore lands within the reserves deemed suitable for agriculture to entry under the homestead and related acts. Finally, it would have authorized the military to protect the reserves where necessary.

McRae's bill gained the support of the Interior secretary and the American Forestry Association. But there was opposition. Some who favored the strict preservation of watersheds, including a number of members of Congress from the West, objected that McRae's bill could open the reserves to destructive logging. Indeed, Congressman Binger Hermann (R-Ore.) told his House colleagues that McRae's bill should be called a "bill to denude the public forest reservations." Some complained that the bill might curtail the widespread practice of obtaining free timber from public lands. Some wanted the secretary to have authority to excise from the reserves lands that had value for grazing or mining. Mining interests wanted to preserve the leverage that the Mining Law of 1872 gave them on public lands outside the reserves. Some, like Populist congressman Jerry Simpson of Kansas, opposed opening the forest reserves to mining and other forms of development. Some opposed the use of the military for what was essentially a civilian task. Amid all these crosscurrents, the Fifty-Second Congress adjourned in early March 1893 without taking a vote on McRae's bill.[14]

McRae fine-tuned his legislation and reintroduced it in the Fifty-Third Congress. This time he came closer to succeeding. Although it still attracted opposition, both from those who thought it was too strict and those who thought it was not strict enough, the House approved it in December 1894 by a comfortable margin. It then went to the Senate, where it was assigned to a new Select Committee on Forest Reservations, created the year before. That committee, chaired by former Interior secretary Henry Teller of Colorado, made McRae's bill considerably less restrictive, and added a so-called in lieu provision allowing those with lands or claims inside the reserves to swap them for tracts of public land "of like area" outside the reserves. The full Senate approved the select committee's bill without debate in February 1895.

A conference was never held to reconcile the differences between the House and Senate versions because an illness in his family made McRae unavailable. As a result, the Fifty-Third Congress ended in early March 1895 without taking further action. In the Fifty-Fourth Congress, the House again passed the McRae bill, in June 1896, but this time no bill emerged from the Senate committee, which in March had become the Committee on Forest Reservations and the Protection of Game. Searching for a path forward, President Cleveland and Congress agreed to establish a special committee of experts to address the situation and recommend suitable legislation.

Despite Congress's difficulty in pushing the legislation over the finish line, it showed no appetite for rolling back the nearly 18 million acres of forest reserves that had already been created. In 1892, when it extended the provisions of the Timber and Stone Act—which had authorized the sale of public forested lands in 160-acre parcels in three western states—to all states with public lands, it specifically excluded lands in forest reserves. Only a handful of bills were introduced between 1891 and 1897 to modify existing forest reserves, and they went nowhere, with one minor exception. In 1896, Congress opened three forest reserves in Colorado to mining claims for gold, silver, and cinnabar (mercury sulfide) under certain restrictions.[15]

CHAPTER TWENTY-ONE

The General Land Office Struggles and Cleveland Spurs Congress into Action

THE LACK OF GUIDANCE FROM Congress left the Interior Department to wrestle with many questions. Should or must it prohibit all uses in the forest reserves that could not claim prior vested rights? Some of those uses, like livestock grazing—the most widespread single use—were not expressly authorized by existing law even outside the reserves. And it was questionable whether some uses that were legal outside the reserves, like mining, could be conducted inside the reserves. The Mining Law of 1872 gave miners the opportunity to gain title to the lands they claimed, which seemed antithetical to the idea that the reserves would stay in U.S. ownership.

In their annual reports from 1891 on, the Interior secretary and the General Land Office commissioner repeatedly called on Congress to enact legislation providing answers to such questions. Expecting Congress to do so, Interior secretary Noble did nothing on the subject before he left office in early March 1893. In April 1894, as congressional deliberations dragged on, the GLO issued its first formal regulations regarding the reserves, prohibiting their use for mining, farming, grazing, logging, or other business purposes.[1]

Many livestock, timber, and mining interests simply defied the prohibition. Livestock operators in particular tended to be locally influential, and knew that the GLO lacked the funds and personnel to challenge them. "Little has been done with respect to forest reservations," GLO commissioner Lamoureux wrote in his *Annual Report* for 1894, because of Congress's inaction. Although he decried the "spirit of lawlessness prevailing among those" who were exploiting the resources of the reserved lands, he noted that these were the actions of relatively few, and were more than offset by petitions for additional reserves from governors, state legislatures, local communities, forestry organizations, and others.[2]

The GLO did bring some trespass cases to test its authority, and won a notable victory in 1896 when a federal court in Oregon drew a "clear distinction" between ordinary public lands—on which the Supreme Court had recognized an "implied license" to graze livestock arising from customary use—and lands in the forest reserves. The latter, the court said, had been set aside for "special public use" to serve the "public good," namely, "the preservation of the forests." For that reason, it was not appropriate to imply the existence of a license for uses that could cause their "destruction or injury."[3]

Still, enforcement resources were scanty, and prosecutions, especially of nomadic sheepherders, not easy to pursue. All in all, as Commissioner Lamoreux noted in his 1895 report, the failure of Congress to enact "much-needed legislation" regarding management of the forest reserves caused "serious embarrassment" to the GLO's efforts to protect them. In his *Annual Report* that same year, Interior secretary Hoke Smith lamented that the forest reserves were "no more protected" than other public lands, except for the important fact that no new entries or claims could be made on lands within the reserves that could lead to transfer of ownership.[4]

THE NATIONAL FORESTRY COMMITTEE RECOMMENDS NEW FOREST RESERVES

As Congress dawdled, Wolcott Gibbs, the president of the National Academy of Sciences, and Charles S. Sargent, the head of Harvard's Arnold Arboretum and publisher of *Garden and Forest,* began to explore the possibility of forming a blue-ribbon committee to study the issues and make recommendations to Congress. A young man named Gifford Pinchot attended their meetings. A child of wealth derived from, among other things, lumbering, he had been given a copy of George Perkins Marsh's *Man and Nature* on his twenty-first birthday, in 1886, and later described it as "epoch-making." After graduating from Yale in 1889, he studied forestry in France for a year. Upon his return to the United States, the well-connected Pinchot obtained, with the help of Frederick Law Olmsted, the position of forester at George W. Vanderbilt's Biltmore Estate near Asheville, North Carolina.[5]

Interior secretary Smith supported the idea, Congress made $25,000 available for it, and in the spring of 1896 the National Forestry Committee was formed, with Sargent as chair and Pinchot as secretary, along with four other experts. Most of its members, including Pinchot, toured the West in the summer and early fall of that year. Although not a member, John Muir traveled with them. Pinchot made a separate trip in June through the northern Rockies and Oregon's Cascades, where sheepherders were continuing to protest the large reserve that Cleveland had established in 1893.[6]

Meanwhile, petitions to establish new reserves continued to be submitted. For example, a Montana group sought to protect forests around the Bitterroot Valley. The Sierra Club, which Muir helped establish in 1892 and led, sought to protect the scenic Lake Tahoe basin, along the California-Nevada border, with its remarkable deep lake of outstanding clarity. (Mark Twain had visited the area not long after arriving in the Nevada Territory in 1861, and celebrated it in *Roughing It* in 1872 as presenting "the fairest picture the whole earth affords.") In 1894, California senator George Hearst went even further. He supported "reserving the whole of the Sierra top" that had not been included in Harrison's reservation of February 1893, from Mount Shasta to below Bakersfield, because it had very little land suitable for agriculture and its mineral potential had been thoroughly prospected.[7]

As 1896 drew to a close, the committee proposed that President Cleveland, soon to leave office, create new forest reserves. Cleveland had never regained popularity after the nation's economy sank into a depression early in his second term. The midterm elections of November 1894 were a huge defeat for his party, with control of the House shifting from 217–123 Democratic to 252–94 Republican. In the presidential election of 1896, the Democratic nominee, William Jennings Bryan, was defeated by former Ohio governor William McKinley, and the Republican Party retained firm control of both houses of Congress. In the West, the picture was more mixed, because Bryan's strong support for coining silver to expand the money supply carried him to victory in all of the intermountain states as well as Washington.

On February 1, 1897, the National Forestry Committee forwarded its list of recommended new reserves to the Interior secretary, David Francis. Sargent's accompanying letter acknowledged that creating new reserves might be controversial, but noted that it would increase "pressure on Congress to enact laws permitting their proper administration." The committee, he wrote, was unanimous in supporting the setting aside of more reserves as a "matter of utmost importance to the development and welfare of the whole country."

(Many years later, Pinchot sought to distance himself from the committee's recommendation.)[8]

Francis endorsed the committee's recommendation, and Cleveland took action. With ten days to go in his term, on February 22, 1897, Washington's Birthday, he proclaimed thirteen new reserves in seven states. Altogether they included some 21 million acres, about two-thirds of which were in Montana and Washington. In a few strokes of his pen, Cleveland had more than doubled the amount of public land in the reserves.

CONGRESS FINALLY TAKES ACTION

Sargent's prediction was borne out, because the new reserves did stimulate Congress finally to complete action on forest reserve legislation. Still, it took three more months and the convening of another Congress to do it. The late-term proclamations of the deeply unpopular president understandably produced negative reactions in some of the affected regions, including predictable objections from mining, lumber, and livestock interests. Initial complaints from western political leaders tended to be narrowly targeted. Typical was the reaction of Governor W. A. Richards of Wyoming, where Cleveland's new reserves covered 2 million acres. He called the president's decision-making process flawed and said that it was premature to add more reserves before a system for protecting them was in place, but he also acknowledged that 90 percent of the people in his state favored forest reserves.[9]

On February 28, an amendment to rescind the Cleveland proclamations was added to an appropriations bill then making its way through Congress. It was offered by Senator Clarence Clark (R-Wyo.), who called Cleveland's proclamations hasty and arbitrarily done, though agreeing that westerners were "anxious" that the forests and watersheds of their region be "properly preserved."[10]

The next move was made by the chair of the House Public Lands Committee, John F. Lacey (R-Iowa). Born in a one-room log cabin in what is now West Virginia in 1841, he moved to Iowa with his family in 1855, served in the Union Army, and eventually became an expert in railroad law. He served eight terms in Congress, beginning in 1889, with a two-year interruption after his first term. A lover of history, science, and nature, Lacey chaired the House Public Lands Committee from 1895 to 1907, where he was a powerful advocate for the forest reserves as well as for preserving wildlife and historic and scientific resources on public lands.

Lacey quickly crafted a compromise alternative, the core of which left the Cleveland proclamations in place and simply gave the president authority to "modify or vacate" any order creating a reserve. While Cleveland's actions may not have been flawless, Lacey told his colleagues, the system of forest reserves "is a highly beneficial one" that "has been working well." Besides giving the new president the power to abolish or modify reserves, his compromise would also, drawing on Thomas McRae's forest reserve bill, open the forest reserves to mining and authorize the president to sell timber from them for domestic or mining purposes. After a brief debate, the House accepted the Lacey compromise, and so did the conference called to reconcile the House and Senate bills. The next day, the last one of the Fifty-Fourth Congress, the bill was approved and sent to Cleveland.[11]

Congress's action showed that the forest reserves continued to enjoy wide support. Rather than undoing the dramatic eleventh-hour action of an unpopular president, or even limiting the president's authority going forward, Congress chose instead simply to clarify that the new president could modify or abolish reserves, and to open the reserves to mining and limited timber sales.[12]

Despite this mild congressional response, President Cleveland apparently resented the criticisms that some in Congress had made of his actions and refused to sign the appropriations bill into law before he stepped down. Because the Fifty-Fourth Congress had by that time adjourned, his pocket veto nullified the compromise.

His action gave the incoming McKinley administration and the new Fifty-Fifth Congress a rude welcome. Unlike the more modern practice, in which Congress's failure to enact funding bills requires the government to shut down except for functions determined to be "essential," in that earlier era the government simply continued to operate on the assumption that Congress would eventually provide an appropriation. (The modern practice stems from a stricter reading of so-called antideficiency laws that implement Article I, section 9 of the Constitution, which prohibits drawing money from the U.S. Treasury without a congressional appropriation.)[13]

McKinley called a special session to address the problem. Members of the new administration and key senators worked to craft acceptable forest reserve legislation, drawing heavily on Congressmen Lacey's and McRae's earlier work. A key part of this new proposal was simply to suspend most of the Cleveland proclamations (except those creating new reserves in California) until March 1, 1898, at which time they would once again become fully effective unless President McKinley had modified them in the interim.

This compromise was politically clever, offering something to practically all affected interests. It gave those who objected to the lack of advance notice of

Cleveland's proclamations an opportunity to enter and file claims to these public lands before they once again became reserved. It gave those who opposed the reservations altogether the opportunity to persuade President McKinley to rescind the Cleveland proclamations. It consoled supporters of forest reserves by automatically reinstating Cleveland's actions in the near future unless McKinley modified them. Perhaps most important, the effort that Congress devoted to the Cleveland proclamations deflected attention from other, more far-reaching parts of the bill, thus smoothing the path to its enactment.[14]

The proposal was debated on the Senate floor in the first week of May. Some westerners continued to criticize Cleveland's action while emphasizing the region's support for, as Senator Shoup (R-Mont.) put it, "forest reserves if they are well and properly located." His Montana colleague, Senator Carter, the former GLO commissioner, urged the president to consult closely with local interests so that boundaries of future reserves would be drawn "with the least possible friction." Senator White (D-Calif.), while wanting to make sure the reserves were open to mineral development, thought Cleveland had not gone far enough, noting that the land around Lake Tahoe had a "character of country that ought to be reserved for the people for all time."[15]

A few senators took a harder line. Senator John Lockwood Wilson (R-Wash.), in whose state the timber industry was particularly powerful, called the Cleveland reserves "ghastly," the work of "scientific gentlemen from Harvard College" who had committed a "great injustice." He scoffed at the watershed protection argument, saying his state had an "everlasting supply" of water from the glaciers found on Mount Rainier.[16] Eventually the Senate accepted an amendment offered by Senator Pettigrew (R-S.D.) to suspend the Cleveland proclamations indefinitely, which would have required action by President McKinley to reinstate them.

Debate in the House a few days later continued the focus on Cleveland's proclamations. A few westerners called his action "villainous" and "the parting shot of the worst enemy that the American people have ever had." But defenders of forest reserves pushed back vigorously, led by the Iowa Republican Lacey and the Arkansas Democrat McRae, carrying on the tradition of bipartisanship that had long marked the movement for reserves. Lacey endorsed the idea of merely suspending the Cleveland reservations until March 1, 1898, and making clear that the president could revoke, modify, or suspend section 24 reservations. He reminded his colleagues that section 24 had a "wise and beneficent" purpose,

namely, "to look out for the future; to endeavor to take care of the next generation." McRae's appeal echoed George Perkins Marsh, claiming that the destructive floods that had occurred earlier that year were in "large measure due to the
reckless destruction of our mountain forests." "If we can learn nothing from
Italy, France, and countries of the Old World," McRae told his colleagues, we
should look to the destruction visited on "New England and other parts of our
own beloved country" and work to "save the South and West from the same
fate."[17]

Lacey and McRae succeeded in getting their version not only through the
House, but also much of it into the version produced by the conference called
to reconcile the House and Senate bills. When the conference bill came to the
Senate for final passage, that personification of the Gilded Age, Silver Senator
Stewart, unleashed a tirade. He called the very notion of forest reserves—none
of which at that point included public lands in his state—a "great blunder." It
was very well, he said, for the national government to protect places with "novel-
ties, curiosities, and strange developments of nature as places of resort, such as
Yosemite," but to make reserves for other purposes was "a most absurd proposition on its face." Stewart scoffed at the idea of permitting "theorists" who had
"studied botany and other things, perhaps, in the Old World," to influence U.S.
forest policy. The Cleveland proclamations were "barbarous," an "outrage upon
the West" and a "disgrace to American civilization."[18]

But Stewart's was a voice from a bygone era. The Senate approved the
conference report by a margin of seven votes, and the House followed suit by a
wide margin. On June 4, 1897, the general appropriations bill including the
forest reserve legislation was signed into law by President McKinley. It would,
without significant amendment, govern the management of what would soon
come to be known as the national forests for the next eight decades.[19]

CHAPTER TWENTY-TWO

An Organic Act for the Forest Reserves

THE LEGISLATION ENACTED IN 1897, eventually known as the National Forest Organic Act, left intact the 18 million acres of forest reserves established before Washington's Birthday, and allowed Cleveland's proclamations of that date—covering 21 million acres—to take effect automatically nine months later if President McKinley took no action to alter them. It also confirmed broad presidential authority to make new forest reserves. Altogether, it cemented into the nation's culture the idea that vast amounts of land would be retained permanently in national ownership.[1]

The Organic Act articulated the reasons for establishing new forest reserves—"to improve and protect the forest within the reservation, or for the purpose of securing favorable conditions of water flows, and to furnish a continuous supply of timber for the use and necessities of citizens of the United States." Each reason held important implications for the future.

The objective of improving and protecting forests put the government deeply into the business of managing landscapes for healthy outcomes.

The goal of "securing favorable conditions of water flows" prodded the executive to regulate activities on the reserves that might interfere with those flows. It also helped open the way for the U.S. government to become involved in constructing projects to store and regulate those flows for irrigation and other purposes. Five years later, Congress did just that by approving the Reclamation Act.

Furnishing a "continuous" timber supply was the seed of an idea that would eventually become a broad policy: managing the renewable resources of the public lands to ensure sustainability, or what eventually came to be called "sustained yield."

While the Organic Act cautioned that Congress did not intend to "authorize the inclusion" in forest reserves of "lands more valuable for the mineral therein, or for agricultural purposes, than for forest purposes," it gave the executive great leeway to decide what lands to include or exclude. It also allowed the president, without redrawing reservation boundaries, to restore tracts of public lands within the reserves to privatization under the homestead or mining laws upon a finding that they were "better adapted for mining or for agricultural purposes." But Congress installed a process to try to ensure that such a step, which would create private inholdings in the reserves, would not be taken lightly, requiring "personal inspection" by a "competent person" appointed by the Interior secretary, ample public notice, and the secretary's recommendation.

McKinley's new General Land Office commissioner, former Oregon congressman Binger Hermann (who had not sought reelection in 1896), cautioned in his *Annual Report* of 1899 that this authority ought to be exercised sparingly. Congress did not, he wrote, contemplate eliminating from the reserves or opening to homesteading "every small isolated tract" that might be farmed. Instead, the act should be administered to protect the integrity of the reserves and their watershed-protection purpose.[2]

THE "IN LIEU" PROVISION

The Organic Act contained one significant giveaway to the beneficiaries of the national government's largesse regarding the public lands. Originating in the bill approved in early 1895 by the Senate Select Committee on Forest Reservations, chaired by Henry Teller of Colorado, the "in lieu" provision became a kind of coda to the Gilded Age. To the extent that the forest reserves could be said to mark the end of the era when railroads and other powerful speculative interests dominated public land policy, the "in lieu" provision was a profligate final gift. It allowed those interests to upgrade the already generous land grants that Congress had earlier bestowed on them and take control of some of the richest stands of timber in the nation.

On the surface it seemed perfectly fair, allowing the "owner" of an "unperfected bona fide claim" to a tract of public land inside a reserve to relinquish it to the United States and in return—"in lieu" thereof—to obtain the right to select and gain title to a tract of public land elsewhere. (The Organic Act made the same offer to "settlers" who owned private inholdings in the reserves.) But the devil was, as it usually is in such matters, in the details. And in crafting those details, packed in a single sentence in the legislation, the advocates for the railroads and other powerful interests did their work exceedingly well.[3]

First, the legislation did not define "unperfected bona fide claim," allowing for creative arguments about what might qualify as one. Second, its bland reference to "owners" of such claims masked the fact that they could be large corporate interests and speculators that hardly fit the Jeffersonian model of yeoman settlers. Third, it allowed these "owners" to select any "vacant" public-domain land outside the reserves, which was interpreted to mean that, first, mineral land could be selected, which was not the usual case, and second, that the land need not be surveyed first. That allowed "in lieu" claimants to jump ahead of potential homesteaders, to whom only surveyed land was available. (Congress closed this loophole in 1900, but only after giving those who sought to exploit it four additional months to take advantage of it.) Fourth, the provision did not require the public land being acquired in the swap to be in the same state as the land being relinquished. This also favored more mobile corporate interests and speculators over genuine settlers. Even more significantly, it vastly enlarged the pool of lands that could be selected, creating the possibility that rich timberlands on the public domain along the Pacific coast might be obtained "in lieu of" claims to arid lands in the intermountain West.[4]

Fifth, and most egregious, the "in lieu" provision did not require a value-for-value match between the land subject to the "claim" that was being relinquished and the land outside the reserve that was being acquired. Instead, it specified only that the land selected not exceed the land *area* of the relinquished claim. Public land outside reserves could be much more valuable than land inside the reserves if, for example, claimants had already logged or otherwise exploited the resources of the latter, or if it had fewer resources or was more isolated.

These details led to a predictable result, one that GLO commissioner Hermann succinctly laid it out in his *Annual Report* for 1898. The "in lieu" provision, he wrote, allowed claimants to "select compact bodies of fine agricultural or timbered lands outside the reserves" and compel the United States to accept "denuded and worthless scattered tracts in the reserves." The deal could be so attractive that speculators and railroad and timber companies would sometimes petition the executive branch to establish forest reserves where they held lands or claims, just so that they could later exchange them for more valu-able public lands elsewhere.[5]

Not long after the Organic Act became law, Hermann and McKinley's Interior secretary, Ethan Allen Hitchcock, asked Congress to repeal or tighten the "in lieu" provision. Congress was slow to respond, but finally repealed it in 1905, though only after validating swaps previously undertaken. While the provision reduced the number of inholdings inside the reserves, its cost was high; among other things, the odor of corruption that surrounded the swaps undermined public confidence in the GLO's administration of the public lands.[6]

REGULATING USES INSIDE THE RESERVES

The Organic Act gave the Interior Department broad authority to formulate rules and regulations governing "occupancy and use" of the forest reserves in order to "insure the objects of such reservations" and "preserve the forests thereon from destruction."

Parts of the act were aimed at making life easier for settlers and other users of the reserves, but Congressman McRae had carefully crafted the legislation to limit opportunities for abuse (other than the "in lieu" provision, which had been added to his bill in the Senate). Thus the Interior secretary could permit "bona fide settlers" to make free use of timber and stone from the reserves for "domestic purposes," and prospectors and miners could make use of these materials in mining, but only under regulations the secretary would prescribe. Moreover, any timber so logged had to be used within the state or territory where the reserve was located. In the House debates, McRae's frustration with miners and others who sought free rein in the reserves was palpable; they must, he warned, "be fair to the Government if they expect the Government to be liberal toward them." John Lacey also pushed back at those who objected to such restrictions, sardonically observing that nothing "is so sacred as an abuse."[7]

Another provision allowed "actual settlers residing within" reserve bound-aries to build roads and other improvements to facilitate the use of their prop-erty, but again only under regulations that may be prescribed by the secretary. Another permitted settlers residing within or near the reserves to "maintain schools and churches" within the reservations, not exceeding two acres per school and one acre per church. Still another allowed "waters" on the reserves to be used for various purposes under either state or federal regulation; presum-ably, state regulation would apply until and unless preempted by federal regulation.[8]

TIMBER HARVESTING

The act contained detailed guidance regarding commercial timber harvesting in the reserves. It permitted the Interior secretary to sell timber, but only for its appraised value or higher, and only for use within the state where it was harvested, not for export. Any timber the government offered for sale had to be "dead, matured, or large growth," in keeping with the objective of providing a "continuous supply" of timber while still "preserving living and growing timber and promoting the younger growth." Finally, trees offered for sale had to be "marked" and "designated."

All these limitations made clear that the Organic Act was not geared to maximize wood production. In fact, per capita consumption of wood was already beginning to decline across the nation as fossil fuels, iron, steel, and cement were increasingly being substituted for it in many applications. Altogether, the limitations on logging underscored that Congress's primary goals in the Organic Act were to protect watersheds and the long-term viability of forests.[9]

GRAZING

Some background is necessary to appreciate what the Organic Act said—or more precisely, did not say—about livestock grazing on the reserves. In 1890, a few months before Congress gave the president the general authority to establish forest reserves, Senator Francis Warren from the then brand-new state of Wyoming had introduced legislation to cede all public lands with value for irrigation and grazing to the states, and to require the states in turn to convey the irrigable lands to actual settlers in small tracts, and to lease the grazing land to owners of contiguous irrigated farms. Warren had a large grazing operation that ran both cattle and sheep; a Senate colleague once referred to him as the "greatest shepherd since Abraham."

Warren's proposal gained no political traction. One important reason was that the livestock operators using public lands were far from united. Even some of those who agreed with Warren that public lands suitable for grazing ought to be transferred to the states did not support his requirement that the state lease rather than give the lands away, because that meant they might have to pay for the privilege of grazing. Some supported legislation that would simply privatize public grazing lands. Some supported legislation that would have the United States issue leases or permits for grazing, to give their operations a more stable foundation, including protection against homesteaders and other grazers. And some preferred the status quo, with the national government continuing to own the lands and the livestock operators taking their chances on being able to continue to graze them under an "implied license."[10]

Another reason that Warren's idea never found favor was that home-steading advocates saw most ranching enterprises as competitors. They viewed industrial-scale livestock grazing as at most a temporary use, to be closely regulated or excluded outright from public land that could be irrigated or dry-farmed successfully enough to qualify for title under the Homestead Act. The most notable conflict between homesteaders and livestock operators was the famous Johnson County War, which was taking place in Wyoming while Warren made his proposal. (That conflict was later given literary and Hollywood treatment in George Stevens's classic movie *Shane* from 1952, based on Jack Schaefer's 1949 novel. The future Supreme Court justice Willis Van Devanter represented ranchers in litigation that grew out of it.)

As long as Congress did not prohibit livestock grazing in forest reserves, their establishment gave grazers protection against homesteaders and speculators, because the divestment laws did not apply within them. For this reason, many livestock interests, especially those not engaged in itinerant sheep-herding, welcomed or at least did not much resist the movement to create forest reserves.

Uncontrolled livestock use could, however, threaten the health of forests and the water supplies they produced. Thomas McRae had told his colleagues in 1894 that his bill was intended, among other things, to keep "cattle and sheep from destroying the young growth" in forest reserves. The act that finally emerged from Congress instructed the Interior secretary to protect forest reserves from "depredations" and to regulate reserve uses in order to carry out the purposes of the reserves and to "preserve the forests thereon from destruction." But it did not specifically mention livestock grazing nor provide any details about how it should be controlled.[11]

It might seem remarkable that although the Organic Act addressed, with considerable specificity, timber harvesting and the actions of ordinary settlers in and around the reserves, it offered no specific guidance on what was then the reserves' single most intensive use—grazing by domestic cows and sheep. There was, however, a political logic to it, because of the complex array of interests involved.

Supporters of the forest reserves, including many in the scientific forestry community, generally regarded livestock grazing as a nuisance at best, and at worst a serious threat. This was particularly so regarding nomadic sheep-herding. Sheep were the dominant consumer of forage in the early years of the forest reserves. Overgrazing was common because sheep would, if not constantly herded, strip all the forage from the land. The National Forestry Committee had adopted John Muir's famous description of sheep as "hoofed locusts," noting that nomadic herders carried "desolation with them," making the damage from illegal timber cutting "insignificant" by comparison. Herders sometimes set fires to encourage new grass growth and clear the land of downed timber and brush, which impeded the movement of flocks. Complicating matters even more, the livestock industry was split between cattle ranchers and sheepherders (although some operators had both kinds of animals), and ethnic tensions sometimes surfaced, because many sheep-herders were immigrants, especially Basques from the Pyrenees.[12]

Irrigation advocates tended to side with the scientists. For one thing, they worried that soil erosion from intensive grazing by sheep or cattle could impair irrigation projects. And they expressed broader cultural concerns. A leading irrigation advocate, William E. Smythe, once contrasted what he called the "civilization of irrigated America" with the "barbarism of cattle ranching."[13]

Given the many disparate interests and positions, it was not surprising that in the Organic Act, Congress essentially handed the problem off to the GLO, leaving it with the daunting task of trying to regulate an ongoing wide-spread use of public lands where there previously had been no regulation, where no consensus existed on what should be done, where the grazing industry, though vocal and politically influential, lacked unity, and where the GLO had such limited supervisory and enforcement capacity. When the Organic Act was signed into law, it had, according to Commissioner Hermann, a total of six persons to patrol some 40 million acres of forest reserves.[14]

While the Organic Act did not provide any specific guidance on how grazing on the forest reserves should be regulated, it did spell the end of the government's tacit laissez-faire policy of allowing livestock interests free range on the many millions of acres of public land in the forest reserves. From now on, that grazing would be overseen by the U.S. government. And even though laissez-faire would continue for a few more decades on even more tens of millions of acres of public land outside the forest reserves, its demise there too was now almost inevitable. As William Voigt put it, "once the national forests were no longer free" to ranging livestock, the "rest of the federal West simply had to follow; the two were but separate organs of the same animal."[15]

MINING

The Organic Act did explicitly identified mining as an authorized use. It allowed people to enter the reserves for "prospecting, locating, and developing" minerals and gave them free use of timber and stone for these purposes. But it also specifically required them, like all other authorized users, to "comply with rules and regulations" adopted by the Interior secretary to "insure the objects of such reservations" and "preserve the forests thereon from destruction." It also gave the secretary the option of simply restoring land deemed "better adapted for mining" to the public domain.

Despite the seemingly clear direction to regulate mining to safeguard the purposes of the reserves, for decades thereafter the executive branch proved unwilling or unable to challenge the political power of the mining industry and its allies. As a result, the mining industry generally acted as if the reserves and the Organic Act put no restrictions on its activities.[16]

CHAPTER TWENTY-THREE

Parks, Forests, and Public Land Policy in the McKinley Administration

CONGRESSMAN McRAE'S DICTUM THAT forest reserves were established "for economic reasons," as distinguished from "parks set aside for nonuse," became a kind of catchphrase. It was not, however, entirely accurate. The Organic Act of 1897 made clear that forest reserves were established to control and even prohibit "economic" activities on them in order to fulfill its objectives, which included improving and protecting the forests. And railroad support for Yellowstone and the parks established in California in 1890 showed that parks were established in part "for economic reasons."

In fact, distinctions between parks and forests were far from clear during the founding era of forest reserves. Congressional and executive branch reports on President Harrison's first use of section 24 authority, which protected areas around Yellowstone Park, variously described his action as "enlarging the boundaries of the Yellowstone Park," or establishing either a "Yellowstone Park extension" or, even less helpfully, a "Yellowstone National Park timber land reserve." In his *Annual Report* for 1891, Interior secretary Noble used the term "parks" to describe section 24 reserves, which he said would "preserve the fauna, fish and flora of our country, and become resorts for the people seeking instruction and recreation," as well as safeguard water supplies.[1]

The same ambiguity was reflected in measures that New York adopted around the same time to protect parts of the Adirondacks. The law establishing the "Forest Preserve," which the New York legislature passed in 1885, called for the state-owned lands within it to "be forever kept as wild forest lands" but did not outlaw timber harvesting. The same was true of the law that established the "Adirondack Park" in 1892. In 1894, voters in New York added to the muddle by approving a new state constitution that included a provision repeating the "forever wild" language applied to the "Forest Preserve" and going on to specify that timber on those lands should not be "sold, removed or destroyed."[2]

Bernhard Fernow, an intellectual leader of science-based forestry and the head of the Division of Forestry at the U.S. Department of Agriculture, sought to clarify matters in 1897. The "movement for open spaces, for parks, for protection of historic or picturesque and interesting places, for reservations in general," was, he wrote, a "hopeful sign of the arrival of a more highly civilized condition in our communities." That said, a park was "for pleasure and recreation," while a forest reservation was for "timber and protection." The former was "attended to by park commissioners and landscape gardeners, the other by foresters and loggers." That helped a little, but forest reservations were often magnets for recreation, and park designations outside urban areas usually did not contemplate "landscape gardening."[3]

In fact, "park" and "forest" reservations shared a common core. Both rested on the notion that government should hold title to the lands, and that public institutions should ultimately be responsible for managing them with a long-term perspective—as Fernow put it in his 1897 article, "a view of permanence." Or to borrow from Thomas Jefferson's expression from more than a century earlier, all reserved lands belonged "in *usufruct* to the living generation," which could derive value from them only so long as they were not depleted or damaged.

While the distinctions that McRae and Fernow put forward had a good deal of influence, Congress and the executive continued to wrestle with what to allow in reserves. A good illustration came with the establishment of Mount Rainier National Park in 1899, the only national park established during the McKinley administration. The nation's fifth-highest mountain outside Alaska, Rainier was a picturesque, relatively isolated volcano, heavily glaciated, with remarkable forests and wildflowers. It was the first national park established substantially through the efforts of scientific groups.

A national park at Rainier had been talked about as far back as 1883. The nearly million-acre Pacific Forest Reserve, which President Harrison had established in 1893, included part of the mountain, leaving out a portion of its western slope. Within a year, members of the Washington congressional delegation introduced legislation to establish a Washington National Park, borrowing language from the Yellowstone National Park legislation and applying it just to that part of the mountain within Harrison's forest reserve. Not long after that, the geologist Bailey Willis of the U.S. Geological Survey assembled a coalition of prominent scientists, scientific groups, and outdoor recreation advocates that worked to enlarge the proposed park's boundaries, extolling the area's "many features of unique interest and wonderful grandeur," including the fact that it was "an arctic island in a temperate zone." They soon gained the support of Seattle newspapers and commercial interests looking to promote tourism.[4]

There was little organized opposition from mining or livestock interests, and the Northern Pacific Railroad Company welcomed the opportunity to swap out its land grants on the mountain for more valuable public land elsewhere. As Congress continued to debate the park idea, one of Cleveland's Washington's Birthday reserves from 1897 more than doubled the size of Harrison's Pacific Forest Reserve and renamed it the Mount Rainier Forest Reserve.

Finally on March 2, 1899, at the end of the Fifty-Fifth Congress, President McKinley signed the legislation establishing a 222,000-acre Mount Rainier National Park. Because the park was composed of land that had already been reserved, it was no longer open to entry under laws like the Homestead Act. The most important, indeed just about the only, thing added by giving it national park status was permanence, because while the Organic Act had made clear that the president could modify or even rescind a forest reserve, a national park could be undone only by Congress.[5]

The legislation included details to placate politically powerful economic interests. For one thing, to avoid a lengthy controversy like the one that had arisen at Yellowstone over whether to allow a railroad to be built in the park, the Rainier legislation contained open-ended grants of rights-of-way into both the park and the adjacent forest reserve to "any railway or tramway company or companies" that might need them, albeit "under such restrictions and regulations as the Secretary of the Interior may establish."

There was more. At the behest of Northern Pacific, the legislation included an "in lieu" provision similar to the one that had been included in the Organic Act two years earlier. It allowed the railroad to exchange the checkerboard sections of land it owned within the park and the surrounding forest reserve (which was almost ten times the size of the national park) for an "equal quantity" of unclaimed nonmineral public lands in any state "into or through which" the railroad operated. Because the Northern Pacific operated a spur line to Portland, Oregon, the inclusion of the single word "into" made timber-rich public land anywhere in Oregon available to it ahead of prospective settlers or anyone else.

The mining industry's political muscle was also on display, for the legislation made the Mining Law of 1872 specifically applicable to lands within the park. Interior secretary Hitchcock called for repeal of the mining provision, writing in his *Annual Report* of 1899 that the provision made it impossible for him to carry out the legislation's mandate that he protect the park resources from "injury or spoliation." It took nine years for Congress to agree.[6]

The Mount Rainier park legislation was the first example of layering reservations or designations of public land on top of one another, a technique that became more and more common over the years. Designations proliferated to include things such as national monuments, wildlife refuges, recreation areas, conservation areas, and wilderness areas. Labels could be cumulative; for example, a forest reserve could become a national park and then a wilderness area. As a result of such actions, many areas of public lands have a complex history, and several layers of management guidance, with new layers usually (though not always) providing additional legal protections, accreting over time like geological strata. When a forest reserve was made a national park, for example, sport hunting was prohibited.

PRESIDENT MCKINLEY AND FOREST RESERVES

The ruckus kicked up by Cleveland's Washington's Birthday reserves quickly faded almost everywhere. John Muir published widely read articles extolling forest reserves in the August 1897 and January 1898 issues of the *Atlantic Monthly*. The first contained his famous admonition that "only Uncle Sam," and not God, could save trees from being destroyed by fools. McKinley took no action to rescind or modify any of the Cleveland reserves, and so, on March 1, 1898, they were automatically reinstated by the terms of the Organic Act. Diehard opponents persuaded the Senate to attach an amendment to an appropriations bill to rescind them, but the House refused to go along, heeding the arguments of John Lacey and future Speaker Joseph Cannon (R-Ill.) that the Organic Act had really settled the matter.[7]

The day after the suspended Cleveland reserves had once again taken effect, President McKinley established a new 1.65-million-acre forest reserve in Southern California. During his remaining time in office, he added nearly a dozen more, totaling more than 7 million acres in five states and two territories. Eight of these were in states where Cleveland had established reserves on Washington's Birthday in 1897, and most, like many earlier reserves, had been sought by local and regional interests. Meanwhile, requests for more forest reserves continued to be submitted.

The only Washington's Birthday reserve that was seriously and persistently resisted was on the timber-rich Olympic Peninsula in Washington. Gifford Pinchot visited the area at the request of McKinley's first Interior secretary, Cornelius Bliss, a few months after it was established. He reported that few of its lands had potential for farming, and that while it did include abundant stands of timber, lands outside the reserve already in private ownership contained copious amounts of timber "sufficient to meet all commercial demands for several years to come."[8]

Railroad and timber interests nevertheless pressed to reduce the reserve's size. When new Washington senator Addison G. Foster, a former railroad and mining executive, took office in March 1899, he demanded that his fellow Republican McKinley shrink the reserve substantially, claiming that "vast agricultural lands" had been included by Cleveland's "outrageous act." Although the reserve's defenders pointed out that Foster's proposed exclusions contained billions of board feet of timber and few settlers, McKinley acceded, excising nearly 265,000 acres from the reserve in April 1900 and another 457,000 acres fifteen months later. His actions, premised on the lands being, in the language of the Organic Act, "better adapted" for "agricultural purposes than for forest usage," shrank the reserve by about a third and excluded about three-quarters of its timber inventory by volume.

Subsequent investigations revealed that most of the excluded lands ended up in the hands of speculators under the Timber and Stone Act, which required taking an oath that the land was "unfit for cultivation" and "valuable chiefly for timber," giving the entire episode the appearance of a rip-off. The controversy over how much of the remaining public lands on the Olympic Peninsula to protect continued for many more decades, with many twists and turns.

In April 1899, McKinley established a "forestry reserve and public park" on some 136,000 acres in the southwestern portion of the Lake Tahoe basin. Years earlier, the Sierra Club had led a campaign to have the GLO study possibilities for forest reserves in the area. In late 1897, the GLO recommended the establishment of large reserve that would include most of the west side of the Tahoe basin as well as 80,000 acres of public land farther west, across the crest of the Sierra Nevada. McKinley's reserve was more modest. Around the same time, Nevada's Silver Senator Stewart proposed to establish a vastly larger national park with Lake Tahoe at its heart. The proposal by the ever devious Stewart seemed mostly designed to use the lake's waters to irrigate lands in

Nevada and to give generous "in lieu" land-selection rights to the Central Pacific Railroad and other interests that had already harvested much of the basin's timber for use in developing the Comstock Lode. His tainted proposal never gained traction, and it was only after Congress repealed the "in lieu" provision in 1905 that President Theodore Roosevelt established a new forest reserve in the area.[9]

A TURF BATTLE IN THE EXECUTIVE BRANCH HEATS UP

On July 1, 1898, Gifford Pinchot succeeded Bernhard Fernow as head of the Department of Agriculture's Division of Forestry. The ambitious Pinchot had many advantages—intelligence, passion, energy, personal wealth, influential friends, public relations skills. The division under his supervision became a beehive of research and recommendations on forest policy, but it managed no land. As he admitted in his autobiography, written several decades later, his "chief object in life" from that moment forward was to "get charge of" the forest reserves. The Interior Department now had a serious rival.

The turf battle that followed was a major factor in public land management for decades. To say Pinchot had sharp elbows and could be overbearing understates the matter. He made no effort in his autobiography to conceal his contempt for the GLO, using words such as "pathetic" and "awful" and describing many of its staff as "human rubbish." Within three years, he had persuaded Congress to expand his budget more than sixfold, and the number of people who worked for him from thirteen to nearly two hundred.[10]

Pinchot quickly grasped that because livestock grazing was the most important use of the reserves, livestock operators were a key constituency, and he spent considerable time and effort wooing them. He sided with sheep interests that wanted continued access to forest reserves in Oregon and Washington, in the process alienating John Muir, who wanted them excluded. He did the same with the forest reserves in the Southwest after touring them in June 1900 with Albert Potter of the Arizona Wool Growers. Overall, Pinchot wrote later, livestock grazing was the "most ticklish question" and the "center of the bitterest controversy" he faced. He understood that livestock could cause serious damage, but he also feared that if the executive simply banned grazing on the reserves, livestock owners might ignore the prohibition, the GLO would have difficulty enforcing it, and Congress might reverse it. In his autobiography, he described the choice facing the executive in stark terms: "Shut out all grazing and lose the Forest Reserves, or let stock in under control and save the Reserves for the Nation." For the time being, his position in the Agriculture

Department afforded him the space to claim simply that his division could manage the reserves better than the GLO.[11]

Pinchot also worked hard to gain the support of the mining industry, especially in South Dakota's Black Hills, where President Cleveland had established a large forest reserve and where the powerful Homestake Mining Company and other mining enterprises were heavy users of timber. He visited the area in the fall of 1897 at the request of Interior secretary Bliss and worked with Homestake and the GLO, leading the latter to approve what was the first timber sale under the Organic Act. Overall, Pinchot worked to persuade the timber and mining industries that forest reserves, properly managed, could help protect against forest fires (which he called a "giant evil") and stabilize timber supplies.

Over at the Interior Department, the GLO was not passive. Since becoming GLO commissioner in March 1897, Binger Hermann had displayed an ambition that nearly matched Pinchot's. His *Annual Report* for 1900 noted that ever since the days of Carl Schurz and James Williamson in the late 1870s, the Interior Department and the GLO had promoted what he called "rational administration of the forests on the public domain." He claimed that the Interior Department had played an instrumental role in inserting section 24 in the 1891 legislation, emphasized its role in the events leading to enactment of the Organic Act in 1897, and called for the "prompt withdrawal" of "all the remaining lands now held by the Government which are more valuable for forest uses than for other purposes." Properly managing the forest reserves, he wrote, required an "organized forest force" that he presciently called a "forest service." The GLO was already calling its field representatives in the reserves "forest rangers." Pinchot later appropriated both terms.[12]

Hermann's 1900 report also noted the "rapidly increasing demands from various quarters for protection" of areas on public lands that contained "objects of world-wide interest." By then, the GLO had examined and reported on five park proposals—Petrified Forest in Arizona, Mammoth Tree in California, Shoshone Falls in Idaho, Pajarito Plateau in New Mexico, and Wind Cave in South Dakota. It withdrew public lands in these and other areas from the homestead and similar acts while they were being considered for protection, often after being asked to do so by local interests. At the request of the Arizona territorial legislature, for example, the Interior Department withdrew public land containing the fossilized remains of trees (so-called petrified forests) in northeastern Arizona in 1896 and 1899. It did the same with public lands in the Catalina Mountains near Tucson at the request of the president of the University of Arizona and other local officials, and with public lands in a mountainous watershed east of Seattle at the city's request, which considered the area a future source of municipal water.

Congress remained miserly in funding the GLO. At the turn of the century, the agency was being given about $175,000 to manage more than 40 million acres of forest reserves—less than half a cent an acre. Even more troubling to Hermann was the fact that Pinchot's relentless lobbying had gained the ear of Hermann's boss, Interior secretary Ethan Allen Hitchcock, whom McKinley had named to succeed Bliss in early 1899. In his 1901 *Annual Report,* Hitchcock wholeheartedly embraced Pinchot's argument that forestry "is properly an agricultural subject," that the Department of Agriculture had "properly trained foresters," and that therefore, if "practicable," administration of the forest reserves ought to be transferred to that department. He even appended to his report an outline of guiding principles that Pinchot had drafted for administering the forest reserves.[13]

Early in 1901, Hitchcock outlined a plan whereby, pending congressional approval of the transfer, Pinchot and his staff would assume primary responsibility for managing the reserves, with Pinchot wearing a second hat, as "Forester" in the Interior Department, while retaining the same position in Agriculture. When Hermann balked at the arrangement, a new forestry division was created inside the GLO, but was staffed mostly by people from Pinchot's office. Over the next several years, the struggle for control of the forest reserves commanded much attention in both departments.[14]

CHAPTER TWENTY-FOUR

National Authority over Public Lands Expanded and Confirmed

IN 1895, CONGRESS FINALLY STOPPED considering the proposal to carve several hundred thousand acres out of Yellowstone National Park in order to allow a railroad to be built to serve the mines at Cooke City, just outside the park's northeastern corner. Three years earlier, the Senate had finally approved the idea, leading Senator Vest, the proposal's longtime critic, to register a tart complaint about the power of the "persistent and unscrupulous" railroad lobby. But then, just as the effort was on the verge of succeeding, it was thwarted in the House after an effective last-minute campaign led by *Forest and Stream* editor George Bird Grinnell. Among other things, Grinnell publicized a letter from Theodore Roosevelt, then serving on the U.S. Civil Service Commission, that called on Congress to keep the park "a great forestry preserve and a National pleasure ground, the like of which is not to be found on any other continent."[1]

The defeat of this bill in 1892 proved to be a turning point, and support for the proposal gradually withered, with Thomas McRae finally pronouncing the idea dead in February 1895. His House Public Lands Committee issued a report concluding that, after "thorough examination of the arguments of both sides," Congress should not "recede" from the "wise policy by which this park was dedicated for the benefit and enjoyment of the entire country." In the end, the episode showed the growing political clout of the national park label.[2]

In the meantime, Senator Vest continued his efforts to establish the legal machinery for punishing violators of park rules. The American bison's spiral toward extinction was still capturing public attention. Poaching of the Yellowstone herd, one of the handful remaining anywhere, was a significant concern, and on March 13, 1894, federal authorities arrested a poacher as he was skinning nearly a dozen bison he had killed in the park. Photographs of the slaughter were circulated in a report from a *Forest and Stream* correspondent.

On Capitol Hill, John F. Lacey seized the opportunity and quickly crafted a bill to strengthen law enforcement's authority over Yellowstone and to protect its wildlife. He secured its passage in the Public Lands Committee on April 4 and in the full House two days later. Vest promptly shepherded Lacey's bill through the Senate with some changes, a conference with the House quickly ironed out the differences, and on May 7, 1894, less than eight weeks after the poacher's arrest, the bill was signed into law by President Cleveland.[3]

The legislation prohibited all hunting of birds and wild animals in the park for commerce or sport. It was supported by sport-hunting advocates such as Grinnell, reflecting his continuing concern to align the interests of sport hunters and more preservation-minded members of the public where possible—an alliance that continues to have significant influence on public land policy to this day. The legislation did allow sportfishing, by hook and line, under Interior Department regulation. Those 1894 policies on hunting and fishing, which included outlawing trade in unlawfully taken fish and wildlife, have been applied to national parks ever since. (In national forests, by contrast, sport hunting is generally permitted.)

In addition, the 1894 legislation finally gave the Interior secretary broad authority to promulgate and enforce any regulations "deemed necessary and proper for the management and care" of the park and its resources, not just those dealing with fish and wildlife, and to punish violators with sanctions including fines, imprisonment, and the forfeiture of guns, traps and other equipment. It also authorized the appointment of resident law enforcement agents, a court commissioner, and the construction of a jail in the park.

Lacey and Vest's work paid off. The park's bison population eventually rebounded from its low of a couple of hundred animals, and today bison are a prime attraction for Yellowstone's millions of visitors.

THE SUPREME COURT CONFIRMS NATIONAL AUTHORITY

During the eventful 1890s, as the legislative and executive branches were making more and larger reservations of public land, the head of the third branch of the national government, the U.S. Supreme Court, issued a series of unanimous decisions that found no obstacles in the U.S. Constitution to this policy. The Court's readiness to defer to acquiring and holding public land to serve noneconomic objectives was in decided contrast to its more skeptical attitude toward many of Congress's decisions regarding regulation of the economy.[4]

In an 1893 decision, *Shoemaker v. United States,* the Court rejected a challenge to the 1890 legislation authorizing the United States to acquire private property in order to establish Rock Creek Park in the District of Columbia. The Court began by noting that not long before, the idea that government could acquire private property for a public park would have been regarded as a "novel exercise of legislative power." But more recently, the Court observed, courts around the country had generally upheld the power of government to make such acquisitions, even over the objection of landowners to whom it paid just compensation, and practically all cities around the country had established parks "for rest and exercise in the open air."[5]

Because *Shoemaker* arose in the District of Columbia, an area over which the Constitution's Enclave Clause gave Congress exclusive jurisdiction, the decision left open the question whether the U.S. government possessed similarly broad authority to acquire private property for a park within a state's boundaries. Three years later, the Court answered that question in the affirmative. The case arose when a landowner challenged the national government's effort to buy its private land at the site of the pivotal Civil War battle at Gettysburg, Pennsylvania. Although the government was prepared to provide "just compensation" as required by the Constitution, the landowner argued that preservation of the site did not qualify as a "public use" entitling the United States to acquire its land.

Writing for the Court in *U.S. v. Gettysburg Electric Railway,* Justice Rufus Peckham noted that the battlefield's preservation was related to Congress's explicit constitutional powers over war and national defense, but went on to put the government's interest on a higher level. The Gettysburg conflict was "one of the great battles of the world," he wrote, with bravery, heroism, and dreadful sacrifice, whose outcome was vital to the "existence of the government itself" and to the "perpetuity of our institutions." The government's acquisition of the battlefield "for the benefit of all the citizens of the country, for the present and for the future" would "show a proper recognition of the great things that were done there" and enhance the "love and respect for those institutions" on the part of every citizen.[6]

The next year, 1897, the Court took a similarly sweeping view of Congress's power to protect public lands it already owned, in its decision in *Camfield v. United States*. The government had sued two Colorado livestock operators to enforce the Unlawful Inclosures Act of 1885. They had acquired the rights to all of Union Pacific's odd-numbered sections of a checkerboarded railroad land grant that encompassed two adjacent townships, and had constructed a fence around the entire periphery of the two townships. Although the fence was physically located on the sections of land they owned, it extended to the very corners of those sections and thus effectively enclosed not only their land, but also the 23,000 acres of public land in the even-numbered sections interspersed with it.

The livestock operators argued, first, that the Unlawful Inclosures Act should not be interpreted to apply to fences located exclusively on private land and, second, if it was nonetheless interpreted to apply to such fences, it was unconstitutional, because, they argued, the Constitution's Property Clause gave Congress no authority to regulate activities on private lands inside a state.

Justice Henry Brown's opinion for the Court rejected both arguments. First, he noted, the statute forbade "inclosures" of public lands, regardless of whether the enclosing fence was on private or public land. If it were construed to apply only to public lands, the law would have been unnecessary, because the national government, like any landowner, had a right to prevent trespass or unconsented occupancy of its land.

Regarding the constitutional issue, Brown wrote that the United States "doubtless has a power over its own property analogous to the police power of the several States," and that power included the right to limit activities on private property where those activities interfered with its use of its property. Otherwise, it could not faithfully perform "its duties as trustee for the people of the United States," who owned those lands. The admission of Colorado into the union had not deprived Congress of its "power of legislating for the protection of the public lands," Brown declared, because "the public domain of the United States" could not be left "completely at the mercy of state legislation."[7]

The Court also rejected the operators' argument that Congress's decision to transfer ownership of public lands in a checkerboard pattern, and its "tacit acquiescence" in the use of its lands as a grazing commons, prevented the United States from now seeking to remove their fence. The national government could stop tolerating livestock grazing on its lands "at any moment," for its "long acquiescence" in the grazers' "appropriation of public lands" did not give them a protected property interest in those lands unless Congress said so, and it plainly had not.

In its decision in *United States v. Rio Grande Dam & Irrigation Co.* (1899), the Court, speaking through Justice David Brewer, confirmed broad national authority over rivers, including the maintenance of stream flows to protect public lands. The United States had sued to stop an irrigation company from constructing a dam across the Rio Grande in New Mexico without seeking its permission. Brewer's opinion confirmed that the United States had the authority to prevent the dam construction if the dam would "substantially diminish the navigability" of the river. The United States could, moreover, assert a right to the "continued flow" of waters in a stream if it were "necessary for the beneficial uses of" public lands bordering the stream. This statement laid the basis for the Court to decide, within a few years, that the United States could reserve waters as well as lands in public ownership in order to meet national objectives.[8]

In decisions in 1893 and 1900, the Court rejected the idea that admitting new states on an "equal footing" with other states limited U.S. authority over public lands. In the second of these, *Stearns v. Minnesota,* Justice Brewer noted that the national government retained ownership and control of a "large amount" of public land when it admitted Minnesota to the union in 1857. The "equal footing" language in the state's enabling act was irrelevant because it applied only to a state's "political rights and obligations," and not to arrangements that Congress might thereafter choose to make regarding those lands it retained.[9]

Collectively, these decisions erased all doubt whether the flourishing movement to have the United States reserve or acquire lands and manage them to serve national purposes rested on a solid constitutional foundation.

PUBLIC LAND RESERVATIONS ON THE EVE OF THEODORE ROOSEVELT'S PRESIDENCY

By the late summer of 1901, nearly 50 million acres of public land had been reserved more or less permanently in U.S. ownership, not including public lands in Indian and military reservations. Most of these were in forest reserves—18 million acres were reserved between 1891 and 1893, President Cleveland's Washington's Birthday proclamations added another 21 million acres, and President McKinley added 7 million more. (The remaining acres were in a handful of national parks.) In addition, many millions of acres had been provisionally withdrawn by the GLO in anticipation of Congress or the president making new permanent reservations.

The program to keep more public lands in national ownership had clearly found favor across the country. While more than 500 million acres of public lands outside Alaska were still open to entry and privatization under laws such as the Homestead Act, the GLO had petitions in hand calling for the establishment of more than 50 million acres of new forest reserves. Both major political parties and all three branches of the national government were in tune with the movement, and there were relatively few vocal opponents of making new reserves.[10]

PART FIVE   THE GREAT TRANSITION, PHASE TWO,
1902–1913

CHAPTER TWENTY-FIVE

Theodore Roosevelt, Public Lands, and the Reclamation Act

AS THE SUMMER OF 1901 FADED into autumn, Theodore Roosevelt became president as the result of an assassin's bullet. One can scarcely imagine an individual better equipped to assume leadership of the nation's public land policy. He straddled two currents of American life. He was a child of the aristocracy, born and raised in the epicenter of the urban East, and educated at Harvard. But in his twenties, seeking solace from the death of his wife and his mother on the same day, he became a rancher in the Dakota Territory, an experience that both helped shape his attitude toward the public lands and gave him credibility on the subject. Henry Teller, a Colorado senator and former Interior secretary, told the *Denver Republican* in October that because Roosevelt had "lived in our country," he "knows what our needs are."[1]

Roosevelt, a devoted naturalist from an early age, loved the outdoors; indeed, he learned of McKinley's impending death in September 1901 when he was descending from the summit of Mount Marcy, New York's highest peak. He knew fauna, and not just from a gun sight, though he was an enthusiastic hunter. He had written books on birds and animal life. With his gregarious disposition and prodigious output as a correspondent, he was already on good terms with many of the officials, scientists, and others who were shaping the new era of public land policy. His brash enthusiasm allowed him to relate to people of all walks of life. He made great copy for journalists, and he appreciated their power to influence public opinion.[2]

He believed in an activist government. Despite being the youngest president ever, the forty-two-year-old Roosevelt had accumulated governmental experience at every level from the local (New York City police commissioner) through the state (legislative leader and governor) to the federal executive branch (U.S. Civil Service commissioner, assistant secretary of the navy, vice president). Altogether, Roosevelt brought to public lands policy a unique combination of knowledge, experience, political savvy, boldness, and boundless energy.

Roosevelt was also favored by timing and circumstance. Euro-American advancement across the continent was by then substantially complete. Except in Alaska, Indian title had been almost completely resolved, leaving most public lands unencumbered by Indian claims. As memories of the brutal struggle over slavery and the bloody Civil War receded, an era of optimism had dawned with the new century. Prosperity had returned after the depression that followed the Panic of 1893. Unemployment had fallen from 14 percent in 1896 to 4 percent by 1901, a level maintained over most of his administration. In the fifteen years that followed 1896, the national economy more than doubled in size.

In his two years as governor of New York, Roosevelt had been a vigorous advocate for protecting land and other natural resources. His second annual message to the state legislature, delivered in January 1900, illustrated the breadth of his concerns. He called for forest and watershed protection; for making the Adirondacks and the Catskills "great parks kept in perpetuity for the benefit and enjoyment of our people"; for continuing the "great good" that was being done to restore the natural beauty of the Niagara Falls Reservation; for logging only in accord with "strictly scientific principles"; for promoting "hardy outdoor sports, like hunting," which are "of no small value to the national character"; for a state ban on factories that used bird skins and feathers for fashion and apparel; for hunting game birds sustainably; and for the "rigid protection" of ordinary birds, especially songbirds.[3]

AN OVERVIEW OF ROOSEVELT'S PUBLIC LAND LEGACY

Roosevelt grasped many of the opportunities presented to him with both hands and left a huge imprint on national public land policy. During his seven-plus years in office, the amount of public land permanently reserved in national ownership more than tripled, and he set in motion or accelerated policy changes that led to much more being reserved in the decades to come.

The era's many initiatives to protect public lands commanded bipartisan support. In fact, while Roosevelt enjoyed Republican control of both houses of

Congress during his time in office, most of the relatively few opponents of his public land initiatives were members of his own party. Furthermore, although executive vigor was the hallmark of his administration, Congress did not remain on the sidelines. Some of its laws corrected mistakes of the past, such as finally repealing, in 1905, the "in lieu" provision of the Organic Act of 1897. Others opened new pathways for protecting public lands, such as the Antiquities Act in 1906, which gave the president broad authority to reserve public lands to protect cultural, historic, and scientific resources. Also, although Roosevelt unilaterally established many of the early public land reservations aimed specifically at protecting wildlife, Congress was quick to jump in and work with him in that endeavor.

Roosevelt broke new ground by driving the development of a public-lands-based energy policy. The rapidly industrializing American economy was becoming more dependent on electricity, primarily produced from fossil fuels and by hydroelectric dams. Public lands contained numerous dam sites and fossil fuel deposits, and when Roosevelt took office, existing law made both resources freely available to developers. Judging that it was foolish simply to give these energy resources to private interests and put them beyond governmental control, he and his successor, William Howard Taft, demanded fundamental changes.

They called on Congress to enact legislation making these resources available only through leasing, which would allow them to be developed under the watchful eye of government and would provide financial return to the national treasury. In the meantime, to increase the pressure on Congress to act, Roosevelt and Taft withdrew many millions of acres of public lands thought to contain energy sources from existing divestment laws. Their vigorous efforts established a momentum for reform that ultimately proved impossible to stop. Although opposition from the energy industry and its sympathizers in Congress delayed enactment for years, the Roosevelt-Taft executive withdrawals remained in place until finally, in 1920, Woodrow Wilson signed the Mineral Leasing Act and the Federal Power Act into law.

Roosevelt and Taft also supported enactment of a new program to bring into public ownership large areas of rugged, privately owned lands that contained, or had contained, forests. This idea had been advanced before Roosevelt took office, nurtured by the same concerns—about the effects of logging on soils, water flows, scenery, and overall quality of life—that had led Congress to enact the original forest reserve legislation in 1891. Success was not achieved until 1911, with the enactment of legislation named after its chief congressional sponsor, John Weeks of Massachusetts. Its program to acquire and, where necessary, restore lands was focused initially on the Appalachian South and New England. Over time, it led to the establishment of more than fifty national forests embracing nearly 20 million acres in forty states.

Although the Roosevelt-Taft era accelerated the trend toward public ownership, hundreds of millions of acres of public land remained subject to divestment under the Homestead Act and other nineteenth-century laws. The idea of using public lands to establish new small farms and settlements and other economic opportunities for ordinary Americans retained political appeal, and Roosevelt and Taft never backed away from it. Indeed, new divestiture programs were enacted during the Roosevelt administration, principally the Reclamation Act of 1902 and the Forest Homestead Act of 1906.

Although millions more acres would pass out of U.S. ownership via divestiture measures, by the end of the Roosevelt era the idea was practically beyond questioning that the national government should own a significant proportion of the nation's land and manage it primarily to serve a wide range of values, of which providing inspiration, wildlife habitat, and recreation were on a par with furnishing commodities such as water, minerals, and timber.

This was not an embrace of socialism. The private sector continued to play the leading role in developing many of the resources that these lands contained. But ownership gave the national government the commanding role in determining whether, when, and under what conditions much of that activity would take place. Compared to situations where public lands were *not* involved, the national government's role was much less constrained by limitations that the Supreme Court was finding in the Constitution.

SETTING THE AGENDA: ROOSEVELT'S FIRST STATE OF THE UNION MESSAGE TO CONGRESS

Even before the new president took up residence in the White House, his friend Gifford Pinchot called on him. Historians of public land policy have described the Pinchot-Roosevelt relationship as an "ideological and political symbiosis," growing out of their shared enthusiasm for power, a good scrap, the outdoors, and reforming natural resource policy. In his autobiography in 1913, Roosevelt identified Pinchot as the one who, "on the whole, stood first" among all the officials who played a part in his administration's accomplishments.[4]

Roosevelt wasted little time serving notice that public land policy would be a major focus of his administration, and that he would be an activist. His first annual message to Congress, in December 1901, drew on drafts prepared by

Pinchot and others to lay out an ambitious agenda that called forest and water issues "perhaps the most vital internal questions of the United States." The forest reserves should be "better protected from fires," and controls were needed on livestock grazing, "above all by sheep." He also made clear that he regarded the forest reserves as supplying more than commodities like timber. At least some of them, he wrote, "should afford perpetual protection to the native fauna and flora, safe havens of refuge to our rapidly diminishing wild animals of the larger kinds, and free camping grounds for the ever increasing numbers of men and women who have learned to find rest, health, and recreation in the splendid forests and flower-clad meadows of our mountains." The fundamental idea, he told Congress, was that the forest reserves should be "set apart forever for the use and benefit of our people as a whole and not sacrificed to the shortsighted greed of a few."[5]

"RECLAIMING" THE ARID PUBLIC LANDS BY IRRIGATION: THE RECLAMATION ACT OF 1902

In that same message, Roosevelt strongly endorsed a federal program to develop irrigation projects in the West. Although some irrigation projects had been built with private capital both before and after the Irrigation Survey debacle in 1890, few were under the illusion that public lands in the most arid regions would be irrigated and privatized in significant amounts without some kind of federal support to build the dams and delivery facilities required to serve them.

A group promoting governmental aid for irrigation had periodically sponsored "Irrigation Congresses," beginning with one in Salt Lake City in September 1891, a few months after Congress gave the president the authority to establish forest reserves on public lands. Its first initiative was to petition Congress to convey arid public lands to the states so that they could undertake irrigation projects. In 1894, Congress took a step in that direction, enacting what became known as the Carey Act, after its chief sponsor, Senator Joseph Carey (R-Wyo.). It offered 1 million acres of public land to each western state (other than California, where a number of irrigation projects were already in the works and where most irrigable lands were already in private ownership) that would contract with the U.S. government to develop irrigation projects at the state's expense and commit to convey the granted land in small tracts to genuine settlers.[6]

Ardent irrigation promoters such as Congressman Francis G. Newlands (D-Nev.) doubted that states could bear the expense of such projects. That prediction proved accurate. By 1902, only four of the ten eligible states had elected to participate, fewer than 700,000 acres had been earmarked for inclusion in Carey Act projects, and only about 10,000 acres had been transferred out of U.S. ownership. Eventually, about a million acres were divested under the Carey Act, more than 60 percent of it in Idaho and 20 percent in Wyoming. Meanwhile, projects built by private enterprise and, to a much lesser extent, the states, were irrigating only a few million acres of arid western lands—far fewer than the 100 million acres that John Wesley Powell had suggested were potentially irrigable in 1890.[7]

The disappointing results of the Carey Act made Congress unenthusiastic about ceding potentially irrigable arid public lands to states. In the Organic Act, Congress had underscored the relationship between public lands and water supplies by describing a primary purpose of the forest reserves as securing "favorable conditions of water flows." Because most of the arid lands that remained in U.S. ownership could not be settled by farmers unless they were irrigated, the irrigation lobby looked to the U.S. government for direct assistance. In a deft bit of political messaging, it characterized its objective as the "reclaiming" of arid lands to advance the ideal of homesteading.[8]

When John Wesley Powell was still politically influential, the forest reserve movement and the irrigation movement had not always seen eye to eye. After Congress marginalized him in 1890, the two movements gradually aligned. When the American Forestry Association held its annual meeting in Los Angeles in July 1899, Gifford Pinchot was in attendance. Southern California was in a drought, and the AFA decided to support a national government program of irrigation assistance. It soon changed the name of its monthly magazine, the *Forester*, to *Forestry and Irrigation*. In their 1900 platforms, both political parties supported legislation to aid the irrigation of arid lands in the West to make them available to settlers.[9]

All this gave the new president a political opportunity, and Roosevelt skillfully seized it by proposing a kind of grand bargain in his first State of the Union message. Describing forests as great "natural reservoirs," he characterized forest reserves as deposits in a water bank account, and irrigation projects carried out with federal assistance as a way to withdraw some of that currency. The "reclamation of the arid unsettled public lands," he told Congress, required the construction of waterworks that were "impracticable for private enterprise" and plainly beyond the capacity of states. So the U.S. government should build them and then make "reclaimed" lands available to "actual settlers" in small plots, with the construction costs repaid "so far as possible" by the new landowners. The western part of the nation could support more than 75 million people, Roosevelt wrote, "if the waters that now run to waste were saved and used for irrigation."[10]

Roosevelt was updating John Wesley Powell's vision, but this time with a deft politician's touch. He did not deny the existence of the natural limits that Powell had emphasized, but at the same time he showed how the program he endorsed had something for everyone. By helping the West and the nation realize the promise of the forest reserves, the reclamation program that he envisioned, Roosevelt said, justified reserving in permanent national ownership practically all headwaters areas. The settlement of formerly public lands, made possible by federally supported irrigation, would provide an economic stimulus that the region needed. In many parts of the West, mining and logging were not sufficient to sustain a local or regional economy. The livestock industry already established on arid public grasslands had no ability to expand; indeed, the number of livestock had long exceeded the lands' carrying capacity. The economic benefits that might come from tourists enjoying the public lands were also variable, and before the advent of the automobile, tourism was limited by the remoteness of many reserves. A commitment to undertake irrigation projects also fit Roosevelt's conception of a muscular national government and his personality—he liked to build things. In that same message to Congress, he called for constructing a canal across the isthmus connecting North and South America.

Congress was already considering legislation to establish such an irrigation and settlement program, but after his strong endorsement, its enactment was a foregone conclusion. In the Senate, westerners of both parties supported it, and in February 1902 what came to be called the Reclamation Act passed on a voice vote.

There was opposition in the House, mainly from fiscal conservatives in Roosevelt's own party. Public lands were still being privatized at a rapid rate (more than 10 million acres per year on average in the 1890s, mostly in the Great Plains region) without federal irrigation assistance. Joseph Cannon, the powerful, tightfisted chair of the House Appropriations Committee, expressed concern—later proved correct—that the initiative to "reclaim" arid lands would evolve into a big and relatively open-ended public works program funded mostly by taxpayers across the nation. Cannon often clashed with his fellow Republican Roosevelt, once describing him as having "no more use for the Constitution than a tomcat has for a marriage license."[11]

When some questioned whether the Constitution gave Congress the authority to enact such a program, westerners such as Congressman George

Sutherland (R-Utah) vigorously pushed back. Sutherland eventually served for
more than fifteen years on the U.S. Supreme Court, where he voted to strike
down a number of federal programs, including much New Deal legislation, as
exceeding Congress's constitutional power to enact. But that was later. Now, he
told his colleagues, the U.S. Constitution was "written in broad and comprehensive terms" that were "never intended to chain the hands of future generations," nor to bind the United States to "condemn this vast domain" of public
lands to "perpetual aridity."[12]

With Francis Newlands leading the charge, the House approved the
measure by nearly a 3–1 margin. Most of the House Democrats and western
Republicans voted for it, and most of the no votes came from eastern and
midwestern Republicans, concerned about the government subsidizing the
expansion of farmland and earmarking revenues from public land sales for
the exclusive benefit of western states. Roosevelt signed what became known as
the Newlands Act into law on June 17, 1902. In their respective platforms in
1904, both political parties took credit for it.[13]

The Reclamation Act applied just to the eleven western states plus the
Dakotas, Nebraska, Kansas, and Oklahoma—states where nearly all the established forest reserves could be found. It authorized the Interior secretary to use
revenues from the sale of public lands—other than revenues shared with all
states under the Morrill Act to support land-grant colleges—to construct and
maintain projects to capture, store, and deliver water to irrigate public lands in
those states. Persons could enter and gain title to the lands made irrigable by
such projects by meeting the requirements of the Homestead Act and paying a
commensurate share of the project's cost, over a maximum of ten years,
without interest. The act also gave the Interior secretary broad discretion to
withdraw public lands from divestment under all laws except the homestead
laws. Over the next few years, more than 40 million acres of public land were
withdrawn, all that was "considered remotely susceptible of irrigation," in the
historian Louise Peffer's description. Much of it adjoined or was downstream
of forest reserves.[14]

Significantly, although reclamation advocates emphasized that the
program would facilitate the transfer of arid public lands into productive private
ownership, from the beginning the Reclamation Act allowed project water to be
delivered to lands *already* in private ownership, with a catch. Reclamation-
project water could not be furnished to tracts of private land in excess of 160
acres held by "any one landowner," who also had to be "an actual bona fide resident on such land, or occupant thereof residing in the neighborhood." The

acreage limitation and the residency requirement—by limiting the project's benefits to "homeseekers in small tracts" and thus "rigidly guarding against land monopoly," as the Democratic Party platform of 1904 put it—were integral parts of the decision to extend the benefits of the reclamation program to privately owned lands.

These restrictions "excited active and powerful hostility," Roosevelt noted, but he called for their "wide and firm enforcement." His call was not heeded. Over the following decades, Congress exempted some projects entirely from the restrictions. Even when it did not, "wide and firm enforcement" by the executive proved to be, by far, more the exception than the rule. In 1977, the Carter administration, prodded by a court order, adopted regulations to tighten enforcement, but after the Reagan administration took office, Congress enacted legislation that essentially ratified the status quo by repealing the residency requirement altogether and greatly relaxing the acreage limitation.[15]

Soon after the Reclamation Act became law, Interior secretary Hitchcock (a McKinley appointee whom Roosevelt had kept on) established the Reclamation Service, initially housed within the U.S. Geological Survey, to administer it. A number of its early projects involved the national government rescuing—that is, taking over and completing—floundering irrigation ventures that had been begun earlier with state or private capital. By the end of 1906, the Reclamation Service was working on twenty-three projects in thirteen states and the New Mexico and Arizona Territories. Within two decades, more than 2 million acres were being irrigated with federal reclamation-project water. But the hope that the act would promote the privatization of significant amounts of public land went mostly unrealized. Most of the lands being irrigated (for example, in the Salt River project near Phoenix and the Truckee-Carson project east of Reno, Nevada, the first two Reclamation Service undertakings) had already passed into private ownership before the projects were built.[16]

The Roosevelt administration was still in office when Congress began enlarging the reclamation program's objectives. In 1906, it authorized the Interior secretary to provide reclamation-project water to "towns or cities on or in the immediate vicinity" of the irrigation projects, and to market electricity generated by project works that was not needed to facilitate irrigation. It was also not long before Congress began to increase the amount of the subsidy that the program provided to irrigators. Over the next few decades, the subsidies grew larger and larger. All this "mission creep" turned the reclamation program into a general public works program in the nation's western region, just as Congressman Cannon had feared.[17]

The Reclamation Act of 1902 helped justify the creation of more forest reserves; total reserve acreage tripled in the first seven years following its enactment. Some of this expansion included public land that had previously been withdrawn with the idea of supporting irrigation projects under the Reclamation Act to benefit to local areas. A notable example was Roosevelt's establishment of the nearly 2-million-acre Inyo National Forest in 1907 on mostly treeless uplands flanking the Owens Valley in eastern California. There, Pinchot helped persuade the president to reject a proposal to build a reclamation project to promote agricultural growth in the valley, in favor of allowing the Los Angeles Department of Water and Power to build a project to capture and export most of the water to the rapidly growing urban areas in Southern California. This was the first, but hardly the last, large water project in the West that captured water furnished by reserved public lands to fuel urban growth. Even by this time, the West had become the most urbanized region in the nation and included five of the nation's twenty-eight largest cities.[18]

CHAPTER TWENTY-SIX

Forest Reserves Expand in Roosevelt's First Term

IN HIS DECEMBER 1901 MESSAGE to Congress, Roosevelt reported that the "practical usefulness of the national forest reserves" had "led to a widespread demand by the people of the West for their protection and extension," and he committed to meet that demand "whenever practicable." He kept his word. Between April 1902 and the end of 1904, he proclaimed forest reserves on nearly 14 million acres of public land in five states and the territories of Alaska, Arizona, New Mexico, and Puerto Rico. As with previous reserves, most were strongly supported by locals, with little outright opposition.[1]

One of these, a 5,000-acre forest reserve on Puerto Rico, demonstrated the breadth of his geographic vision and his interest in tropical wildlife, which had been nurtured by his time in Cuba as a Rough Rider. The island had come under U.S. control in 1899 through the treaty ending the Spanish-American War. Rather than relying on section 24, Roosevelt used authority that Congress had given him in 1902 to reserve public lands and buildings on Puerto Rico for unspecified "public uses." Now known as the El Yunque National Forest, it is the only tropical rainforest in the national forest system and, having grown to more than 28,000 acres, is the largest bloc of public land on the island.[2]

His 4.5-million-acre Alexander Archipelago Forest Reserve in southeastern Alaska also deserves mention, for it illustrated both his passion for action and his tendency to draw on a large circle of friends outside the government for advice. Not long after taking office, Roosevelt requested George Thornton

Emmons, a retired naval officer who had been stationed in Alaska, to investigate opportunities for forest reserves there. Emmons submitted a report that recommended the creation of a forest reserve, and Roosevelt sent it to Interior secretary Hitchcock in April 1902 with the notation that it "strikes me favorably." In August, having received no response from Hitchcock, Roosevelt had an assistant send him a note expressing the "President's desire" that a reserve "be established at once." Ten days later, Hitchcock sent Roosevelt a draft proclamation, and he signed it the next day. (It is now part of the Tongass National Forest.)[3]

In the spring of 1903, Roosevelt embarked on a sixty-six-day, fourteen-thousand-mile trip through twenty-five states, the longest journey ever made by a sitting president. He spent two weeks in Yellowstone in the company of the naturalist John Burroughs, visited the Grand Canyon, and camped with John Muir at Yosemite after visiting the Big Tree Grove of giant sequoias. Many of the dozens of speeches he made to hundreds of thousands of people on this trip included exhortations to protect the marvelous resources found on public lands. Both while traveling and upon his return, he continued to establish new forest reserves.[4]

PINCHOT CAMPAIGNS TO GAIN CONTROL
OF THE FOREST RESERVES

Roosevelt called on Congress to transfer responsibility for the forest reserves to the Agriculture Department soon after taking office, but it took more than three years for Congress to act. In the interim, Pinchot devoted considerable effort to winning over livestock interests, since they were a primary constituency, grazing their herds on tens of millions of acres in the reserves. Pinchot emphasized the importance of framing grazing rules "to meet local conditions," but his most effective move was to hire Albert Potter, a prominent rancher in the Arizona Territory, to head a new grazing branch within the Bureau of Forestry. Potter, whom Pinchot later called the "cornerstone" of the grazing program in the national forests, began work in late 1901 and persuaded his former ranch partner in Arizona, Will C. Barnes, to join him. In his memoir, published in 1941, Barnes, who ran the agency's grazing program from 1915 to 1928, described the grazing branch under Pinchot as "the shock troops who won the West for forestry."[5]

Meanwhile, the General Land Office was gamely attempting to implement the Organic Act of 1897. It was a huge management challenge, complicated by the rapid expansion of forest-reserve acreage and by the knowledge that the ambitious Pinchot and his growing staff were poised to find fault with its performance whenever possible. To complicate things further, lower federal courts were sending inconsistent signals about the GLO's authority to regulate grazing under the Organic Act. Congress continued to leave it to the GLO to wrestle with the subject with but one exception—in 1904, it prohibited "stock of any kind" from grazing in the Bull Run Forest Reserve that President Harrison had established in 1892 in the Cascade Range to protect the city of Portland's water supply.[6]

To deal with the increasing number of sheep being herded on many reserves, the GLO briefly experimented with allowing local woolgrowers' associations to decide who should receive grazing permits, in return for the associations' help in policing their members' grazing operations. Unsurprisingly, the practice failed to bring damage from overgrazing under control, and so the GLO took back authority after a few months. But a seed had been planted, and the idea of giving local livestock associations a leading role in the governance of grazing operations on public land over time embedded itself in grazing administration.

In early 1902, the Interior Department formulated a policy that would also have lasting significance—a "preference" system for issuing grazing permits that favored, in descending order, stockowners who resided within the reserve; who resided outside the reserve, but maintained ranching facilities within a reserve; who resided in the vicinity of the reserve; and who were outsiders but had some fair claim to graze the reserve. Favoring local residents and property owners disfavored nomadic herders, who usually ran sheep rather than cattle. The preference system was not supposed to affect the government's authority to decide whether and on what terms to issue permits to graze the reserves, which had to be renewed each year.[7]

Pinchot's campaign to take over the forest reserves suffered a setback in June 1902 when the House voted down a bill sponsored by John Lacey, chair of the Public Lands Committee, to transfer management of the forest reserves to the Agriculture Department. Opponents of the transfer, led by Joseph Cannon, were critical of Pinchot's "so-called scientific forestry." Just two weeks later, however, Pinchot began his comeback when Congress gave final approval to a bill that established a forest reserve and authorized timber harvesting on 200,000 acres of former Indian land in Minnesota that had come under the control of the Interior Department. The legislation, drafted with Pinchot's help, gave the "forester" in the Agriculture Department considerable supervisory authority, including the power to make and enforce rules regarding timber harvesting so long as the rules were approved by the Interior secretary. This forest reserve was the first one established directly by Congress, and it marked the first time the Agriculture Department was given frontline management authority. It was also the culmination of a years-long campaign to open to logging lands in Minnesota that had been cleared of Indian title not long before, a move that caused controversy in Indian country.[8]

SCANDAL

Pinchot's case to transfer the forest reserves to the Agriculture Department got a critical boost when reports began to surface in late 1902 of widespread abuses of divestment laws under the GLO's administration in Oregon and California. President Roosevelt reacted with characteristic vigor, instructing his attorney general to name a special prosecutor with a mandate to identify the culprits and bring them to justice. An Oregon grand jury heard evidence for eleven months between 1903 and 1905 that eventually resulted in numerous indictments and a number of convictions. One of those convicted, Stephen A. Puter, was persuaded to testify against others, and while in jail he co-wrote a tell-all book about the scandal with the sensational title *Looters of the Public Domain*.[9]

Prominent officials were caught up in the scandal. Oregon senator John Mitchell was indicted, convicted, and sentenced to jail, but died before his appeal could be decided. By some accounts, the other Oregon senator, Charles William Fulton, escaped indictment only because the statute of limitations had run out. Oregon congressman J. N. Williams, who operated a sheep ranch near Prineville, was convicted of conspiring to fraudulently obtain title to several thousand acres of public grazing land; the impression of wrongdoing was not dispelled when his conviction was ultimately set aside on a technicality. Several other public officials, including the U.S. Attorney for Oregon, were indicted, and some were convicted. All this added to the odor of corruption that had long hovered over the GLO's administration of public land divestment and accelerated the momentum for transferring the forest reserves to the Agriculture Department.[10]

As the scandal began to unfold in 1903, GLO commissioner Binger Hermann resigned under pressure from Secretary Hitchcock. Hermann returned to Oregon and promptly won back his congressional seat in a special election called when the incumbent died. Hermann's successor as commissioner was W. A. Richards, who had served a term as governor of Wyoming before becoming assistant commissioner in 1899. Richards became a strong proponent of stripping his own agency of authority over the forest reserves, writing in his 1904 *Annual Report* that the GLO was "neither organized nor equipped" for the job, because it required "special scientific and practical training."[11]

Meanwhile, Pinchot "shamelessly courted the leading grazing interests," as the historian Donald Pisani put it, and made headway. Some livestock operators, especially larger ones, became convinced that they would fare better under his and the Agriculture Department's control than Interior's. In late 1903, Congressman Frank Mondell (R-Wyo.), who had opposed the transfer, changed his mind and became a supporter, as did the Idaho Wool Growers Association.[12]

For some time, Roosevelt had been urging Congress to establish a commission to address what he called the many "complicated questions" involved in public land policy. When it failed to do so, he appointed his own Public Lands Commission in 1903, named Pinchot to head it, and gave it a sweeping mandate. Its other two members were GLO commissioner Richards and Frederick H. Newell, the first director of the Reclamation Service, who was charged with implementing the Reclamation Act. To no one's surprise, the first of the commission's two reports, issued in March 1904, endorsed the transfer of the forest reserves to the Department of Agriculture. Most of its other recommendations were also predictable, including ones to repeal the notorious "in lieu" provision of the Organic Act, as well as the Timber and Stone Act of 1878, the latter repeating a recommendation that the first Public Land Commission, headed by John Wesley Powell, had made more than twenty years earlier.[13]

Proceeding almost parallel to the Public Land Commission was a separate body that Roosevelt had appointed, the Committee on the Organization of Government Scientific Work. Pinchot was a prominent member of this panel as well, so, unsurprisingly, one of its recommendations was to give the Agriculture Department responsibility for not only the forest reserves but also—showing the reach of Pinchot's ambition—the handful of national parks that Congress had established. In his autobiography, Pinchot acknowledged that an "ulterior motive" for his work on both commissions was to advance his campaign to get control of the forest reserves.[14]

PINCHOT PREVAILS: THE FOREST RESERVES ARE TRANSFERRED TO THE DEPARTMENT OF AGRICULTURE

Theodore Roosevelt won a smashing victory in the presidential election of November 1904, winning the popular vote by nearly twenty percentage points, the widest margin in a presidential contest since 1820. Roosevelt's robust expansion of forest reserves and his vigorous championing of other public land policy reforms seemed to resonate with voters in the region most impacted, the West, where he carried every state. That unanimity significantly improved on the mark of his predecessor, McKinley, who lost several western states to William Jennings Bryan in both 1896 and 1900. Indeed, Roosevelt carried eleven of the twelve Colorado counties where forest reserves had been established, losing the twelfth by a mere 25 votes, whereas McKinley lost every one of those counties in 1896 and all but one in 1900.

The election results did not influence historians like John Ise, who in his account of the establishment and growth of the forest reserve system greatly magnified western opposition to it. His view had lasting influence. In 1978, for example, William Rehnquist wrote an opinion for a slim majority of the U.S. Supreme Court that narrowly construed the Organic Act and cited Ise for the proposition that forest reserves caused much "anguish" and protest in the West, including from western members of Congress who "had objected since 1891 to what they viewed to be frequently indiscriminate creation of federal forest reserves."[15]

After the election, Pinchot redoubled his efforts to gain control of the forest reserves. He secured the support of the National Board of Trade, a business organization resembling the modern U.S. Chamber of Commerce, and in early January 1905, turned a weeklong meeting of the American Forest Congress in Washington, D.C., into a pep rally for the transfer legislation. Sponsored by the American Forestry Association, the congress was only the second such national gathering, and the first since 1882. It drew more than a thousand people, including members of Congress, educators, and nearly four hundred executives from timber, railroad, irrigation, and ranching interests. President Roosevelt gave the keynote address. The Forest Congress concluded by endorsing the transfer legislation.

Late that month, Congress approved the transfer legislation, and Roosevelt signed it into law on February 1, 1905. At that point the forest reserves encompassed more than 85 million acres of land. Nearly six hundred employees of the General Land Office were transferred to the Bureau of Forestry at the Agriculture Department, joining the eight hundred already there, and it was not long before the agency's name was changed to the U.S. Forest Service.[16]

The Transfer Act marked the high-water mark of Gifford Pinchot's political influence. One of its provisions gave the Agriculture Department control, for the next five years, of all money received from the sale or use of the reserves or any products from them, with the money to be used for the "protection, administration, improvement, and extension" of the reserves. This so-called revolving fund resembled ones that Congress had included in national park legislation dating back to Yosemite in 1864. Compared to the parks, the forest reserves were a much bigger platform for a revolving fund. Congress had taken a small step in this direction in 1899 when it authorized the Interior secretary to lease land around mineral springs within forest reserves to accommodate visitors seeking "health and pleasure," with the revenue to be held in a special fund in the Treasury for the "care of public forest reservations."[17] The revolving fund included in the Transfer Act meant that compared with the GLO, Pinchot's Forest Service would not be so dependent on the congressional appropriations process, nor so starved of funds.

CHAPTER TWENTY-SEVEN

The Forest Service Takes Control of the Forest Reserves

PINCHOT WASTED NO TIME IN taking command. The day that Roosevelt signed the transfer legislation, Agriculture secretary James Wilson signed a letter to Pinchot—drafted by Pinchot himself—setting forth the agency's guiding philosophy in nine artfully crafted sentences. Reassuringly positive, it was a masterly political stroke, calling for forest reserves to be "devoted" to their "most productive use for the permanent good of the whole people, and not for the temporary benefit of individuals or companies."[1]

Those resources were, it repeated, "for *use*," emphasizing with italics a word taken from Congressman McRae's description of his proposal that formed the core of the Organic Act of 1897. As McRae had done, the Wilson-Pinchot letter qualified "use" with the adjective "permanent," linking it with what is, in modern times, called sustainability. It also promised that "local questions will be decided upon local grounds," with the administration of each reserve "left very largely in the hands of the local officers, under the eye of thoroughly trained and competent inspectors." This echoed a provision that Congress had included in the Transfer Act calling for forest reserve administrators, where "practicable," to be "qualified citizens of the States or Territories" where the reserves were situated. In its most famous phrase, the letter promised that "where conflicting interests must be reconciled," it would be done "from the standpoint of the greatest good of the greatest number in the long run."

Congress soon took other steps to facilitate the Forest Service's new role. On February 6, Roosevelt signed a measure giving "all persons employed in the forest reserve and national park service of the United States" authority to make arrests for violations of laws and regulations relating to the forest reserves and national parks. On March 3, Roosevelt signed bills that repealed the Organic Act's notorious "in lieu" provision, and that authorized the Forest Service to aid in the enforcement of state and territorial laws concerning "the prevention and extinguishment of forest fires" as well as the protection of fish and game.[2]

THE PUBLIC LANDS AND CIVIL SERVICE REFORM

The Wilson-Pinchot letter celebrated a "thoroughly trained and competent" cadre of administrators.[3] This was not a casual reference. A movement to reform the federal civil service had grown up since the Civil War, with the objective of establishing a stable, professional class of governmental managers to temper the spoils system, which rewarded the party faithful with government jobs. Proponents of a reformed civil service saw it as a tool to fight the corruption of the Gilded Age, when alliances between politicians and large corporations and the wealthy threatened the interests of the poor and the growing middle class. Like many of the reform movements of this era, the campaign for civil service reform was helped by articles and editorials in national magazines such as the *Nation, Atlantic Monthly, Century,* and *Harper's Weekly,* which catered to the growing number of educated citizens and an expanding professional class of lawyers and scientists. Through such means, more and more politicians were coming to believe, in the words of Steven Skowronek, a leading chronicler of the movement, that "increasing demands for a national center of authority could not ultimately be met within the confines of American party government," but required a professional class of civil servants.[4]

Still, the movement's success came in fits and starts. Politicians were, after all, beholden to the political parties that worked to elect them, and the parties expected patronage rewards in return. By 1871, after the demobilization of the Union Army, the federal government had a little more than 50,000 civilian employees. That year, Congress gave President Grant sweeping authority to institute civil service reform, but his halfhearted attempts to implement it failed, and were abandoned in 1875.

Over the next quarter of a century, as the nation's population grew and its government assumed more responsibilities, the number of federal civilian employees increased fivefold. Carl Schurz, Interior secretary under President Hayes, emerged as a leading advocate for civil service reform. "As the functions of government grow in extent, importance and complexity," he wrote, "the necessity grows of their being administered not only with honesty, but also with trained ability and knowledge."[5] Other advanced nations had already seen the merit of the idea. Prussia, where Schurz had grown up, adopted a merit system for some public employees in 1873, three years after Great Britain and nine years before Canada.

A tragedy gave the movement an unexpected assist when Hayes's successor, James A. Garfield, was assassinated in 1881 by Charles Guiteau, a deranged lawyer, apparently in retaliation for his failure to secure a federal post after allegedly helping the president's campaign. Two years later, Garfield's successor, Chester A. Arthur, signed major civil service legislation into law. That same year, New York became the first state to adopt similar legislation, steered to passage by a twenty-five-year-old state assemblyman named Theodore Roosevelt.

The federal legislation created a three-person commission to establish and oversee a system of merit selection. Initially, it covered only about 10 percent of the 130,000 executive positions, mostly those in larger post offices and custom-houses. But the act gave the president the authority to extend the system, and successive presidents did, gradually. Theodore Roosevelt was a member of the U.S. Civil Service Commission from 1889 to 1895.

Although the public lands were never at the leading edge in the campaign for civil service reform, they were far from the margins. The shift in public land policy toward reserving more and more lands from divestment changed the question from *whether* the national government would develop an institutional capacity to manage these lands in the national interest to *how* it would do so. The army might be recruited to administer areas such as Yellowstone as a kind of stopgap measure, but few believed that was a permanent solution.

Handing over much of the ordinary business of administering the public lands to a nonpartisan, relatively permanent bureaucracy did not happen quickly. The GLO had long suffered under a patronage system of appointments and a decentralized structure that made it subject to constant pressure from local interests and their representatives in Congress. The political machines and other interests that had long wielded powerful influence did not easily relinquish it.

But the transition went hand in hand with the growing strength of the movement to retain substantial amounts of public land permanently in national ownership. As that happened, those private interests most directly affected—railroad, mining, timber, and livestock enterprises—gradually came to accept the value of a professional civil service. By 1900, nearly half of the more than 200,000 employees in the executive branch, including several thousand in the Interior Department, were covered by civil service laws. In that year Congress specifically provided that all personnel who would be administering the forest reserves should be selected "wholly with reference to their fitness and without regard for their political affiliations."[6]

BUILDING A PROFESSIONAL FOREST SERVICE

In late 1904, Roosevelt ordered that all employees involved in the "protection and administration of Forestry Reserves" be henceforth put under the requirements and protections of the civil service laws, and the Wilson-Pinchot letter confirmed that they would all remain in that status once transferred to the Agriculture Department. With that as a foundation, Roosevelt and Pinchot aimed to show Congress and the nation that an executive branch given broad responsibility for managing public lands could be entrusted to handle it professionally, in a fair and nonpartisan way.

Pinchot was a strong manager and an inspiring leader. According to William Greeley, who served under him and later became the agency's third chief, he was an "outstanding evangelist and a great leader of men," giving the organization a culture of pride and efficiency, with an esprit de corps rare in any bureaucratic organization, in or out of government. Among his many innovations, Pinchot set up a committee under the direction of Assistant Chief Frederick E. Olmsted, the nephew of the great landscape architect, to prepare a simply written manual of policy and procedure. Called *The Use of the National Forest Reserves,* and formatted small enough to fit into a forest ranger's shirt pocket, its first edition was distributed in June 1905. It quickly came to be known simply as the *Use Book.*[7]

An early adopter of now familiar techniques of public relations and communications, Pinchot worked tirelessly to direct the attention of journalists and the general public to the work of the Forest Service. He had the agency prepare educational materials on forestry concerns and encouraged his field officials to disseminate them to newspapers and opinion leaders. Annual reports carefully noted the progress made; for example, Forest Service officials in 1909 delivered 359 public addresses, and the agency distributed more than 1.2 million copies of sixty-three publications and maintained a mailing list of 750,000.[8]

Pinchot brought uniforms and military-like discipline to the Forest Service, giving it a bureaucratic structure on the European model. He sought to staff it with trained foresters, drawing upon his extensive contacts, including the forestry schools he and his family had privately helped establish and nurture; in 1910, there were seventeen such schools. Forestry was emerging as a genuine profession, with a technical literature, research, and applied findings. The Society of American Foresters was organized in 1900 in Pinchot's office at the Agriculture Department. It helped train foresters, but Pinchot also made sure that prominent public officials could become associate members, in order to heighten its visibility. In 1905 the society began publishing its annual proceedings.[9]

SHARING PUBLIC LAND REVENUES WITH STATE
AND LOCAL GOVERNMENTS

Not long after transferring the forest reserves to the Agriculture Department, Congress took a small but precedent-setting step to bolster public support for them. At the time, much state and local government revenue was derived from taxes on land. This tax base was threatened by U.S. retention of ownership of public lands, because of the long-accepted legal principle that made land owned by any government—local, state, or national—immune from property taxation by any other government. It was (and remains) difficult to calculate the serious-ness of this threat. For example, reserving public land in a national forest or park or military base could increase rather than decrease tax revenues to local governments, by enhancing the value of private land in the vicinity and by generating new economic activity taxable by local governments.

State and local governments have always wielded considerable influence in Congress, which guaranteed that it would pay close attention to their concerns that proliferating reservations of public land might adversely affect their governmental revenues. It was, then, no surprise that Congress responded to the growth in forest reserves by doing what it often does when a policy moves in a new direction—namely, by cushioning possible adverse effects that might result from the change. A common way to do that was, as here, through money.

The Agriculture Department appropriations bill that Roosevelt signed into law on June 30, 1906, accepted the idea that if the U.S. Treasury was going to derive revenue from the forest reserves, it should share some of it with state and local governments, as long as the money was directed to purposes that Congress deemed important. Specifically, it gave 10 percent of each forest reserve's annual receipts to the state or territory where the reserve was located, to be spent "for the benefit of the public schools and public roads of the county or counties in which the forest reserve was situated." The share that any county could receive was capped at 40 percent of its income from other sources.[10]

It was a toe in the door. Two years later, as the acreage in forest reserves continued to grow, Congress increased the counties' share to 25 percent of gross federal receipts and eliminated the 40 percent cap. In 1910, the Senate approved a proposal to raise the minimum share still further, but the idea went no further after non-westerners objected, reminding their western colleagues that taxpayers across the nation were paying for managing what were now called national forests. Western members then devised a different way to direct more federal receipts to local projects, persuading Congress in 1912 to mandate that at least 10 percent of a forest reserve's receipts be used to build roads and trails within the reserve.[11]

National forest revenue-sharing programs have endured, and they paved the way for similar programs to be adopted with respect to some—but not all—other public lands. Revenues that the federal government derives from national park lands, for example, have never been shared with local governments. This seems to be because parks do not produce much revenue for the U.S. Treasury, foster considerable economic activity that is taxable by state and local governments, and generally require more federal dollars to manage per acre than forests.

Revenue-sharing programs reduce, though they will never eliminate, complaints about the tax immunity of public lands. They also incentivize state and local governments to lobby for activities on public lands—such as selling timber or leasing minerals—that generate receipts to be shared with them. State and local governmental efforts to maintain and expand public-lands-based revenue sharing have become a permanent part of public land policy. Many studies have examined the impact that the presence of public lands has on the fiscal health of state and local governments. Whether the impact is seen as positive or negative often lies in the eye of the beholder.[12]

The same appropriations bill that inaugurated public land revenue sharing also dropped the five-year expiration date on the revolving fund that Congress had created for Pinchot's Forest Service in the 1905 transfer legislation. This was another significant, but in this case short-lived, win for Pinchot. He had envisioned—dreamed might be a better word—that his agency would support itself mostly through a revolving fund fed by resource-development revenues and gain substantial independence from Congress, which otherwise controlled its purse strings.

THE FOREST SERVICE'S LIVESTOCK-GRAZING POLICIES

Once in control, Pinchot moved carefully on the delicate subject of livestock grazing. The GLO's administration of grazing on the reserves had put in place a number of policies and practices on which Pinchot would build. He and his grazing chief, Albert Potter, moved quickly to reassure ranchers that the Forest Service was sympathetic to their interests. In the 1905 grazing season, the Forest Service issued almost 8,000 permits to graze more than 1.7 million sheep, 630,000 cattle, and nearly 60,000 horses on the forest reserves. It also issued permits for stock "driveways," or passageways to allow animals, mostly sheep, to move across forests to other public or private grazing land, and it worked with the Agriculture Department's Division of Biological Survey to exterminate animals, such as wolves and coyotes, that preyed on livestock.[13]

Most importantly, Pinchot continued the GLO's "preference" system, with some fine-tuning. The *Use Book* listed three classes of grazing permittees, in priority order: those who owned property within or adjacent to a forest reserve; those who owned ranch property elsewhere, but had traditionally grazed in the reserve; and transient herders with no claim of local property ownership, who were mainly itinerant sheepherders with less political power. Absentee owners fared somewhat better under the Forest Service policy, because the GLO policy that it replaced had looked more to residency than property ownership. Overall, the most important effect of the preference system was to disfavor nomadic herders. If excluded from the national forests, they often moved their herds to unreserved public lands, many of which were already overstocked.[14]

Late in 1905, Pinchot decided to establish a fee for grazing, something the GLO had not done. To him, it was both a matter of principle, because the forage was a public resource being converted to private advantage, and a pragmatic move, because the Transfer Act made fee receipts immediately available for Forest Service use, bypassing the congressional appropriations process. Set at a maximum of fifty cents per year for each cow and horse, and eight cents per summer for each sheep, the fee was estimated to be less than one-third of the amount that private landowners charged for comparable grazing.[15]

Unsurprisingly, ranchers resisted paying a fee for a privilege they had long been enjoying for free. Their chief advocate, a Colorado state legislator named Edward Taylor, attacked the very idea of the government putting what he called "a tax upon the people of the West" by charging for "government grass" that "did not cost Uncle Sam a dollar" to produce and "would otherwise go to waste." The ranchers also argued that the government lacked legal authority to charge a fee because neither the Organic Act of 1897 nor the Transfer Act expressly authorized it, although the latter did give the Forest Service control of "all money received" from the "use of any land or resources" in the reserves.[16]

Pinchot met with a number of ranchers in Denver in late 1905 and again in January 1906 and appeared to win them over; in early February, the National Livestock Association endorsed the grazing-fee proposal. Some of the opposition was tamped down by Pinchot's decision to establish forest advisory boards, which gave livestock interests a direct way to express their views on grazing regulations. This effort built on the GLO's earlier, short-lived, and largely unsuccessful experiment of relying heavily on local woolgrowers' associations to administer sheep grazing.

But some livestock interests would not yield on fees, or anything else, without a fight, and filed lawsuits in several courts around the West to challenge the government's authority not only to charge fees but even to require permits for grazing on the forest reserves. Lower courts rendered inconsistent decisions, and the Supreme Court did not settle the matter until well after Roosevelt and Pinchot had left office.[17]

Although some other conflicts, especially involving nomadic sheep-herding, continued to fester, many larger livestock operators gradually came to welcome the stability provided by Forest Service administration, and the protection it gave their operations from competition from homesteaders, irrigation advocates, and nomadic sheepherders. Smaller ranching enterprises were slower to accept the system, and before too long, Frank Mondell complained that the Forest Service was too cozy with rich and powerful ranchers at the expense of their smaller counterparts. The grazing program remained the Forest Service's primary land management concern for the next few decades.[18]

TIMBER HARVESTING ON THE FOREST RESERVES

Timber harvesting on the forest reserves increased almost tenfold, to a little more than 1 billion board feet annually, during Pinchot's years as chief. Still, even after the reserves had tripled in size to more than 150 million acres by the end of Roosevelt's presidency, they were producing only about 1 percent of the 40 billion board feet of timber harvested across the nation. In fact, the relatively low grazing fee produced more receipts than timber sales did every year Pinchot was in office.[19]

Although the Organic Act made furnishing a "continuous supply of timber" one of the major reasons to establish forest reserves, annual wood production from the national forests made up but a small percentage of national wood production for the next four decades. Several factors helped explain this. Large enterprises that supplied timber to national markets operated mostly on private land and did not welcome competition from publicly owned timber. The Organic Act limited timber harvests on the forest reserves to "dead, matured, or large growth" timber and required it to be sold for not less than appraised value. Some of the forests in the reserves had been logged before the reserves were established, and the Organic Act's notorious "in lieu" provision had allowed railroads and others to gain title to valuable timberlands outside the reserves in exchange for cutover lands inside the reserves. Many reserves, particularly in more arid regions, had relatively little commercial timber. Relatively isolated reserves furnished timber mostly for local use. A national economic downturn that began in 1907 reduced the national demand for wood. Longer term, per capita national wood consumption steadily declined as wood was displaced by substitute sources of energy and building materials.[20]

MINING ON THE FOREST RESERVES: USE AND ABUSE OF THE MINING LAW OF 1872

Although the Organic Act authorized the government to regulate mining activities on the forest reserves, Pinchot's Forest Service, like the General Land Office before it, was not eager to take on the mining industry. Its passivity was facilitated by ambiguity in the transfer legislation, which gave the Interior Department a role in administering "such laws as affect" activities like "prospecting" on such lands. The combination of agency inertia and the industry's political influence was so strong that almost three-quarters of a century elapsed before the Forest Service adopted comprehensive regulations governing mining on the reserves. Despite this friendly attitude, miners and their allies occasionally complained, with scant evidence, that the Forest Service was hostile to mining.[21]

Neither the Forest Service nor the Interior Department ever attempted to halt the practice of giving mining claimants in forest reserves "patents" conveying full ownership of their claimed land in the reserves for payment of no more than $5 per acre. Not giving miners fee title would have had no effect on mining, because the Supreme Court had long made clear that miners could extract minerals from public lands for free without bothering to obtain full ownership via a patent. But not giving them "patents" would have avoided creating new inholdings and reduced the opportunities for abuse.[22]

The Mining Law was very attractive to speculators. Anyone who staked a mining claim in a forest reserve gained a legal toehold for occupancy, even if it was for purposes such as harvesting timber; monopolizing water sources for grazing purposes; securing sites for hydroelectric projects, towns, or summerhouses; or gaining control of popular recreational sites in order to extract payment from visitors. Fee title turned the toehold into a permanent right to occupy, and the government often did not pay close attention to whether the claimant had made a "discovery" of a "valuable mineral deposit," which was the Mining Law's touchstone for obtaining title.

Reports by the GLO and the chief forester referred to such abuses of the Mining Law with depressing regularity. In 1908, a longtime Interior Department official named Edward C. Finney lamented how the Mining Law had been applied on such "exceedingly liberal" terms that it allowed large tracts of timber to be harvested on forest reserves. The chief forester's *Annual Report* of 1912 described how a "large livestock company" in an unnamed western state used mining claims to gain control of the only available local water sources, giving it a "complete monopoly" of some "500,000 acres of valuable range." The same report described how a hydroelectric power company used mining claims to gain control of a "valuable power site," and how another enterprise had located mining claims in a scenic mountainous area as part of a scheme to sell "building sites for summer homes."[23]

The government sometimes cranked up the cumbersome legal machinery to challenge some of the more notorious abuses. In 1909, after a protracted struggle, it thwarted efforts to use the Mining Law to gain title to many thousands of acres of land in forest reserves in Northern California that contained valuable timber and hydroelectric sites. In 1910, it secured an injunction against an enterprising person who operated a saloon on his mining claim in the Coeur d'Alene National Forest in Idaho, even though his lawyer had argued, with "much earnestness," according to the federal judge hearing the case, that it "has become customary to erect valuable buildings" on mining claims "for purposes having no necessary relation to mining operations." The court had none of it, explaining that, custom notwithstanding, the Mining Law was concerned with mining, not saloons.[24]

A court in 1914 went so far as to invalidate an already-issued patent in order to correct a particularly flagrant abuse, but that was only after the claimant boasted to its stockholders about its successful thievery. Much more often, courts put obstacles in the path of the government's attempts to rein in abuses. If an entity that gained fee title by abusing the Mining Law sold the land to someone else, the purchaser's title could not be drawn into question by the fact that the land had never seen any mining activity, because, as one court wrote, it was "common knowledge" that many mining claims were patented without ever seeing mining activity.[25]

BOUNDARY ADJUSTMENTS AND RELIEF VALVES FOR HOMESTEADING

Congress recognized that with many millions of acres involved, some adjustments in reserve boundaries might be advisable, so the Organic Act had given the president general authority to redraw reserve boundaries and to restore lands "to the public domain" that were found to be "better adapted for mining or for agricultural purposes than for forest usage." Over the first few decades, redrawing reserve boundaries was not uncommon. Theodore Roosevelt, for example, carved some 61,000 acres from the White River Reserve in Colorado in 1902, where he had been hunting the year before, and another 159,000 acres two years later.[26]

The Forest Homestead Act, enacted in June 1906, provided another relief valve, permitting the Agriculture Department to open lands inside reserves to homesteading if it found that they were "chiefly valuable for agriculture" and could be so used "without injury to the forest reserves." If a homesteader gained ownership under this statute, the land would remain inside the reserve boundaries as a private inholding. The Pinchot-led Public Land Commission of 1903 had recommended this legislation, but because inholdings could complicate management, the Forest Service usually preferred, where feasible, to redraw reserve boundaries to exclude potential agricultural land, and otherwise considered opening forest reserve lands to homesteading only on specific request. In 1912, Congress tweaked the 1906 act to prod the Forest Service to open more reserved lands to homesteading, and by 1915 the act had resulted in the creation of about 2 million acres of inholdings.[27]

RECREATION AND THE FOREST RESERVES

Forest reserves were used for recreation from the beginning, but Pinchot regarded recreational use as distinctly subordinate to other uses. The original *Use Book* had almost nothing to say on the subject, but the 1907 version advised that recreational values were "well worth considering" and that the reserves "quite incidentally" serve a "good purpose as great playgrounds" for a "very large part of the people of the West." In fact, recreation was already the primary human activity on some of the reserves. The most obvious example was the Grand Canyon, where tourism was already beginning to flourish when President Harrison established the forest reserve there in early 1893. It grew even more rapidly after the Santa Fe Railroad opened a spur from its main line to the canyon's south rim in 1901, and the grand El Tovar Hotel opened nearby four years later. It was not until 1915, however, that Congress explicitly acknowledged recreational use in the law governing forest reserves.[28]

Roosevelt and Congress Use Public Lands to Protect Wildlife Habitat

BEFORE ROOSEVELT TOOK OFFICE, the United States had taken only modest steps to protect wildlife on public lands. Congress made the Pribilof Islands in the Alaska Territory a special reservation to protect fur seals in 1869, and prohibited hunting in Yellowstone National Park in 1894. But wildlife had received little attention on forest reserves. President McKinley had established the Afognak Forest and Fish Culture Reserve in the Alaska Territory in 1892, but wildlife was hardly mentioned in the discussions leading to the Organic Act of 1897.[1]

In a decision in 1896 that did not involve the public lands, the U.S. Supreme Court suggested that states "owned" wildlife found within their borders. Three years later, Congress authorized federal employees to "aid in the enforcement of" state fish and game laws on forest reserves, suggesting that, for the most part, Congress was content to let states take the lead on the subject, even on public lands.[2]

That attitude soon began to change. In May 1900, after four years of effort by Congressman John Lacey, President McKinley signed what came to be known as the Lacey Act into law. Although it did not specifically address public lands, it "enlarged" the responsibilities of the Department of Agriculture to "include the preservation, distribution, introduction, and restoration of game birds and other wild birds," and required a federal permit to import "any foreign wild animal or bird." The reference to nongame birds—those not hunted for sport or food—was significant, because they made up four-fifths of all known bird species. The legislation also added a layer of federal law over state laws protecting wildlife by prohibiting the transport across state lines of birds or other animals that had been killed in violation of state law.[3]

In his first message to Congress, in 1901, Roosevelt recommended that certain forest reserves be made "preserves for the wild forest creatures." Lacey incorporated this idea in his 1902 bill to transfer the forest reserves to the Agriculture Department. The "immensity of man's power to slay," Lacey told his colleagues—citing the bison, the passenger pigeon, and declining salmon runs—"imposes great responsibilities." Although the U.S. attorney general had opined that Congress could protect wildlife "in the people's forests"—that is, the forest reserves—without the consent of the states where the reserves were found, Lacey's bill proposed, in a gesture of comity, to require the consent of the pertinent state's governor before the United States converted a forest reserve into a game preserve.[4]

After Lacey's bill was defeated on the House floor, Roosevelt renewed his appeal for legislation to protect wildlife in the forest reserves, calling the "senseless slaughter of game" offensive to "our national good sense." The Senate soon passed a bill authorizing the president to designate a limited number of areas in forest reserves "for the protection of game animals, birds, and fish," without requiring state approval. When it got to the House, Lacey's Public Lands Committee promptly reported it to the floor. Although he had not objected to Lacey's bill the previous year, Frank Mondell of Wyoming—apparently incensed that the new version dropped the requirement to obtain state consent—filed a blistering dissent. Turning public lands that had been "set apart for timber preservation and water conservation into jungles of wild beasts," he said, would allow predatory animals to "become a terror by night and a menace by day to the families, the flocks, and the herds of the people of all the surrounding region," and would be nothing short of "the fad of game preservation run stark raving mad." Mondell did concede there was a "lively and growing public sentiment throughout the entire West favorable to game preservation," but he maintained that state laws and policies were sufficient to satisfy it. His lurid portrayal of the threat posed by predatory animals became a common refrain of livestock operators.[5]

Lacey's bill was never considered by the full House. For his part, Gifford Pinchot never supported making wildlife protection a goal of forest management, preferring to focus on controlling predators in order to gain favor with livestock-grazing advocates like Mondell. The 1908 version of the *Use Book,* for example, instructed forest rangers to report predation by "wolves, cougars, coyotes, bobcats," and other such animals, and to recommend "such action as is necessary to get rid of them."[6]

PELICAN ISLAND PRESERVE

As Congress was deliberating over his idea to dedicate some parts of forest reserves to wildlife, Roosevelt saw an opportunity to protect wildlife on public lands outside forest reserves. For several decades, naturalists had been working to protect Florida's amazing variety of bird species, which were being destroyed in large numbers by market hunters while their habitats were being steadily shrunk by agricultural and urban development. A prized surviving bit of habitat was Pelican Island, little more than five acres in size, located in the Indian River Lagoon about halfway down Florida's eastern coast. It was, remarkably, still public land, having remained free from claims under divestment laws since 1819, when the United States acquired Florida from Spain.

A key player in the campaign to protect Pelican Island was Frank Chapman, an amateur ornithologist who in the 1880s had made a name for himself with his strident criticism in *Forest and Stream* of the "vulgar" and "unconscionable" destruction of birds for fashion. (In 1886, he reported identifying feathers from forty different species in a single hour of observation in Manhattan's fashion district.)[7] Birds killed for fashion were mostly nongame species of no interest to sport hunters, and their harvesting was particularly damaging because it usually occurred during the birds' breeding season, when their plumes were on peak display. *Forest and Stream*'s editor, George Bird Grinnell, encouraged women to lead the struggle for reform of the millinery trade in order to protect birds. Many women's groups eventually engaged more broadly on issues of wildlife and habitat protection.[8]

In 1888, Chapman left his career in banking to work for the American Museum of Natural History in New York, where he met Theodore Roosevelt, whose father had helped found the museum. Chapman visited Pelican Island on his honeymoon in 1898, and in 1901 he published a book called *Bird Studies with a Camera*, which argued that photography rather than slaughter was the best way to appreciate bird life. He also established the Christmas bird count, which, by enlisting thousands of volunteers to report annually on bird populations, remains to this day an important tool for bird conservation efforts.[9]

Chapman soon found sympathizers in the U.S. government, including Theodore Palmer of the Agriculture Department's Division of Economic Ornithology and Mammalogy, who was an expert on and advocate for legislation protecting wildlife, especially birds. The division's longtime chief was C. Hart Merriam, an outstanding naturalist and friend of Theodore Roosevelt's who had been a member of the Hayden survey of Yellowstone in 1872 and one of the founders of the American Ornithological Union (AOU) in 1883.[10]

The AOU formed a Bird Protection Committee, which was headed first by Chapman and then by William Dutcher, an activist whose day job was in insurance, and decided to try to raise money to buy Pelican Island from the United States. To that end, Dutcher arranged to have the land surveyed, the first step toward putting the land up for sale. Putting the land up for sale carried some risk, because bird lovers could be outbid by suppliers to the lucrative fashion trade.

On February 21, 1903, Palmer met with the new commissioner of the General Land Office, William Richards, and other GLO officials, one of whom suggested that the best approach was simply to reserve the island from divestment. Things moved quickly after that. Dutcher wrote Agriculture secretary Wilson, urging quick action, and in early March, Chapman and Dutcher obtained a meeting with Roosevelt. On March 14, the president issued a terse order that Pelican Island be "reserved and set apart" as a "preserve and breeding ground for native birds." It cited no legal authority.[11]

While Roosevelt's boldness was characteristic, he had ample legal grounds to act. Pelican Island easily fit within the terms of section 24 of the 1891 act because it was "wholly or in part covered with timber or undergrowth, whether of commercial value or not," and Harrison's wildlife-oriented Afognak Island reserve was precedent for such a use of section 24. Roosevelt could have also relied on the Lacey Act of 1900, which provided general authority to the Agriculture Department "to adopt such measures as may be necessary for the preservation of game and other wild birds." Indeed, Dutcher had referred to the Lacey Act in his earlier letter to Secretary Wilson, and Roosevelt's order explicitly gave the Agriculture Department "use" of the island as a bird preserve.[12]

RESERVATIONS OF PUBLIC LAND FOR WILDLIFE HABITAT PROLIFERATE

As was often the case, Roosevelt's timing was excellent. There was general public support, other than in parts of the livestock-grazing industry, for the idea that the United States should protect wildlife habitat on lands it already owned. And so, over the next few years, the national government adopted numerous measures to that end, sometimes through executive acts like Roosevelt's at Pelican Island, and sometimes through congressional action.

In November 1904, using language identical to that in his Pelican Island order, Roosevelt reserved Breton Island on Louisiana's Gulf Coast, southeast of New Orleans. In March 1905, he did the same with islands in Stump Lake in North Dakota; and in October with Passage Key, an island in Florida's Tampa Bay, and two groups of islands in Lake Superior along Michigan's Upper Peninsula. He added more islands in Louisiana and Florida in November 1905 and February 1906. Sport hunting was generally prohibited on these reservations, making Roosevelt's leadership even more meaningful, because he was an avid hunter. A new National Association of Audubon Societies established under William Dutcher raised funds to pay wardens to police the reservations during breeding season.[13]

His protective actions were not solely focused on birds. In his December 1904 message to Congress, Roosevelt renewed and broadened his earlier request for clear authority to reserve public lands as game refuges for the preservation of "bison, wapiti, and other large beasts" that were "once so abundant" and now were "tending toward extinction." "We owe it to future generations to keep alive the noble and beautiful creatures which by their presence add such distinctive character to the American wilderness," he wrote, noting that public lands "wholly unsuited to agricultural settlement" can be used for such purposes "at very little expense."[14]

Congress wasted no time in jumping on the bandwagon. In January 1905, it authorized Roosevelt to safeguard "such areas of" the 59,000-acre Wichita Forest Reserve in the Oklahoma Territory, which McKinley had established in 1901, as "should, in his opinion, be set aside for the protection of game animals and birds and be recognized as a breeding place therefor." The legislation also prohibited the "hunting, trapping, killing or capturing" of protected species unless allowed by regulations adopted by the secretary of Agriculture. Later that spring, Roosevelt designated the entire forest reserve the Wichita Mountains Forest and Game Preserve.[15]

While neither the legislation nor Roosevelt's proclamation mentioned bison, the Oklahoma City Commercial Club, soon joined by the Boone and Crockett Club and the New York Zoological Society, mounted a campaign to use the reserve to protect that symbol of the plains, whose numbers were still hovering near extinction. In 1907, a predecessor of the Bronx Zoo in New York City and the American Bison Society (founded in 1905 by Roosevelt, among others) donated fifteen bison to start a herd in the reserves. A contingent of Native Americans headed by the legendary Comanche chief Quanah Parker welcomed the bison to the reserve.[16]

In June 1906, Congress enacted nearly identical legislation authorizing the president to "set aside" areas he deemed suitable "for the protection of game animals" in the Grand Canyon Forest Reserve, which Harrison had established in 1892. Five months later, President Roosevelt issued a proclamation designating the Grand Canyon Game Preserve to include all the lands within the forest reserve that lay west and north of the Colorado River.[17]

Like Congress's designation of Mount Rainier National Park in 1899 on public lands that were already part of the Pacific Forest Reserve, the Oklahoma and Grand Canyon statutes and proclamations layered a new public land designation on top of an earlier one, and with it came some additional protection. Designation of the Grand Canyon Game Preserve, for example, effectively prohibited new mining claims from being located there because, a federal court of appeals ruled decades later, such claims "would interfere with the protection and propagation of game animals."[18]

Also in 1906, Congress enacted the Game and Bird Preserves Protection Act. It made it a violation of federal law, punishable by fine and/or imprisonment for up to six months, for anyone to "hunt, trap, capture, willfully disturb, or kill any bird of any kind whatever or take the eggs of such birds" on any public land "set apart or reserved as breeding grounds for birds by law, proclamation, or Executive Order," except in accordance with regulations adopted by the Agriculture secretary. The act's reference to lands set apart by "proclamation" or "Executive Order" bestowed Congress's blessing on President Roosevelt's Pelican Island order and subsequent similar actions, putting to rest any doubts about their legality.[19]

In May 1908, Congress broke new ground by authorizing the purchase of 12,800 acres—enlarged to 20,000 acres the following year—to establish a "permanent national bison range" in northern Montana. It was the first time Congress authorized the purchase of land specifically for wildlife preservation. The United States had recognized the land as belonging to the Confederated Salish and Kootenai Tribes (CSKT) in a treaty from 1855, but Congress declared the land surplus and available for purchase in 1904 after individual CSKT members were allotted parcels of land. Decades later the CSKT sued and won compensation for the loss of their lands, and in modern times made a determined and ultimately successful effort to recover ownership of the land in the bison range.[20]

While these measures showed how much Congress was in sync with the president on such matters, the irrepressible Roosevelt would not relinquish his lead. In August 1908, he established the Klamath Lake Reservation, encompassing more than 80,000 acres of lakes and marshes in southern Oregon and Northern California, as a "preserve and breeding-ground for native birds" to be administered by the Department of Agriculture. The Reclamation Service had established an irrigation project nearby, and Roosevelt's order specified that the bird reservation was "not intended to interfere" with the use of the reserved area for the Reclamation Act project. A naturalist like Roosevelt could keenly appreciate how important water bodies were for birds, especially migratory waterfowl, and he established many other bird reservations around Reclamation Act projects in his remaining months in office. Indeed, on a single day a week before he left office in 1909, he established seventeen bird reserves in seven states and the territories of Arizona and New Mexico. Roosevelt's actions set the stage for a number of future conflicts between wildlife advocates and farmers who irrigated with Reclamation Act project water.[21]

By the time he left office, Roosevelt had established more than fifty bird reserves and four game reserves on public land. A number of these were outside the West, in places such as Florida, Michigan, and Louisiana, and in territories such as Alaska, Hawaii, and on the Culebra Archipelago in Puerto Rico.[22]

After a century of little action in this area, public lands came to be used to protect wildlife and habitat in the Roosevelt era at an astounding rate. That the executive and Congress moved in tandem and protected many areas outside the West showed how popular these measures were across the nation. Appealing as much to the heart as to the mind, the movement to establish refuges for wildlife reached Americans in ways that more abstract concerns, like the need to protect watersheds, could not.

Hostility to such measures was largely confined to a handful of western politicians aligned with the livestock industry. Senator Weldon Heyburn (R-Idaho) scorned the efforts of the U.S. government to establish "great game preserves" to protect "the beautiful deer." He would, he said, rather have one "cow than all the herds of deer" such preserves could support. Senator William Borah (R-Idaho) complained to his colleagues how the Forest Service was displacing sheep from the forest reserves in favor of elk.[23]

These early wildlife refuges contained many fewer acres of public land than the forest reserves, and it would be another couple of decades before the United States began to acquire significant amounts of private land for national wildlife refuges. The government also moved rather slowly to develop the institutional capacity to handle the increasing federal responsibility for wildlife. In 1905, the newly named Bureau of the Biological Survey took the lead in managing wildlife reservations on public land outside the forest reserves. Though housed in the Agriculture Department, it was completely distinct from Gifford Pinchot's Forest Service; indeed, in his autobiography, Pinchot paid scant attention to reservations of public land for wildlife or to wildlife in general. Eventually, in counterpoint to the shift of the forest reserves from the Interior Department to the Department of Agriculture, management of wildlife reserves on public land would be transferred from Agriculture to Interior.[24]

CHAPTER TWENTY-NINE

Public Lands, Science, and History

THE ANTIQUITIES ACT

THE FIRST DECADE OF THE twentieth century saw public land set aside for cultural and historic preservation at a rapid rate. Interest in such matters had steadily grown since the mid-1870s. William Henry Jackson's pioneering photographs of ancient stone cliff dwellings in southwestern Colorado gained national attention when they were made available in the report of 1876 on the Hayden survey. Congress authorized the establishment of the Bureau of Ethnology in the Smithsonian Institution in 1879, thirty years after the Smithsonian had published its landmark report *Ancient Monuments of the Mississippi Valley*. That same year, Frederick Ward Putnam of Harvard, generally considered the father of American archaeology, edited the Wheeler survey's detailed reports, with illustrations, on archaeological sites in the New Mexico and Arizona Territories. Also that year, the Archaeological Institute of America was founded. (It was given a congressional charter in 1906.)[1]

The institute's first grant went to Adolph Bandelier to study archeological sites in the Southwest and Mexico. Bandelier's report in 1881 lamented that the remnants of ancient pueblo structures on public lands had been "thoroughly ransacked" and "recklessly and ruthlessly" destroyed by relic hunters. Senator Preston B. Plumb (R-Kans.), chair of the Senate Committee on Public Lands, who had visited some of the sites, lamented in 1882 that enacting laws to protect sites from plundering would be useless, and that the only thing advocates of protection could do was to "avail themselves of the license which now exists of going to the different localities and gathering up the relics"—in other words, to beat the vandals to the punch.[2]

Congress failed to act on a bill that Congressman William Holman introduced in 1888 to direct that steps be taken to protect sites "from injury and spoliation," but it did approve a measure the next year to protect Casa Grande, a prominent ruin on public land in the Arizona Territory. Around the same time, the Interior Department began to approve supervised excavations of archeological sites on public lands in the Southwest in an attempt to discourage vandalism, and its General Land Office started withdrawing specific sites from divestment laws even though Congress had not given it specific authority to do so.[3]

The best-known artifact hunters of the era were members of the Wetherill family. They operated a ranch near Mancos, Colorado, and ran cattle through southwestern canyons where archeological sites were abundant. In late 1888, Richard Wetherill and some associates visited some of the largest cliff dwellings, at Mesa Verde in southwestern Colorado, most of which was within the Southern Ute Indian Reservation, established in 1873. The richness of the sites that Wetherill described, to which he gave names like "Cliff Palace," so captured public attention that the Colorado legislature petitioned Congress in 1892 to establish a national park at Mesa Verde.

In the mid-1890s, the Wetherills filed homestead claims on public land containing some of the biggest ruins yet found, in Chaco Canyon in the New Mexico Territory, halfway between their ranch and Albuquerque. With funding from private philanthropists and working with the American Museum of Natural History in New York, they made extensive excavations and shipped wagonloads of artifacts to the museum. Eventually, the GLO began investigating the Wetherills' activities and the validity of their homestead entries and ordered them to cease their excavations.

Overall, the Wetherills' motives were mixed, as was their impact. They helped bring public attention to archaeological sites, sometimes advocated governmental protection of them, and, as they gained better understanding of the science, often cooperated with and donated some of their finds to museums. But they also engaged in extensive unsupervised gathering and sale of large numbers of artifacts.

In 1900, a New York journalist, Virginia McClurg, who had been reporting on the subject for more than a decade, cofounded the Colorado Cliff Dwellings Association with Lucy Davison Peabody, who had worked for years in the Bureau of Ethnology in Washington, D.C., before moving to Colorado. They gained the support of Colorado congressman (and future governor and senator)

John Shafroth, who helped obtain a provision in a sundry appropriations act in March 1901 authorizing the association to lease the Mesa Verde site from the Ute Indians, with the approval of the Interior secretary, in order to protect it from "depredations."[4] Shafroth also introduced bills in 1901, 1902, and 1903 to establish the "Colorado Cliff Dwellings National Park" at the Mesa Verde site, but none made it out of the House Public Lands Committee.

JOHN LACEY AND EDGAR LEE HEWETT TAKE CHARGE

Shortly before the turn of the twentieth century, an educator, anthropologist, and avid archaeologist named Edgar Lee Hewett joined the effort to have the U.S. government act more forcefully to protect archeological sites on public lands. Hewett, who as a farm boy in Illinois had been captivated by books about vanished civilizations, had just become president of New Mexico Normal University (now New Mexico Highlands) in Las Vegas, New Mexico. He helped persuade House Public Lands Committee chair John Lacey to take up the cause.

In 1900, Lacey's committee began to consider a range of proposals. One would have established a national park to protect the ruins and other features of the Pajarito Plateau near Santa Fe. Another would have provided penalties for destroying, injuring, or carrying away any ruin or antiquity found on any public land. Others would have given the president the authority to reserve public lands containing particular features of interest. In April, the committee reported out a modest bill that gave the Interior secretary the authority to reserve tracts of public land up to 320 acres that contained "cliff dwellings and other prehistoric remains." It did not advance. In the fall of 1902, Lacey traveled to New Mexico and visited various sites with Hewett; he returned to Washington, D.C., more determined than ever to pass protective legislation.

Meanwhile, the GLO did not wait for Congress to act. It continued to withdraw tracts of public land containing features of scientific and cultural interest. In 1900, GLO commissioner Binger Hermann reserved public lands containing El Morro, a rock abutment bearing petroglyphs and inscriptions of travelers going back centuries, and 153,000 acres on the Pajarito Plateau, both in New Mexico. His successor, W. A. Richards, a former governor of Wyoming, continued along the same path. He directed the GLO to take steps to preserve ruins at Walnut Canyon and Montezuma's Well, both of which were in forest reserves in the Arizona Territory. He also withdrew public lands containing a prehistoric cliff dwelling, the so-called Montezuma Castle, in the Verde River Valley, and enlarged withdrawals of public lands made earlier to safeguard the fossilized remains of trees, also in the Arizona Territory.[5]

John Lacey, 1841–1913 (Courtesy of the
Library of Congress, LC-B2-5813-3)

To bolster the case for congressional action, Richards asked Edgar Lee
Hewett to prepare a report on the vandalism that threatened sites in the
Southwest. Hewett's report, issued in September 1904, used blunt language,
calling the "extensive traffic" in the "priceless" relics taken from the ruins
"outrageous," and underscoring the loss to science when objects were taken
from public lands by destructive means and scattered about in private collections and museums. It would, he concluded, "be a lasting reproach upon our
government if it does not use its power to restrain" the plunder. His report,
which included a remarkably prescient list of major archaeological sites in the
region that deserved protection, was widely distributed by the GLO, and
Richards included it in its entirety in his *Annual Report* for 1905.[6]

Congressman Lacey then asked Hewett to consult with interested parties
and draft a new bill. Hewett made the shrewd judgment that each agency with
responsibility for lands that could contain archaeological resources—the
General Land Office, the U.S. Forest Service (which in early 1905 had gained
control of the forest reserves), the War Department, and the Bureau of Indian
Affairs (which oversaw Indian reservations)—should be made responsible for
protecting sites within their jurisdictions. Using that approach, Hewett
unveiled his draft in late 1905.

Lacey introduced it in the House, and Senator Thomas Patterson (D-Colo.) introduced it in the Senate. Hewett had consulted carefully and drafted skillfully, because neither the House nor the Senate made any significant textual changes to his draft before approving it on voice vote. Roosevelt signed it into law on June 8, 1906. It was Lacey's last major contribution to public land policy as a member of Congress. In November, he was defeated in his bid for a ninth term.

THE ANTIQUITIES ACT OF 1906

The Antiquities Act was a landmark in public land policy comparable to section 24 of the General Revision Act of 1891. Although it followed the well-worn path of giving the executive the authority to reserve public lands from divestment in order to serve national objectives, its four hundred words contained several important new features. Its first section required any person seeking to "appropriate, excavate, injure, or destroy" any "historic or prehistoric ruin or monument, or any object of antiquity" found on public lands to obtain permission from the head of the governmental agency with jurisdiction over those lands or face fine and imprisonment. This was one of the earliest examples of Congress legislating a uniform approach to public lands regardless of which governmental agency was responsible for managing them, an approach that would become much more common, beginning in the latter half of the twentieth century.[7]

Its second section authorized the president, "in his discretion, to declare by public proclamation historic landmarks, historic and prehistoric structures, and other objects of historic or scientific interest" on public lands to be "national monuments," which would safeguard them from transfer out of U.S. ownership. Hewett's use of the term "monument" was an implicit recognition that only Congress could label an area of public land a "national park."

The act applied to all land "owned or controlled by" the United States. But its second section also established a pathway for protecting worthy sites located on private or state lands—by authorizing the national government to accept donations of land for that purpose. This broke new ground, opening the door for state and local governments and public-spirited private individuals to help the United States protect areas of historic or scientific interest by making them public lands.

The legislation cautioned that national monuments "in all cases shall be confined to the smallest area compatible with the proper care and management of the objects to be protected." Hewett's language here was particularly adroit.

It suggested restraint without imposing a meaningful limit on executive discretion, because it left it up to the president to determine how small an area was compatible with the "proper care and management" of the "objects" to be protected. The answer would depend not only on what kind of "care and management" the executive determined was "proper," but also on how the executive chose to characterize the "objects" to be protected. The act made clear that such "objects" were not confined to specific items of antiquity like artifacts or structures, because Hewett shrewdly borrowed language from one of the broader bills that had been introduced in 1900 to allow the president to reserve public land to protect not only "historic landmarks" and "historic and prehistoric structures," but also "other objects of historic or scientific interest."

By this time, Congress had several times endorsed the holding of historic sites in public ownership for contemplation and study. Some of these were of considerable size—each of the Civil War battlefield parks that Congress established in the 1890s covered several thousand acres. Scientific concerns had also played an important role in some decisions to hold land in public ownership, whether made by the executive, as at Crater Lake in Oregon, Mount Whitney in California, or the Petrified Forest in Arizona, or by Congress, as at Mount Rainier. Some of these reservations included many tens of thousands of acres.

But the Antiquities Act was the first time that Congress unequivocally declared, in legislation of general application, that scientific inquiry was a sufficient reason by itself to hold lands in public ownership. From that point forward, science played an increasing role in public land policy, and eventually, Congress made heeding the teachings of science part of the mandate of all agencies managing public lands.

INITIAL IMPLEMENTATION OF THE ANTIQUITIES ACT

Theodore Roosevelt wasted no time in using this new authority, taking advantage of the spadework that the General Land Office had done by withdrawing public lands from divestment laws. Devil's Tower, an igneous monolith rising 1,300 feet above the surrounding terrain in northeastern Wyoming, was the first, in September 1906. This "lofty and isolated rock," Roosevelt's proclamation noted, was an object of "great scientific interest." Congressman Frank Mondell had expressed support for using the Antiquities Act here, and the GLO had reserved the land from divestment in the early 1890s at the request of Senator Francis Warren (R-Wyo.). Before the year was out, Roosevelt used the same rationale to establish the 7,000-acre Petrified Forest National Monument in the Arizona Territory.[8]

It also did not take long for Roosevelt to use the act's authority to accept donations of land for preservation. A wealthy businessman named William Kent had purchased a parcel of land containing a grove of magnificent coastal redwood trees in Marin County a few miles north of San Francisco in order to preserve it from development. When the North Coast Water Company sought to condemn part of his land as a reservoir site, Kent mailed the deed to the land to Interior secretary James R. Garfield in late December 1907 and requested that a national monument be established and named after John Muir, whom he admired but had never met. Never one to dawdle, President Roosevelt established the Muir Woods National Monument on January 9, 1908. The gift brought Kent national attention and helped him gain a seat in the U.S. House of Representatives in 1910, where, in his three terms, he played an important role in public lands matters.[9]

Muir Woods was not only the first national monument to be established on donated land, but also the first established primarily to protect features other than geologic and archeological ones, and the first near a major urban area. Each of these precedents was followed many times in the future.

A number of Roosevelt's national monuments—Montezuma Castle (1906) and Tonto (1907) in the Arizona Territory; El Morro and Chaco Canyon (1906) and Gila Cliff Dwellings (1907) in the New Mexico Territory—protected remnants of earlier Native American civilizations. Chaco Canyon was the largest of these, at more than 20,000 acres. In using the act to protect Native Americans' imprints on the land, Roosevelt was fulfilling a commitment, suggested by the act, to make modest and indirect gestures to atone for the Euro-American dispossession of Indians from much of their lands.

These early monuments, none exceeding 20,000 acres and most in places with little value for agriculture or mining, were not controversial. But not all the eighteen national monuments that Roosevelt established before he left office were small. His two largest were large indeed—the 808,000-acre Grand Canyon National Monument (1908) and the 639,000-acre Mount Olympus National Monument in Washington (1909).

GRAND CANYON NATIONAL MONUMENT

Roosevelt's Grand Canyon monument proclamation described it as "the greatest eroded canyon within the United States" and thus an object—a very large one—of "unusual scientific interest." The Antiquities Act enabled Roosevelt to act on his own famous admonition, delivered on his visit to the canyon five years earlier, to "keep this great wonder of nature as it now is," for "your children, your children's children, and all who come after you, as the one great sight which every American should see." John Muir had spent time at the Grand Canyon, and his description of it in the *Century* magazine in 1902 noted that it was "once said that the Grand Canyon could put a dozen Yosemites in its vest pocket."[10]

Grand Canyon was by far the largest national monument proclaimed up to that time. Its lands had been included in the nearly 2-million-acre forest reserve that President Harrison had established in 1893, and it remained under the management of the U.S. Forest Service. Land in forest reserves remained open to divestment under the Mining Law and the Forest Homestead Act, but Roosevelt's Grand Canyon proclamation rendered these laws inoperative in the new monument by providing that it "shall be the dominant reservation." Subsequent Antiquities Act proclamations have incorporated this language.

Before Roosevelt proclaimed the Grand Canyon monument, a local entrepreneur, promoter, and politician named Ralph Cameron had staked bogus mining claims at key sites on the canyon's south rim, where most visitors congregated, as well as along the Bright Angel Trail, the most popular route into the canyon's depths. He operated a hotel and livery business and charged tolls for use of the trail, preferring to mine visitors' pockets rather than pretend to prospect for minerals. When Roosevelt proclaimed the monument, the validity of Cameron's mining claims was being contested in legal proceedings that had dragged on for years, and Cameron countered by contesting Roosevelt's use of the Antiquities Act. Eventually, in 1920, the Supreme Court rejected his challenge in a unanimous decision written by Justice Willis Van Devanter, who stated the obvious: the canyon was indeed an "object" of "scientific interest" because it has "attracted wide attention among explorers and scientists, affords an unexampled field for geologic study, is regarded as one of the great natural wonders, and annually draws to its borders thousands of visitors."[11]

Later that same year, Arizona voters elected Cameron to the U.S. Senate, where he spent most of his single term denouncing the U.S. government's interference with his business ventures at the canyon. Finally tiring of such antics, Arizona voters called him home in the 1926 election.[12]

MOUNT OLYMPUS NATIONAL MONUMENT

Efforts to protect public lands on Washington's Olympic Peninsula had a tangled history. As far back as 1890, a national park had been proposed to protect the area's wildlife, especially elk. In 1897, President Cleveland established a 2-million-plus-acre forest reserve. After President McKinley reduced the reserve by a third in 1900–1901, much of the excised land ended up in the hands of large timber companies. In 1904, Congressman Francis Cushman (R-Wash.) introduced a bill to establish a national park of nearly 400,000 acres in the center of the forest reserve that remained. Although that bill made no progress, Congressman William E. Humphrey (R-Wash.) eventually took up the cause and sponsored a bill authorizing the president to establish a "game preserve" on up to 750,000 acres of land within the existing forest reserve. In March 1907, Roosevelt added back nearly 128,000 acres to the forest reserve. Humphrey's "game preserve" proposal passed the House in 1908, but the Seattle Chamber of Commerce persuaded Senator Samuel Piles (R-Wash.) to stop its advance.

Humphrey then turned to Roosevelt, who, on his next-to-last day in office, in March 1909, established the Mount Olympus National Monument on more than 600,000 acres of the forest reserve. His proclamation noted that the area embraced "objects of unusual scientific interest, including numerous glaciers," and that from time immemorial it had "formed the summer range and breeding grounds of the Olympic Elk (Cervus roosevelti), a species peculiar to these mountains and rapidly decreasing in numbers." The species (now considered a subspecies) had been named in honor of Roosevelt in 1898 by his friend C. Hart Merriam, the chief of the Division of Economic Ornithology and Mammalogy in the Agriculture Department.

Mount Olympus was the first but hardly the last national monument to identify wildlife and habitat as core objects of protection. While the Mount Olympus proclamation left the lands under the jurisdiction of the Forest Service, and did not explicitly prohibit timber harvesting, its emphasis on the need to protect the declining elk population, and its warning that the monument reservation was dominant, pointed unmistakably in that direction.[13]

Mount Olympus was Theodore Roosevelt's last use of the Antiquities Act. Here, as elsewhere, his legacy was large. GLO commissioner Fred Dennett noted in his *Annual Report* for 1908 that the act's operative words "fix practically no limits as to the character of the object to be reserved, and therefore the monuments vary greatly in their physical characteristics." Roosevelt demonstrated the act's protean character by using it to protect large landscapes, deeming such action necessary for the "proper care and management" of geological and biological features of interest, as well as to protect objects of cultural and archaeological interest.[14]

Building on that foundation, nearly every subsequent president, Republican and Democrat, has used the Antiquities Act to proclaim national monuments on well over 100 million acres of public land onshore, and hundreds of millions of acres in the oceans over which the United States has jurisdiction. National-monument status ensures that the lands are safeguarded in public ownership and managed to protect the objects of "historic or scientific interest" identified in the proclamations.

CHAPTER THIRTY

Roosevelt and National Parks

ALTHOUGH THEODORE ROOSEVELT was enormously effective in expanding protections for America's public lands, his administration's record on national parks is thin, even though he strongly supported the concept. In dedicating the gateway arch at the northern entrance to Yellowstone in April 1903, he told the crowd that preservation of the park reflected "wise foresight," and he warned that the "only way" people can secure such resources "in perpetuity" is through "ownership in the name of the nation," and by "jealously safeguarding and preserving the scenery, the forests, and the wild creatures."[1]

An obvious explanation for the Roosevelt administration's relative inaction on national parks is that they were managed by the Interior Department (though in some cases, as at Yellowstone, with the help of the army), and Gifford Pinchot was not eager to see its domain expanded. Interior had already made a play for more parks. Not long before Roosevelt became president, GLO commissioner Hermann, responding to a request from John Lacey, had drafted legislation that would authorize the president to protect, as "national parks," areas of public land containing "scenic beauty" or "natural wonders or curiosities, ancient ruins or relics, or other objects of scientific or historic interest, or springs of medicinal or other properties." Hermann's successor, William Richards, appointed by Roosevelt in 1903, supported the proposal, arguing that the government had the duty to protect such places "from spoliation and injury of all kinds," and that the executive was in a better position than Congress to take prompt action.[2]

The Public Land Commission, which Gifford Pinchot had chaired in 1903–4, made no recommendations about national parks. Sensitive to the turf battle being waged, Roosevelt sent mixed messages. In his December 1904 annual message to Congress, he called for expanding the boundaries of Yellowstone National Park and making the "Canyon of the Colorado" River a national park, along with "the Yosemite and as many as possible of the groves of giant trees in California." After Congress transferred the forest reserves to the Agriculture Department in 1905, Roosevelt included in his next annual message a sentence advocating putting the Forest Service in charge of national parks that were "adjacent to forest reserves." The sentence was probably a defensive move engineered by Pinchot, who knew that some forest reserve lands were prime candidates for national-park status, which threatened to shrink Pinchot's domain and enlarge the Interior Department's.[3]

Roosevelt's impact on the national parks cannot be measured solely by the number of parks established during his time in office, because a goodly number of the many forest reserves, game ranges, and national monuments he established eventually became national parks. For example, Roosevelt established the nearly 900,000-acre Lassen Peak Forest Reserve in northern California in 1905. Two years later, he proclaimed two national monuments that included Lassen Peak and a nearby cinder cone, both in the forest reserve. In 1916, Congress established the 100,000-acre Lassen Volcanic National Park, which incorporated both monuments and other parts of the forest reserve. This was the first but far from the last national park to include national-monument lands.[4]

NEW NATIONAL PARKS: CRATER LAKE (1902) AND MESA VERDE (1906)

A few national parks were established during Roosevelt's presidency, some notable and some less so. In 1902, he signed into law a measure establishing Crater Lake National Park in Oregon. As was usually the case in public land protection, many deserved some credit, including local activists and Grover Cleveland, who withdrew the lake and thousands of acres around it from divestment laws in 1886 and seven years later included it in the Cascade Range Forest Reserve. The 1902 legislation made the park available "to all scientists" as well as "pleasure seekers," showing that scientific inquiry was now regarded as an important objective of park management.[5]

In June 1906, Roosevelt approved a bill establishing Mesa Verde National Park in Colorado. Like the Antiquities Act, which he had signed into law just three weeks earlier, it had had a years-long trek through Congress, but its final passage provoked little discussion. Along that journey, proposals had been made to allow coal mining and livestock grazing within its borders, and to follow the Yosemite model of giving the park to the state to be administered under federal law. Congress's rejection of these proposals showed how the national-park idea was maturing.[6]

Mesa Verde was initially an awkward arrangement. The new park embraced about 42,000 acres of public land, but the most notable ruins were on lands in the nearby Southern Ute Indian Reservation. The legislation provided some vague protection for them by putting "all prehistoric ruins" on Indian lands located within five miles of the park boundary (an area of 175,000 acres) "under the custodianship of the Secretary of the Interior." Only in 1913, after several years of Interior-tribal negotiations, did Congress approve an agreement giving the United States fee title to more than 14,000 acres of Indian land containing the most important ruins. In return, the Southern Utes received title to more than 30,000 acres of public land in the vicinity, including land on Sleeping Ute Mountain that was regarded as sacred by tribal members. Historians have offered differing assessments of the fairness of that deal.[7]

YOSEMITE VALLEY COMES BACK INTO U.S. OWNERSHIP

By the time Roosevelt became president, California's management of the Yosemite Valley and the Mariposa Big Tree Grove—now surrounded by the large national park that Congress created in 1890—had come in for withering criticism. For years, John Muir had urged California to cede the lands back to the national government so they could be made part of the national park. California governor George Pardee, a Republican who had won the office in 1902 by defeating San Francisco Democrat Franklin Lane (who later became Woodrow Wilson's secretary of the Interior), favored the idea because management had proved to be a political headache as well as a financial burden.[8]

Muir lobbied Theodore Roosevelt directly when they camped together near Yosemite's Glacier Point in the spring of 1903, but the president proceeded cautiously. Pardee, a Roosevelt ally, first had to overcome opposition from interests vested in state management, including those who believed that state pride was at stake—the *San Francisco Chronicle* thundered that those who favored retrocession were "traitors." Just the year before, California had used state funds to purchase stands of coastal redwoods between San Jose and Santa Cruz from private owners and there establish Big Basin Redwoods as its first state park.

The Yosemite retrocession became even more complicated when Pinchot, always alert to opportunities to add to his domain, worked with John P. Irish, the former head of the state's Yosemite Commission, to have both the state and the federal Yosemite parks transferred to the Agriculture Department. His effort failed, in part because it was opposed by the local army officials then protecting the federal park.

To cut through the tangle, Muir sought the help of the chief executive of the Southern Pacific Railroad, Edward H. Harriman, with whom he had become friendly while a member of an expedition to Alaska that Harriman had led in 1899. William Colby, Muir's lieutenant at the Sierra Club, worked with a Southern Pacific attorney to craft the necessary legislation, and the railroad helped push the bill through the state legislature in March 1905. Congress still needed to enact a law accepting the state's offer, which took two tries, but finally succeeded in June 1906.

From that point on, the Yosemite Valley and the Mariposa Big Tree Grove would be part of a full-fledged and much larger national park, one comparable in size to Yellowstone. The national-park designation came a little more than a year after Congress had, following the recommendation of a commission it had established, made significant adjustments to the boundaries of the 1890 Yosemite Park. The legislation added acreage on the north to include more of the Tuolumne River watershed and made significant reductions along the southern and western boundaries, designed in part to limit the amount of private land inside its borders.

A FEW LESS REMARKABLE PARKS

The other national parks established during Roosevelt's presidency were a curious assemblage of places where Congress succumbed to what a longtime leader of the National Park Service once described as the "parochial enthusiasm of local politicians." Wind Cave, Sully's Hill, and Platt National Parks were small, and at least the last two lacked natural wonders of national significance. This was not the first time such a thing had happened. In 1875, three years after Yellowstone was established, Congress created an eight-hundred-acre national park adjacent to a U.S. Army garrison on Mackinac Island in Michigan at the instigation of Senator Thomas Ferry (R-Mich.). He had been born on the island, and it had become a popular summer resort. Since it lacked features of national interest, Congress simply turned it over to the State of Michigan in 1895, with no strings attached.[9]

The nine-hundred-acre Wind Cave National Park, in the eastern Black Hills of South Dakota, was the first cave to be made a national park. Sully's Hill, encompassing some low wooded hills in eastern North Dakota, was called by one historian the "most unworthy national park ever created." Not much was ever done with it, and Congress redesignated it a national game preserve in 1931 and transferred it to the Department of Agriculture. Platt National Park, about eight hundred acres of mineral springs in south-central Oklahoma, was established in 1906 on land that had been purchased from the Chickasaw and Choctaw tribes a few years earlier. It too was generally treated as a kind of bastard child by the Interior Department as well as Congress (except for the Oklahoma congressional delegation). In 1976, it was combined with other public land and renamed the Chickasaw National Recreation Area.[10]

While these places paled in comparison with the magnificence of Yellowstone, Yosemite, Mount Rainier, and Crater Lake, the park idea was still in its formative stages. No agency inside the Interior Department was made responsible for managing them, let alone developing and enforcing standards to try to ensure that new national parks genuinely served a national rather than merely a parochial interest. The line between the two has never been distinct, leaving considerable room for members of Congress to try to curry favor with constituencies back home by sponsoring bills to create new national parks.

Over in the Agriculture Department, Pinchot was never very interested in park and recreation issues, especially as long as the Interior Department remained in control of parks. Roosevelt was not inclined to use up political capital by vetoing dubious park bills. Not much attention was given to the need to establish standards for designating national parks until a new agency was formed and given exclusive responsibility for the parks, and that did not come about until seven years after Roosevelt left office.

With monuments too, the problem of where to draw the line was a chronic headache, and a few of the early national monuments were also of questionable merit. In May 1908, for example, Roosevelt proclaimed the 160-acre Lewis and Clark Cavern National Monument on land donated by the Northern Pacific Railway high up a mountainside along the Jefferson River in Montana. Lewis and Clark's party had traveled there in 1805, but no evidence suggests that any of its members knew of the cavern's existence. Taft added acreage to the monument in 1911, but Congress enacted legislation in 1937 turning it over to the state, and it became Montana's first state park.

By 1928, eight limestone caves had been protected as national monuments under the Antiquities Act. At that point, the journalist-conservationist Robert Sterling Yard pointedly observed that the nation's public lands might possess one hundred thousand such caves, "each of which appears very wonderful to local imaginations."[11]

RESERVATION LABELS AND USE RESTRICTIONS

As reasons for keeping lands in permanent national ownership proliferated, and as new labels such as "monuments," "bird reserves," and "game reserves" began to be employed, questions were continually raised about what kinds of limits on uses like logging or mining or grazing or dam building might attach to any particular label. Sometimes the answers were slow in coming. Even when answers were supplied, they might not have been permanent, because use restrictions were often adjusted over time. Also, new labels were, and still are, invented with some regularity.

Those in Congress and the executive branch who made the decisions in this era to hold on to significant amounts of land had no standard definition of "park," "forest," "monument," "bird reserve," or "game range" to guide them. They invented and gave content to labels through improvisation. In hindsight, it can sometimes seem as if they had no clear vision of what they wanted to do. But they were adjusting the recipe as they went along, as any good cook might do.

Compromises among competing interests sometimes produced messy results, but they often showed the political process at its most successful. They implemented the strong national consensus favoring national management of large amounts of land, and they produced results that future generations of Americans could treasure. Developing and adjusting the guidelines for governing that immense resource became a major focus of public land policy going forward, constantly requiring judgment calls about just what was in the national interest.

CHAPTER THIRTY-ONE

Making New Forest Reserves

CONGRESS CHALLENGES THE PRESIDENT

THE PROBLEM POSED BY UNSANCTIONED, unregulated livestock grazing on public lands outside the forest reserves and the few national parks became increasingly intertwined with Roosevelt's robust expansion of the forest reserves. Some months before Roosevelt became president, Congressman Justin Bowersock (R-Kans.) had introduced a bill, supported by many large livestock operators, to authorize the Interior secretary to issue grazing leases on these unreserved public lands. Most smaller operators opposed this, fearing that large grazing enterprises would have an inside track to obtain leases. Opposition also came from homesteading and irrigation advocates as well as from Interior secretary Hitchcock, who feared such leasing would allow ranchers to monopolize the range, defeat the irrigation program that Congress was then considering, and end homesteading as a practical matter. As a result, Bowersock's bill failed to gain political traction.[1]

Around this time, Hitchcock was stepping up enforcement against illegal fencing of public lands; his *Annual Report* for 1903 described how livestock operators in Kansas used threats and other forms of intimidation to thwart homesteaders. Such actions helped make the term "cattle baron," as Louise Peffer put it, as despised in some quarters as the term "robber baron."[2]

Congress put another approach on the table in April 1904 by enacting a law named after its chief sponsor, Moses Kinkaid (R-Neb.), that applied only to public lands in the western two-thirds of Nebraska. It gave homesteaders the opportunity to acquire title to up to 640 acres of public land there (quadruple the usual amount) that the Interior secretary had determined was not "reasonably practicable to irrigate." The Kinkaid Act attracted attention as a possible way to privatize public lands suitable primarily for livestock grazing on the Jeffersonian model of small, family-sized enterprises, while at the same time preserving opportunities to irrigate and privatize 160-acre tracts via the Reclamation Act of 1902 and the Homestead Act.[3]

After Roosevelt was elected to a full term in November of 1904, Pinchot decided to stir the pot. Almost immediately after he gained control of the forest reserves in February 1905, he released the second report of the Public Land Commission, which he had been heading. It proposed to establish a system of grazing reserves that would sit alongside the forest reserves, with both programs to be under Pinchot's control at the Agriculture Department. The report found that the "general lack of control" of grazing on the remaining unreserved public land had "resulted, naturally and inevitably, in overgrazing and the ruin of millions of acres." It called on Congress to give the president authority to establish "grazing districts or reserves" to be supervised by the secretary of Agriculture, who would be empowered to "collect a moderate fee for grazing permits" and to regulate grazing according to the needs of a particular locality. It included an appendix prepared by the Forest Service's grazing chief, Albert Potter, reporting that a survey of 1,400 ranchers across the western states showed that the overwhelming majority supported governmental control, with reasonable regulation, to stem the deterioration of the rangelands.[4]

The idea provoked the usual range of reactions, mostly negative, like those that had greeted the Bowersock bill four years earlier. Never inclined to dawdle, Roosevelt continued to use his authority under section 24 of the General Revision Act and the Organic Act to put many more millions of acres of public lands, a good many of which were being grazed by domestic livestock, into forest reserves, where the grazing would be regulated for the first time. Moving lands into forest reserves limited the opportunities for speculators and others who sought to abuse divestment laws, especially once Congress repealed the notorious "in lieu" exchange provision of the Organic Act in March 1905. It also made it more difficult to homestead and privatize public lands.

Since the early 1890s, bills had occasionally been introduced to curb the president's authority to create new forest reserves, but none had made headway. Now, as Roosevelt continued to expand the forest reserves, stirrings of discontent were heard on Capitol Hill, particularly in the Senate. Over several months in 1904 and 1905, Senator Weldon Heyburn engaged Roosevelt and Pinchot in an extensive correspondence, soon collected and published in a Forest Service bulletin, regarding whether more public lands in Idaho ought to be put in forest reserves.

At that point, relatively few western senators supported Heyburn. Most, such as Frank Flint (R-Calif.), Francis Newlands, George Perkins (R-Calif.), Reed Smoot (R-Utah), and Francis Warren, supported establishing more forest reserves. Even Heyburn's Idaho colleague, Fred Dubois, a Republican turned Democrat, sided with the administration, calling Heyburn "utterly oblivious to or careless of facts."[5]

In 1905 and 1906, Roosevelt established several dozen new forest reserves across the West, including on nearly 10 million acres in Idaho and on 7 million each in Montana, Colorado, and Oregon. He established seven new forest reserves in Northern California, including a major extension of the Tahoe Forest Reserve to include most of the California side of the lake's basin. That brought the total reserve acreage to well over 100 million acres, more than double what it was when he took office. Most of these new reserves grew out of surveys undertaken by the General Land Office in response to local petitions submitted before the forest reserves were transferred to the Agriculture Department, and most continued to enjoy local support. The movement for adding reserves was also being fueled by, among other things, the growing advocacy by women's clubs for protecting forests and wildlife. (While women could not vote across the nation until the Nineteenth Amendment to the U.S. Constitution was ratified in 1920, several western territories and states had already taken that step.) Still, on public lands, as in most public matters, as Pinchot later observed in his autobiography, "those who were for made far less noise than those who were against."[6]

As Roosevelt was putting more acres into forest reserves with characteristic vigor, he pushed back on the notion that many of those arid lands could be privatized by homesteading. He showed his deep understanding of the problem in his December 1905 message to Congress, calling it unwise simply to extend the Kinkaid Act's model of 640-acre homesteads across the entire West. The remaining unreserved public lands were mostly too arid to support a viable family homestead on that limited acreage, which would result in "needless suffering and failure" by "bona fide settlers" who relied on the "implied assurance of the Government that such an area is sufficient." On the other hand, he warned, raising the acreage cap across the board would most likely simply increase the holdings of what he called "the great land owners."[7]

Given all this, Roosevelt recommended a more fine-grained, tailored approach to homesteading. He asked Congress to empower the executive to examine and classify the lands with the objective of giving each settler, whether livestock operator or farmer, "land enough to support his family and no more." While this was being done, grazing on these lands should be regulated, as was already being done on the forest reserves. This more calibrated approach would, he argued, bring stability, restore grasslands to health, and increase their value. The United States had paid a high price for tolerating a grazing "commons" on its lands, he wrote, because their present value was "scarcely more than half what it once was or what it might easily be again under careful regulation."

Roosevelt's recommendation could have been implemented by putting the vast majority of public lands in the West into forest reserves and tweaking the requirement of the Organic Act that allowed the president to open reserved land that was "better adapted to . . . agricultural purposes" to homesteading, by instead authorizing the president to set an acreage cap above 160 acres, according to local conditions. Instead, Congress enacted the Forest Homestead Act in June 1906. It authorized the president to open some lands in forest reserves to homesteading under certain conditions, but kept in place the 160-acre cap, and thus did little to facilitate livestock-based homesteading on more arid public lands.[8]

THE POLITICAL LANDSCAPE IN CONGRESS BEGINS TO SHIFT

In the congressional elections of 1906, Republicans held on to every seat in the West except for Nevada's single member. Even though they lost 26 House seats overall, they still enjoyed a comfortable 223–167 majority in the Sixtieth Congress convening in 1907. They also picked up three Senate seats, holding every Senate seat in the West except for one in Colorado and one in Nevada.

As 1906 was drawing to a close, Roosevelt's public lands agenda finally encountered serious headwinds. It was then that, as Doris Kearns Goodwin put it, Roosevelt's "long-standing apprehension over his waning influence on domestic legislation proved justified."[9]

Viewed through a long lens, the West had seen dramatic changes in public land policy in just a decade and a half. Well over 100 million acres had been put under a new regime of governmental supervision. While the forest reserves had been generally welcomed by local and regional interests, they did restrict opportunities for homesteading, ended free and unregulated access for livestock, and reduced opportunities for speculation and the abuse of public land laws, which had a long history. They also threatened to bring regulation to other customary practices, such as gathering free timber and prospecting for minerals, and they made more uncertain the status of unperfected homestead and other types of claims to public lands, and the use of nonfederal inholdings, within their boundaries.

Pinchot had worked to mitigate such concerns. The Forest Service had fleshed out the management directives that Congress provided in the Organic Act, in order to provide clearer guidance on what could and could not be done in the reserves. It had adjusted some reserve boundaries, excising lands found better suited for agriculture or dominated by inholdings. But those actions were not enough to eliminate all complaints, and perhaps Roosevelt and Pinchot underestimated the fatigue that some parts of the West were experiencing from the rapid changes.

As the second session of the Fifty-Ninth Congress was convening in December 1906, Roosevelt renewed his campaign to end unregulated livestock grazing on public lands outside the forest reserves. He described the Forest Service's administration of grazing on the reserves as "an assured success," with range conditions "improving rapidly" and opposition to the grazing fee "practically at an end." He renewed his call for legislation that would provide for similar control of the public lands outside the reserves while protecting the "rights of the settler and homemaker." He also called for modifying the Unlawful Inclosures Act of 1885 to permit reasonable fencing on public lands where it "promotes the use of the range and yet interferes neither with settlement nor with other range rights." Finally, he advocated that the program be administered by the Agriculture Department, because it "alone is equipped for that work."[10]

SHOWDOWN OVER THE 1907–8 AGRICULTURE APPROPRIATIONS BILL

Roosevelt's plan enjoyed the support of some leading, mostly larger western cattle raisers, who desired the stability that governmental regulation could provide, and it was promptly attached to the agricultural appropriations bill that was moving through Congress. But it reignited long-simmering conflicts among the disparate interests involved, garnering criticism from homestead advocates, irrigation project supporters, and some smaller-scale ranchers. Supporters of the Roosevelt plan counterattacked, charging that some supposed homestead advocates were speculators rather than genuine settlers.[11]

On the House side, debate on the appropriations bill was limited. Some westerners, such as Eben Martin (R-S.D.), strongly defended the Forest Service. When the Black Hills Forest Reserve was established in 1898, he said, "you could scarcely find one man in a thousand who was not opposed to the idea [but it] has been so successful that I challenge anyone to find now one man in a thousand in that immediate vicinity who does not recognize its great benefits."[12]

Debate on the Senate floor was much more intense. Larger livestock enterprises running mostly cattle, which were among the chief backers of Roosevelt's proposal, were still thought of by many as industrial operations bent on monopolizing the public lands, rather than as akin to homesteaders merely seeking to make a living through agriculture. The administration's proposal also became intertwined with general questions about the management of the Forest Service, including how much money and how much discretion it ought to be given.

Even Pinchot's salary was a target, because by this time he had become a polarizing figure. Pinchot had his defenders, such as Henry Cabot Lodge (R-Mass.), who said a "more accomplished, a more devoted, a better servant" could not be found. But his critics shrewdly took aim at the revolving fund, which gave him some fiscal independence from Congress, because many members generally supportive of forest reserves, like Lodge, were uneasy at Congress relinquishing its historic power of the purse. The tactic worked; the appropriations bill was amended not only to abolish the revolving fund but also to require Pinchot to submit a detailed report of receipts and estimated expenditures annually.[13]

Charles Fulton (R-Ore.) emerged as Pinchot's leading opponent while offering a paean to the homesteader-settler. "While these chiefs of the Bureau of Forestry sit within their marble halls and theorize and dream of waters conserved, forests and streams protected and preserved throughout the ages and the ages," he told his colleagues, "the lowly pioneer is climbing the mountain side where he will erect his humble cabin, and within the shadow of the whispering pines and the lofty firs of the western forest engage in the laborious work of carving out for himself and his loved ones a home and a dwelling-place."[14]

By that point, the Senate had heard enough about Roosevelt's proposal to give the Agriculture Department control over livestock grazing on public lands outside the forest reserves. On February 22, it stripped the idea from the appropriations bill. That still left a path open for Roosevelt and Pinchot to bring grazing on those lands under governmental control, simply by continuing to put more of them in forest reserves, under the liberal terms of the General Revision Act of 1891 and the Organic Act of 1897.

On February 23, to limit that possibility, Charles Fulton proposed an amendment taken from a separate bill that Senator Heyburn had introduced earlier: "Hereafter no forest reserve shall be created, nor shall any additions be made to one heretofore created within the limits of the States of Oregon, Washington, Idaho, Montana, Colorado or Wyoming, except by Act of Congress." (According to Peffer, sheep interests, which had the most to lose from new reserves, were strongest in those states.)[15]

The Fulton amendment had no effect on existing reserves in those states. Almost immediately, Senator Thomas Carter of Montana jumped in to propose modifying it to prohibit any forest reserve, existing or new, from having exterior boundaries that extended more than one mile "beyond the timber line of the forest embraced therein." Carter, the former GLO commissioner who had helped launch the forest reserve program in the early 1890s, explained that while he and other westerners had strongly supported the 1891 and 1897 forest reserve legislation, and wanted "these forest reservations continued," he opposed extending reserves "to vast areas of agricultural land," which is what he feared Roosevelt and Pinchot would do.

Carter's proposal precipitated a confusing discussion about what was meant by "timber line" and whether it was feasible to excise pockets of untimbered land from forest reserves without destroying their utility. Senator John Spooner (R-Wisc.) warned that Carter's proposal would effectively dismantle the forest reserves and cause great harm. Senator Thomas Patterson offered an amendment that tried to clarify Carter's amendment, but that only confused matters more, so he eventually withdrew it.

At that point, "Copper King" William Andrews Clark (D-Mont.), a Gilded Age symbol whom the historian Michael Malone called an "especially virulent example of the unrestrained capitalist on the frontier," and who was about to leave the Senate after a single term, chimed in to offer his perspective on the whole idea of forest reserves. "We all deplore the denudation of the forest lands," he said, but the harvests had been "demanded for beneficial use in the interests of industrial progress." "Those who succeed us," Clark concluded, "can well take care of themselves."[16]

With that, debate on the Fulton amendment was suspended. Sometime over the next two days, a backroom deal was struck, and when the Senate took the matter up again on February 25, the Carter amendment to the Fulton amendment had been withdrawn. This would leave intact all existing forest reserves, including those in the six states covered by the Fulton amendment. In the brief discussion that followed, only Senator Patterson of Colorado offered a substantive comment. Pointing to the many millions of acres already in forest reserves in those six states, and opining that the administration would not have "the audacity to attempt to set apart any more lands in the States mentioned in the amendment than it already has done," Patterson likened the Fulton amendment to "shutting the stable door after the horse had been stolen." The amendment was then approved by a voice vote. The House quickly concurred without further discussion, and the appropriations bill containing it was sent to the president.[17]

ROOSEVELT HAS THE LAST WORD

The historical record does not reveal whether Pinchot and Roosevelt were parties to the deal that led to Congress's abrupt, last-minute acceptance of the Fulton amendment in its original form. Whether or not they were, Roosevelt had a few days to expand the forest reserves in the six states covered by the amendment, assuming he chose not to veto the bill. Because Congress adjourned on March 4, he could simply have withheld his signature and the bill would have died as a result of the pocket veto. Doing so would have left the Department of Agriculture programs without a congressional appropriation of funds to operate. Almost exactly ten years earlier, the outgoing President Cleveland had exercised just such a veto over a version of what became the 1897 Organic Act for the forest reserves, leaving the mess on his successor's plate.[18]

In his *Autobiography*, published six years later, Roosevelt recounted what happened next with obvious relish. Fulton's amendment, he wrote, would have allowed millions of acres of public lands in those six states "to be exploited by land grabbers and by the representatives of the great special interests, at the expense of the public interest." This made it "equally undesirable" to veto the entire appropriation bill or simply to sign it with the Fulton amendment included.[19]

Accordingly, Roosevelt and Pinchot sprang into action. The Forest Service (building on earlier work in the General Land Office) had for years "been gathering field notes as to what forests ought to be set aside in these States," Roosevelt wrote, and so the "necessary papers were immediately prepared." On March 1 and 2, Roosevelt signed proclamations establishing twelve new reserves and enlarging fifteen existing ones, altogether covering 16 million acres, in the six states subject to Fulton's amendment. On March 4, he signed the appropriations bill containing the Fulton amendment into law.[20]

Looking back, Roosevelt could hardly contain his glee in recounting these events. Noting that Fulton had apparently barely escaped indictment for land fraud in Oregon, he wrote the "opponents of the Forest Service turned handsprings in their wrath; and dire were their threats against the Executive; but their threats could not be carried out, and were really only a tribute to the efficiency of our action."[21]

In taking this seemingly bold step, Roosevelt made a shrewd political calculation. As he had told Congress in his annual message in December 1904: "[The] forest reserve policy can be successful only when it has the full support of the people of the West. It can not safely, and should not in any case, be imposed upon them against their will." A year or so later, he had underscored the point, writing that "westerners who live in the neighborhood of the forest preserves" are those "who in the last resort will determine whether or not [they] are to be permanent."[22]

Roosevelt's excellent political instincts served him well. There was no widespread uproar, in Congress or outside it, calling for reversal of his action. This was in sharp contrast to the reception given Cleveland's Washington's Birthday proclamations—which, covering 22 million acres, were only modestly larger in scope—a decade earlier. Cleveland, plagued by a lingering economic downturn, was widely unpopular toward the end of his second term, and Republicans were about to assume control of both the White House and Congress. Roosevelt, by contrast, enjoyed wide popularity and had two years left in his term, and the Republicans would remain in firm control of the next Congress.

But there was more to it than that. The outcome showed just how fully public opinion across the country had embraced the idea of forest reserves. Indeed, the legislation that contained the Fulton amendment also ordered the Agriculture Department to report on the "advisability" of the U.S. government "purchasing and setting apart," as a "natural forest reserve," watersheds in the Appalachian and White Mountains, in the Southeast and Northeast, "for the purpose of conserving and regulating" stream flow and water supply. It was therefore entirely fitting that in this same legislation Congress directed that the forest reserves "shall be known hereafter as national forests."[23]

Popular support for the forest reserves was about as strong in the West as it was elsewhere. Roosevelt's early-March reservation of an additional 4 million acres in Oregon, for example, was supported by both Portland newspapers and most of the state's timber industry, presumably because it made their private timberland more valuable. In Colorado, where Roosevelt enlarged numerous reserves, the reaction was somewhat more mixed. Democrats, who controlled the legislature, demanded that the new Republican governor, Henry Buchtel, call a "Public Lands Convention" in Denver to air their concerns. Held in June 1907, it attracted nearly one thousand delegates—the majority from Colorado and most of the rest from Wyoming—and was dominated by livestock inter-ests. After incendiary speeches critical of Roosevelt's recent actions by Colorado senator Henry Teller (who had switched parties in 1903 to become a Democrat) and Congressman Mondell of Wyoming, Pinchot addressed the gathering, along with Roosevelt's new GLO commissioner, Richard Ballinger. Pinchot defended the president's actions so effectively that he largely defused the oppo-sition. Before adjourning, the attendees adopted numerous resolutions, but tellingly, none called for abolishing the reserves that Roosevelt had created three months earlier. In fact, within a couple of years, ranchers whose livestock grazed public-domain land near a national forest in northwestern Colorado petitioned Congress to extend its boundaries to include the lands their livestock grazed in order to limit the competition from large nonresident cattle outfits.[24]

The Fulton rider left Roosevelt completely free to create more national forests outside the six states it covered, and he did so at a rapid rate. He also used the Antiquities Act and other authorities to reserve additional public land from divestment. In April 1907, for example, he established four national forests and enlarged seven others in California, Nevada, Utah, and the New Mexico Territory. In May, he established two national monuments in California and two national forests in California and the Arizona Territory, and enlarged two others. That same month, he enlarged the Alexander Archipelago National Forest, which he had created in the Alaska Territory in 1902, and established (over the objection of GLO commissioner Ballinger) the Chugach and Tongass National Forests. The next year, he enlarged the Tongass. He did considerably more in his last few months in office.

CHAPTER THIRTY-TWO

Roosevelt, Public Lands, and Energy Development

ALTHOUGH IT IS A LESS APPRECIATED part of his public lands legacy than his work on forest and wildlife reserves, Theodore Roosevelt set in motion a fundamental reevaluation of U.S. public land policy in relation to energy development. In at least one respect, his impact in this area was even greater. The movement to reserve forests was well under way before he took office; Roosevelt just accelerated it. The same was true, though to a lesser extent, regarding the movement to use public lands to protect wildlife. But the idea that the United States should retain ownership of energy resources found on public lands in order to control and guide their development, a policy he strongly advocated, was almost entirely new.[1]

When Roosevelt became president, America was in the midst of a revolution in the development and use of energy. Fossil fuels were rapidly displacing wood as the primary means of heating homes and powering locomotives, ships, and the newfangled motor vehicles. Technological advances in the generation, transmission, and use of electricity were giving birth to the electrical age. All this spurred a quest for coal, oil, and natural gas, and for sites where the power of falling water could be harnessed to turn turbines and generate electricity.

A few statistics capture the rate of change. More coal was mined in the United States in the ten years before 1908 than had been mined from 1776 to 1896. Annual coal production tripled, to 400 million tons, between 1890 and 1910. Crude oil production increased from 23 million barrels in 1883 to 183 million barrels in 1909. Before 1900, almost no American dwellings were wired for electricity; by 1910 about 10 percent were, mostly in large cities; by 1930, 70 percent were.

It was inevitable that the nation's public lands—which contained large quantities of fossil fuels and many of the best sites for hydroelectric generation—would play a major role in this massive economic transformation. But until Roosevelt came along, with his usual relish for taking on new challenges, fashioning new approaches, and thinking in the longer term, few advocated that the United States should retain ownership of these resources. Roosevelt did, and in so doing, he triggered a national debate about how energy and public land policy ought to intersect. His two immediate successors, William Howard Taft and Woodrow Wilson, followed his lead, and Congress concluded the debate by enacting the Mineral Leasing Act and the Federal Power Act in 1920.

By the time Roosevelt took office, it was becoming increasingly clear that each of the pertinent legal regimes on public lands—the Coal Land Law, the Mining Law, and a hodgepodge of others—contained features that were fundamentally incompatible with orderly, efficient energy development. As that unhappy truth became more apparent, energy developers often simply followed a well-worn path of ignoring or evading those laws. But that course put large capital investments at risk, because it depended on public land managers and the courts looking the other way.

The intersection of energy policy and public land policy raised some big questions. The threshold question was whether the United States should retain or privatize public lands containing these resources. Assuming that was answered in favor of retention, the next question was whether it should use the socialist model of the government itself developing their energy resources, or instead should make them available for private development under federal supervision, such as through a leasing system. Another question was whether the United States should capture some of the value of these resources for their owners—the American people—such as by auctioning development rights to the highest bidder and requiring producers to pay royalties on minerals or electricity they produced. A fourth question was whether it should give energy development priority over other uses of the public lands.

The answers to these questions might vary depending on the energy resource. For example, on the question whether energy development should be given priority, the best sites for hydroelectric dams and associated facilities were often found in national forests and parks, which had been reserved to protect values such as safeguarding watersheds and preserving scenery for recreation. By contrast, coal and petroleum were often found on public lands outside these reservations, where extraction posed conflicts mainly with live-stock-grazing operations and homesteading.

Congress grappled with all these knotty issues for years. Until it resolved them, the executive was left with the challenge of administering public land laws that were not well suited to demands being put on them. More specifically, it was left with a choice between standing aside and letting energy developers have their way on public lands, or instead trying to force congressional action, either by stringently enforcing existing, inadequate laws or by withdrawing public lands from the laws' operation.

When Roosevelt and then Congress began to take up these questions, they faced a national mood that had changed significantly. The libertarian paradigm of freewheeling capitalism, which had dominated American political economy since the beginning of the Industrial Revolution, had fallen out of favor. Helped along by generous public land policies, railroad and mining enterprises had become among the most powerful corporations in the nation. Along with corporate combines called trusts, they exercised monopoly power and often exploited the consumer. Wealth disparities grew to levels never before seen. More and more Americans were coming to believe that a powerful national government was needed to check the excesses of unbridled capitalism.

Theodore Roosevelt was a leading proponent of the need for a counter-vailing power. As he put it in his last message to Congress, in December 1908, because "centralization has already come in business," the only way to protect the general public interest was to empower the central government to "thor-oughly and adequately control and supervise the large corporations." By the end of his administration, a mostly bipartisan Progressive movement had come to dominate domestic politics and demand that government, and particu-larly the national government, play a larger role in American life.[2]

With the emergence of the Progressive movement, the U.S. Supreme Court sometimes waffled on the extent to which the U.S. Constitution constrained the power of Congress and the executive to regulate private enter-prise. But where the public lands were involved, the Court did not waffle. It continued down the path it had consistently taken since the Civil War, namely, firmly rejecting constitutional arguments that would limit the power of the United States to direct how the lands and the resources that it owned were to be used. The vast public lands, in other words, gave Progressives a favorable arena in which to implement their policy objectives and help meet the growing public demand for energy.

SITING AND REGULATING HYDROELECTRIC
FACILITIES ON PUBLIC LANDS

Electrification spurred great interest in hydroelectric generation because its fuel, falling water, was free. Many public lands, particularly in the mountains, contained prime sites for such facilities. Between 1896 and 1901, Congress enacted three somewhat inconsistent laws that allowed hydroelectric projects to be located on public lands. All contained limitations—such as not giving developers much security for their investment—that hobbled their effectiveness. Once it assumed control of the forest reserves in 1905, Gifford Pinchot's Forest Service developed a standard agreement permitting hydroelectric projects to be sited on the reserves for a limited term and requiring payment of an annual rental subject to periodic adjustment. Some in the industry objected to these conditions and instead sought special legislation that would give them ownership of, or at least permanent tenure on, the public lands where they wanted to build their projects. Sometimes Congress went along with them.[3]

The Roosevelt administration pushed back. James R. Garfield, the son of President James A. Garfield and a Pinchot ally, had succeeded Hitchcock as Interior secretary in March 1907. Almost immediately, he started putting public lands outside the national forests that had potential as waterpower sites off-limits to such projects unless they obtained a right-of-way permit under the 1901 law. (Because that law gave the government the authority to revoke permits at any time, most in the industry refused to use it.) The Garfield withdrawals eventually encompassed nearly 4 million acres.

In early 1908, Roosevelt announced that he would sign no more bills authorizing specific dams, whether on or off public lands, if they gave the owners unlimited tenure and did not require them to pay for the privilege. He noted that appropriate compensation was particularly justifiable with regard to the "mountain streams of the West, where the jurisdiction of the Federal Government as the owner of the public lands and national forests is not open to question." He made good on his threat, but by the time he left office, Congress had still not crafted a general policy regarding hydropower development on the nation's rivers, whether public lands were involved or not.[4]

ROOSEVELT AND COAL POLICY: SPLITTING THE MINERAL
ESTATE FROM THE SURFACE ESTATE

Areas of public land containing coal deposits could be sold in tracts no larger than 160 acres under laws that Congress adopted in 1864 and 1873. As the West's population grew and the demand for coal increased, industrial enterprises and speculators sought to evade the 160-acre limitation in time-honored ways—hiring people to make "dummy" entries under the Coal Land Act or to pose as farmers and seek title under agricultural laws such as the Homestead Act. The Interior Department tried to contain such abuses, but with limited success. In June 1906, Senator Robert La Follette (R-Wisc.), a leading Progressive, proposed legislation giving the president authority to withdraw public lands that might contain coal or petroleum from the mineral laws until those laws could be reformed.

Roosevelt was too impatient to wait for Congress to act. At his direction, between July and the end of November, the Interior Department withdrew 66 million acres of public land in Colorado, Montana, Oregon, Utah, Washington, and Wyoming, and the territories of Alaska and New Mexico, from entry under the mineral laws and under nonmineral public land divestment laws such as the Homestead Act. Roosevelt and his successor, Taft, later expanded these withdrawals so that they eventually covered more than 140 million acres.[5]

Withdrawing these vast tracts from entry under the Homestead Act and similar laws was premised on the assumption that until the U.S. Geological Survey determined otherwise, "workable coal [was] known to occur" on them. This presumption marked a radical departure from past practice. The General Land Office had traditionally assumed that public lands were *not* mineral in character unless they were actually producing minerals or were in an area where mining was common. That traditional approach had left most public lands, even those thought likely to contain coal and other minerals, open to divestment to railroad companies, whose land grants excluded mineral lands, as well as to speculators who manipulated divestment laws like the Homestead Act.

This newfound willingness to enlarge the category of lands deemed mineral in character, thereby putting them off-limits to divestment under the nonmineral public land laws, had staying power. From that point forward, the government was usually vigorous in trying to keep public lands that might contain fossil fuels in public ownership, and the federal courts generally cooperated. In 1919, for example, the United States persuaded the Supreme Court to void the Southern Pacific Railroad's title to certain lands in California's Elk Hills where the evidence showed that the railroad knew the land was mineral in character at the time it obtained title from the United States as part of a railroad land grant.[6]

In his special message to Congress on public land policy in December 1906, Roosevelt called for permanently reserving all public lands that might contain coal, and to make the coal available for development under governmental supervision by leasing it to private entities. In the meantime, his administration began selling coal lands at auction to the highest bidder rather than, as had previously been the custom, selling the lands upon request at the modest minimum price that Congress had set in the Coal Lands Act of 1873.[7]

These steps provoked a heated reaction from Congressman Frank Mondell. In a February 1907 speech on the House floor, Mondell likened the search for coal to the search for gold in the early mineral rushes. The president, he said, was practicing "centralization, State socialism and paternalism," as a result of which, the "prospector with his pick and shovel, his grub stake, and his pack mule, is to be banished from the public lands of the United States." Mondell conceded that in the past the executive had many times withdrawn public lands without express authority from Congress. But Roosevelt's coal withdrawals, he argued, were so sweeping as to be unconstitutional. Congressman John Lacey of Iowa contested Mondell's narrow view of the executive withdrawal authority.[8]

Shortly after that, Roosevelt modified his approach in a way that had lasting significance for public land law. He called on Congress to enact legislation that would split ownership of the public lands into two parts—or "estates," in the terminology of property law—one covering minerals that might be found on the land and the other covering everything else. (Although the split is commonly characterized as between owners of the "surface" and the "subsurface," in reality, the owner of the mineral estate owns nothing of the subsurface except minerals.) This splitting of the estates would, Roosevelt wrote, "encourage the separate and independent development of the surface lands for agricultural purposes and the extraction of the mineral fuels in such manner as will best meet the needs of the people." He urged Congress to adopt a leasing system for these minerals, noting that many British colonies and former colonies (such as Australia), as well as most European coal-producing countries, had adopted such systems, and that they were "working satisfactorily." (In those countries, by long tradition, the central government owned all minerals, regardless of who owned the surface.) The matter was urgent, he wrote, because the demand for coal was increasing exponentially.[9]

The idea of splitting estates was not uncommon in the United States. As Roosevelt himself noted, in the East and Midwest, "these two great industries, agriculture and mining, are conducted within the same boundaries, and the country thus attains its highest dual development without conflict of interest." But it was a new idea in American public land law.

His proposal was politically astute. It would allow the United States to continue to make public lands outside forest reserves and parks available for divestment under the Homestead Act, while at the same time preserving public ownership of, and supervisory power over, the minerals those lands contained. Of course, giving farmers and miners a property interest in the same land might lead to conflicts between the two, but Roosevelt did not address how they might be resolved.

Several members of Congress, including Senator La Follette and Congressman Lacey, promptly introduced bills to implement Roosevelt's recommendations. Roosevelt's idea of separating the surface estate from the mineral estate gained immediate traction because it kept more public lands available for homesteading. His idea of leasing rather than selling or giving away the reserved minerals took longer to gain wide acceptance. Until it did, simply splitting the surface estate from the coal estate became an acceptable compromise between the defenders of the status quo like Congressman Mondell and advocates of a mineral-leasing system. In the meantime, as long as Roosevelt's mineral withdrawals stayed in effect, no coal could be developed on those lands where the United States retained ownership of the mineral estate.

On his last full day in office in March 1909, Roosevelt signed the first "split-estate" law in the history of the public lands. It reserved to the United States "all coal" found in a narrowly defined segment of public lands entered by homesteaders. The next year, Congress broadened the reservation to include coal on all public lands entered under the Homestead Act and related laws such as the Desert Land Act. Both the 1909 and 1910 laws reserved to the owner of the minerals the "right to prospect for, mine, and remove the same," but also required compensation to the surface owner for damage caused by the mineral-extraction activity.[10]

The split-estate policy meant that conflicts between mining and home-steading needed to be addressed only if and when mining activity occurred. Until surface mining became common, coal mining usually did not greatly interfere with a homesteader's use of the surface, allowing a kind of peaceful coexistence. Because coal mining was generally far more lucrative than farming, the miner could readily afford to compensate the homesteader for any damage caused by mining activity.

OIL AND GAS POLICY

Demand for petroleum was also growing rapidly, stimulated by the develop-ment of motorized vehicles. For several years after Colonel Edwin Drake drilled the first oil well in western Pennsylvania, in 1859, nearly all oil and gas activity was on private land. When, in the 1870s and 1880s, petroleum began to be extracted from public lands in California, those doing the drilling were quick to assume that the liberal terms of the Mining Law of 1872—which allowed mineral extraction without compensating the United States—governed. But because Senator Stewart had crafted the Mining Law with precious metals like gold and silver in mind, it was far from certain whether it would apply to liquid and gaseous fossil fuels, and if it did not apply, then no law on the books authorized the extraction of petroleum from the public lands.

For years the Interior Department stood to one side and let petroleum extraction go forward unimpeded on public lands, although Interior secretary Teller cautioned in 1883 that it was "undetermined" whether the Mining Law applied. In 1892, Edward Doheny struck oil near the site of present-day Dodger Stadium in Los Angeles. This kicked off a boom that quickly spread to public lands in the region and compelled the Interior Department to address the question. It waffled, first ruling that the Mining Law did not apply, and then reversing itself a year later.

By that time, Congress had had enough. The so-called Oil Placer Act, enacted in 1897, made oil and gas on public lands subject to the Mining Law. The House committee report on the bill conceded that the Interior Department was likely correct that Stewart's law was "not originally intended to extend to" petroleum. But it regarded the Mining Law's provisions as "calculated to aid in the development" of petroleum deposits on public land, and the full Congress agreed, without much discussion.[11]

That proved to be a huge misjudgment. The Silver Senator's arcane law, drafted mostly with prospecting for near-surface deposits of precious metals in mind, did not accommodate the far different needs of an industry that required expensive, time-consuming drilling to find fluids and gases hidden in the bowels of the earth. Indeed, it soon became clear that the Mining Law, far from being "calculated to aid" petroleum development, posed serious challenges for it.

Most problematically, the Mining Law unequivocally prohibited even locating a mining claim on public land until a "discovery" of a valuable mineral deposit had been made, and only a discovery gave the locator an exclusive right to develop minerals. Practically the only way to show a petroleum discovery was by drilling, because, as the Supreme Court put it in a 1905 decision, "indications" of oil seeping out of springs "merely suggested a possibility that the ground contained oil," which was not enough to establish a discovery. But drilling took time and money and could not be done secretly.[12]

The result was predictable. Whenever oil prospectors showed interest in a particular area, all public lands in the vicinity were quickly blanketed with mining claims, often overlapping, from many different entities. In this free-for-all, prospectors drilled as fast as they could to be the first to establish a "discovery." Until then, no claimant had any rights against the United States or anyone else.

That was hardly the only problem. While a single petroleum deposit might extend under thousands of acres, the Mining Law limited the size of claims to approximately twenty acres, and required a discovery to be shown on each claim. This resulted in a madcap proliferation of wells that was highly inefficient, leading to premature production and other ills. As a U.S. Geological Survey report from that era dryly put it, a law that "demands discovery and restricts . . . acreage" does not "encourage prudent or careful development." Moreover, the limitation on claim size, here as elsewhere in public land law, invited evasion through the use of such fraudulent devices as dummy entries.[13]

As with coal, there could also be competition from persons making entry under the Homestead Act and similar nonmineral laws. So that drilling might proceed without interference from homesteaders (or persons posing as such), petroleum companies asked the GLO to withdraw public lands they had targeted for exploration from entry under such laws. The GLO initially agreed and, beginning in 1900, issued more than twenty separate withdrawal orders covering millions of acres of public land in California, Oregon, and Wyoming. This move aroused the ire of homestead advocates and their allies, and the GLO soon retreated, restoring many of the withdrawn lands to agricultural entry in 1902.

In 1907, after petroleum companies and geologists with the U.S. Geological Survey protested that oil operators needed "protection against agricultural filings during the drilling period," the GLO again reversed course and, with the support of new Interior secretary Garfield, reinstated some of its earlier withdrawals. This time there was less pushback because, as the USGS noted, these newer withdrawals were "more closely confined to prospective oil territory" and included less land of interest to agriculturalists, and also because the large coal withdrawals the Roosevelt administration had made in 1906 "had accustomed the public to the withdrawal idea." But these petroleum withdrawals were only from homestead and similar entries, and therefore did not end the free-for-all among those who located mining claims.[14]

The leasing system that Roosevelt called for in his December 1906 message to Congress would apply to oil and gas as well as coal, and would require lessees to pay the United States a royalty on the minerals extracted. He sought to persuade westerners that this system could directly benefit them, because a portion of the revenue that the United States would receive would be earmarked for funding irrigation projects. This arrangement was preferable, he argued, to continuing to give away these resources for free.[15]

There was also a powerful national security argument for the government to assert more control over petroleum. The navy was beginning to convert from coal to petroleum as the fuel of choice for its vessels. This led U.S. Geological Survey director George Otis Smith to recommend in February 1908 that all the remaining public oil lands in California simply be withdrawn and reserved in public ownership, because otherwise, he noted, "the Government will be obliged to repurchase the very oil that it has practically given away."[16]

Freewheeling petroleum enterprises resisted calls for congressional action. Like their counterparts that had extracted precious metals from public lands in the first two decades after the 1848 discovery of gold in California, they preferred the status quo of an untenable legal situation rather than face the prospect of paying the U.S. government something for the privilege of extracting petroleum from public lands. As a result, an atmosphere of lawlessness reigned in the petroleum fields. Congress was not inclined to buck the industry, especially because by 1910 California was accounting for nearly a quarter of the world's petroleum production.[17] In contrast to his vigorous actions in withdrawing public lands containing hydropower sites in order to pressure Congress to bring that industry under governmental control, Interior secretary Garfield did not act on USGS director Smith's comparable recommendation to withdraw all public lands thought to contain petroleum. Roosevelt was uncharacteristically silent on the matter, even though keeping public control of petroleum supplies for his beloved navy ought to have appealed to him. Roosevelt had published a well-regarded history, *The Naval War of 1812* (1882), when he was twenty-four, had served as assistant secretary of the navy, and in late 1907 had sent the (still coal-powered) "Great White Fleet" of sixteen battleships around the world.[18]

At the time, the United States was asking the courts to break up the Standard Oil Trust for violating antitrust laws, which might have factored into Garfield's and Roosevelt's thinking. Also, the national economy had begun to experience turmoil. The stock market had started to decline substantially in September 1906, and in October 1907 a full-scale economic panic ensued, which famously required the stabilizing intervention of the Wall Street financier J. P. Morgan. The ripple effects were felt for years afterward as industrial production plunged and unemployment tripled. As a result, Congress had not acted on the proposal to establish a leasing system for publicly owned fossil fuels by the time Roosevelt left office in March 1909. Indeed, it would not adopt such a system until 1920. In the interim, many acres of public oil lands in California were divested for next to nothing, either under the Mining Law, the Homestead Act, or some other divestment law.

CHAPTER THIRTY-THREE

Public Lands in the Handoff from Roosevelt to Taft

ROOSEVELT'S PUBLIC LAND POLICIES remained popular across the nation despite economic turmoil and Congress's increasing fatigue with his unceasing calls for action. In 1908, the Republican Party platform confidently claimed that no policies other than the president's could bring "greater blessings to posterity." The Democratic platform endorsed "conservation of our natural resources," which, it said, in a dig at congressional Republicans, the president had "vainly sought" from his own "reluctant party." Its only criticism of Roosevelt was a vague reference to unspecified "abuses" that had arisen in the "administration"—but not the establishment—of the forest reserves.[1]

Because Roosevelt had long been a friend and political ally of his anointed successor, William Howard Taft, it was generally expected that Taft would continue along the same path. To the extent that the election of 1908 was a referendum on Roosevelt's policies, it showed the country was still strongly supportive. Taft won the popular vote nationally against William Jennings Bryan by almost ten percentage points and carried every western state handily except Nevada and Colorado, where he lost by narrow margins. It is doubtful that public land policies had much to do with Taft's loss in those two states, which had been strongholds for Bryan in his presidential runs in 1896 and 1900, thanks to his embrace of "free silver."

As the end of his term approached, Roosevelt accelerated his drive to reserve more public lands from divestiture laws. Between Election Day and

Taft's inauguration, he issued forty proclamations establishing or enlarging national forests in fifteen states, including more than doubling the size of the Tongass and Chugach National Forests in Alaska (to well over 15 million and 12 million acres, respectively). He also issued twenty-six executive orders creating bird reservations in thirteen states and proclaimed two new national monuments. On March 2, 1909, his next-to-last full day in office, he established the Mount Olympus National Monument in Washington (one of the states covered by the Fulton amendment) and enlarged thirteen national forests in California, Nevada, and the Arizona and New Mexico Territories.[2]

FOREST RESERVES TANGLE WITH INDIAN POLICY

Seven of Roosevelt's proclamations on March 2 added lands to national forests from Indian reservations in California and the Arizona and New Mexico Territories. These Indian reservations (the Tule River and Hoopa Valley in California, and the Navajo, Jicarilla Apache, Mescalero Apache, White Mountain Apache, and Zuni in Arizona and New Mexico) had been previously established by executive order.

These actions by Roosevelt were a variation on the approach that Congress had adopted for selected Indian reservations in the so-called Dawes Act, enacted in 1887. That act established a process to break up communally owned Indian lands by allotting small parcels to individual Indians. Its passage was the result of, as William deBuys put it, an "unholy alliance of greed and idealism." Dawes Act proponents included those who sought to encourage Indians to assimilate into the larger American society through farming small plots of land that they would own outright, and those who sought to reduce Indian landholdings and make "surplus" lands left over from the allotment process available for non-Indian purposes.[3]

In his first annual message to Congress, Roosevelt celebrated the allotment policy, famously calling it a "mighty pulverizing engine to break up the tribal mass." Roosevelt had long been dismissive of Indian interests, writing in the late 1880s that the "settler and the pioneer have at bottom justice on their side: This great continent could not have been kept as nothing but a game preserve for squalid savages." The Dawes Act and its progeny were the primary reason that the amount of Indian land in the lower forty-eight states continued to shrink: to 78 million acres by 1900 and to about 48 million acres when the act was repealed in 1934.[4]

Roosevelt's proclamations of March 2 put Pinchot's Forest Service in charge of these former Indian lands, but did preserve the right of the Interior secretary and the commissioner of Indian affairs to allot any of them to individual Indians under the Dawes Act. In addition, each proclamation authorized the Interior Department to use the former Indian reservation lands in ways beneficial to the Indians, and gave individual Indians free use of timber and stone from the lands for domestic use on their allotments. All of these rights terminated after twenty-five years, and their exercise was made subject to regulation by the Agriculture secretary (although any allotments made to individual Indians would be permanent). The tribes were not consulted on any of this. Roosevelt's land grab did not survive, because on February 17, 1912, President Taft rescinded these seven proclamations and restored the lands to the Indian reservations.[5]

Like Congress's legislation in 1902 establishing a forest reserve on former Chippewa lands in northern Minnesota, and its 1908 legislation authorizing the acquisition of the National Bison Range on the Confederated Salish and Kootenai Tribes reservation in northern Montana, these last-minute forest reserve proclamations by Roosevelt showed how the national policy to reserve public lands in national ownership for broad public purposes could sometimes become tangled with national policy regarding Indian lands. Such entanglements were, however, the exception rather than the norm. In the vast majority of situations, Indian lands declared surplus through the Dawes Act allotment program were made subject to the public land divestment laws and ended up in private hands, rather than being put in forest reserves or other kinds of reservations. Still, as the historian Theodore Catton noted, the "rise of conservation dovetailed" with the Dawes Act's "national closeout sale on the Indians' landed heritage" and tended to "cast a pall over Forest Service–tribal relations" in the early decades of the twentieth century.[6]

ROOSEVELT AND RESERVATIONS OF PUBLIC LANDS: A SUMMARY

Roosevelt's impact on the public lands was enormous. He more than tripled the amount of public land in various kinds of reservations (and that does not count his tens of millions of acres of mineral withdrawals). He also worked to make public land reservations national in scope. In his last two years in office, he established or enlarged national forests in Arkansas, Kansas, Michigan, and Minnesota. Because fewer public lands remained in states outside the West and Alaska, the reserves there were smaller. Nevertheless, by the time he left office, there were more than 3 million acres of national forests in Arkansas, well over 1 million acres in Minnesota, and smaller amounts in several other states and Puerto Rico. These helped pave the way for the Weeks Act of 1911, which launched a major program to acquire land for national forests across the nation.

Roosevelt's vast expansion of the national forest system brought many tens of millions of acres of public land primarily used for livestock grazing under the control of the Forest Service. Still, when he left the presidency, his administration had made almost no progress in dealing with livestock grazing on public-domain lands outside the forest reserves. Congress's refusal to act on his recommendation to take control of grazing on those lands through a permit-leasing system under the supervision of the Agriculture Department left the future of the lands unresolved. Those lands remained a commons open to all grazers, without any U.S. supervision other than the possibility of limiting fencing through enforcing the Unlawful Inclosures Act.

The regime that Roosevelt advocated was in fact not very different from the one Congress ultimately adopted in the Taylor Grazing Act of 1934, except that the Interior Department, not Agriculture, administered it. But before that happened, Congress in 1916 tried a different approach, promoting rancher-based privatization by enlarging the acreage limit for homesteading.

A number of factors contributed to Congress's failure to adopt Roosevelt's recommendation and put in place a program to control grazing on public lands outside the forest reserves. There was, for one thing, the ongoing turf battle between the Interior and Agriculture Departments, which was magnified by growing resistance to Pinchot's imperious ambition. Because of the sentimental regard many people have for trees, it was also much easier to mobilize public concern about the destruction of forests than about the overgrazing of grasslands. Livestock grazing also brought into play the romance that Americans were developing with the cowboy and an idealized version of ranch life.

Roosevelt contributed to this cultural phenomenon, and the enduring political influence of livestock operators on public land policy. While he was in office, images of the rugged rancher and his cowboy employees were just emerging as cultural symbols. Owen Wister's novel *The Virginian*, widely considered the first western, was published in 1902. Wister, a graduate of Harvard College and Harvard Law School, had spent several summers in the West, making his first trip to Wyoming, where the novel was set, in 1885 and later visiting Yellowstone. He dedicated the book to his friend and Harvard classmate Theodore Roosevelt, and it became an instant success, going through fourteen printings in eight months. Its enormous popularity helped create a genre, leading to countless books, films, and, eventually, television shows. Wister never again wrote about the West.[7]

Wister and Roosevelt—along with the western painter, illustrator, and sculptor Frederic Remington, also enormously popular in this era—were unusual in that they were products of the eastern establishment, yet made reputations as exponents of a western life centered on livestock operations. For many decades to come, the American public's romance with western ranch life complicated the ability of Congress and the executive to grapple with managing public lands heavily used by livestock.[8]

The blizzard of activity that Roosevelt undertook toward the end of his presidency was fully in keeping with his character, for as Robert Sterling Yard later put it, Roosevelt "was perpetually aggressive, forcing the fight at many points at the same time." Roosevelt once privately said that he was just like everyone else, except that "when there is anything to do, I do it with all the power I possess."[9]

But Roosevelt's energy and commitment, aided by Pinchot, were hardly the only, or even the primary, explanations for the vast enlargement in the amount of land retained in national ownership while he was president. The fact was, a clear majority of Americans favored these national reserves. Roosevelt understood that his initiative could carry policy only so far. As he once counseled George Bird Grinnell, it might sometimes be appropriate to "disregard local sentiment entirely," but "in the long run the success of a governmental policy" in the United States "must depend upon the native good will of those sections of the people who take the greatest interest in the matter."[10]

That did not stop reservation opponents such as Elias M. Ammons, a cattleman and Democrat who served in the Colorado legislature, from attacking the "gigantic feudal landlord" that he said was "ruling over unwilling tenants by the agency of irresponsible bureaus, traversing every local right, meddling with every private enterprise." Ammons, who served as Colorado's governor from 1913 to 1915, in which office he was known mostly for siding with mine owners in several bloody conflicts with mineworkers, considered the public lands a bastard offspring of "monarchical Europe" that was "wholly out of harmony with American institutions." He said of the people of the West that "their souls are not their own; their American manhood is subdued; there is ringing in their very souls a hatred of this government." That attitude has never disappeared entirely in the West or, for that matter, in the nation at large.[11]

THE TAFT ADMINISTRATION TAKES OVER

On major questions of public land policy, William Howard Taft did not differ much from Roosevelt. In a special message to Congress in early 1910 on the conservation of natural resources, Taft vowed to continue many of his predecessor's policies, including pressing for legislation to permanently reserve fossil fuels in U.S. ownership when public lands containing them were privatized. He also generally resisted efforts to make more grants of public land to states.[12]

But Taft did not share Roosevelt's passion for nature and the land, and possessed a very different temperament. He once described conservation as "something of a fad and a hobby with some of its advocates." His legalistic approach led him to consider conservation "rather abstruse," wryly observing that "a great many people" favor it, "no matter what it means." Moreover, he lacked his predecessor's appetite for taking vigorous action, especially when his legal authority to do so was less than clear. Finally, unlike his predecessor, he was not close to the chief forester. An early signal of this came when he declined the offer of Pinchot's ally Garfield to remain as Interior secretary, and instead appointed Richard Ballinger, who as GLO commissioner had tangled more than once with Pinchot.[13]

THE BALLINGER-PINCHOT DISPUTE AND THE FIRING OF GIFFORD PINCHOT

The Taft administration's biggest splash on public land policy was an unhappy one. It came about when Pinchot mounted a campaign that charged Ballinger with wrongdoing arising out of the GLO's handling of private claims to public coal lands in Alaska while he was commissioner. The claims had been made by persons with whom Ballinger had previously been associated. After the campaign went public, President Taft sided with Ballinger and fired Pinchot.

It has long been a matter of dispute whether there was any wrongdoing and, if so, whether Ballinger was involved in it. But some things were clear. The notoriety surrounding the controversy impaired the political reputations of just about everyone involved. It helped pave the way for Roosevelt to run for the presidency on the Progressive ticket in 1912, ensuring the defeat of William Howard Taft and the election of Woodrow Wilson.

Despite this profound impact, it is hard to make a case that the Ballinger-Pinchot controversy altered the course of public land policy. It underscored the political toxicity of allegations of corruption in the handling of public lands and resources, but that had been demonstrated by several earlier scandals. It undermined relations between the Interior Department and the Agriculture Department's Forest Service, but they were already somewhat frayed. After firing Pinchot, Taft quickly signaled that the direction of national forest policy would not change; he named Henry Graves, a Pinchot protégé, to succeed him.

All in all, after the dust settled, public land policy traveled on a path that it almost certainly would have followed had the Ballinger-Pinchot controversy never taken place.

Ballinger emerged as a rather sympathetic figure. On some issues, he was a stronger advocate for a progressive policy than the Roosevelt administration had been, and he did no lasting damage to the Roosevelt public land agenda. While there was a long and colorful history of skullduggery involving public land claims at the Interior Department, it is telling that neither a lengthy congressional investigation nor vigorous press scrutiny ever produced decisive evidence that Ballinger had done anything wrong. In the end, the Ballinger-Pinchot controversy was, as a Buffalo newspaper put it, "a quarrel rather than a scandal."[14]

GIFFORD PINCHOT'S PUBLIC LAND LEGACY

Pinchot eventually served two terms as governor of Pennsylvania (1923–27, 1931–35) and actively supported the national forests and conservation initiatives until his death in 1946. Most of his public land legacy grew out of the role that he played on forest issues between 1896 and 1910, when his impact was profound. He was a strong supporter of the national forest system and of the importance of public oversight of the private exploitation of natural resources. He made the national forests a household word and the U.S. Forest Service a paradigm of an effective public bureaucracy, one that, by the time he left office, had more than twice as many employees as the General Land Office even though the acreage it oversaw was less than a quarter of the GLO's.[15]

Part of Pinchot's enduring legacy was a side of governmental administration that hardly ever figures in histories. Along with James R. Garfield and Theodore Roosevelt, he devoted much effort to professionalizing the civil service. While he served in government, the number of civil service system positions in the federal executive branch more than tripled. Pinchot and Garfield also worked to improve governmental administration in less visible ways. In 1905, Roosevelt named both men to a five-member executive commission with the soporific name Committee on Department Methods. It made many farsighted recommendations for improving governmental performance that were no less important for being relatively invisible. Most were ultimately adopted, including centralized federal purchasing, standardized federal employee personnel policies and systems, a retirement plan for civil servants, and better governmental information gathering and records management through, among other things, establishing a national archive.

In his autobiography, published posthumously in 1948, Pinchot criticized the multiplicity of government agencies dealing with public lands and natural resources, charging that they competed "for place and credit and funds and jurisdiction" and paid insufficient attention to the bigger picture. Some of those turf battles were of his own making, for he had two of the sharpest elbows in Washington. His relentless drive for power led him to undervalue the benefits that could flow from competition among government agencies.[16]

For all of Pinchot's vision, leadership, and political skill, he seriously underestimated the increasing appetite of the public, mobilized by John Muir and others, for preserving large tracts of public land in something approximating their natural condition, and the growing political and economic power of recreation-based tourism. He also devoted scant attention to wildlife issues, which loomed ever larger in public land policy in the decades to come. Moreover, his uncompromising attitude often undercut his effectiveness, especially after he lost the political shield that Theodore Roosevelt had provided him.

Still, for many, Pinchot remains an inspirational figure. His forceful advocacy for taking the long view about public land policy—indeed, about policy toward all lands and natural resources—informed the attitudes of Americans for generations to come. The questions he posed, such as those in an article he wrote in 1908, remain highly relevant today:

> This nation has, on the continent of North America, three and a half million square miles. What shall we do with it? How can we make ourselves and our children happiest, most vigorous and efficient, and our civilization the highest and most influential, as we use that splendid heritage? . . . On the way in which we decide to handle this great possession which has been given us . . . hangs the welfare of those who are to come after us. . . . As we accept or ignore our responsibility as trustees of the nation's welfare, our children and our children's children for uncounted generations will call us blessed, or will lay their suffering at our doors.[17]

CHAPTER THIRTY-FOUR

Taft's Undervalued Record on Public Land Conservation

ALTHOUGH TAFT'S RECORD ON public lands was marred by the Ballinger-Pinchot controversy and paled overall in comparison with his predecessor's, his term was not without some notable accomplishments. On September 27, 1909, acting on Ballinger's recommendation, Taft upped the pressure on Congress to bring order to petroleum development on public lands by withdrawing 3 million acres in California and Wyoming from all divestiture laws, including the Mining Law. This action went considerably beyond what Roosevelt had done, because while Roosevelt's withdrawals had protected oil companies from competing claims by homesteaders, they had not protected the lands themselves from being privatized under the Mining Law. Nor did Taft stop there. In the nine months that followed, he made thirteen additional withdrawals covering another almost 3 million acres.[1]

Taft's boldness was ironic, because ordinarily he was much more reluctant than his predecessor to push the boundaries of executive power. In his *Autobiography*, Roosevelt mean-spiritedly oversimplified the comparison, likening his own approach to that of Andrew Jackson and Abraham Lincoln, to "serve the people affirmatively" unless the Constitution "explicitly forbid[s]" it, whereas Taft, he wrote, was like James Buchanan, believing the president "can do nothing, no matter how necessary it be to act, unless the Constitution explicitly commands the action."[2]

Taft did have qualms about taking bold action. In January 1910, a week after he fired Pinchot, he sent Congress a special message asking it to enact a law that would confirm the millions of acres of withdrawals that he and Roosevelt had already made, and would give the executive clear authority to make temporary withdrawals of public lands in the future "to meet conditions or emergencies as they arise." The problem, as he saw it, was that the executive authority needed to avoid outcomes "detrimental to the public interest" on the public lands was "not clear or satisfactory."[3]

Congressman Charles E. Pickett (R-Iowa) introduced a bill to carry out Taft's recommendations. Surprisingly, in light of his earlier heated criticism of Roosevelt's coal land withdrawals, Frank Mondell supported the measure and promptly reported it out of the House Public Lands Committee, which he chaired. Mondell credited public opinion for the change. "We must recognize," he told his colleagues on the House floor on April 13, that "in the country at large public sentiment was behind" the vigorous use of the withdrawal tool. The "principal complaints" of the people, he said, were "not that there was too much withdrawal, but that there was not enough withdrawal."[4]

In the bill's relatively swift journey through Congress, some members spoke in favor even though they regarded the executive's withdrawal power as already well established. One was George Chamberlain (D-Ore.), a former state attorney general, who said his "only regret" was that the "power has not been more frequently and fully used in the past" to control Congress's sometimes "improvident" legislation affecting the public lands.[5]

Not all members favored the bill. Senator Weldon Heyburn of Idaho, Roosevelt's and Pinchot's nemesis, called the proposal "socialistic." First-term congressman Edward Taylor (D-Colo.) complained that bill gave the president the power to "nullify all of our public-land laws whenever he pleases," and that authority would, he warned, "create a permanent federal landed estate" likely to put much of the West "under the control of federal bureaus." Taylor foresaw part of the future, because Franklin Delano Roosevelt used the withdrawal authority to do just that a quarter century later. What he did not anticipate was that his own mind would change to favor keeping the remaining unreserved arid public lands in U.S. ownership. In fact, FDR took action only after Taylor, still serving in the House, laid the basis for it by steering the Taylor Grazing Act through Congress in 1934.

Although congressional discussions of the bill extended over many days, the outcome was never in doubt. The fears voiced by the likes of Heyburn and

Taylor fell on deaf ears; indeed, they were made to mostly empty chambers. On June 25, 1910, President Taft signed the Pickett Act into law.[6]

THE PICKETT ACT AND ITS IMPLICATIONS

The Pickett Act was a nearly complete victory for advocates of public land reservations. Its core provision allowed the president, "at any time in his discretion," to "temporarily withdraw from settlement, location, sale, or entry any of the public lands of the United States," and to "reserve" them for "public purposes to be specified in the orders of withdrawals."

The adverb "temporarily" meant little because that same sentence went on to make clear that "such withdrawals or reservations shall remain in force until revoked by him or by an Act of Congress." A Pickett Act withdrawal could last for eternity, in other words, unless a president or Congress revoked it. In 1912, for example, President Taft made a Pickett Act withdrawal in Oregon (one of the six states covered by the 1907 Fulton amendment forbidding the president from making new forest reserves) in order to give Congress the opportunity to enact a bill to put the withdrawn lands in a national forest. More than a dozen years later, even though Congress had still taken no action on the idea, a federal court of appeals had no difficulty ruling that the Taft withdrawal remained in effect.[7]

The Pickett Act gave the president the authority to reserve *all* public lands, not just those "wholly or in part covered with timber or undergrowth," as section 24 of the 1891 forest reserve legislation had provided. And it gave the president the power to reserve those lands for "public purposes" that the president would determine, in contrast to the somewhat more limiting purposes that Congress specified in the Organic Act of 1897—"to improve and protect the forest," to secure "favorable conditions of water flows, and to furnish a continuous supply of timber."

Indeed, the Pickett Act was so broad that it practically nullified the Fulton amendment, which Congress had put into law a little more than three years earlier. To allow members who voted for both the Fulton amendment and the Pickett Act to save some face, the Pickett Act included a proviso that no "forest reserve" should be created or enlarged in those six states (plus California, which the Pickett Act added to the list) except by an act of Congress. There was much less to the proviso than met the eye. All it meant was that while the president now had nearly unlimited authority to reserve public lands in those states, the same as he did everywhere else, in those states the president could not formally designate the withdrawn lands as "forest reserves."

The Pickett Act did include one meaningful limit, thanks to the political power of the metal-mining industry. Any lands withdrawn under it would "at all times be open to exploration, discovery, occupation, and purchase" under the Mining Law of 1872 with regard to "minerals *other than* coal, oil, gas, and phosphates." In 1912, Congress narrowed this exception down to "metalliferous minerals"—metals such as copper, gold, and silver.[8]

The Pickett Act left open the validity of withdrawals made before it was enacted, so Taft reissued his pre–Pickett Act withdrawals of millions of acres of public lands almost immediately after signing the legislation into law. Some three months earlier, however, prospectors had filed mining claims on public lands in Wyoming subject to Taft's withdrawal order of 1909, and later sold their claims to the Midwest Oil Company, which extracted about fifty thousand barrels of oil from the land. The United States sued Midwest Oil to recover the value of the oil extracted, arguing that Taft's withdrawal meant that the claims were invalid. Midwest Oil countered by arguing that the 1909 withdrawal, lacking the explicit sanction of Congress when it was done, exceeded presidential authority and was unconstitutional.

In a decision issued in 1915, the U.S. Supreme Court ruled against Midwest Oil, with three justices dissenting. The majority found Taft's withdrawal of 1909 lawful because Congress had implicitly approved the executive's long-standing practice of withdrawing particular tracts of public lands from the divestment laws even when it lacked explicit congressional authority to do so. That practice dated back to the earliest days of the nation and had increased in frequency in the years leading up to the Pickett Act, underscoring the executive's role as a maker as well as an executor of public land policy. As the majority put it, the executive's "multitude of orders extending over a long period of time and affecting vast bodies of land in many States and Territories" had withdrawn "large areas in the public interest." These orders were "known to Congress," yet "in not a single instance" had it "disapproved." This long congressional acquiescence "operated as an implied grant of power" that "did not interfere" with any legally vested right.[9] The Pickett Act was a powerful congressional statement about the future of the public lands. It allowed the president, "at any time in his discretion," to reverse a general assumption embodied in many public land laws enacted since early in the nation's history—that a primary thrust of public land policy was to transfer ownership to states or private entities. Now, going forward, the executive branch would have nearly unlimited authority (subject to being overruled by Congress) to keep lands in public ownership and to specify the purposes for doing so.

Of course, having such broad power and exercising it were not the same thing. Politically powerful interests like the fossil fuel and hydroelectric industries could be counted on to resist executive withdrawals that threatened their interests. But the Pickett Act gave the executive an important means of checking their power and persuading Congress to reform public land laws that had outlived their usefulness.

Although the Pickett Act gave the president the power to withdraw some or all of the remaining unreserved public lands from homesteading, the Jeffersonian idea that public lands ought to be used to promote modest, family-sized farms still packed a good deal of political punch. Another two decades passed before that idea finally lost its grip, and then only when it finally came up hard against the most arid and rugged western public lands, and when the livestock industry that operated on many of those lands faced ruin from overgrazing, punishing drought, and economic hard times.

The Pickett Act did not, then, bring an abrupt end to the idea that the national government might divest itself of ownership of public lands that lay outside national forests and other reservations. In fact, over the next couple of decades, well over 100 million acres of public land were privatized in the lower forty-eight states, although the United States retained ownership of the minerals in most of them. Nevertheless, by confirming and leaving nearly unfettered the executive's authority to end large-scale divestments, the Pickett Act brought that end clearly into view.

THE TAFT ADMINISTRATION'S RESERVATIONS
OF PUBLIC LAND

In his message to Congress in January 1910, Taft noted that the amount of public lands outside national forests that had significant stands of trees was now "comparatively small." He established only one national forest during his tenure, the 300,000-acre Santa Rosa National Forest in Nevada, in April 1911, and the next year he added nearly 400,000 acres to the Superior National Forest in northern Minnesota. Generally more comfortable with fine-tuning than taking bold action, Taft adjusted the boundaries of a number of national forests that Roosevelt had created. Mostly this was done to exclude areas with agricultural potential. (Congress attached a rider to the agricultural appropriation bill in 1912 that encouraged such adjustments.) He also reversed all the additions to national forests that Roosevelt had made from Indian reservations in 1909. As a result of these and other actions, the total area of national forests actually shrank by a few million acres while Taft was in office.[10]

In 1911, asserting that public lands outside the national forests that were a livestock-grazing commons were being "destroyed," Taft's second Interior secretary, Walter Fisher, revived the Roosevelt-Pinchot proposal to bring that grazing under control through a leasing system. (He proposed to put the Interior Department, not the Agriculture Department, in control.) Fisher asserted that livestock operators were "coming more and more to the conviction that their own interests would be better subserved by leasing law." As before, some livestock interests favored a leasing system, but also as before, it went nowhere, largely because of opposition from homestead advocates.[11]

The Taft administration moved with some vigor to prevent large grazing enterprises from monopolizing arid public lands by controlling access to scarce water resources. This concern had led Congress to enact the Unlawful Inclosures Act in 1885. It had also led Congress to insist, when in 1897 it authorized livestock enterprises to build reservoirs on unoccupied and unreserved public lands to water their animals, that these reservoir sites remain in public ownership and be held "open to the free use of any person desiring to water animals of any kind." Once the Pickett Act confirmed a broad executive power to reserve public lands for "public purposes," the General Land Office began identifying and reserving from divestment public lands containing springs and other water sources. Within a few years nearly 200,000 acres had been so reserved.[12]

Only one national park was established during Taft's term—Glacier, in northwestern Montana along the Canadian border. It had a long and complicated history. In the early 1880s, Senator George Edmunds (R-Vt.) introduced legislation to protect the public lands in the mountains contributing headwaters to the Missouri and Columbia Rivers. In 1885, George Bird Grinnell began visiting the region both to hunt and to investigate conditions on the reservation where the Blackfeet Indians had been confined in 1883–84. His subsequent articles in *Forest and Stream* and the *Century* drew attention to the area's natural beauty, and he eventually promoted the establishment of a national park.[13]

In 1895, as prospecting for minerals was increasing and as funds the tribe had received from an earlier land cession were dwindling, the commissioner of Indian affairs asked Grinnell to help negotiate a further land cession from the Blackfeet. In an agreement approved by Congress in 1896, the Indians sold lands in the area to the United States for $1.5 million and retained the right to hunt and fish on them as long as they remained publicly owned and "unoccupied." Grinnell, having decades earlier seen the Black Hills wrested from the Sioux after a gold rush, had a legitimate concern that something similar might happen here, although he also engaged in what his biographer called "wishful thinking" in presuming that the area had little value for the Indians. On Washington's Birthday the next year, President Cleveland established a forest reserve in the area that included lands the tribe ceded, but also provided that the "rights and privileges" that the Blackfeet had earlier reserved on those lands should be "in no way infringed or modified."[14]

Legislation to bestow national-park status on what Grinnell had labeled the "Crown of the Continent" began to advance in Congress in the Roosevelt administration, with the Interior and Agriculture Departments competing for control. Illustrating that the national-park concept was still somewhat elastic, Senator Thomas Carter of Montana introduced two different Glacier National Park bills. One would have prohibited all commodity use in the park, which was to be managed by the Interior Department. The other, prepared with the help of Pinchot's Forest Service, would have permitted logging, water development, and railroad construction in the park, which was to be administered by the Agriculture Department.

In 1908, the Senate approved a version of the latter bill. In the House, it was amended to allow irrigation projects as well, but the Sixtieth Congress adjourned in March 1909 without taking final action. In the next Congress, a proposal to have the State of Montana administer the park was beaten back with the argument that because Canada had established its fourth national park just across the international boundary in 1895, a state-administered park would make it harder to establish a binational park that straddled the international border. (The U.S. and Canada approved a binational park there in 1932.)[15]

Finally, in May 1910, Congress sent a hybrid bill to President Taft, who signed it into law. It established a 1-million-acre national park to be administered by the Interior Department, but like the legislation establishing Mount Rainier National Park eleven years earlier, it was shot through with compromises to development interests. Thus, while it directed the Interior secretary to adopt regulations providing for the "preservation of the park in a state of nature," and "for the care and protection of the fish and game" within its boundaries, it authorized the Reclamation Service to build irrigation projects within its borders, and the Interior secretary to grant rights-of-way for railroads, to issue leases for up to twenty years for summerhouses, and to sell dead and downed timber.[16]

Although the legislation proved not to be a lasting prototype for preserving scenic grandeur, the park was almost instantly popular, facilitated by convenient access to the Great Northern Railroad, which ran along its southern boundary and whose president, Louis W. Hill, was a champion of the park. In 1912, it attracted more than six thousand visitors, more than triple the number who went to Yosemite.[17]

Taft established ten national monuments, in the process showing the variety of "objects of historic or scientific interest" that qualified for protection under the Antiquities Act. Most of the lands he protected as monuments had previously been open to divestment laws. Within three weeks of taking office, he established the Navajo National Monument to preserve forty-acre plots of land on the Navajo Reservation in Arizona that contained "prehistoric cliff dwellings, pueblo and other ruins and relics" of "extraordinary" interest. Because these had not been located with precision, the proclamation originally covered an area of more than 100,000 acres, but that was reduced in 1912 to a few hundred acres. In 1909, Taft established Mukuntuweap National Monument, covering 16,000 acres of scenic red-rock desert canyons in southwestern Utah, the most prominent of which was later described by Interior secretary Franklin Lane as "Yosemite in oils." (John Wesley Powell had given the area this name, apparently garbling a Paiute word of unknown meaning.) Its establishment was strongly supported by Senator Reed Smoot of Utah, who a few years later led an effort in Congress to significantly enlarge it and make it a national park. In the process, the Indian-derived name was changed to "Zion," a term frequently used by Mormons who had settled in the vicinity.[18]

Rainbow Bridge National Monument reserved a tract of remote public land in southern Utah that contained a huge natural stone arch. The 13,000-acre Colorado National Monument protected spectacular red-rock canyons in the western part of the state, near Grand Junction, ending a five-year campaign led by an indefatigable local eccentric named John Otto. The Big Hole National Monument in Montana protected the site of the largest battle of the Nez Perce War in 1877, where the legendary Chief Joseph led the Indians on an unsuccessful trek to reach Canada rather than accept relocation from lands promised them by treaties with the United States in 1855 and 1863. Big Hole, on land controlled by the War Department, was the first western battlefield national monument, an ironic twist on the concern with protecting artifacts of Native American culture that had fueled enactment of the Antiquities Act. Sitka National Monument preserved the remains of a Russian settlement on an island in southeastern Alaska. Gran Quivira National Monument protected the ruins of an ancient Indian pueblo and an uncompleted Spanish mission in New Mexico. Two of Taft's proclamations preserved limestone caves in Wyoming and Oregon.[19]

One of Taft's monuments illustrated the Antiquities Act's usefulness in providing nearly instant protection to threatened, publicly owned resources. The so-called Devils Postpile in the Upper San Joaquin River watershed in California's Sierra Nevada contained picturesque sixty-foot-tall basalt columns formed when an ancient lava lake rapidly cooled. Congress had included the unusual geologic feature, whose glacier-polished top has the appearance of a tiled floor, in Yosemite National Park in 1890. In 1905, mining, grazing, and water interests persuaded Congress to cut the area out of the park and restore it to the Sierra Forest Reserve. When water developers unveiled a plan to dam the Middle Fork of the Upper San Joaquin and destroy the formation in the process, John Muir and others protested, and in July 1911, President Taft put a stop to the plan by declaring the area a national monument.[20]

The day before he left office, in 1913, Taft made a Roosevelt-like gesture by reserving nearly 3 million acres of public land from Unimak and Sannak Islands west to Attu Island in the Alaska Territory's Aleutian Island chain. In his last few days in office four years before, Roosevelt had established five wildlife reservations there totaling less than 100,000 acres. Taft had added three more reservations in 1912 before deciding to protect all the remaining islands in the archipelago as a "preserve and breeding ground for native birds" as well as "for the propagation of reindeer and fur-bearing animals, and for the encouragement and development of the fisheries." Jurisdiction was divided between the Department of Agriculture (for terrestrial species) and the Department of Commerce and Labor, as it was then called (for marine species).[21]

CHAPTER THIRTY-FIVE

National Forests Become National with Enactment of the Weeks Act

AS THE MOVEMENT TO RESERVE public lands in the West was gaining strength in the 1880s, a parallel movement began to develop in the eastern part of the country. New England had seen logging for generations, but in the decades after the Civil War, forest clearing proceeded on an industrial scale and penetrated the South. With few attempts made at reforestation, the ill effects that George Perkins Marsh warned about—erosion, water pollution, and increased risk of flooding—were manifesting themselves.[1]

Because nearly all the lands were in private ownership, both politics and law stood in the way of trying to mitigate logging's detrimental effects by regulation. Private landowners resisted controls and had political clout, and courts were not very welcoming to the government asserting regulatory authority over activities on private property. On the other hand, after clearing timber from their land, owners were often more than willing to sell it to the government; indeed, it was not uncommon for them simply to relinquish title to cutover land to state or local governments rather than pay property taxes.

Toward the end of the nineteenth century, a couple of prosperous eastern states took steps to conserve forests. New York spent several million dollars to buy more than 1 million acres in the Adirondacks. Pennsylvania, whose concern on the matter dated from the time of William Penn (*sylvania* being Latin for "forest land"), launched a program in 1895 that resulted in the state acquiring nearly half a million acres of mostly cutover land to reestablish forests and restore watershed function.

Proposals to have the national government acquire lands in eastern mountains emerged from both New England and the southern Appalachians. Their champions had the same mix of objectives as those advocating for forest reserves in the West—protecting water supplies and water quality, reducing soil erosion and the risk of damaging floods, providing for future timber needs, and preserving scenery and outdoor recreational opportunities.

Calls to establish a national park to protect southern Appalachian forests began in the mid-1880s. The North Carolina legislature endorsed the idea in 1893. In late 1899, the Appalachian National Park Association was organized in Asheville, North Carolina, to preserve forests "as a heritage and blessing to unborn generations." In early 1900, the American Forestry Association (AFA) endorsed "the establishment of National Parks and Forest Reservations" along the "crest of the southern Alleghenies." By that point, Gifford Pinchot, who had managed more than 100,000 acres of mostly cutover land that George Washington Vanderbilt II had acquired near Asheville, had succeeded Bernhard Fernow as chief of the Division of Forestry in the Department of Agriculture. Pinchot helped shift the movement's objective from establishing a park for scenery and recreation toward creating a forest reserve that would permit logging.[2]

In May 1900, Congress authorized Agriculture secretary James Wilson to "investigate the forest conditions" in the southern Appalachians. His report, submitted early the next year, endorsed a program of U.S. acquisitions for forest reserves. It noted that the region contained some of the best hardwood forests in the nation, that land was available at a good price, and that management costs could be covered by timber sales. It also highlighted the beauty of the region, which contained the largest and highest mountain mass east of the Rockies. The report included photographs underscoring the connection between heavy logging and flooding and estimated that recent floods had caused millions of dollars of damage.[3]

By the end of 1901, North Carolina and four other southern states had formally consented to the United States acquiring land for such a program, and Theodore Roosevelt pledged his support in his first annual message to Congress. In 1902, bills were introduced into both houses empowering the secretary of Agriculture to spend up to $10 million on forestland acquisitions in the region.[4]

Then the effort stalled. More than three dozen similar bills were introduced in Congress over the next several years, and while some were reported out of committee, and one passed the Senate, none gained final approval. Opposition came from several quarters—from fiscal conservatives, from those who thought the matter should be left to the states, from some who doubted the national government's constitutional authority to undertake the program, and from some in the West who saw it as competition for federal dollars, a fear stoked when one such bill was referred to as the "twin brother" of the Reclamation Act.

Meanwhile, a parallel movement to acquire and preserve forested watersheds in the White Mountains of New Hampshire was also developing, fueled by criticism of logging practices that damaged watersheds and exacerbated flood damage in the late 1890s. In early 1901, the Society for the Protection of New Hampshire Forests was formed, and it helped launch a campaign that led to acquisition bills being introduced in Congress. One, reported out of the Senate Committee on Agriculture and Forestry in 1904, would have authorized the Agriculture secretary to purchase up to 1 million acres to establish a forest reserve in the White Mountains. The committee report called the area the "Switzerland of America," noted that it offered "unrivaled opportunities for rest and recreation" to more than 10 million people "within a day's easy travel," and cited the role of healthy forests in reducing flood risk. While state governments in New York and Pennsylvania had forest acquisition programs, the committee expressed the view that the national government had to spearhead such a program in the White Mountains because New Hampshire was relatively poor and could not feasibly call on the downstream states of Massachusetts and Connecticut to contribute to the protection of watersheds upstream, even though they directly benefited.[5]

At that point, advocates in southern Appalachia and New England began to join forces. The influential *Century* magazine asked in 1904: "Almost the whole of the higher Sierra has been reserved: why not reserve the whole of the higher Appalachians?" The movement spread even further—between 1905 and 1908, bills were introduced in Congress to purchase land in the headwaters of the Mississippi in Minnesota, in the Ozarks in Arkansas, and in Texas.[6]

In 1906, the Senate approved a bill to authorize $3 million to buy land in the Appalachian South and the White Mountains. Although its progress was halted by Speaker Joseph Cannon, proponents kept pressing the case. The agricultural appropriations bill that Roosevelt signed into law in March 1907—the one that included the Fulton amendment curtailing the president's power to proclaim new forest reserves in six western states—directed the secretary of Agriculture to examine and report on the purchase of lands for forest reserves in the Appalachian and White Mountains. During the House floor debate,

Frank Mondell complained of what he called the hypocrisy of its southern supporters, those "gallant defenders of State rights" and "strict constructionists of the Constitution" who were, he said, now eager to have the United States acquire and establish jurisdiction over "vast areas of territory" within their borders, leading to "Federal bureaucratic control." Congressmen Charles Littlefield (R-Me.) and Asbury Lever (D-S.C.) responded by turning the hypocrisy charge around, pointing out that federal financial assistance for irrigation projects under the Reclamation Act of 1902 went only to western states.[7]

A few days after the bill became law, a disastrous flood hit the Monongahela River valley, inundating Pittsburgh, taking lives, devastating agricultural land, and causing more than $100 million in damage. In its wake, the West Virginia legislature asked Congress to purchase flood-ruined lands for reforestation. Several months later, Agriculture secretary Wilson issued his report. It recommended the immediate purchase of 5 million acres in the southern Appalachians and 600,000 acres in the White Mountains, at an estimated total cost of $21 million, and suggested that, ultimately, 23 million acres in the South and 2 million acres in New England should be protected.[8]

The coalition supporting federal acquisition of forestland in the eastern mountains steadily expanded to include such disparate interests as retail lumber dealers, carriage builders, the Daughters of the American Revolution, the National Federation of Women's Clubs, and even the U.S. Hay Fever Association. Logging enterprises in the region came to perceive that they would do better by selling their cutover lands to the government rather than simply abandoning them. More easterners came to grasp that western states were economically helped by the national forests being established in their region. The budding hydropower industry, which was seeking to dam mountain streams, realized that dealing with a single government could be more advantageous than dealing with a multiplicity of private landowners.[9]

At this juncture, a relatively junior member of Congress joined the fray, and his influence would prove pivotal. John W. Weeks (R-Mass.) had graduated from the U.S. Naval Academy, spent two years at sea, worked as a civil engineer in Florida, and then made a fortune in banking in Boston. After serving as the mayor of Newton, Massachusetts, he was elected to Congress in 1905. Weeks, who had grown up in New Hampshire, still spent summers in its White Mountains. He developed a good relationship with Speaker Cannon, who in 1907 put him on the Agriculture Committee and told him that if he could "frame a forestry bill" that was acceptable to him "as a business man," Cannon would let it go to the floor.[10]

Now considerably on the defensive, opponents of the reserves relied heavily on the argument that Congress lacked the constitutional authority to enact such legislation. For opponents from the West, the constitutional issue was a double-edged sword, because the same argument could be made regarding programs popular in their region. A Supreme Court decision in 1907 cast doubt on the constitutionality of the Reclamation Act of 1902, insofar as it authorized the United States to build projects to supply water to irrigate privately owned lands in the West.[11]

Eventually, a consensus formed on Capitol Hill around the idea that the Constitution's clause empowering Congress to regulate commerce "among the several states" authorized the U.S. acquisition of lands that had a direct and substantial connection with navigation, upon which a great deal of interstate commerce depended. If the United States could dredge rivers and harbors to improve navigability—a popular program that Congress had supported for years—it should, so the reasoning went, be able to take measures that, as George Perkins Marsh had pointed out decades before, could reduce erosion from the mountains, thereby lessening the need to dredge.

Hearings held in early 1909 by the House Agriculture Committee began to loosen the gridlock, and John Weeks played an increasingly important role. Democratic governor Hoke Smith of Georgia, who had been involved in establishing forest reserves in the West while serving as Interior secretary under Cleveland in the 1890s, emerged as a leader among southern politicians promoting the legislation. He was joined by former governors of Oregon and California, who cited the popularity and success of forest reservations in their states, as well as by the current governors of Connecticut, Louisiana, Massachusetts, Minnesota, and South Carolina, some Republicans and some Democrats. In a notable demonstration of the capacity of public lands to unite historic adversaries, Republican governor Curtis Guild of Massachusetts suggested it was the first time that governors from the South and New England had ever appeared jointly before Congress "to ask for something for the common welfare of the United States."[12]

After these hearings, the Agriculture Committee adjusted the bill to emphasize the connection to navigation, and to include a provision to pay for the land purchases with revenues from existing national forests. Its report described this feature as a way to promote "national equity," a kind of updated version of the "distribution" policy advocated by older states before the Civil War. Had the United States sold public lands in the western national forests, instead of retaining them in part to facilitate the U.S. construction of irrigation projects to benefit the West, the revenue derived from those sales would have benefited all the states. That made it fair, the report maintained, for the government to invest revenues derived from western national forests in an equivalent "conservation enterprise" in the mountains of the South and East.[13]

Fulfilling his earlier commitment to Weeks, Speaker Cannon permitted the bill to come to the House floor. On March 1, 1909, three days before Roosevelt left office, the House approved what had come to be known as the Weeks Act by a vote of 157–147. The vote reflected regional divisions, with New England and the South in favor and the West solidly opposed because of its "distribution" feature. This split signaled that proponents still had more work to do, because westerners had sufficient clout to prevent the Senate from taking up the bill before Congress adjourned.[14]

At first, the incoming Taft administration did not press the new Congress to resume work on the legislation, but that changed after Taft dismissed Pinchot in early 1910. Pinchot's successor as chief forester, Henry Graves, wasted no time in expressing support for the legislation, perhaps trying to reduce the political damage inflicted by Pinchot's firing. Around the same time, in an effort to reduce western opposition, Weeks scrapped the idea of earmarking national forest revenues to pay for the acquisitions. This modified version passed the House by nineteen votes on June 24, 1910, after which Speaker Cannon congratulated the victors by doffing his hat and saying, "Well, gentlemen, you have my scalp."[15]

Outside events once again intervened before the bill was voted on by the Senate. In the dramatic "Big Burn" during the late summer of 1910, giant wildfires moved through millions of acres of drought-stricken forests in Washington, Idaho, and Montana, riveting national attention on forest conditions. Combined with Weeks's modification regarding how the acquisitions would be paid for, the disaster effectively ended the opposition of western senators, only one of which voted no when the Senate approved the legislation by a wide margin on February 15, 1911.

The Weeks Act was the first major national-forest legislation enacted as a stand-alone law; the forest-reserve bills that Congress passed in 1891, 1897, and 1907 were components of large legislative packages. Like support for forest reserves in the West, the coalition of interests that pushed the Weeks Act through Congress was thoroughly bipartisan.

Reaction to the vote varied. The *San Francisco Chronicle* played the provincial victim card: "The nation robs the West for the benefit of the East." In his *Annual Report* for 1911, Interior secretary Walter Fisher, who had succeeded

Richard Ballinger in March, drew a much different conclusion. The program to purchase forested or cutover lands not adapted to agricultural uses showed, he said, "how unwise it is for the government to dispose of such lands to private individuals." President Taft cautiously described the measure as "authorizing experimental forestation on a large scale."[16]

THE PARTICULARS

The Weeks Act gave the secretary of Agriculture the authority to "examine, locate, and recommend for purchase such lands as in his judgment may be necessary to the regulation of the flow of navigable streams," and to proceed with such purchases if certain conditions were met. Lands so acquired were to be "permanently reserved, held, and administered as national forest lands" just like other lands in the system. The act was not geographically limited, although the widely shared expectation was that the first purchases would be in the southern Appalachians and the White Mountains, and in fact they were. The program eventually expanded across many other states.[17]

One of the preconditions for purchases was for the U.S. Geological Survey to determine that "control of such lands will promote or protect the navigation of streams on whose watersheds they lie." It was hardly a surprise that the USGS apparently never failed to make such a determination. It was not difficult to show some connection—which the act did not require to be quantified—between the use of uplands and the navigability of downstream waters. Once Congress authorized and funded the acquisitions, government scientists had no incentive to put roadblocks in its path.

Another precondition was to secure the consent of the legislature of the state where lands were to be purchased. This feature was not constitutionally required, and in many states it turned out to be a formality—indeed, by the time Congress approved the act, nine states from Alabama to Maine had enacted the necessary legislation. This action too was not surprising. The acquisition and, particularly, the restoration of cutover lands tended to have significant local benefits, and state and local governments hardly minded that Uncle Sam would foot the bill. This was not to say that every state was supportive; for example, Maryland initially gave its consent but withdrew it some years later. Pennsylvania limited its consent to a specific part of the state, and Wisconsin capped the acreage that the United States could acquire.[18]

The United States did not need to find willing sellers, for it could acquire land by exercising its general power of condemnation or eminent domain. The General Condemnation Act of 1888 permitted any federal agency authorized to acquire land for "public uses" to use condemnation whenever it was deemed "necessary or advantageous to the Government." It was rare, however, for the United States to acquire lands under the Weeks Act over the objection of a land-owner. Usually there were more willing sellers than there were appropriated funds from Congress, and condemnation could be controversial. This pattern of rarely resorting to condemnation held true for practically all future programs to acquire land into U.S. ownership. Even when the government instituted condemnation proceedings, it was often done by agreement with the land-owner, simply to determine the amount of "just compensation" owed when the parties could not agree.[19]

The act allowed the United States to purchase less than complete title to land in situations where the purposes of the act would not be compromised. Partial title came about in one of two ways. First, the seller might reserve "minerals," "merchantable timber," and the like (including, by an amendment adopted in 1913, "easements"). These became known as "reserved" interests. Second, sometimes the seller lacked, and thus could not convey, complete title because minerals, timber, or easements were owned by someone who was not party to the transaction with the United States. These third-party interests came to be known as "outstanding" interests.[20]

It became quite common for the United States to acquire less than complete title when implementing the Weeks Act. Doing so facilitated acquisi-tions and, at least in theory, lowered the purchase price by the value of the "reserved" or "outstanding" property interests not being bought. The result was often a kind of mirror image of the program that Congress had authorized regarding public lands in the West starting in 1909, whereby public land could be transferred to homesteader-farmers while the United States reserved owner-ship of minerals.

"Splitting" full title into partial "estates" became, from this point forward, an increasingly common feature of public land policy in general. Its downside was the possibility of future controversy in the event of disagreement between the owners of the separate property interests. In the case of the Weeks Act, for example, the United States often purchased land without purchasing the right to any coal that might be found on it. If the coal owner mined it, especially by the increasingly common technique of surface mining (rather than tunneling), it could greatly impair or even destroy the value of the U.S. interest. The Weeks Act sought to head off future conflicts involving "reserved" interests by directing the parties to negotiate, and include in the deed of conveyance, "rules and regulations" prescribing how those interests could be used. That approach was not available for "outstanding" interests, because they were held by someone other than the seller. Several court decisions show how complicated it can be to resolve these conflicts.[21]

The Weeks Act included a revenue-sharing provision resembling the one that Congress had adopted in 1905 for the forest reserves. It called for five percent of the revenue that the United States derived from lands it acquired under the act to be sent to the state where the lands were located, "for the benefit of the public schools and public roads of the county or counties in which such national forest is situated." As with the 1905 legislation, it did not take long for Congress to make the distribution more generous; in 1914, it increased the state share eightfold, to 40 percent.[22]

THE WEEKS ACT'S IMPACT ON PUBLIC LAND POLICY

An editorial in *American Forestry* in 1911 described the Weeks Act as making "our national forest policy really national." A landmark in public land as well as forest policy, its long journey through the political process helped strengthen the bipartisan national consensus favoring the federal acquisition of land throughout the nation to protect forests and the values they serve. More of the lands eventually acquired under the Weeks Act had already been logged than was typically the case with public lands put into forest reserves in the West. For that reason, the Weeks Act could be said to be the first significant environmental-restoration program ever undertaken by the national government.[23]

The Weeks Act also demonstrated the suppleness of the Constitution. Finally, it showed how the political system could work successfully in allowing states—even, less than a half century after the bloody Civil War, states with a history of fierce resistance to any federal presence—to invite the U.S. government to buy and hold substantial amounts of land within their borders. To date, it has made possible the acquisition of some 20 million acres in more than fifty national forests and national grasslands in forty-one states and Puerto Rico.

CHAPTER THIRTY-SIX

Public Lands at the End of the Age of Theodore Roosevelt

TWO MONTHS AFTER THE WEEKS ACT was signed into law, the Supreme Court issued two significant decisions on the same day, both confirming that the U.S. Constitution gave the national government broad authority to regulate the activities of private industries operating on public lands. As before, the Court's action was in considerable contrast to its rulings in this era that showed a more skeptical attitude toward the national government's constitutional power to regulate economic affairs where public lands were not involved.[1]

Both cases grew out of resistance to grazing regulations in the national forests. One began in California when a federal grand jury indicted Pierre Grimaud and J. P. Carajous for criminal trespass for pasturing sheep without a permit in the Sierra National Forest. As in a number of national forests, livestock grazing was then its primary use, but its greatest resource was water. Downstream water users persuaded the Interior Department to ban sheep grazing on the forest even before its transfer to the Agriculture Department in 1905, and the Forest Service had continued the ban. Trespassing sheep remained a problem, however, consuming forage that the Forest Service had allotted to cattle grazers by permit. The Sierra forest supervisor, William Greeley, who later became the third chief of the Forest Service, described how the sheepherders played "hide-and-seek with the forest rangers all summer," bringing the entire "system of controlled grazing in disrepute."[2]

Grimaud and Carajous were itinerant Basques, but once they were charged, according to Greeley, "top-flight attorneys from San Francisco" who represented "some of the largest land companies in the state" suddenly "magically appeared" as their lawyers to challenge the Forest Service's authority to regulate and charge a fee for livestock grazing. The argument had superficial appeal, because the Organic Act of 1897 had not specifically mentioned livestock grazing. The herders' lawyers also argued that if the act were interpreted to give the Forest Service the authority to regulate grazing, Congress had violated the Constitution's separation of powers by handing the executive branch a kind of blank check to regulate without any congressional guidance as to its exercise, allowing the executive to "legislate," as it were, when the Constitution reserved that power to Congress. That argument had been raised in several previous grazing-trespass cases, and the lower courts had split, some ruling for the government and some for the grazers.[3]

In May 1911, the Court unanimously ruled in favor of the government in an opinion by Joseph Lamar, a recent Taft appointee. Congress's failure to mention livestock grazing was inconsequential, Lamar wrote, because the Organic Act explicitly vested the executive with power to regulate the "occupancy and use" of the national forests, and it could not be doubted that defendants and their sheep were occupying and using the lands. The Organic Act also required anyone exercising what Lamar pointedly called the "privilege" of using the national forests to comply with applicable rules and regulations or be subject to punishment. By these means, Lamar wrote, Congress had "curtailed and qualified" the "implied license" to use public lands that livestock operators had taken advantage of before the forest reserves were established.[4]

The Court also rejected the sheepherders' argument that Congress had unconstitutionally delegated legislative power to the executive branch. It was only in the 1890s that the Court had begun to entertain the idea that the Constitution might give it the authority to invalidate an act of Congress for this reason. As Justice Lamar noted, the Court had never seriously questioned whether Congress could give the executive the power "to fill up the details" in carrying out its general laws, quoting a decision by the Court's legendary chief justice John Marshall in 1825. Giving the executive broad discretion in administering the law was particularly appropriate regarding livestock grazing on public lands because, Lamar observed, details could vary considerably from case to case: "[What] might be harmless in one forest might be harmful in another. What might be injurious at one stage of timber growth, or at one season of the year, might not be so at another."[5]

Finally, Lamar addressed whether the Forest Service could charge a fee for allowing livestock to graze on public land. The Organic Act did not specifically mention fees, but the 1905 act transferring the reserves to the Agriculture Department did, indirectly, when it established a revolving fund supplied by "all money received from," among other things, "the use of any land or resources of said forest reserves." The Agriculture Department's grazing fee—which had, Lamar explained, been "fixed to prevent excessive grazing, and thereby protect the young growth and native grasses from destruction, and to make a slight income with which to meet the expenses of management"—was thus within the authority that Congress had given the executive.[6]

The second decision the Court handed down that day was also a sweeping affirmation of U.S. authority to regulate private activities on the national forests. Fred Light had homesteaded land in Colorado's Roaring Fork Valley a couple of miles from the boundary of a forest reserve that Theodore Roosevelt had established in 1905. Between Light's land and the national forest was other, unreserved, so-called public domain land. When Light turned out his five hundred cattle in the spring, they moved across the unfenced public domain land and grazed in the national forest all summer. Light refused to apply to the Forest Service for a grazing permit, and in 1908 the United States sued him for trespass.[7]

Livestock associations and the Colorado legislature supplied funds to pay Light's attorneys, who made a bold argument. Section 24 of the General Revision Act was unconstitutional, they maintained, because "the public lands are held in trust for the people of the several states," and because Congress could not—either on its own or by empowering the executive to do so—constitutionally withdraw large amounts of those lands "from settlement" without the consent of the pertinent state. They also argued that state law, not federal law, applied to the use of public lands by Light's cattle. At that time, Colorado law immunized livestock owners from trespass claims, in effect requiring rural landowners to fence out others' livestock, rather than holding livestock owners liable for failing to prevent their animals from wandering onto the property of others.

The Court rejected Light's arguments in another unanimous decision written by Justice Lamar. Regarding the assertion that public lands were held in trust for the people of the states, Lamar turned the proposition around, quoting a case from 1890: "All the public lands of the nation are held in trust for the people of the whole country," and then adding, "It is not for the courts to say how that trust shall be administered. That is for Congress to determine." Indeed, the United States "can prohibit absolutely or fix the terms on which its property may be used," Lamar wrote. "As it can withhold or reserve the land, it can do so indefinitely."[8]

The government's past "failure to object" to the use of public lands by livestock "did not confer any vested right" on the livestock owners, because the government could at any time "cancel its tacit consent," which it had done by instituting the permit requirement. Finally, Lamar wrote, the Court's *Camfield* decision in 1897 upholding the Unlawful Inclosures Act had effectively acknowledged that Congress could preempt state law where public lands were concerned. Because Fred Light refused to obtain a permit from the Forest Service, he could be prohibited from turning out his cattle "under circumstances which showed that he expected and intended that they would go" onto the national forest to graze.[9]

POLITICAL CONSTRAINTS ON U.S. REGULATORY AUTHORITY REMAINED

The Court's decisions in *Grimaud* and *Light* were unqualified endorsements of Congress's broad authority over whether and how public land could be used. They made it clearer than ever that there were no constitutional obstacles to Congress or the executive deciding to hold on to and manage large tracts of public land for various public purposes. Moreover, by confirming that Congress could delegate much of that authority to the executive branch, the *Grimaud* decision removed any doubt about the constitutionality of the Pickett Act, which Congress had enacted the year before. The bottom-line message was that the courts would leave it largely up to the executive branch—subject to being overruled by Congress—to decide whether particular tracts of public land would be maintained in public ownership, and if so, how they would be managed.

The Court's decisions did not disturb the political constraints that often operated to limit the government's regulation of private uses of public lands. Although it had broad authority to go after trespassing grazers, the Forest Service continued to give livestock operators, like miners, considerable latitude in using the national forests.[10]

In both mining and grazing, tradition and expectations played a huge role. Both industries had firmly established themselves on the public lands in fact, even if not in law, before the U.S. government began to assert control and before Congress gave the executive branch firm management direction. Both industries were well connected locally and in Congress, as shown by rancher-members such as Wyoming's Congressman Frank Mondell and Senator

Francis Warren, and senators with deep roots in mining such as Nevada's William Stewart and Colorado's Simon Guggenheim. That kind of political power guaranteed that any executive branch regulation of either industry would be closely scrutinized.

But the era when the national government would be largely passive regarding the private use of public lands was fading, symbolized by Henry Teller's representation of Fred Light in his losing cause. Teller was then in the twilight of a long career, having moved to the Colorado Territory in 1861 at the age of thirty-one, built a successful law practice representing mining and railroad interests, and become one of Colorado's first senators upon its admission to the union in 1876. After one term, he served as Interior secretary from 1882 to 1885 under President Arthur, and then returned to the Senate for four more terms, retiring in early 1909. Along the way, he switched parties, leaving the Republicans in 1892 to become a Silver Republican and then a Democrat in 1903.

Teller's public land record was mixed. He was usually friendly to livestock, railroad, and mining interests, but he also occasionally spoke out against abuses of divestment laws, was a strong supporter of the civil service system, and supported the establishment of Mesa Verde National Park. By the end of his Senate career, however, he had become a strident opponent of forest reserves and many of Roosevelt's public lands policies. In his last year in the Senate, he complained about how the people had "gone wild about the forest reserves," had set loose a "great army" of "caretakers in the forests," and were now pressing to establish similar reserves in the East. Echoing the valedictory remarks of Montana's "Copper King" senator, William Andrews Clark, two years earlier, he denounced the idea that there was "a moral or any other claim upon me to postpone the use of what nature has given me, so that the next generation or generations yet unborn may have an opportunity to get what I myself ought to get."[11]

THE END OF THE AGE OF ROOSEVELT
In early 1912, New Mexico and Arizona became the forty-seventh and forty-eighth states, filling out the continental map and giving the West full representation in Congress. In their enabling acts, Congress followed the precedent it had established in authorizing the admission of Utah in 1894, of doubling the percentage of public lands that the new state would receive for public schools—from two sections in every township to four, or 11 percent of the new state's total area. But the enabling acts also reflected Congress's growing dissatisfaction

with how new states had administered grants of public land, because both acts contained an unprecedented number of detailed, stringent restrictions on how the grants should be used. The enabling acts also followed the long-standard practice of requiring the people of the new states to "forever disclaim all right and title to the public lands within their borders," leaving such lands "under the absolute jurisdiction and control of the Congress of the United States."[12]

On May 15, 1912, Senator Weldon Heyburn offered an amendment to an agricultural appropriations bill that would require the United States to transfer all public lands, whether reserved or unreserved, and including mineral rights, to willing states, with the sole exception of lands "held in connection with actual government use." Heyburn told his colleagues that this move would allow private enterprise to operate with "convenience and efficiency," while being regulated as needed by local government, and save the U.S. government millions of dollars every year. "I am presenting a great question," he said, and expressed confidence that if not now, it "will be the law of the land in the near future." In the discussion that followed, only William Borah (R-Idaho) expressed support for his proposal, and it was eventually ruled out of order. The episode spoke volumes about the dominant mood of Congress and the country as the age of Roosevelt drew to a close. Heyburn died that October.[13]

PART SIX   PUBLIC LAND POLICY BETWEEN THE
ROOSEVELTS, 1913–1933

CHAPTER THIRTY-SEVEN

National Parks Take Center Stage

IN THE 1912 CAMPAIGN FOR THE presidency, public land policy was not an issue. Progressives divided their votes among the three major candidates, including Theodore Roosevelt running on the Progressive Party ticket. Woodrow Wilson won decisively, receiving 42 percent of the popular vote and carrying every state along and west of the Mississippi except Utah, which Taft carried, and California, Washington, South Dakota, and Minnesota, where Roosevelt prevailed.[1]

Wilson, the first Democratic president in sixteen years, had little personal interest in public lands. Much of the attention given the subject during his time in office was spent wrapping up unfinished business from the Roosevelt-Taft era. The relationship between national parks and national forests still needed to be worked out. Congress still needed to develop a workable policy regarding fossil fuel extraction and hydropower projects on public lands, and to decide what to do with the more than 150 million acres of mostly very arid western public lands outside the forest reserves. Although most of these lands remained open to homesteading, only a small portion was suitable for crop farming, even if irrigation water were made available. Most were being grazed by livestock without the government's official approval.

During Wilson's eight years in office, Congress made what proved to be its final effort to privatize public lands through homesteading, this time with the U.S. retaining ownership of the minerals found on them. It also created a durable regime for developing federally owned fossil fuels and a few other minerals through leasing by the Interior Department, and a new, separate regime for exploiting hydropower potential on (as well as off) public lands through a new executive branch agency. While these were each significant, the most prominent public lands accomplishment during Wilson's presidency was the creation of the National Park Service to administer the growing number of parks in what would become a national park system.

THE HETCH HETCHY CONTROVERSY

Wilson named as his Interior secretary Franklin K. Lane, a prominent Progressive who had been San Francisco's city attorney and then served on the Interstate Commerce Commission under Roosevelt and Taft. Lane almost immediately faced a controversy left over from the Roosevelt and Taft administrations.

By 1900, San Francisco, the leading city in the western half of the nation, had outstripped its local water supplies and had begun planning a project to tap high-quality water in the glacier-carved Hetch Hetchy Valley in the Sierra Nevada, 175 miles to the east. The project included a dam that would inundate the valley floor, generate electricity, and store water that would be delivered to the city via a pipeline. Hetch Hetchy, which resembled the fabled Yosemite Valley, twenty miles to its south, had been included in the national park that Congress established in 1890 around Yosemite at the urging of John Muir. Muir's article from 1890 in *Century* magazine extolling the values of the proposed national park around Yosemite had spent pages lauding Hetch Hetchy, calling it a "Yosemite Valley end to end" that could be traversed on foot without "a dull step all the way." Including it in the park could, Muir wrote, allow it to "escape" the "ravages" that had been visited on Yosemite Valley under state stewardship. Although the Interior secretary had the authority to issue the city a right-of-way for the project, Secretary Hitchcock had denied the city's application in 1903 for being "not in keeping with the public interest."[2]

In April 1906, much of San Francisco was destroyed in a major earthquake, and the city's inadequate water system made it difficult to fight the ensuing fires. Riding an outpouring of national sympathy, San Francisco renewed its application. Interior secretary James R. Garfield, who had succeeded Hitchcock in 1907, issued the permit, but stipulated that a smaller natural lake (Eleanor) on another tributary of the Tuolumne River northwest of Hetch Hetchy (but still within the national park) be dammed first, and Hetch Hetchy developed later and only if necessary. John Muir appealed to President

Roosevelt to reverse Garfield's decision, but Roosevelt refused to interfere because, he told Muir, most Californians favored the development.[3]

After Taft took office a few months later, his Interior secretary, Richard Ballinger, after visiting the area with John Muir, withdrew Garfield's approval of Hetch Hetchy on the ground that an enlarged Lake Eleanor would be sufficient to meet the city's needs. His successor, Walter Fisher, took the same position, and Taft, having toured the Yosemite region with Muir in October 1909, refused to intercede.[4]

By the time the Wilson administration took office, the proposed inundation of Hetch Hetchy, now framed as a stark choice between developing or preserving a beautiful national park area, had captured national attention. Interior secretary Lane supported his home city, but the project had become so contentious that congressional approval would be needed to move forward. Prominent figures across the country, including members of Congress from both political parties, weighed in on both sides. Most of the California congressional delegation supported San Francisco, along with the secretary of Agriculture, the Forest Service, Gifford Pinchot (now a private citizen), and the president of Stanford University. The opposition included, besides John Muir, Senators John D. Works (California), Key Pittman (Nevada), and Reed Smoot (Utah), along with former Interior secretaries Noble and Hitchcock, the president of the University of California, Berkeley, and the private Pacific Gas & Electric Company, which opposed public ownership of such projects.[5]

As the battle intensified in 1911, Muir, now seventy-three, worked fifteen hours a day to finish his book on Yosemite, which ended with a spirited defense of Hetch Hetchy. Characteristically putting the struggle in spiritual terms, he railed against the "temple destroyers, devotees of ravaging commercialism" who, with their "perfect contempt for nature," lifted their eyes to "the almighty dollar" rather than the "God of the Mountains." His conclusion became famous: "Dam Hetch Hetchy! As well dam for water tanks the people's cathedrals and churches; for no holier temple has ever been consecrated by the heart of man."[6]

Muir's appeal failed. Congressman John Raker (D-Calif.) introduced legislation in June 1913 to allow San Francisco to use public lands for the project. It passed the House easily, and the Senate by an eighteen-vote margin, but only after James A. Reed (D-Mo.) complained about how the "trivial matter" of putting a reservoir in a small remote area had thrown the entire nation in a "condition of hysteria," which increased in "direct proportion" to the distance from the site. President Wilson signed it into law in December 1913.[7]

THE CAMPAIGN FOR A NATIONAL PARK ORGANIC ACT

What the historian Andrea Wulf called the first "national protest movement on behalf of nature" had a lasting impact on public land policy. Its most immediate effect was to help spur Congress to enact legislation establishing a management framework or organic act for a system of national parks, and a new federal agency, the National Park Service, to operate it.[8]

By this time, the nation had a loose collection of fourteen national parks, each created by an act of Congress, along with nearly two dozen national monuments, each created by presidential proclamation, altogether embracing more than 4 million acres. Most were the responsibility of the Interior Department, but administration was decentralized, with the Interior secretary providing little direction. The Forest Service administered a few national monuments, including large ones at Grand Canyon and Mount Olympus. The army looked after the Civil War battlefield parks as well as helping Interior at Yellowstone, Yosemite, and Sequoia National Parks.

The Roosevelt administration had not been keen on the idea of a national park service, mostly because the turf-conscious Pinchot thought it was "no more needed than two tails to a cat." Pinchot had campaigned to have the larger parks transferred to the care of the Agriculture Department. In May 1910, with Pinchot out, J. Horace McFarland, head of the progressive American Civic Association, suggested to Interior secretary Ballinger that the national parks needed "general, intelligent and logical supervision," and he recruited Frederick Law Olmsted, Jr., son of the legendary landscape architect, to help craft and promote the necessary legislation.[9]

Their assiduous lobbying soon produced results. Before 1910 ended, Ballinger, looking to bolster his conservation credentials after his bruising fight with Pinchot, called for establishing a "bureau of national parks and resorts" in the Interior Department. His successor, Walter Fisher, added momentum by holding a conference of influential people inside and outside the government at Yellowstone in 1911 to discuss park issues. Similar gatherings were held annually thereafter. In February 1912, President Taft endorsed the idea.

The timing was propitious. The slogan "See America First" had been coined in 1905, and within a few years the Great Northern Railway made it the center of its corporate identity, playing on the proximity of its rail line to Glacier National Park. With the advent of the automobile age and more leisure time available to the nation's burgeoning middle class, conditions were ripe for a vast increase in tourism in the parks. Canada had established a national parks office in 1911, giving rise to the claim that the United States was falling behind its northern neighbor. The call to "See America First" took on new power as war clouds gathered in Europe, which also led the War Department to withdraw its troops from the California parks in 1914.[10]

After Congress approved the Hetch Hetchy project in late 1913, Interior secretary Lane threw his support behind the campaign. He saw a national park service as a way not only to bring some unifying order to park management, but also to repair relations with park advocates and to head off the threat of the Interior Department losing turf to Agriculture. The connection between the park service campaign and the recent fight over the Hetch Hetchy project was underscored when John Raker and his colleague William Kent (R-Calif.) enlisted in the effort. Indeed, Kent's home in Washington, D.C., was often the site of its strategy sessions, just as it had been in the earlier battle for San Francisco's project. Proponents made common cause with Hetch Hetchy opponents such as Utah senator Reed Smoot, who, with Raker and Kent, played a key role in steering the legislation through Congress.[11]

In December 1914, Lane persuaded Stephen T. Mather, whose family had deep New England roots, to join the Interior Department. Then forty-seven, Mather had been born and raised in San Francisco and graduated from the University of California, Berkeley. After working as a journalist in New York, he became a sales manager for the Pacific Coast Borax Company, where he proved exceptionally talented at marketing and branding the company's chief product, Twenty Mule Team Borax, before co-founding a competing borax company and making a fortune. Mather was an outdoors enthusiast. He had climbed Mount Rainier with the Sierra Club in 1905, and on an expedition in the Kings River Canyon in 1912, had had an encounter of lasting influence with John Muir.

During visits to Yosemite and Sequoia National Parks two years later, Mather was appalled by the deficient management. Not long after that, Interior secretary Lane arranged a meeting with Mather at which—according to Horace Albright, another Californian who had joined Interior not long after graduating from UC Berkeley—Lane asked Mather to give him a report on conditions in the national parks. When Mather followed up with a report, Lane supposedly wrote back, "Dear Steve, if you don't like the way the national parks are being run, come on down to Washington and run them yourself." And so he did.[12]

Mather was the first director of the National Park Service, a position he held for nearly twelve years. A 1920s journalist described Mather this way: "He preached parks, pictured parks, planned parks, played parks on the clangorous cymbals and cooing lute until one is afraid not to go see parks. One dreads a parkless death." Overall, he was as instrumental in giving the National Park

Service as stellar a reputation with the public as Pinchot had been at the U.S. Forest Service.[13]

The two shared a number of attributes. Both had considerable vision and enormous energy, both were skilled in public relations and politics, both loved the outdoors, and neither hesitated to spend his personal wealth to advance favorite causes. But Mather had a more winning personality and made fewer enemies, although he was afflicted with bipolar disorder, which periodically caused him to be unavailable for months at a time. Mather was also less politically partisan, serving under a Democratic and two Republican presidents, none of whom took as intense an interest in public lands matters as Theodore Roosevelt had.[14]

Mather took charge of the campaign for the legislation, beginning with a national park conference held in Berkeley, California, in March 1915, which was attended by members of Congress and other notables. Afterward, he led a camping trip through the Sierra, including Sequoia and Yosemite National Parks, with writers, publishers, and legislators, including future Speaker of the House Frederick H. Gillett (R-Mass.). Then he and Albright went on a well-publicized tour of the northwestern parks, after which he went to Denver to dedicate the new Rocky Mountain National Park. Congress had established it in January 1915 after zealous efforts by its chief promoter, Enos A. Mills (a protégé of John Muir), who was supported by an array of local groups, including the Denver Chamber of Commerce and the Colorado Mountain Club.[15]

The publicity campaign hit a high point when *National Parks Portfolio,* an elegant book of photographs, was published in early 1916 and distributed free of charge to 250,000 people by the General Federation of Women's Clubs. Mather, using his personal funds, had earlier hired Robert Sterling Yard away from the *Century* magazine, and Yard persuaded railroads to underwrite the cost of the book. The popular *Saturday Evening Post* and many other magazines and newspapers editorialized in favor of the legislation, with *National Geographic* devoting its entire April 1916 issue to America's scenic grandeur, with an emphasis on the national parks.[16]

The campaign had what the historian Richard Sellars described as a "pervasive utilitarian tenor," presenting parks not as reservoirs of biodiversity or laboratories for scientific inquiry but rather as "scenic recreation areas that should be vigorously developed for public use and enjoyment to help the national economy and improve the public's mental and physical well-being, thereby enhancing citizenship and patriotism." Yard underscored the economic angle by publishing an article entitled "Making a Business of Scenery" in the June 1916 issue of the *Nation's Business,* the magazine of the United States Chamber of Commerce. The emphasis on patriotism had particular resonance as World War I enveloped Europe. The campaign's success demonstrated how preserving and showcasing the natural beauty of public lands was replacing the nineteenth-century dogma that public lands were a key to producing a virtuous agrarian society.[17]

THE ORGANIC ACT FOR THE NATIONAL PARK SERVICE

The legislation that Wilson signed into law in August 1916 was remarkably brief. Like the Organic Act for the national forests, it put no additional acres of public land off-limits to divestment. It simply created a system out of what had heretofore been a loose assemblage of individual units. The system would be managed by a new agency, the National Park Service (NPS), underscoring the idea that all these units would now serve a common national interest.

The vision for that system, expressed in the act's first section, was broader and somewhat more democratic than that in the Organic Act for the national forest system. The "fundamental purpose" of the park system, it said in words that most NPS employees know by heart, is "to conserve the scenery and the natural and historic objects and the wild life therein and to provide for the enjoyment of the same in such manner and by such means as will leave them unimpaired for the enjoyment of future generations." Over time, those few words came to describe the role that many public lands, and not just those inside the park system, play in American culture.[18]

Frederick Law Olmsted, Jr., was deeply involved in crafting this language, which went through innumerable drafts over several years. Its core mandate was remarkably consonant with the Yellowstone legislation that Congress had enacted nearly a half century earlier, which had referred to that park as a "pleasuring-ground" that was "for the benefit and enjoyment of the people," and which called for the Interior secretary to preserve its "wonders" in "their natural condition." Like the Yellowstone legislation, the National Park Service Act's twinning of "conserving" and "enjoying" park resources glossed over the tension that lurked between those two objectives. Ever since, much ink has been spilled over the question whether these goals are of equal stature or whether "conserving . . . unimpaired" trumps "enjoying" when the two conflict.

The reference to "historic objects" mimicked the language of the Antiquities Act. Olmsted lobbied hard for including the reference to "scenery." Earlier drafts had also contained the phrases "public recreation" and "public health." While these did not survive, "enjoyment" is capacious enough to embrace both ideas. The legislation did not, however, mention science.[19]

The act's second section gave the new National Park Service responsibility for the national monuments over which Interior already had jurisdiction, as well as the Hot Springs Reservation in Arkansas, which Congress had reserved in national ownership nearly a century before. Earlier drafts would have transferred national monuments administered by the Forest Service to the new bureau, but the idea was excised after the Forest Service objected. Instead, the act merely encouraged the Interior and Agriculture Departments to cooperate when Interior-managed monuments were contiguous to national forests.

There was considerable discussion about how loose or tight-fitting the management mandate should be. Horace McFarland of the American Civic Association wanted the legislation to be a "Gibraltar" for defending the parks against future Hetch Hetchy–like projects, but others argued that the Interior Department needed considerable management discretion. The issue was entangled with the question of how much the management of national parks and national forests should differ. The more dam building, grazing, mining, or logging that was allowed in the parks, the more difficult it would be to distinguish them from forests.

The act's third section furnished some answers. It allowed the secretary to issue leases or permits for the use of park land "for the accommodation of visitors," but only for periods "not exceeding twenty years," and cautioned that "no natural curiosities, wonders, or objects of interest shall be leased, rented, or granted to anyone on such terms as to interfere with the free access to them by the public." It contemplated the possibility that logging, livestock grazing, and the destruction of flora and fauna might occur in the parks, but only where the Interior secretary determined that such activities were compatible with or not detrimental to the fundamental purposes of the system. It allowed the secretary to "sell or dispose of timber," but only where "in his judgment" it was required to "control the attacks of insects or diseases or otherwise conserve the scenery or the natural or historic objects" in the park unit. It gave the secretary the discretion to destroy "animals" and "plant life" where they were "detrimental to the use of any" park unit. Mining and dam building were not mentioned.

The act's language addressing livestock grazing had a curious history. It was championed by Congressman Kent, who owned a ranch in Nevada. He told his colleagues that some parks had "large areas where the grass goes to waste" and where a "certain amount" of grazing might therefore be "beneficial." Kent's avocation as a wealthy gentleman rancher called to mind the English aristocrats who had operated ranches in some parts of the West in the latter part of the nineteenth century and prefigured the rise in modern times of so-called amenity ranchers, who seek a lifestyle rather than a livelihood. In the Senate, Kent's language allowing limited grazing was struck from the bill at the behest of Clarence Clark of Wyoming, who explained that he did not want Yellowstone to "become a grazing ground of great sheep and cattle industries," because the "habitat of wild game" must be "very carefully preserved."

The grazing provision was restored in the conference called to reconcile the House and Senate versions, except, in deference to Senator Clark, it was made inapplicable to Yellowstone. The House conferees included a champion of western livestock interests, Edward Taylor of Colorado, who claimed that it "has long been recognized that live-stock grazing in the mountains protects forests from fire." Taylor also contended that charging livestock operators a fee for grazing in remote sections of parks not visited by tourists could produce revenue for park administration, and he emphasized that the practice could be ended by the secretary should the "needs of tourists" dictate otherwise."[20]

While it did not entirely rule out all conventional economic uses of park system lands, the National Park Service Act certainly discouraged them. Over time, the act's fundamental thrust—that national parks are not places where resources should be extracted, but rather places where people go to be inspired and learn and recreate, and where safeguarding those opportunities for future generations was at least as important as providing them to current generations—would leave no room for mining, dam building, commercial logging, or livestock grazing.

CHAPTER THIRTY-EIGHT

The National Park System's Early Years

IN THE YEARS LEADING UP TO 1933, the national park system soaked up a good deal of the political attention devoted to public land issues at the national level, even though its total area was a small fraction of that in the national forest system, and a tiny fraction of all public lands. In the spring of 1918, following the model of the Wilson-Pinchot letter sent when the Agriculture Department gained control of the national forests in 1905, Interior secretary Lane sent Stephen Mather a comprehensive statement of national park policies. Horace Albright claimed primary credit for its drafting, vetting it through Mather and other park advocates.

What came to be known as the Lane letter provided a somewhat sharper vision than that found in the Organic Act regarding the role of the National Park Service, especially in relation to national forests. It began by setting forth three principles that would govern NPS decision making. The first was to maintain the parks "in absolutely unimpaired form for the use of future generations as well as those of our own time." The second was that the parks "are set apart for the use, observation, health, and pleasure of the people." The third was that "the national interest must dictate all decisions affecting public or private enterprise in the parks," with no mention of deciding "local questions on local grounds" such as appeared in the Wilson-Pinchot letter.[1]

It called for maintaining "strict . . . control" over leasing lands for visitor facilities, in tracts that were "no larger than absolutely necessary." Emphasizing public enjoyment over private advantage, the Lane letter specifically prohibited leasing plots for summerhouses because of the risk that the practice could exclude the public from "convenient access" to natural features. Particular attention should be paid to "harmonizing" buildings, roads, trails, and other facilities with the landscape. Hunting would be prohibited, as would grazing by sheep. The cooperation of the government's "scientific bureaus" should be sought, and interpretation and education should be encouraged "in every practicable way." Entrance fees were never mentioned, and apparently never considered.[2]

At the time, some parks had considerable acreage not owned by the United States, a legacy of railroad land grants and other divestment laws. Because these inholdings could "seriously hamper the administration of these reservations," the Lane letter advocated their elimination over time, through purchase or donation.

It also addressed system expansion. Without mentioning the smaller, lower-quality parks that Congress had previously approved, it cautioned against adding areas that "express in less than the highest terms the particular class or kind of exhibit which they represent." While it noted that the national forests contained many areas that might qualify for park status, it diplomatically called for investigating them "jointly with officers of the Forest Service."[3]

ACCOMMODATING VISITORS TO THE NATIONAL PARKS

Stephen Mather concentrated his considerable talents of promotion and persuasion on building a political constituency for the system. The primary way to do that, he believed, was to get people into the parks, which meant not only publicizing them but also building the infrastructure to facilitate visitation. For that, Mather needed congressional funding, because the parks, unlike the national forests, were never expected to bring in revenue through sale of resources like grass and timber.

Whether to build roads to allow motor vehicle access to the parks had already been the subject of discussion. In 1912, addressing the annual convention of J. Horace MacFarland's American Civic Association, James Bryce, the British ambassador to the United States and a prominent advocate of protecting large open spaces, expressed alarm about allowing automobiles free access to places such as the Yosemite Valley. Their noise, pollution, and very speed, he said, interfered with appreciation of the "sentimental charm of the landscape." Even allowing the auto to carry visitors to places of accommodation in scenic parks was a slippery slope, Bryce warned, since the car would "soon be allowed to go wherever else there is a road to bear it." Thus, he counseled, it was better not to "let the serpent enter Eden at all."[4]

Bryce's advice fell largely on deaf ears. When he wrote those words, the growing American middle class was already becoming captivated by the mobility that automobiles could provide and had purchased nearly 1 million of them. That number grew to 10 million by 1922 and 23 million by 1929. Park advocates such as Mather did not object to admitting automobiles to the big parks, and neither did Congress. The 1915 statute establishing Rocky Mountain National Park specifically directed that provision be made for automobile use. Although the National Park Service Act was silent on the subject, the Lane letter announced that automobiles and motorcycles would be permitted in all national parks.[5]

By 1919, two-thirds of Yellowstone's more than 60,000 visitors were arriving by private car. In 1920, the NPS opened a road to the high country twelve thousand feet above sea level in Rocky Mountain National Park. That same year, almost 1 million people visited national parks and monuments. Soon thereafter, the NPS approved, and Congress funded, the famous Going-to-the-Sun Road through Glacier National Park. In 1922, Mather contracted with the Alaska Road Commission to build a highway to Mount McKinley. In 1924, Congress approved a three-year program to build new roads and to upgrade existing ones in the national parks and monuments. Yosemite's visitors more than doubled within two years after a new, all-year road was completed into the valley in 1925. By 1927, park-system visitation had nearly tripled from the figure from seven years earlier.[6]

Although the primary attraction of the parks was their natural scenery, overseers of some parks sought to entertain visitors in ways that would not meet modern standards. Practices that had developed in Yellowstone, such as fish stocking with non-native species and the winter feeding of charismatic animals, spread to other parks after the NPS was created. Some parks offered stunts such as bear shows at garbage dumps and "firefalls," in which burning embers were thrown over cliffs to appear like a waterfall, to the delight of tourists. With public visitation seen as essential to sustaining political support for a national park system, the NPS practiced what Richard Sellars called a "selective kind of preservation, promoting some elements of nature and opposing others—altering natural conditions largely in an attempt to serve the other part of its mandate, the public's enjoyment of the parks."[7]

A FLOOD OF NEW PARKS AND MONUMENTS

The strong public support that led to the Organic Act for the National Park Service also led Congress to designate several new parks. A few weeks before the Organic Act was signed into law, Congress established Lassen Volcanic

National Park in Northern California (Mount Lassen had erupted for the first time in recorded history a couple years earlier) and Hawaii National Park, comprising units on both Maui and the Big Island. Because some of the Hawaii land was privately owned, the legislation authorized the territorial government to acquire needed lands.

In 1917, Congress established Mount McKinley National Park in the Alaska Territory. It encompassed North America's highest peak (the mountain's Native Alaskan name, Denali, was restored in 2015), magnificent scenery, and what one of its primary advocates, the naturalist and activist Charles Sheldon, described as a "vast reservoir of game." (In 1917, Congress rejected Sheldon's recommendation that the park be named Denali, but changed its mind in 1980.) In 1919, Congress established the first national park in the East, in Maine (originally called Lafayette, Congress changed its name to Acadia in 1929), as well as Grand Canyon National Park in Arizona and Zion National Park in southwestern Utah.[8]

Several of these parks—Lassen, Grand Canyon, Zion, and what became Acadia—grew out of national monuments that presidents had established using the Antiquities Act, and the first two had been forest reserves before that. Legislating the conversion of a national monument or part of a national forest to a national park became a common practice, attractive because it added prominence and allowed Congress to claim political credit. Congress itself sometimes established national monuments and installed them in the national park system, beginning in 1929 with Badlands National Monument, on lands acquired and donated to the United States by the State of South Dakota.[9]

Mather and Albright strategically used the establishment of monuments by the executive as a gateway to areas eventually receiving national-park status, especially in the scenic Colorado Plateau region. Four years after Congress established Zion National Park, for example, President Harding—urged on by the Utah legislature—established a national monument encompassing scenic natural amphitheaters of eroded red-rock spires some fifty miles to its northeast. The area was already part of a national forest, and Harding left it under Forest Service management. The following year, at the urging of Congressman Don Colton (R-Utah) and over the opposition of the Agriculture Department, Congress authorized its conversion to what it called Utah National Park, contingent on the United States first acquiring all the land within the boundaries that Congress drew. Eventually, Congress enlarged the park and changed its name to honor the local Mormon pioneer Ebenezer Bryce, who grazed livestock in the rugged area and supposedly described it as "a Hell of a place to lose a cow."[10]

In 1918, Woodrow Wilson established what was the largest national monument up to that time—the 1.1-million-acre Katmai in the Alaska Territory, where a large volcanic eruption had occurred six years earlier—and put it under the control of the National Park Service. Wilson had in 1915 succumbed to entreaties from timber and mining interests and reduced the size of Theodore Roosevelt's Mount Olympus National Monument on Washington's Olympic Peninsula (then still under the control of the Forest Service) by more than half. That move was a very rare departure from what had become a well-established pattern of adding layers of protection to scenic areas of public lands.[11]

The powerful movement to expand the park system was almost completely free from partisan politics and did not slacken when Republicans controlled the levers of power. In 1925, President Coolidge outdid Wilson by establishing the 1.2-million-acre Glacier Bay National Monument, also in Alaska. Although the National Park Service Organic Act had not used the word "science," Coolidge's proclamation characterized Glacier Bay as offering a "unique opportunity" for "scientific study."[12]

Altogether, Coolidge used the Antiquities Act more than a dozen times, to protect such areas as Carlsbad Cave in New Mexico (in 1930, Congress enlarged the 700-acre monument that Coolidge proclaimed in 1923 to 46,000 acres and converted it to Carlsbad Caverns National Park), scenic portions of the Chiricahua Mountains in southeastern Arizona, Craters of the Moon in Idaho, and Lava Beds in California. Chiricahua and Lava Beds were carved out of national forests and initially left in the care of the Forest Service; the others were on previously unreserved public lands. In 1929, shortly before he left office, Coolidge signed legislation establishing Grand Teton National Park in Wyoming. Its boundaries were narrowly drawn to protect only the eastern slopes of the picturesque Teton Range, and efforts to expand the park started almost immediately.[13]

NEW PARKS IN THE EAST

Once Congress established Acadia National Park in Maine, Mather and Albright looked for similar opportunities in the East and South, drawing on the local support for protecting scenery that had helped persuade Congress to enact the Weeks Act in 1911. Interior secretary Hubert Work appointed the Southern Appalachian National Park Commission in 1924 to explore the idea, and the efforts paid off when Congress enacted legislation in the next few years that authorized the establishment of three new national parks—Shenandoah in eastern Virginia, Great Smoky Mountains in North Carolina and Tennessee, and Mammoth Cave in Kentucky.[14]

Then, in 1931, Congress conferred national-park status on Isle Royale in Lake Superior, the largest island in the Great Lakes. It broke new ground for the park system in several respects. Much of the island was owned by private mining and lumber interests. Copper had been mined there for centuries, and while the island was too rugged and remote to support much commercial logging, numerous cabins and resorts dotted its shores. Still, its isolation made it attractive for nature study, and groups such as the National Geographic Society and the Izaak Walton League strongly supported making it a park. Horace Albright found it worthy because of its "utterly distinct" scenery, its "primitiveness, its unusual wild life and interesting flora," and its remnants of "prehistoric occupation." In 1924, President Coolidge had withdrawn nearly all the remaining public land on the island (some 9,000 acres, or about 7 percent of the total) from divestment while its future was being discussed. The authorizing legislation was steered through Congress in 1931 by two influential Michigan Republicans, Senator Arthur Vandenberg, then in his first of four terms, and Congressman Louis Cramton, then finishing his ninth and last term. (Even though closer to Minnesota, Isle Royale is part of Michigan.)[15]

Nearly all the land in these four new parks outside the West was in private ownership. The tight-fisted Congress insisted that no federal dollars be used, and leveraged the political and economic power of national-park status to persuade state and local governments and private interests to secure the needed lands and donate them. In each case, the authorizing legislation fixed the park's boundaries but prohibited formal establishment of the park until ownership of the land had been transferred to the United States.

This acquisition strategy worked, but slowly. Formal park establishment took nine years from authorization at Isle Royale and Shenandoah, fourteen years at Great Smoky Mountains, and fifteen years at Mammoth Cave. Land acquisitions did not follow any particular pattern. At Great Smoky Mountains, thousands of small public donations were matched by a $5 million grant from John D. Rockefeller, Jr., the son of the founder of the Standard Oil Company. At Isle Royale, the state of Michigan donated land it owned and put up funds to acquire private land, and Congress in 1932 facilitated acquisitions there by giving the Interior secretary discretion to lease lands back to donors for twenty years or their remaining lives. (That model would occasionally be followed elsewhere, with mixed results, because lessees sometimes fiercely resisted termination of their use.) At Shenandoah, the State of Virginia bought much of the land, and if a private owner of land was unwilling to sell, the state took title by eminent domain, paying "just compensation." That use of eminent domain sometimes caused lasting bitterness among unwilling sellers, not unlike the experience of some Native Americans who were dispossessed from reservations of public lands in the West.[16]

The expansion of the national park system outside the West worked much as Mather and Albright had envisioned. It gave many more people ready access to protected public lands—Great Smoky Mountains, for example, has been the nation's most visited national park since it was established—and generated much economic activity. It also was a demonstration of how U.S.-owned and protected lands could serve democratizing values by being open to all regardless of income or background, an especially powerful message as the nation's economy took a severe downturn with the onset of the Great Depression. Living up to that ideal sometimes proved challenging for the National Park Service in the era of Jim Crow racial segregation in the South.[17]

Mather, at ease in the world of the wealthy, led by example, devoting some of his own money to building the park system. John D. Rockefeller, Jr., donated substantial sums in support of several parks besides Great Smoky Mountains. Through such efforts, private philanthropy helped, and from time to time continues to help, expand America's system of protected public lands.[18]

PRESERVING STANDARDS AND
FIGHTING OFF DEVELOPMENT

The capsule description that national forests were open to "use" and national parks were not was always an oversimplification, but adoption of the National Park Service Organic Act did produce more differentiation between parks and forests. It also increased uniformity. The park system was different from the national forest system because each national park (though not each national monument) was established by a separate statute, and these individual laws sometimes contained management guidance that differed from that laid out in the Organic Act. The statute establishing Mount McKinley National Park, for example, expressly allowed U.S. mining laws to continue to apply to public lands inside its boundaries, something that Congress had also done at Crater Lake and Mount Rainier before the Organic Act was adopted.[19]

By organizing the individual park units into a system and legislating generic guidelines for park management (though without repealing specific directions that earlier statutes had provided for individual parks), the National Park Service Organic Act promoted more consistent management from unit to unit. Congress took another important step in this direction in 1931 by enacting, with little debate, legislation to "provide for the uniform administration of the national parks," which repealed or limited many, though not all, of the carve-outs for activities such as mining and railroad building that had appeared in earlier park laws. As a result, commercial logging, mining, hydropower, and irrigation projects became rare in parks unless specifically blessed by Congress, as at Hetch Hetchy. The same was true for livestock grazing, although it lingered in some parks for a long time, becoming, in the words of Sellars, an "enduring vexation" for the agency despite the limiting language in both the Organic Act and the Lane letter.[20]

The national park system's spectacular success with the American public attracted many proposals for new parks. Some raised a concern that Bob Keiter described as a "thinning of the blood." Hot Springs, Arkansas, for example, lacked scenic grandeur or unique features. It did, however, have historic cachet as the first tract of public land reserved in national ownership for recreational or health-promotion purposes, and that was enough for Mather to want it in the system. Called merely a "reservation" in the National Park Service Organic Act, which gave the service jurisdiction over it, a rider on civil appropriations legislation in 1921 made it a full-fledged national park.[21]

Mather, Albright, and key park supporters in Congress worked to maintain standards for admitting new parks to the system. Sometimes this required disappointing politicians who sought national recognition for local areas. Perhaps the least meritorious park idea during this era was one championed by Senator Albert Fall (R-N.M.). His proposed Mescalero National Park consisted of a handful of small, relatively isolated tracts in and around the Mescalero Indian Reservation in southern New Mexico, one of which, as it happened, adjoined Fall's ranch. This national park would have remained open to mining, grazing, power and irrigation development, and hunting, and would have included land within the Indian reservation without compensating the tribe. Despite all these shortcomings, the necessary legislation passed the Senate in 1922, the year after Fall became President Harding's Interior secretary, but it never advanced in the House. Another questionable proposal, to establish the Ouachita National Park in Arkansas, made it to President Coolidge's desk in 1928. He vetoed it after strong opposition was mounted by the Interior and Agriculture Departments and by Congressman Don Colton, the chair of the House Public Lands Committee, who warned the president that if the bill were signed, his committee would likely have no recourse but to approve a dozen other similar, inferior park bills.[22]

As its supporters had envisioned, the National Park Service Organic Act helped reduce the number of proposals to invade individual parks with dams and other industrial developments. But it did not end them entirely. Efforts by livestock and lumber interests to gain access to parks in World War I were mostly rebuffed, although some cattle were allowed in Yosemite, over the opposition of the NPS. Interior secretary Franklin Lane supported a legislative proposal to allow two dams to be built in the southwestern portion of Yellowstone National Park to benefit irrigation interests in Idaho. Mather and Albright staunchly opposed the idea; Mather was reportedly ready to resign over the matter, but fate intervened when ill health forced Lane to step down, and his successor, John Barton Payne, sided with Mather. The dam proposal passed the Senate in April 1920 but got no further. Montana and Idaho irrigators continued to push for dams to be built in Yellowstone for almost two more decades but never succeeded. Dam building in other park-system units continued to be an issue for decades.[23]

THE END OF THE MATHER ERA

After nearly twelve years as National Park Service director, Mather resigned after suffering a severe stroke in January 1929; he died within a year. From a modern perspective, Mather overemphasized the building of infrastructure to facilitate visitation, forged too many pragmatic alliances with railroad and highway interests and park concessioners, and paid insufficient attention to science and ecology, tending to see large parks, in Sellars's description, as providing a "rugged, mountainous version of peace and plenty . . . a paradise of beauty and richness, free of fires and predators."[24]

With no established template, the task of building a national park system was full of judgment calls. While hardly flawless, Mather's judgment was often sound, even by demanding modern standards. Sellars's general assessment seems fair: Mather was a "promoter, builder, and developer" who made the national parks "an enduring feature of the American landscape and a source of national pride" that promoted "clean living in God's great out-of-doors" and provided "vast schoolrooms of Americanism" where people could learn to "love more deeply the land in which they live." Mather's personal ethics were beyond reproach, he generally stayed above partisan politics, and his devotion to the parks and the National Park Service was deep. His will left Albright and Arno Cammerer, his immediate successors as director, $25,000 each to promote their independence of thought.

His relentless promotion helped build a constituency for protecting public lands outside as well as inside the national park system, leaving an imprint arguably as significant as Gifford Pinchot's. (He was more modest than Pinchot. Robert Sterling Yard quoted him as saying that he earned his fortune "out of the soil of the country, so why should I be praised for putting a little of it back? That's only decent acknowledgment.") His grasp of how public lands could help build a sense of national pride in the magnificence of the nation's natural bounty, along with an appreciation of the outdoors, had a profound effect that continues to this day. Congressman Louis Cramton, one of his closest allies on Capitol Hill, paid tribute to Mather on the House floor in words that later appeared on memorial plaques mounted in several national parks: "There will never come an end to the good he has done."[25]

CHAPTER THIRTY-NINE

The National Forest System Matures and Evolves

BY 1913, THE UNITED STATES HAD purchased more than 400,000 acres of land in the East and South for national forests. In 1915, not long after George Vanderbilt died unexpectedly, the nation purchased 87,000 acres around his North Carolina estate from his widow. In 1916, President Wilson designated it and other land that the government had purchased in the vicinity as the Pisgah National Forest, the first one in the East.[1]

By 1917, about 1.5 million acres had been approved for purchase under the Weeks Act. A little more than half of this was cutover timberland; less than one-third was old-growth forest. In 1918, Wilson proclaimed two new national forests in Virginia, one in Alabama, and the White Mountain National Forest in New Hampshire, the first in New England. It eventually more than doubled in size to nearly 800,000 acres and draws more visitors annually than either Yellowstone or Yosemite National Park.

Funding constraints kept the acquisition program relatively modest compared to the acreage in western national forests, but Congress enacted two laws in the 1920s that accelerated it. The Clarke-McNary Act of 1924 allowed purchases for timber production as well as watershed protection, and the McNary-Woodruff Act of 1928 authorized increased appropriations. As a result, Weeks Act purchases grew significantly during the Hoover administration. In each of the three years starting with 1929, more acreage was purchased than in any previous year.

Few people who today enjoy Vermont's summer greenery or fall foliage displays are aware that national-forest acquisitions in that state began only after November 1927. It was then that the state experienced massive flooding, exacerbated by deforestation. This caused much devastation, with topsoil scoured from thousands of acres and more than one thousand bridges destroyed, as well as considerable loss of life. It was a forceful reminder of the teachings of George Perkins Marsh, himself a Vermonter. Five years later, enough land had been purchased to allow President Hoover to proclaim the Green Mountain National Forest.

By 1933, about 4.5 million acres in the East and South had been acquired, much of it cutover land where forests would be restored. The Weeks Act led to the establishment of seventeen national forests in twelve states, from Maine to Florida, with the largest holdings in Virginia, New Hampshire, and North Carolina.[2]

Nearly all the timber harvested in the nation during this era came from private lands. Timber harvested from the national forests mostly supplied local needs. Nationally, the demand for wood declined in relation to supply, a trend accelerated by the Great Depression. The net effect was that the national forests never produced more than a small fraction of the nation's demand for wood until after the outbreak of World War II.[3]

CREATING AND ELIMINATING INHOLDINGS

During Wilson's presidency, about 2 million acres of land in the national forests were privatized under divestment laws like the homestead acts and the Mining Law of 1872. Privately owned inholdings in the national forests, as in the national parks, could undermine the objectives that Congress had established for these public lands. They could be eliminated by acquisition, but Congress was often reluctant to supply the needed funds. Another solution was a land swap in which an inholding was exchanged for U.S.-owned land outside the national forests. The Pinchot-led Public Land Commission had recommended in 1903 that Congress provide the executive with generic authority to make such exchanges, but the notorious "in lieu" swap provisions of the Organic Act of 1897 and the Mount Rainier National Park legislation of 1899 had been so badly drawn and administered as to make exchanges involving public land politically toxic.[4]

Finally, Congress enacted the General Exchange Act in 1922. It authorized the Interior secretary to trade unappropriated public lands for nonpublic lands of "equal value" inside national forests that the Agriculture secretary deemed "chiefly valuable for national forest purposes" in the same state. Exchanges were at the discretion of the government, and valuations were determined by appraisal, requiring judgment calls that sometimes became lightning rods for criticism. Despite this, exchanges hold considerable potential for win-win outcomes, and they have remained an important way to consolidate public landholdings. Forest inholdings could also be eliminated by gift after Congress included a provision in the Clarke-McNary Act of 1924 authorizing the Agriculture secretary to accept for incorporation into national forests donations of land "chiefly valuable" for timber.[5]

LIVESTOCK GRAZING BECOMES MORE ENTRENCHED
From the time the Forest Service began administering the national forests in 1905, it had difficulty in setting appropriate grazing levels. Livestock operators were resistant to reducing their grazing, and little science could be brought to bear on the subject. To its credit, the agency took steps to fill that vacuum, establishing an Office of Grazing Studies in 1910 and its first field experiment station in 1912. It was headed by Arthur Sampson, who ten years later became a professor at the University of California, Berkeley, where he became known as the "father of range science" and published the first textbook on the subject.[6]

In 1917, Congress began appropriating federal dollars for making so-called range improvements—fences, windmill-driven wells, water tanks, and corrals— designed to facilitate the livestock use of national forest lands. At the same time, because World War I was raging, the Forest Service abandoned efforts to curb grazing in the national forests, dealing what William Rowley, the leading historian of national forest grazing, called a "staggering blow" to the agency's efforts to restore healthy grasslands. By 1918, about 100 million acres, two of every three acres of national forest land, were being grazed by more than 20 million animals, owned by 33,000 permittees. Shortly after the war ended, the Forest Service lengthened the standard term for a grazing permit from one to five years. At the same time, it modestly increased the grazing fee, although the amount charged remained well below the cost of renting comparable, privately owned pasturage.[7]

The Supreme Court had made crystal clear that livestock operators had no "vested right" to use public lands, but they never gave up asserting that their grazing permits simply confirmed an underlying legal entitlement to graze— even though the permits had a limited tenure, carried no right of renewal, and at least purported to subject their grazing to close and continuing governmental supervision. Oliver Wendell Holmes, Jr., had explained the operators' attitude in his famous essay "The Path of the Law," from 1897, in which he observed that a "thing which you have enjoyed and used as your own for a long time, whether property or an opinion, takes root in your being and cannot be torn away without your resenting the act and trying to defend yourself, however you came by it."[8]

Their sense of entitlement was nurtured by the government's practice, dating back to the General Land Office's administration of the forest reserves, of giving owners of nearby property a "preference" to obtain a permit to graze livestock in the reserves. After 1905, the Forest Service continued the preference system, with some fine-tuning, even as it was insisting that a permit to graze national forest land was a privilege and could not be sold or transferred without agency approval. In this it was, as Rowley put it, "fighting a losing battle" to keep permits from "assuming value in the commercial grazing community." By the early 1920s, when a permit came with a five-year term, a below-market grazing fee, and access to federally funded grazing improvements, it was practically inevitable that the permit preference, no matter its stated limitations, would be built into the market price of the livestock enterprise and serve as collateral when operators wanted to borrow money.

Many other private enterprises had value that was similarly dependent on the government allowing access to public lands, such as timber mills or smelters dependent on timber harvests or mines found on public lands, or owners of places of accommodation dependent on public-lands-based tourism. All of these enterprises, like livestock operators, did not hesitate to exercise what influence they could muster with executive branch land managers and with Congress to preserve access to public lands in order to maintain the value of their enterprise. But livestock operators were almost unique among them in claiming a legal entitlement to that access. Their claim bolstered their already pervasive influence in most of the rural areas across the arid West, as well as in the corridors of the national government.

Even though the Forest Service took pains to formally preserve its legal authority over whether, where, and on what terms to allow livestock to graze in the national forests, the combination of political influence and a bold assertion of legal entitlement allowed livestock operators to strong-arm—perhaps "cow" is a more apt word—the Forest Service. It rarely if ever revoked or failed to renew a grazing permit, even if the holder had violated its terms or pertinent grazing regulations. Moreover, when a permittee sold its livestock operation at a price that reflected the value of the public land grazing permit associated with it, the agency never refused to allow the grazing permit to be transferred to the buyer, even though it had taken pains to reserve the power to do so.[9]

The agency's reluctance to risk antagonizing livestock operators was also apparent in the scant attention the agency paid to what the Organic Act of 1897 had defined as a primary purpose of the national forest system; namely, "securing favorable conditions of water flows" by protecting watersheds that produce them. In 1923, a midlevel Forest Service official called attention to this neglect and the shortcomings of the agency's livestock-grazing policies in a "Watershed Handbook" that he prepared for the agency, drawing on his experiences in administering southwestern national forests. These criticisms by Aldo Leopold, who had joined the agency in 1909 after graduating from the Yale School of Forestry, mostly fell on deaf ears because the Forest Service generally tended, as the historian Samuel Hays put it, to "minimize watershed problems." That was not the last to be heard from Leopold. Over time his on-the-ground experience, combined with his talents for science, philosophy, and expressive writing, gave him enormous influence on how Americans came to regard land, including public land.[10]

THE FOREST SERVICE BECOMES A "MULTIPLE USE" AGENCY

Although in Pinchot's time the Forest Service had conceived of recreation as merely an incidental use of the national forests, that attitude began to change soon after he was fired. The boom in outdoor recreation made it a primary use of many forests, and Congress began to nudge the agency to be more accommodating to it. In 1915, it authorized the Agriculture secretary to issue permits allowing up to five acres in any national forest to be used, for up to thirty years, for "summer homes, hotels, stores, or other structures needed for recreation or public convenience." All of this, plus the rivalry that grew up with the National Park Service after it was established in 1916, made the agency treat recreation more seriously.[11]

In 1917, the Forest Service's annual report mentioned recreation for the first time, with Chief Henry Graves noting that more than eight hundred permits had been issued for summer residences, and more than fifty for hotels and resorts. In less than twenty years, those numbers would grow to nearly thirteen thousand and one thousand, respectively. The issuance of recreational residence permits—which generated income for the Forest Service—contrasted with National Park Service policy, for the Lane letter had flatly prohibited the practice.[12]

A Forest Service report in 1918 frankly acknowledged that recreation "stands on a par with other major uses" of the national forests, because their "wild, interesting, and beautiful" land was attracting, according to its estimate,

3 million people, who spent an average of 2.5 days recreating in the national forests each year. Within a few years, Chief William Greeley was urging that the agency modify timber sales to "protect scenic features, roads, camping places, and the like against loss of attractiveness." The establishment of national forests closer to population centers in the East helped fuel an upsurge of recreational visits in the 1920s to more than 30 million by decade's end.[13]

During this era, the Forest Service slowly began to pay more attention to protecting wildlife and wildlife habitat on forest reserves. Pinchot had resisted moving in this direction, but once again Congress provided a nudge after he was fired. In 1916, it authorized the president to designate areas of national forest lands purchased under the Weeks Act "for the protection of game animals, birds, or fish," and specified penalties for the taking of any wildlife, including nongame birds, on areas so designated without permission from the secretary of Agriculture. (In 1934, Congress extended this authority to the remainder of the national forests.)[14]

The Forest Service was slow to use this power. It did not want to antagonize states, most of which required state licenses to hunt and fish anywhere inside their borders. States derived considerable revenue from license fees and resisted any move by the Forest Service that would curb their programs. The Forest Service also did not want to antagonize livestock interests, and for that reason paid little attention to a recommendation advanced in 1924 by a noted wildlife biologist, the University of California professor Joseph Grinnell, to curtail grazing by domestic livestock in some places in the forests to help preserve "wild animal life."[15]

Still, by the early 1930s the Forest Service was beginning to speak of the forests as having "multiple uses," a term that soon became the commonplace way of describing the objectives of national-forest administration. This evolution happened without any significant adjustment in the terms of the Organic Act of 1897; indeed, it was not until 1960 that Congress gave "multiple use" formal legal recognition on the national forests.[16]

CHAPTER FORTY

The Forest and Park Services Compete and Cooperate

THE FOREST SERVICE, WHICH HAD been managing national forests for barely a decade when Congress created the National Park Service, viewed the new agency as a serious threat to its hegemony over public land reservations. Yet the two agencies managed to fashion some common policies that fostered cooperation between them.[1]

Nowhere was that vacillation between competition and cooperation more apparent than in the area of recreation, which flourished in both systems. (Being much larger, the national forest system attracted far more recreationists than the park system.) President Calvin Coolidge paid attention, issuing a statement in early 1924 describing outdoor recreation as a "great character builder" that should be made available to the poor as well as the rich. Saying that the U.S. government should play a leadership role because the public lands contained "almost unlimited opportunities" for recreation, he called for a national conference on the subject, naming Theodore Roosevelt, Jr., its executive chair. In May, more than three hundred people representing more than one hundred national organizations met for three days in the nation's capital. A follow-up conference was held in early 1926, followed by a report in 1928 consisting of papers on subjects related to recreation.[2]

Both agencies adopted aggressive road-building policies. Although Mather's efforts at the National Park Service attracted more publicity, the Forest Service had a head start. In 1912, Congress began a practice of making

10 percent of the annual receipts from every national forest available for the construction of roads and trails within that forest. In 1916, it enacted the first in a series of Federal-Aid Highway Acts, which earmarked significant sums for national-forest road building. Over the next couple of decades, the road system in the national forests grew from a few thousand to almost 90,000 miles, keeping pace with the growing number of automobiles in the country and contributing to the blossoming use of national forests for recreation.[3]

The Forest Service and the Park Service were also allied in combatting what both considered major threats; namely, fire, insects, and forest diseases. Fire—the "Forest Fiend," Mather called it—was regarded as the worst of these. Firefighting became a kind of crusade on all public lands after the dramatic Big Burn of 1910 in the northern Rockies, and road building to improve access to remote areas became an important component of the effort. The Clarke-McNary Act of 1924 directed the Forest Service to cooperate with local authorities and "other suitable agencies" (like the Park Service) on firefighting, and a major fire in Glacier National Park and adjacent national forests in 1926 helped forge closer cooperation between the two agencies.[4]

With almost no deliberation, the U.S. government assumed lead responsibility for fighting fires in rural parts of the nation where public lands were common, with little regard for jurisdictional boundaries or property ownership. The rationale for federal action was sketched out in 1927 in a terse opinion by Justice Oliver Wendell Holmes for the Supreme Court, in a case involving U.S. enforcement of a federal law prohibiting the building of fires on or "near" public lands and leaving them unextinguished. (Congress enacted the law in June 1910, two months before the Big Burn.) Calling forest fires one of the country's "great economic misfortunes" and emphasizing that the danger "depends upon the nearness of the fire, not upon the ownership of the land where it is built," Holmes reaffirmed that the Constitution gave Congress the authority to control actions on nonfederal lands that "imperil" public lands.[5]

What Peter Matthiessen once called the "uncertain tool of wildlife management" known as predator control was another area where, at least initially, park and forest policy was congruent. Although protecting wildlife was gaining public support in this era, carnivorous mammals such as wolves, mountain lions, and coyotes were exceptions. Mostly to maintain good relations with nearby livestock operators, administrators of early national parks made efforts to control predators, and the Forest Service began hiring hunters for that purpose not long after assuming responsibility for the national forests in 1905. Some states doled out cash for predator destruction: Montana, for example, paid bounties on more than 100,000 wolves and nearly a million coyotes between 1882 and 1928. But the bounty system was inefficient, costly to state governments, and, as Matthiessen once put it, "shot through with fraud." The wily coyote remained a big threat, especially to domestic sheep, which were numerous in the national forests.[6]

Although wild predators have never accounted for more than a very small proportion of livestock losses—paling in comparison to disease, weather, and other causes—influential livestock operators such as Wyoming senator Francis Warren convinced the national government to lead an aggressive program of predator control, arguing that public lands were carnivore breeding grounds. In 1914, Congress began appropriating federal funds to the Agriculture Department's Bureau of Biological Survey specifically for that purpose. The agency soon became, in the historian Thomas Dunlap's words, a "semi-independent extermination company for western ranchers," with predator control accounting for most of its budget by the late 1920s, and its annual reports carefully documenting the numbers of each type of predator killed, mainly through shooting and poisoning by strychnine.[7]

By that time, however, the program had become controversial in the national park system. Nature lovers and scientists began to object, as wolves and cougars disappeared from parks such as Yellowstone, Glacier, and Rocky Mountain, and otters were eradicated from a lake in Yellowstone because they were eating trout (including some introduced, non-native species), a favorite target of sport anglers. Mather, who regarded wildlife matters as secondary, tended to support predator control, but the Park Service eventually banned the Biological Survey from trapping and poisoning on park system lands. Feeling some heat, the Biological Survey also stopped releasing its annual tally.[8]

Sometimes the Park Service and Forest Service found themselves at odds on the subject. The most notorious episode concerned mule deer in the Kaibab National Forest, north of Grand Canyon National Park. By 1920, the year after the park was created, the Forest Service decided that the removal of mountain lions had caused a damaging irruption, or explosion, in the deer population. It called for exterminating half the deer, but Mather objected, arguing the deer were in good shape overall and were a popular attraction for park visitors. The Forest Service's plan was finally carried out, although many more deer died from starvation and disease than shooting. Modern ecologists continue to debate the causes and effects of what at the time was regarded as a political and managerial disaster. Similar conflicts sometimes cropped up elsewhere, made more complicated by the fact that hunting was generally forbidden in parks but allowed in national forests under state law. In 1929, for example, the chief ranger at Yellowstone likened hunters gathering outside the park boundary to a "skirmish line of troops."[9]

Competition between the Park Service and the Forest Service for support among the general public and on Capitol Hill arose in many contexts, and sometimes descended into petty bickering. The Forest Service once published a map of California that left the national parks as blank spaces, for example, and Mather once complained when a Forest Service official promoted recreation on national forests at a national park conference, and he later sought to persuade Congress not to provide funds for national-forest recreation programs.[10]

President Harding's Interior secretary, Albert Fall, made an effort to transfer the Forest Service to the Interior Department. Although he had the support of some livestock and hydropower enterprises, the idea was going nowhere even before Fall resigned in early March 1923. The Forest Service's defenders in Congress counterattacked by including in the Clarke-McNary Act of 1924 a provision authorizing the Agriculture secretary to identify Interior Department–managed public lands that were "chiefly valuable for stream-flow protection or for timber production" and could be "economically administered as parts of national forests." Unsurprisingly, the Agriculture Department found considerable acreage that met the criteria, but Interior opposed transferring any land to the Forest Service, and nothing came of it.[11]

Another interdepartmental wrangle, this one involving public lands rich with cultural and archaeological resources on northern New Mexico's Pajarito Plateau, resulted in a complex series of moves and countermoves. General Land Office withdrawals of public lands on the plateau dated back to 1900, and Edgar Lee Hewett, among others, promoted the idea of establishing a national park in the area. Theodore Roosevelt included the area in the Jemez Forest Reserve, which he established in 1905. Wilson included it in the Bandelier National Monument, which he established in 1916, but kept it under Forest Service management. In the mid-1920s, the Park Service proposed a 300,000-acre national park in the area. The Forest Service fought back, arguing that the Park Service proposed to sully the experience by building paved roads into canyons containing some of the best-preserved ruins. To show that it was more protective, the Forest Service designated a portion of the contested terrain as a "primitive area," where road building was generally forbidden, in 1928. The Forest Service's strategy did not succeed. In 1932 President Hoover enlarged the monument and transferred it to the National Park Service.[12]

Despite the competition—or perhaps as a result of it—both agencies modestly expanded their landholdings in the twenty years ending in 1932. The national park system included about 12.5 million acres by then, while the national forest system remained far larger, embracing more than 160 million acres of land owned by the United States (that is, not counting the inholdings within its boundaries). Competition between them continued to command a good deal of attention, but the agencies' management regimes were not all that different at the ground level. Putting livestock grazing in the national forest system to one side, the predominant active human use of most of the land in both systems was recreation. Most other extractive uses that remained possible in the forests but generally not in the parks—mining, commercial timber harvesting, and dams—occupied a relatively small proportion of national forest lands.[13]

THE EMERGENCE OF THE IDEA OF PROTECTING "WILDERNESS" VALUES

In the first couple of decades of the twentieth century, a few scientists, echoing a suggestion that George Perkins Marsh had made a few decades earlier, began to advocate preserving some tracts of public land in an essentially natural condition. Within days of the National Park Organic Act becoming law in 1916, for example, Joseph Grinnell and Tracy Storer predicted in *Science* magazine that national parks might end up being "the only areas remaining unspoiled for scientific study." As roads began to proliferate in both parks and forests, the idea of preserving "unspoiled" areas began to gain favor in both agencies, and over time it provided some fuel for competition between them.[14]

In 1919, the Forest Service hired Arthur Carhart, a landscape architect, as a "recreation engineer" and assigned him to prepare plans for a road and a group of recreational cabins at a remote lake in Colorado's White River National Forest. After studying the situation, Carhart recommended against the development, and his supervisor agreed. After communicating with Carhart, Aldo Leopold, then an assistant district forester in Albuquerque, in 1922 prepared a plan for a road-free "Wilderness" or "National Hunting Ground" extending over more than half a million acres in the Gila National Forest in southwestern New Mexico. His superiors approved the plan in 1924, and Leopold began advocating for similar plans to be developed in each western state.[15]

Forest Service chief William Greeley supported putting some curbs on road construction. He opposed the construction of a major highway through national forests across the Sierra Nevada in California as well as a toll road to the top of Mount Whitney. Acknowledging that more people would "throng" such highways than would visit the mountain wilderness, Greeley wrote that it was important to prevent "motorized recreation from sweeping wilderness recreation, dear to the souls of many folk, off the face of the map." In the late 1920s, he commissioned the agency's first systematic inventory of its remaining roadless areas. It identified some seventy-five tracts totaling 55 million acres, with the largest single unit covering 7 million acres.[16]

Although some national-park officials continued to advocate for more roads and other visitor facilities, arguing that without them "a national park would be merely a wilderness," Mather sometimes lauded the idea of keeping some backcountry free of "piercing feeder roads," as did his former associate Robert Sterling Yard, who had been the best man at his wedding. Yard, who had left the Park Service in 1919 to become executive secretary of the new nonprofit National Parks Association (founded with Mather's blessing and financial support), became increasingly concerned about the rapid growth in park visitation and the infrastructure needed to accommodate it. Because most visitors stuck close to roads and camps, it was feasible, as he put it in 1928, to preserve the "enormous outlying wilderness" for those "who care enough for it to endure the pleasurable hardships of the trail." Yard himself had urban tastes—the only outdoors area he knew well, he would joke, was Central Park—but his advocacy for preserving backcountry areas from development had influence.[17]

In 1928, the report of a joint committee of the American Forestry Association and the National Parks Association that had studied recreation-related resources on public lands devoted several pages to "wilderness recreation," defining "wilderness" as "a roadless area where pioneer modes of travel and outdoor life may be enjoyed." Because the public lands were where the "remaining wilderness of America, modified as inevitably it has been, is now found," the U.S. government, it said, had a "great responsibility" to husband it. That same year, Congressman Scott Leavitt (R-Mont.) introduced legislation that would authorize the establishment of national recreation areas within national forests, but it never advanced.[18]

In 1929, the Forest Service adopted what were known as "L-Regulations" to govern what was becoming a system of "primitive areas" on national forests that were designed to maintain rudimentary "conditions of environment, transportation, habitation, and subsistence," in order to conserve their value for "public education, inspiration, and recreation." The construction of permanent "improvements" in such areas was prohibited unless authorized by the Forest

Service chief or the Agriculture secretary. By 1933, the agency had formally designated sixty-three "primitive areas" containing more than 8 million acres.[19]

In 1928, Horace Albright, then superintendent at Yellowstone and soon to succeed Mather, published an article in the *Saturday Evening Post* called "The Everlasting Wilderness." He suggested that the Park Service should keep large landscapes in the backcountry of the national parks free of roads or other developments. Once he became director, he issued a policy promoting "research reserves," areas to be kept "in as nearly as possible unmodified condition free from external influences." Their location was not to be publicized, and entry would require a special permit. More than two dozen such areas were created in ten parks, but the idea, according to Richard Sellars, "worked better in theory than in practice," and eventually it became moribund.[20]

For its part, Congress made no attempt to interfere with any of these Forest Service and Park Service initiatives to protect wild areas. In 1930, in fact, it took a step in the same direction by enacting what was called the Shipstead-Nolan Act. It required the preservation, "in an unmodified state of nature," of a large tract of public lands and waters in northern Minnesota along the Canadian border.[21]

Government action to protect those lands dated back nearly three decades. Not long after the turn of the twentieth century, an energetic Minnesota state forestry commissioner, Christopher Andrews, persuaded the General Land Office to withdraw more than 1 million acres of public land in the area from divestment, in pursuit of his vision of establishing an international forest reserve. In 1909, Theodore Roosevelt established the Superior National Forest, which included nearly all the withdrawn land, and across the border, the Ontario government established the Quetico Forest Reserve. In 1910, the Boundary Waters Treaty between the United States and Canada took effect. It committed both nations to protect the waters along their common border, and created a joint commission to enforce it. In 1913, a year after President Taft expanded the Superior National Forest by some 380,000 acres, the Canadian reserve was made a provincial park.

Some years later, the first recreation plan for the Superior National Forest, developed by Arthur Carhart, prioritized primitive recreation. In 1926, the Forest Service banned roads and timber harvesting, along with recreational developments other than "waterway and portage improvements," in part of the forest. Proposals to dam and log in the general area created enough controversy to persuade President Coolidge in 1928 to issue an executive order withdrawing public lands around the national forest from divestment.

Two years later, Congress enacted the legislation named after its sponsors, Senator Henrik Shipstead (Farmer-Labor party, Minn.) and Congressman William Nolan (R-Minn.). Among other things, it prohibited altering natural water levels and logging within four hundred feet of shorelines throughout the border lakes region, an area larger than any single primitive area that the Forest Service had yet established. In 1933, Minnesota enacted similar legislation protecting state lands in the area. The federal public lands remained under Forest Service control even though the National Park Service had long coveted the area.

Over the next few decades, both agencies took increasing interest in the idea of keeping sizable areas of public land undeveloped, and Congress eventually reengaged in a major way. In the historian Roderick Nash's words, protecting "wilderness" grew "from an esoteric notion" into a "broad national sentiment" that took a powerful hold on public land policy in the last half of the twentieth century.[22]

CHAPTER FORTY-ONE

Ranchers, Homesteaders, and Energy Developers Compete for Primacy

ALTHOUGH THE FOREST SERVICE and National Park Service attracted a great deal of attention during the two decades leading up to 1933, the Interior Department's General Land Office remained responsible for more public land in the forty-eight states than both of them combined. In 1916, Congress made one more attempt to promote large-scale privatization of the mostly arid GLO-administered lands by enacting the Stock-Raising Homestead Act (SRHA).

Then, in 1920, Congress completed work on two landmark laws. The Mineral Leasing Act resolved the long struggle over whether fossil fuels on lands overseen by the GLO and the Forest Service should be held and developed via leasing arrangements instead of being privatized under the Mining Law. The Federal Water Power Act gave the Forest Service (as well as other agencies administering public land reservations) the authority to prescribe conditions governing hydropower projects on their lands; this action was part of a general reform that made hydropower projects subject to a new regulatory program administered by a new agency, the Federal Power Commission.

THE STOCK-RAISING HOMESTEAD ACT

On the surface, the SRHA was a substantial victory for those advocating homesteading with modest-size ranches, a small advance for mineral developers, and a near-total defeat for larger livestock enterprises. As it worked out, however, many who tried to make it as rancher-homesteaders were doomed to failure, and many of the public lands privatized under the SRHA ended up being consolidated into larger ranches or reacquired by the United States in rescue operations.[1]

The stage for the SRHA was set by three initiatives launched during the Roosevelt and Taft administrations. The first was when Congress raised the 160-acre cap set in the Homestead Act of 1862 to 320 acres (in the Enlarged Homestead Act of 1909, which was intended to promote dry farming in nine arid western states), or to 640 acres (in the Kinkaid Act of 1904, which was the first homestead law based on raising livestock rather than food crops, and applied only in western Nebraska). The second was Roosevelt's and Taft's withdrawals of enormous tracts of public land thought to be valuable for coal, oil and gas, or hydropower, accompanied by their call for Congress to adopt leasing systems to govern the development of these resources. The third initiative was Congress's splitting the mineral estate off from the rest of the land and handling it under different laws, starting with the Coal Lands Act of 1909.[2]

Enactment of the SRHA came only after larger livestock operators made one more unsuccessful effort to gain a more secure tenure on unreserved public lands. In 1914, the congressman and gentlemen rancher William Kent revived the proposal that Theodore Roosevelt had advanced in 1906 to give the Department of Agriculture the authority to issue grazing leases on those lands. Kent's bill called for leases with ten-year terms. Ranchers would pay a grazing fee, and one-quarter of the fee revenue would be distributed to the states. Owners of nearby private land would be given preference, and local boards of ranchers would help administer the system. As before, the idea drew numerous opponents.[3]

Advocates of homesteading countered by urging Congress to expand the acreage cap along the lines of the Kinkaid Act. By this time, Congress had enacted the Pickett Act, and Taft had used it to confirm his and Roosevelt's massive earlier withdrawals of public lands thought to contain fossil fuels. Their objective, shared by Progressives generally, was to persuade Congress to have the government control the development of fossil fuels that might be found on them. If the United States encouraged homesteading on these lands, the Progressives' agenda could be served by its reserving ownership of the minerals in the homestead conveyance.[4]

Into this tangle stepped Edward Taylor, a Democratic congressman from western Colorado in his fourth term. Having grown up in a cattle-raising family in northwestern Kansas, Taylor had long opposed U.S. ownership of public lands. In 1911, he called the Weeks Act "one of the most amazing outrages that has ever been perpetrated upon the American people," and in a speech on the House floor in 1914, he condemned as "un-American" the idea that the United States should retain title to and lease the "resources of the West."[5]

The proposal he skillfully steered through Congress, the SRHA, permitted prospective homesteaders to occupy 640 acres of GLO-administered public lands that the Interior secretary had deemed "chiefly valuable for grazing and raising forage crops," lacking "merchantable timber," and "not susceptible of irrigation from any known source of water supply." The occupants could gain ownership simply by making valuable "permanent improvements" on the land rather than, as the homestead laws intended, by growing food crops.[6]

The 640-acre figure was borrowed from the Kinkaid Act, which Congress had approved in 1904 for western Nebraska. That program's less-than-smashing success—many who tried to homestead under it abandoned the attempt, and many who gained title went bust and sold out to larger ranching enterprises—did not deter Taylor. The Enlarged Homestead Act of 1909, which had raised the cap to 320 acres, had initially been more successful than the Kinkaid Act as dryland farming spread throughout the northern Great Plains. Indeed, more than twice as many acres of public land were entered for home-steading purposes in 1913 than in any other year since enactment of the Homestead Act in 1862. But ultimately, a good many of these dryland home-steads also failed, with the land ending up back in U.S. ownership.[7]

Unlike the Kinkaid Act and the Enlarged Homestead Act, the SRHA reserved to the United States all the "coal and other minerals" that might there-after be found in these lands, along with "the right to prospect for, mine, and remove the same." The reservation preserved the possibility that the United States could make the minerals available for development through leasing, but did not itself require a leasing system. Because President Wilson had left the Roosevelt-Taft withdrawals in place, Congress would remain under pressure to enact the legislation necessary to put a mineral leasing system in place. The SRHA also established a framework for resolving conflicts that might emerge between the homesteader and the developer of the reserved minerals, by allowing the latter to "occupy" as much of the land surface as was needed "for all purposes reasonably incident to" the removal of the minerals, but also obliging it to compensate the surface owner for any "damages to the crops or tangible improvements."[8]

The thrust of the SRHA was to promote homesteading by modestly sized livestock-grazing operations. While it succeeded in some places, it proved enormously difficult to make a living that way in many other parts of the arid West, where scores or even hundreds of acres of forage might be required to sustain a single animal, and where public lands in the vicinity were being grazed by other livestock operators. Although dozens of millions of acres of public land were entered under the SRHA, and millions of acres were privatized, many of the stock-raising homesteads, like many Kinkaid Act and dryland farming operations, ended in failure. Its enactment showed how Congress and many westerners "sentimentally clung to the homestead idea," as the historian Louise Peffer put it, much longer than conditions on the ground warranted. By the early 1930s, Edward Taylor and his allies were finally persuaded that the United States ought simply to retain ownership of practically all the remaining arid public lands.[9]

Over the longer term, the SRHA's blurring of the distinction between farming and ranching, and its sharp division between ranching and mining, had another, subtler effect—it helped change the image of livestock operators from business barons engaged in a kind of industrial activity to settler-homemakers who resembled Jeffersonian yeoman family farmers in the public eye. This shift, which had earlier been given some momentum by Theodore Roosevelt and his friend Owen Wister, enabled livestock operators to claim some of the hallowed reputation that homesteaders had long enjoyed in public land policy, and to exert political influence far in excess of their numbers or their contribution to the nation's meat production.[10]

THE MINERAL LEASING ACT

Once the Roosevelt-Taft withdrawals thwarted the ability of mining companies to access vast tracts of public lands, numerous bills were introduced in Congress to make at least some of those lands again accessible. Because oil companies were well aware of the difficulties that the arcane requirements of the Mining Law posed, most did not push hard for simply rescinding the withdrawals. There was also little support for selling the withdrawn lands or conveying them to the states. All this helped clear the way for acceptance of the Roosevelt-Taft proposal to retain the minerals in national ownership and make them available by leasing. What became the Mineral Leasing Act (MLA) promised to make mineral development more orderly than the free-for-all that had developed before the Roosevelt-Taft withdrawals. The main concern of most mining enterprises was that Congress not make them pay too much to the government.[11]

The MLA's journey to enactment had several steps. In 1914, in the aftermath of the alleged scandal involving Alaska coal land entries that led to the

Ballinger-Pinchot controversy, Congress enacted legislation calling for leasing, rather than selling, public lands in Alaska thought to contain coal. Three years later, as the United States was preparing to enter World War I, Congress enacted a hybrid sale-leasing system to govern the development of potassium compounds useful in manufacturing explosives. It authorized the Interior secretary to issue permits giving recipients exclusive rights to explore up to 2,560 acres of public land. If they discovered valuable potassium deposits within two years, they could gain ownership of one-quarter of the land included in the permit, with the secretary authorized to lease the remainder by competitive bidding or some other method. Lessees would pay the United States a royalty (capped in the legislation), and the revenue would be shared with the states.[12]

In 1920, Congress finally approved the MLA. It extended leasing to all fossil fuels (coal, oil, gas, and oil shale) and sodium and phosphate (minerals valuable for fertilizer) everywhere they might be found on public lands, except in national forest lands acquired under the Weeks Act and lands in the national park system or on military reservations. The long march toward that landmark reform was little affected by Republicans taking control of both houses of Congress for the first time in a decade in the 1918 elections.

In the end, the most contentious issue was—as is often the case when Congress adopts a new legal paradigm—how to handle the transition from the old system to the new. Oil prospectors had filed many thousands of claims under the Mining Law before and even after President Taft's withdrawals. Although most of these claims were effectively invalidated by the *Midwest Oil* decision of the Supreme Court in 1915, oil was being produced from a good many of them. Furthermore, after the U.S. Geological Survey published a report around the same time noting vast deposits of oil shale in western Colorado, eastern Utah, and southwestern Wyoming, many thousands of mining claims were filed on them. Even though none of these claims was producing oil from the shale in commercial quantities, all these claimants wanted Congress to give them title or at least a preferential right to lease those lands. What to do with these claimants provoked strenuous debate. The U.S. attorney general and the secretary of War opposed giving them anything, but Interior secretary Lane supported the idea of converting the claims to leases.[13]

In the end, Congress compromised by agreeing to provide limited and, unfortunately, ambiguous protection to prior claimants—the lack of specificity provoked nearly a century of litigation. With that, the legislation that reformers such as Roosevelt (who had died the year before) and Taft had long sought was given final congressional approval, and Woodrow Wilson signed it into law on February 25, 1920.[14]

The MLA remains a cornerstone of public land law. It ended a national policy that had prevailed since the 1860s of conveying full title to public lands that might contain fossil fuels or fertilizer minerals. While the United States would retain ownership of the minerals, it would not develop them, but would instead give private industry that opportunity, under governmental supervision. In fact, the socialist idea of the government itself undertaking to develop the minerals was discussed at some length on the Senate floor, and concern that it might gain favor helped convince some in Congress to support the leasing system.[15]

The welter of detail in the act's thirty-eight sections boiled down to giving the Interior secretary broad authority to decide when, where, and under what conditions to issue permits or leases for such development, and to adopt "necessary and proper rules and regulations" to govern the undertaking. It required competitive bidding in cases where lands were believed to contain the targeted minerals; otherwise, the secretary could issue exploration or prospecting permits, which could ripen into leases for at least some of the permitted land if valuable deposits were discovered.

To promote competition and guard against monopoly, the act limited the acreage and the tenure of permits and leases, required lessees to diligently develop their leases or forfeit them, and capped the leased acreage that any one enterprise could hold in a single state. Finally, lessees were required to make royalty payments to the Treasury, expressed as a percentage of the gross value of the minerals extracted, as well as annual rental payments. (The MLA gave the Interior secretary discretion to set the royalty and the rental rates, above a floor it established.) Only ten cents of every dollar of revenue received went into Treasury's general fund. Slightly more than half of the revenues were earmarked to build Reclamation Act water projects in the western states. The remainder was distributed directly to the states where the minerals were found, to be used for roads and public education.[16]

The core concept—that the United States would retain ownership of public resources and, at its discretion, make them available to the private sector through permits or leases, to be developed under governmental supervision, with the developer obliged to pay something for the value received—had been put in place for logging and livestock grazing on the forest reserves around the turn of the twentieth century. But the MLA took the idea to a new level. Fossil fuels were becoming increasingly vital to the national economy and—except for a few precious metals such as gold and copper—had by far the highest market value of any of the natural resources found on the nation's public lands.

The MLA thus was another demonstration of how deeply the idea that the U.S. government should keep control of public lands had become embedded in the nation's political culture. To be sure, not all members of the enacting Congress liked the outcome—although he voted for the bill, Senator Albert Fall of New Mexico decried the government inserting itself deeply "in business matters," where, he said, it had always been and "always will be a failure." But few others shared Fall's view, then or later. In the next few decades, with almost no debate over the basic approach, Congress adopted a similar leasing system for minerals on so-called acquired lands, for geothermal resources, and for resources on public lands submerged off the nation's shores.[17]

THE FEDERAL WATER POWER ACT

President Wilson signed the Federal Water Power Act into law three months after the MLA. It too ended a long policy debate. In the previous couple of decades, hydroelectric projects had become a major source of electricity in a rapidly electrifying nation. Many of these projects, especially in the western states, were on public lands. Indeed, by 1916 nearly half the total electricity supply in the western states came from hydroelectric projects located on national forests.[18]

The Forest Service, applying a policy developed under Pinchot, issued limited-term permits for such projects that required annual rental payments. Some projects—such as Hetch Hetchy, which generated electricity along with storing water and which was in a national park, not a national forest—had been approved by special acts of Congress. Nevertheless, the industry continued to lobby Congress to give it ownership of, or at least free access to, project sites on all public lands.[19]

Following the path that miners and livestock operators had laid down, some developers simply built projects on public lands without asking for permission. When the United States challenged the Utah Power and Light Company for doing that on a national forest in Utah's Bear River valley, one of the company's arguments was that local Forest Service officials were aware of its activities yet had taken no action, a failure that, according to the company's lawyers, prevented the government from complaining. In 1917, the case came before the U.S. Supreme Court.[20]

The Court unanimously ruled against the utility. Its opinion was written by Justice Willis Van Devanter, who was no stranger to public lands matters. As a young lawyer in Wyoming in the 1890s, he had defended ranchers in the so-called Johnson County War before moving to Washington, where he served from 1896 to 1903 as assistant attorney general with responsibility for the Interior Department. During Van Devanter's Interior service, he "did more than any other person to give character and distinction to the administration of the public lands," according to another Supreme Court justice, William O. Douglas. Roosevelt appointed him to the federal circuit court of appeals in 1903, and Taft elevated him to the Supreme Court in 1910.[21]

Those dealing with the government are not, Van Devanter wrote, entitled to rely on informal representations made by its employees regarding matters on which Congress had not given them the authority to act. When the United States seeks to "enforce and maintain its policy respecting lands which it holds in trust for all the people," it cannot be bound by actions of its "officers or agents" when those acts are inconsistent with the applicable law. Even if governmental agents had "impliedly acquiesced" in the company's activities, such a "neglect of duty" gave the company no defense in a case where the government was seeking "to enforce a public right or protect a public interest." Both the "settled course of legislation" and "repeated decisions of this court" had made clear that Congress ultimately controls the public lands.[22]

The *Utah Power & Light* decision helped persuade the hydroelectric industry that new legislation was needed to establish a workable mechanism for the government to give its permission for such projects. But the industry wanted the permission to be open-ended, without a termination date, and it balked at paying very much for it. The House tended to side with the Progressives, and the Senate with the industry, but eventually a compromise was reached.[23]

The Federal Water Power Act of 1920 was not limited to the public lands. It applied to all projects to develop power from or improve navigation on all "navigable waters of the United States" if undertaken by the private sector or by state or local governments. Henceforth, any such project needed to be licensed and regulated by a new entity, the Federal Power Commission, composed of the secretaries of War, Agriculture, and the Interior.

The best sites for hydroelectric projects were usually found on public lands. Indeed, a large majority of all the licenses that the Federal Power Commission issued in the 1920s and 1930s were for projects on national forest lands, not only in the West but also in other parts of the country where the United States had acquired land under the Weeks Act.[24]

The commission could approve a project proposed in any public land "reservation" only after finding that it would "not interfere or be inconsistent with the purpose for which the reservation was created or acquired." Even more importantly, approval was made subject to the conditions that the federal agency managing the reservation required for its "adequate protection and utilization." The act required licensees to compensate the United States for their use of "its lands or other property." Half of the revenues were earmarked to build Reclamation Act projects in the western states, three-eighths were given to the states, and one-eighth went into the U.S. Treasury.[25]

The Federal Water Power Act was generally a big victory for the Progressives, but there was one problem. Its broad reference to projects in public land "reservations" allowed the commission to issue licenses for hydropower projects on national park system lands, thus reopening the door to new Hetch Hetchy–type controversies just four years after the National Park Organic Act appeared to have closed it. Stephen Mather, John Howard Payne (who had succeeded Lane as Interior secretary in March 1920), and the National Parks Association strongly objected and asked Wilson to veto the bill. To defuse the controversy, President Wilson agreed to sign the bill into law only if its sponsors promised to enact corrective legislation in the next session of Congress.

The next Congress did add the prohibition on approving projects in the park system, although the industry insisted that the restriction be limited to projects within the system "as now constituted." Wilson signed the corrective bill on his last full day in office in March 1921. The episode illustrated the national park system's growing political stature, although it would not head off future controversies over whether dams should be built on lands in the system.[26]

CHAPTER FORTY-TWO

The End of the Progressive Era

BOTH POLITICAL PARTIES CLAIMED credit for the Mineral Leasing Act and the Federal Water Power Act, which would, Senator Thomas Walsh (D-Mont.) predicted, come to be regarded as significant for the West as the Homestead Act and the Mining Law of 1872. Their enactment ended the pivotal epoch in policy making that had begun in 1890 and gave lasting shape to the nation's public lands.[1]

They also ended for several decades intense congressional engagement in reforming public land policies, leaving the executive branch as the primary engine of policy development until the 1960s. Although Congress produced a steady stream of legislation on public lands over that time, only a handful of laws had a fundamental impact.

A good example of this rather abrupt loss of appetite for reform on Capitol Hill came in 1922. The Mining Law of 1872 continued to apply to all minerals not covered by the Mineral Leasing Act, the most important of which were gold, silver, and copper. Major mining companies had long understood that they were ill served by the law's obscure complexities, and in the 1910s they began to consider how best to reform it. Eventually, an industry committee recommended a thorough overhaul of the Mining Law, and reform bills were introduced in Congress.

In 1922 the House Committee on Mines and Mining held extensive hearings on reform measures. Industry and governmental officials minced few words in describing the law's shortcomings. Horace Winchell, a mining geologist from California, decried how the Mining Law had to be "stretched and warped and evaded" in order for the industry to operate, which often led to "expensive litigation, dishonesty on the part of the locators, and connivance on the part of land office officials." He called it "defective, inadequate, antiquated and pernicious," said it was "opposed by the majority of mining operators," and recommended that it be "radically changed."[2]

Opposition was led by those who benefited from the status quo, including small-scale prospectors, speculators, and those who feared that reform would deprive them of access to the public lands. The California gold rush and the other rushes around the West had given the lone prospector and small miner an image rivaling that of the homesteader in American political culture. Although they had long been a relatively insignificant part of the mining industry, they had no trouble finding champions on Capitol Hill such as Congressman John Raker of California, who said he did not want them to be "shut out by the engineer."

In the end, Congress took no action. The demise of the reform proposal ended serious deliberations over the future of the Mining Law for several more decades. In the meantime, the industry was left to continue to stretch and warp and evade the Mining Law, and it worked, with considerable success, to persuade public land managers to look the other way while it did so.[3]

ALBERT FALL AND THE TEAPOT DOME SCANDAL

In the fall of 1920, Warren G. Harding, calling for a "return to normalcy," swept to the presidency, carrying every state in the West and everywhere else except the South. Republicans also firmed up their control of Congress, gaining sixty-two House and ten Senate seats. Public lands issues played no role in the campaign. Harding named one of his poker-playing cronies, New Mexico senator Albert B. Fall, as Interior secretary.

Born in Kentucky in 1861, Fall was raised in the South during Reconstruction. His father had served with Confederate general Nathan Bedford Forrest (later the first grand wizard of the Ku Klux Klan), and did time in a military prison after the war. With little formal education, Fall emigrated to the Southwest in 1881, where he dabbled in mining ventures and crossed paths with Edward L. Doheny, who would go on to make a fortune in oil and be a key player in the scandal that brought Fall down.

In 1887, Fall settled in Las Cruces, practiced law, and entered territorial politics as a Democrat, but over time gravitated to the Republican Party. At the outbreak of the Spanish-American War, he joined the outfit that became known as the Rough Riders, organized by Theodore Roosevelt, but he never made it to Cuba. Thereafter, his career path resembled that of William Stewart, Nevada's Silver senator, for he served the New Mexico Territory in its legislature, as its attorney general, as a justice on its supreme court, and as a delegate at the statehood constitutional convention, and then became one of the state's first U.S. senators. Along the way, he invested in several successful mining ventures and acquired a several-thousand-acre ranch east of White Sands.

Early in his Senate career, he called for abolition of the Interior Department and advocated transferring management of New Mexico's national forests to the state. But he admired Theodore Roosevelt, nominating him for president at the 1916 Republican Convention, and voted for the Mineral Leasing Act and the Federal Water Power Act.[4]

As Interior secretary, Fall sought to have the Forest Service transferred to the Interior Department, and vigorously pursued plans to develop Alaska's coal, oil, and timber resources, but his efforts ran into considerable opposition and came to naught. On national parks, Fall compiled a mixed record. He supported Mather in opposing dams in Yellowstone National Park and fighting off attacks by Senator Ralph Cameron (R-Ariz.) on the National Park Service's administration of the Grand Canyon, but he continued to press hard for an ill-conceived national park near his New Mexico ranch.[5]

Fall quietly persuaded President Harding and his Navy secretary, Edwin Denby, to transfer control of the naval petroleum reserves that Presidents Taft and Wilson had created in California and Wyoming to the Interior Department. The Wyoming reserve was called Teapot Dome after a nearby rock formation, and the name soon became synonymous with scandal.

Fall's undoing began in April 1922 when, without competitive bidding, he secretly leased the entire Teapot Dome petroleum reserve to Harry Sinclair's Mammoth Oil Company. A few weeks later, he gave Edward Doheny's Pan American Petroleum Company an option to lease the Elk Hills Reserve in California, an option the company exercised later that year. As word of these deals gradually trickled out, criticism mounted. The Senate Public Lands Committee held investigative hearings on the matter a few months after Fall left Harding's cabinet in early March 1923 to return to New Mexico. It was eventually revealed that Sinclair and Doheny had both "loaned" Fall several hundred thousand dollars in 1921–22, which he used to restore and expand his ranch, and pay back taxes on it. When pressed on the matter, Fall attempted to conceal his "loans" from Sinclair and Doheny by saying he had obtained a loan from someone else.

By then, Calvin Coolidge had succeeded the deceased Harding, and the damning facts emerging about Fall's activities threatened Coolidge's bid to retain the presidency in 1924. To contain the damage, Coolidge appointed two special prosecutors, former senator Atlee Pomerene (D-Ohio) and future Supreme Court justice Owen Roberts, a Republican lawyer from Philadelphia. They eventually won a civil suit in the Supreme Court to cancel the Elk Hills and Teapot Dome leases, and Fall was ultimately found guilty of bribery. The first cabinet officer in American history to be convicted of a felony committed while in office, Fall served nearly ten months in federal prison and afterward lived in relative obscurity, dying in 1944 at the age of eighty-three.[6]

The Teapot Dome scandal had little impact on public land policy overall. It did not help the Interior Department in its competition with the Agriculture Department for primacy over public lands. It did make public land administration a favorite subject for press scrutiny and occasionally led Interior Department officials to express frustration with the multiple layers of review installed to reduce opportunities for fraud. In that way, Albert Fall's ghost stalked the halls of the Interior Department for many years thereafter.[7]

PUBLIC LANDS AND PETROLEUM IN THE AFTERMATH OF TEAPOT DOME

President Harding took a measured approach to exploiting the petroleum and other resources of the public lands. A few days before Fall resigned as secretary in early 1923, Harding created a new naval petroleum reserve in northwestern Alaska on 24 million acres of public land, an area about the size of Indiana. He explained that the future supply of oil for the military "was a matter of national concern" and that current law seemed "imperfectly applicable" to the unique conditions of the area, which was believed to contain substantial petroleum deposits.

In July, shortly before he fell ill and died in San Francisco as he was returning from the first-ever presidential visit to Alaska, Harding gave a speech—drafted by Herbert Hoover, then secretary of Commerce—that showed how much protection of public lands had entered the political mainstream. Extolling Alaska's "preeminence as the empire of scenic wonders," he said it was certain to become "a favored destination in summer travel," and he called for a firm stance against "a program of ruinous exploitation." Forest

Service chief William Greeley later wrote that "Gifford Pinchot himself never packed more conservation into a single speech."[8]

By the mid-1920s, oil production in Southern California, much of it from public lands, had doubled, and huge new discoveries had been made in East Texas and Oklahoma on private and Indian lands. Although the ensuing glut caused oil prices to fall, the Interior Department nevertheless continued to hand out thousands of permits and leases under the Mineral Leasing Act on tens of millions of acres of public land.

Shortly after taking office in 1929, President Hoover put a moratorium on new permits and leases for oil on public lands. The industry filed litigation challenging his decision, but in 1931 the Supreme Court curtly rejected its argument. The Mineral Leasing Act gave the Interior secretary discretion *not* to lease, the Court said, and it pointed to the secretary's "general powers over the public lands as guardian of the people," to the Pickett Act, and to its own *Midwest Oil* decision as leaving no doubt that the president could "withdraw public lands from private appropriation."[9]

That same year, Hoover persuaded Congress to amend the Mineral Leasing Act to allow federal oil and gas lessees to cooperate with others pumping from a common deposit underlying both public and nonpublic lands. Such "unitization" of operations allowed for more efficient production and illustrated how public land policies could be brought to bear to help curb wasteful industry practices.[10]

CHAPTER FORTY-THREE

Debating the Future of Unreserved Public Lands

THE STOCK-RAISING HOMESTEAD ACT showed how homesteading still commanded considerable political power in 1916, but it was obvious to close observers that most remaining unreserved public lands were simply too arid and rugged to support settlement through ranches capped at 640 acres. Will Barnes of the Forest Service estimated in 1917 that a single cow on such lands might need 35–50 acres. As a result, the SRHA, in the words of the historian Paul Gates, was "nothing but a remnant sale."[1]

Initially, the SRHA's objective of promoting homesteading by modest-sized ranching enterprises met with some success. Within a year, more than sixty thousand entries had been made, and Interior secretary Lane wrote Congressman Carl Hayden (D-Ariz.) in 1918 that he expected the SRHA to "leave the Government hardly enough grazing land to be worth consideration." Lane's prediction proved wildly optimistic. SRHA entries were eventually made on more than 56 million acres of public land, but two-thirds of them never led to title being transferred, and privatization never exceeded 3 million acres in any single year.[2]

Still, in the first third of the twentieth century, more public land was privatized under the original Homestead Act, the Enlarged Homestead Act, and the SRHA combined than had been privatized under the Homestead Act in the last third of the nineteenth. In the more arid regions, privatization often increased competition for forage on the commons of the public domain, and that led some livestock operators to seek the greater security provided by governmental administration of grazing in the national forests. In 1919, for example, sheep and cattle interests that were grazing some 400,000 acres of unreserved public land in northeastern California as a commons decided they would be better off if the Forest Service took control and provided order. Congressman John Raker introduced legislation authorizing the president to transfer the land to the Modoc National Forest, and it quickly gained the approval of Congress.[3]

The pace of privatization steadily dwindled throughout the 1920s, falling below 2 million acres in 1928, and below 1 million in 1933. During that same period, numerous dryland farmers and small ranching enterprises went bust, victims of low commodity prices, drought, or both. Some of their land was acquired by larger operators, but a good deal of it was eventually reacquired by the United States.[4] Many westerners saw this coming. In 1920, Congressman Frank Mondell told his colleagues that the idea of homesteading may have been carried "too far," and that the country "may be reaching a time" to "arrange some way" for these lands be leased for grazing, being careful not to "tie them up in great leaseholds." In his *Annual Report* of 1923, the commissioner of the General Land Office, William Spry, a Republican who had been governor of Utah from 1909 to 1917, wrote that 640-acre parcels of public lands could "no longer readily [be] found" that would "justify efforts at stock raising." Therefore, he concluded, Congress ought to direct the Interior secretary to institute a leasing program in order to "insure the preservation of the pasturage." Hubert Work, Albert Fall's successor as Interior secretary, put things more bluntly, warning President Coolidge in 1924 that "unauthorized and unrestricted grazing on the public domain is, I believe, destroying it."[5]

The risk remained that large livestock operators could monopolize public rangelands by controlling vital water sources, and the General Land Office continued to work to prevent it. The SRHA had reaffirmed the president's power to reserve public lands that contained "water holes or other bodies of water needed or used by the public for watering purposes," as well as lands needed to provide public access to them. Any lands so reserved were to be "kept and held open to the public use for such purposes" under rules that the Interior secretary was to prescribe. In 1926, after nearly 400,000 acres of public lands containing identifiable water sources had been reserved, President Coolidge expanded the effort tremendously. He issued an executive order that, without specifying individual tracts, simply withdrew *all* the remaining public lands in the immediate vicinity of *every* "spring or waterhole" *anywhere* on "vacant unappropriated unreserved public land."[6]

The reform pot was stirred in Congress in the mid-1920s. First, congressional appropriations committees, over which western members of Congress had less influence than they did on the committees dealing specifically with national forests and other public lands, began pressing the Forest Service to raise its grazing fee to a level more comparable to what private landowners charged. That pressure eventually led a subcommittee of the Senate Public Lands Committee to conduct a general review of livestock grazing on unreserved public lands as well as on the national forests. It was chaired by Senator Robert Stanfield (R-Ore.), who had gained a measure of fame during World War I by operating what was reputed to be the world's largest sheep ranch, with more than 350,000 head. His subcommittee conducted hearings throughout the West in 1925. Eventually, a reform bill was negotiated with the Coolidge administration that followed the outlines of the proposal that Theodore Roosevelt had made in 1906–7 to create a program in the Agriculture Department for leasing the unreserved public lands. It provoked the usual wide-ranging opposition, including from those who preferred the status quo; those who wanted Interior to be in charge; and those who wanted the grazing lands turned over to the states.[7]

As with several previous efforts, this rich brew of conflicting interests doomed the bill, but not before the SRHA's primary sponsor, Edward Taylor, expressed the hope that a system could be devised to give the Interior Department control of livestock grazing on the public lands outside the national forests, with less "red tape and machinery and expense of leasing." A couple of years later, Scott Leavitt, who had been a Forest Service ranger from 1907 to 1917 before being elected to Congress in 1922, worked with ranchers in southeastern Montana to craft a bill addressing deteriorating local rangeland conditions. Enacted into law in 1928, it established what became known as the Mizpah-Pumpkin Creek Cooperative Grazing Unit, and authorized public lands in the 109,000-acre unit to be leased for up to ten years to ranchers who would work to restore the rangeland to health and graze it under Interior Department regulations. The experiment seemed to have promise, as did a similar one in Custer County, Idaho.[8]

WILDLIFE AND SCENERY ON THE UNRESERVED PUBLIC LANDS ATTRACT ATTENTION

President Coolidge's call for the U.S. government to take the lead in promoting outdoor recreation eventually led a joint committee of the American Forestry Association and the National Parks Association to survey and report on the recreation-related resources available on public lands. Released in 1928, one of its recommendations was to identify areas of remaining unreserved lands that were suitable for protection through the Antiquities Act. It also noted how some unreserved public lands, which tended to be at lower elevations than the national forests or national parks, played a vital role in wildlife conservation, and how some wildlife populations were declining because of intense livestock grazing. "There is no graver conservation problem," it warned, than the "present imperative need to restore the productivity of these lands, to stabilize the livestock industry, and preserve some remnant, at least, of the wild life of the western ranges."[9]

That same year, Robert Sterling Yard published a remarkable book, *Our Federal Lands: A Romance of American Development*. It catalogued areas of unreserved public lands that he recommended be kept in national ownership and managed for recreation and other broad public purposes. Many of his suggestions were prescient. For example, he described the part of the Colorado Plateau centered in southern Utah as the place where "scenically the Public Domain reaches its climax": "No other country of its general nature . . . is nearly its equal in size, ruggedness, diversity, richness and sheer beauty of form and color. For minute detail and heroic example, it challenges the world of erosional spectacles." Its "extraordinary values," he wrote, "may not be measured in dollars." Similarly, he described the Owyhee River country around the intersection of Idaho, Oregon, and Nevada as "invaluable for summer recreation," even though it was currently "overgrazed," and he predicted that it would ultimately be recognized for the recreational opportunities it offered.[10]

THE HOOVER ADMINISTRATION AND THE GARFIELD COMMITTEE

In the late summer of 1929, President Hoover's Interior secretary, Ray Lyman Wilbur, told a gathering of western governors in Boise, Idaho, that it was time for a "new public land policy," one that would transfer control of the "surface rights" to all public lands outside national parks, monuments, and forests to states "willing to accept the responsibility." Hoover and Wilbur had met as undergraduates at Stanford University in the 1890s. Wilbur served as Stanford's president from 1916 until 1943, and did not officially take leave when serving as Interior secretary.[11]

Hoover followed up with a letter providing more details. The "lack of constructive regulation" of public lands chiefly valuable for grazing had, he told the governors, led to "over-grazing and their deterioration," impairing soils and water supplies. States should be given an opportunity to obtain surface rights to these lands, but he added an important qualification—the United States should retain ownership of any lands possessing a "distinctly national as well as local importance." Furthermore, any transfer should protect "homesteaders and the small stockmen," though Hoover supplied no details about how this might be done.[12]

While Hoover—who had made a fortune as a mining engineer—wanted the United States to retain the mineral rights on any transferred lands, doing so would not, he assured the governors, deprive states of any money, because under the terms of the Mineral Leasing Act, the "royalties from mineral rights revert to the Western states either directly or through the Reclamation Fund." Here he exaggerated, but only slightly, since the Mineral Leasing Act of 1920 called for the United States to keep 10 percent of leasing revenue. Anticipating states' concern about how the proposal might affect their share of the federal road fund (whose formula for distribution gave more money to states with larger amounts of public land), Hoover suggested that the current formula remain "undisturbed for at least ten years" as a transition period.

Reaction to the Hoover-Wilbur proposal was decidedly mixed both in the West and nationally, but the idea was not dismissed out of hand. Congressman Don Colton sponsored a congressional resolution creating a "Committee on the Conservation and Administration of the Public Domain" to study Hoover's idea. Colton told his colleagues that something needed to be done because the lack of "supervision or control" on the unreserved public lands had led to their "being ruined" by overgrazing and erosion so severe that it called into question the very "future of the livestock industry in the West."[13]

Nearly all twenty members of what came to be known as the Garfield Committee—after its chair, former Interior secretary James R. Garfield—were Republicans. Because each western state governor selected a member, most were from the intermountain West. By the time of its first meeting, in late 1929, the stock market had crashed and the nation was plunging into the Great Depression.

The committee's report, issued on January 16, 1931, was thoroughly vetted by the states, Congress, and relevant interest groups. The report and that vetting laid bare the complicated ideological and financial considerations involved in making fundamental changes regarding these remaining unreserved public lands. The committee adopted many of Hoover's suggestions, but qualified and limited them in important ways. It noted the steady decline in home-steading under the 1862 and 1909 acts from the peak reached in 1913, and a similar decline in SRHA entries after 1922. It also noted the many failures marked by "abandoned homes," which provided "pitiful evidence of human hopes buried beneath the economic insufficiency of 640 acres in a semiarid section as a stock-raising unit to support a family." There was, it concluded, "no room for disagreement" that "some form of regulation of the range is an immediate necessity."[14]

The committee's first recommendation, therefore, was that all remaining unreserved public land be put under "responsible administration or regulation for the conservation and beneficial use of its resources," and that the states be given the option to accept that responsibility.

Before the United States made any such land transfer, however, it should first reserve those public lands deemed "important for national defense, reclamation purposes, reservoir sites, national forests, national parks, national monuments, and migratory-bird refuges." Boards composed of three U.S. and two state representatives should be formed in each state to make recommendations about which lands the United States should keep. The committee noted that national parks and monuments protected "wilderness areas in their natural state," as well as "archaeological and ethnological remains" and "unusual wonders of nature," and it expressed the desire that the future growth of the National Park Service "be assured." It also recommended that the "conservation of our wild life, including migratory birds," be given "equal consideration" with other possible uses. It also recommended that any grants of land to states "should be safeguarded in that respect."[15]

Only after a comprehensive review to determine which lands ought to be kept in national ownership would the remaining public lands—those believed valuable "chiefly for the production of forage"—be offered to the states. Even that offer had significant strings attached. Any lands conveyed to the states should be "impressed with a trust" that would require their "rehabilitation" and include such other "restrictions as Congress might deem appropriate." (Although the committee did not acknowledge it, this recommendation strongly resembled the Yosemite Valley grant to California in 1864, by which Congress impressed state ownership with a federal trust that significantly limited what California could do with the land.) The report went on to suggest that Congress prohibit states from relinquishing ownership of any land they received except through public auction, with all proceeds being put in a state permanent fund.

States would have ten years to decide whether to accept the offer. If a state declined, the lands would be retained by the United States, with the president having the responsibility of regulating grazing use on them. (The committee's decision to give this authority to the president allowed it to sidestep the delicate issue whether the Interior or Agriculture Department would have control.) The United States would retain mineral rights on any lands it conveyed to the states, unless and until a state developed a program of mineral-land conservation and use similar to that found in the Mineral Leasing Act of 1920. This meant that any state acquiring mineral rights could not sell them, but only lease them for a fair return, and would have to devote a majority of revenues from mineral leases to irrigation projects.[16]

Congress had imposed similar requirements on states less than four years earlier, in the so-called Jones Act of 1927. That law had come in response to a campaign by some western states, led by Utah governor George Dern, asking that they be allowed to obtain public lands considered mineral in character as part of their statehood school-land grants. Up to this time, Congress had never agreed to convey public lands considered mineral in character to states. Some western states had not yet received all the lands granted to them at statehood because surveys required to determine the location of the granted lands had still not been completed. The Jones Act provided that these western states could obtain lands that were mineral in character to complete their statehood grants, but on the "express condition" that the states develop any minerals found on these lands only through leasing, not sale, and use revenues derived from leasing only "in aid of the common or public schools," or otherwise forfeit the grant.[17]

Every member of the Garfield Committee signed its report except William Greeley, who had recently stepped down after eight years as Forest Service chief. Greeley favored simply extending the Forest Service's system of grazing regulation to the unreserved public lands. He noted that President Hoover had, in announcing the committee, emphasized the need for "a great western strategy for the protection of watersheds." Watershed protection had been a primary reason for the creation of the national forests in the first place, and Congress remained aware that livestock grazing could interfere with it. In fact, Hoover soon signed into law a bill that reserved public land along both sides of California's Owens Valley in order to protect a water-export project that the City of Los Angeles had undertaken, and authorized the Interior secretary to regulate livestock grazing on the reserved land in order to "conserve" its "natural forage resources." Although the committee did not endorse Greeley's suggestion, he did not file a formal dissent.[18]

REACTION TO THE GARFIELD COMMITTEE'S REPORT

Initial public reaction to the committee's report ranged from lukewarm to sharply negative. Over the many months that the administration took to develop legislation to implement its recommendations, whatever support had existed for the idea of giving the states more responsibility for the remaining unreserved public lands largely evaporated.

The administration's bill was finally introduced in Congress at the end of 1931. At hearings held on it in both the House and Senate in March 1932, representatives of the affected states expressed opposition based on three concerns. One was that the public lands they might eventually be offered were more a liability than an asset. As Utah's Governor Dern, who led the western states' response, put it: "The states already own, in their school land grants, millions of acres of this same kind of land, which they can neither sell nor lease, and which is yielding no income. Why should they want more of this precious heritage of desert?" States like Nevada, with a small population and vast amounts of unreserved public lands, simply could not take on the costs of administering such a huge amount of territory.[19]

The states' second problem was the loss of the key to the door of the U.S. Treasury that the public lands supplied. Hoover and the committee had foreseen their concern about the loss of federal funds for building and maintaining roads, since the formula for distributing them was based partly on the amount of public land found within a state, but the states were not placated by the committee's recommendation that the existing formula be continued for a "definite period" of transition. Westerners also feared they could lose access to federal funds to build more water projects in the West. Governor Dern told Congress that the western states were "dependent upon reclamation works built by the Federal Government" and feared that "accepting these public lands" would undermine their case for more assistance.[20]

The states' third objection was that mineral rights were not included. They were not satisfied by Hoover's reminder that under the Mineral Leasing Act of 1920, the states already received, directly or indirectly through the Reclamation Fund, 90 percent of the revenue derived from federal mineral leases. They knew that Congress could change that formula in the future, and that states could only influence, but not control, when and under what conditions the United States might lease the minerals it retained.[21]

Reaction from interest groups with a stake in the public lands was almost uniformly negative. The minerals industry and some larger ranching enterprises preferred to deal with a single government rather than with multiple ones. Livestock associations in Nevada, which were composed mostly of large livestock enterprises, preferred to take their chances with the federal government. Defenders of the free ride that the Mining Law of 1872 provided on public lands did not welcome the prospect of states gaining control of minerals with an obligation to administer them through a leasing system that required the payment of royalties. Some smaller-scale ranchers, miners, and homestead advocates worried about being marginalized if state governments had more control of public lands. The Idaho Wool Growers Association protested that its members could be deprived of access to free forage on the public lands.[22]

Livestock interests were concerned that transferring lands to the states might weaken the case for U.S.-sponsored predator control. The connection between U.S. land ownership and federal funding for predator control had been highlighted when President Hoover signed the Animal Damage Control Act into law just weeks after the Garfield Committee's report was released. It authorized the secretary of Agriculture to spend $10 million over ten years on "campaigns for the destruction or control" of predators on the public domain, as well as on national forests and on other lands. It was championed by Congressmen Scott Leavitt and Edward Taylor, the latter voicing the livestock operators' customary complaint that public lands were "breeding grounds and native habitat" for carnivores.[23]

The reaction of Gifford Pinchot–style conservationists was captured in the title of an article written by a Pinchot associate that appeared in *Harper's* in October 1931—"The Handout Magnificent." Supporters of national parks and wildlife refuges voiced fears that transferring the remaining unreserved public lands to the states would drastically curtail opportunities to establish more parks, refuges and monuments.[24]

By May 1932, opposition from across the political spectrum had made it clear that the administration's bill was going nowhere. On May 5, Don Colton and his colleague Burton French (R-Idaho) proposed a substitute bill, based in part on Congressman Leavitt's Mizpah-Pumpkin Creek 1928 legislation, that would direct the Interior Department to take steps to restore the unreserved public lands to health. Although the bill did nothing to advance the Garfield Committee's recommendations, which the administration still claimed to support, the Interior and Agriculture Departments testified in favor of it, on the rationale that the Interior Department should have "immediate authority to regulate grazing" on these public lands even if some of them might eventually be transferred to the states. The Colton-French bill eventually passed in the House but died in the Senate. It was, however, revived by the Congress that was elected in the fall of 1932.[25]

THE GARFIELD COMMITTEE'S IMPACT

The reaction to the Garfield Committee's report in Congress and in the nation as a whole showed wide opposition to transferring the bulk of the remaining public lands out of national ownership. This left only one realistic path forward. As Louise Peffer wrote, it "clarified opinion" and gave an "all-clear signal" for the enactment of comprehensive legislation to control livestock grazing on these lands, with the objectives of rehabilitating them and husbanding their value for the nation while stabilizing the floundering livestock industry dependent on them.[26]

The episode had another, less appreciated effect. Although some histories describe it in simplistic terms—Hoover offered to give the states the remaining unreserved public lands without the mineral rights, and the states refused the offer because they wanted the mineral rights—there was much more to this chapter in public land history than that. Most importantly, the Garfield Committee report helped focus regional and national attention on the fact that these remaining unreserved public lands—mostly lying in the arid regions of intermountain West and Southwest—contained many areas with qualities worthy of protection in national ownership. Public interest in protecting natural scenery, recreational opportunities, wildlife habitat, and historical and other cultural resources had not slackened, despite the Great Depression.

Looking back a couple of decades later, Herbert Hoover expressed bitterness that the western states had rejected what he called the "gorgeous gift" of public lands that he had offered them. In his view, the states simply "wanted Federal money for the improvement and administration of these lands," and thus had only themselves to blame when the Interior Department established a "new bureaucracy directed from Washington" to guide "the cattlemen and the sheepmen toward the paths of sweetness and light." The historian Kenrick Clements suggested that Hoover's "ideological commitment" to his proposal blinded him to the breadth and depth of the opposition.[27]

But Hoover was also an avid angler and outdoorsman. In World War I, appointed by Woodrow Wilson to help ensure food supplies for the war effort, he had worked to keep livestock grazing out of national parks. He promoted a national program of outdoor recreation while heading Robert Sterling Yard's National Parks Association in 1924–25, at the same time that he was serving as secretary of Commerce. His wife, Lou Henry Hoover, also a Stanford graduate, was an advocate for enjoying the outdoors and headed the national Girl Scouts for several years in the mid-1920s. As president, Hoover worked to keep in national ownership significant tracts of previously unreserved public lands to serve purposes other than livestock forage.[28]

Hoover used the Antiquities Act to establish Arches National Monument in Utah (4,500 acres, April 1929); Sunset Crater National Monument near Flagstaff, Arizona (3,000 acres, May 1930); and Great Sand Dunes National Monument in Colorado (36,000 acres, March 1932). In 1929, he established an eccentric national monument called Holy Cross on a mountain about a hundred miles west of Denver, Colorado. On its northeastern face, a horizontal bench intersected a deep gorge, both of which held snow much better than the surrounding terrain, allowing a distinct white cross to emerge in the warmer months. Samuel Bowles had written about it in 1869, and over the next few years William Henry Jackson photographed it, Thomas Moran painted it, and Henry Wadsworth Longfellow wrote a sonnet about it. The area was included in the White River National Forest, the second reserve created under the Forest Reserve Act of 1891, but eventually it attracted enough attention and visitation that Hoover made it a national monument under Forest Service care. (It was transferred to the National Park Service in 1933, but Congress removed the monument designation in 1950 and returned the mountain to Forest Service administration after visitation declined, partly because erosion and rockslides had impaired the projection of the cross.)

In 1930, Hoover signed legislation enlarging and converting the national monument that Coolidge had proclaimed in southern New Mexico into the Carlsbad Caverns National Park. In February 1931, he signed legislation that established, with the agreement of the Navajo Nation, Canyon de Chelly National Monument within the Navajo Reservation, under Park Service management.[29]

After losing decisively to Franklin Delano Roosevelt in the presidential election of November 1932, Hoover ended his term with a Theodore Roosevelt–like exercise of executive power. He used the Antiquities Act to add 273,000 acres to the protected areas around Grand Canyon in December, and to establish new national monuments at White Sands in New Mexico (131,000 acres, January 1933); Death Valley in California (849,000 acres, February 1933); Saguaro in southern Arizona (54,000 acres, March 1933); and Black Canyon of the Gunnison in Colorado (10,000 acres, March 1933). Congress eventually made all of them national parks.[30]

In short, without much fanfare, Hoover made a good start on implementing the Garfield Committee's recommendation that deserving areas of the remaining arid public lands be reserved from divestment and protected in

Herbert Hoover (1874–1964) and Lou Henry Hoover (1874–1944), in 1930 (Harris & Ewing Collection, Prints & Photographs Division, Library of Congress, LC-DIG-hec-35974)

national ownership. Over succeeding decades, as appreciation of their marvelous scenic, archaeological, cultural, biological, and other values steadily grew, presidents and Congresses put many millions more acres in national monuments, national parks, and national wildlife refuges with names such as Bears Ears, Cabeza Prieta, Canyonlands, Capitol Reef, Cascade-Siskiyou, Chiricahua, Grand Canyon–Parashant, Grand Staircase–Escalante, Great Basin, Joshua Tree, Missouri Breaks, and Organ Pipe Cactus.

CHAPTER FORTY-FOUR

Wildlife Protection Gains Prominence

THANKS ESPECIALLY TO THEODORE Roosevelt and Congressman John
Lacey, public lands had become a means for protecting wildlife. But that cause
was still not a central concern of the national government when the Wilson
administration took office. A book published in 1910 with the title *The
Conservation of Natural Resources in the United States,* for example, made no
mention of wildlife.[1]

One reason was that several governmental agencies had some responsibility for wildlife-related matters, but very different objectives, reflecting the
disparate interests of market hunters and other commercial harvesters, sport
hunters and anglers, livestock grazers wanting control of predators, and those
seeking to protect and preserve wildlife. The Biological Survey in the
Department of Agriculture managed most of the first bird and game reserves
located on public land, but also exterminated predators. That department
included the Forest Service. Although its Organic Act had not mentioned wildlife, it managed the Grand Canyon Game Preserve and was also involved in
predator control. Otherwise, the Forest Service paid little attention to wildlife
while Pinchot was in charge. Its interest grew after Pinchot departed, with
Chief Forester William Greeley drawing attention in 1921 to the "considerable
public importance" of fish and wildlife habitat in the national forests. The
Bureau of Fisheries in the Department of Commerce mostly looked after the
needs of the commercial fishing industry. The Interior Department's National

Park Service looked after wildlife in national parks and some national monuments. Further complicating the wildlife picture, wildlife agencies in state governments generally assumed responsibility for licensing hunting and fishing on the national forests and unreserved public lands.[2]

A number of developments between 1913 and 1933 overcame these complications and made wildlife habitat protection a significant concern of public land policy.

PROTECTING MIGRATORY BIRDS BY TREATY AND STATUTE

The first of these developments was a provision in the agriculture appropriations bill enacted in 1913. Sponsored by Senator George P. McLean (R-Conn.) and Congressman John Weeks, it directed the Agriculture secretary to "adopt suitable regulations," after three months' notice to the public and approval by the president, to govern the taking of migratory birds, which it defined as those not remaining "permanently the entire year within the borders of any State or Territory." It applied to both "game and insectivorous birds." Protecting the latter was aimed at enlisting support from farming interests, since some nongame species were believed to help control insect populations that posed threats to crops. The legislation did not command unanimous support. Senator James A. Reed of Missouri scorned the case for it as nothing more than "maudlin sympathy for birds born and reared thousands of miles from our coast," and said the "only purpose" these birds served was to adorn women's hats.[3]

Some years earlier, the Supreme Court had dropped hints that states might "own," and thus have primary authority over, wildlife. The doubt this raised about Congress's constitutional authority to protect wildlife helped stymie action on similar bills, which had been regularly introduced in Congress for nearly a decade. The 1913 law was challenged soon after it was adopted, and lower federal courts in Arkansas and Kansas held it unconstitutional. The U.S. government appealed the Arkansas decision to the U.S. Supreme Court, but the judicial process moved at a glacial pace.[4]

In the meantime, Senator McLean and others suggested that to bolster the case for Congress's power to legislate on the subject, the United States should sign a treaty protecting migratory birds. There was precedent for such an international agreement—in 1911, the nation had entered into a treaty with Great Britain, Japan, and Russia for the preservation and protection of fur seals. The Senate passed a resolution supporting the idea, and the Wilson administration promptly negotiated the Convention for the Protection of Migratory Birds with

Great Britain (which acted for Canada). It was ratified by the U.S. Senate in late 1916.[5]

In 1918, Congress adopted the Migratory Bird Treaty Act (MBTA). Giving sweeping effect to the treaty's simple ban on "hunting" migratory birds during closed seasons, the act made it unlawful to "hunt, take, capture, kill," or attempt to do the same, or to possess, transport, buy, sell, or offer to buy or sell, any bird protected by the treaty, or "any part or nest or egg" thereof. The act did not distinguish between "game" birds, which were targets of hunters, and nongame species such as songbirds prized by birders. Violators could be criminally punished. The MBTA also authorized the Agriculture secretary to adopt regulations providing details about the extent to which hunting, selling, transporting, and carrying out other activities regarding migratory birds were "compatible" with the terms of the treaty. This idea of "compatibility" with wildlife conservation eventually ripened into a generic test for determining what could be permitted on public lands set aside as refuges for wildlife.[6]

The Missouri attorney general, an avid duck hunter, was cited for violating the MBTA, and he promptly filed suit on behalf of his state, challenging its constitutionality. He urged the court to apply its pre–Civil War decision in *Pollard v. Hagan,* which had suggested that new states automatically acquire ownership of public lands simply by virtue of their admission to the Union, and expand it to include ownership of wildlife. When the case came before the Supreme Court, in 1920, the Court turned back the challenge by a vote of 7–2. The majority opinion, written by Justice Oliver Wendell Holmes, Jr., showed how, in Linda Greenhouse's words, a great Supreme Court decision is "an episode in the ongoing dialogue by which the Court engages with the society in which it operates and in which the Justices live."[7]

Holmes seized the occasion to criticize an idea that eventually came to be known as "originalism"—namely, that the U.S. Constitution ought to be interpreted strictly according to the understanding of those who framed it. Whether the Constitution's framers contemplated that its treaty power might be used to protect migratory birds was not important, Holmes wrote, because the Constitution created a governing process, one capable of producing results that "could not have been foreseen completely by the most gifted of its begetters." This case, he wrote, "must be considered in light of our whole experience and not merely in that of what was said a hundred years ago," for it had taken "a century and cost their successors much sweat and blood to prove that they created a nation." Holmes had firsthand experience with blood sacrifice; he had thrice been wounded in the Civil War, in the chest at Ball's Bluff in 1861, in the neck at Antietam in 1862, and in the foot at Chancellorsville in 1863.[8]

The state's argument that it owned migratory birds, Holmes wrote, leaned "upon a slender reed": "Wild birds are not in the possession of anyone; and possession is the beginning of ownership. The whole foundation of the State's rights is the presence within their jurisdiction of birds that yesterday had not arrived, tomorrow may be in another State and in a week a thousand miles away." "Here," he concluded, "a national interest of very nearly the first magnitude is involved," one that can "be protected only by national action in concert with that of another power." Because the birds have "no permanent habitat" in a state, "there soon might be no birds for any powers to deal with" were it not for the treaty and its implementing statute. Nothing in the Constitution required the national government to "sit by while a food supply is cut off and the protectors of our forests and our crops are destroyed. It is not sufficient to rely upon the States."

CONGRESS LAUNCHES A PROGRAM TO ACQUIRE WILDLIFE HABITAT

The regulations that the Agriculture Department adopted to implement the MBTA prohibited the market hunting of waterfowl, limited sport hunting to a few months a year, and imposed daily bag limits for geese and ducks. Although the treaty that these regulations were implementing had been hailed as the "glorious conclusion" to the struggle to protect bird populations, and although the regulations did help stabilize populations of game birds, the good news proved temporary. The problem was that these efforts were focused exclusively on limiting predation by humans and did not protect habitat.[9]

It was not long before bird populations again began to decline, especially in the middle of the nation. A big problem there was the relentless expansion of farmland, which led to the draining of wetlands, especially so-called prairie potholes—small water bodies carved by retreating glaciers that were so heavily used by birds for breeding and nesting that some called them "duck factories." The middle of the country contained the most productive habitat on the continent, responsible for about half the total population of waterfowl.[10]

As the consequences of this habitat destruction became apparent, the scope of efforts to protect wildlife broadened to protect habitat. It also "taught people," in the words of one historian, to "think more ecologically about their relationship to birds." Although the idea of using areas of public land as "refuges" to protect wildlife from predation was by then well accepted, as efforts expanded to protect habitat, it became apparent that much of the most valuable habitat—especially wetlands and lands along rivers and streams—was in private ownership. Thus, a national program to protect wildlife would, in many parts of the nation, necessitate the government acquiring ownership of lands.[11]

Congress took the first step in 1924 when it authorized the establishment of the Upper Mississippi River Wild Life and Fish Refuge in the floodplain of the mighty Mississippi from Illinois to Minnesota. The legislation was drafted by the Biological Survey and the American Game Protection Association, a private advocacy group organized by the firearms industry in 1911. The campaign for the legislation was led by the Izaak Walton League of America, named after the legendary English angler, which had been founded by sport hunters and anglers in 1922. The league was the most influential group advocating for wildlife and habitat protection in this era. By 1924, it had 100,000 members (known as "Ikes"), and its monthly magazine, *Outdoor America*, became what one historian called the "most comprehensive journal" of the conservation movement.[12]

The legislation directed the Agriculture secretary to acquire, by "purchase, gift, or lease," areas of land and water that were "not used for agricultural purposes" and were suitable as a "refuge and breeding place" for all manner of wildlife, not just migratory birds, and for vegetation as well. Specifically, it aimed to protect "wild birds, game animals, fur-bearing animals, and . . . plants," under regulations prescribed by the secretary of Agriculture, and "fish and other aquatic animal life," under regulations prescribed by the secretary of Commerce. As in the Weeks Act, Congress required any acquisition to be approved by the legislature of the state where the lands were found, but that provision did not prove to be an obstacle. The legislation also permitted opening the refuge to hunting and fishing, which over time created considerable controversy among conservation interests. Ultimately, the legislation resulted in the United States acquiring a few hundred thousand acres along nearly three hundred miles of the Upper Mississippi in four states.[13]

In 1928, Congress took similar action farther west, authorizing the creation of the Bear River Migratory Bird Refuge where the river—which flowed in a large loop from Utah through southwestern Wyoming and southeastern Idaho and then back into Utah—emptied into the north end of the Great Salt Lake. Because much of its waters were diverted upstream, the establishing legislation aimed to restore as well as protect wetlands, and so it authorized the acquisition of water rights as well as land. It also authorized the construction of dikes, ditches, and other works, and the acquisition of what came to be known as "flood easements," a legal right to flood privately owned land where doing so would benefit wildlife. (This move was another form of splitting property into different "estates," like the separation of surface and mineral rights.) Agriculture's Biological Survey used all these tools to re-create marshlands that eventually attracted hundreds of species of birds.[14]

That same year, the U.S. Supreme Court dealt another blow to state claims of primacy over wildlife, this time specifically in the context of public land management. In a brief unanimous opinion authored by Justice George Sutherland (who had represented Utah in the U.S. Senate from 1905 to 1917 after earlier serving a term in the House of Representatives), it rejected a challenge by the governor of Arizona to the Forest Service's decision to shoot deer to reduce their numbers on the Kaibab National Forest north of the Grand Canyon without securing hunting licenses from the state. "The power of the United States" to "protect its lands and property does not admit of doubt," Sutherland wrote, citing several earlier Court decisions construing the Property Clause, "the game laws or any other statute of the state to the contrary notwithstanding."[15]

In February 1929, outgoing president Coolidge signed into law the Migratory Bird Conservation Act (MBCA). Loosely based on the framework of the Weeks Act, it gave the Agriculture secretary generic authority to purchase or rent areas of land and water that were deemed "suitable" for use as "inviolate sanctuaries for migratory birds" and had been approved by a joint congressional-executive commission. As in the Weeks Act, the secretary was obliged to gain the consent of the pertinent state before making any acquisition. By 1931, all but eight states had provided the requisite consent. The MBCA also followed the Weeks Act model by authorizing the United States to acquire lands encumbered with easements and other restrictions as long as the secretary determined that they would "in no manner interfere with" the use of lands for bird protection purposes.

The MBCA's reference to "inviolate sanctuaries" suggested that these areas would see little human use. The Biological Survey did discourage recreational uses on most refuges, but it allowed livestock grazing and even crop farming on some. While the acquisitions initially depended on funds being made available through legislative appropriations, within a few years Congress provided a regular funding stream through the sale of so-called duck stamps.[16]

The MBCA's principal sponsor was Peter Norbeck (R-S.D.). The son of Scandinavian immigrants, he served one term as governor before being elected to the Senate in 1920, where he followed in the footsteps of another Republican

388 LAND POLICY BETWEEN THE ROOSEVELTS

from the middle of the country, Iowa's John Lacey, as a champion of wildlife conservation. His sponsorship of the MBCA did not dampen his popularity at home; he survived the Democrat sweep in 1932, outpolling his opponent by 26,000 votes while Franklin Delano Roosevelt was carrying the state by 84,000 votes.

Meanwhile, new wildlife refuges continued to be created on lands that the United States already owned or had acquired by donation. The support of Presidents Coolidge and Hoover for such actions was not surprising. Both were avid anglers, with Hoover once writing in *Outdoor America* about how the "contemplation of the eternal flow of streams" is a "fine reducing agent for the egotism which we get out of narrow occupations." In early 1931, Hoover established the Charles Sheldon National Wildlife Refuge as a "refuge and breeding ground for wild animals and birds" on a 34,000-acre ranch in northern Nevada along the Oregon border. The land had been purchased and donated by the Audubon Society and the Boone and Crockett Club.[17]

Illustrating how wildlife protection had emerged as an important responsibility of the national government, the 1930 revised edition of *The Conservation of Natural Resources in the United States* contained a major section on wildlife. Overall, between 1921 and 1933, the number of wildlife refuges managed by Agriculture's Biological Survey increased from 70 to 102, through both reservations and acquisitions.[18]

CHAPTER FORTY-FIVE

Public Lands and Multipurpose Water Development

THE DISCUSSIONS THAT TOOK place in the 1920s over the future of the unreserved public lands were related to discussions occurring at the same time over the future of the program inaugurated by the Reclamation Act of 1902. While that program sought to "reclaim" arid public lands by irrigation and then privatize them, by the 1920s it was in considerable trouble. Of the more than two dozen projects completed or under construction in 1924, less than one-quarter had been initiated after 1908.[1]

Two things had become clear. First, rather than facilitating the home-steading of unreserved public lands, most reclamation-project water was being furnished to land already in private ownership. Second, the limited subsidy for farmers contemplated in the original legislation—a ten-year interest-free loan of federal dollars—was not nearly enough to make irrigation projects economically viable. Even though Congress had, in 1906, approved using reclamation-project dams to generate and market electricity to help pay for the projects, as well as authorized making project water available for municipal purposes, whose users could presumably pay more, most were financial failures.[2]

After a "few years of trial and a lot of error," as Marc Reisner put it in *Cadillac Desert*, his classic history of the reclamation program, Congress undertook a "long and remarkable series of 'reforms.' " As early as 1910, it began to pour more money—$20 million of general funds in that year alone—into Reclamation Act projects. In 1914, it relaxed the irrigators' obligation to repay their loans from the Reclamation Fund, doubled the repayment term from ten to twenty years, and lowered the amount due in the early years. Congress also decided that it alone would authorize future projects, recapturing the authority it had delegated to the Interior secretary in 1902.[3]

Despite these measures, the program continued to flounder. In 1920, it accounted for little more than 5 percent of the nearly 19 million acres being irrigated in the West. Meanwhile, not even 10 percent of the money lent to reclamation-project farmers had been repaid. To bolster the program's finances, the Mineral Leasing Act and Federal Water Power Act, both enacted in that year, earmarked about half the revenues they would produce for the reclamation program. That fall, both political parties' platforms supported extending the program. Then a severe depression hit the agricultural sector. With well over half the irrigators defaulting on their repayment obligations, Congress gave them what it called "emergency" relief each year between 1921 and 1924.

In 1923, Interior secretary Hubert Work, who renamed the administering agency the "Bureau of Reclamation" in an attempt to change its image, appointed a committee that came to be known as the Fact Finders to examine the mess. Besides former Interior secretary James R. Garfield, its members included Elwood Mead, who had years of experience in irrigation project development and administration at the state and the federal levels. By the time its report was issued, in 1924, Work had named Mead to lead the bureau. The Fact Finders' sixty-six recommendations were primarily aimed at requiring expert advance planning and tighter controls in order to improve the chances that governmental irrigation projects could succeed, financially and otherwise. As Congress was considering these recommendations, some outside the West— especially farmers concerned about bringing new lands into cultivation while the agricultural economy was seriously depressed—began to question the wisdom of subsidizing agriculture in the arid region.

In late 1924, Congress adopted many of the Fact Finders' recommendations in a rider on an appropriations bill. Just two years later, it further restructured the program, in what was known as the Omnibus Adjustment Act. Commissioner Mead began to turn control of the projects, as well as the responsibility for paying operation and maintenance costs, over to local water users' associations. This devolution somewhat improved things, but the program remained mired in controversy. With the agricultural sector in depression, successive secretaries of Agriculture began publicly sparring with Mead about whether the U.S. government ought to continue to subsidize irrigated agriculture in the West. This exacerbated the long-standing tensions between the

Interior and Agriculture Departments, which had previously been confined to turf battles over administering public lands.

While all this was happening, the Bureau of Reclamation and others were developing proposals to build very large dams and other works primarily intended to serve purposes that went well beyond the Reclamation Act's initial narrow focus on encouraging homesteading on unreserved public lands. These purposes included bringing irrigation water to more privately owned farmlands, supplying more water for municipal and industrial uses, reducing downstream flood risks, generating electricity, and, last but often not least, supplying political and financial grease to facilitate and implement agreements among states regarding how the waters of interstate rivers should be used. Accompanied by the development of construction techniques that made huge high dams possible, this greatly expanded focus fundamentally altered, although it did not sever, the reclamation program's relationship to public land policy.

The reorientation toward high multipurpose dams had its beginnings in a large irrigation project in the Imperial Valley in Southern California just above the Mexican border. That project originally had nothing to do with the reclamation program and little to do with public land policy. The valley, almost all of which is below sea level, had been settled and mostly privatized by the turn of the twentieth century. In 1871, the United States had given the Southern Pacific Railroad one of the last railroad land grants, to build a line from Los Angeles to Yuma, Arizona. Eventually, the railroad sold half a million acres in the Imperial Valley to an irrigation company, financed largely by eastern investors. It built diversion facilities to capture water from the Colorado River at a point below the international border in Mexico, and deliver it by gravity flow along an ancient riverbed west and north to the valley. That company went bust, but another sprang up in its place.

In 1905, high Colorado River flows overwhelmed the crude barrier that the company had built at the site of its diversion, and so for nearly two years the entire river flowed into the valley, inundating more than 200,000 acres and creating the Salton Sea. Only through strenuous efforts by the Southern Pacific, then controlled by E. H. Harriman, was the flow redirected back to the river's outlet in the Gulf of California. Valley irrigators then built levees along the river to try to prevent a recurrence, but the river carried so much silt that the levees had to be continually raised. The growing expense led the valley to seek help from Congress. At the same time, developers along the Southern California coast, which had already outstripped its local water sources, became increasingly interested in tapping the waters of the Colorado River.[4]

The Reclamation Service, seeking new sources of political support, responded to these events by proposing, in 1922, to build the world's first high dam on the Colorado River in a deep canyon on public land along the Arizona-Nevada border. The idea was to reduce downstream flood risks, generate copious amounts of electricity, and capture and make a massive amount of water available for multiple uses.

Meanwhile, the seven states in the Colorado River basin (Arizona, California, Colorado, Nevada, New Mexico, Utah, and Wyoming) discussed the possibility of an interstate agreement to allocate the river's waters among them. In 1921, President Harding appointed Commerce secretary Hoover to be the federal government's representative at the talks, and under Hoover's energetic prodding, the famous Colorado River Compact was announced in November 1922. It was the first time that states and the nation had agreed to allocate the waters of an interstate river. Unable to reach an agreement on each state's share, the negotiators divided the river's watershed into an upper and a lower basin—the dividing line being a place called Lee's Ferry in Arizona, just below the Utah border—and allocated approximately half the river's average annual flow to each basin. Although Arizona refused to go along with the compact, the other states and Congress agreed to move forward with it while setting aside a share for Arizona.

These developments were embodied in the Boulder Canyon Project Act, which Congress approved in December 1928. Besides the high dam (which was actually built in Black Canyon, after investigation revealed it to be a better location), the act authorized construction of a more secure diversion and delivery facility—all to be located within the United States, and hence named the "All-American Canal"—to deliver Colorado River water to California's Imperial Valley. The farmland there was practically all in private ownership and being irrigated already. For that reason, the Boulder Canyon Project Act did not itself result in the privatization of many public lands, which had been the primary motivation for the reclamation program.[5]

The Boulder Canyon Project Act fundamentally changed the direction of the reclamation program, which ever after had little to do with privatizing public lands, but still had considerable effect on public lands and public land policy. For one thing, the project works—what became known as Hoover Dam and the huge reservoir it created, named after Commissioner Elwood Mead, which extended more than 100 miles upstream, nearly into the Grand Canyon, as well as the 80-mile-long All-American Canal—were almost all on public lands. The engineering techniques developed to build Hoover Dam helped pave the way for Congress to authorize many more large multipurpose dams and reservoirs over the next few decades.

In the 1930s, the four largest dams in the world were in the West, and all were built by the U.S. government—Hoover on the Colorado, Shasta on the Sacramento, and Bonneville and Grand Coulee on the Columbia. The first two were built by the Bureau of Reclamation, and the last two by its rival agency, the Army Corps of Engineers. All told, between 1930 and 1980 the United States built more than a thousand dams. Most of the larger ones were located on, and inundated hundreds of miles of canyons on, public lands. They stored large amounts of water and produced large amounts of electricity for use in the region—in 1936, more than one million people crowded together in downtown Los Angeles for a spectacular electric parade to celebrate the arrival of power from Hoover Dam. The dams also collectively altered the hydrologic regime of nearly all the significant rivers in the West, with destructive effects on riverine environments, particularly iconic salmon runs.[6]

Over time, large areas of public land around many of these reservoirs were reserved and managed primarily for recreation, open space, and related public values, almost always in so-called national recreation areas administered by the National Park Service. There was more than a little irony in the Park Service's role, since the agency's origins were deeply influenced by the intense political fight over whether the Hetch Hetchy dam would be built in Yosemite National Park.

The model for national recreation areas was set at Hoover Dam, and grew out of recommendations made to Interior secretary Hubert Work in the early 1930s by Louis C. Cramton. In his nine terms in Congress, Cramton had championed the national park system. When he was defeated in 1930, Work hired him and tasked him to make recommendations regarding the 3 million acres of public lands in the region around Lake Mead that President Hoover withdrew from divestiture in April 1930. Cramton recommended that Hoover establish a national monument on nearly 300,000 acres near Grand Canyon National Park, which he did in December 1932. Well over 1 million acres, Cramton recommended, should be managed primarily for recreation under the administration of the Park Service. This was done, first by means of a cooperative agreement between the Park Service and the Bureau of Reclamation, and decades later by an act of Congress.[7]

Finally, and most importantly, the Boulder Canyon Project Act helped cement in place a profound shift in public land policy in relation to the settling of the West. For most of the nation's history, Congress had used grants of public lands to various entities to advance settlement. By the late 1920s, the experience with the SRHA and the reclamation program had made clear that practically none of the remaining arid public lands would be settled on that model.

For the next few decades, the arid West's remaining public lands became sites for locating federally funded projects to generate power and water to meet the demands of its burgeoning urban areas, where most of the land had long been in private ownership. The public lands also furnished large amounts of open space for recreation and inspiration, which contributed to the quality of life in western urban oases.

Over those decades, Congress made more federal dollars available to build and operate reclamation-project works than it did for managing national forests, parks, and all other public lands combined. As the western states' reaction to the Garfield Committee's recommendation had made clear, this transformation in the reclamation program made it easy for most western politicians to accept, indeed to welcome, the continued ownership by the national government of vast expanses of mostly arid public lands in their midst.[8]

PART SEVEN FILLING IN THE GAPS IN PUBLIC LAND POLICY, 1933–1960

CHAPTER FORTY-SIX

The Taylor Grazing Act

FRANKLIN DELANO ROOSEVELT WAS elected the nation's thirty-second president in November 1932 with 57 percent of the popular vote, losing only a handful of northeastern states. Democrats gained ninety-seven seats in the House and twelve in the Senate and took overwhelming command of the Seventy-Third Congress, which began work in March 1933.

Born in 1882, an only child, a distant cousin of the twenty-sixth president, and an avid birder and sailor from an early age, FDR was tutored at his family's estate along the Hudson River in Hyde Park, New York. After earning degrees from Harvard College and Columbia Law School, he quickly became bored with the practice of law and entered politics. Elected a state senator in 1910, he chaired the Forest, Fish, and Game Committee and promoted a number of forestry and wildlife protection measures.[1]

In 1913, Woodrow Wilson named him assistant secretary of the Navy, a position that Theodore Roosevelt had held in 1897–98. There he became a close friend of Interior secretary Franklin Lane and, because he strongly supported public ownership of hydroelectric dams, did not oppose San Francisco's Hetch Hetchy project. In 1920 he ran for vice president on the Democratic ticket with Ohio governor James Cox. Soon after their decisive defeat, he contracted polio, permanently lost the use of his legs, and dropped out of public life for a time. After reentering politics, he was elected governor of New York in 1928 by a narrow margin and reelected in 1930.

Public land policy was not an issue in the 1932 presidential campaign, which was dominated by whether the national government was doing enough to tackle the nation's economic miseries. In FDR's acceptance speech at the Democratic National Convention, he not only pledged a "new deal for the American people," but also called for employing a million men to restore forests and curb soil erosion on millions of acres of land, along the lines of a program he had supported as governor that promoted the state's purchase and restoration of cutover forest lands.[2]

The measures enacted in the famous first Hundred Days of Roosevelt's presidency included the creation of the Civilian Conservation Corps (CCC), staffed by unemployed, unmarried young men. On March 21, he asked Congress to enact the necessary legislation; it had done so by March 31, the first person was enrolled on April 8, and the first camp was opened on April 17. Within a few months, more than 300,000 men were working out of nearly 15,000 camps. Over the next eight years, three million men participated. In conjunction with the National Park Service and the Forest Service, corps members planted trees and built roads, trails, bridges, campgrounds, and other visitor facilities.

The Public Works Administration (PWA, originally the Federal Emergency Administration of Public Works), another agency that Congress established in the early days of FDR's administration, carried out other projects on lands in the national park system, such as the Skyline Drive and the Blue Ridge Parkway in Virginia and North Carolina. Both the CCC and PWA ended with U.S. entry into World War II, despite FDR's effort to persuade Congress to make them permanent, but not before their highly visible activities helped educate millions about the public lands and the government's role with regard to them.[3]

During his eventful twelve years as president, FDR took a more "personal interest in the details of conservation policy" than any president other than his distant cousin Theodore, according to the historian Stephen Fox. He gave the Democratic Party bragging rights for protecting public lands, just as Theodore had done for the Republican Party, but the achievements of both in this arena generally enjoyed bipartisan support. FDR gave prominent roles on public land matters to two Republicans who had drifted toward the Democrats and supported him in 1932. Henry A. Wallace was named secretary of Agriculture, a position his father had held in the Harding and Coolidge administrations, and Harold Ickes was named Interior secretary.[4]

Ickes was born and raised in Pennsylvania, earned bachelor's and law degrees at the University of Chicago, became involved in progressive politics as a Republican, and supported Theodore Roosevelt's Bull Moose campaign in 1912. A strong supporter of civil rights and civil liberties, Ickes went on to serve more than thirteen years as Interior secretary, the longest tenure in the department's history, and simultaneously directed the Public Works Administration. An incorruptible workaholic with a grasp for power and what Fox called a "ferocious integrity" that sometimes expressed itself in "self-righteous posturings," he so delighted in cultivating a reputation as a contentious personality that he named his life story, published in 1943, *The Autobiography of a Curmudgeon.* His tenure was marked by conflict, internal and external, most notably growing out of his unrelenting efforts to turn the Interior Department into a Department of Conservation that would include the Forest Service.[5]

ENACTMENT OF THE TAYLOR GRAZING ACT

By the time FDR took office in March 1933, there remained, in the forty-eight states, more than 170 million acres of unreserved public lands, nearly a third of which were in Nevada. Nearly as much land was in the national forest system, and 12 million acres or so were in the national park system and in scattered wildlife refuges and game ranges.[6]

Most of the unreserved lands continued to be grazed by domestic livestock without federal supervision. Many were in poor condition. Attempts to privatize these lands under the SRHA had dwindled, and many small farms and ranches in the more arid regions had failed. In the two years before FDR took office, influential Republican congressmen—Colton of Utah, French of Idaho, and Leavitt of Montana—had been making considerable progress toward ending the long stalemate over the future of these lands, but they were swept from office in the Democratic landslide. Edward Taylor, the Colorado Democrat who had been a principal sponsor of the Stock-Raising Homestead Act in 1916, took charge of the effort in 1933. Although Taylor had earlier strongly opposed the United States retaining ownership of these grazing lands, he had gradually changed his position as he came to the realization, he later reported, that "waste, competition, overuse, and abuse of" these lands threatened the "basic economy of entire communities," leaving only the national government to "cope with the situation," because the job was "too big" for "even the States to handle." The western states' rejection of the Garfield Committee's recommendation, he told his colleagues, clearly demonstrated that the idea of states taking ownership of these lands was merely "an iridescent dream." Although westerners once "couldn't find words vehement enough to express [their] denunciation of the Roosevelt-Pinchot policy" that sought to take over "control of the

Edward Taylor, 1858–1941 (Courtesy of the Library of Congress, LC-USZ62-125771)

public domain," they "have slowly and reluctantly come to see the wisdom" of governmental regulation of grazing as was taking place on the national forests, and hope "to repeat that policy on the fast deteriorating" public domain. Once convinced, Taylor pursued legislative reform with the "zeal," in Louise Peffer's words, "of a convert."[7]

In the first Hundred Days, Interior secretary Ickes sent FDR a memorandum asking him to support legislation like Taylor's. Roosevelt, aware of the mishmash of interests that had long produced a stalemate on the question, wrote in longhand at the bottom, "Yes, but there will be a howl." When Taylor's bill did not advance during the first session of the Seventy-Third Congress, which ended in June 1933, Ickes sought to raise the cost of continuing inaction. He ordered stepped-up enforcement of the Unlawful Inclosures Act, which prohibited fencing public lands without governmental permission. He also seriously considered instituting a leasing system by executive action, through the mechanism of withdrawing all unreserved lands from entry except by operators who had obtained leases from the Interior Department. His chief lawyer advised him in January 1934 that the Pickett Act authorized such action, but he decided to hold off in order to give Congress one more opportunity to act. In his zeal to convince Congress that his department, and not the Department of Agriculture, should be given the responsibility of administering grazing on these lands, Ickes claimed that Interior could do the job with a minimal bureaucracy and at a low cost that could be covered by a small grazing fee. (Ickes's rash claim led Congress to starve Interior's grazing-supervision program of funds for years, with predictable results.)[8]

In Congress, the debates covered the same ground that they had traversed for decades, with paeans to the homesteader, protests that big livestock operators would dominate a leasing system, and a few calls for states to take charge. But as Peffer put it, all those "old, familiar strains" were now merely "faint echoes" of earlier debates, "diluted by time and the hopelessness of the cause they represented."[9]

On April 11, 1934, what was now called the Taylor Grazing Act (TGA) passed the House by a margin of nearly 3–1. In June, the Senate made some adjustments before approving the bill by a voice vote. Colorado senator Alva Adams summed up western sentiment this way on the Senate floor: "None of us like[s] to be regulated, and that is probably more true in western areas than anywhere else," but regulation "is preferable to overgrazing and lack of regulation," which was the current situation. The House quickly accepted the Senate's amendments, and on June 28, 1934, President Roosevelt signed into law what Taylor later immodestly called "the *magna carta* of American conservation."[10]

THE DETAILS

The TGA was a landmark achievement in public land history. Its fundamental purposes were expressed in its title—to "stop injury to the public grazing lands by preventing overgrazing and soil deterioration, to provide for their orderly use, improvement, and development, [and] to stabilize the livestock industry dependent upon the range, and for other purposes." Although most of it focused on controlling livestock grazing, those last three words were significant, for the act recognized that these lands could have many different uses, and it directed the Interior Department to accommodate them as far as reasonably possible.

Its first section authorized the Interior secretary to establish "grazing districts" on unreserved public land thought to be "chiefly valuable for grazing and raising forage crops." The descriptor "chiefly valuable" has created some confusion ever since, and deserves a brief explanation. Throughout, the TGA makes clear that this reference was not intended to make livestock grazing the dominant use of grazing district lands at the expense of other values; that is, it does not prevent the secretary from devoting lands in grazing districts to other uses in addition to, or even instead of, livestock grazing. Section 3, for example, says that the Interior secretary "is authorized"—not required—to issue permits for livestock grazing in the districts. In section 15, the secretary is "further authorized" to issue *leases* allowing livestock grazing on public lands *outside* grazing districts, on largely the same terms as the *permits* the secretary was authorized to issue for livestock grazing inside the districts.

Read in the context of the entire act, in other words, the first section's reference to lands in grazing "districts" as being "chiefly valuable for grazing" has little legal significance. This fact has never prevented supporters of the livestock industry on public land (including federal administrators) from believing, and repeatedly asserting, that Congress decided, in enacting the TGA, to make grazing the preferred use of public lands in grazing districts.[11]

The TGA's second section directed the secretary to "do any and all things necessary to accomplish the purposes of this Act and to insure the objects of such grazing districts, namely, to regulate their occupancy and use, to preserve the land and its resources from destruction or unnecessary injury, [and] to provide for the orderly use, improvement, and development of the range." The third section permitted the secretary to issue livestock grazing permits to eligible stock owners upon payment of "reasonable fees" for terms not to exceed ten years. It directed the secretary to "specify" both "numbers of stock and seasons of use" and to give "preference" in issuing grazing permits to "those within or near a district" who are "landowners engaged in the livestock business, *bona fide* occupants or settlers, or owners of water or water rights." (The fifteenth section, authorizing the secretary to issue grazing leases on public lands outside grazing districts, followed the same approach, with some minor differences, calling on the secretary to give preference to "owners, homesteaders, lessees, or other lawful occupants of contiguous lands.")

The preference idea was borrowed from the system first devised by the General Land Office in the early 1900s and refined by the Forest Service after it assumed control of the reserves in 1905. The TGA was, however, the first time that a grazing "preference" had been embodied in legislation. The act went on to address whether this "preference" included any legal entitlement to graze livestock on public lands; specifically: "so far as consistent with the purposes and provisions of this Act, grazing privileges recognized and acknowledged shall be adequately safeguarded, but the creation of a grazing district or the issuance of a permit shall not create any right, title, interest, or estate in or to the lands."

The first clause quoted, up to "but," was drawn from language added in the House at the instigation of Congressman James Scrugham (D-Nev.), although, notably, his amendment referred to "grazing rights" rather than "privileges." Nevada's livestock operators, a relatively small number, grazed more than 50 million acres of unreserved public lands, or three-quarters of the entire state.

Administration officials strongly opposed Scrugham's language. The Interior Department warned that Ickes would ask FDR to veto the bill if it was included. As an Interior witness at a Senate committee hearing explained, "ruinous" overgrazing made "some reduction or redistribution" of existing grazing uses necessary, and that made the idea of giving "users of the public range a vested right to its use" problematic, to say the least. Forest Service chief F. A. Silcox agreed that the Scrugham amendment would open "the door to endless controversies, misunderstandings, and footless litigation." In response to the administration's concerns, the Senate committee rewrote Scrugham's amendment to limit its reach by changing "rights" to "privileges" and adding the clause beginning with "but."[12]

Two other textual changes made in the Senate and eventually included in the final version had far less content than met the eye. One, offered by Senator Pat McCarran of Nevada, prevented the Interior Department, once it issued a grazing permit, from refusing to renew it if the permittee could show two things: first, that it was in compliance with "the rules and regulations laid down by the Secretary," and second, that a failure to renew would "impair the value of" a grazing unit "pledged as security for any bona fide loan." McCarran's amendment did not convey a right to renewal, because it did not curtail the Interior secretary's broad power to make rules to prevent overgrazing and otherwise protect and improve the public lands, which rules could effectively prevent renewal of grazing permits in particular situations.[13]

The other amendment inserted the words "pending its final disposal" in the act's first section, which authorized the secretary to establish grazing districts. Like the word "temporary" modifying "withdrawal" in the Pickett Act, the word "final" meant nothing in context, because there really is no such thing as a "final" disposal of public lands. Were Congress to make what it called a "final" decision to reserve land in public ownership or to transfer ownership to some other entity, Congress could always change its mind and, in the first case, transfer ownership to someone else, or in the second case, reacquire the land for some public purpose. The word "disposal" also meant little, because many things besides relinquishing ownership could constitute a "disposal" of public lands, including putting them in national parks, monuments, forests, or other reservations. Nevertheless, the phrase "pending final disposal" would allow opponents of public landholdings to claim—despite overwhelming evidence to the contrary—that Congress in 1934 believed that the United States would ultimately relinquish ownership of these lands.[14]

Section 4 of the TGA gave the Interior secretary authority to permit the construction of fences, wells, reservoirs, "and other improvements necessary to the care and management of" livestock authorized by grazing permits, and also required a new permittee to pay the previous permittee the "reasonable value" (as determined by the secretary) of its investment in order to use them. Decades later, Congress incorporated this idea of successor permit holders compensating their predecessors for investments made on the public lands into legislation governing private concessions in the national parks.[15]

Other provisions in the TGA were a miscellany. One made clear that the public lands included in grazing districts were to remain open to access by others "for all proper and lawful purposes," which included everything from recreation to locating claims under the Mining Law. Another directed the secretary, in administering the grazing districts, to "provide, by suitable rules and regulations, for cooperation with local associations of stockmen, State land officials, and official State agencies engaged in conservation or propagation of wild life." Another prohibited holders of grazing permits from interfering with hunting and fishing on the public lands within the district. Another authorized the secretary to accept donations of land and to exchange lands on an equal-value basis. Another gave the president limited authority to transfer lands between Interior and the Agriculture Department's Forest Service in order to simplify administration. Other sections allocated half the revenue from grazing fees to the pertinent states for distribution to the pertinent counties, with the remaining half held in the U.S. Treasury (but half of that earmarked for the Interior secretary to use for constructing or maintaining range improvements).[16]

Altogether, the TGA created a framework for Interior to hold and protect these formerly unreserved public lands in public ownership indefinitely and manage them for a variety of purposes.

INITIAL IMPLEMENTATION OF THE TGA

In late November 1934, FDR issued a sweeping executive order withdrawing "all" unreserved public lands in all the western states except Washington from "settlement, location, sale or entry," pending their "classification" according to their "most useful purpose." In early February 1935, he signed a second sweeping withdrawal of all unreserved public lands in twelve other states (including Washington) in order to help implement economic recovery programs that contemplated using public lands for "projects concerning the conservation and development of forests, soil, and other natural resources, the creation of grazing districts, and the establishment of game preserves and bird refuges."[17]

Along with the TGA itself, these two executive orders spelled the end of large-scale divestitures of the nation's public lands outside Alaska. That this came without significant controversy—indeed, without much attention being paid at all—showed how deeply the idea of the U.S. owning and managing vast landscapes for broad public purposes had become ingrained in the nation's political culture. As a leading member of Roosevelt's so-called Brain Trust, Rexford Tugwell, put it in a 1936 magazine article, the TGA "laid in its grave" a policy toward public lands "which had long since been dead and which walked abroad only as a troublesome ghost within a living world." Tugwell's description was apt. Ever since, proposals to disinter the policy of divesting significant amounts of public lands have failed to gain significant political traction.[18]

All this is not to say that the initial implementation of the TGA was easy. To the contrary, it was an enormously challenging task to rehabilitate vast amounts of public lands badly damaged by overgrazing while also dealing with, and trying to bring some order to, an entrenched industry whose thousands of members had been grazing these lands with no governmental oversight for many decades.[19]

Hammered by the Depression and by deteriorating range conditions, many livestock operators were eager to embrace the change as long as they could continue to graze the public lands and would not have to pay too much for the privilege. The TGA initially capped at 80 million acres the amount of public land that could be included in organized grazing districts. Although the legal difference between the administration of grazing on public lands inside districts (by "permits") and outside districts (by "leases") was not significant, operators preferred to be in districts, and applications for grazing permits flooded in. To accommodate them, Congress amended the TGA in 1936 to increase the acreage cap on grazing districts to 142 million, and in 1954 it eliminated the cap altogether.[20]

Ickes selected Farrington "Ferry" Carpenter, a Princeton- and Harvard-educated lawyer from northwestern Colorado who had some ranching experience, as the Interior Department's first director of grazing. After holding meetings all over the West, Carpenter organized thirty-two grazing districts covering 75 million acres of public land. The Civilian Conservation Corps was enlisted to undertake range rehabilitation and improvements. Steps were taken to address jumbled ownership patterns of intermingled private, state, and U.S. public land, through land exchanges or cooperative agreements.

Following the TGA's direction that the department cooperate with "local associations of stockmen," Carpenter quickly established groups of what were initially called "advisors" (later, "boards"), who were elected by permittees. Because many smaller operators did not participate in elections, larger operators tended to win. These advisors determined grazing district boundaries, oversaw implementation of the preference system, and otherwise played a large, even decisive role in the act's early implementation. Indeed, one of the department's first regulations unabashedly provided that district advisors would be "the local governing agency as to all matters of a range regulatory nature." In part, this delegation ("abdication" is a more apt word) of federal responsibility was simply a practical necessity. Two years after the TGA became law, Interior had only one grazing administrator in the field for every 4 million acres of public rangeland.[21]

Determining who qualified for the statutory preference for grazing permits was a source of much conflict in the early years. The statute referred to several qualifications—"landowners engaged in the livestock business, *bona fide* occupants or settlers, or owners of water or water rights"—without prioritizing them. This left the secretary considerable discretion. After some waffling, Interior decided to give first preference to those who owned land in the vicinity and had an existing use. It considered fences on public lands to be evidence of use, even if the fences violated the Unlawful Inclosures Act. And it defined existing use as having put livestock on public land sometime between 1929 and 1934, a time period that favored larger operators who had survived the droughts and economic downturn that had begun to plague the range livestock industry well before the stock market crash. Itinerant sheepherders were disfavored, accelerating their disappearance from many parts of the western range.[22]

Another problem was to determine how many animals each permittee should be permitted to turn out on the public rangelands. There was wide agreement in Congress that some reduction would be necessary if the act's express purpose of ending "injury" to the public lands by "preventing overgrazing and soil deterioration" was to be achieved. Not long into the job, however, Carpenter decided that making operators comfortable with the new regime was a higher priority. As he told a statewide meeting in Oregon in December 1934, installing regulatory controls "as hastily as many people think we should" would "hamstring the livestock and hammer the heads of the operators unmercifully." On the other hand, he said, if "we go at it slow, we will continue to hammer the public domain." He described his approach with cold candor: "Well, as the public domain range is less articulate than the stockmen, we have chosen to hammer the public domain."[23]

Other factors complicated the task of restoring rangeland health. In some places, efforts to curb grazing to rehabilitate national-forest grasslands increased the demand for grazing on lands overseen by Interior. Almost everywhere, there was a paucity of systematically gathered information about conditions on the ground, and a limited amount of science that could be brought to bear to determine appropriate grazing levels. For all these reasons it was perhaps inevitable that, as Wesley Calef noted in his comprehensive 1960 study, permits were often "issued for many more livestock than the range could properly support."[24]

The Agriculture Department had recommended that FDR veto the Taylor Grazing Act, ostensibly because the bill did not give the Interior Department enough authority to control grazing, but more likely because it did not put Agriculture in charge. Still smarting from that setback, and increasingly concerned by Harold Ickes's campaign to convert the Interior Department into a Department of Conservation that would include the Forest Service, the Agriculture Department released a comprehensive report on public rangelands in 1936, at a time when Congress had before it the bill to amend the TGA to enlarge the amount of public lands that could be put in grazing districts. Prepared by the Forest Service and titled "The Western Range," it was the first broad overview of the status of livestock grazing on the public lands. It concluded that practically none of the grazing lands administered by Interior were in "reasonably satisfactory condition," with about two-thirds suffering forage depletion. (Forest Service administration of grazing on the national forests got only somewhat better marks, the report finding that only about half were in "reasonably satisfactory condition," and one-third having depleted forage.) The report called the Taylor Grazing Act inadequate, and recommended that the Agriculture Department take control from Interior. (It failed to note that Interior's deference to the livestock industry bore more than a passing resemblance to early efforts by Pinchot's Forest Service to manage grazing on the forest reserves after the 1905 transfer.)[25]

Both Ickes and the western ranching industry vigorously contested the conclusions of "The Western Range." In 1937, Congress gave Ickes a win when it provided his department with additional authority to manage the timber-rich, so-called O&C lands (named after the Oregon & California Railroad) in western Oregon, which the Forest Service had long coveted. Emboldened, he resumed his campaign to persuade Roosevelt to create a Department of Conservation. This time, livestock interests joined the Forest Service in opposition, and FDR threw cold water on the idea in early 1939 when he wrote Senator Key Pittman (D-Nev.) that he had "no thought" of transferring the Forest Service to Interior.[26]

Meanwhile, Ickes finally lost patience with Carpenter's livestock-friendly perspective and summarily fired him in November 1938. A few months later, to ward off a loss of influence, livestock interests worked with Nevada's Senator McCarran to write the role of rancher-dominated elected advisory boards into the TGA. Interior got the message; although the 1939 amendment allowed the secretary to remove any member elected by permittees, no secretary ever took such an action. Board members sometimes included bankers, lawyers, and other urban types. Not long after, the permittees organized a national council of advisory boards, mostly composed of representatives of larger ranching operations, to advocate before the executive branch and Congress.[27]

The operators' strategy worked. A Senate report in 1943 noted that the recommendations of the advisory boards were "accepted and carried out" in the "vast majority of cases." The Interior Department's decisions resolving claims of preference by livestock operators came to be referred to as "adjudications," which seemed to imply that a property right was being determined, even though it was not. Similarly, a couple of lower-court decisions, ignoring the plain language of the TGA, spoke of ranchers being "entitled" to grazing permits under certain conditions. Congress muddled matters even further in 1942 by enacting legislation compensating operators when the public lands they were grazing were appropriated for "war purposes."[28]

The political scientist Grant McConnell later used Interior's administration of the Taylor Grazing Act as a prominent example in his classic study of the "capture" of administrative agencies by interest groups. He found that the advisory boards behaved like a "public body when it was convenient and a private lobby when that was expedient." There was, he concluded, "probably no other public program of substantial size" in which "the elements of power and control" were "so stark."[29]

Livestock grazing remained the most prominent use of arid public lands in the sparsely populated rural West for generations, though its contribution to the nation's meat supply was never more than very modest. Operators continued to command considerable political power in the halls of Congress and in the Interior and Agriculture Departments.

CHAPTER FORTY-SEVEN

National Parks in the New Deal

FRANKLIN ROOSEVELT WAS A STRONG and vocal supporter of national parks. In a radio address in 1934, he expressed hope that every American could visit them, because they were "not for the rich alone." He went on well-publicized trips to national parks that year and in 1937 and 1938. The system's acreage doubled in the 1930s, and the number of visitors surged from around 6 million in 1934 to more than 16 million in 1938; FDR cited this increase as an "accurate barometer" of a recovering economy.[1]

Urged on by Harold Ickes and Horace Albright, Mather's successor as head of the Park Service, FDR looked for opportunities to add land to the system. He had been in office scarcely three months when, exercising authority that Congress had recently given him to reorganize the executive branch, he signed an executive order that paved the way for the Park Service to take responsibility for fifteen national monuments formerly overseen by the Forest Service, along with military parks, cemeteries, and other federal areas. It was a significant expansion of the park system.[2]

Altogether, FDR signed legislation establishing four new national parks, proclaimed eleven new national monuments, oversaw the enlargement of many existing parks and monuments, and took numerous other steps that enlarged the vision of how public land ownership could protect the nation's natural and cultural heritage and make it accessible to all.[3]

OLYMPIC NATIONAL PARK

One of the national monuments that FDR's 1933 reorganization order transferred to the Park Service was on the scenic, timber-rich Olympic Peninsula in the state of Washington. In 1909, Theodore Roosevelt had layered a 615,000-acre national monument onto a 1.5 million-acre forest reserve that Grover Cleveland had established in 1897 (but President McKinley later shrank). In 1915, Woodrow Wilson shrank the monument by more than half.

Public support for enlarging the national monument and redesignating it a national park grew when, beginning in 1933 and for several years thereafter, hunters killed several hundred rare Olympic elk on national forest land adjacent to the monument. In 1935, Congressman Monrad Wallgren (D-Wash.) introduced a bill to create a 700,000-acre Olympic National Park, mostly by adding land from the national forest. When Congress failed to act, Roosevelt considered expanding the monument. Trying to prevent loss of land to the Park Service while trying to appease those who sought more protection, the Forest Service enlarged a "primitive area" that it had established on the national forest.[4]

In the early fall of 1937, FDR visited the Olympic Peninsula to promote Wallgren's park legislation. It was eventually modified to create a park of 650,000 acres and to authorize the president to add up to 250,000 more acres from the national forest. As a small consolation, it gave the Forest Service control of a few thousand acres formerly in the monument. Roosevelt signed Wallgren's bill into law at the end of June 1938.

In early 1940, following more negotiations between the Forest Service and the Park Service, FDR, exercising the authority that Wallgren's legislation gave him, enlarged the park by some 187,000 acres, taking in rainforests in the river valleys on the west and the Elwha River headwaters and valley on the north. In addition, he authorized the acquisition of a corridor down the Queets River valley on the west all the way to the Pacific Ocean, along with a strip of land along the Pacific shore. This produced some grumbling locally, but it did not prevent FDR from carrying the Olympic Peninsula as well as the rest of the state in the election that fall, one that also saw Washington voters elect Wallgren to the U.S. Senate. (He was later elected the state's governor.) During World War II, the timber industry attempted to persuade FDR to emulate Woodrow Wilson and waive the protections to give it access to some of the area's timber, but FDR refused. The Queets corridor and ocean-strip acquisitions were finally completed and added to the park in 1953.[5]

NEW NATIONAL PARKS OUTSIDE THE WEST

Each of the four national parks that Congress had authorized in the East during the Coolidge and Hoover administrations required that the necessary lands be "secured by the United States only by public and private donations." Roosevelt was finally able to dedicate them in 1935 (Shenandoah), 1940 (Isle Royale and Great Smoky Mountains), and 1941 (Mammoth Cave). For Great Smoky Mountains, Congress appropriated several hundred thousand dollars in 1938 to accelerate land acquisitions. It was the first time that Congress appropriated federal dollars specifically to acquire lands for the national park system. (The Civil War battlefield parks had been acquired by the War Department and managed by it until FDR put them in the national park system in 1933.)[6]

The Great Smoky Mountains and Shenandoah National Parks required the Interior Department to face the challenge of enforcing the democratic ideal of equal access for all in the face of Jim Crow racial segregation, then at its zenith in the former Confederacy. Initially, the Park Service and even Ickes took the position that the agency would "conform generally to the State customs" in the accommodation of park visitors. That mandated racial segregation, and effectively meant that facilities for nonwhites were either inferior or nonexistent. When African Americans sought campsites that the "separate but equal" principle was supposed to furnish them, the Park Service often responded with the dodge that it would consider doing so only when "sufficient demand" existed. Ickes, long a committed crusader for civil rights, eventually became more insistent that the Park Service do more to make the parks welcoming to African Americans, but it took years to make much progress.[7]

In 1935, Congress authorized Big Bend National Park in Texas on the condition that, as with earlier parks outside the West, the lands involved be donated to the nation. The state already owned a good deal of the area and had put some of it in a state park in 1933. When the House member representing the area and both Texas senators proposed to enlarge the protected area and convert it into a national park, FDR was strongly supportive. The necessary legislation went swiftly through Congress without debate. When Roosevelt signed it into law, he expressed the hope it would one day become part of "one great international park," modeled on the Glacier-Waterton Peace Park, established with Canada in 1932. A 708,000-acre tract that formed the core of the park was deeded to the United States, and Big Bend National Park was formally established on June 12, 1944, six days after D-Day.[8]

PARKS FOR BIOLOGY AND WILDERNESS

While these new parks followed existing models, other New Deal–era parks broke new ground, with lasting impact. One initiative was to protect places with rich biological resources. A second, strongly supported by Secretary Ickes, was to establish "wilderness parks," which would have few roads or visitor accommodations other than primitive campgrounds.

Both ideas were nurtured by a scientist, George Melendez Wright, who had joined the Park Service in 1927 at age twenty-three, not long after graduating from the University of California, Berkeley. Dismayed that parks lacked essential scientific information, he began to direct a monumental survey of park wildlife populations. (From a wealthy family, he largely funded the study himself.) The result was a landmark series of monographs. Wright's work and that of other conservationists such as Aldo Leopold, Olaus Murie, and Margaret Murie cast new light on the tension, embedded in the National Park Organic Act, between managing parks for scenery-enjoying visitors and managing them to preserve ecological conditions. Among other things, the survey's results helped the Park Service move away from controlling predators. While it was "impossible to keep any area in the United States in an absolutely primeval condition," Wright wrote, there are "reasonable objectives that we can strive for." His influence was felt long after he was killed in a car accident in 1936.[9]

The idea of protecting the enormous diversity of birds and other biological resources of South Florida from the powerful forces of development dated back to the turn of the twentieth century. Not everyone identified with conservation was in favor; the dogmatic wildlife advocate William T. Hornaday regarded the area as "only a swamp" that was not "fit to elevate into a national park." In 1929, at the instigation of Senator Park Trammell (D-Fla.), Congress directed the Interior secretary to examine and report on the "desirability and practicability" of establishing a "Tropic Everglades National Park," not simply for the people's "enjoyment" but also "to preserve said area in its natural state."[10]

The report, issued in June 1930, was favorable, but Congress did not finish work on the necessary legislation for four more years. With Trammell and his colleague Duncan Fletcher (D-Fla.) in support, the bill passed the Senate without difficulty. In the House, the debate was not only spirited but also unusually partisan, with Republicans leading the opposition. FDR strongly supported the bill, having advocated for protecting the area since he had explored it while recovering from polio in the early 1920s, and his endorsement helped push the bill across the finish line in 1934.[11]

It authorized an Everglades National Park of more than 1 million acres and required the United States to acquire the lands only by donation. Much of the land in South Florida had been claimed by the state under the notoriously abused Swampland Act of 1850, and a good deal of it had been sold off to developers. That state of affairs lent a certain poetic justice to the state's reacquiring and donating large areas back to the United States in order to establish a new national park primarily for preservation and scientific study. The legislation required the area to be "permanently reserved as a wilderness," with no visitor facilities allowed that would "interfere with the preservation intact of the unique flora and fauna and the essential primitive natural conditions now prevailing in this area."

It took more than a dozen years to complete the land acquisition. The process was complicated by nearby oil discoveries, which led Congress in 1944 to enact legislation allowing the Interior secretary to accept land for the park subject to reservations of minerals, and to "furnish such protection" as "may be necessary" to protect the park until the reservations were extinguished. The park was dedicated in 1947, almost simultaneously with the publication of Marjory Stoneman Douglas's book *The Everglades: River of Grass,* considered a classic of nature writing. Douglas had been a staunch advocate for the park for years, and the last chapter of her book highlighted its continuing vulnerabilities. A primary reason for this was that the park protected only the downstream portion of the complex South Florida ecosystem. Today the park comprises about 1.5 million acres.[12]

Kings Canyon in the southern Sierra Nevada was another wilderness park established during FDR's administration. Efforts to create a park in the region dated back to 1881 and continued after Congress created the Sequoia and General Grant National Parks nearby in 1890. In 1919, both of California's senators and the local member of Congress proposed, with Mather and Albright's support, establishing a large park—which they would have named after Theodore Roosevelt—to include the watershed of the south and middle forks of the Kings River. The idea did not advance, even after renewed attempts were made in 1921 and 1923. Opponents included usual suspects such as livestock grazers, irrigation interests, power companies (which did not want potential dam sites included), and the Forest Service, because nearly all the land proposed for inclusion was in the national forest system.

In 1926, Congress extended the boundary of Sequoia National Park eastward to the crest of the Sierras without incorporating Kings Canyon. Finally, in March 1940, Congress enacted legislation establishing Kings Canyon National

Park (at one point, the bill would have named it after John Muir) on more than 450,000 acres abutting Sequoia National Park. It prohibited dams and power projects, and while it did not flatly prohibit road building, it authorized the Interior secretary to limit motor vehicles, "to insure the permanent preservation of" the park's "wilderness character." Thereafter, Congress prohibited using funds appropriated for park operations for the construction of new roads, underscoring the idea that Kings Canyon would be a wilderness park.[13]

Ickes often complained about the proliferation of roads and other creature comforts in the national parks. The Park Service leadership, influenced by Mather's legacy of promoting easy access to parks, did not always sing the same tune. For example, Arno Cammerer, the third director of the Park Service, published an article in 1936 in which he argued that roads can "make many friends" for a wilderness park because visitors may not "know what a wilderness is until they have a chance to go through it." Around the same time, the National Parks Association promoted the idea of establishing a separate "National Primeval Park System." While it never attracted political support, opponents of road building and other developments wielded increasing influence over time, and within three decades a powerful movement coalesced around the notion that areas of "wilderness" on the public lands ought to be protected by legislation regardless of the agency managing them.[14]

NATIONAL SEASHORES

Congress and FDR's administration collaborated to authorize the first park-system unit along the nation's coastline. As early as 1917, Stephen Mather had promoted the establishment of a national park on the Indiana Dunes, along the shore of Lake Michigan east of Chicago, urged on by botanists at the University of Chicago who were pioneers in the study of ecology. Sand dunes had originally occupied most of Indiana's forty miles of shoreline, but were being demolished to make way for steel mills, ports, and other industrial enterprises. Mather's idea went nowhere in Congress, although in 1926 the State of Indiana established a 2,100-acre state park in the area. (In 1966, Congress established a national lakeshore there and made it the nation's sixty-first national park in 2019.)[15]

Not long after FDR took office, the head of the Park Service's Civilian Conservation Corps operations, Conrad Wirth, oversaw the preparation of a report on "potential shoreline parks." In June 1936, Congress directed the Interior Department agency to study, in cooperation with state and local entities, "public park, parkway and recreational-area programs" in places other than national forests, and three days later declared it to be national policy to improve and protect beaches on the coasts in order to foster "healthful recreation of the people."[16]

In 1937, Congress authorized creation of the Cape Hatteras National Seashore, to be administered by the National Park Service, at the site of a large CCC camp along the North Carolina coast. Congress set its boundaries to include some 64,000 acres, with lands that the United States did not own to be secured only by donation. The legislation allowed portions of the seashore "especially adaptable for recreational uses" to be "developed for such uses as needed," but called for the remainder to "be permanently reserved as a primitive wilderness," with no development for "visitor convenience" permitted unless it would be compatible with "the preservation of the unique flora and fauna or the physiographic conditions now prevailing in the area."[17]

In a visionary speech in October 1938, Ickes made a powerful case for putting much more land along seashores into public ownership. He expressed dismay that the nation' s people, then numbering well over 100 million, could not "set foot upon the thousands of miles of beaches" along its coasts "except by permission of those who monopolize the ocean front." It was, he said, "the prerogative and the duty" of both the national and state governments to take measures to acquire "solid blocks of ocean front hundreds of miles in length," because "the people have a right to a fair share of it." It took another quarter century for the idea to take firm root, helped along by Wirth, who became director of the Park Service in 1951.[18]

CONGRESS GIVES THE PARK SERVICE A
MANDATE TO PROMOTE HISTORY

In 1935, Congress enacted the Historic Sites Act. It built on Congress's establishment of Civil War battlefield parks in the 1890s and on the 1906 Antiquities Act's focus on objects of "historic interest." Sponsored by Senator Harry Byrd (D-Va.) and enthusiastically supported by FDR, the law made it "national policy to preserve for public use historic sites, buildings, and objects of national significance for the inspiration and benefit of the people of the United States." It directed the Park Service to conduct a survey of "historic and archaeologic sites, buildings, and objects" in order to identify those possessing "exceptional value as commemorating or illustrating the history of the United States." Finally, it gave the Interior secretary broad authority to acquire, "by gift, purchase, or otherwise," land and other property for such purposes. The Historic Sites Act helped make public lands a prominent means of educating Americans about their history. It also laid the groundwork for Congress, three decades later, to give all federal agencies an obligation to consider historic values that might be affected by their actions.[19]

RECREATIONAL DEMONSTRATION AREAS, PARKWAYS, AND SCENIC EASEMENTS

Another New Deal program established parks on lands, mostly near urban areas, purchased from failing farmers or donated by states and restored with the help of the CCC or other relief agencies. Nearly four dozen areas covering some 400,000 acres in twenty-four states were eventually involved, with a dozen becoming part of the national park system, including Prince William Forest Park in Virginia and the Catoctin Mountain Park in Maryland. The latter included a presidential retreat that FDR dubbed "Shangri-La" and Dwight Eisenhower later named "Camp David."[20]

Another park-system initiative built on FDR's involvement in New York's Taconic State Parkway in the mid-1920s and Herbert Hoover's promotion of Skyline Drive in Shenandoah National Park in Virginia a few years later. Both were elongated parks containing a highway open only to noncommercial vehicles for travel at moderate speeds. The idea was to encourage automobile-based, scenery-inspired tourism as well to provide economic stimulus. Hoover had funded Skyline Drive with emergency economic recovery funds that Congress made available in the early years of the Depression. FDR immediately put money provided by the National Industrial Recovery Act of 1933 to work in building the Blue Ridge National Parkway. Running nearly five hundred miles along the crest of the Appalachians, connecting Skyline Drive to the Great Smoky Mountains, it was formally authorized by Congress in 1936. Two years later, Congress authorized the Natchez Trace Parkway, also administered by the Park Service, which ran from Nashville, Tennessee, to Natchez, Mississippi. Harold Ickes was not enthusiastic about, as he put it, "scarring" a "wonderful mountainside" with a road, but for FDR having a disability made him more supportive.[21]

In an attempt to limit the cost of these parkway units, the Park Service began to acquire what came to be called "scenic easements," which involved purchasing from nearby landowners the right to prevent intrusions, such as new buildings, that could impair views from the parkway. (This action was another example of splitting the ownership of property into different segments or estates.) Ultimately, scenic easements were acquired on thousands of acres along the Blue Ridge and Natchez Trace Parkways. They were the forerunner of the modern "conservation easement."[22]

FDR AND THE ANTIQUITIES ACT

FDR used the Antiquities Act to establish almost a dozen new national monuments and enlarge numerous others, all administered by the Park Service. Nearly all of them protected previously unreserved public lands, in effect implementing a recommendation of the Garfield Committee in 1931 to hold in national ownership areas of public land of national significance. Several were in more arid parts of the country even though FDR was not personally attracted to arid landscapes. Most had strong local support.

Not long after FDR took office, Minerva Hamilton Hoyt, a leader of the Garden Clubs of America and the founder of the International Deserts Conservation League, began lobbying the president and Ickes to protect a large area in the southeastern California desert where a picturesque species of yucca called the Joshua tree was found. Intrigued, FDR withdrew 1.1 million acres of public land between Palm Springs and Twenty-Nine Palms from divestment in October 1933. It took a few years to untangle complications involving the landholdings of the Southern Pacific Railroad, but in 1936 Roosevelt proclaimed the 825,000-acre Joshua Tree National Monument. The next year, he established the 331,000-acre Organ Pipe Cactus National Monument in southern Arizona, and that same year added more than 300,000 acres to the Death Valley National Monument, which Hoover had established less than a month before leaving office.[23]

Outside the West, Roosevelt used the Antiquities Act to protect Fort Jefferson in the Dry Tortugas off South Florida in 1935 and the Channel Islands off Southern California in 1938, and to add more than 900,000 acres to Glacier Bay National Monument, which Calvin Coolidge had established in Alaska in 1925. He also used the Antiquities Act to protect several historic sites, including Harpers Ferry in West Virginia and the boyhood home of the scientist George Washington Carver in Missouri, which was the first time the act was used to honor an African American. None of these stirred controversy. Congress established a few other national monuments by legislation in the same era and later converted several of FDR's monuments to national parks.[24]

Not all the national monument ideas in FDR's administration came to fruition. A proposal to establish a vast national monument in southern Utah attracted enough opposition to derail it. As early as 1914, prominent local officials had proposed to protect public lands along the Waterpocket Fold, a distinctive hundred-mile-long geological formation running north-south to the west of the Colorado River. The idea attracted interest from state officials and members of the Utah congressional delegation in the early 1930s. A Park

Service report around the same time called the "great canyons, gorges, and cliffs" of the Colorado River country between Moab, Utah, and Lees Ferry, Arizona, one of the "great wilderness areas of the United States," a place of, as one writer put it, "otherworldly" landscapes where "one geological miracle succeeds another" over many miles. Seeing an opportunity, in the spring of 1936 the Park Service proposed a 4-million-acre Escalante National Monument, named after a Spanish priest who had traveled through the region in the late eighteenth century. It would extend along both sides of the Colorado and Green Rivers from the Moab area almost to the Arizona state line.[25]

In hindsight, the Park Service's boldness was the project's undoing. The inclusion of so much of the Colorado River system triggered opposition from proponents of dams, who did not want new protected areas of public lands to interfere with their ambitions. Local ranchers were also not keen on the idea.

While this idea was simmering, FDR established the 37,000-acre Capitol Reef National Monument on part of the Waterpocket Fold in August 1937. The next year, he greatly increased the size of two existing national monuments in the region, adding more than 200,000 acres of scenic red-rock canyons to the 80-acre Dinosaur National Monument, which Woodrow Wilson had established in 1915 along the Utah-Colorado border, and enlarging eightfold the 4,500-acre Arches National Monument, which Herbert Hoover had established in 1929 near Moab.[26]

Around the same time, the Park Service decided to reduce the size of the proposed Escalante monument by nearly two-thirds, but it still would include nearly 1.6 million acres along both sides of the Colorado River. The local reaction to the smaller proposed monument was somewhat less hostile, and in late 1938 the Interior Department circulated a draft monument proclamation for discussion. Eventually, however, Secretary Ickes lost enthusiasm for the idea, leaving it for Presidents Clinton and Obama, many decades later, to revive the use of the Antiquities Act to protect large areas of the canyonlands of southern Utah.[27]

THE TETON NATIONAL MONUMENT CONTROVERSY

FDR's last use of the Antiquities Act, to protect land along the eastern foot of the Teton Range in northwestern Wyoming, raised a ruckus. The magnificent scenery of the Tetons and the adjacent Jackson Hole—a "hole" being, in the parlance of early nineteenth-century fur-trapping mountain men like David Jackson, a valley ringed by mountains—had long been prized, but protecting it in public ownership would involve a complex series of actions extending over many decades.

Not long after Congress established Yellowstone National Park, in 1872, proposals were made to extend the park southward to include some of the Tetons and adjacent areas, but it was not long before much of the valley floor had been privatized under various divestment laws. In early 1897, President Cleveland put some of the public land that remained into the Teton Forest Reserve, which he established. In 1912, after a massive die-off of elk caused in part by disruption of their traditional migration routes by homesteading and livestock ranching, and after a request from the Wyoming legislature, Congress established an elk refuge in Jackson Hole on nearly three thousand acres, much of it acquired from local landowners. Additional reservations of public land and further acquisitions of private land eventually expanded the refuge to more than twenty thousand acres.[28]

In the early 1920s, some local landowners approached Horace Albright about the possibility of the U.S. government acquiring their lands to establish a national park. Not long afterward, when John D. Rockefeller, Jr., was vacationing in the area with his family, Albright suggested that he purchase these lands, with the idea of donating them to the government for permanent protection. Rockefeller agreed, formed the Snake River Land Company, and in 1928 began quietly making purchases. While this was happening, Congress enacted legislation establishing Grand Teton National Park, which included only the peaks and the eastern mountain front down to, but not onto, the valley floor. Calvin Coolidge signed it into law shortly before leaving office in 1929; earlier, he had withdrawn the remaining public lands in the area from divestiture.

By 1933, Rockefeller's company had acquired more than 32,000 acres. The Hoover administration supported extending the park's boundaries into the valley floor to include the Rockefeller lands and a chunk of the Teton National Forest, and Wyoming's senators introduced the necessary legislation. It passed the Senate in 1934 but was stymied when the Treasury Department objected to paying Teton County a few thousand dollars a year to make up for the property tax revenue it would lose once the lands passed into U.S. ownership.

At this point, the politics got very complicated, stalling congressional action. The Forest Service did not want to lose more ground to the Park Service. Some dude ranchers and hunters opposed enlarging the park, and park advocates such as the National Parks Association objected to including man-made reservoirs on the valley floor in the park, and to extending the terms of the grazing permits and summerhouse leases the Forest Service had issued. In February 1943, Rockefeller advised Roosevelt that because of continuing congressional inaction, he intended to divest himself of his Jackson Hole lands. To secure their donation to the United States, Roosevelt exercised his authority under the Antiquities Act in March 1943 to establish the 221,000-acre Jackson Hole National Monument.[29]

Wyoming officials protested loudly, one calling it a "foul Pearl Harbor blow"—this barely fifteen months after the attack that killed more than two thousand Americans in Honolulu. The actor Wallace Beery and a young local rancher, Clifford Hansen, who was later elected governor of the state and then served two terms in the U.S. Senate, led a protest cattle drive across the monument, and the State of Wyoming filed suit in federal court to overturn Roosevelt's action. Ickes offered the Wyoming congressional delegation assurances that livestock grazing and other uses on the affected lands would be maintained, but Congressman Frank Barrett (R-Wyo.) was not placated, and pushed a bill through Congress to overturn Roosevelt's action. When it arrived on his desk shortly before the Seventy-Eighth Congress adjourned in December 1944, Roosevelt pocket vetoed it.

The next year, the Wyoming district court upheld Roosevelt's action, and the state did not appeal. Barrett continued to press his bill in subsequent Congresses without success. Finally, the Wyoming congressional delegation and the Truman administration reached an agreement on a compromise bill that became law in September 1950. It more than tripled the size of Grand Teton National Park to nearly 300,000 acres, which included most of the monument lands, and added 6,000 acres to the National Elk Refuge and 3,000 acres to the Teton National Forest. It also modified the Antiquities Act to prevent future presidents from using it in Wyoming without the consent of Congress, the first time the act had ever been amended. The existence of so much protected public land has helped Teton County, Wyoming, which embraces the park and the southern part of Yellowstone, to rank first in per capita income among the nation's counties in recent years.[30]

Altogether, FDR's national-park legacy was richer than his cousin Theodore's. Visitation to the national park system went up sixfold, to about 21 million, in the nine years between the time Roosevelt took office and Pearl Harbor. A good deal of this was because of the system's expansion—its acreage more than doubled during FDR's tenure—especially in the East and South near population centers. But some was because ordinary Americans, increasingly mobile, visited park-system lands in increasing numbers, a development that Roosevelt and Ickes, following in the footsteps of Stephen Mather, had worked hard to encourage. The new directions they charted for the system not only established a solid foundation for its future growth, but also provided new rationales for acquiring and protecting additional public lands.[31]

CHAPTER FORTY-EIGHT

A System of Wildlife Refuges Begins to Emerge

BY THE TIME FDR TOOK OFFICE, the federal government was managing a few million acres (most of it owned by the United States; it leased the remainder) primarily for wildlife protection. The Biological Survey in the Department of Agriculture was looking after more than one hundred wildlife refuges, sixty-five of which were for migratory birds. The Migratory Bird Treaty Act of 1918 and the Migratory Bird Conservation Act of 1929 were the primary legal bases for this effort. Other federal agencies administered twenty-four game ranges.[1]

But all was far from well, especially with waterfowl populations. As a result of laws like the swampland acts and the development accompanying a growing human population, marshes and wetlands vital to bird life had, by some estimates, been reduced by three-quarters over the previous century, to some 30 million acres. There were now several million bird hunters, and proliferating roads and motor vehicles made hunting grounds much more accessible. In the early 1930s, drought in the central part of the continent caused waterfowl numbers to plummet to historic lows. By one estimate, the duck population dropped from 100 million in 1930 to 20 million in 1934.[2]

In early 1934, the alarm sounded by hunters and biologists led FDR to establish a three-person Committee on Wild Life Restoration. It was led by Thomas Beck, a friend of Roosevelt's and publisher of *Collier's Weekly*, and its other members were Jay N. "Ding" Darling, a prize-winning editorial cartoonist and hunter-conservationist from Iowa who was a Republican critic of the New Deal, and Aldo Leopold, who had left the Forest Service to become a professor of wildlife management at the University of Wisconsin and had just published a landmark book, *Game Management*. Darling's cartoons appeared in hundreds of newspapers and "made him a kind of visual Will Rogers," according to Stephen Fox.[3]

Working fast, the committee produced a succinct, hard-hitting report in February 1934 that recommended numerous measures to reverse the "critical and continuing decline" in wildlife resources. Its most important recommendation was to spend up to $50 million in federal funds to acquire several million acres of land to restore and protect habitat not only of migratory waterfowl but also upland game and nongame birds. It also called for the retirement of marginal livestock grazing on "extensive tracts" of public lands, and for the appointment of a "restoration commissioner" under the direction of the secretaries of Agriculture, Interior, and Commerce, who would drive wildlife restoration projects across the executive branch.[4]

Well received by states as well as by wildlife advocates and hunters, the report helped spur quick congressional action. On March 10, FDR signed what became known as the Fish and Wildlife Coordination Act into law. Among other things, it called for the national government and the states to cooperate in developing a "nation-wide program of wild-life conservation and rehabilitation," and instructed the Biological Survey and the Bureau of Fisheries to "conduct such investigations as may be necessary" to develop a "program for the maintenance of an adequate supply of wild life" on all public lands. It directed U.S. agencies that operated water projects (primarily, the Bureau of Reclamation and the Army Corps of Engineers) to allow the federal wildlife agencies to use project water for "migratory bird resting and nesting areas" where doing so was consistent with the projects' "primary use." By strengthening a link between water projects and migratory-bird habitat that Theodore Roosevelt had first forged a quarter of a century earlier, the Coordination Act helped establish, according to one estimate, more than 2 million acres of wildlife refuges.[5]

The Coordination Act also required builders of federally licensed dams to consult in advance with the Bureau of Fisheries and provide ways for migrating fish like salmon to bypass the dams "by means of fish lifts, ladders, or other devices," if "economically practicable." This did not noticeably curb the economically depressed nation's—and FDR's—enthusiasm for dam building. Nor, unfortunately, did it reduce by much the toll that dams visited on migratory fish. Congress later overhauled the act twice, in 1946 and again in 1958, to make it somewhat more protective.[6]

This was the start of what would prove to be a momentous year for wildlife protection. On March 16, FDR signed into law what became known as the Duck Stamp Act. It created the first pot of federal money to be used exclusively for wildlife conservation, by requiring the purchase of a stamp (obtainable from the Post Office for one dollar, and good for a year) in order to legally take migratory waterfowl. This hit a sweet spot for FDR, an avid stamp collector. Ding Darling, whom FDR had named director of the Biological Survey in 1935, designed the first one, a brush and ink drawing of two mallards.

The act called for the revenue raised from duck stamp sales to be put into a "migratory bird conservation fund" administered by the Agriculture secretary, 90 percent of which was to be spent on acquiring, developing, and maintaining "inviolate migratory-bird sanctuaries." (Under the Migratory Bird Conservation Act of 1929, the executive could establish new refuges without the specific approval of Congress.) In the early years, revenues from duck stamp sales were relatively small—1939 was the first year they exceeded $1 million—so FDR supplemented them with funds that Congress had made available to fight the Great Depression.[7]

These moves marked the beginning of what would eventually become a genuine national system of wildlife refuges. J. Clark Salyer II, a Missourian who had been a professor of biology before Darling hired him, was its primary architect in its formative years. In the first two years, four dozen new refuges, which covered about 1.5 million acres of land, were established. By the time Salyer retired, in 1961, nearly 29 million acres were in national wildlife refuges.[8]

Three other notable wildlife-related developments occurred in 1934. First, the U.S. Senate formed a Special Committee on the Conservation of Wildlife Resources. (The House of Representatives followed suit four years later.) Second, Roger Tory Peterson published his *Field Guide to the Birds,* which quickly became a best seller and one of the most influential naturalist guides in the twentieth century. According to one commentator, Peterson did more than anyone to "introduce" Americans who no longer made their living on the land "to their natural environment," by supplying them with "simple, comprehensive tools" to make sense of what they see and hear in the outdoors. And last but not least, Frederick C. Lincoln, who had been in charge of bird banding at the Bureau of Biological Survey since 1920, published two pioneering works. Using empirical data gained through bird banding, he systematically mapped their "flyways"—the routes connecting breeding, migration, and wintering areas. Lincoln's efforts proved invaluable in guiding U.S. land acquisitions and other bird conservation efforts on a continental scale—a prime example, though hardly the only one, of meticulous government-led science informing national public land policy.[9]

In 1935, Congress amended the Duck Stamp Act to inaugurate a revenue-sharing program. It transferred to counties where refuges were located one-quarter of all revenue from the sale of "timber, hay, grass, or other spontaneous products of the soil" or any other "privileges" on the refuges, requiring them to use the funds for public schools and roads. As with other public-lands-based revenue-sharing programs, this was a double-edged sword. While it helped garner support for establishing new refuges, it also, once they were established, incentivized counties to lobby for more revenue-generating activities on them.

To lower the cost of land acquisition, the 1935 legislation authorized the Agriculture secretary to work out arrangements with landowners that would permit them to use the land where such use was compatible with, and subordinate to, the overriding wildlife protection purpose. The Biological Survey already tolerated "compatible" uses on many of the areas it managed, and "compatibility" gradually ripened into a general management standard used across all wildlife refuges. Finally, the legislation also authorized the United States to acquire lands deemed "chiefly valuable for wildlife" by swapping them for unreserved public lands of equal value elsewhere in the same state.[10]

In February 1936, FDR hosted the North American Wildlife Conference in the nation's capital. More than two thousand representatives from federal and state wildlife agencies, hunter and angler groups, wildlife and conservation organizations, and other wildlife enthusiasts met for five days to discuss ways to promote wildlife protection. The conference idea was Ding Darling's, but by the time of the event, he had been succeeded as director of the Biological Survey by his deputy, Ira N. Gabrielson, who would remain in the post for eleven years. The National Wildlife Federation, which remains a prominent nongovernmental advocate for wildlife, was organized at this meeting. Later that year, the United States entered into a treaty with Mexico for the protection of migratory birds, following on the 1916 treaty with Canada. It included numerous species not addressed by the earlier treaty.[11]

The nation's growing enthusiasm for protecting wildlife during the 1930s mostly submerged long-standing tensions among hunters, scientists who studied wildlife, those who treasured wildlife for observation, those who opposed animal cruelty, and livestock interests, who wanted predators to be controlled. Occasionally, however, disputes broke into the open, more often than not triggered by a group called the Emergency Conservation Committee, led by a prominent activist, Rosalie Edge. It had organized in 1930 to target the

Audubon Society for its support of hunting and trapping, and the Biological Survey for its predator-poisoning program.[12]

During his time in office, FDR established more than 150 areas on public lands in thirty-six states specifically to protect wildlife. Acreage in wildlife refuges tripled, from less than 6 million in 1933 (more than two-thirds of which was in Alaska) to more than 17 million in 1945 (less than half in Alaska). Eleven new areas in nine states were each larger than 100,000 acres, including the Kenai and Kodiak Refuges, which FDR established in Alaska in 1941, primarily to protect moose and brown bear populations. Some refuges were the product of interagency collaboration; for example, the Biological Survey and the National Park Service worked to establish a refuge in Montana's Centennial Valley to protect the breeding grounds of the trumpeter swan, a charismatic species that frequented Yellowstone National Park not far away.[13]

Two noteworthy wildlife-protecting actions were taken in eastern Oregon. The 250,000-acre Hart Mountain National Antelope Refuge was established in 1936, and a 100,000-acre bird reservation that Theodore Roosevelt had established in 1908 was significantly expanded. The latter, renamed the Malheur Wildlife Refuge, originally included two large lakes and many small, shallow lakes and wetlands, but not the rivers that fed them. That omission spelled trouble for the refuge's water supply, especially when the meatpacking giant Swift & Company bought up much of the land in the area, intending to establish a cattle empire. But when the Great Depression brought the company to the brink of bankruptcy in 1935, it persuaded the United States to buy its 65,000 acres in the area. Another 14,000 acres was added in another rescue buyout in 1942. And so in "a wonderful irony," wrote the historian Nancy Langston, "the West's grandest cattle empire became its grandest duck and wetland empire." Local newspapers criticized this turn of events, while Portland newspapers were more welcoming. (The refuge was the scene of an armed takeover in 2016 by a right-wing group that claimed the United States had no constitutional authority to own public lands.)[14]

The considerable efforts that Congress and FDR's administration made to protect wildlife paid off. According to some estimates, waterfowl numbers quadrupled across the continent between 1935 and 1946.

At the same time, continuing a trend that had begun in the 1920s, the Biological Survey tolerated more nonwildlife uses on refuges. Some, like the vast Desert Game Range that FDR established in Nevada in 1936, were kept open to livestock grazing and put under the joint jurisdiction of the Interior and Agriculture Departments. Originally 2.2 million acres—since reduced to 1.6

million acres, but still the largest refuge in the lower forty-eight states—the Desert Game Range was "set apart" both for the "conservation and development of natural wildlife resources" and for the "protection and improvement of public grazing lands and natural forage resources." Pairing these objectives reflected a hope that giving wildlife a coequal status with domestic livestock might advance the rehabilitation goals of the Taylor Grazing Act. As a government report noted in 1934, some areas of public land "would be valuable for wildlife production if the present overgrazing by domestic stock were prevented." Livestock operators usually did not welcome efforts to curb grazing on these dual-purpose game ranges, so they proved to be, unsurprisingly, a recipe for conflict.[15]

While the amount of public land devoted primarily to wildlife protection grew substantially during FDR's tenure, it was not yet formally organized into a full-fledged system like the national forest and national park systems, for which Congress had provided overarching organic legislation to guide their management. The refuges varied greatly in size and had somewhat varied purposes. Some were supposed to protect the habitat of particular species or types of species—the largest number (though not the largest in size) were located along flyways to protect habitat for migratory waterfowl—while others were to protect wildlife generally. In July 1940, FDR took a symbolic step toward making this jumble of areas (with labels such as "reservations," "bird refuges," and "migratory waterfowl refuges") a system by renaming all of them "national wildlife refuges." "Game ranges," which had grazing by domestic livestock as a coequal purpose, were not included.[16]

FDR had one other important impact on public land wildlife policy. On July 1, 1939, using the reorganization authority that Congress had renewed a few months earlier, he transferred the Bureau of Biological Survey and the Bureau of Fisheries from the Departments of Agriculture and Commerce, respectively, to the Department of the Interior. On June 1, 1940, the two bureaus were combined to form the U.S. Fish & Wildlife Service (FWS), with Ira Gabrielson its first director. The FWS has administered the national wildlife refuges ever since. The move to Interior was a major step toward realizing Harold Ickes's long-held dream of heading a Department of Conservation, and it sparked rumors that Roosevelt would soon move the U.S. Forest Service to Interior, but opposition from key members of Congress effectively quashed that idea for the remainder of FDR's tenure.[17]

Later that June, FDR signed legislation that for the first time gave the protection of U.S. law to the bald eagle. Even though the Continental Congress had made it the national symbol in 1782, the Migratory Bird Treaty and related protective legislation that followed excluded eagles and other raptors. With its numbers in serious decline and patriotic sentiment stirring as Europe plunged into war, Congress forbade any taking of the bald eagle on or off public lands without a permit from the Interior secretary. The legislation excluded the Territory of Alaska, however, where a government bounty led to the slaughter of an estimated 100,000 bald eagles before Congress repealed the exemption in 1959.[18]

In 1942, the FWS published its first refuge *Manual,* setting out national policies and guidelines for managing refuges. This was a landmark step in welding the collection of refuges into a genuine system. In the 1940s and 1950s, Congress made modest changes in the pertinent statutes, mostly designed to increase the amount of public lands available for wildlife protection. In 1949, it increased the price of duck stamps and gave the Interior secretary the discretion to allow sport hunting on as much as one-quarter of the area of any migratory bird refuge. In the Fish and Wildlife Act of 1956, Congress established separate bureaus of Sport Fisheries and Wildlife and Commercial Fisheries, but kept both within Interior's Fish & Wildlife Service. That same act directed the Interior secretary to "take such steps as may be required" to, among other things, conserve and protect "wildlife resources" in general, not just migratory birds, including the "acquisition of refuge lands," the latter basically confirming authority the secretary already possessed.[19]

In 1958, Congress approved another increase in the price of duck stamps and raised to 40 percent the maximum area the Interior secretary could open to hunting on any refuge. It also specifically authorized duck stamp revenues to be used to acquire "small wetland and pothole areas." To date, more than 1.5 million acres of these "waterfowl production areas" have been protected in several states in the northern Great Plains, usually by easement or lease, rather than full fee ownership.[20]

Overall, the collection of national wildlife refuges steadily grew through the 1940s and 1950s, with some huge additions in Alaska made at the end of the Eisenhower administration.[21]

CHAPTER FORTY-NINE

Other New Deal Public Land Policies

AS FDR WAS PREPARING TO TAKE office in early 1933, the Forest Service released a lengthy report on the nation's forests, *A National Plan for American Forestry*, that came to be known as the Copeland Report. It proposed more than doubling the size of the national forest system through acquisitions. A committee of the National Planning Board issued a report in 1934 containing even more ambitious recommendations for land purchases.[1]

The new administration never endorsed these recommendations, but FDR, who had rehabilitated the forests on his family's estate in Hyde Park, New York, and once reported his occupation to *Who's Who* as "tree grower," moved quickly to ramp up Weeks Act purchases, with a focus on the South. During his first term, enough land had been purchased to enable him to establish new national forests in Alabama, Florida, Georgia, Louisiana, Mississippi, North Carolina, Ohio, South Carolina, Texas, Virginia, and Wisconsin. Pointing to deforestation as a factor exacerbating destructive floods along the Ohio River in March 1937, he kept up the pace in his second term, proclaiming two national forests in Missouri, and one each in Illinois, Kentucky, and Michigan.[2]

During Roosevelt's twelve-plus years in office, about 11 million acres were added to national forests by Weeks Act purchases, more than twice the amount purchased in the first two decades after it became law. After that, the Weeks Act gradually declined in importance, supplanted by other programs for acquiring public lands. Overall, it brought more than 20 million acres into the national forest system, mostly in the East and South. Because the program relied almost entirely on willing sellers, nearly half the land within the outer boundaries of the national forests in those regions is still privately owned. On about a third of the land that the United States acquired, the mineral rights are privately owned.[3]

BUYING FAILED HOMESTEADS BACK INTO NATIONAL OWNERSHIP

FDR's New Deal included an initiative, unveiled early in 1934, to use funds appropriated for federal economic emergency relief to buy millions of acres of damaged land, mostly former farmland, back into national ownership. The objective was to restore these lands to a healthy condition and to provide habitat for wildlife and recreational opportunities. It built on groundwork laid by Hoover's Agriculture secretary, Arthur Hyde, who in late 1931 convened a national conference to address agricultural land policy, including the growing problem of abandoned farmland. The effort got a boost in 1935 when the ecologist Paul Bigelow Sears, following in the tradition of George Perkins Marsh, published his study *Deserts on the March*. Also in that year, Congress established the Soil Conservation Service and installed it in the Department of Agriculture.[4]

Altogether, upward of 11 million acres were purchased in some thirty states at a total cost of less than $50 million, or about $4 per acre. All sales to the United States were voluntary. A good deal of the land targeted for purchase was in the Great Plains, where many overoptimistic settlers had gone bust after gaining title to public land under various homestead laws. Nearly 4 million of the purchased acres were eventually included in twenty "National Grasslands" in twelve western and plains states; the grasslands were managed by the Forest Service primarily for wildlife, recreation, and livestock grazing. A little more than 2 million acres, mostly in Montana, was transferred to the Interior Department in 1958 and managed for similar purposes. About 1.4 million acres were added to national forests or used to establish new national forests in Alabama, Arkansas, Georgia, and Mississippi. A few hundred thousand acres were transferred to the Fish & Wildlife Service to become wildlife refuges.[5]

EVOLVING NOTIONS OF "MULTIPLE USE" AND "SUSTAINED YIELD"

During this era, the term "multiple use" became part of the lexicon of public land policy, and was mostly applied to national forests. The concept did not have much shape. Practically all public lands permitted recreation and paid some attention to watershed and wildlife protection. Limited mining and logging occurred in wildlife refuges and even in the national park system. While more mining was found in national forests and on lands that Interior managed under the Taylor Grazing Act, those mining activities occupied only a small portion of the total acreage. The national forests saw more logging than national parks and wildlife refuges, but most national forest acreage had never been logged.

The Forest Service paid increasing attention to recreation and wildlife during the New Deal. In 1935, it established an administrative unit focused on recreation. In 1936, it approved the first downhill ski area on national forest land, at Sun Valley in Idaho; over the next four decades, it approved more than two hundred. Also in 1936, it established a division of wildlife management. From time to time, it made special efforts to protect endangered wildlife; for example, by closing an area of the Los Padres National Forest in California to protect a nesting colony of condors. By 1938, about 4 million acres of national forests were designated as federal game refuges, and about 3 million acres had been closed to domestic livestock in the "interest of wildlife production."[6]

The Forest Service still did not give prominence to the safeguarding of watersheds, even though that was a primary motivation for creating the national forest system in the first place, was given statutory recognition in the Organic Act of 1897 ("securing favorable conditions of water flows"), and helped pave the way for the Reclamation Act of 1902. This indifference was highlighted in a curious law that Congress adopted in 1940. It authorized the Agriculture secretary to enter into cooperative agreements with municipalities obtaining water supplies from national forest lands that would allow the lands to be withdrawn from all uses, even from casual entry by the general public, if those uses might interfere with "protection of the watershed." But the statute also obliged municipalities to reimburse the Forest Service for the "loss of net annual revenues" that would otherwise be "derived" from timber or other resources withdrawn from "utilization." That financial penalty discouraged municipalities from pursuing such cooperative agreements, and none was ever executed.[7]

The notion that the renewable resources found on national forests, especially timber, should be managed on the basis of "sustained yield" gained favor in rough parallel with "multiple use." Its origins were in the 1897 Organic Act's reference to furnishing a "continuous supply" of timber. In 1937, Congress adopted a version of "sustained yield" in legislation directing the Interior Department to manage more than 2.5 million acres of timber-rich "O&C lands" in Oregon.

These lands had a complex history. In 1866, Congress granted the Oregon & California Railroad 4 million acres of land to build a rail line from Portland south to the California border. The company built the line but never sold all the granted lands to bona fide settlers, as Congress had required it to do, in part because many of the lands were too rugged and heavily timbered to be suitable for agriculture. Southern Pacific acquired the railroad in 1887, and after Edward Harriman took over the company in 1901, he stopped all further land sales, saying the railroad needed lumber for ties and bridges. In 1916, after years of litigation and several further acts of Congress, the United States took back title to the unsold lands, compensating Southern Pacific. The 1916 legislation authorized the Interior secretary to sell timber from the lands "in cooperation with the Secretary of Agriculture," and then to open them to homesteading. That plan did not work out well, and most of the lands remained in U.S. ownership, under Interior Department supervision. (Congress did something similar with 75,000 acres of adjacent land forfeited by the Coos Bay Wagon Road Company for similar reasons.)[8]

The 1937 legislation directed Interior to manage these "revested" lands for "permanent forest production." Timber was to be harvested on a "sustained yield" basis. At the same time, Interior was to protect watersheds, regulate stream flow, provide recreation, and contribute to local "economic stability." Revenue derived from timber sales was to be shared with eighteen local counties through a complex formula. While the legislation allowed for livestock grazing, it was made subordinate to these other uses. Some O&C lands were within national-forest boundaries, leading to years of confusion as to which agency would manage them, which Congress finally settled in 1953 in favor of the Forest Service.[9]

While the goals that Congress set out in the O&C legislation had political appeal, they left many questions unanswered, such as how much room the goal of "permanent forest production" left for protecting wildlife and other values the legislation did not mention. Congress also left unclear how Interior should schedule its sales of timber to help achieve local "economic stability," especially in relation to timber harvesting from other lands in the region.

In 1944, Congress enacted the Sustained-Yield Forest Management Act. Its primary thrust was to authorize the Departments of Agriculture and the Interior to establish "cooperative sustained-yield units" that could include private as well as public land, and to enter into agreements with private landowners that would help provide stability to timber-dependent communities. The promise was never realized; only one such "cooperative" unit was ever formed. The broad objective set forth in the act was to encourage the Forest Service and the Interior Department to coordinate the management of public forested lands to furnish a "continuous and ample supply of forest products" and secure "the benefits of forests in maintenance of water supply, regulation of stream flow, prevention of soil erosion, amelioration of climate, and preservation of wildlife." This something-for-everybody character left a great deal to agency discretion, and the legislation had no discernible impact.[10]

INTERAGENCY COOPERATION ON THE APPALACHIAN TRAIL

Another New Deal innovation with enduring implications for public land policy came in 1938 when the chiefs of the Forest and Park Services signed a cooperative agreement with the Appalachian Trail Conference. The trail had been promoted by Benton MacKaye, an ardent advocate for the outdoors who had worked in Pinchot's Forest Service in its early years. In an engagingly written, influential article in 1921 titled "An Appalachian Trail: A Project in Regional Planning," he proposed a footpath from New Hampshire's Mount Washington (New England's highest peak) to North Carolina's Mount Mitchell (the highest point in the United States east of the Mississippi), to be built and maintained by volunteers. More than half of the nation's population, MacKaye wrote, was within a day's travel of the proposed route, and national forests had already been established along parts of it.[11]

MacKaye ended the article by predicting that the idea was "something to be dramatized," and he was right. Outdoor clubs along its route—some of which had developed local trails that would be incorporated into the long trail—launched the Appalachian Trail Conference to carry it out. In the 1930s, the Civilian Conservation Corps helped with the task, and the route was eventually extended to Mount Katahdin in Maine and Springer Mountain in Georgia. The trail was essentially complete in 1937.[12]

Its 2,200 miles wound through fourteen states. By 1938, nearly half of it was on land in either the national forest system or the national park system, acquired either through the Weeks Act or through donations by states and private interests. The cooperative agreement obligated the federal agencies to maintain, on the public lands traversed by the trail, a two-mile-wide buffer strip where roads and most other incompatible developments would be prohibited. The agreement did not extend to state or private land, but all the states involved eventually legislated similar buffer strips. The development of the Appalachian Trail helped deepen the practice of public land management agencies partnering with states, localities, and nonprofit organizations, a practice that has persisted in many parts of the nation.[13]

Even before MacKaye wrote his article, multiday hiking trails had been built in the West, taking advantage of the fact that much suitable public land had been reserved in the systems of national forests and parks. Construction of a 210-mile trail from Yosemite to the summit of Mount Whitney in California's Sierra Nevada had been initiated in 1915 in a collaboration between the state and the Sierra Club, and named after John Muir. The Forest Service built a trail stretching over four hundred miles between Mount Hood and Crater Lake in Oregon in 1920. In the early 1930s, Clinton Clarke of Pasadena promoted the idea of the Pacific Crest Trail, which would link these and other trails into one stretching nearly 2,700 miles from Canada to Mexico. In 1945, the first bill was introduced in Congress to create a national system of hiking trails and provide a funding mechanism for their acquisition and maintenance, but it would be another couple of decades before it would become law.

ROADS AND WILDERNESS

The competition that had emerged between the Forest Service and the Park Service in the 1920s around the idea that some public lands ought to be kept roadless, in a "wilderness" condition, continued through the New Deal, though FDR's administration was somewhat conflicted on the subject. The president, with his extremely limited mobility, looked with favor on building roads to bring more people closer to nature. Harold Ickes was much less enthusiastic, as was Bob Marshall, a scientist and prominent wilderness enthusiast who had worked for the Forest Service and was in charge of forestry at the Bureau of Indian Affairs under Ickes.[14]

The national forest system offered the most opportunities for "preserving the primeval," as a Park Service report put it in 1934, while noting that the Forest Service's "emphasis on use" was an obstacle, as were the widespread practices of livestock grazing and predator extermination. To provide more focused advocacy, Benton MacKaye, Bob Marshall, Aldo Leopold, and others founded the Wilderness Society in 1935. Its advocacy concentrated on preserving such areas from significant conventional development like roads and other major intrusions.[15]

Marshall rejoined the Forest Service in 1937, where, shortly before his death in 1939 at the age of thirty-eight, he oversaw the development of new regulations to govern the Forest Service's growing system of "primitive areas," which by then included more than 13 million acres in ten western states. These "U-Regulations" were more restrictive than the "L-Regulations" adopted a decade earlier. Most importantly, they prohibited timber harvesting and all road building except for what might be necessary for access to private inholdings (and then only with "appropriate conditions").[16]

Although Congress occasionally enacted legislation protecting "wilderness" values on specific tracts of public lands (such as parts of the Superior National Forest in Minnesota in 1930, the Everglades in 1934, and Kings Canyon in 1940), it did not adopt generic legislation creating a national system of wilderness areas for another quarter century.[17]

DAMS AND NATIONAL RECREATION AREAS

Dam projects were popular in the New Deal era. Many of the best sites for larger dams were on rivers and streams flowing through highly scenic public lands. In national forests, project advocates could argue that dams were helpful in "securing favorable conditions of water flows," an objective that Congress had identified in the 1897 Organic Act. Dams were much harder to reconcile with the purposes of the national park system, but that did not stop water-project advocates from trying to make the case, and once in a while Congress allowed water projects to invade parks. In 1937, for example, it approved a tunnel through Rocky Mountain National Park to convey water from the headwaters of the Colorado River eastward across the Continental Divide to irrigate lands north of Denver. Water-project advocates also sometimes thwarted suggestions to include particular areas into the national park system, such as the proposed Escalante National Monument in Utah in the late 1930s.[18]

From time to time, dams and reservoirs built on public lands outside the national park system led to lands being added to the system. Hoover Dam on the Lower Colorado River, the first high multipurpose dam in the West, created a narrow 115-mile-long reservoir behind it. In 1930, President Hoover withdrew 3 million acres of public land in the area, with the idea that at least some of it should be permanently reserved because of its recreational potential. In 1936, Congress asked the National Park Service and the Bureau of Reclamation, the dam's builder and operator, to decide how to handle the matter, which led to an interagency agreement that the Park Service would manage more than 1 million acres in what was then called the Boulder Canyon Recreation Area.[19]

Something similar was done at other federal reservoirs built in scenic parts of the West—for example, around Lake Shasta in California and around the reservoir (eventually named after FDR) formed by the Grand Coulee Dam on the Columbia River in eastern Washington. These actions took place with congressional knowledge and funding, but without formal legislation. Beginning in the 1960s, those arrangements ripened into a new formal category of public lands—national recreation areas—each legislated by Congress. One of them was established around Lake Powell, a huge reservoir on the

Colorado River named after John Wesley Powell, in the heart of what would have been the Escalante National Monument, which was created by the giant Glen Canyon dam that Congress authorized in 1956.[20]

NEW DEAL PUBLIC LAND POLICIES AT THE POLLS

FDR's vigorous efforts to hold more lands in national ownership generally met with favor across the country. When he ran for a third term, in 1940, the Democratic Party platform claimed credit for positive impacts in the "public land states under the wise and constructive legislation of this Administration." The Republican Party platform endorsed the program to reacquire nonproductive farmlands from willing sellers and use them for such purposes as "watershed protection and flood prevention, reforestation, recreation, erosion control, and the conservation of wild life." FDR rolled to victory, winning 55 percent of the popular vote nationally and carrying all eleven western states except Colorado.

Four years later, with the world engulfed in war, the political picture regarding public lands had changed little. The Republican Party platform endorsed the "withdrawal or acquisition of lands for establishment of national parks, monuments, and wildlife refuges," though "only after due regard to local problems and under closer controls to be established by the Congress." On the campaign trail, its presidential candidate, Thomas E. Dewey, accused the president of making "land grabs" without "respect for the rights and opinions of the people affected," an apparent reference to the Jackson Hole National Monument. In the presidential election, FDR nearly duplicated his 1940 margin in the popular vote, and in the West lost only Wyoming in addition to Colorado.[21]

SUMMARIZING THE IMPACT

FDR's administration did much to give shape to today's public lands. The national park and national forest systems continued to expand, and what would become a system of national wildlife refuges was being assembled. More public lands were acquired or reacquired for a widening array of purposes, especially outside the West. The Taylor Grazing Act and FDR's subsequent executive orders retained practically all the remaining arid public lands in the intermountain West and Southwest in national ownership. It was a central part of an incipient fourth system of public lands administered by the Interior Department, with livestock grazing finally being managed through a permit-leasing system. Finally, the idea of protecting large areas of public lands in something approximating their natural condition, where road building and resource extraction would be precluded, was taking firm root. Although the

Democrats had firm control of Congress as well as the presidency, the tradition of bipartisan public-land policy making on all these matters persisted.

As economic miseries mounted in the Great Depression, public-land-based recreation and tourism provided glue that helped bind the nation together. At the same time, Congress forged new links between public lands and state treasuries. The Federal Highway Act of 1936, which authorized millions of additional federal dollars to construct and improve "roads and trails" on public lands, allowed states for the first time to tax gasoline sales made on military and other federal "reservations." Four years later, in the so-called Buck Act, Congress allowed states to levy income, sales, and use taxes on activities in any "Federal area" (defined broadly to include all public lands) within their boundaries. It cautioned, however, that giving the states taxing authority did not "limit the jurisdiction of" the United States over these lands.[22]

The scientific study of nature, and particularly of wildlife and wildlife habitats, began to inform public land policy as never before. By the 1930s, there was growing agreement that human actions were the primary cause of species extinction and that the preservation of habitat was essential. In the mid-1930s, Aldo Leopold promoted the idea of inventorying species facing extinction. The challenge was not easily met. In 1941, the United States balked at the price of acquiring a tract of land in Louisiana that was habitat for the ivory-billed woodpecker, which had already become scarce, and the land was later logged by German prisoners-of-war to make crates and chests for the war effort. The last ivory-billed woodpecker was spotted there in 1944.[23]

The year before, the Interior Department's Fish & Wildlife and National Park Services had collaborated on a book designed to bring public attention to endangered species. With chapters devoted to creatures as diverse as birds, grizzly bears, and marine life, it foreshadowed the future by calling the movement to save as much as possible of America's wildlife "heritage"—including nongame as well as game species—a "powerful, moving force."[24]

CHAPTER FIFTY

Grazing and Logging the Public Lands in the Postwar Era

IN 1940, SOON AFTER HE JOINED the Public Lands Committee, Senator Pat McCarran launched a campaign to showcase alleged abuses of authority by governmental overseers of livestock operators on public lands. The campaign lasted until his death in 1954. He had tangled with Interior secretary Harold Ickes ever since joining the Senate in 1933; both men were, in the words of McCarran's biographer, "stubborn, bellicose brawlers, who elevated minor disagreements to matters of principle and demonized opponents." Besides making a lot of noise, McCarran wielded power effectively, and officials in the executive branch feared his wrath. The Interior Department was McCarran's primary focus. Whereas the Forest Service managed relatively few acres in Nevada, the state was home to the five largest livestock operations that Interior supervised, and two of the next five largest. Louise Peffer called McCarran's campaign the "lengthiest, most concerted, and in some respects, the most successful attempt made in the twentieth century by one person" to skew public land policy in favor of one category of users.[1]

Trouble began to brew in 1944. Livestock prices had risen significantly, but Interior's grazing fee had not been raised from the rate that Ferry Carpenter had set in 1936—a nickel a month per cow-calf unit and a penny a month per sheep. The House Committee on Appropriations pressed Interior to increase grazing fees, reprising a controversy that had erupted over fees for grazing on the national forests twenty years earlier. Although Interior's fee was only about one-third of the Forest Service's, McCarran and his allies opposed any increase.

Interior was caught in the middle, especially Clarence Forsling, who, before he became Interior's new director of grazing in May 1944, had long been director of research for the Forest Service. When Forsling proposed to triple Interior's grazing fee to match the Forest Service's, McCarran conducted hearings in several western states over the next several months and insisted that Forsling testify at each one. The proceedings were not even interrupted to celebrate the Allied victory in Europe in May 1945; livestock interests were, as William Voigt, the executive director of the Izaak Walton League, put it, "fighting their own war and were not to be diverted by the collapse of the Hitler regime." The next month, Secretary Ickes capitulated and withdrew the proposed fee increase.[2]

The year 1946 was an even more tumultuous one for Interior's grazing program. In February, Ickes abruptly resigned after almost thirteen years in the job. In March, the House Committee on Appropriations retaliated against Interior's abandonment of the grazing fee increase by drastically cutting the department's funding for grazing administration. In May, President Harry Truman submitted a reorganization plan to Congress, one component of which proposed to establish a new Bureau of Land Management (BLM) by merging Interior's Grazing Service, established by Ickes in 1939, with the old General Land Office. (The plan eliminated the awkward arrangement whereby the Grazing Service was responsible for grazing districts, while the GLO was responsible for so-called section 15 leases, which permitted grazing on public lands outside the districts.) The plan took effect sixty days later when Congress lodged no objection to it.[3]

The cut in federal funding engineered by the House meant that the BLM began its existence by having to cope with a nearly two-thirds drop in its grazing administration personnel. This crippled its capacity to supervise livestock grazing, for it now had but fifty field representatives to look after more than 140 million acres of public land. Senator McCarran effectively vetoed Forsling as a candidate to be the BLM's first director, which left GLO commissioner Fred Johnson serving as acting director for nearly two years. It was hardly a propitious beginning for an agency that was responsible for managing more acres of public land than any other.[4]

THE ADMINISTRATIVE PROCEDURE ACT

At practically the same time that the BLM came into being, Congress was enacting the Administrative Procedure Act (APA). Although it applied to agencies across the executive branch, it would have significant impact on decision making by agencies overseeing public land, especially by inviting federal courts to give more scrutiny to those decisions.[5]

Senator McCarran was one of the APA's primary sponsors, and some of the impetus behind it came from his concern to protect livestock operators on public lands. As the Interior Department began regulating them under the Taylor Grazing Act, McCarran and some of the operators' other congressional allies complained that grazing permittees were being denied "due process." Similar complaints were sometimes voiced by others in the private sector as the federal government extended its regulatory reach, first in the Progressive era and then in the New Deal.

The APA, the product of ten years of deliberation and negotiation, was Congress's response. It provided a governing framework that sought to regularize both decision making by executive branch agencies and judicial review of those decisions. It applied to agencies that managed public lands, with one small exception. Its requirement that agencies follow certain procedures when adopting formal regulations curiously exempted matters relating to, among other things, "public property," which included public lands. The exemption, which did not apply to the act's other provisions, has never been important; public land management agencies have nearly always chosen to follow the APA's rule-making procedures anyway.[6]

Senator McCarran described the APA as a "bill of rights" for all those "whose affairs are controlled or regulated" by federal agencies. The legislation invited those "aggrieved" by agency decisions to seek review of them in federal court in order to ensure they are not, in its words, "arbitrary, capricious, or otherwise not in accordance with law." Federal courts had long played a role, usually a rather minor one, in public land policy as miners, railroad companies, and livestock operators, along with the national government, occasionally sought the assistance of the courts in resolving disputes involving public lands. The APA opened the door for more regular judicial oversight, which became much more common when the modern environmental movement gained strength in the 1960s.

LIVESTOCK OPERATORS TRY AGAIN FOR OWNERSHIP
Amid the turmoil surrounding the BLM's birth, Senator Edward Robertson (R-Wyo.), a rancher, introduced a bill to give states ownership of all public grazing lands. It went nowhere, but in the late summer of 1946, livestock operators began to formulate a strategy aimed at persuading the next Congress to give grazing permittees ownership of the public lands they grazed, including even those in the national forests.[7]

This move got the attention of increasingly well-organized conservation interests, especially after Republicans won fifty-four seats in the House and twelve in the Senate in the November 1946 elections, taking control of both chambers. Bernard DeVoto, a native of Ogden, Utah, who had gained national prominence as a historian, novelist, and essayist, sounded an alarm. In January 1947, *Harper's Magazine* published his essay "The West Against Itself," in which he attacked livestock grazers, among others, as prominent abusers whose overgrazing caused massive erosion on public lands. In one caustic passage, DeVoto wrote that observing the Missouri River flow "greasily past Kansas City" was to watch "those gallant horsemen out of Owen Wister shovel Wyoming into the Gulf of Mexico," and he warned that their heirs "hope to shovel most of the remaining West into its rivers." Conservationists gave particular prominence to the targeting of the national forests; the future Oregon senator Richard Neuberger published an essay in the *Nation* in April 1947 titled "Looting the National Forests."[8]

Livestock-industry allies tried to stay on the offensive. From August to early October 1947, Congressman (and future senator and Wyoming governor) Frank Barrett led a wide-ranging subcommittee investigation into public land administration, conducting hearings in Montana, Wyoming, Colorado, Utah, and Nevada. The field hearings were supposed to give proponents of divestment the opportunity to air their complaints and make their case.

But the hearings produced something that Barrett and his allies were not expecting; namely, a lot of opposition to the divestment proposal, a good deal of it from the grass roots. Editorial reaction, particularly from cities, was disparaging— the *Denver Post* scorned what it called "Stockman Barrett's Wild West Show." (As had been true since before the turn of the twentieth century, the West had the highest proportion of urban residents of any region of the country.) The open space and recreational opportunities the public lands supplied were increasingly valued. Even more important, many westerners continued to believe, as they did when responding to the Garfield Committee's 1931 report, that the federal support they considered vital for water and power projects in the region was very much linked to maintaining U.S. ownership of much of the region's land.[9]

Barrett's subcommittee did not hold a hearing in Idaho, presumably because its state legislature had approved a resolution earlier in 1947 listing nine reasons why the United States should continue to own public lands despite the "persistent effort" being made by "certain western Congressmen." Among those reasons were that "watersheds vital to our agricultural economy would be jeopardized and reclamation development imperiled under private ownership," as would "recreational values and privileges." In addition, the resolution continued, U.S. revenue sharing was "commensurate with or exceed[ed] potential tax revenues" that might be realized if those lands were privatized. Finally, it warned that privatization would produce "feudal ownership and restriction of human liberties similar to that now existent in European countries."[10]

In early October, a subdued Congressman Barrett sent Agriculture secretary Clinton Anderson some bland recommendations on how grazing management on the national forests might be improved and suggested that the agency refrain from reducing authorized levels of grazing for three years. Anderson—who early in his career had been a crusading journalist in Albuquerque, where his articles about Interior secretary Albert Fall's unsavory dealings helped uncover the Teapot Dome scandal—firmly rejected the suggestion. He was, he informed Barrett, "convinced the overgrazed conditions" on many forests were so serious that no delay was advisable. Anderson also denied that reducing grazing levels would lead to higher beef prices, noting that animals grazed in the national forests provided less than 1 percent of the nation's meat supply.[11]

The ineffectual effort to transfer ownership of public lands to livestock interests demonstrated once again the depth of support for keeping these lands in national ownership. Before Barrett brought the hearings to a close, the chief of the Forest Service, Lyle Watts, called the idea to divest the United States of significant amounts of public lands "dead" and predicted that it would "hardly be a major issue again for many years to come." A Colorado correspondent for the *Economist* magazine supplied this succinct postmortem: livestock operators badly underestimated the "vigour of the opposition" out of a mistaken belief that the takeover of Congress in the 1946 elections by Republicans "supposedly dedicated to the strengthening of private enterprise" had handed them a political opportunity.[12]

Even before Barrett's subcommittee toured the West, Congress had confirmed that the BLM was here to stay. In July 1947, it enacted legislation that enlarged the BLM's management authority by authorizing it to sell timber, vegetative resources, and common minerals like sand and gravel from the public lands that it managed, when that was not "detrimental to the public interest" and was done by competitive bidding or for "adequate compensation."[13]

The BLM finally began to stabilize when, in March 1948, the Senate confirmed Truman's nomination of Marion Clawson—whose father had operated a small ranch in Nevada, and who wrote his Harvard Ph.D. dissertation on the economics of the western livestock industry—to become BLM director. In July of that year, DeVoto supplied more acerbic commentary in his *Harper's* essay "Sacred Cows and Public Lands," in which he noted that the industry's biggest defenders in Congress themselves held permits to graze livestock on public lands.[14]

Agriculture secretary Anderson put the issue of federal administration of public land grazing to a more direct popular test. In May 1948, he resigned and returned to New Mexico to run for an open U.S. Senate seat. The Republican nominee was Patrick J. Hurley, a former cowboy, decorated soldier, diplomat, and secretary of War under Herbert Hoover, who was on record as supporting a "thorough investigation" of the Forest Service's "unreasonable domineering bureaucratic management" of what he called ranchers' "grazing rights." In the November election, Anderson prevailed handily, by a 57–42 percent margin, President Truman won a full term, and the Democrats regained control of both the House and the Senate, picking up Senate seats in Idaho and Wyoming.

That same year the Society for Range Management, a professional organization, was formed, signaling the growing maturity of the science of grassland ecology. Meanwhile, the number of hobby or amenity ranches, which Marion Clawson described in 1950 as being "operated chiefly for their owner's pleasure rather than for profit," was beginning to increase in several parts of the West.[15]

PERMITTEES NEVERTHELESS STRENGTHEN THEIR HOLD ON PUBLIC RANGELANDS

Despite public land livestock operators having lost badly in their bid to gain ownership—or perhaps because of it—they managed to tighten their grip on the public range. For one thing, the BLM was appropriated only about $7 million in 1949, less than one-tenth of the Forest Service's appropriation, even though it managed more acres. As the *Economist* correspondent noted, slashing the agency's budget could "break down the barrier to exploitation almost as effectively and much less conspicuously than a new law."[16]

Livestock operators also had success in persuading the U.S. government to underwrite more of the cost of their use of public rangelands. Before it was disbanded in World War II, the Civilian Conservation Corps had substantially enlarged the U.S. contribution to the business of livestock grazing on public lands by constructing numerous range "improvements"—fencing, water tanks, pipelines, and the like. Now ranchers sought to have the U.S. government carry on that work and do more to restore rangelands damaged by overgrazing, which would lessen the pressure to reduce numbers of grazing livestock.

An important step in this direction came with enactment of the Anderson-Mansfield Act in 1949, sponsored by the new senator Clinton Anderson and Congressman Mike Mansfield (D-Mont.). It authorized a $133 million, fifteen-year program to reseed 4 million acres of national forest grazing lands that it described as "seriously depleted." Conservation advocates did not offer much resistance, even though they recognized, as William Voigt noted, it was a "momentous policy shift," because it transferred "much of the burden of reha-bilitating damaged forest ranges from individual permittees to the taxpayer at large." Around the same time, the Forest Service indicated it would lower the grazing fees of permittees who made improvements on their allotments.[17]

In 1950, Congress gave livestock operators on the national forests another victory. The Granger-Thye Act, sponsored by Congressman Walker Granger (D-Utah) and Senator Edward Thye (R-Minn.), finally gave the Forest Service's grazing program an explicit statutory foundation, while authorizing the expen-diture of federal funds for, among other forms of assistance, range improve-ments, reseeding, and the eradication of rodents, poisonous plants, and noxious weeds.[18]

The Granger-Thye Act also confirmed the role of local advisory boards of permittees, which were to offer their "advice and recommendations" on just about every grazing decision the Forest Service would make, including crafting regulations and determining whether and on what terms to issue individual grazing permits. The Agriculture secretary or his "duly authorized representa-tive" could reject such advice only if the local advisory board was informed "in writing" of the "reasons for such action." While the act cautioned that it should not be "construed as limiting or restricting any right, title, or interest of the United States in any land or resources," its practical effect was to give operators influence over national-forest rangelands comparable to what they had estab-lished over BLM-managed public lands.[19]

In the 1952 election campaign, the Republican platform called for "restora-tion of the traditional Republican public lands policy," without providing any clues about what that was. As the campaign heated up, some business interests suggested that the United States owned too much land, and advocated priva-tizing some of it. Eisenhower swept to a convincing victory, 55–42 percent over Adlai Stevenson, carrying every western state as well as most of the rest of the nation. Republicans made modest gains in both the House and the Senate, enough to win a bare majority in both bodies.

Their victory did not rekindle any efforts to divest the United States of ownership of public lands. While Eisenhower's Interior secretary, Douglas McKay, told the western governors in November 1953 that the administration intended to gradually transfer public-domain land into private hands (though he left vague whether that would happen through leasing or an outright transfer of ownership), nothing came of it. And even though Eisenhower's Agriculture secretary, Ezra Taft Benson, expressed strong opposition to expanding public landholdings, the total acreage in the national forest system grew modestly from about 181 million acres to nearly 186 million acres in 1960.[20]

Livestock operators tried other ways to bolster their legal hold on public rangelands. In 1953, Senator Barrett of Wyoming and Congressman Wesley D'Ewart (R-Mont.) introduced legislation to give Forest Service grazing permittees a legal right to transfer their permits. It was opposed by the American Forestry Association and went nowhere, but a watered-down version was introduced by Senator George Aiken (R-Vt.) and Congressman Clifford Hope (R-Kans.) the next year. In an effort to attract more support, it eliminated the section giving operators the right to transfer their permits, added recognition of wildlife and recreation as proper objectives of national forest management, and created advisory boards made up of representatives of wildlife advocates and others to parallel the livestock operators' advisory boards. Although it won the endorsement of President Eisenhower in August, the changes were not enough to defuse opposition, in the West and elsewhere, from those who feared the domination of public lands by livestock grazers, to the detriment of other users. Opponents included supporters of irrigation projects as well as hunters and other recreationists. The Aiken-Hope bill passed the Senate but died in the House.[21]

TIMBER HARVESTING AND ROAD BUILDING ESCALATE ON THE NATIONAL FORESTS

The big story on the national forests in the years following World War II was the rapid expansion in timber harvesting and road building. During the war, the proportion of the nation's wood supplies that came from the national forests doubled from 5 to 10 percent as the annual harvest grew from 1.3 billion board feet (BBF) in 1939 to 3.1 BBF in 1945. This increase began a trend that continued for four more decades. By 1950, more than 6 BBF were being harvested on the national forests; by 1960, more than 9 BBF. Thereafter, the cut hovered between 10 and 12 BBF annually until the late 1980s. (Harvesting levels on the O&C lands in western Oregon, managed by Interior's BLM, followed suit, more than quadrupling after 1950 to 1.66 BBF in 1970.)

The increase was initially fueled by the postwar housing boom, particularly in the suburbs, as returning soldiers resumed their pursuit of the American dream. The impact was felt in national forests across the nation, but the bulk of the increase came from the timber-rich national forests along the Pacific coast, from Northern California into southeastern Alaska.[22]

This burst of timber harvesting relied more and more heavily on the economically efficient practice of clear-cutting, or removing all standing trees regardless of age. It also took place without any change in the law that governed the national forests, which meant that the restrictions in the Organic Act—confining timber harvesting to "large growth" or "mature trees" that had first been "marked and designated"—had to be, and were, ignored. The surge in timber harvesting also sharpened the distinction between the U.S. Forest Service and the National Park Service, giving rise to the quip that while both agencies like big trees, the Park Service likes them vertical while the Forest Service prefers them horizontal.[23]

In 1948, the Forest Service signed a fifty-year contract calling for the harvest of nearly 20 BBF of timber from the Tongass National Forest in southeastern Alaska. The contract included numerous economic incentives designed to establish a pulp and paper industry in the region. The agency had four more similarly huge deals on the drawing board. In 1953, Agriculture secretary Benson told the American Forestry Association that "conservation means management," and he expressed the hope that "we no longer have any citizens who look upon conservation and preservation as synonymous terms."[24]

The Columbia National Forest, located between the Columbia River and Mount Rainier in Washington, provided a thumbnail portrait of the unrelenting pressure to increase timber harvests. In 1949, when it was renamed the Gifford Pinchot National Forest, the Forest Service projected that its timber stands could produce 200 million board feet (MBF) annually in perpetuity. By 1960, about 440 MBF were being cut every year, and in 1968 the cut reached almost 560 MBF.[25]

The emphasis on harvesting timber required what the historian Paul Hirt described as a "veritable orgy of road-building." The network of mostly unpaved roads threading through the national forests grew from fewer than 100,000 miles in 1945 to more than 160,000 miles in 1960. (By contrast, the interstate highway system, which Congress authorized in 1956, contains somewhat less than 50,000 miles.) The road network in the national forest system was concentrated in those 80 million acres that the Forest Service classified as commercial timberland, where there was well over one mile of road for every square mile of forest.

The emphasis on timber production adversely affected soils and most wildlife and increased the amount of land needing reforestation. The Anderson-Mansfield Act, which noted that more than 4 million acres of commercial timberlands were "denuded," authorized more federal funds for reforestation. But appropriations did not keep up with the demand, and the backlog of lands needing reforestation steadily grew. Hirt summed up the first decade and a half following the end of World War II this way: the "breakneck acceleration of timber sales and old-growth forest liquidation vastly outstripped related programs in reforestation, erosion control, and wildlife habitat management."[26]

CONGRESS ADDRESSES SKYROCKETING RECREATIONAL USE OF THE NATIONAL FORESTS

Meanwhile, recreational use of the national forests grew dramatically. Gasoline rationing and the military buildup had severely limited such use during World War II, but the number of recreational visitors grew fivefold in the first decade after the war ended, to more than 50 million every year. Because roads built primarily for logging allowed greater access to forests, and because timber harvesting could boost deer and elk numbers, hunters and other recreationists did not always resist stepped-up timber harvesting.

In the early years of the Eisenhower administration, Representative Howard Baker (R-Tenn.) and Senator Lee Metcalf (D-Mont.) worked to dedicate a small portion of the Forest Service's timber receipts to support recreation. Although they were supported by a broad coalition that included state game and fish commissioners and the American Automobile Association, Agriculture secretary Benson opposed the legislation, and it failed.[27]

Benson soon changed his tune. Not long after the National Park Service rolled out its "Mission 66" in 1955—a program consisting mostly of capital improvements for visitor accommodations to be completed by that agency's fiftieth anniversary in 1966—he directed the Forest Service to prepare a five-year plan for recreation development, dubbed Operation Outdoors. Released in 1957, it predicted that the annual number of recreation visitors should climb to 66 million within five years. That number was exceeded the very next year, and Congress soon tripled the agency's funding for recreation.

THE MULTIPLE USE–SUSTAINED YIELD ACT

In 1960, Congress enacted the first generic legislation addressing management of the national forests since the Organic Act of 1897. It came about mostly because the surges in timber harvesting and recreation were on a collision course. Its roots traced back to the early 1950s, when livestock operators were working to shore up their legal status on the national forests. The Aiken-Hope bill, which the Senate approved in 1954, contained a bland recognition of various uses of lands in the national forest system, and although the bill died in the House, it came to be a vehicle for deliberations over how the Forest Service should handle competing uses. The discussions that followed over the next few years, and the ultimate legislative outcome, provided an illuminating snapshot of the relative political strength of disparate users of national forests.[28]

In 1956, Democratic senator Hubert Humphrey of Minnesota, acting on a recommendation from a consortium of wildlife and recreation advocates, introduced legislation to protect and preserve "multiple uses" on the national forests, listing range, timber, water, mineral, wildlife, and recreation as resources to be protected. Humphrey's bill initially perturbed most other interests. Comfortable with the status quo, the Forest Service was initially reluctant to support the legislation. The timber industry and supporters of dam building and irrigation were concerned about naming more authorized uses, believing it weakened their preferential position: in the Organic Act, Congress had identified furnishing a "continuous supply of timber" and "securing favorable conditions of water flows" as primary national forest purposes. The mining industry likewise wanted to protect what it thought was its preferred position, because the 1897 act allowed the Mining Law of 1872 to continue to apply to the national forests, though it did make mineral activity subject to regulation. State fish and game authorities worried that giving the Forest Service a mandate to provide for wildlife uses might impinge on the authority they had long exercised to regulate hunting and fishing on the national forests. The National Park Service was concerned that giving the Forest Service a mandate to provide for recreation would make it a stronger competitor for public funds. Advocates for preserving natural or "wilderness" values on public lands were troubled by the emphasis on the word "use."

Over the next four years, Humphrey surgically adjusted the bill's language to address each of these concerns. The timber industry and the dam builders were mollified by added language cautioning that the new purposes were "supplemental to, but not in derogation of," the purposes established in the 1897 act. The mining industry was appeased by a provision that nothing in the act "shall be construed so as to affect the use or administration of the mineral resources of national forest lands." State fish and game agencies were assuaged by a clause noting that nothing in the act "shall be construed as affecting the jurisdiction or responsibilities of the several States with respect to wildlife and fish in the national forests." To placate the Park Service, new wording provided that nothing in the act would "affect the use or administration of Federal lands not within national forests." Wilderness advocates were reassured by new language providing that the "establishment or maintenance of areas of wilderness are consistent with the purposes and provisions" of the legislation.

In 1958, the Forest Service drafted its own version of the legislation. It added the concept of "sustained yield," an idea rooted in the Organic Act's reference to a "continuous" supply of timber. The agency's draft also furnished definitions of both key concepts. Its definition of "multiple use" very carefully avoided acknowledging how competing uses could conflict with one another, and used multiple phrases designed to preserve the agency's discretion. Specifically, it called for the "various renewable resources of the national forests" to be "utilized in the combination that will best meet the needs of the American people," and for the agency to make the "most judicious use of the land for some or all of these resources or related services over areas large enough to provide sufficient latitude for periodic adjustments in use to conform to changing needs and conditions," while recognizing that some national forest land "will be used for less than all of the resources" it contained.[29]

President Eisenhower signed the Multiple Use–Sustained Yield (MUSY) Act into law in June 1960. By the time it emerged from the legislative wringer, the guidance it was supposed to have provided had become so hedged and watered down that it was nearly meaningless. Indeed, since it has been on the books, one would be hard-pressed to point to any particular management decision that would have been made differently had the act not existed.

Nevertheless, the act was a noteworthy development. It provided confirmation, at the highest political level, that the interests of wildlife and recreation and of preserving some national forest lands as "wilderness" were now firmly in the mainstream of public land policy. Equally important, it radiated with instructions to the Forest Service to take the long term into account, and not to let the marketplace slavishly dictate decisions about how public lands are managed. Thus, the definitions of both "multiple use" and "sustained yield" included the admonition that the national forests should be used "without impairment of the productivity of the land." The definition of "sustained yield" also spoke of achieving and maintaining outputs of the system's renewable resources "in perpetuity." While the definition of "multiple use" required considering the "relative values" of various resources, in the same breath it cautioned that the result should "not necessarily be" a "combination of uses that will give the greatest dollar return or the greatest unit output."[30]

On its face, the MUSY Act applied only to the 180 million–plus acres of public land that were in the national forests. But principles embedded in it— that the government should manage public lands without affecting their productivity over the long run, and without simply following marketplace signals—became increasingly important to how all public land was managed.

Six weeks after passing the MUSY Act, Congress gave final approval to the Public Land Administration Act. The law gave the BLM basic governing authority—such as the power to accept donations of property and establish fees and charges—as needed for, in its words, the "improvement, management, use, and protection" of the enormous system of public lands it managed. It helped pave the way for Congress finally to give the BLM its own organic act. The Federal Land Policy and Management Act, enacted in 1976, not only directed the BLM to manage its lands for multiple use and sustained yield (updating the definitions of those terms to require that more attention be paid to cultural resources and the environment), but also contained a wealth of specific instructions regarding how the BLM was to manage those lands.[31]

In one important respect, the MUSY Act marked the end of an era. It was the last time that Congress left so much discretion to executive branch agencies that managed public lands. Within a very few years, Congress began to legislate much more prescriptively, ruling out or restricting particular uses on many areas of public land, most prominently through the Wilderness Act and similar measures.

CHAPTER FIFTY-ONE

Mineral Policy Developments Onshore and Offshore

IN THE AFTERMATH OF WORLD WAR II, Congress took some modest steps to curb the reach of the Mining Law of 1872. At that point, it generally applied to all minerals found on public lands except fossil fuels and a few fertilizer minerals (such as sodium, sulfur, and potash), which were governed by the Mineral Leasing Act of 1920. The basic structure of the Mining Law remained unchanged from when Senator Stewart had crafted it, even though esoteric details of its application—especially how easy it was to locate mining claims and how difficult it was to determine whether they were legitimate—continued to cause many problems. Besides creating difficulties for governmental managers and other users of public lands, counterfeit claims were a problem for the legitimate mining industry.[1]

As other avenues for privatizing public lands were closed off, the Mining Law became more prized by speculators and scoundrels who had no thought of extracting minerals. Some simply wanted to be paid to relinquish their claims. Others used claims as covers for logging, for dwellings, for gaining access to water (including prime fishing streams), or for other purposes. The Mining Law's broad reach—it applied even to common substances such as sand, stone, and clay—made such abuses hard to deal with.[2]

The abuse—documented in numerous reports done by and for the Forest Service and the Interior Department—put the agencies between a rock and a hard place. Mining-industry representatives blamed the government for not exerting more effort to weed out spurious claims, and in practically the same breath condemned it for its "tendency" to look at "every mining claim with suspicion," an attitude, they said, that was "contrary to" the Mining Law's "intent and purpose."[3]

In 1947 and 1955, Congress finally tried to deal with some of these problems. The Materials Sales Act of 1947 authorized the Interior secretary to sell common minerals found on public lands (sand, stone, gravel, and common clay; the law also covered vegetative materials such as yucca, mesquite, and cactus), but not the land itself. The secretary could sell such materials if doing so would not be "detrimental to the public interest." But Congress did not rule out locating claims under the Mining Law for these substances, leaving it to the Interior Department and the courts to decide whether such claims could lawfully be made, and thus the act did little to rein in abuses.

Eight years later, Congress did prevent new claims from being located under the Mining Law for "common varieties" of such widespread minerals. While this action was helpful, it likewise had limited impact on abuses. For one thing, it did not affect existing claims, estimates of which ran into the millions— but no one really knew how many, because Congress had never required mining claims to be recorded with the BLM or its predecessor, the GLO. For another, new mining claims could be located for any "uncommon variety" of these common substances, which the 1955 act vaguely defined as having "some property giving it distinct and special value." This left plenty of room for argument, and there were powerful incentives for locators to argue that they had found an "uncommon variety," because if they succeeded, the Mining Law gave them complete ownership not only of the minerals, but also of the public lands they claimed, for a maximum of five dollars an acre.[4]

Unsurprisingly, abuses continued. The master was a colorful scoundrel named Merle Zweifel. He freely admitted to locating counterfeit mining claims on 30 million acres of public land in the postwar era for the sole purpose of being bought out by genuine mining enterprises or the government. His ploy worked more often than the industry or the government cared to admit in circumstances where they needed to establish clear title, and it made more sense to buy his spurious claims rather than go to the time and expense of contesting them. He never disturbed the public lands he claimed, Zweifel said, because doing so would have damaged the scenery. He admitted that plaguing mining companies was "an enjoyment [he couldn't] pass up," and that he had "a lust for money." Zweifel eventually ran into considerable legal trouble, but mainly because of his flamboyance.[5]

Other practitioners of this technique were more circumspect. Occasionally, situations where the Mining Law supplied a convenient way to exploit other public land resources made national news. In 1955, controversy erupted when the Interior Department approved patents to mining claims that transferred ownership of a valuable old-growth forest in Oregon's Rogue River National Forest. The mining claimant proceeded to log 2 million board feet, leading the newspaper columnist Drew Pearson to dub Interior secretary Douglas MacKay "Giveaway McKay." It was only in the 1960s that the executive branch and Congress began to take meaningful steps to curb such abuses.[6]

PUBLIC LANDS AND URANIUM

As the United States entered the nuclear age at the end of World War II, uranium was thought to be a scarce mineral, and public lands were thought to be the most likely place to find it. At first, as part of the Atomic Energy Act of 1946, Congress reserved all uranium that might be found on public lands. This step proved ineffectual. Uranium could still be extracted from preexisting mining claims or mineral leases—indeed, by one estimate, most public land with uranium potential was already under oil and gas lease. Furthermore, neither the Mining Law nor the Mineral Leasing Act addressed how to reconcile conflicts between claims and leases. In 1954, Congress tried again, in the Multiple Mineral Development Act. It repealed, retroactively, the uranium reservation, made uranium subject to location under the Mining Law, and adopted a complicated process for untangling locatable from leasable minerals.[7]

An old-fashioned "rush" of exploration on public lands in the 1950s and 1960s showed that uranium was much more common than previously believed. The resulting "U-Boom" saw large quantities produced from public and Indian lands on the Colorado Plateau and in New Mexico and Wyoming. Regulation to protect the environment was foreign to the government's administration of the Mining Law, and the mining and processing of the radioactive element produced a tragic legacy of lung cancer among miners from small, poorly ventilated underground mines, several hundred of which were on the Navajo Nation. Water contaminated by runoff from the mountains of radioactive mill tailings left behind required expensive cleanup efforts, some of which continued into the third decade of the twenty-first century.[8]

Although the idea was raised from time to time, Congress showed no interest in replacing the Mining Law altogether. Interior secretary Ickes wanted to replace it with a leasing system, but the mining industry was firmly opposed, arguing that reform would "result in locking up the treasures of our western mining areas." In a report from 1949, the Hoover Commission—appointed by President Truman to recommend improvements in the executive branch (and headed by the former president, who had made a fortune in the mining industry)—pointed out serious defects in the law and recommended several reforms, but stopped short of endorsing a leasing system. The report of the President's Materials Policy Commission (the Paley Commission) in 1952 also documented numerous problems and did endorse a leasing system. Nothing came of either report.[9]

SETTLING THE OWNERSHIP OF SUBMERGED
LANDS OFFSHORE

Public lands underneath the oceans and seas along the nation's shores often escape attention, but they became an important part of the public lands story after World War II. When the nation was founded, no norms of international law addressed how far off its shores a country could assert territorial rights. In a letter to the British minister in 1793, Secretary of State Thomas Jefferson officially claimed U.S. jurisdiction over a three-mile zone from its shoreline. Jefferson's position, based on national defense considerations, eventually won acceptance as a general principle of international law.[10]

This left open a question of domestic law—whether the United States, as opposed to its constituent coastal states, owned the natural resources in that coastal zone. For many decades, neither the U.S. government nor coastal states made any effort to interfere with harvesting fish or other resources found in that coastal zone. Ownership began to matter when private companies started developing petroleum on submerged lands offshore. Natural oil seepage from the ocean floor off Santa Barbara, California, led some companies to construct crude platforms to drill for oil in shallow water there as early as 1897. In 1921, California adopted legislation (closely modeled on the Mineral Leasing Act of 1920) authorizing the issuance of permits to its own residents to mine for petroleum off its coast. The national government did not advance a claim to own all submerged lands offshore until well into 1930s.[11]

Interior secretary Harold Ickes eventually decided that the United States should make such a claim, but when in 1942 he asked the attorney general to go to court to protect it, President Franklin D. Roosevelt put the matter on hold. Ickes tried again in 1944 and again was told to stand down; at the time, he wrote in his diary that Edwin Pauley, a California oilman and fund-raiser for the Democratic Party, had derailed the proposal, apparently because oil companies preferred dealing with states rather than the national government.

Harry Truman, who became president following Roosevelt's death in April 1945, authorized the attorney general to file suit against California in the U.S. Supreme Court to settle the ownership question. The oil industry and the coastal states then asked Congress to short-circuit the litigation by formally renouncing any claim to offshore lands (except any the United States had previously acquired by purchase or donation). The House adopted a joint resolution to that effect in September 1945 and sent it to the Senate. Truman, undeterred, promptly issued a proclamation asserting national control of the entire continental shelf and the waters over it.[12]

In early January 1946, Truman nominated Edwin Pauley to be secretary of the Navy, a position that gave him control over the naval petroleum reserves on public lands. Ickes, concerned by that prospect, testified at Pauley's confirmation hearing that Pauley had opposed the United States claiming ownership of offshore lands, on the grounds that it could dry up oil industry contributions to the Democratic Party. The news media feasted on this story, especially after Ickes made available excerpts from his diary recounting the episode. At his next press conference, Truman suggested that Ickes might be mistaken. On February 12, an enraged Ickes sent a letter to Truman resigning as Interior secretary, effective March 31. The next day, the president accepted his resignation but advanced his departure date to February 15. Thus ended Ickes's long tenure at Interior, the result of a personal quarrel, much like the end of Gifford Pinchot's career at the Forest Service thirty-five years earlier.[13]

Truman remained resolute that the Supreme Court should resolve the ownership question. In July 1946, the Senate passed the joint resolution disclaiming U.S. ownership that the House had passed the previous September, but only after amending it to make clear that the United States was not relinquishing its claim to the continental shelf beyond three miles. The House quickly accepted the Senate amendment and sent the joint resolution to the White House. Truman promptly vetoed it, explaining that Congress was "not an appropriate forum to determine the legal issues" then pending before the Supreme Court.[14]

In June 1947, the Supreme Court upheld the national government's claim in *United States v. California*. There was some symmetry in the fact that the Court's majority opinion was written by Justice Hugo Black, a former senator from Alabama. California's principal legal claim for ownership was based on an opinion written for the Court in 1845 by another former Alabama senator, Justice John McKinley. In his opinion in *Pollard v. Hagan*, McKinley had embraced the idea that because the thirteen original states owned the lands underneath inland navigable waters inside their borders, all of the succeeding states gained ownership of lands of that character when they were admitted to the union on an "equal footing" with the original states. In several decisions after *Pollard,* the Court had put several important limitations on McKinley's reasoning and had never extended it to submerged lands offshore.[15]

Justice Black's opinion simply assumed McKinley was correct in applying the "equal footing" idea to determine the ownership of submerged lands in *inland* waters, rejecting the U.S. attorney general's invitation to overturn *Pollard* altogether. Black's conclusion was that *Pollard* did not support state ownership of submerged lands off the nation's coasts, because there the interests of national defense and international relations were too intimately involved. Only one justice was persuaded by California's argument.[16]

United States v. California's strong endorsement of a broad definition of public lands under national control was consistent with how the Court had generally ruled on such matters since the Civil War. Only a month before, for example, the Court had unanimously rejected Wyoming's claim that its 1890 statehood grant of a section of public land in every township for schools vested immediately, even before surveys had located those grants on the ground. Approving the state's argument would, Chief Justice Vinson wrote, unacceptably "complicate the performance of the Government's obligation with respect to the public lands," for at the same time that Congress authorized statehood for Wyoming, it was reserving tracts of public lands to "accomplish such important purposes as preserving the national forests and mineral resources, establishing public parks, and the like."[17]

The Court's decision in *United States v. California* did not question Congress's authority under the Constitution's Property Clause to relinquish ownership of these submerged lands to the states. The matter was not an issue in the 1948 presidential campaign, but the coastal states and the oil industry persuaded Congress to enact a joint resolution in May 1952 that would confirm state title to submerged lands in a belt of lands offshore. Truman promptly vetoed it. The issue then took on a somewhat partisan cast in the 1952 elections. In contrast to the Democrats' silence, the Republican platform called for the "restoration to the States of their rights to all lands and resources beneath navigable inland and offshore waters within their historic boundaries." Even after Eisenhower won the presidency and the Republicans regained control of Congress, Truman refused to yield on the matter. Four days before he left office, he issued an executive order setting aside submerged lands on the continental shelf as a naval petroleum reserve. The political tide had turned, however, and his order was short-lived.[18]

On May 22, 1953, Eisenhower signed the Submerged Lands Act into law. The Senate passed it by a vote of 56–35 on May 5, and the House by a vote of 278–116 on May 13. It annulled Truman's executive order and generally gave the coastal states (including states bordering the Great Lakes) title to submerged lands from the mean high-tide line out to three nautical miles offshore (or in the case of Texas and the Gulf coast of Florida, three marine leagues, or about ten nautical miles). (It was not a coincidence that the beneficiary states were a majority of the states and contained most of the nation's population.)[19]

The act made clear that its primary aim was to give the beneficiary states the right to develop the resources of that belt of lands off the coasts, for it explicitly reserved to the United States all its "rights in and powers of regulation and control of" the lands the act confirmed to the states, along with the waters above them, for its "paramount" purposes of "commerce, navigation, national defense, and international affairs." Finally, the act "hereby confirmed" the rights that Truman had claimed for the United States in his 1945 proclamation, namely, to natural resources in a vastly larger area, some nine times the area granted to the coastal states, that lay farther offshore. The Supreme Court upheld the Submerged Lands Act the following year in a brief, unsigned opinion.[20]

On August 7, 1953, Eisenhower signed the Outer Continental Shelf Lands Act (OCSLA) into law. Warren Christopher, a future secretary of state, called it "epochal" because it was Congress's first assertion of jurisdiction over a vast area whose "mineral resources and food potential" had been said to "make its acquisition more important to the nation than the Louisiana Purchase." The House version of the Submerged Lands Act had contained the nucleus of what became the OCSLA, but it had been dropped out of the Senate version, with the promise of promptly addressing the matter in a separate bill.[21]

The OCSLA gave the Interior secretary the authority to lease minerals and other resources on the outer continental shelf that lay seaward of the lands that Congress had just granted to the coastal states. The OCSLA generally followed the model of the Mineral Leasing Act of 1920, except that it required all leases to be issued competitively, and it did not share with the coastal states any revenues that the United States derived from mineral leasing on the federal outer continental shelf. The legislative history showed that both of these differences were the result of careful deliberation.[22]

The OCSLA also authorized the president to "withdraw from disposition" any unleased lands of the outer continental shelf, thus giving the chief executive a tool to protect offshore resources comparable to that provided by the Pickett Act of 1910 for public lands onshore. President Eisenhower used this authority in 1960 to establish the Key Largo Coral Reef Preserve near Miami, in order to, in the words of his withdrawal order, "protect and preserve this natural wonder for the benefit of future generations." The Interior Department promptly adopted regulations prohibiting disturbance of the resources on the withdrawn lands, and Florida established a state park on adjacent state submerged lands at the same time. Eisenhower's action proved to be a model for future presidents to protect offshore public lands.[23]

Today, the United States owns submerged lands generally lying from three to twelve nautical miles offshore (although determining exact boundaries requires the application of complicated rules). Moreover, through the OCSLA, the United States exercises jurisdiction that strongly resembles ownership over a vastly larger area out to the limit of the outer continental shelf. Altogether, offshore public lands cover an area significantly larger than the 2.3 billion acres that make up the total area of the fifty states.[24]

PART EIGHT PUBLIC LANDS IN MODERN TIMES, 1961–PRESENT

CHAPTER FIFTY-TWO

The Wilderness Act Reshapes Public Land Policy

THE BOULDER CANYON PROJECT ACT led to seventeen years of bickering about what to call the giant dam it authorized. Interior secretary Wilbur had named it after President Hoover in 1929. Ickes renamed it Boulder Dam in 1933. When, in 1946, the Republicans gained control of Congress for the first time since Hoover's presidency, they restored his name, leading one observer to propose that it be called "Hoogivza Dam." More importantly, Hoover Dam's dazzling engineering achievement not only boosted the nation's confidence in the depths of the Great Depression (it was finished ahead of schedule and under budget), but also led to a proliferation of similar projects all across the West.

Because almost all of the region's significant rivers crossed state lines, most of these projects related to arrangements that the states and the United States made to allocate their waters among the affected states. The Boulder Canyon project, for example, helped California realize its share of the water that the pathbreaking Colorado River Compact of 1922 allocated to the river's lower basin. (The compact gave the lower basin somewhat more than half of the river's total estimated annual flow, and California claimed more than half of the lower basin's allocation.)[1]

After World War II, the states in the river's upper basin worked with the U.S. Bureau of Reclamation to secure congressional authorization for projects that would facilitate their capture and use of the water that the compact allocated to them. One such project was to build two dams on the Green River, the Colorado's largest tributary, at a place called Echo Park. The site of the proposed dams—along the Colorado-Utah border just below where the Yampa River flowed into the Green—lay in Dinosaur National Monument, which was administered by the National Park Service. In 1938, with the support of local interests looking to promote scenery-based tourism, FDR had vastly expanded an eighty-acre national monument that Woodrow Wilson had established there in 1915.[2]

Echo Park was the first proposed dam project to capture national attention since Hetch Hetchy four decades earlier. The Park Service opposed it, but was overruled by the Interior secretary. Opponents outside the government, led by Howard Zahniser, of the Wilderness Society, and David Brower, the young new leader of the Sierra Club, launched a campaign to defeat it. Bernard DeVoto kicked it off with an essay in the *Saturday Evening Post* in 1950. Over the next few years, it attracted many prominent supporters, including Ulysses Grant III, the grandson of the former president and also a West Point graduate and retired major general. The campaign eventually succeeded in persuading Congress to remove the Echo Park dams from the suite of projects included in the 1956 Colorado River Storage Project (CRSP) Act.[3]

The battle over Echo Park showed how more and more Americans were coming to regard an attack on one protected area of public land as an attack on all of them. Approving the Echo Park project would, opponents emphasized, "open the door to similar invasion" of other protected areas of public lands. The message reverberated politically and helped nationalize the issue.

This focus on what Zahniser called the "sanctity of dedicated areas" of public lands did make scenic areas of public lands that lay outside protected systems more vulnerable to development. One of the dams that Congress authorized in the CRSP Act would be located near, and named after, a little-known place called Glen Canyon, farther downstream on the Colorado River. Glen Canyon, on BLM-managed public land in Utah just north of the Arizona border, was not in any "dedicated area" because the water project lobby had thwarted the Park Service's proposal to establish the large Escalante National Monument there in the late 1930s.[4]

The opponents of the Echo Park dams did not strenuously object to the proposed Glen Canyon dam, and almost certainly lacked the political strength to defeat it. The mid-1950s marked the acme of the big-dam-building era, which was promoted by a powerful bipartisan coalition of states, irrigation and power interests, congressional committees, and executive branch agencies such as the Bureau of Reclamation and Army Corps of Engineers. In hindsight, the Glen Canyon dam was a high price to pay for preserving Echo Park, because it inundated a much larger and even more scenic expanse of public land. As awareness of that loss grew, it fed the movement to put additional worthy areas of public land into protected systems.

THE LONG BATTLE FOR THE WILDERNESS ACT

Advocates for protecting public lands with few obvious marks of human activity sought to build on the Echo Park campaign's success by establishing a new national system of protected public lands. On the very day in 1956 that President Eisenhower signed the CRSP legislation into law, Zahniser sent a letter to key members of Congress asking them to support legislation to institute a network of "wilderness" areas on public lands.[5]

The idea had been around for decades. From their earliest days, both the Forest Service and the Park Service had limited the use of some lands under their control in order to preserve their natural values. Beginning in the 1920s, the Forest Service had begun to formally protect some areas with labels such as "primitive area." Beginning in 1930, Congress started enacting legislation that specifically preserved "wilderness" values in the Boundary Waters in northern Minnesota (managed by the Forest Service), and in the Everglades in Florida and Kings Canyon in California (both managed by the Park Service).

The first version of the bill that became the Wilderness Act was introduced by Senator Hubert Humphrey in June 1956. Its journey to enactment took more than eight years and involved five Congresses, nine committee hearings, more than six thousand pages of testimony, and several dozen legislative drafts.

At the time the first wilderness bill was introduced, most public lands remained little touched by road building, dam building, logging, or mining. Most of those lands were, however, legally open to most such activities. (The National Park Organic Act had never been interpreted to limit road building, for example.) Depending on how Congress chose to define "wilderness," up to 200 million acres of public land in the forty-eight states could likely qualify, although proponents of the Wilderness Act generally avoided speculating about its potential reach.

Early versions of the Wilderness Act would have allowed lands on Indian reservations to be included, with the consent of the affected tribe. Decades earlier, the wilderness advocate Bob Marshall had promoted the idea as a way to help preserve traditional tribal culture. While serving as director of forestry for the Bureau of Indian Affairs in 1937, he persuaded Interior secretary Ickes to issue an order forbidding road construction on nearly 5 million acres of land on sixteen Indian reservations for the stated purpose of protecting tribal privacy. Although Marshall was regarded as a progressive on Indian matters, he did not consult the affected tribes. Ickes's order stirred some resentment and over time was largely rescinded. Eventually, the Indian-lands provision was dropped from the proposed legislation.[6]

The champions of the Wilderness Act in and out of Congress were seasoned operatives, pragmatic as well as visionary. Besides Zahniser, who had grown up exploring the Allegheny National Forest near his home in Pennsylvania, they numbered several members of Congress from the West, the region most affected. These included Senators Clinton Anderson (D-N.M., who chaired the conference committee that ironed out the differences between the House- and Senate-passed versions in 1964), Frank Church (D-Idaho), James Murray (D-Mont.), and then-congressman Lee Metcalf (D-Mont.).

Not all were from the West, and not all were Democrats; four of the ten co-sponsors of Humphrey's original bill were Republicans. The leading champion in the House was John Saylor (R-Pa.), who had opposed the dam at Glen Canyon and told his colleagues in July 1956 that "we Americans are the people we are largely because we have had the influence of the wilderness on our lives." Saylor, a political conservative, was the ranking member on the House Interior Committee from 1959 until his death at age sixty-five in 1973, and was an influential proponent of numerous measures protecting public lands.[7]

The act's long trek through Congress was fueled by other development-versus-preservation controversies that erupted in the wake of Echo Park. An example was the Forest Service's decision in 1957 to rescind its 1938 designation of the French Pete Valley in Oregon's central Cascade Mountains as a "primitive area," thus making it available for logging. The resulting grassroots protest helped convince Oregon senators Wayne Morse and Richard Neuberger to support the Wilderness Act. The massive postwar increase in road building and clear-cutting on the national forests also helped fuel the campaign.[8]

The deliberations leading up to the Wilderness Act helped submerge the decades-long rivalry between the Forest Service and the National Park Service. Both agencies initially resisted the legislation, fearing the loss of management discretion. By 1958, however, each had been persuaded to come around, both by the popularity of the cause and by the shrewd decision of the act's proponents not to establish a new agency to administer designated wilderness areas, or to make wilderness designation a tool for moving lands from one agency to another.

Public lands were not a significant issue in the tight contest for the presidency in 1960, when the Californian Richard Nixon won all the western states except Nevada and New Mexico. As a senator, the new president, John F. Kennedy, had opposed the Echo Park dams and supported wilderness legislation. Shortly after taking office, he called on Congress to pass a wilderness act. The Senate responded by approving the legislation later that year by a wide margin, but it did not advance further. Meanwhile, the Sierra Club published two influential books celebrating beautiful American wild landscapes that, as Stephen Fox put it, "brought the wilderness to people": *This Is the American Earth* (1960, with photographs by Ansel Adams) and *In Wildness Is the Preservation of the World* (1962, with color photographs by Eliot Porter).[9]

Kennedy appointed Stewart Udall, just forty-one, to be his Interior secretary. Udall had grown up in the pioneer Mormon community of St. John's, Arizona, interrupted his college education to enlist in the air force, and flew fifty combat missions over western Europe before returning to finish college and law school. He then practiced law in Tucson before winning a seat in Congress in 1954. Over his eight years as Interior secretary, Udall left a prominent mark on public land policy. He laid out the reasons for wilderness legislation in an essay in the *New York Times Magazine* in May 1962, and in 1963 he published *The Quiet Crisis*, a popular book with an introduction by President Kennedy that William deBuys called a "turning point in American conservation history."[10]

The release in 1962 of *Outdoor Recreation for America*, the report of the Outdoor Recreation Resources Review Commission chartered by Congress and chaired by Laurance Rockefeller, helped boost the effort. All eight of the commission's congressional members (out of fifteen total) were on the House and Senate committees responsible for public lands, including Senator Anderson and Congressman Saylor. Without singling out any agency or land system, the report called for Congress to enact legislation to preserve "certain primitive areas as 'wilderness areas.' "[11]

The campaign for the Wilderness Act was helped immeasurably by the tenor of the late 1950s and early 1960s. An expanding middle class enjoyed unprecedented economic prosperity and leisure time. Americans had confidence in their governmental institutions and were optimistic about the future. The Vietnam War had not yet begun to divide the country and give rise to a counterculture. As the nation rallied after the tragic assassination of John F. Kennedy, Lyndon Johnson, master legislative strategist, was at the peak of his power.

The final votes on the Wilderness Act were not close; 373–1 in the House and 73–12 in the Senate, with the twelve Senate dissenters equally divided between

Lyndon Johnson signing the Wilderness Act, September 3, 1964. Among those pictured are Margaret "Mardy" Murie (*third from left*), Frank Church (*fifth from left*), Alice Zahniser (*sixth from left*), Wayne Aspinall (*eighth from left*), Clinton Anderson (*directly behind Johnson*), John Saylor (*second from right*), and (*right*) Stewart Udall. (Photograph by Abbie Rowe, National Park Service Historic Photograph Collection)

Republicans and Democrats. On September 3, 1964, just six weeks after Senator Barry Goldwater (one of the no votes) accepted the Republican Party's nomination for the presidency in a speech brimming with hostility toward government, Johnson signed the Wilderness Act into law. Two months later, Johnson won a full term as president in a landslide of historic dimensions.[12]

THE WILDERNESS ACT: THE DETAILS

The Wilderness Act's uncommonly eloquent language defines "wilderness" as "an area where the earth and its community of life are untrammeled by man, where man himself is a visitor who does not remain"; an area that retains "its primeval character and influence, without permanent improvements or human habitation," and that "(1) generally appears to have been affected primarily by the forces of nature, with the imprint of man's work substantially unnoticeable; (2) has outstanding opportunities for solitude or a primitive and unconfined type of recreation; (3) has at least five thousand acres of land or is of sufficient size as to make practicable its preservation and use in an unimpaired condition; and (4) may also contain ecological, geological, or other features of scientific, educational, scenic, or historical value."[13]

The qualifiers "generally," "primarily," and "substantially" convey that wilderness lands are not necessarily free of human imprint, but "untrammeled" signals that humans do not constrain the operation of natural forces there. The definition focuses more on what is seen than what might be revealed by a detailed examination, informed by scientific understanding. It focuses on protecting public lands *from* development, rather than *for* particular purposes. Thus, wilderness "may" (not "must") have "features of scientific, educational, scenic, or historical value."

The Wilderness Act established the national wilderness preservation system (NWPS). Any public lands meeting its definition of "wilderness"— regardless of which agency manages them—are eligible for inclusion. Once lands are in the system, the act's legal protections overlie and limit the operation of other laws that apply to particular agencies. The act allows the managing agency to continue to administer designated wilderness "for such other purposes" as are within the agency's legal mandate, but only as long as "its wilderness character" is preserved. While the act imposes sharp limits on use regardless of which agency manages the area, a few differences among agencies are still possible. Hunting is permitted in wilderness areas managed by the Forest Service, for example, but not in those managed by the Park Service.[14]

Public lands included in the NWPS are subject to some of the most stringent protections found anywhere. Building roads, harvesting timber, and mining are generally forbidden, as are, with narrowly drawn exceptions, most other forms of "commercial enterprise," as well as "motorized equipment" and "mechanical transport." At the time the act was adopted, there were relatively few off-road or all-terrain vehicles, such as war-surplus Jeeps, that could penetrate the backcountry without any need for roads. Within a decade, an explosion in the types, number, and popularity of off-road vehicles began to spark conflicts that heavily influenced proposals to expand the NWPS.[15]

Their threat to wilderness values helped persuade Presidents Nixon and Carter to mandate efforts to regulate off-road-vehicle use on all public lands. In February 1972, Nixon issued an executive order directing each public land agency to designate which of their lands were open and which were closed to such use. When agencies were slow to comply, Carter provided firmer direction five years later. Considerable litigation and controversy resulted, but over time all the agencies instituted management plans to control the use of such vehicles.

Congress was content to remain mostly on the sidelines while all this occurred, but off-road-vehicle use remains a major point of contention when Congress considers whether to add areas to the NWPS. In recent years, mountain biking and e-biking have been added to the mix. Although they are mechanical means of transportation currently forbidden by the Wilderness Act, proposals have been made in Congress to give their users access to NWPS areas. Another vehicular-related campaign is a decades-long effort by the State of Utah to claim rights to thousands of miles of rights-of-way under a nineteenth-century statute, RS 2477, that Congress repealed in 1976. Its undisguised objective has been to disqualify millions of acres of public lands from wilderness consideration. The result so far has been lengthy and mostly inconclusive litigation.[16]

The Wilderness Act put 9 million acres of national forest lands in thirteen states into the NWPS—less than 2 percent of the public lands. The Forest Service was already protecting these 9 million acres through "wilderness," "wild," or "canoe" designations that it had invented. Enactment of the Wilderness Act simply gave those protections statutory backing and more permanence. Although many more public lands met the act's definition of wilderness, its champions settled for this relatively modest amount of acreage in order to get the legislation establishing the architecture of the system through Congress.

Water-project advocates, miners, and other developers of resources found on public lands had considerable political power and—fearing this new restrictive system could thwart their ambitions—did not go quietly. To accommodate them, the Wilderness Act was shot through with political concessions—on water projects, on mineral development, on livestock grazing, and on other matters.

Although the act's compromises opened the door for constructing water projects and carrying on mining operations in NWPS areas, that almost never happened. Topography, climate, remoteness, market forces, and public opposition all stood in the way and could not be overcome. Livestock grazing was a different story; it continues in many wilderness areas to this day.

With one narrow exception, the Wilderness Act made Congress the exclusive gatekeeper of the NWPS. Section 6 of the law allows donations or bequests of land within or "adjacent to" NWPS areas to be added without further action by Congress; otherwise, lands can be added to the system only through legislation.

In hindsight, making itself the gatekeeper was the most important decision Congress made in the act. It was particularly important to curmudgeonly Representative Wayne Aspinall (D-Colo.), who had chaired the House Interior Committee since 1959. First elected to Congress in 1948 to fill the seat Edward Taylor once held, Aspinall had long advocated that Congress reclaim some of the authority over public lands that it had delegated to the executive branch. When Eisenhower used the Antiquities Act shortly before he left office in early 1961 to protect a popular recreational area of public land along the historic C&O Canal near Washington, D.C., Aspinall was incensed by what he regarded as the president's invasion of Congress's prerogative.[17]

Aspinall saw himself as a traditional "conservationist" in the Pinchot mold, opposing the "waste" of natural resources. He was decidedly not in the camp of those he called "purist preservationists," who wanted areas saved "merely for the sake of saving." In Congress, he was a dependable defender of livestock operators, dam builders, and the mining industry. He was, therefore, not keen to have a system of wilderness areas grow very much. John Saylor and his allies, such as John Dingell (D-Mich.), reluctantly acquiesced in his insistence that Congress be the gatekeeper.[18]

The need to obtain congressional approval in order to expand the NWPS beyond its modest beginnings in the Wilderness Act challenged wilderness advocates to organize politically. Grassroots campaigns were imperative because of the internal dynamics of the congressional process. A deeply embedded characteristic of that process is that bills addressing the management of particular tracts of public land in one state or locale—whether the objective is a wilderness designation or something else—almost always need the support, or at least not the active opposition, of the most directly affected members. If a particular area of public land is to be designated wilderness, in other words, it almost always needs the sign-off of the local congressional delegation.[19]

The act directed the Interior secretary to review every "roadless" area (though it did not define "road") of at least 5,000 contiguous acres in the national park and national wildlife refuge systems (and roadless islands of any size in the latter) and to recommend to the president, who in turn would recommend to Congress, whether they should be put in the NWPS. At the time, a few tens of millions of acres in those two systems qualified for the review. The act directed the Agriculture secretary to conduct a similar review of about 5.6 million acres of national forest lands classified as "primitive." Congress gave the three agencies several years to complete these reviews.

The act was silent, however, regarding any review of the many more tens of millions of acres of potentially eligible lands on national forests outside "primitive areas." It was also silent regarding public lands managed by the Bureau of Land Management.[20]

THE WILDERNESS ACT IN PRACTICE

In acquiescing in the idea that only Congress could add acres to the national wilderness preservation system, wilderness advocates were, in effect, wagering that their movement would continue to gain political strength, including at the grass roots. It turned out to be a good bet. The idea of keeping many areas of public land free from conventional development resonated deeply in American culture. The Wilderness Society and other groups built coalitions and campaigned locally and nationally for enlarging the NWPS, with great success. They were helped by the fact that most eligible areas, besides being roadless, contained rugged terrain that would be costly to access for development.[21]

One issue that commanded considerable attention in the early days of the act's implementation was how "pure" an area had to be to qualify for inclusion in the NWPS. Much public land, especially outside the West, had seen some logging, contained primitive roads, or otherwise bore some often-faint imprint of human use. Some purist wilderness champions believed that such signs were enough to disqualify areas from consideration, no matter how "natural" they might appear. The Forest Service's leadership took this position in the act's first few years, presumably seeking to minimize congressional intrusions on its management discretion. Congress never bought into that philosophy; it made national-forest areas in New Hampshire and North Carolina charter members of the NWPS, and in 1968 put a portion of the Great Swamp National Wildlife Refuge, twenty-six miles west of New York's Times Square, into the system, the first Interior Department–managed lands to be included. Over time, Congress designated many areas outside the West as wilderness, most notably in the Eastern Wilderness Areas Act, signed into law in 1975 by President Gerald Ford. ("Purists" diminished in number as more scientific evidence emerged showing the effect of indigenous peoples on landscapes dating back millennia.)[22]

Measured by acreage, the golden age of wilderness legislation was from the late 1970s to 1995. The early 1980s supplied an indication of how rapidly the idea of protecting many millions of acres of public lands as wilderness had gained purchase. The conservative Heritage Foundation recommended to the Reagan administration that it make mineral exploration the "dominant use" of lands that were already in the National Wilderness Preservation System. The idea was to take advantage of the twenty-year window for issuing new mineral leases and locating new mining claims that had been included in the 1964 legislation at the insistence of Wayne Aspinall and the fossil fuel and mining industry. But when Reagan's Interior secretary, James Watt, proposed to issue oil and gas leases in wilderness areas, it triggered an outcry. Congressman Don Edwards (D-Calif.) memorably characterized Watt's idea of wilderness as "a parking lot without stripes," and Congress closed the leasing window before Watt could act. Although the Senate was then in Republican control, even Western senators such as Alan Simpson and Malcolm Wallop, both Wyoming Republicans, thought Watt had gone too far.[23]

During this golden age, Congress and wilderness advocates concentrated on lands managed by the Forest Service and, to a lesser extent, by the BLM. These were viewed as the areas most threatened with development, compared with lands managed by the Park Service and the Fish & Wildlife Service. These last two agencies were both less inclined, and less empowered by the laws under which they operated, to approve wilderness-impairing development.

Wilderness champions outside the government often conducted more detailed and systematic surveys of candidate areas than the executive branch agencies did, and Congress often put more acres in the NWPS than the agencies recommended. In 1978, for example, Congress put Oregon's French Pete Valley, whose downgrade from "primitive area" status by the Forest Service had helped stoke support for the Wilderness Act, into the NWPS. In recent decades, the system has continued to expand, albeit at a considerably slower pace.[24]

The results tell the story. From its relatively humble beginnings in 1964, the NWPS has now grown to include more than 111 million acres—more than one of every six acres of public land—in more than 800 separate wilderness areas in forty-four states and Puerto Rico. (A little more than half this acreage is in Alaska.) Forty-four million acres of the NWPS are managed by the National Park Service, 36 million acres are managed by the Forest Service, 21 million acres are managed by the U.S. Fish & Wildlife Service, and 9 million acres are managed by the BLM. Until and unless Congress says so, road building, mining, logging, and other intensive kinds of development are not permitted on these lands.

The wilderness protection movement has also remained thoroughly bipartisan. Six Republican presidents signed legislation that accounts for about half of the approximately 54 million acres currently in the NWPS outside Alaska. About 14 million of those acres were moved through Congresses in which

Republicans controlled at least one house. Because legislation designating wilderness generally needs the acquiescence of local members of Congress, inclusion in the NWPS is considered permanent. Proposals to shrink the NWPS have never gained traction in Congress and are almost never even made.[25]

The amount of land held permanently in national ownership, when plotted in graph form over time, shows a steady upward line of growth beginning in 1890, with especially large jumps in acreage from 1900 to 1910, in the 1930s, and the 1970s. The amount of those lands secured in the national wilderness preservation system shows a steep increase beginning in 1970, and then approximately leveling off after 1980. The acres of reserved public lands include those that were, beginning with the Weeks Act of 1911, acquired by purchase or donation from states or private owners. These now total more than 60 million acres. It does not include submerged lands off the nation's coasts, or minerals that the United States reserved when it conveyed the land surface to others.[26]

THE PENUMBRA OF THE WILDERNESS ACT

The amount of land in the NWPS is hardly the only measure of the act's enormous influence on public land policy. Nearly the same amount of public land outside the system is being managed as if it were part of the system. For example, not a single acre of the 2.2-million-acre Yellowstone National Park is in the NWPS, but it is generally understood that any proposal to build roads there or otherwise develop its backcountry would trigger calls for "preserving the wilderness" and encounter fierce opposition. That has proved to be a potent rallying cry even against developments on private land, and has sometimes resulted in an area ending up in U.S. ownership and being protected much as if it were in the NWPS. A proposal in the early 1970s to build a large airport near Everglades National Park in South Florida, for example, led Congress to enact legislation in 1974 authorizing the United States to purchase more than 700,000 acres of land to establish the Big Cypress National Preserve (only the second time Congress had used that label) as part of the national park system.[27]

There are many other examples of Congress requiring wilderness-like protection of areas of public land without including them in the NWPS. Sometimes Congress does it, as at Big Cypress, by appending to a tract of public land a label (national preserve, reserve, conservation area, recreation area, scenic area, and many others) and directing that it be managed to give primary emphasis to protecting natural values. Congress also often directs agencies to

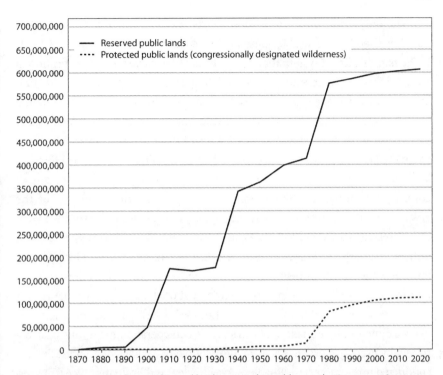

Land reserved in national ownership and land protected as wilderness by Congress, 1870–2020. The units shown on the vertical axis at left are acres. The changes in acreage are graphed in ten-year increments, not year by year. (Chart by Stephanie Smith, Grand Canyon Trust, and Bill Nelson)

inventory their landholdings, identify candidate areas, and submit recommendations to Congress regarding their possible inclusion in the NWPS.

In the Federal Land Policy and Management Act enacted in 1976 (the so-called BLM organic act), Congress instructed the Interior secretary to identify all roadless areas larger than 5,000 acres (and all roadless islands) managed by the BLM and to recommend whether Congress should include them in the NWPS. It also prohibited the Interior secretary from doing anything on these lands that could impair wilderness values until Congress provided otherwise. On other public lands eligible for NWPS inclusion where Congress has not required interim protection, the agencies themselves—sometimes with nudging from the courts as well as from wilderness champions—have provided it. This has been done to preserve Congress's gatekeeper role; that is, its power to decide which areas of public land should be included in the NWPS.[28]

The only 5,000-plus-acre roadless tracts of public land that Congress has never insisted be reviewed for possible inclusion in the NWPS are those lands in the national forest system that did not bear a "primitive area" classification in 1964. This is a very large amount of land, many tens of millions of acres, a third or more of the acreage in the national forest system. In the deliberations leading up to passage of the Wilderness Act, wilderness champions decided not to press for a congressionally mandated study of these areas. This was at a time when the Forest Service regarded logging as the dominant use of most forested lands under its care, and had classified at least half this roadless acreage as commercial forestland. By contrast, many of the charter members of the NWPS, and the "primitive" areas that the act did require to be studied, were little-forested "rocks and ice" areas, and practically all were in rugged terrain, difficult to access, and thus not especially coveted by the timber industry.[29]

Even though Congress had not required it, in 1971 the Forest Service decided, after some hesitation, to review all national-forest roadless areas over 5,000 acres for possible inclusion in the NWPS. (The agency decision was likely influenced by President Nixon's giving consideration to requiring such a review by executive order.) Over the next couple of decades, the Forest Service conducted three successive Roadless Area Review and Evaluation (RARE) exercises. The results provided a barometer of the rapid rise in popular support for wilderness protection. RARE I, completed in 1973, recommended that Congress include a little more than 12 million acres in the NWPS. Two years later, in the Eastern Wilderness Areas Act, Congress put a number of areas in the NWPS that the agency had recommended against protecting. RARE II, completed in 1979, recommended that Congress include 15 million acres in the NWPS, with 11 million more acres considered for further study. In the 1980s, Congress again followed up by putting millions more acres in the NWPS that the agency had recommended against protecting.[30]

In 1999, the Clinton administration promulgated a "roadless rule" that protected 58.5 million acres of national forest land from nearly all wilderness-disqualifying development until Congress acted either to include them in the NWPS or to remove them from further consideration. It was adopted after extensive public outreach that included six hundred public meetings around the country and elicited 1.6 million public comments.

The roadless rule has survived mostly intact, although it has produced a tangle of litigation and other maneuvering. The State of Wyoming tried but failed to persuade the federal courts that the rule was inconsistent with the Wilderness Act. The George W. Bush administration proposed to repeal much of the Clinton rule, citing concerns about its scope (although 95 percent of the public comments it received were in support of the rule). To prevent its repeal, California, Oregon, and New Mexico sued, alongside wilderness groups, and persuaded the courts to halt the Bush process, by which time Barack Obama had become president. In the meantime, Idaho and Colorado petitioned to change the roadless rule as it applied in their states, which led to some relatively minor adjustments. More recently, Utah and Alaska petitioned the Trump administration to repeal or limit the rule in their states. In late 2020, the administration removed 9 million acres of the 17-million-acre Tongass National Forest, the nation's largest, from the protections of the roadless rule.[31]

In the BLM's initial wilderness review in the late 1970s, mandated by the Federal Land Policy and Management Act, the bureau overlooked millions of acres of potential NWPS lands. Subsequently, it came to identify many of them as "lands with wilderness characteristics" in its planning process. It manages most of these lands in ways that protect their wilderness values. Other areas of public lands have remained undeveloped and eligible for wilderness status, though often without any kind of formal protective designation.[32]

Although Indian lands have never been put in the NWPS, a few tribes, most notably the Confederated Salish and Kootenai Tribes (CSKT) in northwestern Montana, manage some tribal lands as wilderness. In 1936, the CSKT proposed to establish a tribally maintained national park on tribal lands on the west side of the Mission Mountains. That idea never advanced, but the next year the area was one of those included in Secretary Ickes's order, promoted by Bob Marshall, preserving roadless areas on several reservations. Because the CSKT had not been consulted, the tribe protested this action, and the designation was eventually withdrawn. The eastern portion of the Mission Mountains is managed by the Forest Service, which designated much of it a "primitive area" in the 1930s. In 1975, Congress put 75,000 acres in the NWPS. In 1982, the CSKT established a 92,000-acre wilderness area on the western portion, and the tribe and the Forest Service cooperate closely in managing adjoining wilderness areas. The driving force behind the tribal wilderness was CSKT member Thurman Trosper, who had been a marine officer at Guadalcanal and served in the Forest Service, in the National Park Service, and as president of the governing council of the Wilderness Society.[33]

All told, perhaps as many as 100 million acres of public land that meet the criteria to be included in the NWPS remain outside it, but in fact are managed much as if they were in it. These areas, plus the 111 million acres already in the NWPS, mean that today about one-third of all public lands—substantial amounts of them managed by each of the four principal public land agencies—are under some form of wilderness-like protection.

Although Congress or, in some cases, executive branch agencies could open these lands to road building, logging, or other such developments, there is little appetite in the body politic to do so. Proposals to develop these areas are practically guaranteed to create controversy and thus are rarely made. This state of affairs reflects widespread acceptance of the idea that, generally speaking, roadless public lands outside as well as in the NWPS should not be developed.

All these means, complicated though they may be, show how the Wilderness Act has fundamentally changed the management of a significant portion of the nation's public lands, mostly without regard for which government agency is responsible for managing them.

CHAPTER FIFTY-THREE

New Labels and New Means of Protecting Public Values in Public Lands

ON THE SAME DAY HE SIGNED the Wilderness Act into law, President Johnson signed legislation creating the Land and Water Conservation Fund (LWCF). Like the Wilderness Act, the LWCF was also influenced by the *Outdoor Recreation for America* report, which had called for increased governmental funding for outdoor recreation programs. The LWCF's purpose is to improve the "quality and quantity" as well as the "accessibility" of outdoor recreation resources across the nation.

The fund receives money from a variety of sources. By far the most important is royalties paid by federal lessees extracting petroleum on the outer continental shelf. Until 2020, Congress had to appropriate funds distributed from the LWCF, and it usually appropriated only a fraction of the amount coming in. That changed when President Trump signed the Great American Outdoors Act into law. It made the LWCF a genuine revolving fund—what comes in, goes out. It passed both Houses of Congress with strong bipartisan support; the vote was 310–107 in the House and 73–25 in the Senate.[1]

LWCF money is distributed to state as well as federal agencies. Since its establishment, the fund has provided more than $11 billion to federal agencies for land acquisition. The funds are distributed to all four major land management agencies, with the National Park Service ordinarily receiving the largest share. The LWCF remains a primary, though not the only, source of funds for U.S. acquisition of land for conservation and recreation.[2]

NATIONAL RECREATION AREAS

The Wilderness Act was the first public land legislation that significantly limited how certain public lands could be used regardless of which agency was managing them. It was soon followed by others. Indeed, within a month, Congress established the first of what has become a significant and growing collection of "national recreation areas" (NRAs) on public lands.

This idea had its origins in a recommendation made by Louis C. Cramton, a former congressman from Michigan and strong supporter of the national park system, to Interior secretary Work in 1932 regarding what to do with a large area of public land around Lake Mead, the reservoir formed behind Boulder Dam. It led to an interagency agreement between the Bureau of Reclamation and the National Park Service in 1936 that gave the NPS management authority over what was called the Boulder Dam Recreation Area in Nevada and Arizona. Similar interagency agreements followed for other large areas of public land around several Bureau of Reclamation and Army Corps of Engineer reservoirs. For many years, Congress neither objected to the practice nor incorporated it into law.[3]

In 1963, the year after *Outdoor Recreation for America* had underscored the role of public lands in meeting the nation's growing appetite for outdoor recreation, the Kennedy administration announced a policy to govern the selection, establishment, and administration of recreation areas on public lands. It called for them to be "spacious" and "strategically located within easy driving distance" of urban centers, and to be places where outdoor recreation would be the "dominant or primary" purpose. Other uses might be permitted if "compatible" with—that is, not "significantly detrimental to"—the "recreation mission." Bowing to Wayne Aspinall's eagerness to restore congressional primacy in public land policy making, the policy left the establishment of every NRA up to Congress.[4]

On October 8, 1964, President Johnson signed the first NRA legislation into law. It enlarged the former Boulder Dam Recreation Area (which Interior had renamed the Lake Mead National Recreation Area in 1947) to 1.5 million acres, and directed the Park Service to manage it for "public recreation, benefit, and use," in a "manner that will preserve the scenic, historic, scientific, and other important features of the area." It followed the recommendation of *Outdoor Recreation for America* and the Kennedy administration policy by establishing a "dominant use" management regime, leaving the door open for other uses such as livestock grazing and even some kinds of mineral development, but only if consistent with recreational use.[5]

Congress subsequently established several NRAs that followed the Lake Mead model of protecting lands around large federal dam and reservoir projects. But Congress also created NRAs that were aimed at protecting areas of public lands *from* dam building and related developments. The first of these was the Hells Canyon NRA, established in 1975 on more than 600,000 acres of public land along the Idaho-Oregon border in the deepest gorge in North America (2,000 feet deeper than the Grand Canyon). It was downstream of three large dams built on the Snake River by the Idaho Power Company after World War II.

The controversy at Hells Canyon evolved from an initial battle over whether private or public entities should build a fourth dam, to whether another dam should be built at all. A pivotal moment came in 1967 when the Supreme Court, in an opinion written by Justice William O. Douglas, set aside a Federal Power Commission decision to license the fourth dam. The Federal Power Act, Douglas wrote, required the commission to consider "the public interest in preserving reaches of wild rivers and wilderness areas, the preservation of anadromous fish for commercial and recreational purposes, and the protection of wildlife." The Hells Canyon NRA legislation protected the area from dams but kept the lands in the national forest system. It had bipartisan support in both states' congressional delegations.[6]

The Sawtooth NRA, established in 1972 to protect more than 700,000 acres of public lands in the mountains of central Idaho, illustrated the versatility of the protective NRA designation—showing how it offered a politically attractive compromise between the "something for everybody" tenor of "multiple use" and the "no roads or any development" command of the Wilderness Act. As early as 1911, local women's clubs had proposed to establish a national park in the Sawtooth. In 1966, Senator Frank Church introduced two bills to protect the area—one would make it a national park and the other an NRA, the latter keeping the land in Forest Service hands and at least somewhat available to uses such as livestock grazing and timber harvesting.

In 1970, controversy over a proposed molybdenum mine in the area resulted in Cecil Andrus, a vocal opponent of the mine (and future Interior secretary), defeating the incumbent governor, a mine supporter. Not long after, the Republican and Democratic members of the congressional delegation came together to push the NRA legislation through Congress. It banned mining, authorized the United States to acquire "scenic easements" to protect "esthetic values," and even told the Agriculture secretary to regulate the "use, subdivision, and development of" *private* inholdings within the NRA's boundaries to ensure consistency with the act's purposes. Illustrating Congress's increasing appetite for fine-tuning public lands protections by overlay designations, the 1972 legislation put some Sawtooth NRA lands in the NWPS; in 2015, Congress added more NRA lands to the NWPS.[7]

Over the years, the NRA designation has been applied to public lands in many different settings. Some, like the Gateway NRA in metropolitan New York City and the Golden Gate NRA in California's Bay Area, follow the Kennedy administration's suggestion by being located close to urban centers. (In recent years the Golden Gate NRA has been the most visited unit of the national park system, with more than 15 million visitors annually.) The Santa Monica Mountains NRA in Los Angeles, consisting of about 24,000 acres of public land, 42,000 acres of state parks, and some 95,000 acres of local parks, study reserves, and private property restricted by conservation easements, may be the largest urban park in the world.

There are now more than forty NRAs in nearly two dozen states from Alaska to Vermont to Georgia. About half are administered by the National Park Service, and the rest are divided between the Forest Service and the Bureau of Land Management.[8]

WILD AND SCENIC RIVERS ACT

Outdoor Recreation for America called on Congress to enact legislation that would maintain rivers of "unusual scientific, aesthetic, and recreation value" in their "free-flowing and natural setting without man-made alterations." The Park Service had made a similar recommendation a couple of years earlier, and with the strong support of Interior secretary Udall, had persuaded Congress to protect two rivers in the Ozarks in Missouri under Park Service supervision. All this, along with President Johnson's endorsement of the idea in his special message to Congress titled "Conservation and Restoration of Natural Beauty" in February 1965, paved the way for Congress, with strong bipartisan support, to enact the Wild and Scenic Rivers Act (WSRA) in 1968.[9]

Sponsored by Senator Frank Church and Congressman John Saylor, the WSRA declared that it was national policy to preserve selected river segments that "possess outstandingly remarkable scenic, recreational, geologic, fish and wildlife, historic, cultural, or other similar values" in "free-flowing condition" and to protect them and their "immediate environments" to benefit "present and future generations."[10]

The WSRA established a system of protected free-flowing rivers and streams and "related adjacent land areas"—corridors that averaged one-quarter mile back from each side of the river (with the coverage capped at 320 acres per mile). Eight river segments in California, Idaho, Minnesota, Missouri, Oregon, and Wisconsin were the charter members. Some were overseen by Interior and some by the Agriculture Department. Most river segments in the system contain substantial amounts of public land, but because settlements and agriculture historically tended to concentrate along rivers, it is not uncommon for considerable land in WSRA corridors to be privately owned, even in parts of the country rich with public lands. The WSRA authorizes but does not require the United States to acquire ownership of nonpublic lands along the designated rivers.

The act prohibits all federal agencies from assisting in the construction of any water project that would "have a direct and adverse effect on the values for which the river was" put in the system, and from assisting developments outside the designated segment that would "unreasonably diminish" its "scenic, recreational, and fish and wildlife values." It also prohibits the Federal Power Commission from licensing any project on or "directly affecting" a designated river, and constrains all new diversions of water upstream that could diminish water flows in the designated river segment. Land uses and developments in the river corridor are to be controlled by a plan prepared by the administering federal agency and are permitted only if they do not "substantially interfere with public use and enjoyment" of the values for which the area was included in the WSRA system.

As with the Wilderness Act and NRAs, Congress is the gatekeeper for adding new areas to the system, but the WSRA makes one important exception. If a state legislature designates a river segment for permanent protection and the state's governor requests that it be added to the national system, the WSRA empowers the Interior secretary to put it in the national system if it meets the act's criteria. This has happened a few times, most notably when, at the request of California governor Jerry Brown, Secretary Cecil Andrus protected more than a thousand miles of several rivers along California's northern coast hours before he left office in early 1981. A federal court of appeals upheld his action against a challenge brought by timber and water development interests and several counties.[11]

The WSRA mandated a study of more than two dozen specific river segments in twenty-four states for possible inclusion in the national system. It also directed all federal agencies to consider potentially eligible river areas in all their future planning and to "consider and discuss" the possibility of expanding the system in any river basin and project plan report they submitted to Congress.[12]

Over the more than half century since the WSRA became law, the system has expanded to include segments totaling 13,000-plus miles of more than 200 rivers in forty states and Puerto Rico. The strong public support for free-flowing rivers that produced the WSRA effectively marked the end of the nation's dam-building era. (More than 75,000 significant dams had been built since the nation's founding, directly affecting an estimated 600,000 miles of American rivers.)[13]

Sometimes Congress has added areas to the system without waiting for agencies to complete studies, most notably in Oregon in 1988, when Senator Mark Hatfield (R-Ore.) championed legislation that put nearly 1,500 miles in the system. Congress has occasionally used somewhat similar labels for the same end, designating certain river segments to be administered by the National Park Service as national scenic riverways (southern Missouri, 1964) or national rivers (the Buffalo in Arkansas, 1972, and New River Gorge in West Virginia, 1978).[14]

PUBLIC LANDS AND THE MODERN ENVIRONMENTAL MOVEMENT

Shortly after the Nixon administration took office in 1969, Congress produced a series of comprehensive environmental laws, an outpouring of environmental regulatory lawmaking unmatched before or since. The first, signed into law January 1, 1970, was the National Environmental Policy Act (NEPA). Its core requirement is that federal agencies formally consider, in an environmental impact statement, the environmental consequences of their decisions before acting—looking before leaping, as it were. NEPA has had considerable impact on public lands, both in influencing agency decisions and by giving litigants a ready tool to wield in court to obtain careful consideration of environmental impacts. Later that same year, following the first Earth Day celebration, Congress enacted a comprehensive Clean Air Act, followed in 1972 by an equally comprehensive Clean Water Act. These two laws have affected public land management to a much lesser extent.

These new comprehensive pieces of legislation marked the emergence of a powerful political movement aimed at protecting the environment. Culturally and politically, it was somewhat distinct from the movement to protect public lands. There were commonalities—a primary objective of many modern public land statutes is, after all, protecting the environment. But there were important differences. The environmental movement focused more on protecting public health and the urban environment, and on regulating private activities. The movement to protect public lands, which had a longer history, was aimed more at protecting natural values and recreational opportunities, and focused more on guiding decisions by public agencies. Each movement involved somewhat different constituencies, executive branch agencies, congressional committees, regional impacts, and relationships with states.

THE ENDANGERED SPECIES ACT

The annihilation of the Carolina parakeet and the passenger pigeon and the precarious decline of the bison around the turn of the twentieth century had kindled public concern about protecting wildlife species from extinction. Over the years since, growing appreciation of biodiversity and species interdependence has underlined that concern, captured in Aldo Leopold's aphorism that "to keep every cog and wheel is the first precaution of intelligent tinkering."[15]

In 1962, Rachel Carson's *Silent Spring* was published. It sold more than a half million hardcover copies and was on the *New York Times* best-seller list for thirty-one weeks. At a Senate hearing in June 1963, Senator Ernest Gruening (D-Alaska) predicted that, like *Uncle Tom's Cabin,* it would change the course of history. In E. O. Wilson's description, it delivered a "galvanic jolt to public consciousness" that not only reignited national concern about species loss but also advanced many other efforts to conserve nature. Her message was, as Peter Matthiessen wrote, "what threatens our fellow creatures must ultimately threaten ourselves, since our lives are inescapably intertwined with theirs." Carson's sixteen years with the Fish & Wildlife Service (she left in the early 1950s to write full-time) informed the alarm her expressive prose sounded about the effects of the increasing use of synthetic pesticides, particularly DDT, on wildlife. This put her at odds with the Agriculture Department, which spearheaded the use of pesticides on private as well as public lands.[16]

Carson's book did not focus specifically on public lands, but she had earlier written in opposition to the Echo Park dams and to a proposed six-lane highway through Rock Creek Park in Washington, D.C., and her warning in *Silent Spring,* like George Perkins Marsh's a century earlier, had a significant impact on public land policy. The year after her book appeared, Stewart Udall issued a call in the *New York Times* for more action to protect wildlife because they "have a claim to life as valid as our own," one that should be honored "as much for our preservation as for theirs."[17]

In 1966, Congress enacted the first version of the Endangered Species Act (ESA), as part of a larger bill focused on public lands managed primarily for wildlife. It instructed the Interior secretary to maintain a list of species of fish and wildlife believed to be threatened with extinction, and to use existing authorities to carry out a program for "conserving, protecting, restoring, and propagating" them, including habitat acquisition. Udall championed the legislation and put the first seventy-eight species on the list, including such icons as the grizzly bear, the timber wolf, the manatee, and the whooping crane.[18]

After modestly adjusting the ESA in 1969, Congress enacted a new, much beefed-up version in 1973, with strong bipartisan support and almost no dissent. "Nothing is more priceless and more worthy of preservation than the rich array of animal life with which our country has been blessed," President Nixon said in signing it into law. It set forth a comprehensive framework for identifying and protecting species of fish, wildlife, and plants that were facing extinction. Sometimes called the "pit bull" of environmental statutes, its ambitious goal of preserving biological diversity straddled the movement to protect the environment and the movement to protect public lands. While it protects endangered fish and wildlife species on private land as well as on public lands (its protections for listed species of plants apply only to public lands), much of its power has been focused on limiting habitat loss on public lands, especially those managed by the Forest Service and the BLM.[19]

The core of the act is found in two of its sections. Section 7 requires all agencies of the U.S. government to "seek to conserve endangered species," to "utilize their authorities in furtherance of" the ESA's purposes, and to "insure" that any actions they authorize, fund, or carry out do not "jeopardize the continued existence of" such species. Section 7 also requires every U.S. agency proposing actions that could affect listed species to consult with the Interior Department's Fish & Wildlife Service (and the Commerce Department's National Marine Fisheries Service, or NMFS, for certain fish species) before acting. Altogether, section 7 makes endangered-species conservation an important part of every public land management agency's mission.[20]

Section 9 of the ESA makes it unlawful for "any person" (defined broadly to include public-land-managing agencies) to "take" (defined broadly to include "harm" as well as "capture" or "kill") any individual member of a listed species. The Fish & Wildlife Service followed this up in President Ford's administration by adopting a regulation making clear that "harm" could include "significant habitat modification or degradation" by such practices as logging or livestock grazing. The Supreme Court upheld this regulation in its landmark decision in *Babbitt v. Sweet Home* (1995).[21]

The ESA accelerated some trends that were already moving forward in public land management. One was to take biology, and particularly biodiversity, into account in decision making. It reflected what the environmental historian Richard N. L. Andrews described as a "new public consciousness," whose "most revolutionary element" was to recognize the environment "as a living system—a 'web of life,' or ecosystem." The Wilderness Act mentioned science, but mostly in passing. When a "listed" species is involved, by contrast, the ESA dictates that science play a commanding role, taking precedence over more conventional considerations such as economics, consumer demand, and the concerns of state and local governments.[22]

Another trend was to blur distinctions and responsibilities among the different agencies managing public lands. Much like the Wilderness Act, the ESA applies to all agencies managing public land without distinguishing among them. Moreover, the consultation requirement in section 7 gives the wildlife agencies (FWS and NMFS) considerable influence over how agencies such as the Forest Service and the BLM must shape their actions in order to avoid jeopardizing listed species.[23]

THE COURTS BECOME MORE INVOLVED

A third trend that the ESA accelerated was the growing involvement of the judicial branch. The ESA's relatively broad and inflexible commands gave federal courts a broad license to scrutinize public land decisions that might affect listed species. This was dramatized in 1978 when the U.S. Supreme Court enforced the ESA to halt the Tennessee Valley Authority's work on the almost-finished Tellico Dam because a small fish called the snail darter, previously unknown, was found just downstream of the dam site and at the time it was believed to exist nowhere else.[24]

The groundwork for greater judicial involvement in public lands matters had been laid in the 1960s. It was then, as public lands were becoming increasingly prized for what was then commonly called "noneconomic" values such as recreation and wildlife, that the federal courts began to grapple with whether champions of these values could obtain court review of agency decisions that threatened them. The question had two dimensions. One was constitutional—whether such a dispute presented a "case" or "controversy" over which the federal courts had jurisdiction under Article III of the Constitution, and whether judicial involvement was consistent with the "separation of powers" doctrine that governs the relationship of the government's legislative, executive, and judicial branches. The second dimension was statutory—whether champions of those values could be considered legally "aggrieved" within the meaning of the Administrative Procedure Act (1946).

The breakthrough came in the Supreme Court's 1972 decision in *Sierra Club v. Morton*. The club had challenged decisions by the Forest Service and the Interior Department authorizing Walt Disney Productions to build a ski resort on national forest land in the scenic Mineral King Valley in the southern Sierras in California, along with an access road through the adjacent Sequoia National Park. Justice Potter Stewart's opinion for the 7–2 majority ruled against the Sierra Club on a narrow, technical ground, but made clear that the club could obtain judicial review once it properly framed its case. "Aesthetic and environmental well-being, like economic well-being," Stewart wrote, "are important ingredients of the quality of life in our society," and the fact that such interests are "shared by the many rather than the few does not make them less deserving of legal protection through the judicial process."[25]

The Court's decision opened federal courthouse doors across the nation to cases testing whether decisions by public land management agencies were consistent with congressionally imposed standards and safeguards. It came at almost exactly the same time that Congress was strengthening those safeguards and providing more legal footholds for those trying to challenge public land decision making, and recreational users and nonprofit watchdogs of public lands were developing the capacity to litigate. Congress mostly welcomed judicial involvement, because the courts would help ensure that its laws were properly implemented. Indeed, it included in some modern laws features that encourage so-called citizen suits.

In the realm of public lands, the result was a surge in litigation, mostly against the Forest Service and the BLM. The overall effect added momentum to the movement, long under way, to preserve many public lands for such broad purposes as inspiration, recreation, and preservation.

PROTECTING PUBLIC LAND VALUES THROUGH INTERGOVERNMENTAL ARRANGEMENTS AND PUBLIC-PRIVATE PARTNERSHIPS

Congress took numerous steps to promote collaboration between federal land-management agencies and state and local governments and the private sector. One example was the National Trails System Act, which President Johnson signed into law the same day as the Wild and Scenic Rivers Act. Its roots were in the disarray that the Appalachian Trail began experiencing in the 1950s as more development intruded and forced the relocation of trail segments. Then, as Bill Bryson put it in his classic book *A Walk in the Woods*, the nation got an Interior secretary, Stewart Udall, "who actually liked hiking." Udall laid the groundwork for the trails act by overseeing the completion and publication of a comprehensive interagency study, *Trails for America,* in 1966.[26]

The act established a national system of trails—originally, "recreation" and "scenic" trails, with "historic" trails added by a 1978 amendment. The Appalachian and Pacific Crest Trails were the charter members, the former primarily administered by the Park Service and the latter by the Forest Service. It also required fourteen other candidate trails around the nation to be studied. So far, eleven national scenic trails and nineteen national historic trails have been designated, totaling more than 50,000 miles; they are administered by the Park Service, the Forest Service, or the BLM. In 2009 a new category, national geologic trail, was added. Trail segments are found in nearly every state, and public lands are an important component of many of them. On the act's fortieth anniversary, the eighty-eight-year-old Udall described a national trail as "a gateway into nature's secret beauties, a portal to the past, a way into solitude and community" as well as an "inroad to our national character."[27]

Congress legislated other ad hoc intergovernmental arrangements to protect publicly owned lands and others. Examples include the New Jersey Pinelands National Reserve, established in 1978, which encompasses more than 1 million acres, only about 90,000 of which are public lands. It is managed by a unique commission applying both federal and state laws, with some involvement by the Department of the Interior. The Columbia River Gorge National Scenic Area in Oregon and Washington, established in 1986, also includes considerable nonpublic land and is administered by a bistate commission as well as by the Forest Service. The City of Rocks National Reserve in Idaho, established in 1988, includes a mixture of public, state, and private land and is managed by the Park Service cooperatively with the State of Idaho.[28]

PROTECTING PUBLIC VALUES IN LAND WITHOUT
FORMAL PUBLIC OWNERSHIP

While the National Park Service helped pioneer the concept of scenic easements in the 1930s by acquiring a right to prevent inappropriate development along the publicly owned Blue Ridge and Natchez Trace Scenic Parkways, its easement acquisition had a problematic history. As one analyst put it, the easements "breed misunderstandings, cause administrative difficulties, are difficult to enforce, and cost only a little less than" what full ownership would cost. As a result, the Park Service stopped acquiring new scenic easements along the parkways in the 1950s.

Despite these difficulties, the idea of what came to be known as "conservation easements" began to take hold across the country. Held either by governmental agencies (including public land management agencies) or by private nonprofit entities, these easements restrict development of the property that they encumber in order to serve the interests of recreation, scenic preservation, and environmental protection. Depending on how they are drafted, they may prohibit nearly all or only some uses of land, and they usually do not require the owner of the easement-encumbered land to give the public access to it.

Helped along by generous tax subsidies in the Internal Revenue Code and in some state laws, conservation easements have flourished in recent years, and now apply to dozens of millions of acres of land across the nation. The problems that the Park Service encountered early on still exist. Moreover, the tool has been subject to abuses, such as being used where conservation values are suspect or inflated, or where the easement holder is a captive of the property developer and not interested in enforcing the restrictions. The latter problem can be particularly difficult to remedy, because third parties usually have limited ability to enforce the easements.[29]

"Rails to trails" is another kind of private-public partnership that has flourished in the past few decades (and is much less subject to abuse). These partnerships seek to preserve recreational opportunities where railroad networks—many built on public or formerly public lands—have fallen into disuse as a result of increasing competition from truck and air transportation. Rail lines reached a peak of 275,000 miles in 1916, but trains stopped operating along some 40,000 miles of railroad corridors between 1930 and 1975, and another 65,000 miles in the fifteen years after that. In 1983, Congress enacted innovative legislation that facilitated the development of recreational trails in these railroad corridors. Although it stopped short of claiming these corridors as public lands, it asserted a strong public interest in them by mandating that public recreational use "shall not be treated" under federal or state law as an "abandonment" of the railroad right-of-way so long as it retains the potential for future rail transport. The result has been spectacular, with many thousands of miles of rail-trails used by tens of millions each year for walking, running, cycling, and similar pursuits.[30]

IMPLICATIONS OF LAYERING PROTECTIONS ON PUBLIC LANDS

The operation of laws such as the Wilderness Act and the Endangered Species Act on the management charters of public land management agencies has added considerable complexity. The proliferation of labels and layers of management prescriptions are untidy and sometimes confusing. This outcome was probably inevitable, the result of our political system grappling pragmatically with the need, in a vast and populous country, to accommodate evolving public values while satisfying an array of local, regional, and national interests.

The most noteworthy feature of this burgeoning modern practice is its overall objective. Congress has not seen fit to legislate national systems of public lands devoted to mining, grazing, timber harvesting, or off-road-vehicle recreation. Indeed, in the long history of public lands, the Tongass National Forest in southeastern Alaska, which has been described as the nation's "most contested national forest," is just about the only place where Congress has experimented with setting specific goals for the production of commodities like timber.

With very few exceptions, public land legislation in the modern era has a common core; namely, to add protections for natural and cultural resources, to encourage non-motorized recreation, and to promote an enhanced appreciation of nature. A good illustration of this is found in the "Collaborative Forest Landscape Restoration Program," which Congress directed the Forest Service to establish in 2009. The program targets projects covering at least fifty thousand acres, and can include land managed by other agencies. Project criteria include objectives such as prohibiting permanent roads, maintaining or restoring old-growth forests, promoting the return of more natural fire regimes, and improving watershed conditions and wildlife habitat.[31]

A kind of paradox has emerged from this modern practice of layering protections on areas of public land. The American public has more and more come to value public lands not simply as individual features or places, or even as components of systems, managed by specific agencies. Everything is linked to everything else, as John Muir pointed out well over a century ago, and so it is that public lands in general are increasingly regarded as a single democratizing institution, America's common ground.[32]

CHAPTER FIFTY-FOUR

Making the Modern Bureau of Land Management

ONE OF THE DEALS THAT PAVED the way to enacting the Wilderness Act was an agreement between the Kennedy administration and House Interior Committee chair Wayne Aspinall on three other pieces of legislation. All became law on September 19, 1964, sixteen days after the Wilderness Act. The first launched a pet project of Aspinall's, the Public Land Law Review Commission (PLLRC), to study and recommend reforms in the nation's laws dealing with public lands (other than military lands and those in the national park system).[1]

The second, the Classification and Multiple Use Act (CMUA), had been promoted by the administration. It directed the Interior secretary to classify BLM-managed public lands for either retention or divestment. The latter, it specified, was appropriate only for public land that was "required for the orderly growth and development of a community" or that was "chiefly valuable for residential, commercial, agricultural (exclusive of lands chiefly valuable for grazing and raising forage crops), industrial, or public uses or development." The parenthetical exclusion of public lands chiefly valuable for stock raising was Congress's reaffirmation of the decisions that it and FDR made in 1934–36 to retain those lands in national ownership.[2]

Retention, according to the CMUA, was appropriate to serve a wide variety of purposes. These included (in addition to traditional activities such as stock raising, logging, and mining) "fish and wildlife development and utilization," "outdoor recreation," "watershed protection," "wilderness preservation," and a kind of circular catchall, "public values that would be lost if the land passed from federal ownership." The reference to "wilderness preservation" was the first explicit acknowledgment by Congress that BLM-managed lands might be put in the national wilderness preservation system. The CMUA went on to specify that lands classified for retention should be administered in accordance with the "multiple use–sustained yield" principles Congress had adopted for the Forest Service four years earlier.

The third part of the package was the Public Land Sales Act. A companion to the CMUA, it authorized the Interior secretary to sell those public lands classified for divestment in tracts not to exceed 5,120 acres. Sales were to be made to "qualified governmental agencies" at appraised fair-market value, or to "qualified individuals" at auction at "not less than" that value.[3]

Over the next several years, the Interior Department, in consultation with state and local governments, carried out the CMUA. Focusing almost entirely on BLM-managed lands outside of Alaska, it classified some 175 million acres for retention and only 3.4 million acres as suitable for divestment. Of the latter, a mere few thousand acres were sold under the Public Land Sales Act. By its own terms, the CMUA expired in 1969, but classifications under it could remain in force indefinitely. The results of the CMUA were further confirmation—if any were needed—that nearly all BLM lands would remain in national ownership.[4]

The Kennedy and Johnson administrations enthusiastically supported revamping how the BLM was to manage the public lands under its care. Early in his term, Kennedy had called on the Interior Department to develop a program of "balanced usage" for the BLM lands that fully took into account recreation and wildlife values. After he was appointed to lead the agency in 1963, Charles Stoddard launched a systematic inventory to identify special "natural areas" worthy of protection. Over the next several years, more than a hundred areas encompassing several hundred thousand acres were so designated.

Although but a tiny fraction of the BLM's vast domain, these designations paved the way for more ambitious steps. Some places protected by executive action in this era, such as the Red Rock Recreation Lands near Las Vegas, and Paria Canyon, Aravaipa Canyon, and the Vermillion Cliffs in Arizona, eventually became part of a network of dozens of millions of acres that BLM manages primarily for recreation and preservation. In 1964, to symbolize this reorientation, the agency's original emblem, depicting a miner, logger, rancher,

Bureau of Land Management logo, 1953
(Drawing by Bill Nelson)

Bureau of Land Management logo, 1964
(Drawing by Bill Nelson)

engineer, and surveyor looking out on an industrial landscape, was changed to portray mountains, meadows, a river, and a tree.[5]

THE PUBLIC LAND LAW REVIEW COMMISSION REPORT AND ITS AFTERMATH

Modeled on the 1958 legislation that Aspinall had sponsored to establish the Outdoor Recreation Resources Review Commission, the PLLRC had nineteen members—three Republicans and three Democrats from both the House and the Senate Interior Committees, six persons appointed by the president, and a chair elected by majority vote of the other eighteen. By prearrangement, Aspinall became chair. Thirteen of the nineteen commissioners were members of Congress, and sixteen were from western states. The commission's bipartisan, congressional, and western-dominated membership helped account for its great success in translating its recommendations into law.

The PLLRC was thorough and deliberate. It directed the preparation of dozens of substantial background reports, established a thirty-four-member advisory council and a liaison with each state's governor, and heard testimony from nearly a thousand people at sixteen public meetings. Congress extended its initial deadline by three years, and its report, *One Third of the Nation's Land,* was issued in June 1970. Most of its 137 principal recommendations, and hundreds of others sprinkled throughout its text, were unanimous. Environmental protection was a consistent theme; for example, on grazing, the most extensive extractive use of public lands, it called for taking into account forage necessary for the "support of wildlife" and for excluding livestock from "frail lands where necessary to protect and conserve the natural environment."

Two aspects of its report were immediately controversial. One was its recommendation merely to reform the antiquated Mining Law of 1872—which it acknowledged had been "abused" and had "many deficiencies"—rather than replacing it with a leasing system. This was one of its few recommendations that was not unanimous. Commissioner Morris Udall (D-Ariz.), who had been elected to fill his brother Stewart's seat in Congress, and three of the noncongressional members dissented, calling for a leasing system, noting it had worked satisfactorily in the Mineral Leasing Act of 1920 and on state and Indian lands. The majority's recommendation also drew protests from mainstream media such as *Life* and *Sports Illustrated* magazines.[6]

The second was its overarching recommendation that public lands be managed to "recognize the highest and best use of particular areas of land as dominant over other authorized uses." Critics feared that traditional extractive uses long favored by Aspinall would remain "dominant" ones. Aspinall was bruised by this criticism, believing it the product of what he described as an "emotional environmental binge" that was sweeping the nation. A careful reading suggests he had a legitimate beef. The report made clear that it did "not intend" to "place emphasis on" traditional extraction "to the exclusion of other uses and values." Moreover, it readily acknowledged that on some public lands the primary objective might well be to promote "nonmarket values" such as fish, wildlife, and watershed protection.[7]

Around the time the PLLRC report was released, Aspinall found an occasion to expound his vision of a modern, environmentally sensitive public land policy. Congress had before it a bill to establish the King Range National Conservation Area (NCA) on some 60,000 acres of rugged and scenic BLM land along the Northern California coast. The bill, sponsored by the local congressman, Don Clausen (R-Calif.), made clear that conservation and recreation were to be dominant uses of the area. Aspinall strongly supported the bill while expressing the hope that grazing, mining, and timber harvesting might be able to continue in the NCA under "safeguards" to protect "environmental and scenic values." President Nixon signed the bill creating the nation's first NCA into law in October 1970. Over the next several decades, the NCA concept became a popular way for Congress to make conservation and recreation the dominant uses of a considerable amount of BLM land.[8]

In 1971, Congress complicated the BLM's mandate, especially in Nevada and a few other parts of the intermountain West, by enacting the Wild, Free-Roaming Horses and Burros Act. These animals were descendants of domesticated horses and burros that had been released or escaped into the wild. Their capture and slaughter, often by inhumane means and mostly for pet food and to reduce competition for forage by livestock, attracted considerable negative public attention. Interior secretary Udall had established wild horse ranges in Nevada (on Nellis Air Force Base in 1963) and Idaho (on BLM lands, in 1968), but that was not enough for wild-horse advocates such as Velma Johnston of Nevada. Known as "Wild Horse Annie," she led an effective national letter-writing campaign that resulted in the legislation being sponsored or supported by western members of both parties and passing both houses with little dissent. Calling them "living symbols of the historic and pioneer spirit of the West," the act protected "all unbranded and unclaimed horses and burros on public lands" (which it defined to include national forests as well as BLM lands) from "capture, branding, harassment, or death."9

The act left the BLM with the nearly impossible task of finding a middle ground between animal-rights activists and livestock operators and their allies in the horse meat industry. Acting at the behest of the operators, New Mexico challenged Congress's authority to enact it. In 1976, the Supreme Court rejected its claim, finding the act a proper exercise of Congress's power under the Constitution's Property Clause. While the "furthest reaches" of that power "have not yet been definitively resolved," Justice Thurgood Marshall wrote for the unanimous Court, "we have repeatedly observed that 'the power over the public land thus entrusted to Congress is without limitations.'" The Court rebuffed the state's contentions that "traditional state power over wild animals" put this case on a "different footing," and that the Constitution's Enclave Clause required state consent before Congress could take such a step.10

Meanwhile, the century-old tradition of bipartisanship in public land policy continued to hold. Republican Richard Nixon waxed eloquent about the public lands in his environmental message to Congress in 1971, arguing that their "spectacular scenery, mineral and timber resources, major wildlife habitat, ecological significance, and tremendous recreational importance" made them the "breathing space" of the nation. His second Interior secretary, Rogers Morton, added protection to BLM lands in several places, including along the Snake River in Idaho, where many birds of prey were known to gather; in New Mexico's Organ Mountains; and on more than 1 million acres in the California Desert. The platforms of both parties in 1972 pledged to continue public land conservation efforts. That same year Aspinall was defeated by a liberal in the Democratic primary (who went on to lose in the general election), but his departure did not derail Congress's efforts to implement the PLLRC report he had championed.11

THE FEDERAL LAND POLICY AND
MANAGEMENT ACT OF 1976

The Federal Land Policy and Management Act of 1976, or FLPMA, and called "flip-ma," signed by President Ford two weeks before the 1976 election, incorporated many of the PLLRC's recommendations. It was an amalgam of several bills—one drafted by the Nixon administration, another crafted under the leadership of Henry "Scoop" Jackson, chair of the Senate Interior Committee (who had been a member of the PLLRC), and a third initially introduced in the House by Aspinall. Final floor votes were not recorded, but the Senate had twice approved earlier versions by lopsided votes. The vote on the House bill was much closer, 169–155, with most opposition coming from liberal Democrats and others who regarded the bill as too reflective of Aspinall's tenderheartedness toward traditional extractive uses. As with the PLLRC, westerners dominated the conference between the House and the Senate that hammered out the final version, supplying sixteen of its nineteen members.

FLPMA began with a policy declaration once again reaffirming that public lands managed by the BLM "be retained in Federal ownership," except under very narrow circumstances. It directed that BLM-managed public lands be managed on a "multiple use" and "sustained yield" basis.

Reflecting a shift in values since 1960, FLPMA defined these concepts more broadly and more ecologically than did the MUSY (Multiple Use–Sustained Yield) Act, enacted sixteen years earlier. The FLPMA definition of multiple use, for example, added a requirement to take into account "the long-term needs of future generations" for resources such as "natural scenic, scientific and historical values" in addition to "recreation, range, timber, minerals, watershed, wildlife and fish." It also called for management "without *permanent* impairment of the productivity of the land *and the quality of the environment*" (differences from the MUSY Act italicized). (In its introductory statement of policy, FLPMA called on public lands to be managed "in a manner that will protect," among other things, "atmospheric" values. This may have been an indirect reference to a report issued eleven years earlier that noted the adverse effects of climate change tied to fossil fuel emissions.)[12]

FLPMA made "land and resource planning" a central focus of BLM's management process. This built on a system that BLM had put in place a few years earlier. Around the same time, Congress instructed the Forest Service to use a similar process to guide its decision making, and it eventually applied the same idea to the Fish & Wildlife Service and the National Park Service.

This congressional embrace of planning as a tool for managing public lands embodied an approach to land management that married scientific expertise and democratic values. It resembled Gifford Pinchot's call in 1905 for managing the national forests in a "businesslike manner" after giving "due notice" to those affected, a system in which the resolution of conflicting interests would be "decided from the standpoint of the greatest good of the greatest number in the long run." The process of preparing these plans involved consultation with other governmental agencies (federal, state, and local), users of public lands, and the general public, and was supposed to add transparency to executive decisions.

FLPMA repealed some 3,500 public land laws—most of them oriented toward divestment—that had accumulated since the nation's founding. Many of these were truly dead letters, but some were mischievous engines of uncertainty and litigation. For example, an incoherent mishmash of laws authorized the Interior Department to issue permits allowing occupation or use of public lands for various purposes. FLPMA repealed all these and its title 5 installed a single, uniform process. Applying to both the BLM and the Forest Service, it required paying careful attention to the environment and in most cases required users of the public lands to pay a market-based fee. This was a substantial improvement, as were FLPMA's comparable provisions governing exchanges and sales of public land.

FLPMA followed the PLLRC majority recommendation to reform but not replace the Mining Law of 1872. Congress for the first time required all mining claims to be recorded with the BLM, and expressly made all mining activities on public lands subject to FLPMA's generic command that the Interior secretary "shall, by regulation or otherwise, take any action necessary to prevent unnecessary or undue degradation of" the public lands.

FLPMA replaced the Pickett Act's presidential withdrawal authority with a new, broader version. In another step that limited the operation of the Mining Law of 1872, it did away with the Pickett Act's prohibition on withdrawals from "metalliferous mining." It also repealed the "implied authority of the President to make withdrawals and reservations resulting from the acquiescence of the Congress," taking the unusual step of naming the Supreme Court decision (*United States v. Midwest Oil Co.*) that had blessed that practice. It put a twenty-year limit on new executive withdrawals but imposed no limit on how many times they could be renewed. It called for the Interior secretary to review all existing withdrawals except any made by Congress, and any executive withdrawal that established national monuments or added lands to the national wildlife refuge system. It also purported to give either house of Congress or its public land committees authority to initiate or reverse executive withdrawals, but the Supreme Court later ruled that the Constitution did not permit Congress to delegate its legislative authority to one of its houses or committees.[13]

FLPMA required the BLM to review all its lands and identify roadless tracts over 5,000 acres that might be included in the National Wilderness Preservation System. With limited exceptions, it prohibited the BLM from taking any action that would "impair the suitability of such areas for preservation as wilderness," until Congress decided their future. To the same protective end, FLPMA established the California Desert Conservation Area. About one-quarter of California fell within its outer boundaries (which included private, military, and national park system lands). It called for the BLM-managed lands that make up nearly half the conservation area, or more than 10 percent of the Golden State, to be managed with special attention to natural values.

FLPMA left the Taylor Grazing Act mostly in place, but adjusted provisions dealing with grazing leases, permits, and advisory boards, and applied these changes to the Forest Service as well. For example, it gave holders of expiring existing permits "first priority" to obtain new ones, but only as long as (a) the lands "remain[ed] available" for grazing in accordance with BLM or Forest Service plans; (b) the permittee was in compliance with all rules, regulations, and permit terms and conditions; and (c) the permittee accepted terms and conditions that the government decided to include in the new permit. Just two years later, in 1978, Congress enacted the Public Rangeland Improvement Act. Finding that "vast segments of the public rangelands" remained in "unsatisfactory condition," it called for a twenty-year program of additional funding for range improvements to deal with the problem. The law was largely exhortatory and had almost no effect on the ground.[14]

The so-called Payment in Lieu of Taxes Act, a companion measure, was signed into law the day before FLPMA. It carried out another PLLRC recommendation by authorizing the national government to make payments to units of local government to mitigate BLM lands' immunity from property taxes, with the amounts to be set in the annual congressional appropriations process.[15]

Earlier in 1976, Congress had enlarged the BLM's domain by giving it authority to manage more than 22 million acres of public land in northwestern Alaska that President Harding had put in a naval petroleum reserve in 1923. The transfer act called for Interior to study and report on the "values of, and best uses for," the reserve lands. In December 1980, following completion of the study, Congress authorized Interior to carry out a program of competitive oil and gas leasing there that would include "conditions, restrictions, and prohibitions" Interior deemed appropriate to protect the reserve's surface resources from significant adverse effects.[16]

JIMMY CARTER AND THE "SAGEBRUSH REBELLION"

In the election held two weeks after FLPMA was signed into law, Jimmy Carter won the presidency. All eleven western states went for his opponent, the incumbent Gerald Ford, though in several cases by small margins. The Vietnam War and the Watergate scandal had left the nation in turmoil, made worse by severe inflation and gasoline shortages that stemmed from an oil embargo by the Organization of Petroleum Exporting Countries, or OPEC.

In March 1977, Carter's Interior secretary, Cecil Andrus, hailed the enactment of FLPMA by proclaiming that the "initials BLM no longer stand for Bureau of Livestock and Mining." Instead, he said, the lands it managed would be stewarded "in a manner that will make the 'three R's'—rape, ruin and run—a thing of the past."[17]

Carter early on threatened to withdraw support for dozens of water projects that Congress had authorized. The press quickly dubbed this a "hit list." Because many of these projects were in the West, and because, in response to a court order, his administration proposed regulations to enforce mostly ignored provisions of the Reclamation Act of 1902 forbidding the delivery of project water to farms larger than 160 acres, he was accused of making "war" on the region. Within a couple of years, he added ammunition to that charge by supporting crash programs to develop "synthetic fuels" from fossil fuel deposits found mostly on public lands in Colorado, Utah, and Wyoming, and to build a mobile intercontinental ballistic missile system on public lands in Nevada and Utah that were being used primarily for livestock grazing.[18]

In June 1979, the Nevada legislature launched what came to be dubbed the "sagebrush rebellion" by enacting a statute claiming ownership of BLM lands. Over the next couple of years, Arizona, New Mexico, Utah, and Wyoming followed suit, with Wyoming claiming ownership of Forest Service lands as well. These measures were promoted largely by livestock operators concerned that grazing might be restricted on public lands, a concern magnified when the BLM settled NEPA litigation brought by environmental groups by agreeing to conduct detailed environmental assessments of livestock grazing throughout the West. The state laws were portrayed in the media as a reaction to the administration's purported "War on the West."

The interior West was undergoing dramatic demographic and economic changes as urban areas boomed and rural economies lagged. While FLPMA's confirmation that most BLM-managed public lands would remain in national ownership merely continued a policy that had been in place for many decades, its repeal of thousands of laws from a bygone era underscored that the national government would remain in charge. Although FLPMA had been heavily shaped and supported by western members of Congress of both parties, some of them, such as Congressman James Santini (D-Nev.), lent their support to the sagebrush rebels, blaming faulty implementation by Carter's executive branch.[19]

The sagebrush rebellion was, from start to finish, a gesture of discontent rather than a serious political movement aimed at divesting the United States of ownership of public lands. None of the five states that passed sagebrush rebellion laws ever filed litigation or took any other concrete step to enforce their claims to ownership. Indeed, the first thing the State of Nevada did after enacting its legislation laying claim to ownership of public lands was to seek assurance from the Interior Department that the federal money it received under the "payments in lieu of taxes" program—which depended on continuing U.S. ownership—would not be interrupted. Similar bills introduced in other western states were all defeated or vetoed, and a handful of bills introduced in Congress calling for the United States to relinquish title to some public lands went nowhere.[20]

Ronald Reagan, whose 1980 campaign manager was Senator Paul Laxalt (R-Nev.) and who allowed a few cattle to run seasonally on his 680-acre ranch in California's scenic Santa Ynez Valley near Santa Barbara, shrewdly exploited the rebels' discontent, telling audiences in the interior West to "count me in as a sagebrush rebel." He soundly defeated Carter's bid for reelection in 1980 and helped Republicans pick up enough seats to gain control of the U.S. Senate. Critics of public lands took heart from his famous inaugural address pronouncement in 1981 that "government is not the solution to our problem; government is the problem"—although he was referring to high inflation, unemployment, and the budget deficit, and did not mention public lands.[21]

The sagebrush rebellion quickly fizzled. Reagan's Interior secretary, James Watt, did work to hand over effective control—but not ownership—of many public lands to fossil fuel enterprises and livestock operators, but the courts and Congress stymied most of his initiatives. Undeterred, Attorney General Edwin Meese and David Stockman, head of the Office of Management and Budget, persuaded Reagan to propose an "asset management program" that would involve selling 35 million acres of "surplus" public lands, including several million acres in national forests, over five years, ostensibly to help reduce the budget deficit. Introduced in 1982, the idea was stoutly opposed by most

Republicans as well as Democrats on Capitol Hill, and went nowhere. Several years of relative quiet on public land policy followed Watt's resignation under fire in late 1983.[22]

When the Clinton administration took office in early 1993, its Office of Management and Budget almost immediately proposed to increase fees for public land grazing and mining. This triggered a backlash that faintly echoed the sagebrush rebellion. Senator Harry Reid (D-Nev.) attempted to engineer a legislative compromise, but was stymied by a filibuster led by Senator Pete Domenici (R-N.M.). Then Clinton's Interior secretary, former Arizona governor Bruce Babbitt, launched a years-long effort to improve the BLM's grazing administration through a series of regulatory changes dubbed "rangeland reform." Babbitt's program was eventually implemented and mostly upheld by the courts, with the Supreme Court rejecting challenges to it by livestock operators in a unanimous decision in 2000.[23]

While this was happening, Nevada ranchers and a handful of rural western counties tried once again to claim ownership of western public lands. The political winds in an increasingly urban West had, however, shifted even more against them. When a Nevadan who turned his livestock on public lands without a permit defended himself against a trespassing suit brought by the United States by arguing that the public lands were unconstitutional, the attorneys general of Alaska, Montana, Nevada, New Mexico, and Oregon filed an amicus brief on the side of the United States, finding it "well-established that the United States is the lawful owner of the public lands." The federal court of appeals agreed.[24]

Meanwhile, the character of the grazing industry on public lands continued to change. Studies suggest that half or more of the grazing permittees in the modern era are so-called amenity ranchers, who earn most of their income elsewhere. Although agency statistics show a decline in the number of animals authorized to use the public lands since World War II, this paints a misleading picture. As a result of selective breeding and other measures, the average cow is considerably heavier, and consumes more forage, than in the past.[25]

BLM CONSERVATION LANDS GROW
INTO A GENUINE SYSTEM

The attention that the media lavished on these so-called western rebellions did not distract Congress or the executive branch from putting more BLM-managed public land under protective management. Starting in 1978, Congress enacted numerous bills that added nearly 9 million acres of BLM land, in more than two hundred separate areas in ten states, to the national wilderness preservation system. Congress left nearly 13 million other BLM-managed acres protected as "wilderness study areas."

Congress also established more than a dozen national conservation areas on nearly 4 million acres of BLM land, including two national riparian conservation areas in Arizona, and other NCAs in Arizona, Colorado, and Nevada. It legislated a national monument in the Santa Rosa Mountains behind Palm Springs, California, and established the Headwaters Forest Reserve in Northern California, under BLM management, to preserve some 7,500 acres of ancient redwoods purchased from a private owner by the United States (which put up $250 million) and the State of California ($130 million). In 2000, it added significant protections, including wilderness designations, to nearly a half-million acres of BLM land around Steens Mountain in the Oregon desert. Nearly all these actions had strong bipartisan support.[26]

The executive branch chimed in with several actions of its own, underscoring how the "Bureau of Livestock and Mining" was no more. In 1996, President Clinton established the nearly 2-million-acre Grand Staircase–Escalante National Monument on public lands in southern Utah and put BLM in charge of it, the first time it had been given responsibility to manage a national monument. Clinton went on to create several more BLM-managed national monuments. President Obama followed suit, adding more than 5 million acres to the BLM's conservation portfolio. The most prominent of these was the 1.3-million-acre Bears Ears National Monument in southeastern Utah. (In 2017, President Trump issued proclamations reducing Bears Ears by 85 percent and Grand Staircase–Escalante by nearly half.)

To give the BLM's network of lands managed for conservation a stronger identity, Interior secretary Babbitt in 1999 created the National Landscape Conservation System, later shortened to National Conservation Lands. Babbitt called BLM lands "essential, defining landscapes of the American West," "connective tissue" that furnishes migration pathways for wildlife and "maintains complex desert ecosystems." He predicted that the BLM would soon "be better known as the Bureau of Landscapes and Monuments." In 2009, Congress gave the system a statutory underpinning. It now includes more than 34 million acres across the eleven western states and Alaska, or about 15 percent of the BLM's total acreage. Livestock grazing is still permitted on many of these lands, but most other nonrecreational uses are either excluded or sharply limited.[27]

The BLM's evolution into an agency that gives much attention to recreation, wildlife, ecological protection, and cultural resources is one of the most important developments in public land policy in the last half century. No doubt Wayne Aspinall would have been surprised to see nonextractive uses become dominant objectives for so much BLM land, but it was the dominant-use framework that he espoused and helped put in place—combined with evolving public opinion in an increasingly urbanized, recreation- and preservation-oriented West—that made it possible.

CHAPTER FIFTY-FIVE

Making the Modern Forest Service

TIMBER HARVESTING IN THE national forests continued at high levels from the 1960s through most of the 1980s, averaging between 10 and 12 billion board feet annually. In the first Reagan term, John Crowell, a former timber industry executive who supervised the Forest Service as assistant secretary of Agriculture, called for plans to increase the annual cut to 20 billion board feet over the next several decades.[1]

Thanks in part to advances in lumbering technology, most of the harvesting was now done by clear-cutting, or the wholesale removal of all trees regardless of age, as opposed to selectively cutting individual trees. More benignly dubbed "even-aged management" by the Forest Service and the industry, it essentially replaced natural forests with wood fiber farms, and provoked controversy. Although it tended to be an efficient harvesting method, it was also unsightly, increased soil erosion and flooding, was increasingly done in tandem with extensive herbicide spraying, negatively affected many wildlife species, and fostered boom-and-bust cycles in the local economies where it was practiced.

As accessible high-quality timber supplies were depleted, the Forest Service had to build more roads to reach what remained. That construction led to an upsurge in what came to be known as "below-cost" timber sales, in which the revenues the United States derived from the sales were exceeded by the government's management outlays, including road-building costs, attributable to carrying them out.[2]

Nevertheless, the Forest Service plunged ahead at full throttle. In 1964, it announced that clear-cutting would become the standard practice on West Virginia's Monongahela National Forest. It also promoted clear-cutting in the Northern Rockies, the Pacific Northwest, and southeastern Alaska.[3]

By the early 1970s, a backlash was well in place. Congressman Lee Metcalf asked the University of Montana School of Forestry to examine the agency's practices on the Bitterroot National Forest. The West Virginia legislature established a commission to do the same on the Monongahela. A subcommittee of the Senate Interior Committee chaired by Senator Frank Church held extensive oversight hearings on clear-cutting, and President Nixon established the Advisory Panel on Timber and the Environment. All were, in varying degrees, critical of the agency's extensive use of clear-cutting. Church's subcommittee suggested guidelines to curb the practice.[4]

Around this time, a coalition of nonprofit groups sued the Forest Service in West Virginia, arguing that clear-cutting violated the explicit command of the 1897 Organic Act to harvest only "dead, matured, or large growth of trees," in order to promote "younger growth," and only after trees that met this standard were "marked and designated." While the 1960 Multiple Use–Sustained Yield Act had acknowledged that timber harvesting was an appropriate use of the national forests, it had also made clear it was "supplemental to, but not in derogation of," the 1897 act, and did not mention clear-cutting.

In 1975, in what came to be known as the *Monongahela* decision, a federal court of appeals agreed that clear-cutting was indeed inconsistent with the requirements of the Organic Act. The court acknowledged that after World War II, the Forest Service had changed from a "custodian" to a "production agency" in order to help satisfy a rising global demand for timber. But, it said, the judiciary had no authority to rewrite the 1897 statute to accommodate that change. The "appropriate forum to resolve this complex and controversial issue," the court concluded, "is not the courts but the Congress." A few months later, a federal court in Alaska handed down a similar ruling.[5]

THE NATIONAL FOREST MANAGEMENT ACT

Meanwhile, Congress had already made one attempt to update the Organic Act while sidestepping the clear-cutting controversy. The Forest and Rangeland Renewable Resources Planning Act of 1974—which came to be known as the RPA—called on the Forest Service to prepare, and periodically update, layers of plans to guide its future decision making. The most important of these were management plans to be prepared for each unit in the national forest system, using an interdisciplinary approach to achieve "integrated consideration of physical, biological, economic, and other sciences."[6]

Requiring the Forest Service to engage in elaborate planning had some political appeal because it allowed Congress to avoid making hard choices. By leaving the criteria for the agency's decision making relatively amorphous, the RPA ultimately produced much paper but had little impact on agency or congressional practices. Its lack of meaningful, substantive standards left the courts reluctant, as one put it, to "intrude on" what it called the "shared responsibilities" of the executive and legislative branches.[7]

The first response of the Forest Service and the timber industry to the *Monongahela* decision was to ask Congress simply to repeal the 1897 act's limitations on clear-cutting. Those advocating restricting the practice pushed back, seeking a more thorough overhaul of the agency's legal charter. The effort ultimately engaged the Interior and the Agriculture Committees of both houses of Congress. Senator Hubert Humphrey, who had been a primary architect of the Wilderness Act, captured the sentiments of many when he noted that national forests could no longer "be viewed only as trees and the trees viewed only as timber." Instead, he said, the "soil and the water, the grasses and the shrubs, the fish and the wildlife, and the beauty that is in the forest must become integral parts of resources managers' thinking and actions."[8]

After much bargaining, the National Forest Management Act of 1976 was signed into law in the fall of 1976, one day after FLPMA. The complex act substituted a new set of timber-harvesting standards for the strictures on timber harvesting in the 1897 act. These incorporated much of the Church committee's suggested guidelines and had the effect of allowing clear-cutting to continue with some restrictions.[9]

But the NFMA did more than that; indeed, it crafted what amounted to a new organic charter for the Forest Service, the first fundamental change since 1897. At bottom, underneath much verbiage that pushed the agency to pay more attention to science and other values besides wood, Congress left the Forest Service considerable discretion. In most places where the act announced restrictions, it also provided escape hatches. Thus, for example, it directed the Agriculture secretary to identify lands "not suited for timber production," but qualified it enough to preserve some agency discretion to continue below-cost timber sales. It tightened the definition of "sustained yield" by directing the Agriculture secretary to limit sales of timber from each national forest to an amount that could be removed "annually in perpetuity," but allowed the secretary to depart from that standard for various reasons, including simply to meet "overall multiple-use objectives."[10]

The NFMA put the planning process that Congress had established in the RPA two years previously at the center of Forest Service decision making. It required the agency to prepare detailed regulations, informed by advice from a committee of scientists, to govern the development and periodic revision of forest plans. Permits, contracts, and other agency management actions had to be consistent with the forest plans. In the end, however, the planning process operated more to narrow agency choices rather than to make them. As the Supreme Court noted in a 2004 decision addressing the similar BLM planning system, an agency plan "is generally a statement of priorities; it guides and constrains actions but does not (at least in the usual case) prescribe them."[11]

THE SPOTTED OWL AND THE NORTHWEST FOREST PLAN

Although the 1974 and 1976 laws added complexity to Forest Service decision making, the first generation of plans produced under the NFMA did little to change national forest management. Clear-cutting declined somewhat, but inertia and pressure from inside and outside the Forest Service kept timber production levels high, especially in the timber-rich Northwest, which had long produced more than half of the total national forest timber output. (BLM's management of the timber-rich O&C lands in Oregon followed a similar pattern.) As late as 1990, two-thirds of the Forest Service's professional staff were engaged in activities designed to facilitate the harvest.[12]

The NFMA required forest plans to "provide for diversity of plant and animal communities." To implement this vague command, the Forest Service's regulations required maintaining "viable populations" of existing species in each planning area. In the early 1980s, the agency designated the northern spotted owl as a "management indicator species," making it a proxy for many species. The owl's few thousand breeding pairs were thought to occupy several million acres of ancient Douglas fir forests in the Pacific Northwest, about two-thirds of which lay in national forests.[13]

This designation eventually triggered a mighty conflict, marked by divisions inside and outside the Forest Service over whether it was overemphasizing timber harvesting, by intense press coverage across the nation, and by a cascade of court decisions. In 1988, a federal judge in Seattle brought the Endangered Species Act's demanding requirements into play by determining that the Fish & Wildlife Service had no grounds for refusing to list the northern spotted owl as an imperiled species. Not long after, another federal judge in

Seattle, finding what he called a "remarkable series of violations" of laws such as the NFMA and the National Environmental Policy Act, effectively halted most harvesting of ancient forests on both national forest and BLM-managed public land in the region.[14]

As the controversy intensified, congressional committees held hearings that aired contentious issues and solicited recommendations from forest management experts. In 1990, Congress included a rider in an appropriations act (upheld by the U.S. Supreme Court in 1992) that opened up some old-growth timber on public lands in Oregon and Washington to the timber industry. Soon after, the BLM succeeded in exempting from the ESA forty-four timber sales it had proposed on the O&C lands in Oregon, using a process that Congress had created after the Supreme Court's Tellico Dam decision of 1978. It allowed a cabinet-level committee—informally dubbed the "God Squad"—to lift ESA strictures under certain narrowly defined circumstances. The move backfired. Exempting these BLM timber sales simply tightened the grip of the ESA on harvesting ancient forest timber elsewhere, including on national forest lands, and thus provided no relief for the industry.[15]

During the 1992 presidential campaign, the incumbent, George H. W. Bush, argued that the ESA was broken and needed to be fixed, but his challenger, Bill Clinton, promised only to hold a "timber summit" to consult all stakeholders before crafting a solution. In a race that included the third-party candidate Ross Perot, Clinton prevailed, carrying Washington, Oregon, and California (although gaining a majority of the popular vote only in California). Within a few months, Clinton and Vice President Al Gore and three cabinet members held a widely publicized gathering in Portland, Oregon, with a number of forest experts and affected residents. The administration succeeded, in the words of a prominent scientist, in "explicitly reframing the controversy," making the key question "how to protect a broad range of environmental values" within the old-growth ecosystem, including politically iconic salmon runs adversely affected by extensive timber harvests. Equally important, the "timber summit" explored ways of cushioning the economic impacts of reduced timber harvests.[16]

Eventually, the administration adopted the Northwest Forest Plan, which covered more than 24 million acres of BLM and Forest Service lands across the three states. Applying an ecosystem-based approach, it put well over half these public lands off-limits to practically all timber harvesting and furnished transitional economic assistance to loggers and timber-dependent communities. The plan mostly survived court scrutiny, and hostilities in the timber wars gradually receded, although litigation continued for more than two decades over aspects of the plan's implementation. Across the entire national forest system, timber production declined by more than three-quarters from 1980s levels. (Those levels were generally regarded as unsustainable even if the ESA had never come into play.)[17]

The timber wars had some political fallout. Democrats lost several House seats in the Northwest in the 1994 elections as the Republicans gained control of both chambers for the first time in forty years. The new Congress tried to provide the industry some transitional relief by adding a controversial "salvage rider" on a 1995 appropriations bill. President Clinton approved it over objections from conservationists. It modestly increased timber sales in the short run, but lost effectiveness over time.[18]

In the end, the spotted owl controversy held several lessons for public land policy in the modern era. It furnished a dramatic demonstration of the influence courts could have on public land decision making. It showed the depth of public support for protecting endangered species. Indeed, during the entire episode, Congress never seriously considered simply abolishing the limits that the ESA and related public land laws imposed on timber harvesting. It exposed the shortcomings of the ESA's "God Squad" exemption process. Perhaps most important, the controversy showed how public lands could facilitate a regional transition to a more sustainable resource policy. The Northwest Forest Plan deliberately put most of the burden of protecting the habitat of endangered species on public lands, thus allowing more timber harvesting and other development to proceed on private and state-owned land.[19]

The ESA continues to affect the management of many public lands. Because its protections for listed species are so strict, landowners and other stakeholders potentially affected by the restrictions that come with listing increasingly make efforts to protect species in decline before their condition becomes dire enough to qualify for listing. The most ambitious of these plans, comparable in scale and complexity to the Northwest Forest Plan, was launched by the Obama administration to protect the sage grouse. The historic habitat of this showy bird included millions of acres of mostly BLM-managed public land from northeastern California to southeastern Montana. Federal agencies worked with several states and interest groups to devise a plan that involved numerous agency commitments to restrict activities in sage grouse habitat in order to avoid it being listed. The Trump administration backed off some of those commitments. The jury is still out on whether listing can be avoided.

WILDFIRES AND PUBLIC LAND POLICY

Public land management agencies, especially the Forest Service, have long played a leading role in fighting wildfires in most places where public lands are common. Wildfires have been increasing in size and intensity. A destabilizing climate accentuates droughts, which, assisted by forest pests that thrive in warmer temperatures, lead to increased tree mortality. The problem is made worse by the proliferation of home building in the "wildland-urban interface" and by a buildup of flammable vegetation across many landscapes. Both are legacies of a century of aggressive fire suppression nearly everywhere.

Public land policy can play only a limited role in addressing the problem. The vast majority of dwellings and other structures threatened by wildfire are not on public lands. Building codes and associated restrictions on the use of nonpublic lands can reduce the risk to structures from wildfires, but those matters have historically been regarded as the responsibility of state and local governments.

The cost of dealing with wildfires has consumed an increasing share of the budgets of the land management agencies in the last couple of decades, leading to Congress becoming more involved. Agencies are doing more "fuel reduction projects" such as controlled burns and removing flammable brush and trees. Proposals to exempt such projects from public land and environmental laws have gained some favor in Congress, though there is concern that such projects can provide an excuse for promoting timber harvests at the expense of other values. In 2003, President Bush signed the Healthy Forests Restoration Act into law. It streamlined the process for approving such projects (including providing limited exemptions from NEPA) on up to 20 million acres of public land, other than lands subject to specific protections such as the Wilderness Act. It has since been amended several times. Such projects continue to spark litigation.[20]

THE DECLINE OF MULTIPLE USE THROUGH
RESTRICTIVE ZONING

Over the last several decades, an ever increasing amount of land in the national forest system, just like that in the other public land systems, has come to be managed primarily to protect its natural values. Wilderness designations by Congress and the Forest Service's "roadless rule" together now include well over one-third of the acreage in the system. Many millions of acres of national forest lands are mostly off-limits to timber harvesting as a result of the Northwest Forest Plan or other ESA-inspired restrictions. Commercial logging has been limited in other areas, such as the Bull Run watershed, which supplies

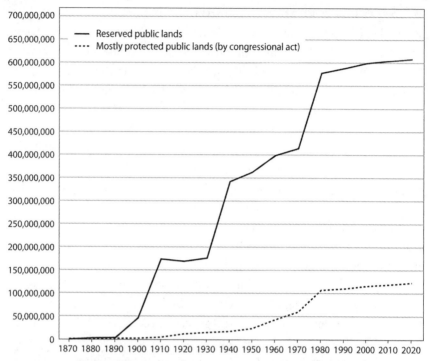

Land reserved in national ownership and land mostly protected by acts of Congress, in acres, 1870–2020 (Chart by Stephanie Smith, Grand Canyon Trust, and Bill Nelson)

water to Portland, Oregon, through a combination of court decisions and congressional action.[21]

More than 3 million acres of national forest land are in thirteen national monuments. Most of these were established by presidents, although Congress legislated the 110,000-acre Mount St. Helens National Volcanic Monument in Washington, primarily for scientific study and recreation, two years after its massive 1980 eruption. Congress has also established national scenic areas in the national forest system. Similar to national conservation areas on BLM lands, they make protection and low-impact recreation dominant objectives, and either forbid or strongly discourage traditional extractive uses such as mining and timber harvesting. The first of these, the Mono Basin National Forest Scenic Area in California, was established in 1984. It has been followed by more than a half dozen others in Oklahoma, Virginia, Georgia, and Michigan.[22]

Through these diverse mechanisms, and reflecting changing public attitudes, the amount of public land available for traditional "multiple uses" has sharply declined. Today the national forests are managed for objectives that are considerably different from those that predominated in earlier eras, and that are

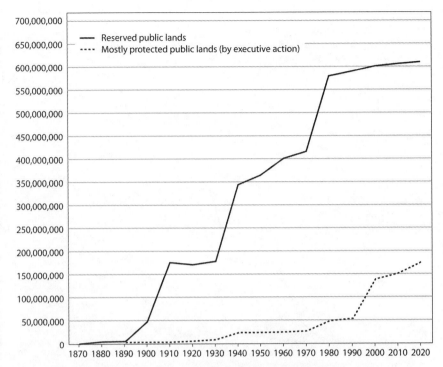

Land reserved in national ownership and land mostly protected by executive action, in acres, 1870–2020 (Chart by Stephanie Smith, Grand Canyon Trust, and Bill Nelson)

increasingly similar to those pursued by other public land management agencies. The change has been heralded by modern Forest Service chiefs such as Jack Ward Thomas and Michael Dombeck, experts in wildlife and fisheries and similar disciplines; Dombeck formerly led the Bureau of Land Management.[23]

The overall scope of these changes is captured in three graphs. The first shows the growth over time of the amount of public lands that are mostly protected as a result of action by Congress (but not including lands in the NWPS). These are areas where Congress has discouraged—but not entirely forbidden—road building and other intensive development. Included in this category are all lands in the national park and national wildlife refuge systems that Congress has not included in the NWPS, all national recreation areas and national scenic areas managed by the Forest Service, and all national conservation areas and wilderness study areas managed by the BLM. Altogether this category includes about 125 million acres, or a little more than 20 percent of all public lands.[24]

The second graph shows the growth over time of the amount of public land that is mostly protected as a result of actions by the executive branch. On these

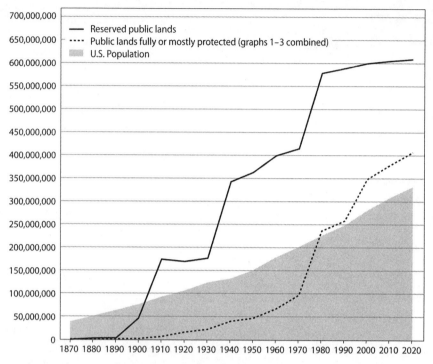

Land reserved in national ownership (in acres), land completely or mostly protected (in acres), and U.S. population, 1870–2020 (Chart by Stephanie Smith, Grand Canyon Trust, and Bill Nelson)

lands, the executive has—by exercising discretion that Congress has given it—imposed sharp limits on road building, mining, logging, and similar activities. A prominent example is the nearly 60 million acres protected by the Forest Service's "roadless rule." The executive could reverse any of these decisions without further action by Congress. In this category are almost 200 million acres, or a little less than 33 percent, of the total. A comparison of this with the preceding graph shows how the executive branch has tended to be somewhat out in front of Congress in increasing protections for public land areas.

The third graph adds together the data from the first two graphs to show the cumulative amount of public lands currently protected from most kinds of intensive development. It also shows U.S. population growth over the same period, using the numbers in the vertical axis on the left to refer to people as well as acres. What it reveals is a considerable correlation between growth in population and growth in the amount of public lands protected from most forms of intensive development.

CHAPTER FIFTY-SIX

Charting the Future of Public Lands in Alaska

AT SOME 365 MILLION ACRES (plus another 60 million acres of inland waters), Alaska is by far the largest state—bigger than the next three biggest states (Texas, California, and Montana) combined. When it was admitted to the union in 1959, nearly all of it was public land, subject to unresolved rights of Indians, Aleuts, and Eskimos. At statehood, these Alaska Natives, most of whom lived in small, remote rural villages, made up about one-fifth of the state's total population of around 225,000. Alaska's Native population had not changed much since the 1880s, but the non-native population increased sharply after World War II, spurred by a growing military presence.[1]

Congress's decisions regarding these vast holdings of public lands, the most fundamental of which it made between 1958 and 1980, reflected the experience that the United States had accumulated since its founding. Alaska gave the nation, as Interior secretary Rogers Morton reportedly said in 1971, the opportunity to avoid past mistakes and "do things right the first time."[2]

The legislation that Congress approved in 1958 to admit Alaska into the union gave the state the right to select and own more than 100 million acres of public lands. The Alaska Native Claims Settlement Act of 1971, or ANCSA, gave Alaska Native corporations the right to select and own more than 40 million acres of public lands. The Alaska National Interest Lands Conservation Act of 1980, or ANILCA, set the course for most of the remaining public lands in the state. Most important, it put more than 100 million acres of formerly

BLM-managed public lands into the national park and national wildlife refuge systems, and more than 56 million acres in the national wilderness preservation system.[3]

PUBLIC LANDS IN THE PERIOD BEFORE STATEHOOD

U.S. government actions to protect Alaska's rich natural resources from unregulated plunder dated back almost to the time it purchased the Alaska territory from Russia in 1867. Alaska was a military district until 1884, and thereafter simply a district until 1912, when Congress organized it as a formal territory.

John Muir made the first of his several trips there in 1879. The descriptions he and others published sparked a kind of science-based tourism, especially along the "inside passage" in southeastern Alaska. In 1899, the railroad tycoon Edward Harriman led such an excursion. Its participants included, besides Muir, several other scientists and authors. One was Henry Gannett, who earlier had helped found the National Geographic Society. Writing in *National Geographic* in 1901, Gannett presciently called Alaska's scenery "more valuable than the gold or fish or the timber, for it will never be exhausted," and its worth will be "measured in direct returns in money received from tourists."[4]

President Harrison established one of the nation's first forest reserves in 1892 on Afognak Island, the second-largest island of the Kodiak Archipelago, southwest of Anchorage. Between 1902 and 1909, Theodore Roosevelt issued a series of orders establishing the nearly 17-million-acre Tongass National Forest in southeastern Alaska and the 5-million-acre Chugach National Forest around Prince William Sound east of Anchorage. As he was leaving office, in 1913, William Howard Taft reserved nearly 3 million acres in the Aleutian Islands for fish and wildlife, especially birds.

In 1917, Congress established Mount McKinley (now Denali) National Park around North America's highest peak. In 1918, Woodrow Wilson established a large national monument, also in the care of the National Park Service, at Katmai, southwest of Anchorage. In 1925, Calvin Coolidge did the same at Glacier Bay, in southeastern Alaska. The scale of these three units reflected Alaska's immense size; at the time, they accounted for more than 40 percent of the acreage in the entire national park system. The impetus for these actions came mostly from scientists. Travel being so difficult, these three units saw only a few thousand visitors through the 1920s; by comparison, Yellowstone attracted nearly 2 million in the same period. No Park Service representative visited Katmai for more than two decades after the monument was established.[5]

In the 1930s, the Park Service studied several large areas for possible addition to the national park system, including Admiralty Island, in the southeast, and the Wrangell–Saint Elias Mountains, along the Canadian border east of Anchorage. The wilderness advocate Bob Marshall—who had lived in a remote Native village in the Brooks Range of northern Alaska for more than a year in the late 1920s and published a best-selling book about his experiences—advocated keeping the state "largely a wilderness," as he put it in a dissent to a 1938 congressionally commissioned report on Alaska resources.[6]

In addition to the actions noted in the preceding paragraphs, Theodore Roosevelt, Herbert Hoover, and FDR all set aside large amounts of land in Alaska to protect birds and other wildlife. In 1941, FDR established the Kodiak National Wildlife Refuge on Kodiak Island, and the National Moose Range on the Kenai Peninsula, south of Anchorage, each encompassing nearly 2 million acres.

In 1957, President Eisenhower's Interior secretary, Fred Seaton, withdrew 9 million acres of public land in far northeastern Alaska, including the calving ground of the immense Porcupine caribou herd, after a campaign spearheaded by the longtime conservation advocates Olaus and Margaret "Mardy" Murie. In December 1960, Seaton formally established the Arctic National Wildlife Range there, extolling its "priceless" and "unparalleled" wildlife, wilderness, and scenic values. That same day, he established two more large protected areas, the 1.8-million-acre Kuskokwim National Wildlife Refuge in southwestern Alaska—which he called "probably the greatest waterfowl breeding ground" in North America—and the nearly half-million-acre Izembek National Wildlife Refuge in the Aleutian Islands. All these actions came almost two years after Alaska became a state, and shortly before the Eisenhower administration left office.

Although these U.S. efforts were aimed at preserving nature, some of Alaska's public lands saw intensive development. There were gold rushes around Juneau in 1880 and Nome in 1899. Large copper mines were operated in the Wrangell Mountains of south-central Alaska from 1909 to 1938. In 1914, Congress authorized the construction of an all-weather railroad line, operated by the Interior Department, from Seward north through Anchorage to Fairbanks, as well as the leasing of Alaska public lands for coal development. The United States also reserved large tracts of public land as possible future energy sources. Besides President Harding's establishment in 1923 of a 23-million-acre naval petroleum reserve in the far northwestern part of the state, about 27 million acres were reserved over the years as potential sites for hydropower projects, although few were built.[7]

NATIVE RIGHTS TO ALASKA LANDS

None of these actions by Congress or the executive purported to resolve the rights of Alaska Natives to public lands. The congressional act of 1884 that brought civil government to Alaska provided that they would "not be disturbed in the possession of any lands actually in their use or occupation or now claimed by them" until Congress provided otherwise. Congress's only land reservation for Indians in the territory was made in 1891, on the 130,000-acre Annette Island in southeastern Alaska, after a group of Tsimshian Indians migrated from British Columbia with a Scottish missionary and settled there.[8]

In the New Deal era, Interior secretary Ickes and his Indian commissioner, John Collier, worked toward establishing reservations for Alaska Natives. One focus was to firm up the land rights of the Tlingit and Haida Indians, who lived in villages mostly inside the boundaries of the Tongass National Forest in southeastern Alaska. But they made only limited progress, clashing with B. Frank Heintzleman, who was a top official of the Forest Service in Alaska from the end of World War I until he became territorial governor in 1953.[9]

World War II brought much military activity to the territory, and its population increased significantly. After the war, national Indian policy began shifting toward what was called "termination," that is, ending the traditional federal trustee relationship with Indians. One of the first steps that Congress took in that direction was in 1947. A national shortage of newsprint and a growing demand for timber to rebuild Japan as an American ally led the timber industry and its congressional boosters to look to southeastern Alaska. With Heintzleman's enthusiastic support, a plan was worked out to establish a public-lands-based lumber and pulp industry through long-term deals that, besides selling huge amounts of timber, called for building several mills locally to process it.

In enacting what came to be known as the Tongass Timber Act, Congress brushed off protests from the Tlingit and Haida Indians and from Ickes, who had left the government by then. The legislation authorized the Agriculture secretary to sell timber from the Tongass, and the Interior secretary to sell lands in the national forest for timber mills and other processing facilities—all to be done "notwithstanding any [Native] claim of possessory rights." The Alaska Native Brotherhood and the National Conference of American Indians condemned the act as "Alaska's Teapot Dome," and they turned to the courts, seeking compensation.[10]

In the early 1950s, while the case was making its way through the courts, the Forest Service implemented the Tongass Timber Act by signing several fifty-year contracts that altogether sold more than 13 billion board feet of timber. Controversy about these contracts continued for decades; in the end, only two mills were built, and the contracts were eventually either significantly reformed or abandoned.[11]

In 1955, the U.S. Supreme Court, in a 5–3 decision, rejected the Tlingit Indians' claim for compensation for the loss of their lands inside the Tongass National Forest. Their title had never been "recognized" by the United States, the Court's majority found. Therefore, the majority held, it was appropriate to leave to "Congress, where it belongs," the decision whether to give the Indians what it called "gratuities for the termination of Indian occupancy of Government-owned land," instead of "making compensation for its value a rigid constitutional principle." Though a bitter defeat for the Natives, the Court's decision did not, as it turned out, deter Congress from seeking to devise a just solution to Native claims to Alaskan lands. Sixteen years later, it approved a deal that involved giving Alaska Natives a considerable amount of land as well as money.[12]

THE STATEHOOD ACT AND PUBLIC LANDS

When Alaska was admitted to the union in 1959, less than 1 million acres of its land, or well under 1 percent, was in private ownership, and more than 80 million acres were in various federal reservations, including forests, parks, monuments, and wildlife refuges. In the statehood act, Congress followed its historic practice of giving the new state grants of public land while requiring it to renounce any claim to lands not granted. The renunciation extended both to lands that the United States retained and to lands that "may be held by any Indians, Eskimos, or Aleuts."[13]

The scale of Congress's gift to the new state was, by any measure, extraordinary. Alaska was given the right to select nearly 104 million acres of public land over twenty-five years. This was an area larger than California, and more land than Congress had given all eleven western states in the lower forty-eight combined. There was more. Congress permitted the new state to select public lands valuable for minerals, a privilege it had mostly denied earlier-admitted states. And it gave the new state a much larger share than other states had received of mineral revenues the United States might receive from public lands that it retained.[14]

In the first few years after statehood, Alaska moved deliberately in making its land selections, concentrating on places believed to be valuable for minerals and other forms of economic development. Native groups felt increasingly threatened by these land selections and by proposals to industrialize parts of rural Alaska. The biggest such proposal, put forward by the Army Corps of Engineers in 1954, was to build the Rampart Dam on the Yukon River north-west of Fairbanks. It would have created a Lake Erie–sized impoundment, the largest man-made reservoir in the world, primarily to generate electricity. Large water projects still had allure in that era, and Kennedy and Nixon both endorsed the project during campaign swings in Alaska in 1960. (Plans for the dam were shelved in the late 1960s.) Another notable proposal, championed by Edward Teller and the Atomic Energy Commission, called for exploding nuclear bombs on the state's northwestern coast to create a harbor from which minerals extracted in the interior could be shipped.[15]

To meet these threats, Native groups organized the Alaska Federation of Natives and began pressing their land claims more vigorously in the Interior Department and Congress. Around the same time, advocates for protecting more of Alaska's public lands became increasingly active, because they shared some of the Natives' concerns. Rampart Dam, for example, would have flooded vast wetlands that were breeding grounds for many millions of waterfowl.[16]

THE ALASKA NATIVE CLAIMS SETTLEMENT ACT AND THE PUBLIC LANDS

Alaska Natives found a sympathetic ear in Interior secretary Stewart Udall. In December 1966, he halted most transfers of public land in Alaska until Congress addressed the matter of Native claims. In 1967, bills to resolve Native claims were introduced in Congress.

Before Udall's "freeze," the United States had transferred ownership to the state of 2 million acres on the North Slope, which borders the Arctic Ocean between the Arctic National Wildlife Refuge on the east and the Naval Petroleum Reserve on the west. The state leased some of these lands to oil companies, and in early 1968, on leased acreage at a place called Prudhoe Bay, the Atlantic Richfield Company struck a rich petroleum deposit. Drilling on other nearby leases soon confirmed it as a major find. The oil company lessees promptly formed a consortium to build the 789-mile-long Trans-Alaska Pipeline System (TAPS) to ship the oil southward across the state to Valdez, a small fishing village with an ice-free harbor on Prince William Sound. There, the oil could be loaded on tankers and shipped to markets.[17]

In 1969, Walter Hickel, a wealthy developer who had been elected governor of Alaska in 1966, was named Interior secretary by the new president, Richard Nixon. At his confirmation hearing, he agreed not to end the Udall freeze on conveying lands to the state without the approval of the pertinent congressional committees. He did, however, issue permits giving TAPS the use of a corridor of public lands 200–500 feet wide for the pipeline. The oil companies moved forward with the project and, later in 1969, bid nearly $1 billion for additional state leases on the North Slope.[18]

In April 1970, Native villages with claims to land along the pipeline's route persuaded a federal judge in Washington, D.C., to temporarily halt work on the project while he considered their claims. That upped the pressure on Congress to resolve Native claims, and it took up the challenge with considerable dispatch.

In the summer of 1971, major conservation groups formed what they called the Alaska Coalition to spearhead a national campaign to provide permanent protection to more of Alaska's public lands. As a first step toward that goal, working with the Alaska Federation of Natives and the National Park Service director, George Hartzog, the coalition helped persuade Congress to include, in the legislation settling Native claims, a mechanism to review unreserved public lands in Alaska for the purpose of identifying areas that Congress ought to protect permanently.[19]

In December 1971, President Nixon signed into law the Alaska Native Claims Settlement Act (ANCSA). It laid out what it called a "fair and just settlement" of all "aboriginal land claims" by giving Alaska Natives nearly $1 billion and the right to select and obtain ownership of more than 40 million acres of public land.

ANCSA involved a complicated mechanism, never used before or since. It called for the land to be selected by and distributed to local village and regional Native corporations that were to be organized under state law, as distinguished from the tribal form of organization common in the lower forty-eight states. ANCSA allowed village corporations (but not regional corporations, which were established mainly for economic development) to select lands immediately surrounding their settlements without regard for whether they were within the external boundaries of existing wildlife refuges.[20]

ANCSA's section 17(d)(2) provided the framework for the review of unreserved public lands sought by conservationists. Known simply as "D2," it authorized the Interior secretary to withdraw, from nearly all actions that could lead to a loss of ownership—including most state and Native selections—up to 80 million acres of public land that the secretary deemed "suitable for addition to or creation as units of the National Park, Forest, Wildlife Refuge, and Wild and Scenic Rivers Systems." To give Congress time to consider the matter, the withdrawal would remain in effect for seven years and then automatically expire. ANCSA's section 17(d)(1) ("D1") supplemented D2 by broadly empowering the Interior secretary to withdraw an unlimited amount of public land in the state whenever it was deemed necessary to protect "the public interest."[21]

THE ROAD TO ANILCA, PART ONE: 1971–76

The statehood act and ANCSA left Congress with the challenge of making decisions regarding management of the remaining public lands in the state. This it did in the Alaska National Interest Lands Conservation Act (ANILCA) of 1980. The path to its enactment was strewn with obstacles.

The first order of business after ANCSA was to clear the path for the construction of the pipeline to get the North Slope oil to markets. The Wilderness Society and other conservation groups had sued the United States in 1970, contending that Hickel's pipeline permits violated the Mineral Leasing Act of 1920. That statute unequivocally limited the width of rights-of-way across public lands for petroleum pipelines to twenty-five feet on either side of the pipeline. TAPS admittedly required a much wider swath of public land. The United States argued that it could issue "special land use permits"—which Congress had not specifically authorized—in order to allow TAPS to use the public lands it needed outside the statutorily prescribed width.

In February 1973, in a dramatic illustration of the increasing judicial engagement in public land matters, the U.S. Court of Appeals for the D.C. Circuit found that the Interior Department could not evade the width limitation spelled out in the Mineral Leasing Act of 1920 by the contrivance of a "special land use permit," and halted pipeline construction. At the same time, it declined to rule on the conservationists' claim that the Interior Department had violated the National Environmental Policy Act by not seriously considering the alternative of routing the pipeline through Canada to the Midwest, where the risk of oil spills from tanker traffic could be avoided and where refinery capacity and domestic demand for oil were the greatest. That issue was not, the court decided, ripe for decision until and unless Congress fixed the width-limitation problem. In April, the Supreme Court declined to review the circuit court decision.[22]

The oil companies and the administration sought, and promptly got, a workaround from Congress. Within months, Congress amended the Mineral Leasing Act to relax the statutory width limitation. It also immunized the TAPS project from further review under NEPA, with Vice President Spiro Agnew providing the decisive vote after the Senate deadlocked on the issue in July. Congress's decision to foreclose further consideration of routing the pipeline through Canada meant that North Slope oil would be carried by tankers through the pristine Gulf of Alaska. There, in 1989, the *Exxon Valdez* ran aground, spilling 260,000 barrels of oil and fouling more than a thousand miles of coastline.

In early 1972, Interior secretary Rogers Morton, who had replaced Hickel in 1970, withdrew 80 million acres under ANCSA's D2, and another 45 million acres under D1. At the same time, he made many millions of acres of public land available immediately for selection by the state and the Native corporations. He issued the necessary TAPS permits in January 1974, and the pipeline began operation in 1977. It provided a strong boost to the state's economy and, because state and Native corporation land selections were now moving forward, eased the way for Alaska's congressional representatives to acquiesce in providing stronger protections for more public lands elsewhere in the state.[23]

The fundamental questions Congress resolved in ANILCA were how much land to put in various categories of national stewardship and which agency would be given management responsibility for each area. Many other related matters also had to be addressed, including traditional subsistence uses of public lands by rural, mostly Native residents, and management of the rich timber supplies in the national forests of southeastern Alaska.

The state, the Alaska Federation of Natives, the Alaska Coalition, and each of the federal land management agencies had a stake in these issues, and each engaged closely in the congressional process. No one interest had an absolute veto over the outcome, so coalition building was essential. A particularly powerful one was forged by the Native community, the Alaska Coalition, and the state to allow rural subsistence uses to continue on most public lands.

In late 1973, Morton recommended that Congress put nearly 33 million acres in the national park system, 32 million acres in national wildlife refuges (sharing management with the BLM on two of them), and 19 million acres in the national forest system. In November 1974, Alaska voters narrowly ousted William Egan, a Democrat who had been the state's first governor and was then in his third (nonconsecutive) term. The winner was Republican Jay Hammond, who had been a marine fighter pilot in World War II and campaigned as a supporter of land conservation.

The Tongass National Forest gained some attention when, in December 1975, timber harvesting there was halted by a federal judge in Anchorage, who followed the court of appeals decision in the *Monongahela* case. While Congress cured that problem by enacting the National Forest Management Act in 1976, its resolution did not quiet the controversy about the future of timber harvesting in the Tongass.[24]

Meanwhile, the Alaska Coalition put together a massive national campaign—unparalleled in the history of public lands—aimed at persuading voters in every congressional district across the nation to urge their elected representatives to support a strong protection bill. As was the case when many other places on public lands now regarded as "crown jewels" were first protected, most Americans had never visited Alaska. Advocates brought to bear every lesson learned from past campaigns, such as those to protect Hetch Hetchy and Echo Park and those used to enact the Wilderness Act and expand the wilderness system. They emphasized the unique opportunity of the decision before Congress, describing Alaska's public lands as "the nation's last wilderness." They linked the effort to patriotic sentiments fanned by celebration of the nation's bicentennial in 1976. Much more than any previous campaign to protect public lands, they emphasized ecological issues, speaking of the need to preserve a "fragile and delicate" landscape and "complete ecosystems."[25]

The timber and mining industry and others who wanted less protection organized the Citizens for the Management of Alaskan Lands (CMAL), and were eventually joined by others, including the National Rifle Association and some labor unions. (Other labor unions, including the United Auto Workers, supported the Alaska Coalition.) CMAL was significantly less effective than its rival at mobilizing national opinion.[26]

THE ROAD TO ANILCA, PART TWO: 1977–80

Neither political party's 1976 platform specifically addressed Alaska lands. On winning the presidency, Jimmy Carter, who had a deep personal commitment to protecting the environment, named Idaho governor Cecil Andrus, a veteran of several battles to protect public lands in his home state, his Interior secretary. At his confirmation hearing, Andrus indicated that the Alaska lands bill was a top priority for the administration.[27]

Although Republicans made some gains in the Senate, Democrats still commanded a majority in both chambers. Morris Udall, who became chair of the House Interior Committee, created a special subcommittee on Alaska lands chaired by Congressman John Seiberling (D-Ohio). Seiberling and Udall played major roles in crafting ANILCA. On the Senate side, the key players were Henry "Scoop" Jackson, who was generally supportive of protecting public lands but was also close to the Seattle business community, which had long favored resource development in Alaska, and the two senators from Alaska, Ted Stevens (R) and Mike Gravel (D).

The bill that emerged from the House in May 1978 came after Seiberling's special subcommittee held numerous field hearings in cities in the lower forty-eight states and in Alaska communities, giving legislators firsthand knowledge of the lands at issue. The Alaska Coalition made sure the hearings were well attended and received extensive press coverage. A considerably less ambitious bill emerged from Jackson's committee in the Senate in the early fall of 1978.

With the expiration of the D2 withdrawal looming in December 1978, a last-minute effort was made to craft a compromise bill, or at least to extend the D2 withdrawal, before Congress adjourned ahead of the November 1978 elections. The effort was doomed when Senator Mike Gravel threatened to filibuster any bill. Gravel's obstruction irritated many of his colleagues. In a rare departure from senatorial courtesy, Ted Stevens criticized him on the Senate floor, saying his behavior put at risk the long tradition of the Senate never approving a bill that affected only one state when both senators opposed it. In those fall elections, the Democrats lost fifteen seats in the House and three in the Senate but remained in control of both houses.[28]

The D2 withdrawal would expire in early December. To maintain the status quo until Congress could finish work on a comprehensive land bill, the Carter administration was planning to use its D1 authority, which was not expiring, to make new emergency withdrawals. A few days before the D2 withdrawal expired, the state jumped the gun by filing land selections in areas earmarked for national-park status in the bills that Congress was considering. This aggressive step helped persuade the administration to take stronger protective action.

On December 1, 1978, President Carter used his Antiquities Act authority to establish fifteen national monuments on 56 million acres of Alaska public land. Most of the acreage was put in the national park system, more than 10 million acres were put in the national wildlife refuge system (the first national monuments administered by the Fish & Wildlife Service), and 3 million acres were put in the national forest system. Carter's proclamations contained eloquent, detailed descriptions of the ecological and cultural values being protected. At the same time, Interior secretary Andrus made emergency withdrawals to protect another 40 million acres that the administration had recommended for permanent protection. A mining company filed suit to annul the executive actions. (An Alaska federal court ruled against the company in 1980, and it did not appeal.) These dramatic events brought even more national attention to the future of Alaska lands and put the matter squarely back in front of the legislative branch.[29]

As the new Ninety-Sixth Congress took the matter up early in 1979, a number of issues became bargaining chips. One involved the future of timber harvesting in the Tongass. A second was whether petroleum development would be allowed on the coastal plain of the Arctic National Wildlife Refuge east of the Prudhoe Bay oil field. A third was whether hunting would be permitted in newly protected areas of public lands.

In early 1979, Udall introduced a new bill that was more protective than the one the House had passed the previous year. In March, however, with the national economy beginning to falter, his committee rejected the bill by a one-vote margin, approving a weaker bill instead. Udall and his allies regrouped and persuaded the House to reject that weaker bill and eventually, in the summer of 1979, to approve a revised bill that Udall and Seiberling had crafted with John Anderson (R-Ill.).[30]

The action then shifted to the Senate. Jackson's committee produced a bill in October 1979, but floor debate did not begin until the summer of 1980. In August, the Senate approved, by a wide margin, a bill that was less protective than the House bill, but stronger than the committee bill. As negotiators for the House and Senate worked to reconcile the two versions, the Iranian hostage crisis and the presidential contest between Carter and Ronald Reagan dominated the political landscape, and in early October, negotiators called a halt until after the election.[31]

In November, Ronald Reagan swept to victory and the Republicans gained control of the Senate. That ended the bargaining. In the lame-duck congressional session, the House simply accepted the Senate-passed bill, and on December 2, 1980, President Carter signed into law the most sweeping public lands protection bill in American history. It gave him a credible claim to being, as his chief domestic policy advisor, Stuart Eizenstat, later wrote, the "greatest presidential protector of our nation's natural bounty since Theodore Roosevelt."[32]

THE ALASKA NATIONAL INTEREST LANDS CONSERVATION ACT

The scale of the law, like the state itself, was stunning. It added more than 56 million acres to the national wilderness preservation system, nearly 54 million acres to the national wildlife refuge system, and nearly 44 million acres to the national park system—tripling the size of the wilderness and refuge systems and doubling the size of the park system. While it rescinded most of the Carter-created national monuments, ANILCA protected nearly all the lands they had protected. It confirmed the Admiralty Island and Misty Fjords national

Jimmy Carter at signing of the Alaska National Interest Lands Conservation Act, December 2, 1980. Among those pictured are John Seiberling (*left*), Mo Udall (*second from left*), Phillip Burton (*third from left*), Ted Stevens (*second to the right of Carter*), and (*right*) Interior secretary Cecil Andrus. (Courtesy of the Jimmy Carter Presidential Library and Museum and the U.S. Fish & Wildlife Service)

monuments in southeastern Alaska, with a few modifications, and left them under Forest Service management.[33]

Many dozens of pages of dense text included a jumble of details and exemptions spelling out what was permissible in the various units. Some of these were different from what would have been allowed on comparable lands in the lower forty-eight, reflecting the peculiarities, political and otherwise, that prevailed in Alaska. The most important generic directive was to permit subsistence hunting and fishing, including motorized access, on many of the protected lands.

The subsistence provision was primarily for the benefit of the Alaska Native community, although at the insistence of Senator Stevens, it was extended to all "rural residents," both Native and non-Native. The legislation also included compromises to allow particular developments to go forward, such as carving nearly 150,000 acres from the Misty Fjords monument for a molybdenum mining project.[34]

The legislation did not put every issue to rest. Two of the most hotly contested—whether to allow petroleum development on the coastal plain of the Arctic National Wildlife Refuge, and how much timber harvesting to allow in the Tongass National Forest—continued to be debated for decades. ANILCA did not put the refuge into the wilderness system, but it did require a further act of Congress before any of it could be leased for oil and gas development. It put some Tongass lands in the national wilderness preservation system, but also set a target timber harvest of 450 million board feet annually, and included a $40 million annual federal subsidy to facilitate reaching it.

Several things were noteworthy about how the political process played out in ANILCA. One was that—contrary to the political dynamic that usually operates on Capitol Hill—the Alaska congressional delegation could not stop a Congress determined to protect a vast amount of public land in their state. Although the state had major influence on the legislation, an unprecedented national campaign by protection advocates persuaded Congress to assert, as pronounced in the title of the legislation, a strong "national interest" in these lands. Another was how the executive branch was able to shape the outcome through its detailed studies of the resources and values at stake, and actions such as national-monument proclamations and other withdrawals.

A third involved the relationships among the land management agencies. While there was some jockeying for turf, such maneuvering did not play a dominant role in the outcome. Partly this was because the Forest Service had a presence only east and southeast of Anchorage, with Interior dominant everywhere else. Partly it was because all agencies shared the objective of protecting these vast landscapes, including but not limited to wilderness designations. If one were keeping score, the national wildlife refuge system gained the most, followed closely by the national park system, with the national forests and the BLM gaining the least. ANILCA did give the BLM management of the 1.2-million-acre Steese National Conservation Area, one hundred miles northeast of Fairbanks, and left it in charge of more than 70 million acres in the state outside the ANILCA-designated units, including the large national petroleum reserve in northwestern Alaska.

Crucial to ANILCA's success were the formation of coalitions and the crafting of compromises among disparate interests. The Alaska Coalition and the Alaska Federation of Natives forged a fruitful, though occasionally uneasy, relationship, with a key component being agreement on the terms of subsistence hunting and fishing on conservation-oriented lands. Something similar happened when Udall, Seiberling, and the Alaska Coalition, eager to have sport hunters support the legislation, agreed to put more of the lands earmarked for the national park system into "park preserves" (where sport hunting is permitted) rather than simply in "parks" (where it is not).[35]

Like practically all public land policy making over the nation's long history, ANILCA also reflected considerable bipartisanship. Republican senator Ted Stevens played a constructive role throughout and had great influence on the final product. Yet ANILCA also marked a decline in that tradition, once the political Right began to portray national assertion of authority over public lands as government overreach. That line of attack contributed to Reagan's rise to power and helped Republicans unseat incumbent Democrats in the Senate between 1974 and 1980 in California, Colorado, Idaho, New Mexico, Utah, Washington, and Wyoming. Since ANILCA became law, Alaska has experienced a boom in public-lands-based tourism, and little effort has been made in Congress to undo or modify its basic terms, except those for petroleum drilling in the Arctic National Wildlife Refuge.

Public lands legislation of ANILCA's breadth is almost certain never to happen again. It was a fitting culmination of nearly two centuries of national experience in making policy for public lands, for it showed once again, this time on a grand scale, how the American political system could reconcile a complex mixture of interests in a way that afforded considerable protection for nature and for the interests of future generations.

CHAPTER FIFTY-SEVEN

Making the Modern U.S. Fish & Wildlife Service

IN 1961, CONGRESS DECIDED TO boost the program to protect waterfowl habitat by giving the Fish & Wildlife Service an interest-free loan of up to $200 million as an advance on the duck stamp fund. (It forgave the loan twenty-five years later.) The following year, its enactment of the Refuge Recreation Act took a long step toward organizing areas of public land devoted primarily to wildlife into a national system. It came in response to a spurt in the recreational use of refuges, which more than doubled to 11 million visitor days between 1954 and 1960.[1]

The act authorized the Interior Department to allow recreation on refuges, and on "other conservation areas" that it administered for "fish and wildlife purposes," as an "appropriate incidental or secondary use" where it was "not inconsistent with" the "primary objectives for which each particular area is established." This compatibility test—demanding that such a "secondary" use not interfere with "primary" refuge purposes—reflected long-standing agency practice, and had been mentioned in the 1935 amendments to the Duck Stamp Act. Congress's decision to apply a "dominant use" standard to Interior-administered wildlife conservation areas across the nation was in contrast to its decision, two years earlier, to apply a "multiple-use standard"—which gave the managing agency considerably greater leeway—to national forests.

The Refuge Recreation Act also limited recreational uses to places where the secretary determined that "funds [were] available" for the agency to handle "permitted forms of recreation." This idea of tying the use of public lands to available funds had never before appeared in any law dealing with public lands. It turned out not to have a demonstrable impact on Congress. Congressional appropriations committees, which are the primary holders of agency purse strings, often regard agency complaints of poverty as attempts at extortion. Likewise, it had no demonstrable impact on the courts whenever they had occasion to examine FWS recreational management, because courts are not equipped to make judgments about funding adequacy. Still, the idea does draw a useful link between agency management and funding, and may provide some encouragement for the FWS to curb recreation where funds to manage it are not "available."

The Refuge Recreation Act gave the secretary useful general management authorities. These included the power to issue permits, charge fees, and issue regulations governing all "public use." The act also authorized the secretary to accept donations of funds and property, including property burdened by agreements that limited how it could be used (so-called restrictive covenants), if they were "compatible" with refuge purposes. Finally, it authorized the secretary to acquire "limited areas of land for recreational development adjacent to" refuges, though it forbade the use of duck stamp revenue for that purpose.

In 1964, Congress made modest adjustments in the program that it had adopted in 1935 to share refuge revenues with counties where refuges were located. It expanded the pool of revenue to be shared to include money that the FWS derived from timber harvesting and livestock grazing on the refuges, and limited counties' use of the shared funds to public schools and roads. Refuge system revenues—which are mostly derived from the sale of forest products and petroleum extraction where the United States owns the mineral rights—have never amounted to more than a few million dollars a year, far below the amount generated by activities on national forests and BLM lands.[2]

THE NATIONAL WILDLIFE REFUGE SYSTEM
ADMINISTRATION ACT

The National Wildlife Refuge System Administration Act of 1966 marked a major advance by finally formally establishing the National Wildlife Refuge System (NWRS). It was defined to include all areas that the FWS administered as "wildlife refuges, areas for the protection and conservation of fish and wildlife that are threatened with extinction, wildlife ranges, game ranges, wildlife management areas or waterfowl production areas." The same act extended the

Refuge Recreation Act's compatibility standard to cover all uses, not just recreation.[3]

The NWRS Administration Act also included the first version of the Endangered Species Act, making the preservation of biodiversity an important national objective. Pairing that with the administration of wildlife refuges underlined the close connection between the two. Before this, most refuges had been established to protect waterfowl and charismatic mammals. Henceforth, more refuges—fifty to date—would be established specifically to protect species threatened with extinction. The 1966 act drove that point home by authorizing the purchase and establishment of the Mason Neck National Wildlife Refuge in Virginia—since renamed in honor of Elizabeth Hartwell, the leader of the campaign to establish it—to restore bald eagle habitat. Today, national wildlife refuges help protect hundreds of ESA-listed species.[4]

THE REFUGE SYSTEM GAINS STRENGTH

Over his eight years in office, Stewart Udall did much to advance the cause of wildlife protection on public lands. Through his role as chair of the Migratory Bird Conservation Commission, he worked with members of Congress such as Silvio Conte (R-Mass.) and Roman Hruska (R-Neb.) to establish more than five dozen new refuges in thirty states. He also banned the aerial shooting of bald and golden eagles on all lands administered by the Interior Department, and in 1967 announced his opposition to the giant Rampart Dam project in Alaska, citing its devastating impacts on wildlife as well as the concerns of Alaska Natives.[5]

That same year, Robert H. MacArthur and E. O. Wilson published *The Theory of Island Biogeography.* Its analysis of factors influencing species diversity in an isolated setting helped revolutionize understanding of how biodiversity evolved and how it might be protected. Out of this work emerged a new applied science, conservation biology, that came to influence the management of many public lands. The next year, a report that Udall had commissioned on the long-range goals of the national wildlife refuge system, prepared by a committee chaired by Professor A. Starker Leopold, Aldo's son, endorsed the idea of adding a "natural ecosystem" component to refuge management.[6]

In the mid-1970s, a controversy erupted that demonstrated growing support for giving the Fish & Wildlife Service a more prominent role on public lands. It began when Interior secretary Rogers Morton—displaying the department's traditional tilt toward the livestock industry—proposed to give the BLM sole management authority over three public land "game ranges" that the BLM and the FWS had been jointly managing in a not very successful effort to balance livestock grazing with wildlife protection. In response, Congressman John Dingell, who had been a primary sponsor of the NWRS Administration Act, pushed a bill through Congress that not only gave the FWS exclusive control over those three ranges, but also put sharp limits on the power of the executive to transfer lands acquired for refuge purposes away from the FWS. President Ford signed it into law in early 1976.[7]

The Dingell legislation followed on a report that documented numerous instances of executive actions that shrank refuge-system units. It specifically prohibited removing any lands from the wildlife refuge system, including any lands the executive might add in the future, without the consent of Congress. The Federal Land Policy and Management Act, enacted later in 1976, reaffirmed the Interior secretary's power to establish wildlife refuges on lands managed by the BLM by using the withdrawal tool to transfer them to the FWS, and it forbade the secretary from modifying or revoking any such withdrawal. Together, these acts strengthened executive authority to grow—but not shrink—the refuge system.[8]

The growing prominence of the FWS was on full display in the landmark Alaska lands legislation of 1980, which tripled the acreage in the NWR system. Its reach was further extended in 1986 when the United States and Canada adopted the North American Waterfowl Management Plan, which called for protecting another 2 million acres of waterfowl habitat in the United States. Later that same year, Congress adopted the Emergency Wetlands Resources Act to implement the plan, primarily through the FWS. The North American Wetlands Conservation Act, enacted in 1989, took more steps in that direction, and in 1996, the FWS and its counterparts in Canada and Mexico signed a tripartite agreement that consolidated efforts to conserve wildlife on a continental scale.[9]

THE PROBLEM OF INCOMPATIBLE SECONDARY USES GROWS

The 1968 Leopold report cautioned that once they were established, uses of refuges that turned out to be incompatible with wildlife would be difficult to dislodge. The warning had little effect. Ten years later, a federal court roundly condemned the FWS's decision to allow recreational motorboating and water-skiing to proliferate on a refuge established in Nevada to protect migratory waterfowl. That also had little effect, and a stream of critical reports, both internal and external, documented festering problems. A study by the General Accounting Office in 1989 found that well over half the refuges tolerated incompatible uses such as mining, logging, powerboating, off-road-vehicle use, and livestock grazing. This triggered a series of congressional hearings, and by 1990 bills were being introduced in Congress to not only tighten the compatibility standard but also to generally overhaul refuge administration.[10]

To ramp up pressure for action, wildlife protection advocates sued the Interior secretary in 1992, alleging a system-wide failure to prevent incompatible use. The Clinton administration settled the litigation in late 1993 by agreeing to undertake a comprehensive review of secondary uses and to promptly terminate those found not compatible. Meanwhile, reform legislation was slowly advancing in Congress. In 1996, President Clinton issued an executive order to reform NWRS administration, the terms of which heavily influenced the legislation that Congress adopted the following year.[11]

THE NATIONAL WILDLIFE REFUGE SYSTEM IMPROVEMENT ACT OF 1997

The congressional leaders in the reform effort were Senator Bob Graham (D-Fla.), Representatives John Dingell, Gerry E. Studds (D-Mass.), George Miller (D-Calif.) and—after the elections in the fall of 1994 put the Republicans in control of both Houses of Congress—Don Young (R-Alaska), who succeeded Miller as chair of the House Natural Resources Committee, and Senators John Chaffee (R-R.I.) and Dirk Kempthorne (R-Idaho).

Although there was broad bipartisan support for reform, a dispute between "bleeding hearts and gunners," as Wallace Stegner once described them, threatened to derail the entire effort. Sport hunters wanted protection from efforts by humane organizations to stop sport hunting on refuges, but a bill that Congressman Young pushed through the House in 1995 tilted so far in favor of sport hunting that many wildlife conservation advocates opposed it. The result was a stalemate. Young eventually asked Interior secretary Babbitt to try to engineer a compromise. After more than two months of meetings with interested groups, Babbitt succeeded, and Congress swiftly enacted it into law.[12]

The NWRS Improvement Act of 1997 was a landmark in public land policy. It requires the FWS to manage the refuge system in accordance with cutting-edge ecological understanding, including the rapidly advancing science of conservation biology. It declared the system's "mission" to be to provide a "national network of lands and waters for the conservation, management, and where appropriate, restoration of the fish, wildlife, and plant resources and their habitats." The reference to "plants" underscored the intent to include entire ecosystems. Most far-reaching was the act's mandate that the Interior secretary "ensure that the biological integrity, diversity, and environmental health of the System are maintained for the benefit of present and future generations of Americans." This gave the FWS the most ecologically oriented mandate of the four land management agencies.[13]

The NWRS Improvement Act contained a major overhaul of the primary purpose–secondary use framework. The compromise that Babbitt engineered on sport hunting created a new, third category of authorized refuge use called "wildlife-dependent recreation." This was defined to include "wildlife observation and photography" and "environmental education and interpretation" as well as sport hunting and fishing. The act positioned this new category between core wildlife-protection purposes and disfavored economic uses such as grazing, mining, and logging, as well as other forms of recreation such as powerboating.

Most refuge system visitors—more than 50 million annually in recent years—engage in wildlife observation and photography. Hunters (more than 2 million) and anglers (nearly 7 million) have political clout that belies their numbers, and sport hunting and fishing are permitted on most of the units in the refuge system and on most of its acreage. (Fishing and hunting account for only 10 and 4 percent, respectively, of total recreation-related expenditures; nonconsumptive uses account for the rest.) The tension between sport hunters and other wildlife advocates that the Babbitt-engineered compromise abated has never disappeared. The Trump administration stoked the coals by requiring artists who entered the annual duck stamp contest to celebrate hunting and not just waterfowl. This sparked protests that the new requirement could discourage non-hunters from purchasing stamps and thereby shrink the amount of money available to acquire new refuges.[14]

The NWRS Improvement Act put new teeth in the compatibility standard and more process in its application. Secondary uses can be permitted only if, "in the sound professional judgment of" the FWS director, they would not "materially interfere with or detract from the fulfillment of the mission of the System or the purposes of the refuge." But the law draws sharp distinctions between "wildlife-dependent recreational uses" and other, less-favored secondary uses. Determining whether the former are compatible can be done through a streamlined process, whereas compatibility determinations regarding the latter follow a much more exacting process that includes, among other things, written findings that must be updated periodically.[15]

The act's effect on the ground has been consistent with the congressional intent to disfavor economic uses such as petroleum or mineral extraction, timber harvesting, and livestock grazing. Petroleum extraction in refuges now occurs primarily in situations where the United States does not own the mineral rights. In those few cases in which drilling occurs on land where the United States does own the mineral rights, oil and gas leases either predated the refuge's establishment, or the Interior Department issued leases in order to capture revenue where U.S.-owned oil and gas was being drained from a refuge by means of wells located on nonpublic land outside its boundaries. (Leases in the latter situation typically prohibit wells from occupying the surface of refuge lands.) Hard-rock mining is almost unknown in the refuge system. Although nearly 20 percent of the system's acreage is forested, timber harvesting occurs on only a few thousand acres annually. Livestock grazing takes place on more than 1 million acres in the refuge system, but more than half of this is on a single unit, the Charles M. Russell NWR in Montana.

There are, however, some refuges where the FWS does not have exclusive jurisdiction, which can mean that more secondary uses occur. On these "overlay refuges," the FWS exercises management authority over land under the jurisdiction of another agency by means of a cooperative agreement. FWS has entered such agreements with agencies like the BLM, components of the Department of Defense, and the National Aeronautics and Space Administration. A particularly complicated case is the Merritt Island NWR, which is adjacent to the Kennedy Space Center and also within the 67,500-acre Canaveral National Seashore, which is managed by the National Park Service. Any such cooperative agreement can be terminated by the other agency unless Congress puts its imprimatur on it. Another variant occurs when the FWS holds conservation easements on land owned by someone else; this situation now exists on more than 4 million acres of land.[16]

SOME COMPLICATIONS IN FWS ADMINISTRATION

The NWRS Improvement Act does not fully resolve a tension inherent in the refuge system's dual nature—that is, where individual units were established with specific purposes that may not exactly square with the system's over-arching mission. The act calls for each refuge to be "managed to fulfill the mission of the System, as well as the specific purposes for which that refuge was established," and provides that conflicts between the two are to "be resolved in a manner that first protects the purposes of the refuge, and, to the extent practicable, that also achieves the mission of the System." Congress's decision to give individual refuge purposes primacy in the event of conflict can enlarge the influence of local interests if, as if often the case, they helped shape the establishment of a specific refuge.

The NWRS Improvement Act's formula for resolving the tension between individual refuge purposes and the national system's objectives leaves room for judgment. Because the act's overall thrust is to promote uniformity throughout the system, however, the conflict between the system's mission and individual units' purposes ought to be relatively clear in order for the latter to prevail. Potential conflicts are mostly addressed in the "comprehensive conservation plan" that the act requires to be prepared for each unit. (In ANILCA, Congress required that a plan be prepared for each Alaska refuge; the NWRS Improvement Act made that requirement system-wide.) As the NWRS Improvement Act shows, Congress can resolve the tension that sometimes exists between the national and local interests in different ways, in the different public land management systems.[17]

The FWS has an array of responsibilities that do not involve public lands, and this, too, can complicate its administration of the refuge system. These include operating fish hatcheries, administering programs that make grants to states for wildlife-related purposes, and regulating trade in various species. Some of these non-public-land duties, such as enforcing the Endangered Species Act on private land, can be especially controversial. Other agencies managing public lands likewise have other responsibilities—for example, the National Park Service maintains the National Register of Historic Places and monitors state and local governments' compliance with Land and Water Conservation Fund grant restrictions. But some observers believe the FWS's other responsibilities help explain why it receives fewer dollars from Congress per acre of land managed than any of the other three major land management agencies.[18]

The FWS's wildlife responsibilities on public lands can also be complicated by the government's activities to control predators. Though the federal program to control predators dates back more than a century, it has been in considerable turmoil in the modern era. Stewart Udall commissioned a review of the program—which at that time was being administered by a unit of the FWS—by an advisory group chaired by A. Starker Leopold, and Udall adopted its recommendations for overhauling the program, including reassessing its goals. In 1972, President Nixon issued an executive order ending the practice of poisoning predators on public lands, and asked Congress to repeal the Animal Damage Control Act of 1931, but opposition by livestock operators on public lands thwarted the effort. Gerald Ford partially reversed Nixon's poisoning ban. President Carter banned killing coyote pups in their dens. In 1982, President

Reagan overturned Carter's and Nixon's bans. In 1985, he transferred the program from Interior to the Department of Agriculture (from which it had been transferred in 1939), where in 1997 it was renamed the Division of Wildlife Services.[19]

THE DELICATE MATTER OF RELATIONS WITH STATE AUTHORITIES

Water, fish, and wildlife are mobile resources that do not respect jurisdictional boundaries. Partly for this reason, states have long been involved in regulating water use and the taking of fish and wildlife on wildlife refuge system units, and tend to oppose any actions that could lessen their role. State fish and wildlife agencies derive revenue from hunting and fishing license fees, sometimes in amounts that make up a significant proportion of their budgets. They generally resist federal actions that could diminish sport hunting and fishing, and support actions that can have the opposite effect. Alaska, for example, has pushed for killing predators in national wildlife refuges in order to boost ungulate and waterfowl populations.[20]

These factors make questions of state-versus-federal authority over fish, wildlife, and water a matter of some political sensitivity. Several Supreme Court decisions have made clear that Congress can, if it chooses, override state authority on such matters. One, handed down in 1976, is illustrative. In 1952, President Truman established the Devil's Hole National Monument (administered by the National Park Service) on public lands in Nevada in order to protect an underground pool that was the only known habitat of a rare species of fish. In 1971, the United States sued a landowner in the vicinity who in 1968 had begun to pump large amounts of groundwater, allowable under Nevada law—a move that threatened to dry up the pool and kill the fish. The Supreme Court ruled that Truman's order preempted state water law, permitting the United States to limit the groundwater pumping to the extent needed to protect the fish.[21]

Eventually, the United States bought much of the land around Devil's Hole and established the Ash Meadows National Wildlife Refuge there to protect an array of rare desert species, including the fish. The National Park Service continues to administer Devil's Hole, and the FWS manages the surrounding refuge, about 40 percent of it under a cooperative agreement with the BLM. Ash Meadows became one of the first places in the nation to be recognized as a "wetlands of international importance" under an international treaty (the Ramsar Convention) that the U.S. Senate ratified during the Reagan administration.

The states' political influence in Congress often persuades it to avoid exercising its authority to preempt state law, and instead to leave somewhat fuzzy how the state-federal balance should be struck. When Congress fails to provide clear direction, it is left to the executive branch and the courts to resolve particular disputes as they arise. Although the devil is in the details, as a general matter, state policies on fish and wildlife and on water use have the least influence on the national park system, somewhat more but still limited influence on the national wildlife refuge system, and considerably more influence on the national forest system and on BLM lands.

With respect to the FWS, an Interior Department regulation directs that refuge system units be managed, "to the extent practicable and compatible with the purposes for which they were established, in accordance with" state laws and policies. The 1997 NWRS Improvement Act did not change that approach. The FWS continues to work closely with states, especially on hunting and fishing regulation, and the relationship between the states and the FWS on such matters continues to be a delicate one.[22]

PROTECTION OF WILDLIFE RESOURCES OFFSHORE

An oil spill off the Southern California coast that began eight days into his presidency in 1969 helped persuade President Richard Nixon to do more to protect marine resources. The next year, he used his reorganization authority to create a new agency, the National Oceanic and Atmospheric Administration (NOAA). He was apparently on track to put it in the Interior Department until a note from his Interior secretary, Walter Hickel, urging him to listen to students protesting the invasion of Cambodia was leaked to the press. Nixon expressed his irritation by installing NOAA in the Department of Commerce instead. One of NOAA's components was the Bureau of Commercial Fisheries, which was transferred out of Interior's Fish & Wildlife Service and renamed the National Marine Fisheries Service. Informally known as NOAA Fisheries, it shares authority with the FWS for enforcing the ESA and related laws off the nation's shores.[23]

In 1972, Congress got into the act by passing two new marine protection laws. One, the Marine Mammal Protection Act, prohibited the "taking"— broadly defined to include harassing, hunting, and capturing as well as killing—of marine mammals, with enforcement jurisdiction shared between the FWS and NOAA. The second, the Marine Protection, Research, and Sanctuaries Act, gave the Commerce secretary broad authority to designate marine sanctuaries offshore (including in the Great Lakes) in order to preserve or restore an area's "conservation, recreational, ecological, or esthetic values." Although this second law grew out of a 1966 recommendation of President Johnson's Scientific Advisory Committee to establish a marine counterpart to the Wilderness Act, it fell considerably short of that goal. It did not prohibit— indeed, it did not even expressly limit—industrial activities such as commercial fishing or oil and gas development in these "sanctuaries." These industries also succeeded in softening the protective purposes of the program as it was being implemented. It was an illustration of how, in such matters, the offshore commercial-fishing industry exercises political influence comparable to that of public land livestock permittees onshore.[24]

Because merely designating particular areas as marine "sanctuaries" does not provide much protection, Presidents George W. Bush and Barack Obama both turned to the Antiquities Act to create vast protected areas offshore. In 2006, Bush established a vast national marine monument on nearly 90 million acres around the Northwestern Hawaiian Islands, a chain of small uninhabited islands and atolls that sprawls across more than a thousand miles of the Pacific Ocean northwest of the inhabited Hawaiian Islands. Shortly before leaving office in 2009, he established two more marine national monuments in the Pacific. One included some 61 million acres in the Marianas Trench in the western Pacific near Guam and the Northern Mariana Islands. The other encompassed nearly 9 million acres around the 39,000-acre Rose Atoll National Wildlife Refuge. The refuge was established in 1973 by a cooperative agreement between the Interior Department and the government of American Samoa. In 2014, Obama more than tripled the size of Bush's Northwestern Hawaiian Islands monument, and two years later established the first Atlantic marine national monument, Northeast Canyons and Seamounts, on more than 3 million acres off the New England coast.[25]

All the marine monuments, which now cover more than 356 million acres, are collaboratively managed by the FWS and NOAA, with the FWS having primary jurisdiction over most of the acreage. Unlike marine "sanctuaries," commercial fishing is generally forbidden in marine monuments, though there are exceptions. The Marianas Trench Marine National Monument includes the seabed but not the water column, which allows commercial fishing to continue. In 2020, President Trump opened the Northeast Canyons and Seamounts monument to commercial fishing, an action that is being tested in court. Oil and gas activities are generally forbidden in marine monuments, as is mining generally. The latter prohibition is important, since large mining companies are gearing up to mine the beds of the seas for polymetallic nodules.[26]

THE REFUGE SYSTEM TODAY

Today the national wildlife refuge system covers nearly 100 million acres onshore and several hundred million acres of submerged lands offshore, making it the world's largest and most diverse system of areas devoted primarily to wildlife protection. Although more than three-quarters of the system's onshore acreage is in its sixteen Alaska units, refuges—which now number more than six hundred—are found in every state in the lower forty-eight. More than a hundred refuges, in thirty-seven states, are within twenty-five miles of a metropolitan area with more than 250,000 people. By some estimates, the refuge system includes about half the major ecosystem types found on the planet. Onshore refuges include land more than two hundred feet below sea level (California's Salton Sea) and more than nine thousand feet above (in the Arctic National Wildlife Refuge in Alaska).

Altogether, the growth of the system in modern times has reflected what Peter Matthiessen described in his book *Wildlife in America* as a "fundamental transformation in public understanding of the world and man's place in it" as well as a "significant redirection of conservation thought and practice."[27]

CHAPTER FIFTY-EIGHT

Making the Modern National Park Service

JOHN F. KENNEDY'S ELECTION IN 1960 helped jump-start a significant expansion of the national park system. An initial emphasis was on seashores, which was not surprising, given Kennedy's affinity for Cape Cod. Conrad Wirth, who headed the National Park Service from 1951 to 1964, had laid the groundwork, overseeing the preparation of reports in the 1950s that advocated purchasing and protecting lands along what the service called "our vanishing shoreline" for public recreation and the conservation of important biological resources. Although Congress had authorized the Cape Hatteras National Seashore Recreational Area in the 1930s, it took nearly two decades for it to be established. It conjoined an existing wildlife refuge with land donated by the State of North Carolina and land that the United States bought with the help of private philanthropy.[1]

While serving in the Senate, Kennedy had co-sponsored a bill with his colleague Leverett Saltonstall (R-Mass.) to establish the Cape Cod National Seashore. A few months after he was inaugurated, Congress sent him the necessary legislation, and that proved a turning point. In the next dozen years, Congress established nine more national seashores and three national lakeshores, together covering nearly 1 million acres in a dozen states. Though accounting for but 1 percent of the park system's acreage, they are among its more heavily visited units.[2]

Two of these, on Assateague Island in Maryland and Fire Island in New York, were slated for intense recreational-homesite development before a series of severe storms in the early 1960s dampened the enthusiasm for such use. At Assateague, Interior secretary Udall worked closely with the local congressman, Republican Rogers Morton, who later became Nixon's second Interior secretary. At Fire Island, he worked with New York's senators, Kenneth Keating and Jacob Javits, and Congressman John Lindsay, all Republicans. To overcome the reluctance of the legendary New York public-works empire builder Robert Moses, Udall invoked the precedent of Frederick Law Olmsted and Central Park, suggesting that Fire Island could become a comparable "seashore sanctuary" for New Yorkers.

In 1966, Congress established the Indiana Dunes National Lakeshore, a half century after Stephen Mather had first proposed it. Its champion was Senator Paul Douglas (D-Ill.), who had to work hard to placate the local congressman, Charles Halleck (R-Ind.), who initially favored giving the land to the steel and shipping industries. (In 2019, Indiana Dunes became the nation's sixty-first national park.)[3]

The legislation protecting these coastal areas used various techniques to control the use of private property within their boundaries, including direct regulation by the Interior Department. Blending private and public ownership became more common as the park system moved into urban areas. George and Martha Washington's estate at Mount Vernon in Virginia had been owned and protected by private philanthropy since before the Civil War, but in 1961, Congress directed the Park Service to acquire lands and scenic easements across the Potomac River in Maryland to protect its viewshed.[4]

Stewart Udall's eight-year tenure as Interior secretary was a dynamic period for the park system. Early on, he appointed two committees to review National Park Service policies. One, chaired by A. Starker Leopold, examined wildlife management in the park system. The other, a team from the National Academy of Sciences headed by William J. Robbins, evaluated the agency's research program. Both reports were submitted in 1963. Leopold's committee recommended that most national parks "should represent a vignette of primitive America" and should use the tools of science to re-create that vision where necessary. Its assumption that the biological resources found in national parks had not been manipulated by Native Americans was later challenged, but its emphasis on maintaining natural appearances remained influential. The Robbins report was critical of the agency's failure to develop a capacity for science and urged it to pay more heed to science in its management decisions. Its recommendations for reform were slower to take hold.[5]

Udall also created an office of international affairs at Interior. He promoted the first World Conference on National Parks, a weeklong gathering in Seattle in 1962, and delivered its keynote address. This pioneering effort spawned what has since become a substantial international movement to establish and expand protected areas around the globe.[6]

Udall elevated the Park Service's presence in his native region. In 1962, Congress converted the Petrified Forest National Monument into a national park, and in that same year, Udall persuaded Kennedy to enlarge the Saguaro National Monument, which President Hoover had established on Tucson's east side thirty years earlier, by adding a unit on the city's west side. (In 1994, Congress combined both units into a single national park.) Early in his tenure, three members of the Utah congressional delegation asked him to explore the possibility of creating a park or recreation area in a scenic expanse southwest of Moab, Utah, that had been part of the Park Service's Escalante National Monument proposal in the 1930s. It took three years to bring to fruition, but in 1964, President Johnson signed legislation creating the 237,000-acre Canyonlands National Park. Seven years later, Congress enlarged it by nearly 100,000 acres, to the size that Udall had originally proposed.[7]

George Hartzog, who headed the Park Service from 1964 to 1973, was a tireless advocate in the Mather mold, although he came from a very different background. After a hardscrabble childhood on South Carolina's coastal plain, he became a preacher at age sixteen, read law, and became a lawyer. He eventually joined the General Land Office and then the Park Service, working his way up the ranks.[8]

Several dozen units were added during his tenure, when he worked not only with Udall but also with his Republican successors, Walter Hickel and Rogers Morton. Among the more notable were Guadalupe Mountains (Texas, 1966), North Cascades (Washington, 1968), Voyageurs (Minnesota, 1971), and Arches and Capitol Reef (both in Utah, and both converted from national monuments, 1971); as well as national recreation areas at Ross Lake and Lake Chelan (both in Washington, 1968), and Golden Gate (San Francisco Bay area, 1972) and Gateway (New York City area, 1972). Not long after Hartzog left office, Congress established the first "national preserve" units in the national park system in Texas (the Big Thicket National Preserve, on nearly 1 million acres of acquired land in an area of notable biological richness in East Texas) and Florida (the Big Cypress National Preserve, on more than 700,000 acres of acquired land adjacent to Everglades National Park).

DÉTENTE WITH THE FOREST SERVICE

Udall and Hartzog worked with Agriculture secretary Orville Freemen to tamp down the rivalry between the Park Service and the Forest Service. Among other things, they cooperatively allocated responsibility between the two agencies for managing the 250,000-acre Whiskeytown-Shasta-Trinity National Recreation Area, which Congress established in 1965 around reclamation reservoirs in Northern California.

The détente between the two agencies has generally been maintained, although public land is still sometimes transferred from the Forest Service to the Park Service. The most recent example involved the Valles Caldera National Preserve in New Mexico. It was established in 2000 when Congress authorized the acquisition of a 90,000-acre privately owned parcel of land in a volcanic basin in north-central New Mexico west of Los Alamos. It was the legacy of a land grant that Congress had made in 1860 to compensate heirs of a Mexican-era land grant that had been wrongfully wrested from the grantee. At the insistence of Senator Pete Domenici, the preserve was made part of the national forest system, but managed primarily by a quasi-independent governmental corporation overseen by nine federally appointed trustees (including one each from the Forest Service and the Park Service). The trust's primary mission was to protect the area's natural and cultural resources while allowing public recreation, logging, and livestock grazing to the extent deemed compatible, under a frankly "experimental management regime" designed to promote "long term financial sustainability." The vision of self-financing proved unattainable, and in 2014, a few years after Domenici left the Senate, Congress put it in the national park system.[9]

REDWOOD NATIONAL PARK

The long struggle to establish Redwood National Park in Northern California, which finally succeeded in 1968, illustrated a number of challenges facing the national park system in the modern era. In contrast to its more vigorous efforts to preserve sequoia groves in California's Sierra Nevada, the United States had done little to limit the privatization of public lands containing old-growth redwood forests along the state's northern coast. The only exception was Theodore Roosevelt's use of the Antiquities Act in 1908 to protect a single grove of redwoods in the Muir Woods National Monument on donated land a few miles north of San Francisco. Some redwood stands had been preserved in California's state park system as early as 1902, supported by private philanthropy and state funds. In 1918, Congress authorized a feasibility study for a redwood national park. That same year, the private Save-the-Redwoods League was founded to coordinate fund-raising to acquire and protect more redwood forests. Over the years, the league's conservative leadership vacillated on whether to support a national park. Dependent on willing sellers, the league refrained from criticizing the industrial logging companies that were busily harvesting the remaining ancient redwood forests.[10]

After World War II, new technology facilitated the harvesting of the giant trees, and by 1960, only about 15 percent of the original 2 million acres of ancient forests remained, and only a small fraction of these had been protected in state parks. Alarmed that the remainder would be gone within two or three decades at the current rate of harvesting, the Sierra Club called on Congress to use federal funds to establish a national park. A few years later, the National Geographic Society joined the campaign to protect what it called the "Mount Everest of All Living Things," and President Johnson and the National Park Service endorsed the objective.

The legislation enjoyed bipartisan support, promoted by Republicans, including Senator Thomas Kuchel (Calif.) and Congressman Don Clausen (Calif.), and Democrats such as Senator Henry Jackson (Wash.). Signing it into law on the same day as he did the Wild and Scenic Rivers Act, the National Trails System Act, and legislation creating the North Cascades National Park in Washington, President Johnson said it "spared what is enduring and ennobling from the hungry and hasty and selfish act of destruction." The law authorized a park of 58,000 acres. About half was to be purchased from private owners; the remainder came from incorporating three state parks. Congress authorized $92 million for the acquisition, but the ultimate cost was several times higher.[11]

One of the features of the 1968 legislation illustrated a growing problem across the national park system—threats to park integrity originating from activities outside park boundaries. As the legislative campaign was gathering momentum in the mid-1960s, the tallest trees then known to exist on earth were discovered in an oxbow of Redwood Creek not far upstream from the proposed park. The park boundary was then redrawn to include a narrow finger of land called the "worm," which extended a few miles upstream to include this "tall trees grove," but to limit the cost of acquisition, ancient redwoods upslope and upstream were excluded. The private timber companies that owned these lands were left free to harvest these trees, even though it was known that the resulting erosion and debris could threaten the tall trees grove. (In late 1955, and again in late 1964, mud slides caused by heavy rains had toppled numerous ancient redwoods in Humboldt Redwoods State Park, located some forty miles to the south.)[12]

In a lame attempt to mitigate the problem, the Redwood National Park legislation authorized the Interior secretary to enter into what it called "cooperative agreements" with the logging companies that owned these lands. The companies were more interested in profit than cooperating, and so logging continued unabated for the next several years just outside the new park's boundaries. The festering problem led to lawsuits from environmental groups, and eventually, in 1978, park advocates led by Congressman Phillip Burton (D-Calif.) persuaded Congress to legislate a near doubling of the park's size. By that time, much of the land in the Redwood Creek watershed had been cleared of old-growth redwoods, making the 1978 expansion more about environmental mitigation and restoration than about protecting old-growth redwoods. All told, Redwood National Park wound up being the most expensive national park in U.S. history, by some measures more costly than all the other national parks combined. The expansion legislation did nudge the Interior Department to pay more attention to threats posed by activities outside park boundaries, directing that the "protection, management, and administration" of all units "be conducted in light of the high public value and integrity of the system."[13]

THE SIERRA CLUB, WALT DISNEY, AND MINERAL KING

The Sierra Club also played a major role in a controversy involving national park and national forest lands in the southern Sierra Nevada. The Forest Service administered most of the land in the scenic Mineral King Valley, which was accessible by a dirt road and surrounded on three sides by Sequoia National Park. In the late 1940s, the agency had proposed to develop a ski area complex there, but the idea remained dormant until the 1960s, when it was revived at the request of Walt Disney Productions.

The politics quickly got complicated. The Disney proposal called for constructing a new paved road to the area, nine miles of which would go through Sequoia National Park. Interior secretary Udall dragged his feet on approving the road, but California's governor, Ronald Reagan, pushed the project, and President Johnson agreed to support it if Reagan would support the creation of Redwood National Park. The Sierra Club's lawsuit to stop the Disney development eventually resulted in the Supreme Court's landmark 1972 decision giving recreational users of public lands standing to challenge agency decisions in federal court on the grounds they did not comply with the governing statutes. As the litigation dragged on, Disney eventually lost interest, and in 1978 Congress added Mineral King to Sequoia National Park and expressly prohibited "permanent facilities for downhill skiing" in it.[14]

DAMS IN PARKS REDUX

In the mid-1960s, yet another controversy like Hetch Hetchy or Echo Park erupted over dams involving the park system. Interior's Bureau of Reclamation zealously campaigned to build two dams in the Grand Canyon as part of its proposed Central Arizona Project. The dams' primary purpose was to generate the electricity needed to pump more than a million acre-feet of water up more than two thousand feet in elevation over a distance of more than three hundred miles, from a diversion point on the Colorado River downstream of the canyon to the burgeoning cities of Phoenix and Tucson. Surplus electricity would be sold to help underwrite the project's multibillion-dollar construction cost.

The 1919 statute establishing Grand Canyon National Park authorized the Interior secretary to use lands in the park for Bureau of Reclamation projects so long as they were "consistent with the primary purposes" of the park. Both of the proposed dams were outside the park boundary, although the reservoir created by the downstream dam would have backed up into the park. The Hualapai tribe, whose reservation included part of the downstream dam site, supported the dam because it would share in the power revenues the dam's turbines generated. Upstream, the Navajo Nation eventually came to oppose both dams.[15]

Initially, Interior secretary Stewart Udall and the Arizona congressional delegation, including Stewart's brother Morris, strongly supported the dams, as did Wayne Aspinall, chair of the House Interior Committee. Park protection advocates led by the Sierra Club mounted a national campaign in opposition. A high point came when—after the Bureau of Reclamation argued that more tourists could enjoy the canyon's grandeur from boats cruising the flatwater reservoirs that the dams would create—the club ran full-page advertisements in national publications with the tagline "Should we also flood the Sistine Chapel so the tourists can get nearer the ceiling?" Another ad quoted Theodore Roosevelt's famous admonition from 1903 to leave the canyon undisturbed. Such clever conservation advocacy helped galvanize nationwide opposition. Stewart Udall withdrew his support in the fall of 1966, and most other dam proponents capitulated a few months later, although Aspinall held out until the spring of 1968. The Central Arizona Project legislation, which LBJ signed into law late that summer, substituted a coal-fired plant as the source of electricity to power the project's pumps. It also, at Aspinall's insistence, authorized several water projects in the Colorado River's upper basin. President Johnson signed it into law two days before signing the Wild and Scenic Rivers Act.[16]

PACKAGING PROTECTIVE PUBLIC LAND LEGISLATION

In 1978, Congress departed from its traditional practice of adding units to the park system through stand-alone legislation. Congressman Burton, a master political strategist, decided instead to follow a long-standing congressional custom of assembling individual bills appealing to different constituencies into a single package. Critics called the National Parks and Recreation Act of 1978, which Burton engineered, a "park barrel" bill—a variant of "pork barrel," the term used to describe legislation funding local projects so that politicians can curry favor with constituents. Burton's handiwork, which enjoyed wide, bipartisan support, established fifteen new units of the park system, from the New River Gorge National River in West Virginia to the Santa Monica Mountains National Recreation Area in Southern California. It also made many additions to the national wilderness preservation and wild and scenic rivers systems.[17]

This success helped launch a modern trend of omnibus public land legislation, one that shows no signs of abating. Such bills usually involve several components and often more than one land management agency, all united by a common central theme of protecting more public lands. ANILCA, passed in 1980, was the quintessential example. In 1988, an omnibus public lands bill created a new national monument (Hagerman Fossil Beds) and national reserve (City of Rocks) in Idaho, and established the Mississippi National River and Recreation Area to coordinate management of the river and adjoining land through Minnesota's Twin Cities. The public lands in all of these units were put under Park Service administration, except the City of Rock National Reserve, which includes a considerable amount of state and private land and is now mostly managed by the Idaho Department of Parks and Recreation under a unique cooperative agreement.[18]

The California Desert Protection Act in 1994, steered through Congress by Senator Dianne Feinstein (D-Calif.), likewise had several components. It converted Death Valley and Joshua Tree from national monuments to national parks (making Death Valley the largest unit of the park system outside Alaska), upgraded protection of the Mojave National Scenic Area by making it a national preserve, and established several dozen wilderness areas on 7 million acres managed by the BLM, the Park Service, and the Fish & Wildlife Service. Although it had the strong support of the other senator from California, Barbara Boxer, and most of the state's congressional delegation, it was a rare example of public lands protection legislation being opposed by local Republican members of Congress and a good many Republican senators.[19]

BOLSTERING THE PARK SERVICE'S AUTHORITY
TO PROTECT PARK RESOURCES

Several modern pieces of legislation have enhanced the Park Service's authority to protect lands in the park system. In 1970, Congress gave the Park Service some direction about how it should resolve tensions between the general guidance in the National Park Organic Act, and specific management instructions in statutes establishing individual park units. Similar to the direction that Congress later gave the Fish & Wildlife Service, it emphasized that individual park-system units, "though distinct in character," were "united" as "cumulative expressions of a single national heritage." Thus, while unit-specific statutes would take priority in the event of outright collision, the system's "general authorities" should govern, to the extent they were "not in conflict with any such specific provision."[20]

In 1976, Congress directed the Park Service to prepare a "general management plan" for each unit of the system, with a primary focus on visitor accommodation. Just two years later, growing more mindful of the prospect that overwhelming numbers of visitors could "love parks to death," it significantly altered the planning mandate. Congressman Burton's "park barrel" bill directed that park plans identify and take into consideration "visitor carrying capacities" and also include "measures for the preservation of" park resources.[21]

Also in 1976, Congress enacted legislation to deal with the lingering problem of hard-rock mining in parks. A few areas had remained open to claim location under the Mining Law of 1872, even after being added to the national park system. Also, some newer units incorporated public lands that were encumbered with mining claims. After several news stories trained a spotlight on mining activities in Death Valley and near Mount McKinley in Alaska, Congress addressed the problem generically in the Mining in the Parks Act of 1976, which was really more of a "no mining in the parks act." It closed all units to the location of new mining claims and directed the Interior secretary to regulate all mining activities within park boundaries—even on inholdings already privatized under the Mining Law—to the extent that the secretary "deem[ed] necessary or desirable" for the "preservation and management" of park units.[22]

Another issue that Congress addressed during this era was overflights. This had been a problem with some public lands as far back as the late 1940s, when President Truman issued an executive order prohibiting flights below four thousand feet over what eventually became the Boundary Waters Wilderness in northern Minnesota. Truman's order, which was upheld by the courts, was apparently the first such ban in a conservation area anywhere. A couple of decades later, commercial tourist overflights were proliferating in the Grand Canyon, raising the ire of visitors on the ground. In the Grand Canyon National Park Enlargement Act of 1975, Congress authorized the Interior secretary to recommend appropriate measures to the Federal Aviation Administration to protect the "natural quiet" of the park experience, but Interior lacked sufficient clout to spur regulatory action by the FAA, which had always focused only on flight safety.[23]

In 1987, the bipartisan efforts of Arizona legislators Mo Udall and John McCain led to the National Parks Overflights Act. It gave the Park Service the authority to craft regulations to regulate tourist overflights, including the establishment of flight-free zones, in order to substantially restore the "natural quiet and experience of" the Grand Canyon. The act directed the FAA to implement the Park Service regulations unless doing so would "adversely affect aviation safety." It also called for studying the overflight problem at other park-system units as well as at national forest wilderness areas.[24]

Finally, in 2000, Congress enacted the National Parks Air Tour Management Act, which called on the FAA and the Park Service together to develop air-tour management plans for most national parks (as well as for Indian reservations subject to commercial air-tour operations). The objective was to prevent or mitigate "significant adverse impacts" on "natural and cultural resources, visitor experiences, and tribal lands." This legislation's ambitious goal has yet to be achieved.[25]

THE NATIONAL PARKS OMNIBUS MANAGEMENT ACT

The National Parks Omnibus Management Act of 1998 was the last of Congress's reforms of the "organic acts"—statutes providing a general framework for management—of the four public land agencies, following the NFMA (Forest Service) and FLPMA (Bureau of Land Management) in 1976 and the NWRS Improvement Act (Fish & Wildlife Service) in 1997.

The 1998 act for the first time directed the Park Service to make science an integral part of its decision making, and gave it an unequivocal mandate to promote scientific research. It implemented, at last, a major recommendation of the Robbins report from 1963, which had been repeated in *Science and the National Parks* (1992), a report generated by another National Academy of Sciences committee. The legislation was also influenced by a critical study of the agency's scientific failures by the historian Richard Sellars, published in 1997.[26]

Although the act called on the Park Service to provide "state-of-the-art management, protection, and interpretation" of the system's resources, it provided few substantive details about how to achieve these goals. It did, however, strengthen and sharpen planning provisions that Congress had adopted in 1976 and 1978. The net result gave the Park Service a planning mandate similar to those that Congress had given the three other major public land management agencies. Altogether, it equipped the Park Service with ample authority to grapple with growing numbers of visitors and modern challenges such as how accessible park-system lands should be made to wireless-networking technology and to new forms of transport such as e-bikes and skateboards. Having the authority does not, of course, mean its exercise will be free from controversy.

The act also made important reforms in the Park Service's concession-management program. Although the practice of contracting with private enterprise to provide services and accommodations for park visitors went all the way back to the Yosemite (1864) and Yellowstone (1872) authorizing acts, Congress did not adopt a comprehensive regulatory scheme for private concessions until the Concessions Policy Act of 1965. It contained protections for concessioners such as thirty-year contracts, a preference for renewal, and a right of compensation (called a "possessory interest") for improvements that a concessioner made, if its contract was not renewed. All these were designed to ensure what the act called "continuity of operation."[27]

Concessions became big business with the continuing growth in park visitation, with several hundred concession contracts in more than one hundred park-system units generating many hundreds of millions of dollars in annual revenues. Seeking to inject more competition into the program, the 1998 act made several reforms. It cut back on protections for larger concession operations, shortening the contract term to twenty years, repealing the renewal preference, and overhauling the right of compensation for what it relabeled the "leasehold surrender interest."

Park concessions gained notoriety in 2016 when it was revealed that an avaricious park concessioner, Delaware North, had quietly trademarked the names of some of Yosemite's most iconic attractions and accommodations during the years it held the park concession contract, and then demanded $51 million for its "intellectual property" when the concession contract expired in 2015 and a new concessioner took over. (Some of the trademarked names, such as "Ahwahnee" and "Wawona," derived from the area's indigenous Miwok Indians.) After years of litigation, the matter was settled in 2019 with the United States paying Delaware North nearly $4 million, and the trademarks going to the new concessioner and—to prevent the situation from recurring—back to the government upon expiration of the concession contract.[28]

None of these enhancements of the Park Service's regulatory authority engendered significant controversy in Congress. The esteem in which the American public holds the park system overcame grumbling from interests that were curbed by such legislative reforms, such as the FAA (which had resisted having its regulatory responsibility enlarged beyond air safety) and the air tour, mining, and concession-hospitality industries. Throughout the modern era, visitation to the park system has grown steadily, exceeding 300 million each year in the period 2015–19.[29]

CHAPTER FIFTY-NINE

Mineral and Energy Development
in the Modern Era

AS HE WAS LEAVING OFFICE IN January 1969, Interior secretary Udall called the repeal of the Mining Law of 1872 and replacing it with a leasing system the "most important piece of unfinished business on the Nation's natural resource agenda." The next year, the Public Land Law Review Commission agreed that the Mining Law needed to be reformed, but only four dissenters, including Congressman Mo Udall, endorsed a leasing system. The Nixon administration eventually came to agree with the dissenters and endorsed a leasing system.[1]

The Federal Land Policy and Management Act, which Congress enacted in the fall of 1976, did not go that far. It modified the Mining Law in important ways but retained its basic structure. Most important, it directed the Interior secretary to regulate activities on mining claims (along with all other activities on public lands) in order to prevent "unnecessary or undue degradation." It also confirmed that the Interior secretary had broad authority to withdraw public lands from the location of new mining claims, and for the first time required locators to record their claims with the BLM. A few hundred thousand claims were recorded by the deadline. (According to some estimates, as many as six million claims had been located on public lands since the first Mining Law was enacted in 1866.)[2]

Proponents of a leasing system were not assuaged, and in early 1977 they appeared to be on the verge of success. President Carter was strongly supportive, as was Scoop Jackson, chair of the Senate Energy and Natural Resources Committee. At that point, fervent defenders of the Mining Law initiated a recall campaign in Arizona against Mo Udall, who had just become chair of the House Interior and Insular Affairs Committee. This persuaded him to back away from the effort. In his inimitable fashion, he explained that he had "felt the heat, if not seen the light." His retreat took Mining Law reform off the congressional agenda for years.

In 1994, three years after Udall retired from Congress, reform nearly made it across the finish line. The House passed a comprehensive reform bill sponsored by Congressmen George Miller and Nick Joe Rahall (D-W.V.), and the Senate passed a much more modest bill. Negotiators came close to crafting a compromise, but time ran out before it could be completed.

One reform did emerge from the near miss in 1994. In May of that year, a court told Interior secretary Babbitt that the Mining Law required him to hand over ownership of public lands in Nevada estimated to contain gold worth $10 billion to a multinational mining company. The law required the company to pay the government a few thousand dollars. At a press conference, Babbitt, standing in front of a large facsimile of a check made out to the company from "the American taxpayer," called it the "biggest gold heist since the days of Butch Cassidy." Public reaction to the stunt persuaded Congress to begin—and to maintain ever since—the practice of including in the annual Interior Department funding bill a prohibition against processing applications to privatize ("patent") public land under the Mining Law.[3]

While mining claimants can no longer obtain complete title to public lands, they continue to extract minerals such as gold, silver, copper, lead, zinc, and molybdenum without paying anything to the landowner, the United States, a benefit not available anywhere else on earth. The favorite target remains gold, most of which becomes jewelry—showing how, just as bird populations were plundered for their plumage more than a century ago, fashion can still drive the demand for public resources.

Although at least 100 million acres of public land remain open to claim staking under the Mining Law, relatively few new big hard-rock mines have been opened in the past few decades. A major reason for this is that proposals to open new mines are almost certain to create controversy, mostly because of their impact on the environment. The concern is not hard to understand. Modern mining is usually conducted on a vast scale, in which hundreds of *tons* of material are moved for every *ounce* of metal extracted. Many mines produce what is called acid mine drainage, which can require treating water runoff in perpetuity. Public lands contain thousands of abandoned mine sites dating back to the nineteenth century. Acid mine drainage contaminates a sizable number of watersheds in the West, which will require billions of dollars to clean up or stabilize.

The industry made few attempts to exploit the compromise in the Wilderness Act of 1964 that kept wilderness areas in national forests open to claim staking through 1984. In his classic *Encounters with the Archdruid* in 1971, John McPhee recounted a debate between Charles Park, a mining engineer, and David Brower, the Sierra Club's president, over whether a hard-rock mineral deposit in the Glacier Peak Wilderness northeast of Seattle should be developed. It has remained unmined, even though the mining claims had already been privatized. (The land was later acquired by the government.) A lesson here is that in addition to sparking controversy, the development of mineral deposits in remote, rugged areas where infrastructure is lacking can be expensive.[4]

Since the 1970s, hard-rock mining on public lands has been regulated by federal land managers, and in some states, by state regulators as well. Disturbed lands must undergo some restoration, and a bond must be posted to cover the costs of reclamation in the event of bankruptcy. Still, regulatory failures are common, and many bonds have proved to be inadequate.

The mining industry continues to stoutly defend the Mining Law because it makes public minerals available for free and because its freewheeling aura has long made the government timid about firmly exercising its regulatory authority. As the industry's contribution to local and regional economies has diminished, and as the scale of its environmental disruption has increased, public support for the industry has declined. A proposed gold mine in a historic mining area upstream of Yellowstone National Park, for example, engendered enough opposition that the Clinton administration negotiated a $65 million buyout in 1996 to stop it. Through it all, repeal and replacement of the Mining Law of 1872 has remained out of reach in Congress.

A COAL BOOM AND BUST ON PUBLIC LANDS

The energy crisis precipitated by the Arab oil embargo of 1973 persuaded electric utilities across the nation to make coal rather than petroleum their preferred fuel. The Clean Air Act of 1970 discouraged the use of high-sulfur coal, so interest in tapping large low-sulfur coal deposits that the United States owned in the West, primarily in Wyoming, rose sharply. Many of these deposits were on lands where the national government did not own the surface, having conveyed it under the Stock-Raising Homestead Act of 1916 while reserving the minerals. The SRHA did not give the surface owner the right to veto mining, but it did require the miner to compensate the surface owner for damage caused by mining.[5]

As the coal industry moved westward, SRHA landowners, primarily ranchers, asked Congress for the power to veto mining on their lands. Their timing was good. For decades, the coal industry had gradually been shifting from underground mining to surface mining—by 1973, more than half the nation's coal was being produced that way. Although surface mining is more efficient and less dangerous, it is more disruptive to the environment, and state laws regulating the practice varied widely. So in the 1970s, Congress began seriously considering legislation to regulate the surface mining of coal throughout the United States, on private as well as public land.

To bolster support for the legislation, its sponsors agreed to give private surface owners a veto over the mining of U.S.-owned coal. Because surface owners could sell their consent, and because prospective miners could factor the cost of buying that consent into their bids to buy U.S.-owned reserved coal, this "surface owner consent" provision effectively transferred a portion of the value of the coal from the United States to the surface owner.

The deal facilitated the passage of what became the Surface Mining Control and Reclamation Act (SMCRA, or "smack-ra"). President Carter signed it into law in 1977; his predecessor, Gerald Ford, had vetoed similar bills in 1974 and 1975. SMCRA prohibited coal surface mining on many categories of public lands, including wildlife refuges and wilderness areas. It also allowed the Interior secretary to declare other public lands "unsuitable" for such mining. In 1976, Congress had enacted separate legislation overhauling the coal-leasing provisions of the Mineral Leasing Act of 1920, primarily to promote more competition in leasing, to better balance coal development against other uses of public lands, and to strengthen protection of the environment.[6]

As clearer ground rules were established, production of federally owned coal boomed, eventually accounting for nearly half of all the coal mined in the nation. It was concentrated along the rich coal seams of the Powder River Basin of Wyoming and Montana; at the height of the boom, nine of the ten largest coal mines in the nation were surface mines extracting federal coal in Campbell County, Wyoming.

In the early 1980s, even though the market was already sated, Interior secretary James Watt made an all-out effort to lease more federal coal. This created considerable controversy, leading Congress to establish a commission to investigate federal leasing policies. This indirectly led to Watt's resignation after he made intemperate remarks about the diversity of the commission's membership. The commission made numerous recommendations for reforming the leasing process, some of which the Interior Department adopted, but these actions did not end criticism of Interior's coal program.[7]

In the second decade of the twenty-first century, growing concern about carbon emissions and climate change caused electrical utilities to shift away from coal. This turned the public land coal boom into a bust. Bankruptcies and defaults on environmental-cleanup obligations followed. The Trump administration tried to revive coal development on public lands, but the disappearing domestic market for coal-fired electricity made the effort futile.

OIL SHALE AND SYNTHETIC FUELS

Immense deposits of oil shale on public lands in western Colorado, eastern Utah, and southern Wyoming gave rise to one of the most peculiar sagas in public land history. Hundreds of billions of barrels of petroleum are locked in these "rocks that burn." For more than a century, all efforts at commercial extraction failed, giving rise to the quip that "oil shale is the fuel of the future, and it always will be." Processing the low-grade resource requires huge amounts of energy and water and causes major environmental disruption.

Oil shale was governed by the Mining Law of 1872 until Congress made it leasable in the Mineral Leasing Act of 1920. The leasing act preserved "valid claims" for oil shale that had previously been located on public lands. In hindsight, it can fairly be said that none of these many thousands of oil shale mining claims were valid. They could not meet the legal test for validity—which was to show that the claimed deposit could be mined at a profit. Litigating the validity of these claims created much demand for lawyers, along with work for federal courts that stretched over nearly a century.

The oil shale claimants' argument for validity was bolstered by Interior secretary Hubert Work's naive decision in 1927 that found—despite the lack of commercial viability—"no possible doubt" of oil shale's value as an "enormously valuable resource for future use by the American people." Work's ruling led the Interior Department to privatize several hundred thousand acres of public land, but resulted in no production of oil shale. In the 1960s, Interior secretary Udall instituted challenges to the validity of the remaining oil shale claims. This move led to inconclusive Supreme Court decisions in 1970 and 1980, a controversial Interior Department decision in the 1980s that privatized several more thousands of acres, and litigation that continued well into the twenty-first century.[8]

Secretary Udall offered to lease unclaimed tracts of public land believed to contain oil shale. He got no industry takers. The Interior Department did issue some leases for oil shale during the energy crisis of the early 1970s, but still no commercial production resulted. In the late 1970s, President Jimmy Carter proposed a program to massively subsidize the development of oil shale and other so-called synthetic fuels, such as natural gas derived from coal. Congress included the program in the Energy Security Act of 1980, and the United States put almost $1 billion into several projects, including one to develop an oil shale deposit in western Colorado. Declining oil prices led to the program's abandonment in 1986.

Despite this forlorn history, Congress remained stubbornly enamored of the possibility that oil shale might be commercially developed. In the Energy Policy Act of 2005, it once again called for a program to lease public lands thought to contain oil shale. As before, nothing tangible resulted. More recently, several things—growing concern about carbon emissions and other environmental impacts, the upending of energy markets by conservation efforts, the rapid emergence of renewable energy sources such as solar and wind, and the development of techniques to extract conventional petroleum more cheaply— have combined to end practically all serious interest in oil shale on public lands, perhaps this time forever.

DEVELOPMENTS INVOLVING PUBLIC LANDS
SUBMERGED OFFSHORE

The extraction of petroleum on the outer continental shelf (OCS) grew steadily in the 1960s and 1970s, aided by improvements in technology. The Santa Barbara oil spill in 1969 eventually led Congress to overhaul the OCS leasing statute in 1978, to strengthen environmental regulation, and to install a more orderly, consultative, and competitive leasing and development process. The reform also extended the leasing system to all minerals—including hard-rock minerals that, onshore, are subject to the Mining Law of 1872. Interest in harvesting metal nodules in the marine seabed has steadily grown, but the Interior Department has not yet issued any leases for this purpose.

In 1983, as developing technology was making petroleum deposits in deeper waters more accessible, President Reagan proclaimed U.S. "sovereign rights and jurisdiction" over an exclusive economic zone that extended two hundred nautical miles offshore. In the years since then, petroleum development has remained the primary use of submerged lands offshore. These lands now account for about a fifth of domestic oil production and a smaller share of gas production.[9]

James Watt sought to vastly expand the OCS leasing program during his tenure as Reagan's first Interior secretary. Although the amount of leased acreage offshore nearly doubled in the 1980s, his efforts triggered a considerable political backlash. Most coastal states persuaded Congress and a succession of presidents from both political parties to rule out petroleum leasing off all or most of their coastlines. After Watt's Interior Department issued oil and gas leases off North Carolina in 1981, Congress enacted a law, the Outer Banks Protection Act, putting obstacles in the path of their development. (Eventually, in 2000, the lessee oil companies persuaded the Supreme Court that Congress's action entitled them to recover the $156 million they had paid for the leases.) Concerns that petroleum extraction might harm the productive Georges Bank fishery off Massachusetts halted leasing efforts there—ironically, the fishing industry then so overexploited the fishery that it collapsed in the early 1990s.[10]

Coastal states also sometimes sought help from the courts. California sued to block U.S. leasing off its shores, arguing that the Coastal Zone Management Act of 1972 required Interior's offshore leasing program to be consistent with the state's stringent regulation of land uses in the coastal zone. When the Supreme Court ruled against California in 1984, the state turned to Congress. It eventually got most of what it was seeking in CZMA amendments that Congress adopted in 1990.[11]

The bottom line is that primarily because of the efforts of most coastal states, petroleum development on the OCS is limited almost entirely to the central Gulf of Mexico. In 1995, to promote development in deeper waters, the industry persuaded Congress to slash the royalties that deepwater lessees had to pay the U.S. Treasury. Then, in 2006, Alabama, Louisiana, Mississippi, and Texas persuaded Congress for the first time to give them a share of the revenue that the United States derived from petroleum production on the OCS, as long as they used it for coastal conservation, restoration, and hurricane protection.[12]

After the Santa Barbara event in 1969, the offshore industry avoided major spills until 2010, when British Petroleum's Deepwater Horizon rig exploded. It killed eleven workers and poured more than 200 million gallons of petroleum into the Gulf of Mexico—several dozen times the amount spilled off Santa Barbara. Not only was it the largest marine oil spill in world history, but a study in 2020 concluded that it spread considerably farther and was more damaging to the marine environment than originally believed. The disaster led to numerous administrative reforms and tougher regulations, but the industry-friendly Trump administration reversed many of these once it took office.[13]

DEVELOPMENTS IN ONSHORE OIL AND GAS

When the energy crisis of the 1970s boosted interest in developing onshore oil and gas, it exposed deficiencies in the Interior Department's leasing program. A primary one stemmed from a decision by Congress decades earlier to require the Interior Department to hand out oil and gas leases to the "person first making application," except in the very narrow circumstance of a "known geological structure of a producing oil or gas field," where leases could be put to auction. In areas not qualifying for auction where speculative interest was high, thousands of applications would pour into the department on the date that a tract was made available for leasing.

The department's solution to the problem was to adopt a lottery, randomly selecting the applicant to receive the lease. A federal appeals court upheld this approach in 1963, wryly noting that the episode "furnishes compelling proof, familiar to the membership of Congress, that the human animal has not changed, that when you determine to give something away, you are going to draw a crowd." Despite mounting criticism, Congress resisted repeated efforts during the 1960s and 1970s to change the law to offer tracts competitively and thereby to produce more revenue for the treasury. James Watt added to the controversy by opening up much more public land to leasing in the early 1980s. So eager was he that he became the first Interior secretary to try to lease lands in the national wilderness preservation system, until a bipartisan coalition in Congress stopped him.[14]

Continuing concerns about the leasing system's failure to promote competition and protect the environment finally led the Republican-controlled Senate to pass an onshore-oil-and-gas leasing reform bill in 1986, and the next year it was included in a giant package of bills that President Reagan signed into law. The 1987 legislation not only required competitive auctions, but also directed the government to "regulate all surface-disturbing activities" on oil and gas leases in order to conserve "surface resources," and to require "complete and timely reclamation" and "restoration of any lands or surface waters adversely affected by lease operations." It also gave the Forest Service a veto over oil and gas leasing on national forests; previously, it could only recommend that the Interior secretary not issue leases.[15]

The Interior Department's intermittent zeal to issue petroleum leases on scenic undeveloped public lands has sometimes triggered enough opposition to persuade Congress or the executive branch to reverse course, and buy back leases in order to foreclose development. In recent years, this has happened on several national forests, including the Badger–Two Medicine area near the Blackfoot Reservation and Glacier National Park in northern Montana, in the Wyoming Range in Wyoming, and in the so-called Thompson Divide in west-central Colorado.[16]

Since 2000, the petroleum industry has greatly improved its ability to drill horizontally and reach many more petroleum deposits from a single well. At the same time, the industry has improved techniques for hydraulic fracturing, or "fracking," which involves injecting water and chemicals along with sand or other "proppants" at high pressure into a well bore to fracture rock and create pathways that facilitate extraction of petroleum. These technological improvements, along with the "Halliburton loophole"—a part of the Energy Policy Act of 2005 that exempts fracking fluids from regulation under the Safe Drinking Water Act—has led to a boom in fracking. Most of it occurs on private land, but some is found on public lands. Some of it exploits mineral rights that the United States did not acquire when it bought land for national forests, wildlife refuges, and even some units of the national park system.[17]

HYDROPOWER ON PUBLIC LANDS IN THE MODERN ERA

Almost no new hydropower projects have been approved on public lands in the past half century. This is primarily because of strong public support for preserving free-flowing rivers and wild places. Instead, in recent years the focus has been on removing existing dams to restore iconic anadromous (migrating from the sea to rivers) fish species such as salmon, along with riverine environments. As Interior secretary Bruce Babbitt, an early leader of the dam removal movement, put it: "My parents' generation gloried in the construction of dams across America's rivers. My generation saw how those rivers were changed, deformed, killed by dams. [The next] generation must help decide if, how and where those dams stand or fall."[18]

Public lands and the hydropower-licensing scheme created by the Federal Power Act of 1920 have been in the forefront of many dam removal efforts. Licenses issued under that act come up for renewal every few decades in a process now conducted by the Federal Energy Regulatory Commission, the successor to the Federal Power Commission. The act has always given the Interior and Agriculture Departments the authority to put conditions in project licenses to limit the damage that hydropower projects can cause to public and Indian lands. In a significant decision in 1984, the Supreme Court breathed new life into this authority, emphasizing the act's "plain command" that licenses contain such conditions as the secretary deems necessary to provide adequate protection for the affected lands. That authority gives public land agencies (as well as affected Indian tribes) substantial leverage over relicensing decisions, and has sometimes led to negotiated settlements with licensees that create pathways for dams to be removed.[19]

RENEWABLE ENERGY RESOURCE DEVELOPMENT
ONSHORE AND OFFSHORE

In the Energy Policy Act of 2005, Congress called on the Interior secretary to approve, within a decade, renewable-energy projects on onshore public lands to generate at least ten thousand megawatts of electricity, enough to power several million homes. The Interior Department crafted a program in the Obama administration to meet this goal, using the Federal Land Policy and Management Act's permit authority. It allows the use of BLM-managed public lands for such purposes, obligates project developers to pay fair-market value (which can be calculated on the basis of energy output), and requires permits to be conditioned to "minimize damage to scenic and aesthetic values and fish and wildlife habitat and otherwise protect the environment." As a result, dozens of solar and wind projects now operate on public lands.[20]

That same legislation gave the Interior secretary broad authority to permit the outer continental shelf to be used for energy projects from sources such as wind, in ways that promote competition and "ensure" both a fair return to the United States and "protection of the environment." The Interior Department has been moving forward with a program to lease tracts on the OCS for wind-power generation. While construction and operating costs are somewhat higher offshore compared to onshore, offshore wind resources are more dependable and, properly located, have fewer conflicts with other uses.[21]

MINING AND ENERGY DEVELOPMENT
ON PUBLIC LAND: A SUMMARY

In recent years, public lands have been responsible for about a quarter of total U.S. oil production (down from 36 percent in 2009) and about 13 percent of total U.S. natural gas production (down from 25 percent in 2008). Most of the oil production is from the OCS; most of the gas production is from onshore public lands. The share from public lands has declined as total domestic oil production increased substantially beginning in 2013.

Although energy development on public lands attracts considerable public attention, only a few tens of millions of acres, nearly all managed by the BLM, are directly affected by these intensive industrial uses. As of 2020, of the nearly 250 million acres that the BLM manages, a little more than 10 percent were leased to oil and gas companies, and about half of the leased acreage was actually producing oil and gas. Coal leases cover less than a million acres, concentrated in Wyoming. A similarly small proportion of public lands is occupied by hard-rock mines and by renewable-resource developments. In sum, measured by acreage, mining and energy development altogether make use of a relatively small amount of the nation's public lands.[22]

CHAPTER SIXTY

Public Lands and Native Americans in the Modern Era

BEGINNING IN THE 1960S, Indian tribes across the nation stepped up efforts to reclaim their sovereignty and revitalize their cultures. As part of this renaissance, some tribes sought to regain title to, or at least control or influence over, those of their ancestral lands that remained in public ownership.[1]

From William Howard Taft's reversal in 1912 of Theodore Roosevelt's attempt to transfer some Indian reservation lands to the national forest system, until the 1960s, Indians rarely intersected with public land policy. In the 1920s, the U.S. government's Indian policy began to move away from promoting the breakup of communally held landholdings and assimilation, and toward redressing past wrongs and revitalizing tribal sovereignty, albeit under the paternal supervision of the Bureau of Indian Affairs. One signal of this shift occurred in 1928 when Congress authorized the California attorney general to sue the United States on behalf of California Indians in the U.S. Court of Claims seeking compensation—but not the land itself—for the wrongful taking of their land dating back to the gold rush. Numerous special laws like this one authorizing lawsuits seeking relief on behalf of tribes for past wrongful governmental actions against them were enacted before 1946. Only a fraction of the two hundred or so claims filed under them resulted in compensation.[2]

In the New Deal era, the Interior Department under Harold Ickes (who, like his solicitor Nathan Margold, was an early champion of protecting Indian rights) laid important groundwork for reviving Indian claims to lost homelands. At their urging, the United States sued the Santa Fe Pacific Railroad to dispute its claim that its 1866 land grant entitled it to nearly half of the million-acre reservation that President Arthur had established for the Hualapai tribe by executive order in 1883. The U.S. ultimately prevailed in the Supreme Court in 1942. The opinion for the unanimous court was written by Justice William O. Douglas (who was not only an avid recreational user but also an advocate for protecting public lands). Douglas's opinion revived and reaffirmed principles of Indian law that had been established more than a century earlier in Supreme Court decisions written by the legendary Chief Justice John Marshall, but that had fallen into desuetude. It concluded that the Hualapai's title had not been extinguished by the terms of the 1866 grant or by subsequent efforts to remove the Hualapai from the area. The principles applied in the decision breathed new life into tribal claims of redress for land dispossessions.[3]

In 1946, Congress abandoned its approach of dealing with Indian claims of wrongdoing piecemeal and sent President Truman legislation that established the Indian Claims Commission. Its core function was to adjudicate claims that the United States had not engaged in "fair and honorable dealings" with Indians in the past, and to award compensation when the evidence showed that to be the case. In signing it into law, Truman noted that the United States had "pledged respect for all Indian property rights" beginning with the Northwest Ordinance of 1787 and had purchased vast amounts of land "from the tribes that once owned this continent," paying them hundreds of millions of dollars. It would, he noted, "be a miracle if in the course of these dealings—the largest real estate transaction in history—we had not made some mistakes and occasionally failed to live up to the precise terms of our treaties and agreements" with tribes. The commission, Truman said, provided a means for correcting "any mistakes we have made."[4]

While the Indian Claims Commission Act generally waived all statute of limitations and similar defenses for wrongs accruing before it took effect in 1946, it did not allow Indians to recover ownership of lands wrongfully taken from them, even if the United States still owned them. It also limited monetary compensation for such losses, because the commission was not authorized to award interest on amounts that the United States owed, and monetary damages could be offset by money and property that the national government had "gratu-itously" given to Indian claimants over the years. Despite these limitations, the Indian Claims Commission process sometimes proved helpful for tribes hoping to make a case to Congress for regaining ownership or control of public lands to which they had ancestral claims.

A few times during this period, Congress approved negotiated arrange-ments with tribes that implicated public lands. In 1931, Congress and the Navajo Nation agreed to establish the Canyon de Chelly National Monument on more than 80,000 acres of land on the Navajo reservation. The tribe retained its rights in the land and influence over its management by the National Park Service. Legislation establishing Everglades National Park in South Florida in 1934 preserved "existing rights of the Seminole Indians" without defining them, but only when they were "not in conflict with the purposes" of the park. In Minnesota in 1958, Congress established the Grand Portage National Monument on 700 acres of land, half of which was donated to the United States by the Minnesota Chippewa Tribe and the Grand Portage Band of Chippewa Indians. The Indians retained the right to regain ownership of the lands as well as preferences regarding visitor services and other rights of use.[5]

In the modern era, the first successful tribal effort to regain lost control over ancestral lands came in 1970 when, after a long struggle, the Taos Pueblo, with the support of the Nixon administration, persuaded Congress to restore its title to the 48,000-acre Blue Lake area in northern New Mexico. Blue Lake, long considered sacred by the pueblo, had been included in a forest reserve in 1905 by Theodore Roosevelt. A key event in the pueblo's campaign was its winning a judgment from the Indian Claims Commission that the area had been wrong-fully taken. The congressional restoration included the limitation that the area be used "for traditional purposes only," and be subject to "such regulations for conservation purposes" as the Interior secretary deemed appropriate.[6]

Not long afterward, another long-standing dispute involving a tribe and a national forest was settled, without congressional intervention. The Indian Claims Commission ruled in 1966 that 21,000 acres intended for the Yakama tribe of Washington in a treaty with the United States from 1855 had later been mistakenly included in a forest reserve. Acting on the advice of the attorney general that he could, in these "exceptional and unique circumstances," restore the land to the tribe without the need for Congress to act, President Nixon did so by executive order in May 1972.[7]

That same year, Congress brought nearly a century of struggle to a close by correcting a survey error from 1871 that had failed to accurately depict the northern boundary of the Warm Springs Indian Reservation in Oregon. The reservation was established in a treaty with the United States in 1855 in return for the Indians ceding their title to a much larger area. The survey error wrong-fully excluded some 78,000 acres from the reservation. Most of the land was later put in national forests, although some became privately owned. The legislation in 1972 excised the land from the national forests, and although it did not alter the private ownership of the remaining lands, it put them inside the reservation as well. The journey to the correction was marked by several acts of Congress and decisions by the Indian Claims Commission and the courts.[8]

THE HAVASUPAI TRIBE SCORES A VICTORY
AT THE GRAND CANYON

Beginning in the late 1960s, the Havasupai tribe, which for millennia had inhabited lands in the watershed of Havasu Creek, a tributary of the Colorado River in the Grand Canyon, fought proposals to enlarge Grand Canyon National Park. Eventually, the tribe won a substantial victory.

The tribe's relationship with the U.S. government regarding land rights had a tangled history. In 1866, a transcontinental railroad land grant infringed on the tribe's homeland. Not long afterward, a mineral rush brought numerous non-Indians to the area. In 1880, President Hayes established a reservation for the tribe consisting of nearly 40,000 acres along Havasu Creek. Two years later, President Arthur downsized the reservation by almost 99 percent, to 518 acres. President Harrison's Grand Canyon Forest Reserve (1893) included public lands that surrounded the small reservation, as did Theodore Roosevelt's Grand Canyon National Monument (1908). The Forest Service eventually agreed to give tribal members free permits to graze livestock in the forest reserve. The legislation establishing Grand Canyon National Park gave the Interior Department the discretion to permit Havasupai tribal members to use and occupy tracts of land in the park "for agricultural purposes."[9]

Some tribal members lived inside the park in two places, one around Indian Gardens along Bright Angel Trail, and the other above the canyon's south rim. The Park Service gradually pushed them out of both, but the tribe continued to run cattle and horses on national park, national monument, and national forest lands under permit. In 1930, a prospector exploited the Mining Law of 1872 to gain ownership of a tract of land in the national forest close to scenic waterfalls along Havasu Creek. Later, the Park Service bought him out and built a campground for visitors to the falls.

In the late 1960s, the Park Service, supported by the Sierra Club, began urging Congress to expand the boundaries of the national park to take in national forest and national monument lands that the tribe had been using. The tribe countered by proposing to enlarge its reservation by transferring some land from the park and forest, thus triggering an unusually direct, and rare, collision between an Indian tribe and public land protection advocates. Over time, the tribe's proposal gained the support of key members of the Arizona congressional delegation (Senator Barry Goldwater and House members Morris Udall and Sam Steiger) as well as President Richard Nixon.

The tribe won a substantial victory when, in January 1975, President Gerald Ford signed the Grand Canyon National Park Enlargement Act into law. Besides adding 400,000 acres to the park, the legislation moved 185,000 acres from the national forest and the national park to the Havasupai reservation. It provided that the lands added to the tribe's reservation were to be kept "forever wild" for the most part, off-limits to mining and other commercial and industrial development. It also designated 93,500 acres of national park land as a "traditional use area" to be under joint control of the tribe and the Park Service, open only to livestock grazing and other "traditional purposes," and subject to regulation by the Interior secretary to protect its "scenic, natural, and wildlife values."[10]

Not long after this, a couple of hundred miles to the east and south, the Pueblo of Zuni's success before the Indian Claims Commission led Congress to enact two laws restoring lands of great cultural significance to it, in 1978 (Zuni Salt Lake, 618 acres) and in 1984 (Zuni Heaven, 8,960 acres).[11]

A POTPOURRI OF MODERN EFFORTS TO ACCOMMODATE INDIAN INTERESTS IN PUBLIC LANDS

Encouraged by these successes, more tribes began to seek title to, or more influence over, public lands from which they had been dispossessed. This in turn led to numerous efforts by both Congress and the executive to accommodate Indian interests in how public lands are managed.

Sometimes Congress's response was generic, adding protections for cultural resources on all public lands. In the 1970s, for example, a federal court of appeals ruled that the prohibition in the Antiquities Act against disturbing any "object of antiquity" on public lands was unconstitutionally vague and thus unenforceable. Congress responded in 1979 by enacting the Archaeological Resources Protection Act. It not only provided much more specific guidance, but also expanded and added more teeth to its protections.[12]

Another congressional action of general application came in 1990 with enactment of the Native American Graves Protection and Repatriation Act. The law added several new legal protections for cultural items, broadly defined, found on lands owned or controlled by the United States.[13]

In 1992, Congress significantly expanded the National Historic Preservation Act (NHPA) by extending its protections to tribal cultural properties. First enacted in 1966, the NHPA illustrated the growing public support for preserving traces of the past. It instructed all federal agencies, including those managing public lands, to "take into account" how their actions would affect historic properties that were listed, or eligible for listing, on the National Register of Historic Places, which Congress had established in the Historic Sites Act (1935).[14]

Congress's expansion of the NHPA in 1992 made "properties" of "traditional religious and cultural importance" to Indian tribes eligible for inclusion on the National Register. ("Properties" could include "districts, sites, buildings, structures, and objects.") This action significantly enlarged the potential for tribes to influence public land management actions that might affect such "properties." While the NHPA does not mandate absolute protection, only that consideration be given to protecting such "properties," it has sometimes, with help from the federal courts, resulted in curtailing activities that threatened "properties" found on public lands.[15]

The Clinton administration built on all these developments to deepen the relationship between public land management agencies and tribes. In May 1996, President Clinton issued an executive order instructing all public land management agencies to "avoid adversely affecting the physical integrity of" Indian sacred sites on the lands they managed, and to "accommodate access to and ceremonial use of" such sites by Indian religious practitioners. While the obligation is not absolute—applying only "to the extent practicable, permitted by law, and not clearly inconsistent with agency functions"—it effectively invited tribes and public land management agencies to engage with one another, and helped spur the agencies to reexamine their management practices. Not long after that, Interior secretary Babbitt and Commerce secretary Daley signed an order that had been negotiated with tribal interests and designed to ensure that implementation of the Endangered Species Act maintained appropriate respect for tribal sovereignty.[16]

A further step along this line came in late 2016, when Interior secretary Sally Jewell issued an order captioned "Identifying Opportunities for Cooperative and Collaborative Partnerships with Federally Recognized Indian Tribes in Management of Federal Lands and Resources." It called on Interior agencies to consider such partnerships because tribes have "special geographical, historical, and cultural connections" with some public lands. The order noted that details of such "arrangements" could "vary widely depending on the circumstances." The order cautioned agencies to be "mindful of legal limits" on their power to delegate "inherently Federal functions" to other entities.[17]

Besides such actions of general applicability, Congress more and more often began to address concerns of tribes when it was enacting legislation that added protections to specific areas of public lands. When Congress established the Mono Basin National Forest Scenic Area along California's eastern Sierras in 1984, for example, it directed the Forest Service, in recognition of Indian peoples' past use of the area, to "insure" their "nonexclusive access" for "traditional cultural and religious purposes." Legislation in 1987 establishing the El Malpais National Monument (more than 100,000 acres, managed by the Park Service) and the El Malpais National Conservation Area (approximately 263,000 acres, including two areas in the national wilderness preservation system, managed by the BLM) in western New Mexico safeguarded Indian access for "traditional cultural and religious purposes." It also authorized temporary closures to protect the privacy of Indians' religious activities, and called for the creation of a tribal advisory committee.[18]

In 1988, Congress enacted legislation transferring nearly 12,000 acres of national forest land on the Olympic Peninsula to the Quinault tribe to correct a surveying error, and put another 5,460 acres that remained in the national forest under special management that afforded the tribe specific rights.[19]

That same year, the U.S. Supreme Court appeared to hand the budding movement to bolster tribal rights a significant setback in a case involving a national forest in California. It ruled, 6–3, that the "free exercise of religion" clause in the First Amendment did not constrain the Forest Service's authority to build a road and harvest timber in an area traditionally used by three nearby tribes for religious purposes. Although the majority opinion, written by Sandra Day O'Connor, concluded that the Constitution did not require that public lands be managed to accommodate Indian religious practices, it acknowledged that public land managers had considerable discretion to do so. The California tribes then worked with wilderness advocates on a political remedy and achieved success in 1990 when Congress included the national forest lands in the national wilderness preservation system, protecting them from road construction and logging.[20]

The Clinton administration negotiated several cooperative arrangements involving tribes and public lands, sometimes with the help of Congress. In converting Death Valley from a national monument to a national park in 1994, for example, Congress directed the Interior secretary to consider establishing a reservation for a band of Timbisha Shoshone Indians who had occupied lands in the valley since time immemorial, mostly seasonally. The United States had not formally acknowledged the Indian presence when President Hoover

established Death Valley National Monument in 1933. During FDR's adminis-
tration, the Civilian Conservation Corps constructed adobe houses for the
Indians on a forty-acre plot near Furnace Creek. In the 1980s, the Timbisha
Band gained official recognition from the Interior Department. In 2000, after
years of negotiation, Congress approved a detailed agreement that gave the
band 300 acres of land at Furnace Creek and designated another 3,000 acres a
"Natural and Cultural Preservation Area" to be managed jointly with the Park
Service.[21]

That same year, Congress established the 271,000-acre Santa Rosa and San
Jacinto Mountains National Monument near Palm Springs, California. It is
jointly managed by the BLM and the Forest Service. The product of the
combined efforts of Congresswoman Mary Bono (R-Calif.) and the Clinton
administration, the legislation acknowledged the area's "special cultural value"
to the Agua Caliente Band of Cahuilla Indians, and included specific provisions
regarding consultation and cooperation with the band, including land
exchanges. The Steens Mountain Cooperative Management and Protection
Act, also enacted in 2000, directed the Interior secretary to "conserve, protect
and to ensure traditional access" by the Burns Paiute Tribe to "cultural, gathering, religious, and archaeological sites" on an area of public lands it protected
in Oregon.[22]

Actions of this kind were not confined to tribes in the West. In 1998,
Congress approved legislation making permanent the Miccosukee Tribe's
occupancy of more than 300 acres in the northern edge of Everglades National
Park. The tribe had occupied the land under permit from the Park Service since
1964. The legislation found that the "amount and location of land allocated to
the Tribe" in this Miccosukee Reserved Area "fulfills the purposes of the
park."[23]

The trend continued in the George W. Bush administration with enactment of the T'uf Shur Bien Preservation Trust Area Act in 2003. It ratified an
agreement between the Sandia Pueblo and the Forest Service that settled the
pueblo's long-standing claim to several thousand acres of land near the crest of
the Sandia Mountains above Albuquerque, New Mexico. The agreement came
in the wake of a ruling by the Interior Department solicitor in early 2001
confirming that pueblo land had been included in a forest reserve early in the
twentieth century as a result of a surveying error. Over the intervening years,
some of the land had been privatized and subdivided into a luxury home development. The legislation did not disturb the private land, and allowed the United
States to retain title to the national forest lands, but it gave the pueblo veto

power over any new uses that the Forest Service might propose, and a permanent right of access for "traditional or cultural uses."[24]

Several other laws enacted during the George W. Bush administration included accommodations of Indian interests while adding protections to areas of public lands. Three in Nevada protected Indian "spiritual, cultural, and traditional food-gathering activities," and one of these also authorized the transfer of 3,500 acres of public land to the Ely Shoshone Tribe. The Ojito Wilderness Act of 2005, besides putting more than 11,000 acres of BLM land in New Mexico in the national wilderness preservation system, authorized the sale of several thousand acres of public land to the Zia Pueblo so that it could consolidate its landholdings and protect religious and cultural sites.[25]

The Obama administration attracted national attention in 2016 when the president established the Bears Ears National Monument on well over a million acres of public land managed by the BLM in southern Utah. Obama's action was heavily influenced by a petition to establish a large monument in the area submitted by several tribes in the region with ancestral ties to these lands, which contain a large number of cultural sites. The head of one of the tribes described how, in assembling the petition, the tribes "focused on the light, not the darkness" of how their ancestors had been dispossessed of these lands. Obama's proclamation broke new ground by creating a tribal commission that would have special influence on the BLM's management of the area. It was by far the largest protected area of public lands where Native Americans were given a meaningful role in its administration. (Obama's establishment the same day of the 300,000-acre Gold Butte National Monument in southern Nevada was also strongly supported by area tribes.) The next year, President Trump issued a new proclamation downsizing the monument by 85 percent; his action was immediately challenged in court.[26]

At the end of 2020, Congress approved legislation sponsored by Montana's senators, Jon Tester (D) and Steve Daines (R), that gives the Confederated Salish and Kootenai Tribes (CSKT) control of the National Bison Range adjacent to their reservation. The United States established the range in 1908 on land it obtained from the CSKT, and it was being managed by the Fish & Wildlife Service. The legislation, which was part of a broader settlement of tribal claims involving water rights, came after many decades of effort by the CSKT, including a victory in the Court of Claims (the successor to the Indian Claims Commission) in 1971. (Regarding bison and public lands, Indian tribes have generally supported the coordinated efforts of the Interior Department's land management agencies to restore bison herds to some of the lands they manage.)[27]

Not all tribal efforts to regain some control over ancestral lands have succeeded. The most notable failure has involved the Black Hills in South Dakota. In 1980, the U.S. Supreme Court affirmed a lower-court judgment that the Sioux Nation was never adequately compensated when Congress coerced it to cede the Black Hills to the United States in 1877, the year after the Battle of the Little Bighorn. Much of the area was made a forest reserve by President Cleveland in 1897. Although the Court's decision confirmed that the Sioux were owed more than $100 million in compensation for the loss, the Indians refused the money and instead pursued legislation to have the land restored. A bill to do that has never advanced very far in Congress; meanwhile, the monetary judgment has grown to more than $1 billion. A somewhat similar situation exists in Nevada. In 2004, Congress authorized federal funds to be distributed to Western Shoshone tribal members to satisfy a decades-old Indian Claims Commission judgment compensating them for loss of their ancestral lands. Some tribal members refused to accept the money, but their effort to persuade Congress to give them title to the public lands instead has made no headway.[28]

COOPERATIVE RESTORATION—WORKS IN PROGRESS

The modern era has produced several examples of tribes working cooperatively with public land management agencies on measures of cultural importance to tribes. Perhaps the biggest success has involved the removal of two dams on the Elwha River on the northern side of Washington's Olympic Peninsula. The dams decimated large salmon runs that the Lower Elwha Klallam Tribe had relied on for millennia. Built in 1913 and 1927, these dams were downstream of what was then the Olympic National Monument. (In 1940, Congress converted the monument to a national park, and enlarged it two years later, bringing the upstream dam within its boundaries.) Decades later, the dams' private owner sought renewal of its operating license by the Federal Energy Regulatory Commission (the successor to the Federal Power Commission). The tribe and conservationists intervened and objected. Negotiations eventually led to a landmark agreement, approved by Congress in 1992, that called for the United States to purchase and remove the dams. Implementation was delayed for years while plans were prepared for managing the 10 million tons of sediment that the dams had captured and held. The dams were finally removed in 2011 and 2014. Salmon runs have returned, and river restoration continues; to date, the total project cost exceeds $300 million.[29]

Inspired by the Elwha agreement, the Klamath, Hoopa, Yurok, and Karuk tribes in Northern California and southern Oregon have helped craft what would be the largest dam removal project in the nation, involving four large structures on the Klamath River. The objective is to rebuild what were once the largest salmon runs between San Francisco Bay and the Columbia River while maintaining a national wildlife refuge that is an important stop on the Pacific flyway and sustains a large raptor population. The complex negotiations have taken several twists and turns. In 2010, the FERC licensee, the States of Oregon and California, and several federal agencies reached an agreement on a plan to remove the dams. It required congressional approval, and when Congress balked—after hearing objections from reclamation project irrigators that the deal did not adequately protect their interests, and from salmon advocates that the deal gave the irrigators too much water and the fish not enough—the parties rewrote the deal to avoid the need to obtain a congressional sign-off. Further proceedings are pending before FERC, with a goal of removing the dams sometime in the next decade, at a cost exceeding $400 million.[30]

Another complicated arrangement, nearly completed, would protect the Badger–Two Medicine area on national forest land adjacent to Glacier National Park and the Blackfeet Nation's reservation in northern Montana. The tribe ceded the land to the United States in 1895 but retained limited rights to hunt, fish, and harvest timber on it. In the early 1980s, Interior secretary Watt issued several dozen oil and gas leases on the ceded lands. The tribe and conservation groups challenged Watt's action, and activity on the leases was suspended. Eventually, in 2006, Congress enacted legislation sponsored by Montana's senators, Max Baucus (D) and Conrad Burns (R), that prohibited further leasing and offered federal tax incentives to leaseholders who retired or donated their leases. Only one leaseholder remains; it has sought, so far unsuccessfully, to persuade the courts to allow it to drill wells on the land instead.[31]

An effort to promote cooperation between Indians and public land managers in South Dakota's Badlands has, like many such efforts, a complicated history. Primarily through the efforts of South Dakota senator Peter Norbeck, Congress established Badlands National Monument in 1929 and expanded it in 1936, putting the Park Service in charge. Most of the land had been acquired by the State of South Dakota and donated to the United States. During World War II, the air force commandeered lands of the Oglala Sioux Tribe immediately south of the monument for a bombing range. When the air force decided in the 1960s that it no longer needed those lands, Congress transferred jurisdiction over them to the Park Service as the south unit of the monument. Through all this, the lands remained in tribal ownership. In 1976, the tribe and the Park Service struck an agreement on how the south unit would be managed, but its implementation was plagued with difficulties. A provision of the National Parks and Recreation Act of 1978 converted both monument units into a single national park. In 2012, the Park Service announced support for converting the south unit into the first tribal national park, but to date Congress has not acted on the proposal.[32]

In Alaska, Alaska Natives are the primary beneficiaries of the subsistence-hunting and fishing preference for rural residents that applies to most public lands in the state by the terms of the Alaska National Interest Lands Conservation Act. Otherwise, Native influence on public lands has been made more complicated by Congress's decision in 1971 to settle Native land claims by vesting title to more than 40 million acres in state-chartered Native village and regional corporations, rather than in traditional tribal entities. For example, traditional tribal interests opposed a Trump administration initiative to roll back protections for roadless areas in the Tongass National Forest, while Sealaska, the regional Native corporation, saw it as a business opportunity.[33]

Other efforts to forge cooperative arrangements among Indians and public land management agencies are moving forward, and more can be expected. Altogether, the growing influence of Native Americans over how their ancestral lands are managed, particularly in order to protect natural and cultural resources, mirrors what has been taking place in many nations around the world in recent decades.

Usually in such situations, much discussion and negotiation are required to establish trust and a shared vision. U.S. public land management agencies are, to varying degrees, growing more comfortable in such undertakings. Success usually produces unique arrangements tailored to particular contexts. It is more politically challenging for tribes to seek outright ownership instead of more protection for, and influence over, areas of public land of special significance to them. Whether they succeed is usually influenced by the strength of their case of past unfair treatment.

CHAPTER SIXTY-ONE

The Politics of Public Lands in the Modern Era

CHANGE OR CONTINUITY?

IN THE 1970S, AS THE NETWORK OF protected public lands was rapidly expanding, rhetoric on the right side of the political spectrum began to change. Along with the usual calls for loose regulation and making more public lands available for mining and logging came demands that the United States simply relinquish ownership of substantial amounts of public land to private interests or state governments.[1]

A small subset of livestock operators had never abandoned what Congressman Edward Taylor once called the "iridescent dream" that the United States would relinquish ownership of the public lands their livestock grazed. What was new was a veneer of intellectual justification claiming that the reason the United States held huge swaths of land was simply that public institutions and officials were self-serving. Rather than genuinely seeking to promote the public good, their primary, or maybe their only, objective was simply to expand and protect their own power and influence. James Buchanan, then a University of Virginia economist, made this notion of government as self-aggrandizing a central part of the "public choice" ideology that he developed in the 1960s, reacting to the U.S. government's efforts to end Jim Crow racial segregation in the South. (Coincidentally, around the same time, Interior secretary Stewart Udall drew a parallel between those who attacked U.S. ownership and management of public lands and those in the South who attacked the U.S. role as a protector of civil rights.) Buchanan's theory gained favor with libertarian academics, philanthropists, and parts of the business community.[2]

The new attack on public lands also drew from a somewhat overlapping movement on the right that celebrated unfettered free enterprise. It was reflected in the writings of Milton Friedman, a libertarian economist whose book *Capitalism and Freedom* (which made no mention of public lands) first appeared in 1962. Its most prominent champion was Senator Barry Goldwater. It was also related to a widely circulated memorandum to the U.S. Chamber of Commerce in 1971 called "The Attack on the Free Enterprise System." This manifesto, written by Lewis F. Powell, Jr. (whom Richard Nixon appointed to the U.S. Supreme Court later that year), was a call to arms for corporate America to undertake direct political action to counter advocacy by Ralph Nader and the budding environmental movement. Of course, criticism of government in this era was hardly confined to the right—a Nader-commissioned book in 1972 characterized the Forest Service as the captive of commercial timber interests.[3]

The Colorado beer magnate Joseph Coors, describing himself as "stirred" by the Powell manifesto, helped fund the establishment of the Heritage Foundation in Washington, D.C., in 1973, as well as the Mountain States Legal Foundation in Denver in 1977. The latter was a counterpart to the Pacific Legal Foundation, founded in 1973, which quoted the manifesto at length in its prospectus. These and similar organizations (funded by, among others, the deep-pocketed Koch brothers) worked with some success to make U.S. ownership of public lands a symbol of distant bureaucratic government that victimized livestock grazers, miners, loggers, and the fossil fuel industry.

Such efforts helped feed the "sagebrush rebellion" that emerged in the intermountain West in the late 1970s. The arguments also found fertile ground in orthodox Republican Party ideology. Ronald Reagan, who had become an ardent advocate of free enterprise while working for General Electric and hosting its television show from 1954 to 1962, shrewdly flirted with the "sagebrush rebels" in his successful campaign for the presidency in 1980. In the process, he helped give political rhetoric about public lands a partisan edge not seen in American politics since before the Civil War.[4]

In the years that followed, Republican Party rhetoric often displayed a kind of generalized hostility to public lands as an institution—but it never challenged iconic components of that institution such as national parks. Moreover, its hostile rhetoric remained mostly just that—rhetoric—almost entirely disconnected from decisions made by Republicans serving in Congress or in leadership positions in the executive branch. Instead, with very few exceptions, they continued to support the broad thrust of public land policy that the nation had followed since before 1900. Goldwater captured this dichotomy. A hero to the Right, he was one of only twelve senators (and six Republicans) to vote against the Wilderness Act, yet in the 1980s he co-sponsored wilderness legislation and called his support for building the Glen Canyon Dam in the 1950s the biggest mistake in his congressional career.[5]

THE POLITICS OF PUBLIC LANDS FROM
REAGAN TO GEORGE W. BUSH

The Republican public lands two-step, employing rhetoric hostile to public lands while at the same time working pragmatically to advance protections for them, often succeeded at the ballot box. A demonstration of its mainstream appeal could be found in the election results for 1980 in the state of Washington. By substantial margins, the state's voters chose Ronald Reagan over Jimmy Carter and replaced a Democratic senator and governor with Republicans, but by a considerably bigger margin they rejected a proposed state constitutional amendment designed to clear the way for the state to lay claim to the public lands within its borders.

An even more concrete test of the divide between hostile rhetoric and popular support for protecting public lands came soon after. Initially, Reagan turned public land policy over to Joseph Coors and his allies. Interior secretary James Watt, who had been the first CEO of the Mountain States Legal Foundation, aggressively sought to give the fossil fuels industry and livestock operators free rein on public lands to the maximum extent allowed by law, and then some. The administration also proposed a program—ostensibly to raise revenue to help close a yawning budget deficit—that would have divested U.S. ownership of 35 million acres of "surplus" BLM and national forest land. In the end, nearly all these efforts were stymied by a bipartisan coalition in Congress, including some western Republicans, and by the judiciary.[6]

After Watt resigned in late 1983, the Reagan administration quickly steered to the middle on public lands issues. In 1984, with Republicans still in control of the Senate, Reagan signed legislation adding more than 8 million acres to the National Wilderness Preservation System—the largest addition in a single year since enactment of the Wilderness Act (other than 1980, the year of the Alaska lands legislation).[7]

Reagan was reelected by a wide margin that fall. The next year, Arizona governor Bruce Babbitt took note of the powerful backlash that the early Reagan policies had engendered. Advocates for protecting public lands, he said, "driven from the Nation's capital, went home" to the grass roots, where they sharpened their message, broadened their base, and gained "energy and strength for a new wave of reform" of public land policies. The backlash would, Babbitt predicted, result in replacing the idea of "multiple use"—which freely tolerated activities such as logging and mining, and which still applied to well over half of the public lands—with "public use." That idea, Babbitt wrote, embraced "the new reality that the highest, best and most productive use of western public land will usually be for public purposes—watershed, wildlife and recreation."[8]

His prediction proved accurate. Republicans and Democrats continued to find common ground on legislation adding protections to many areas of public land, and neither the Reagan nor the George Bush administration stood in their way. Reagan ended up signing legislation that more than doubled the acreage in the wilderness system in the lower forty-eight states. It seemed to show, the former BLM director Frank Gregg later wrote, that the "image of the West as political captive of resource-based industries is nostalgia, not reality."[9]

In 1994, two years after Bill Clinton was elected president, Republicans gained control of both Houses of Congress for the first time in forty years, flipping fifty-four House seats, including seventeen in seven western states, and picking up an open Senate seat in Arizona. Their campaign to gain control of the House, led by Newt Gingrich of Georgia, centered on the "Contract with America," which advocated a number of conservative policies but made no mention of public lands. The Republican ascendancy did, however, lead to a brief hiccup on public land policy reminiscent of the early Reagan administration. A controversial piece of a giant, omnibus budget reconciliation bill that Gingrich steered through Congress opened the Arctic National Wildlife Refuge to petroleum development. Clinton vetoed it in early December 1995, citing the ANWR provision as one of his principal objections.[10]

At that point, congressional Republicans once again retreated to the middle on public lands. In the fall of 1996, less than two months after Clinton irked Republicans in the intermountain West by establishing the nearly 2-million-acre Grand Staircase–Escalante National Monument on BLM lands in southern Utah, he signed into law the Omnibus Parks and Public Lands Management Act. Guided through the Republican-controlled Congress by Congressman Don Young, it modestly expanded the wilderness system and established several other new protected areas. In Clinton's second term, Congress enacted progressive reforms of the organic statutes governing the national park and national wildlife refuge systems, and established more protected areas, and

Clinton himself established more than a dozen new national monuments, many on BLM lands, without much controversy.[11]

The right wing succeeded in inserting a plank in the 1996 Republican platform that called for a "thorough review" of U.S. public lands, with a goal of retaining ownership only of "unique property worthy of national oversight" and transferring the rest to state and local governments. This idea, last seriously urged at the national political level by the Hoover administration, was repeated in the party's platform for 2000. Both were empty gestures. Republicans did not make ownership of public lands a significant issue in the elections of 1996, 1998, or 2000.

THE POLITICS OF PUBLIC LANDS FROM
GEORGE W. BUSH TO TRUMP

In the election of 2000, George W. Bush won a razor-thin victory facilitated by a 5–4 Supreme Court decision, and Republicans remained in control of both Houses of Congress. Bush—who had bought a ranch in Texas in 1999, where, when he was president, it was said that Secret Service agents outnumbered cows—installed another former Mountain States Legal Foundation official, Coloradan Gale Norton, as Interior secretary. When she signaled her receptivity to requests to modify or abolish the Clinton national monuments, she found little appetite in the West or in Congress for doing so. Indeed, in November 2001, Congress prohibited Interior from issuing any oil and gas leases in any national monuments, including the ones Clinton had established, unless a monument proclamation specifically permitted it.[12]

In 2002, Frank Luntz, a Republican messaging strategist who was the principal author of the "Contract with America," bluntly advised the GOP to resist making a head-on challenge to what he called "the most popular federal programs today"—specifically, "conservation of public lands and waters through parks and open spaces." Instead, he recommended attacking "an intrusive federal bureaucracy," in which "some pencil-pushing Washington bureaucrat" dictates rules that ordinary Americans must follow. Norton got the message; her mantra on public lands was her bland "four C's"—"communication, consultation and cooperation in the service of conservation." Norton left all the Clinton monuments unchanged even though her BLM director, Kathleen Clarke, had promised to restore "multiple use" by reversing what she decried as the BLM's recent conversion to a "Bureau of Landscapes and Monuments."[13]

George W. Bush himself had little interest in public lands issues. He did, however, break important new ground by using the Antiquities Act to establish four huge marine national monuments in the Pacific, the first in 2006 and the other three a few days before leaving office in 2009. Otherwise, he too mostly kept to the middle on public lands. He signed legislation crafted by Nevada senators Harry Reid (D) and John Ensign (R) that established a new national conservation area and designated several hundred thousand acres of wilderness in their state; on the less protective side, Bush signed the Healthy Forests Restoration Act of 2003, which lowered barriers to commercial logging in national forests.[14]

Public land policy was not an important issue in the 2008 presidential campaign. Barack Obama carried the Pacific coast states along with Nevada, Colorado, and New Mexico, and the Democrats gained several western seats in both the House and Senate, retaining control of both houses, which they had won in 2006.[15]

Obama's record on public lands generally tracked Clinton's. Another omnibus public land management act, most of whose components had been worked out during the Bush administration, became law early in his first term. It continued the now three-decade-long trend of omnibus public land packages that largely focused on adding protections. It also continued the even longer trend of Congress recovering decision-making authority it had previously delegated to the executive, mostly by curtailing road building and conventional economic development through zoning particular areas of public lands by law. Each of these reflected bipartisan deals involving members of Congress from the affected areas. In the package were designations of new wilderness areas in eight states, new wild and scenic rivers in three states, a new national monument in New Mexico, and new national conservation areas in Utah (two), Colorado, and New Mexico. The new monument and national conservation areas were all administered by the BLM.

The 2009 omnibus package also made several additions to the National Trails System and established the first comprehensive program for protecting paleontological resources found on public lands. On the national forests, the law established a new national recreation area in Oregon and new national scenic areas in Virginia, and protected an ancient bristlecone pine forest area in California. Last but not least, it gave statutory recognition to the BLM's entire system of "national conservation lands," a system that had grown piecemeal since the 1960s, and had been given formal recognition as a system by Interior secretary Babbitt in the late 1990s.[16]

In the midterm elections of 2010, Republicans regained control of the House by picking up sixty-three seats, including several in six western states, after a campaign dominated by economic issues and marked by the emergence of the hard-right Tea Party within the Republican Party. In 2012, the party platform—after being silent on the subject in 2004 and 2008—once again called for a review of U.S. public lands, with a goal of transferring some to state and local governments. Despite this, public lands were not an issue in the fall campaign. Obama was reelected and Republicans kept control of the House.

In his second term, acting on growing public concern about greenhouse gas emissions and a destabilizing climate, Obama took several steps aimed at curbing fossil fuel development on public lands, and promoting their use for solar and wind energy facilities. He also vigorously used his Antiquities Act authority to establish large new national monuments onshore as well as offshore. One, the nearly 1-million-acre Bears Ears National Monument in Utah, was by far the largest protected area of public lands where Native Americans were given a meaningful role in its administration.

Meanwhile, Congress continued to add protections to public lands, with bipartisan support. The Rocky Mountain Front Heritage Act of 2014 (supported by Montana's Republican House member as well as its two Democratic senators) created a 200,000-acre "Conservation Management Area" and designated new wilderness areas. After Republicans gained control of the Senate in the 2014 midterm elections, Obama signed legislation crafted over several years by Congressman Mike Simpson (R-Idaho) that established three new wilderness areas on 275,000 acres of public land in the Boulder–White Clouds area in Idaho. In 2016, in an acknowledgment of the increasing clout of the outdoor recreation industry, much of it centered on public lands, Congress enacted legislation requiring periodic systematic assessments of the industry's contributions to the economy.[17]

THE TRUMP ADMINISTRATION

The Republican Party platform in 2016 called on Congress to "immediately pass universal legislation," with a "timely and orderly mechanism," requiring the United States to convey "certain" (though unspecified) public lands to the states. That demand followed a Republican National Committee resolution in 2014 calling for the United States to transfer title to public lands to all willing western states, in fulfillment of the country's alleged "statehood promise." Yet the standard-bearer that the party chose that summer, Donald Trump, had months earlier explicitly rejected the idea of relinquishing ownership of public lands, most prominently in an interview with *Field and Stream* magazine after Ted Cruz, one of his opponents, had endorsed it. Upon winning election, Trump chose Montana congressman Ryan Zinke, who had resigned from the 2016 plat-form committee rather than endorse the anti-public-lands plank, as Interior secretary.[18]

Once in office, the Trump administration continued to disavow any effort to transfer ownership, but soon took several steps that seemed to lay the groundwork for it. Zinke's successor as Interior secretary, David Bernhardt, named Perry Pendley acting head of the BLM. Pendley was a protégé of James Watt, a prominent advocate of the view that public lands were unconstitutional, and a longtime CEO of the Mountain States Legal Foundation. Bernhardt also moved BLM's headquarters from Washington, D.C., to western Colorado, a step widely perceived as a precursor to a divestment program.

The Trump administration also moved aggressively to reverse the many-decades-long trend of protecting more and more acres of public land from intensive development. In late 2017, Trump signed executive orders severely downsizing the Bears Ears and Grand Staircase–Escalante National Monuments in southern Utah. This lifting of protections against mining and other development on about 2 million acres was the most regressive action in public land policy in well over a century. Trump went on to instruct the Forest Service to roll back roadless-area protections for the Tongass National Forest, in southeastern Alaska.

Taking a page from James Watt's book, the administration moved to turn effective control of many public lands over to fossil fuel companies. It reversed the Obama administration's curtailment of coal leasing. It set in motion an ambitious program to issue oil and gas leases on millions of acres of public lands onshore and offshore. It attacked climate science, and initiated a signifi-cant rewriting of regulations implementing the National Environmental Policy Act, the Endangered Species Act, and the Migratory Bird Treaty Act. It backed away from an Obama administration plan—crafted with several states in the intermountain West—designed to keep the sage grouse off the endangered species list by restricting development in its remaining habitat. Its priorities were dramatized when, during the government shutdown in late 2018 and early 2019, it furloughed national park rangers while keeping in place those who processed permits for oil and gas drilling on public lands.[19]

Almost no Republicans, in or out of Congress, publicly criticized these steps. The silence was in stark contrast to vocal support of public lands among Republicans in earlier years. The sea change was underscored when Arizona senator John McCain—who in 1996 had touted Theodore Roosevelt's legacy in a *New York Times* op-ed titled "Nature Is Not a Liberal Plot"—died in August 2018.[20]

In contrast to their silence, the actions of congressional Republicans sent a somewhat more mixed message. Congress was required to vote on only one Trump initiative to open protected areas of public land to development—to issue oil and gas leases in the coastal plain of the Arctic National Wildlife Refuge, in northeastern Alaska. Alaska's government, which is heavily dependent on petroleum revenues, had long sought to open it to oil and gas leasing after Congress closed it in ANILCA. In late 2017, the Republican-controlled Congress approved it, on a strict party-line vote, in an amendment tucked into legislation making large tax cuts that primarily benefited the wealthiest Americans. On the other hand, that same Congress rebuffed the Trump administration's request to make huge cuts in the budgets of public lands programs not related to fossil fuels.[21]

In the congressional elections in 2018, Democrats picked up forty-one seats (including several in six western states) and regained control of the House. They also flipped Senate seats in Nevada and New Mexico, but lost a net of two nationwide, so the Senate remained in Republican control. In early 2019, the newly divided Congress completed work on yet another omnibus public land protection bill, the latest in a series of bipartisan protection packages dating back decades. This one was named after a recently deceased long-time congressional advocate for protecting public lands, John D. Dingell, Jr., one of the sponsors of the original Wilderness Act. President Trump signed the Dingell Act into law in March 2019 without fanfare. Most of its parts had been agreed upon earlier when the Republicans controlled both houses.[22]

The Dingell Act followed the pattern established in earlier omnibus legislation. It established new wilderness areas in Utah and California and new wild and scenic rivers in Utah and several New England states. It established the San Rafael Swell Recreation Area as well as a national monument and a national conservation area, all on BLM land in Utah—ironically, not far from Obama's Bears Ears National Monument, which President Trump had drastically downsized a little more than a year earlier. The Obama administration's willingness to use the Antiquities Act helped Congress focus on finding alternative paths to add protections to public lands, similar to what Congress did in some places as the Clinton administration was winding down. The Dingell Act capped a decade during which Congress was able to produce, with bipartisan support, legislation adding protections to millions of acres of public land in the politically conservative states of Utah and Idaho.

Some individual components of the Dingell Act, like some in the 2009 omnibus bill, showed how bipartisan bargaining could successfully balance the interests of the nation and of local areas, and those of protection advocates and development interests. Heightening protection for many lands was accompanied by land exchanges, conveyance of small amounts of public lands to local governments, and relaxing management prescriptions on some areas that had been candidates for inclusion in the wilderness system.

The Dingell Act also permanently reauthorized the Land and Water Conservation Fund (LWCF). Since Congress launched it in 1964, the LWCF has provided several billion federal dollars to acquire millions more acres into public ownership (state as well as federal) for conservation and recreation. (At least 40 percent of the funds available in each year must be allocated among the four major federal land management agencies for acquisitions.) The multi-year campaign for its permanent reauthorization had gained the support of a number of congressional Republicans from western states as well as elsewhere, and for good reason. Measures of public opinion such as the annual "Conservation in the West" poll—which surveyed attitudes in the eight states of the intermountain West—continued to show strong bipartisan support for protecting public lands.[23]

In 2020, Congress took an even more significant step, again with bipartisan support. It made the LWCF a true revolving fund, which substantially increased the amount of money available to the fund each year. The Dingell Act and these fundamental modifications in the LWCF showed that although momentum for adding protections to public lands had slowed somewhat, it had not entirely stalled. The nearly unremitting hostility of the Trump administration to protecting public lands, when measured against the mostly contrary actions of Congress and the closeness of the 2020 elections, left no clear answer to the "change or continuity" question posed in this chapter's subtitle.[24]

CHAPTER SIXTY-TWO

Public Lands Today

THE STRONG, LONG-STANDING consensus supporting the national government's ownership of large amounts of land continues. Congress has approved the divestment of significant amounts of public lands only two times since it enacted the Stock-Raising Homestead Act more than a century ago. Both came in the 1950s, and both involved unique circumstances. The first gave coastal states ownership of a three-mile-wide band of submerged lands along their shores. The second gave the new state of Alaska ownership of more than 100 million acres of public lands. (The congressional act giving Alaska Natives 44 million acres of public land in 1971 was of a different character, since it was done to settle their legal claims to Alaska land.) No other significant divestment proposal has gained political traction for more than a century.

Since Alaska joined the union in 1959, the U.S. population has nearly doubled—and nearly tripled in the West, where most public lands are found. The population has also become more urban. Over that time, support has steadily grown for using public lands to provide recreation and inspiration, to protect wildlife and other natural attributes, and to restore abused lands to productive health.

DISTINCTIONS AMONG PUBLIC LAND
AGENCIES CONTINUE TO BLUR

Other than in Alaska, neither the total amount of land in national ownership nor its distribution among the four major land management agencies has changed very much since 1960. (The same became true in Alaska once the state and Native land selections, and ANILCA's redistribution of public lands among the four agencies, were completed.)

What has occurred is an increasing blurring of the historic distinctions differentiating how these four agencies manage public lands. They have long had similar policies in a number of areas, so it was always an oversimplification to regard the Park Service as focused on recreation, the Forest Service on logging, the BLM on livestock and mining, and the Fish & Wildlife Service on waterfowl. Still, those characterizations had some descriptive value, especially in the public mind.

More and more, those identifications no longer hold true. Since 1960, Congress has enacted many laws that determine what uses are allowable on public lands without regard for the agency managing them. Most notably, it has put many millions of acres of land overseen by each of the four agencies into the national wilderness preservation system, where they are, with very few exceptions, managed identically. It has also given ever increasing amounts of land managed by all four agencies designations such as "recreation area," "conservation area," "scenic area," "reserve," "preserve," and the like. These labels carry defined legal constraints that prohibit or discourage many potential uses, and for the most part these specific labels are not strongly associated with a specific agency. One reason labels have proliferated is because the label can be a political bargaining chip, with protection advocates willing to acquiesce in a less familiar label in return for securing stronger protections over a larger area.[1]

Congress has also, in overhauling the organic laws that govern each of the four agencies, given them very similar instructions regarding how they should make management decisions; for example, by using plans and paying close attention to science. Finally, Congress has also, by enacting the Endangered Species Act (ESA), given each agency a mandate to protect imperiled species.

Over the same time period, the executive branch has exercised authority that Congress has given it to the same distinction-blurring effect. As a result of vigorous presidential use of the Antiquities Act, for example, each of the four major public land management agencies now manages, in nearly identical fashion, many millions of acres of public land in national monuments. Each of the four has also adopted management plans for millions of acres that call for broadly similar administration.

These laws and these executive branch actions have limited or prohibited road building and most other kinds of intensive development on most public lands. This is true even on many national forest and BLM lands traditionally regarded as open to "multiple uses." On many public lands, Congress has added a protective designation such as "wilderness" or "national conserva- tion area." On many others, executive actions—such as presidential national- monument proclamations, zoning decisions by agencies in the management plans they prepare and in other policies they adopt, such as the Forest Service's roadless rule—have led to that result.[2]

To be sure, each agency's particular history, institutional culture, and governing laws still influence its public profile and its management of public lands under its control. Most logging on public lands occurs in the national forest system. Most fossil fuel development on public lands occurs in areas managed by the BLM. (In each case, however, such intensive development occurs on a relatively small proportion of the lands managed by that agency.) Most waterfowl on public lands are found in national wildlife refuges. Some of the most iconic scenery is found in the national park system.

As distinctions among the agencies have become blurred at the ground level, general public perceptions of public lands have also gradually changed. People tend to focus less on *which* agency is managing particular tracts of public land (especially because the proliferation of labels such as "conservation area" creates confusion on this score), and more on *why* those lands are being held— and that means, increasingly, focusing on their natural and cultural values.

All these developments mean that the old way of thinking about public lands—that the values and uses they serve are explainable mostly by which agency manages them—is less and less accurate.[3]

This blurring of distinctions has also helped change the nature of competi- tion among the agencies. Before 1960, interagency competition tended to focus on differences in agencies' management goals. In modern times, this is much less the case, because all agencies seek public and congressional support for many of the same things—such as protecting or restoring lands, acquiring inholdings, and accommodating recreation. At the same time, it has become more common for professional land managers to move from one agency to another, as when in the late 1990s Michael Dombeck became chief of the Forest Service after serving as acting director of the BLM for nearly three years. Some, especially committed skeptics of government, have long criticized the competition (and some functional overlap) among the agencies as creating inefficiencies and waste, even as those skeptics celebrate the virtues of competition in free markets. On such matters, competition can, as in the private sector, foster better outcomes.

PUBLIC LANDS AND ENVIRONMENTAL RESTORATION

All public land agencies share a concern for restoring the health of the lands they manage. The idea was an important reason for establishing some of the early forest reserves and was a principal rationale for enacting the Weeks Act. It was also a primary reason for enacting the Taylor Grazing Act and led to New Deal programs such as the one that resulted in establishing national grasslands on failed homesteads. The idea continues to command political support. Congress enacted the Forest Landscape Restoration Act as part of the 2009 omnibus public lands act. It directed the Forest Service to institute "collaborative, science-based ecosystem restoration" of competitively selected landscapes composed mostly of public lands. The first ten projects covered nearly 10 million acres in ten states.[4]

Two notable modern examples of public lands restoration can be found northeast and northwest of downtown Denver, Colorado. There, in a modern version of swords into plowshares, facilities producing military weapons have been converted into national wildlife refuges. Both the Rocky Mountain Arsenal and the nearby Rocky Flats Plant were rehabilitated under the Superfund hazardous waste cleanup program, which Congress established in 1980, and were put in the national wildlife refuge system in 1992 and 2001, respectively.[5]

Perhaps the largest restoration program involving public lands has been taking place for several decades around Everglades National Park, in South Florida. From its inception, the park suffered from upstream water diversions that began when the Army Corps of Engineers built a dike around Lake Okeechobee, upstream of the park. Beginning around 1950, another Army Corps project facilitated the diversion of large amounts of water that would ordinarily have flowed through the park, bringing into being a large agricultural area between the lake and the park. In the early 1970s, both the State of Florida and the United States began to take steps to restore some water flows to the park, and at President Nixon's urging, Congress authorized the Big Cypress National Reserve in 1974, just north of the park. Finally, in a powerful demonstration of state-federal cooperation to protect an iconic area of public lands, Congress and Florida in 2000 each approved a "Comprehensive Ecosystem

Restoration Plan." Although billions of dollars are being spent, its ultimate success is still in question.[6]

REDISTRIBUTING AUTHORITY AMONG THE BRANCHES OF GOVERNMENT

Congressman Wayne Aspinall's crusade to have Congress recapture much of the authority over public land use that it had previously delegated to the land management agencies in the executive branch still has impact. Congress has used three techniques to accomplish this recapture, each of which reallocates decision-making power over public lands.

The first technique is for Congress to enact laws that "zone" or specify what can and cannot be done on particular areas of public land—such as putting lands in the national wilderness preservation system. Such place-based congressional zoning gives local opinion a bigger voice in the political process because Congress finds it nearly impossible to protect a particular area of public land (as wilderness or anything else) if the congressional representatives from that area object. This is because, regardless of party or ideology, members of Congress have always been very uncomfortable dictating how public lands in some other member's district will be managed, for fear the tables could be turned on them. Instances in which this powerful institutional norm does not control the outcome are rare. The principal one was Congress's enactment of the Alaska National Interest Lands Conservation Act (ANILCA) in 1980. In that case, the state's congressional delegation, especially Senator Ted Stevens, had great influence over ANILCA's terms, but could not prevent it from being adopted. A massive national, grassroots campaign persuaded Congress to trump the local interest in determining the future of many of Alaska's magnificent public lands.[7]

This institutional norm operates regardless of which political party controls Congress. Its effect is to promote cooperation and compromise across party and ideological lines. This is especially true when different political parties control one or both houses of Congress and the presidency—which has been the case for most of the past forty years. All this has made Congress's decisions to protect public lands durable. It is almost unheard of for Congress to weaken, much less rescind, protections for public lands once it enacts them.

A second technique Congress has used to recapture authority from the executive is subtler—namely, by revamping each public land management agency's decision-making process. Congress has required each agency to pay attention to science and to the impact of its actions on biodiversity and the environment whenever it exercises the discretion that Congress has given it. It has required each agency to engage in systematic planning, information gathering, and analysis, and to follow a relatively transparent decision-making process, giving states, local governments, and other stakeholders notice and an opportunity to comment on proposed actions. It has also limited each agency's discretion in situations where species listed under the Endangered Species Act may be affected. (The ESA has also operated to redistribute authority among those agencies. Its requirement that all public land managers must, before taking action that may affect a listed species, consult Interior's Fish & Wildlife Service—and for certain fish species, the National Marine Fisheries Service in the Department of Commerce—gives those agencies substantial influence over the way that many public lands are managed.)

A third technique Congress has employed to recapture authority from the executive is by allowing—indeed, inviting—the federal courts to police executive decisions. Modern agencies' organic acts, along with laws such as the ESA and the National Environmental Policy Act, provide a much more secure foothold for judicial intervention than was available in earlier times. The Supreme Court has cooperated by opening federal courthouse doors to recreationists and other noneconomic interests seeking to challenge agency decisions. These noneconomic interests have become better organized and funded, and more willing to use the courts. At the same time, groups with an agenda to fight restrictions on the use of public lands, like the Mountain States Legal Foundation, have sought to enlist the courts to pursue their vision. The involvement of the courts and a wide group of stakeholders has limited the discretion of public land managers and made it more likely that their decisions will conform to congressional directives. (The courts have, however, continued their long-standing deference to Congress when it exercises its constitutional Property Clause authority to make "all needful rules and regulations respecting" the public lands.)

In general, both Congress and the agencies have been very hesitant to give nonfederal entities express decision-making authority over public lands. A major concern is that doing so might upset the balance of national and local interests. Congress has made exceptions in places where public lands make up a relatively small proportion of the targeted lands, as in the New Jersey Pinelands or the Columbia River Gorge. Congress and the executive have been somewhat more receptive to the idea in cases where Indian tribes have strong cultural connections with specific places, as in the Bears Ears National Monument.[8]

The Endangered Species Act has helped forge collaborations between federal land management agencies and state or local governments. Besides the efforts to protect spotted owl habitat in ancient forests in the Pacific Northwest, ESA concerns have resulted in innovative multispecies protection plans being developed by federal, state, and local agencies in California. A precipitous decline in some prominent species that range widely over public lands in the intermountain west—principally, the sage grouse and the desert tortoise— have produced habitat protection plans covering large areas, with management coordinated between federal agencies and state and local governments. The plans generally protect the species' habitat on public lands in order to make it easier to develop private lands. For example, Washington County in southwestern Utah worked with federal and state agencies in the 1990s to craft a plan to conserve desert tortoise habitat. The centerpiece of the plan was the Red Cliffs Desert Reserve, 62,000 acres of prime tortoise habitat. In 2009, Congress put 45,000 acres of the reserve, which was managed by the BLM, into a new national conservation area.

RECONFIGURING PUBLIC LANDHOLDINGS

Another important development in the modern era has been the increasing link between efforts to protect and restore natural values on public lands, and initiatives aimed at consolidating fragmented landholdings. Meeting the growing demand to manage public lands in harmony with ecological principles can be complicated by inappropriate uses of nearby nonpublic lands. Conversely, it can be facilitated by redrawing ownership boundaries to follow watershed or ecosystem lines. Reconfiguring ownerships can also improve access for recreation and promote more efficient or productive use of nonpublic lands.

Land exchanges and acquisitions to reconfigure patterns of ownership date back to the flowering of the reservation movement around 1900. The notorious "in lieu" provision of the Organic Act of 1897 was an early, though badly flawed, example. In modern times, reconfiguration has been pursued much more vigorously, driven especially by the growing demand to protect biodiversity and to provide recreational access. Congress and the executive have addressed this problem both generically and through numerous place-based actions.[9]

The Land and Water Conservation Fund, launched in 1964, is a prime source of funds for federal land acquisitions for conservation and recreation. Another important source is the Forest Legacy Program, established by Congress in 1990 and administered by the Forest Service. It seeks to protect prime forestland threatened by conversion to nonforest uses, either through outright acquisition by the Forest Service or by purchase of conservation easements, in collaboration with state and local governments and land trusts. (The program's funding now comes through the LWCF.) There are several other smaller, more targeted programs for conservation land acquisitions. All the agencies tend to prioritize acquisition of inholdings, because their development can fragment habitat, increase the risk of fire and invasive species, and pose other problems for protected public lands. All such acquisition programs depend almost entirely on willing sellers; condemnation authority is rarely exercised.[10]

In recent years, concern has grown about the amount of public land left unavailable to recreationists because private owners of surrounding lands do not permit access. A Supreme Court decision in 1980 involving checkerboarded land in Wyoming, the legacy of the first transcontinental railroad land grant, highlighted the problem. The Unlawful Inclosures Act, Justice William Rehnquist wrote for a unanimous Court, was not violated when the private owner of checkerboarded sections refused to permit the public to cross the corners of the checkerboard in order to travel from one section of public land to another for recreation. Years later, a report by a nonprofit group showed more than 9 million acres of public land in the western states were inaccessible to recreation because of such problems, including between 1.5 and 3 million acres each in Montana, Nevada, and Wyoming.

A primary solution to this problem is the acquisition of access corridors. The Land and Water Conservation Fund is the main vehicle for funding such purchases. The legislation in 2019 that permanently reauthorized the fund included a directive that all four federal land management agencies identify and prioritize opportunities for acquiring lands in order to foster recreational access to federal land, and spend a specified percentage or amount from the fund for that purpose each year.[11]

Actions to protect specific places on public lands have often drawn attention to problems created by awkward ownership patterns, and have driven efforts to find solutions. A long and only partly successful effort has involved the Lake Tahoe Basin in Nevada and California. Following failed efforts to establish a national park there in the early twentieth century, the National Park Service examined the idea again in the 1930s but concluded that intensive development around the lake's border made it unworkable. Around the same time, the Forest Service began efforts to enlarge national forests in the basin by acquisition. These accelerated after the Land and Water Conservation Fund was established. By 1980, the Forest Service held about two-thirds of the total acreage in the basin, but only about 16 percent of the shoreline.[12]

Tahoe is an excellent example of how federal efforts to protect public land often operate in harmony with state efforts. California began acquiring land in the Tahoe basin as far back as the 1920s to establish state parks. Nevada later did much the same thing. The two states formed an interstate park commission to develop an overall plan in 1961, and in 1969 established the Tahoe Regional Planning Agency to guide further development in the basin. Congress got into the act in 1980 when it approved a bill cosponsored by Congressmen Phil Burton and Jim Santini that authorized the sale of BLM parcels scattered across the booming metropolitan Las Vegas area, and directed that most of the proceeds be used to acquire "environmentally sensitive" lands in the Lake Tahoe basin.[13]

In the modern era, two politicians were leaders in the effort to reconfigure public land ownerships to enhance protection for natural values—Harry Reid and Bruce Babbitt. Reid crafted several pieces of legislation during his Senate career that remade the map of Nevada, primarily in the interest of protecting more public lands. None of these involved state lands, because Nevada had sold off nearly all of its statehood-granted lands decades earlier. In 1998, two years after he spearheaded a successful drive to have Congress establish the first national park in his state (the nearly 80,000-acre Great Basin National Park), he pushed the Southern Nevada Public Land Management Act (SNPLMA) through Congress. Scaling up the idea behind the Burton-Santini 1980 legislation, it accelerated the sale of surplus BLM lands in the fast-growing Las Vegas area and directed that the proceeds be spent to acquire property across the state that would preserve "natural, scientific, aesthetic, historical, cultural, watershed, wildlife, and other values contributing to public enjoyment and biological diversity" as well as "enhance recreational opportunities and public access." So far, more than 40,000 acres have been sold, nearly $4 billion in revenue has been produced, and more than 70,000 acres have been acquired.[14]

In 2000, Congress did something similar in the Federal Land Transaction Facilitation Act (FLTFA). It authorized the sale of isolated tracts of public land throughout the western states and Alaska that BLM management plans had identified as surplus. The proceeds must be used to acquire inholdings within any protected area of public land, and 80 percent must be spent in the state where it was generated. The FLTFA operated at a much smaller scale than the SNPLMA because surplus BLM land outside the Las Vegas area generally had much less value, and because its proceeds were spread across all four agencies.

Still, the FLTFA generated over $100 million for inholding acquisitions before it expired in 2011. In 2018, Congress reauthorized it.[15]

Bruce Babbitt helped engineer large-scale state-federal land exchanges that remade the maps of Arizona and Utah, advancing the federal interest in protecting public lands while enhancing opportunities to develop state lands to benefit public education. Exchanges designed to ameliorate the problem of scattered school land sections have a long history. In 1880, for example, Congress accepted Nevada's offer to exchange its 1864 statehood grant of 4 million acres (two sections in every township) for the right to select 2 million acres from any available nonmineral public lands anywhere in the state. The state chose lands in the Las Vegas valley and around Reno and Carson City as well as elsewhere (and by 1900 had sold nearly all of them).[16]

When Babbitt was governor of Arizona, from 1978 to 1987, he teamed up with then–BLM state director Dean Bibles to engineer several creative land swaps. Arizona, like New Mexico and Utah, had been granted four sections of land in every township, or about 11 percent of the state's entire area, and unlike many states, had held on to most of its school lands. The Babbitt-Bibles deals exchanged scattered state sections for BLM parcels in the fast-growing Phoenix area. One transaction ending up giving the BLM control of a riparian area regarded as one of the premier bird-watching sites in the nation. The land had been privatized in a Mexican land grant in the 1840s, and its owner agreed to a three-way exchange involving the state as well as the BLM. The BLM's acquisition paved the way for Congress in 1990 to establish the San Pedro National Riparian Conservation Area, an early component of the BLM's system of conservation lands.[17]

While serving as Interior secretary, Babbitt had great success in Utah. Its governor, Scott Matheson, had first promoted the idea of a massive state-federal land exchange in the early 1980s, only to see it stymied by opposition from livestock operators on public lands. Congress and the executive eventually took small steps in that direction, but the idea did not come to fruition until President Clinton established the Grand Staircase–Escalante National Monument in southern Utah in 1996. Inside the monument's boundaries were nearly 200,000 acres of Utah school sections.[18]

Babbitt and Utah's Republican governor, Mike Leavitt, crafted a deal that not only removed all the state inholdings from the new monument, but also traded out more than a quarter million acres of state inholdings in national parks, forests, and Indian reservations across the state. In return, the state received a somewhat smaller amount of public land that it sought for mining and other forms of economic development. Congress ratified the agreement in the Utah Schools and Lands Exchange Act of 1998. Building on that success, Congress approved similar deals in 2000 (Utah West Desert Land Exchange Act) and 2009 (Utah Recreational Land Exchange Act). Altogether, these exchanges resulted in the United States conveying nearly 300,000 acres of public land to the state and in return gaining title to nearly 600,000 acres of scattered state lands, most of them inholdings in protected areas of public lands.[19]

A deal of a comparable magnitude was consummated in Montana between 2008 and 2010. It resulted in protecting more than 300,000 acres of checker-boarded land that the United States had granted to the Northern Pacific Railway in 1864. The overall objective of this Montana Legacy Project was to promote conservation management, and much of the land was eventually transferred to the U.S. Forest Service. A significant part of the $500 million purchase price came from private philanthropy, but most of it came through a financing mechanism that Senator Max Baucus inserted in the 2008 Farm Bill.[20]

A few major land exchanges that have improved protection of public lands have had interstate dimensions. One, approved by Congress in 1988, gave a Florida real estate developer a valuable parcel of urban land in central Phoenix, the site of a former Indian school operated by the Bureau of Indian Affairs. In return, the United States acquired more than 100,000 acres of land in South Florida near Everglades National Park and the Big Cypress National Preserve, and a $35 million trust fund was established for Indian education. Interstate exchanges like this are rare because interstate politics make them very challenging.[21]

One other example of reconfiguration has involved the closure of military bases and the conversion of the lands to national wildlife refuges. In the past three decades, this happened on well over a million acres, the bulk of it being in two large marine refuges in the Pacific. Cleanup of contamination is often an issue, and sometimes public access to the refuges has to be restricted. The military has retained ownership of a small percentage of the lands, with the FWS managing them under a cooperative agreement. (Sometimes the process works the other way; in recent years, for example, the navy has sought to expand its presence on public lands in Nevada.)[22]

Practically all of these reconfigurations have come about because of continuing public demand to conserve areas with high public values, for the enjoyment of future as well as present generations, in national ownership. Many more such opportunities exist.

CHAPTER SIXTY-THREE

Public Lands and the Future

THE PUBLIC LANDS FACE MANY challenges to which the political system
has not yet responded effectively. This means their future can only dimly
be seen.[1]

THE CLIMATE CHALLENGE

A destabilizing climate poses countless tests for public lands. It alters natural
qualities that were a primary reason why the United States decided to retain or
acquire them. "Your children's Yellowstone," the headline of an article in the *New
York Times* warned not long ago, "will be radically different." Florida's Everglades
and numerous other protected areas of public land along the coasts—including
nearly one-third of the nation's 550 national wildlife refuges—face inundation as
the seas rise. In many public-land-rich places, droughts are becoming more
frequent, more severe, and longer lasting, and large wildfires more common.[2]

Public land managers must increasingly focus on how to adapt to the new
world that is emerging. The issues range from how to manage vegetation and
accommodate altered migration corridors of charismatic mammals to how to
deal with changing fire regimes.[3]

Public lands are also being called on to help limit greenhouse gas emissions, which is urgently needed if catastrophic climate change is to be avoided.
Many public lands have abundant solar and wind resources. On the other hand,
fossil fuel production from public lands, which now accounts for about

one-quarter of total U.S. carbon emissions, will have to be sharply limited unless carbon-capture technology can be developed and widely applied.[4]

THE BIODIVERSITY CHALLENGE

Closely related to the climate challenge are grave threats to biodiversity. Like climate change, it is a global problem. By some estimates, less than a quarter of the earth's land is now free from substantial human impact. This could drop to 10 percent by 2050, accelerating what is already being called the sixth great extinction in the planet's history. Numerous reports have documented significant declines in wild animal populations worldwide. In the United States, the human footprint continues to expand across the landscape, especially in places where public lands are not plentiful. Bird populations have plummeted by nearly 30 percent in the last half century. A substantial proportion of species listed under the Endangered Species Act depend on habitat found on public lands.[5]

Looming extinctions have led the eminent biologist Edward O. Wilson—who in 1980 called the loss of biodiversity from "careless misuse" and destruction of natural habitats the "folly that our descendants are least likely to forgive"—to advocate setting aside half the earth's surface as a protected natural reserve. As an interim step, a campaign is now under way to have the world's nations commit to protecting 30 percent of the land and marine areas under their jurisdiction by the year 2030. In this country, the public lands are a good start toward that goal. They make up nearly all the 12 percent of U.S. lands and 26 percent of U.S. marine areas that are today considered permanently protected.[6]

The U.S. collection of protected public lands helped persuade nations around the world to do something similar. Global networks of protected lands include biosphere reserves (now numbering more than 700, across more than 120 nations, including a dozen in the United States, all national parks), world heritage sites that celebrate nature (now numbering more than 200, in nearly 100 nations, including 20 in the United States, mostly on public lands), and wetlands of international importance (now numbering well over 2,000, in more than 150 nations, including 40 in the United States, by acreage, nearly all on public lands).[7]

"LOVING THE LANDS TO DEATH": THE RECREATION
EXPLOSION

The recreational use of public lands continues to grow exponentially. A micro-illustration is provided by the history of rafting the Colorado River through the Grand Canyon. From the time of John Wesley Powell's pioneering expedition in 1869 through 1949, a total of fewer than 100 people made the journey. (One was future Arizona senator Barry Goldwater, who wrote a book about his 1940 trip.) By 1961, the total had reached 1,000. Less than two decades later, the National Park Service was capping the number at about 30,000 *per year*.[8]

In 1980, Grand Canyon National Park reported 2 million visitors; in 2011, 4 million; in 2017, 6 million. More and more places on public lands are experiencing what has come to be known as the "Instagram problem." Within months after a scenic viewpoint in Utah overlooking Horseshoe Bend on the Colorado River in the Glen Canyon National Recreation Area was "geotagged" and publicized on social media, visitation skyrocketed from one thousand *a year* to four thousand *a day*.[9]

Besides taxing the infrastructure built to accommodate visitors, and the personnel and budgets of the managing agencies, the huge increase in visitation has made managing public lands much more complicated. Instead of wrestling with questions about logging or mining, managers are now much more likely to weigh how to balance recreational use with the protection of wildlife and cultural resources, and whether and how to accommodate hikers, off-road-vehicle users, mountain bikers and e-bikers, bird-watchers, wild horse lovers, target shooters, sport hunters and anglers, climbers, and myriad other enthusiasts.

THE DECLINE OF COMMODITY EXTRACTION AND THE FUTURE OF LIVESTOCK GRAZING

Extractive uses on public lands have diminished sharply in importance. Coal production has plummeted. Public lands are responsible for a declining share of petroleum exploration and development in the nation. Timber harvesting remains well below levels reached in the 1980s. Proposals to build new dams are almost unheard of; the removal of existing dams is much more likely to be on the table. Few new hard-rock mines are being proposed, and when they are, they attract considerable opposition. With a single exception, traditional extractive uses occupy an ever smaller share of the public lands, a trend that seems unlikely to change.

The one exception is grazing by domesticated livestock. It is still found on well over half the public lands in the lower forty-eight states. In some ways, that industry seems as entrenched as ever. The Trump administration lowered the grazing fee for both BLM and national forest lands to the floor that Congress set more than four decades ago. Yet the industry has changed somewhat. As the economic return from raising livestock on public lands has steadily declined, there has been a substantial, though difficult-to-measure rise in the number of amenity ranchers, persons of substantial means who pursue a lifestyle rather than profit.

The deep regard that Americans have long shown toward livestock ranching has eroded in recent decades, a trend perhaps best illustrated by the public welcoming of the return of wolves to large landscapes. Although wolves account for less than 1 percent of livestock mortality, and various programs compensate ranchers for losses due to predation, livestock operators have mostly, and vehemently, resisted their second coming many decades after they were extirpated. But operators' protests have been in vain. Wolves have expanded across western public lands since their reintroduction in Yellowstone National Park in 1995, and there they have attracted large numbers of visitors.[10]

Livestock grazing on public lands never counted for more than a tiny fraction of the nation's meat production, and today it plays a relatively insignificant role in most local economies across the West. It seems destined to shrink, especially as American diets change and arid regions become hotter and drier with climate change.[11]

Livestock grazing is often least profitable where it causes the most damage, such as in the arid public lands of the intermountain West and the Southwest. Retiring these public lands from grazing through the voluntary sale of grazing permits has considerable potential. Even though such arrangements would seem to offer something for all interests, such deals can be devilishly difficult to pull off. A big problem is that defenders of ranching culture—such as the Public Lands Council, the operators' principal trade association—stoutly resist ending grazing on even a single acre of public land, and their lobbying against such deals is often effective. Much wider use of this market-based tool is possible, but only if Congress gives such retirements legal backing, which it has sometimes done in specific places.[12]

THE FUNDING CHALLENGE

Even though public lands are vast, the cost of managing them is extremely small when measured against other demands on the federal treasury. The combined annual budgets of the four public land management agencies has hovered around $13 billion in recent years, a tiny fraction of total federal outlays. The four principal managing agencies together employ about 3 percent of the total civilian workforce employed by the U.S. government, not counting the U.S. Postal Service.[13]

Nevertheless, funding for public lands has not kept pace with the dramatic increases in visitation and the growing costs of meeting the other challenges described above. In recent years, for example, agency budgets have been severely taxed by the costs of fighting fires—fires that have been made worse by a destabilizing climate and made more threatening by the proliferation of home building in the "wildland-urban interface."[14]

Not the least of the destructive effects of inadequate funding for agencies is how it undermines public support for public lands, by making it harder for agencies to fulfill their stewardship mission while keeping the lands accessible for public use.

CONCLUSION

Like the nation, the institution that is America's public lands has traveled an enormous distance since the Revolutionary War not only created a national government, but also brought a great deal of land into national ownership. Its history shows how the American political system has functioned with considerable success to bridge partisan, regional, and other divisions to make the public lands the nation's "breathing space," as President Richard Nixon put it in 1971—a vast public asset that nurtures national pride, physical and mental health, and a spirit of community in an increasingly diverse nation.[15] A legion of political figures, virtually none of whom will ever be household names, have played important roles in that story.

Because questions of public land policy are ultimately political questions, it is difficult to predict how people will react to the changes now taking place. How will voters respond as more and more iconic places on public lands become crowded? Does a reported decline in interest among younger people in outings in the great outdoors signal an emerging trend that could undermine support for public lands?[16]

Will voters continue to support protecting public lands as a changing climate takes its toll? Will they favor maintaining the strict protections of the Endangered Species Act as extinctions multiply? Already, because relatively few listed species have recovered enough to be removed from the list, there have been calls for radically changing the ESA, leading E. O. Wilson to retort that one might as well call for closing hospital emergency rooms because so many people die there.[17]

How might policy toward public lands change if partisan rhetoric intensifies? If rejection of, rather than respect for, the teachings of science becomes a dominant attitude? If the American political system becomes more dysfunctional? Will candidates for political office, especially in places where public lands are abundant, continue to see that protecting them improves the quality of American life, or the opposite? Will the long-standing, bipartisan consensus on the general direction of public land policy endure, or might it unravel?

The role of our public lands on the global stage is also in question. Over the last century and a half, America's decision to protect a substantial portion of its lands for posterity has served as a model for many nations around the world. It remains to be seen whether the United States will exert similar leadership as the world grapples with the challenges posed by a destabilizing climate, ongoing destruction of natural landscapes, and a grim decline in biodiversity.

All that said, it seems beyond much doubt that if asked, most Americans today would agree that holding and protecting a large amount of land in national ownership, open to all, has been extraordinarily visionary and beneficial. When examined through the long lens of the nation's history, our public lands have shown how our governing process, for all its imperfections, can work to produce a result that most Americans support.

In his seminal work *The Wealth of Nations,* published the same year as the Declaration of Independence, the Scottish philosopher Adam Smith, the classic expositor of free-market capitalism, argued for the private ownership of property with a single exception. That was for lands held "for the purpose of pleasure and magnificence," which, he wrote, a "great and civilized" nation ought to hold for everyone's benefit. More than a century and a quarter later, the president of the American Civic Association, J. Horace MacFarland, delivered a similar message to a gathering of the nation's governors at the White House. The natural beauty of "all the national domain yet remaining," he said, "should be jealously guarded as a distinctly important natural resource, and not as a mere incidental increment." Doing so would, he said, result in a "more beautiful, and therefore a more prosperous America."[18]

That Americans have heeded Smith's and MacFarland's advice is a success story deserving of celebration—one particularly welcome in the sour, polarized political era in which we live.

NOTES

Notes contain shortened citations to principal sources, with full citations contained in the bibliography. Full citations are given for sources not listed in the bibliography.

1. THE NATION'S FOUNDING AND THE PUBLIC LANDS

1. Principal sources for this chapter are Gates, *Public Land Law Development*, 49–57; Hibbard, *Public Lands Policies*, 7–14; Jensen, *Articles of Confederation*, 107–238; Kluger, *Seizing Destiny*, 61–67, 84–122, 189–91; Leshy, "Are Public Lands Unconstitutional?," 504–12.
2. Thomas Jefferson, "Declaration of Independence," 1776; available from the National Archives, www.archives.gov/founding-docs/declaration-transcript.
3. Tocqueville, *Democracy in America*, 372.
4. Gates, *Public Land Law Development*, 50.
5. Mary R. Murrin, "New Jersey and the Two Constitutions," in *A New Jersey Anthology*, compiled and edited by Maxine N. Lurie, 121–44, at 126 (Newark: New Jersey Historical Commission, 1994).
6. James Madison, *Debates on the Adoption of Federal Constitution in the Convention Held at Philadelphia in 1787*, rev. and newly arranged by Jonathan Elliot (Philadelphia, 1836), 5:112; *Fletcher v. Peck*, 10 U.S. 87, 142 (1810) (Marshall, C.J.).
7. Quoted in Kluger, *Seizing Destiny*, 119–22, 189–91.
8. *Journals of the Continental Congress* 17:806 (September 6, 1780), available from the Library of Congress, https://memory.loc.gov/cgi-bin/query/D?hlaw:3:./temp/~ammem_VK4C::.
9. Quoted in Gates, *Public Land Law Development*, 51.
10. Quoted in ibid., 52.

11. Hibbard, *Public Lands Policies*, 9; Thomas LeDuc, "History and Appraisal of U.S. Land Policy to 1862," in Ottoson, *Land Use Policy and Problems*, 3–17, at 3; Feller, *Public Lands in Jacksonian Politics*, 5.

12. Thomas Hutchins, *An Historical Narrative and Topographical Description of Louisiana and West-Florida* (1784), 93, available from the Internet Archive, https://archive.org /details/historicalnarratoohutc.

13. Gregory E. M. Maggs, "A Concise Guide to Using Dictionaries from the Founding Era to Determine the Original Meaning of the Constitution," *George Washington Law Review* 82, no. 2 (April 2014): 358–93; Leshy, "Are Public Lands Unconstitutional?," 506–7.

14. Alan Taylor, *American Revolutions: A Continental History, 1750–1804* (New York: Norton, 2016).

15. J. Hector St. John de Crèvecoeur, *Letters from an American Farmer* (1782; letter 3), available from The Avalon Project, https://avalon.law.yale.edu/18th_century /letter_03.asp.

16. Banner, *How the Indians Lost Their Land*, 112–13.

2. PUBLIC LANDS AND THE ORDINANCES OF 1784, 1785, AND 1787

1. Principal authorities for this chapter are Ellis, *Quartet*, 31–35; Gates, *Public Land Law Development*, 61–74; Jensen, *Articles of Confederation*, 239–45; Onuf, *Statehood and Union*; Rakove, *Beginnings of National Politics*; Wills, *Necessary Evil*.

2. Thomas Jefferson to Edmund Pendleton, August 13, 1776; available from The Avalon Project, http://avalon.law.yale.edu/18th_century/let8.asp.

3. Gates, *Public Land Law Development*, 51.

4. Story, *Commentaries*, vol. 3, §§ 1311–12.

5. The text of the Land Ordinance of 1784 is available from the Library of Congress, http://memory.loc.gov/cgi-bin/query/r?ammem/bdsdcc:@field(DOCID+@lit(bdsdcc13401)).

6. "An Ordinance for Ascertaining the Mode of Disposing of Lands in the Western Territory," May 20, 1785, *Journals of the Continental Congress* 28:375–86, available from the Library of Congress, http://memory.loc.gov/cgi-bin/ampage?collId=lljc&fileName=028/lljc028.db&recNum=386&itemLink=r?ammem /hlaw:@field(DATE+17850520)::%230280388&linkText=1.

7. Andro Linklater, *Measuring America: How the United States Was Shaped by the Greatest Land Sale in History* (New York: Plume, 2003), 174–75.

8. *Cooper v. Roberts*, 59 U.S. 173, 177–78 (1850).

9. George Washington to James Madison, November 5, 1786, available from Founders Online, National Archives, https://founders.archives.gov/documents /Washington/04-04-02-0299; Rakove, *Beginnings of National Politics*, 350–51.

10. "An Ordinance for the Government of the Territory of the United States North West of the River Ohio," July 13, 1787, *Journals of the Continental Congress* 32:334–44, available from the Library of Congress, https://memory.loc.gov/cgi-bin /ampage?collId=lljc&fileName=032/lljc032.db&recNum=343.

11. Jennifer Schuessler, "Alexander Hamilton, Enslaver? New Research Says Yes," *New York Times*, November 9, 2020.

12. Robert W. Fogel and Stanley L. Engerman, *Time on the Cross: The Economics of American Negro Slavery* (New York: Norton, 1989); Farrand, *Framing of the Constitution*, 110–11.

3. THE U.S. CONSTITUTION AND THE PUBLIC LANDS

1. Principal sources for this chapter are Amar, *America's Constitution; The Federalist Papers* (widely available online); Farrand, *Framing of the Constitution*; Farrand, *Federal Convention of 1787*; Leshy, "Are Public Lands Unconstitutional?"; Story, *Commentaries on the Constitution.* The quotation from Madison is in Federalist 38.
2. Federalist 38 (Madison).
3. Ibid.
4. Farrand, *Framing of the Constitution*, 143–45.
5. Joseph Story, *A Familiar Exposition of the Constitution of the United States* (New York: Harper & Brothers, 1840), chap. 25, § 219.
6. Federalists 7 (Hamilton) and 43 (Madison).
7. Amar, *America's Constitution*, 273.
8. Farrand, *Framing of the Constitution*, 143–44; Farrand, *Federal Convention of 1787*, 2:454 (August 29, 1787).
9. Leshy, "Are Public Lands Unconstitutional?," 507–8.
10. Story, *Commentaries*, vol. 3, chap. 23, § 1214.
11. Farrand, *Federal Convention of 1787*, 2:505–6, 510 (September 5, 1787).
12. Federalist 43 (Madison).
13. Leshy, "Are Public Lands Unconstitutional?," 512–16.
14. Ellis, *Quartet*, 150–53, 172.
15. Smith, *Virgin Land*, 6.

4. ADMITTING NEW STATES AND ACQUIRING NEW TERRITORY

1. Principal authorities for this chapter are Ablavsky, "Rise of Federal Title"; Cohen, "Original Indian Title"; Gates, *Public Land Law Development*, 75–120, 285–318; Kluger, *Seizing Destiny*, 270–300; Newton, *Federal Indian Law*, §§ 1.03–7, esp. at 77–79.
2. Thomas B. Jones, "The Public Lands of Tennessee," *Tennessee Historical Quarterly* 27, no. 1 (Spring 1968): 13–36.
3. Walters, *Albert Gallatin*.
4. 2 Stat. 173–175 (1802).
5. 2 Stat. 225 (1803).
6. Gates, *Public Land Law Development*, 804–5 (appendix C).
7. David P. Currie, "The Constitution in Congress: Jefferson and the West, 1801–1809," *William and Mary Law Review* 39, no. 5 (1998): 1456–63.
8. Quoted in Kluger, *Seizing Destiny*, 289.
9. Ibid., 398.
10. Alfred W. Crosby, *Ecological Imperialism: The Biological Expansion of Europe, 900–1900*, 2nd ed. (Cambridge: Cambridge University Press, 2004); Tai S. Edwards and Paul Kelton, "Germs, Genocides, and America's Indigenous Peoples," *Journal of American History* 107, no. 1 (June 2020): 52–76.

11. Cohen, "Original Indian Title"; Newton, *Federal Indian Law*. General works on Indians, the European invasion, and its effects include Cronon, *Changes in the Land;* Charles C. Mann, *1493: Uncovering the New World Columbus Created* (New York: Vintage, 2011).

12. The literature on Indian law and policy is enormous. A good place to start is Charles F. Wilkinson, *American Indians, Time, and the Law: Native Societies in a Modern Constitutional Democracy* (New Haven, Conn.: Yale University Press, 1987).

13. Walsh, *American West,* 29.

14. Washington to James Duane, September 7, 1783, in W. C. Ford, ed., *The Writings of George Washington, 1782–85* (New York: G. P. Putnam's Sons, 1890), 10:311–12.

15. *Annual Report of the Secretary of the Interior* (1862), 9.

16. Cohen "Original Indian Title," 35.

17. 60 Stat. 1049 (1946).

18. Ablavsky, "Rise of Federal Title," 646.

19. Gates, *Public Land Law Development,* 87–119.

20. Paul Sadin, *Managing a Land in Motion: An Administrative History of Point Reyes National Seashore* (National Park Service, October 2007), 17–20 (available online).

5. EXPLORATION, SCIENCE, AND THE APPRECIATION OF NATURE

1. Principal sources for this chapter are Barrow, *Nature's Ghosts,* 17–19, 364; Goetzmann, *Exploration and Empire;* Nash, *Wilderness and American Mind;* Wulf, *Invention of Nature,* 1–9, 95–96, 235–48; Wulf, *Founding Gardeners.* Jefferson's book was *Notes on the State of Virginia* (France, 1785; reprint, New York: Penguin, 1999).

2. Joseph Ellis, *American Creation: Triumph and Tragedies at the Founding of the Republic* (New York: Knopf, 2007), chap. 6.

3. Wulf, *Invention of Nature.*

4. Wulf, *Founding Gardeners,* 205–8.

5. Ibid., 157.

6. Goetzmann, *Exploration and Empire,* xii, 109, 323.

7. Dan Flores, ed., *Southern Counterpart to Lewis and Clark: The Freeman and Custis Expedition of 1806* (Norman: University of Oklahoma Press, 1984).

8. Edgeley W. Todd, ed., *The Adventures of Captain Bonneville, U.S.A. in the Rocky Mountains and the Far West, Digested from His Journal by Washington Irving* (Norman: University of Oklahoma Press, 1961), 372.

9. Nash, *Wilderness and American Mind,* 64, 96–107; Steven Inskeep, *Imperfect Union: How Jessie and John Frémont Mapped the West, Invented Celebrity, and Helped Cause the Civil War* (New York: Penguin, 2020).

10. Joseph C. Ives, *Report Upon the Colorado River of the West* (Washington, D.C.: Government Printing Office, 1861), 110.

11. Lowenthal, *George Perkins Marsh,* 78–89.

12. Walters, *Albert Gallatin,* 328–89, 352–55.

13. Nash, *Wilderness and American Mind,* 45–46, 67–69.

14. Hyde, *American Vision,* 21; Evan Cornog, *The Birth of Empire: Dewitt Clinton and the American Experience, 1769–1828* (New York: Oxford University Press, 1998); Nash, *Wilderness and American Mind,* 70.

15. Zaslowsky and Watkins, *These American Lands,* 254–55.

16. Suzanne Lessard, *The Absent Hand: Reimagining the American Landscape* (Berkeley, Calif.: Counterpoint, 2019), 38–41.

17. Martin, *Genius of Place*, 126–53; Rybczynski, *Clearing in the Distance*, 45, 155–57.

18. Runte, *National Parks*, 5–9.

19. Goetzmann, *Exploration and Empire*, 184–91.

20. Sellars, *Preserving Nature in the National Parks*, 293n2; Jen A. Huntley, *The Making of Yosemite: James Mason Hutchings and the Origin of America's Most Popular Park* (Lawrence: University Press of Kansas, 2011).

21. Mumford, *Brown Decades*, 29–31; Laura Dassow Walls, *Henry David Thoreau: A Life* (Chicago: University of Chicago Press, 2017).

22. Quoted in Hans Huth, "Yosemite: The Story of an Idea," *Sierra Club Bulletin* 33, no. 3 (1948): 47–78; reprint, Yosemite, Calif.: Yosemite Natural History Association (1984), 9.

6. DIVESTING PUBLIC LANDS TO BUILD A NATION

1. Primary authorities for this chapter are Dick, *Lure of the Land*, 213–15, 358; Feller, *Public Lands in Jacksonian Politics*, 45–197; Gates, *Public Land Law Development*, 219–46, 319–86; Hibbard, *Public Land Development*, 269–88; Leshy, "Are Public Lands Unconstitutional?," 501–2, 521–27, 576–80; Rae, *Railway Land Subsidy Policy*; Robbins, *Our Landed Heritage*, 71–92; Treat, *National Land System*, 67–68, 126, 136.

2. 8 Reg. Deb. 1098 (June 20, 1832).

3. 5 Stat. 107 (1836). This law also incorporated the Office of the Surveyor General into the General Land Office.

4. Tocqueville quoted in Skowronek, *Building a New American State*, 6; Lawrence Friedman, *A History of American Law*, 2nd ed. (New York: Simon & Schuster, 1985).

5. 1 Stat. 138, 144 § 22 (1790).

6. LeDuc, "History and Appraisal of U.S. Land Policy to 1862," 5.

7. Feller, *Public Lands in Jacksonian Politics*, 94–96, 109, 111–12, 131–33, 147–55, 165–70, 181–88.

8. See generally Leshy, "Are Public Lands Unconstitutional?," 521–27.

9. Ibid.; Jon Meacham, *American Lion: Andrew Jackson in the White House* (New York: Random House, 2008); Meacham, *Soul of America: The Battle for Our Better Angels* (New York: Random House, 2018), 30–31; Robert V. Remini, *The Life of Andrew Jackson* (reprint, New York: Harper Perennial, 2001), 238–42.

10. Remini, *Life of Andrew Jackson*, 68–70; Theodore Roosevelt, *Thomas H. Benton* (Boston: Houghton Mifflin, 1899), 25–26, 29; 6 Reg. Deb. 23 (January 18, 1830).

11. Feller, *Public Lands in Jacksonian Politics*, 77–78, 92, 109, 126–35, 149.

12. Ablavsky, "Rise of Federal Title," 647–57.

13. 2 Stat. 445 (1807).

14. James Madison, Proclamation 22, Ordering Unauthorized Persons to Remove from the Public Lands (December 12, 1815); Removal of Intruders from Public Lands, 1 Op. Atty. Gen. 471–73 (May 27, 1821).

15. Gates, *Public Land Law Development*, 219–46.

16. Robbins, *Our Landed Heritage*, 71–92; 5 Stat. 453, 455–56 (1841).

17. Dick, *Lure of the Land*, 112.

18. Story, *Commentaries*, vol. 3, chap. 31, § 1321.

19. 4 Stat. 236 (1827); John Bell Rae, "Federal Land Grants in Aid of Canals," *Journal of Economic History* 4, no. 2 (November 1944): 167–77.

20. Remini, *Life of Andrew Jackson*, 172–73, 336; Simon Winchester, *The Men Who Made the States: America's Explorers, Inventors, Eccentrics, and Mavericks, and the Creation of One Nation, Indivisible* (New York: HarperCollins, 2013), 252–55.

21. Gates, *Public Land Law Development*, 360.

22. Cong. Globe, 31st Cong., 1st sess. 850 (1850).

23. Rae, *Railway Land Subsidy Policy*, 2, 5–8, 25–28.

24. Gates, *Public Land Law Development*, 360; *Annual Report of the Commissioner of the General Land Office* (1897), 72; Wilkinson and Anderson, *Land and Resource Planning*, 130.

25. Gates, *Public Land Law Development*, 804–5 (appendix C); LeDuc, "U.S. Land Policy to 1862."

26. Hibbard, *Public Land Development*, 269–88; Gates, *Public Land Law Development*, 328; Dick, *Lure of the Land*, 213–15, 358.

27. Gates, *Public Land Law Development*, 325, 329 (charts showing annual divestitures under the General Swamp Land Act).

28. Reiger, *American Sportsmen*, 29; Fischman, *National Wildlife Refuges*, 100 Stat. 3582 (1986).

29. *Annual Report of the Secretary of the Treasury* (1848), 311–14.

30. Utley and Mackintosh, *Department of Everything Else*.

7. RESERVATIONS AND ACQUISITIONS OF PUBLIC LANDS

1. Principal sources for this chapter are Cameron, *Governmental Forest Control*, 29–155; Dana, *Forest and Range Policy*, 46–53; Gates, *Public Land Law Development*, 531–42; Swenson, "Mineral Resources Exploitation," 702–6.

2. *United States v. Midwest Oil Co.*, 236 U.S. 459, 476 (1915).

3. 2 Stat. 445 (1807).

4. Mark Kurlansky, *Salt: A World History* (New York: Walker, 2002).

5. John A. Jakle, "Salt on the Ohio Valley Frontier, 1770–1820," *Annals of the Association of American Geographers* 59 (1969): 687–709.

6. Blumm and Tebeau, "Antimonopoly in Public Land Law."

7. 1 Stat. 464, 490 (1796); 2 Stat. 173 (1802).

8. 4 Stat. 79 (1824); 19 Stat. 221 (1877).

9. See, for example, Newton, *Federal Indian Law*, §§ 1.03[4]–[9], 45–75.

10. 2 Stat. 748, 750 (1812).

11. Dana, *Forest and Range Policy*, 46–50.

12. 3 Stat. 347 (1817); Cameron, *Governmental Forest Control*, 31, 51; Dana, *Forest and Range Policy*, 46–53; Gates, *Public Land Law Development*, 532–34; William R. Adams, "Florida Live Oak Farm of John Quincy Adams," *Florida Historical Quarterly* 51, no. 2 (October 1972): 129–42.

13. 4 Stat. 472 (1831) (Timber Trespass Act).

14. *United States v. Briggs*, 50 U.S. 351 (1850).

15. 4 Stat. 505 (1932); Fairfax et al., *Buying Nature*, 36.

16. Ise, *Our National Park Policy*, 13, 244–45; David Maraniss, *First in His Class: A Biography of Bill Clinton* (New York: Touchstone, 1996).

17. *Wilcox v. Jackson*, 38 U.S. 498 (1839); Coggins et al., *Federal Public Land and Resources Law*, 382–91.

18. U.S. Constitution, Fifth Amendment and art. I, § 8, cl. 17; Story, *Commentaries*, vol. 3, chap. 18, § 1141.

19. Christian R. Burset, "The Messy History of Federal Eminent Domain Power," *California Law Review Circuit* 4 (December 2013): 187–208; William Baude, "Rethinking Federal Eminent Domain Power," *Yale Law Journal* 122, no. 7 (May 2013): 1738–1825.

20. Cameron, *Governmental Forest Control*, 47–50; 4 Stat. 256 (1828); Gates, *Public Land Law Development*, 533.

21. *Kohl v. United States*, 91 U.S. 367 (1875); Fairfax et al., *Buying Nature*, 14, 26–28.

22. The Virginia Charter can be found at The Avalon Project, http://avalon.law.yale .edu/17th_century/va01.asp.

23. Swenson, "Mineral Resources Exploitation," 701–2.

24. Carl J. Mayer and George Riley, *Public Domain, Private Dominion* (New York: Random House, 1985), 20–39.

25. Wisconsin Historical Society, "Lead Mining in Wisconsin: The Birth of the Badgers," www.wisconsinhistory.org/Records/Article/CS408.

26. 2 Stat. 448 (1807); Swenson, "Mineral Resources Exploitation," 702–4.

27. 2 Stat. 445 (1807).

28. James E. Wright, *The Galena Lead District: Federal Policy and Practice, 1824–1847* (Madison: Historical Society of Wisconsin, 1966).

29. 4 Stat. 364 (1829).

30. *United States v. Gratiot*, 39 U.S. 526, 528–34 (1840).

31. Ibid., 538.

8. PUBLIC LAND POLICY IN CONFUSION IN THE PERIOD BEFORE THE CIVIL WAR

1. Principal sources for this chapter are Fehrenbacher, *Dred Scott Case*; Gates, *Public Land Law Development*; Leshy "Are Public Lands Unconstitutional?," 531–53; Leshy, *Mining Law*, 9–23; Swenson, "Mineral Resources Exploitation," 700–708.

2. John McPhee, *Assembling California* (New York: Noonday Press, 1994), 1–68, esp. 48–49.

3. *United States v. Gratiot*, 39 U.S. 526 (1840); *United States v. Gear*, 44 U.S. 120 (1845); 9 Stat. 37 (1846).

4. Leshy, *Mining Law*, 13.

5. Gates, *Public Land Law Development*, 301–4.

6. Eric Foner, *Gateway to Freedom: The Hidden History of the Underground Railroad* (New York: Norton, 2015); Martin, *Genius of Place*, 74–75.

7. Millard Fillmore, First Annual Message to Congress, 1850.

8. Swenson, "Mineral Resources Exploitation," 712–13.

9. Benjamin Madley, *An American Genocide: The United States and the California Indian Catastrophe, 1846–1873* (New Haven, Conn.: Yale University Press, 2016).

10. 5 Stat. 657 (1844).

11. *Annual Report of the Secretary of the Interior* (1861), 445.

12. 41 *Annals of Congress* 1308 (1824).

13. *Pollard v. Hagan*, 44 U.S. 212 (1845).

14. Ibid., 224. A full discussion of John McKinley and *Pollard* is found in Leshy, "Are Public Lands Unconstitutional?," 521–41.

15. *Dred Scott v. Sandford*, 60 U.S. 393, 407 (1857).

16. Amar, *America's Constitution*, 265; Leshy, "Are Public Lands Unconstitutional?," 543–45.

17. Faust, *This Republic of Suffering*.

9. NEW DIVESTMENT POLICIES SOW SEEDS OF A BACKLASH

1. Principal authorities for this chapter are Dick, *Lure of the Land*, 134–37, 153–58, 191; Gates, *Public Land Law Development*, 219–47, 342–86, 393–98, 490, appendix A, 799–801; Greever, "Railroad Land Grant Policies"; Ise, *United States Forest Policy*, 51, 52, 67, 73, 78, 113, 116, 122; Rae, *Railway Land Subsidy Policy*, 131, 202–3, 233; Roberts, "Federally Granted Railroad Rights-of-Way," 131–44, 154–58; R. White, *Railroaded*.

2. 12 Stat. 392, 12 Stat. 413 (1862); H. Smith, *Virgin Land*, 170 (Jeffersonian yeomen description).

3. James Buchanan, veto message, February 24, 1859; Gordon, *Rise and Fall of American Growth*, 311.

4. Ben Zimmer, "The United States Is . . . or Are?," *Visual Thesaurus*, July 3, 2009, www.visualthesaurus.com/cm/wordroutes/the-united-states-is-or-are.

5. Stegner, *Beyond the Hundredth Meridian*, 219.

6. 13 Stat. 356, 358; 13 Stat. 365 (1864); Greever, "Railroad Land Grant Policies."

7. Dana, *Forest and Range Policy*, 36–37; S. G. Reed, "Land Grants and Other Aids to Texas Railroads," *Southwestern Historical Quarterly* 49 (April 1946): 518–23; Stephen G. Wilson, "Railroad Construction, Public Aid to," *Handbook of Texas*, https://tsha online.org/handbook/online/articles/mpro1.

8. Cong. Globe, 38th Cong., 1st sess., 3021–24 (1864); Cong. Globe, 40th Cong., 2nd sess., 424–35 (1868); Cong. Globe, 41st Cong., 2nd sess., 2095 (1870), 3 Cong. Rec. 78–79 (1874); 3 Cong. Rec. 173–74 (1874); 3 Cong. Rec. 1600 (1875); 4 Cong. Rec. 2603–6 (1876); Gates, *Public Land Law Development*, 380, 456, 461, 474, 483–84; David Maldwyn Ellis, "The Forfeiture of Railroad Land Grants, 1867–1894," *Mississippi Valley Historical Review* 33, no. 1 (June 1946): 38–39, 41, 51–52, 54; Blake, *Holmans of Veraestau*, 101–3, 124, 143–48; Arnold, "Congressman William Holman," 301–13.

9. R. White, *Railroaded*, 63.

10. Chernow, *Grant*, 644; Paul W. Gates, "An Overview of American Land Policy," *Agricultural History* 50, no. 1 (January 1976): 213, 220.

11. 12 Stat. 489, §2 (1862); 13 Stat. 365, §2 (1864); Adams quoted in R. White, *Railroaded*, introduction, n4.

12. Greever, "Railroad Land Grant Policies"; *Wolsey v. Chapman*, 101 U.S. 755 (1879); *Wood v. Beach*, 156 U.S. 548 (1895).

13. Roberts, "Federally Granted Railroad Rights-of-Way," 118–20; 12 Stat. 489, § 7 (1862); 13 Stat. 356, § 4 (1864); Rae, *Railway Land Subsidy Policy*, 123, 125–30, 323–27; Gates, *Public Land Law Development*, 356–86, 396, 457–61; Greever, "Railroad Land Grant Policies," 84.

14. *Schulenberg v. Harriman*, 88 U.S. 44 (1874); *Railroad Land Co. v. Courtright*, 88 U.S. 310 (1874); Rae, *Railway Land Subsidy Policy*, 131, 202–3, 233; Ellis, "Forfeiture of Railroad Land Grants," 30–32, 56.

15. *Platt v. Union Pacific*, 99 U.S. 48 (1878); see also *Railway Co. v. Prescott*, 83 U.S. 603, 607 (1872); *United States v. Union Pacific Railroad Co.* 98 U.S. 569 (1878); Robbins, *Our Landed Heritage*, 255–67; Ellis, "Forfeiture of Railroad Land Grants," 32–33.

16. Thomas quoted in Keila Szpaller, "Signs of the Times: What Are Plum Creek's Plans for Lolo Pass?," *Missoula (Mont.) Independent*, January 30–February 6, 2003. For the Supreme Court's modern look at access issues raised by the checkerboard, see *Leo Sheep v. United States*, 448 U.S. 668 (1979).

10. MORE GIVEAWAYS SOW MORE SEEDS OF DISCONTENT

1. Swenson, "Mineral Resources Exploitation," 724–25. Swenson is a principal source for information about William Stewart and the Mining Law of 1872, along with Russell R. Elliott, *Servant of Power: A Political Biography of Senator William M. Stewart* (Reno: University of Nevada Press, 1983), 1–46, and Leshy, *Mining Law*.

2. James L. Roark, "George W. Julian: Radical Land Reformer," *Indiana Magazine of History* 64, no. 1 (March 1968): 25–38.

3. Leshy, *Mining Law*, 21–22, 386–87.

4. Justin Kaplan, *Mr. Clemens and Mark Twain: A Biography* (New York: Simon & Schuster, 1966), 58; Stegner, *Beyond the Hundredth Meridian*, 304; Mark Twain, "My Late Senatorial Secretaryship," *Galaxy*, May 1868, twainquotes.com/Galaxy/186805.html.

5. Leshy, *Mining Law*, 15; Swenson, "Mineral Resources Exploitation," 716–19; George Julian, *Political Recollections* (Chicago: Jansen, McClurg, 1884), 289, 292.

6. Dan Plazak, *A Hole in the Ground with a Liar at the Top: Fraud and Deceit in the Golden Age of American Mining* (Salt Lake City: University of Utah Press, 2006), 61–66, 69–77; Leshy, *Mining Law*, 95.

7. Wyant, *Westward in Eden*, 127.

8. W. Turrentine Jackson, "The Infamous Emma Mine: A British Interest in the Little Cottonwood District, Utah Territory," *Utah History Quarterly* 23, no. 4 (1955): 339–62.

9. 14 Stat. 253, §9 (1866); Thompson et al., *Legal Control of Water Resources*, 1040–43.

10. 14 Stat. 251, §8 (1866); Coggins et al., *Federal Public Land and Resources Law*, 360–72.

11. Vernon Parrington, *Liberalism, Puritanism, and the Colonial Mind: Main Currents of American Thought* (New York: Harcourt, Brace & World, 1927), 3:23; Noam Maggor, *Brahmin Capitalism: Frontiers of Wealth and Populism in America's First Gilded Age* (Cambridge, Mass.: Harvard University Press, 2017).

12. R. White, *Railroaded*; Chernow, *Grant*, 729.

13. Ben Tarnoff, *The Bohemians: Mark Twain and the San Francisco Writers Who Reinvented American Literature* (New York: Penguin, 2014), 229.

14. Ibid., 162–63.

15. Henry George, *Progress and Poverty* (1879; New York: Robert Schalkenbach Foundation, 2008), 389–92.

16. Mumford, *Brown Decades*, 21; Stegner, *Beyond the Hundredth Meridian*, 219: Fox, *John Muir and His Legacy*, 352–53.

17. 16 Stat. 573–79 (1871); Roberts, "Federally Granted Railroad Rights-of-Way," 133–34.

11. PROTECTING PUBLIC LANDS FOR INSPIRATION: YOSEMITE AND YELLOWSTONE

1. Simon Schama, *Landscape and Memory* (New York: Knopf, 1995), 7.
2. Principal sources for Yosemite are Hans Huth, "Yosemite: The Story of an Idea," *Sierra Club Bulletin* 33, no. 3 (1948): 47–78; reprint, Yosemite, Calif.: Yosemite Natural History Association (1984), 76–77; Huth, *Nature and the American: Three Centuries of Changing Attitudes*, 2nd ed. (Lincoln: University of Nebraska Press, 1990), 26–30; Jen A. Huntley, *The Making of Yosemite: James Mason Hutchings and the Origin of America's Most Popular Park* (Lawrence: University Press of Kansas, 2011); Margaret Sanborn, *Yosemite: Its Discovery, Its Wonders, and Its People* (New York: Random House, 1981), 46–100.
3. Madley, *American Genocide*, 164–70; Spence, *Dispossessing the Wilderness*, 101–5; Rebecca Solnit, *Savage Dreams: A Journey into the Hidden Wars of the American West* (Berkeley: University of California Press, 2014), 219–20.
4. Lafayette Houghton Bunnell, *Discovery of the Yosemite, and the Indian War of 1851, Which Led to that Event* (New York: Revell, 1880), 54; John Muir, *The Yosemite* (New York: Century, 1912; reprint, Martino Fine Books, 2017), 192.
5. Madley, *American Genocide*, 346–53; Banner, *How the Indians Lost Their Land*, 228–56; Keller and Turek, *American Indians and National Parks*, 19–29; Spence, *Dispossessing the Wilderness*, 6.
6. Carol Kramer, *Calaveras Big Trees* (Charleston, S.C.: Arcadia, 2010).
7. Huntley, *Making of Yosemite*, 65–71.
8. Huth, "Yosemite," 26–27.
9. Ibid., 27; Huth, *Nature and the American*, 145–46.
10. Martin, *Genius of Place*, 1, 171; William Deverell, " 'Niagara Magnified': Finding Emerson, Muir, and Adams in Yosemite," in *Yosemite: Art of an American Icon*, ed. Amy Scott (Los Angeles: Autry National Center, 2006), 9–22.
11. 13 Stat. 325 (1864).
12. Ibid.; Robin W. Winks, *Frederick Billings: A Life* (1991; reprint, Berkeley: University of California Press, 1998), 281.
13. Cong. Globe, 38th Cong., 1st sess., 2300–2301 (May 17, 1864).
14. *Hutchings v. Low* (also styled *The Yosemite Valley Case*), 82 U.S. 77 (1872); Sanborn, *Yosemite*, 100.
15. Leshy, "Are the Public Lands Unconstitutional?," 545–46; *Grisar v. McDowell*, 73 U.S. 363 (1867); *Gibson v. Chouteau*, 80 U.S. 92 (1871).
16. Martin, *Genius of Place*, 267.
17. Sears, *Sacred Places*, 122–42; Hyde, *American Vision*, 67–70; Stegner, *Beyond the Hundredth Meridian*, 375.
18. Wolfe, *Son of the Wilderness*, 123–26, 143, 152.
19. Grant McConnell, "The Conservation Movement—Past and Present," *Western Political Quarterly* 7, no. 3 (September 1954): 465; Wolfe, *Son of the Wilderness*, 82–83, 103–4, 116, 145–50, 180–89; Fox, *John Muir and His Legacy*, 20–22, 79, 85.
20. Nash, *Wilderness and the American Mind*, 75; William Cullen Bryant, ed., *Picturesque America*, 2 vols. (New York: Appleton, 1874).
21. Mark Twain, *Roughing It*, 3rd ed. (1872; Berkeley: University of California Press, 1995), 121; Stegner, *Beyond Hundredth Meridian*.

22. Wolfe, *Son of the Wilderness,* 130–36, 186–87; Worster, *Passion for Nature,* 169, 194–96; Sanborn, *Yosemite,* 103–9; Hyde, *American Vision,* 213; Url Lanham, *The Bone Hunters* (New York: Columbia University Press, 1973), 186–87, 215–16; Goetzmann, *Exploration and Empire,* 323.

23. Principal sources for Yellowstone are Haines, *Yellowstone Story,* 1:166, 172; Bartlett, *Nature's Yellowstone,* 194–97; Ise, *Our National Park Policy,* 13–50.

24. Treaty between the U.S. and the Crow Tribe, 15 Stat. 649 (1868); Treaty between the U.S. and the Eastern Band of Shoshone and the Bannock Tribe, 15 Stat. 673 (1868).

25. Haines, *Yellowstone Story,* 1:129–30; Taliaferro, *Grinnell,* 85–86.

26. Nathaniel P. Langford, "The Wonders of the Yellowstone," *Scribner's Monthly,* May 1871, 1–17, 113–28.

27. Black, *Empire of Shadows,* 335–51; Chernow, *Grant,* 659.

28. Bartlett, *Nature's Yellowstone,* 189, 200–201; Haines, *Yellowstone Story,* 1:135–37, 348n119; Henry James, "Niagara," *Nation,* October 12 and 19, 1871.

29. Nash, *Wilderness and the American Mind,* 108–13; Cong. Globe, 42nd Cong., 2nd sess., 159 (1871).

30. Cong. Globe, 42nd Cong., 2nd sess., 1243 (1872).

31. Haines, *Yellowstone Story,* 1:166–69; Cramton, *Early History of Yellowstone.*

32. Cong. Globe, 42nd Cong., 2nd sess., 1243 (1872).

33. 17 Stat. 32 (1872).

12. PILLAGING PUBLIC LANDS FOR WOOD, GRASS, AND MINERALS

1. Principal sources for the wood plunder are Cameron, *Governmental Forest Control,* 100–178; Ise, *United States Forest Policy;* Pisani, "Forests and Conservation."

2. Interior Secretary to the U.S. Attorney in Minnesota, January 16, 1862, quoted in *Annual Report of the Commissioner of the General Land Office* (1877), 25; Wilkinson and Anderson, *Land and Resource Planning,* 131.

3. Cameron, *Governmental Forest Control,* 109.

4. Pisani, "Forests and Conservation," 344–45; 18 Stat. 482 (1875); *Georgetown, Breckenridge and Leadville R.R. Co.,* 1 Interior Lands Decisions 610 (1883); Ise, *United States Forest Policy,* 83–84.

5. Dan DeQuille, *History of the Big Bonanza* (Hartford, Conn.: American Publishing, 1877), 238; Rossiter Raymond, *The Mines of the West: A Report to Secretary of the Treasury* (New York: Ford, 1869), 176; Randall Rohe, "Man and the Land: Mining's Impact in the Far West," *Arizona and the West* 28, no. 4 (Winter 1986): 299–338, at 307; Pisani, "Forests and Conservation," 344–45.

6. 17 Stat. 605 (1873); Dana, *Forest and Range Policy,* 31–33.

7. Principal sources for the grass plunder are Clawson, *Western Range Livestock Industry;* Dick, *Lure of the Land;* Foss, *Politics and Grass;* Gates, *Public Land Law Development;* Knowlton, *Cattle Kingdom;* Osgood, *Day of the Cattleman;* Peffer, *Closing of the Public Domain;* Robbins, *Our Landed Heritage;* Rowley, *Grazing and Rangelands;* Voigt, *Public Grazing Lands.*

8. *Annual Report of the Commissioner of the General Land Office* (1875), 7; Peffer, *Closing of the Public Domain,* 9; Dick, *Lure of the Land,* 227.

9. Wilkinson, *Crossing the Next Meridian,* 82–89; Walter Prescott Webb, *The Great Plains,* new ed. (1931; Lincoln: University of Nebraska Press, 1981), 206, 224.

10. Quoted in Osgood, *Day of the Cattleman*, 189.

11. George Stewart, "History of Range Use," in U.S. Department of Agriculture, *The Western Range: A Great but Neglected Resource* (Washington, D.C.: Government Printing Office, 1936), 119; Gates, *Public Land Law Development*, 482; H.R. Rep. 3415 (Serial No. 2445), 49th Cong., 1st sess. (1886), vol. 11, 2; Osgood, *Day of the Cattleman*, 98; Robbins, *Our Landed Heritage*, 217; Knowlton, *Cattle Kingdom*, xiv, 96–97, 118–19, 135–39, 219–24; Laurence M. Woods, *British Gentlemen in the Wild West: The Era of the Intensely English Cowboy* (New York: Free Press, 1989); Clawson, *Western Range Livestock Industry*, 260–61; Rowley, *Grazing and Rangelands*, 17.

12. *Buford v. Houtz*, 133 U.S. 320 (1890).

13. R. White, *"It's Your Misfortune,"* 225.

14. *Mackay v. Uinta Dev. Co.*, 219 Fed. 116 (8th Cir. 1914).

15. Clawson, *Western Range Livestock Industry*, 260–62 (engine-vehicle analogy).

16. Desert Land Act, 19 Stat. 377 (1877).

17. *Annual Report of the Commissioner of the General Land Office* (1885), 46–48; Gates, *Public Land Law Development*, 638–43.

18. deBuys, *Seeing Things Whole*, 6.

19. Gates, *Public Land Law Development*, 422–34.

20. Osgood, *Day of the Cattleman*, 198–99.

21. Ibid., 190; Knowlton, *Cattle Kingdom*, 135–41, 220–24.

22. Unlawful Inclosures Act, 23 Stat. 321 (1885); Peffer, *Closing of the Public Domain*, 25; Gates, *Public Land Law Development*, 466–68.

23. Potter quoted in Rowley, *Grazing and Rangelands*, 15–16; Foss, *Politics and Grass*, 4; Peffer, *Closing of the Public Domain*, 26.

24. Voigt, *Public Grazing Lands*, 30–32.

25. Stewart, "History of Range Use," 123; Voigt, *Public Grazing Lands*, 29–30; Dick, *Lure of the Land*, 246–54; Wilkinson, *Crossing the Next Meridian*, 89–90; Knowlton, *Cattle Kingdom*, xv; Worster, *Under Western Skies*, 45.

26. Peffer, *Closing of the Public Domain*, 26; Stewart, "History of Range Use," 123; Gates, *Public Land Law Development*, 482–83; quoting H.R. Rep. 3415 (1886), 2; Alien Property Act, 24 Stat. 476–77 (1887); Knowlton, *Cattle Kingdom*, 177, 219–26, 310.

27. Gates, *Public Land Law Development*, 394–95, 470; Osgood, *Day of the Cattleman*; Ise, *United States Forest Policy*, 80; Knowlton, *Cattle Kingdom*, 187; Donahue, "Western Grazing," 738–43; Voigt, *Public Grazing Lands*, 30.

28. Donahue, "Federal Rangeland Policy," 303, 318, 323, 345; Laitos and Carr, "Transformation on Public Lands," 169; Wilkinson, *Crossing the Next Meridian*, 81; R. White, *Railroaded*, 475–81.

29. Robert L. Kelley, *Gold vs. Grain: The Hydraulic Mining Controversy in California's Sacramento Valley* (Glendale, Calif.: Clark, 1959), 27–28, 57–60; McPhee, *Assembling California*, 42–45; White, *"It's Your Misfortune,"* 232–34; Randall Rohe, "Man and the Land: Mining's Impact in the Far West," *Arizona and the West* 28, no. 4 (Winter 1986): 299–338, at 331–32.

30. *Woodruff v. North Bloomfield Gravel Mining Co.* 18 F. 753, 768–72, 774, 775–76, 779–80, 783, 787, 800, 806 (C.C.A. 1884).

31. *Woodruff*; *People v. Gold Run Ditch & Mining Co.*, 66 Cal. 138 (1884); *National Audubon Society v. Superior Court*, 33 Cal. 3d 419, 658 P.2d 709 (1983).

32. Kelley, *Gold vs. Grain*.

33. Isabella Bird, *A Lady's Life in the Rocky Mountains* (1879; reprint, Oxford: Beaufoy, 2017), 133; Helen Hunt Jackson, "O-Be-Joyful Creek and Poverty Gulch," *Atlantic Monthly*, December 1883, 753–62.

34. Comprehensive Environmental Response, Compensation and Liability Act, 94 Stat. 2767 (1980); Duane A. Smith, *Mining America: The Industry and the Environment, 1800–1980* (Lawrence: University Press of Kansas, 1987); Government Accountability Office, *Hardrock Mining: Information on Abandoned Mines and Value and Coverage of Financial Assurances on BLM Land* (2008), www.gao.gov /assets/120/119391.pdf.

13. EFFORTS LAUNCHED TO PROTECT PUBLIC FOREST LAND

1. Wulf, *Founding Gardeners*, 207–11; Lewis Mumford, "Audubon: Passionate Naturalist," in *Interpretations and Forecasts, 1922–1972* (New York: Harcourt Brace Jovanovich, 1973), 74. Principal authorities for this chapter are Dana, *Forest and Range Policy*; Gates, *Public Land Law Development*; Ise, *United States Forest Policy*; Pisani, "Forests and Conservation"; Williams, *Americans and Their Forests*.

2. Mumford, *Brown Decades*, 32–36; Lowenthal, *George Perkins Marsh*, preface.

3. David Lowenthal, "Marsh's *Man and Nature* at 150," *George Wright Forum* 32, no. 3 (2015): 229–35.

4. William Cronon, foreword to Lowenthal, *George Perkins Marsh*; George Perkins Marsh, *Man and Nature, or, Physical Geography as Modified by Human Action* (New York: Scribner, 1864), 44, 55.

5. Marsh, *Man and Nature*, 35, 55.

6. George Perkins Marsh, *The Earth as Modified by Human Action* (New York: Scriber, Armstrong, 1874), 326–27.

7. Wulf, *Invention of Nature*; Mumford, *Brown Decades*, 32–36, quotation on 35.

8. Cong. Globe, 42nd Cong., 2nd sess., 2140 (1872); Cong. Globe, 42nd Cong., 3rd sess., 15 (Dec. 3, 1872); Ise, *United States Forest Policy*, 42.

9. John Muir, "God's First Temples: How Shall We Preserve Our Forests?," *Sacramento Record-Union*, February 5, 1876; Wolfe, *Son of the Wilderness*, 191; H.R. 2075, 44th Cong., 2d sess. (1876); Ise, *United States Forest Policy*, 112–14.

10. Pisani, "Forests and Conservation," 352–55.

11. *Annual Report of the Commissioner of the General Land Office* (1877), 25.

12. *Annual Report of the Secretary of the Interior* (1877), xv–xx; Rutherford B. Hayes, First Annual Message to Congress, December 3, 1877.

13. 20 Stat. 89 (1878); *Budd v. United States*, 144 U.S. 154, 161 (1892); Ise, *United States Forest Policy*, 74–78.

14. 20 Stat. 88 (1878); Gates, *Public Land Law Development*, 552–54; Williams, *Americans and Their Forests*, 398–99.

15. 8 Cong. Rec. 6 (1878); *Annual Reports of the Secretary of the Interior* (1878–80).

16. Stegner, *Beyond the Hundredth Meridian*; Pisani, "Forests and Conservation," 346–49; "American Forestry," *Nation*, January 1879, 87–88.

17. *Wooden-Ware Co. v. United States*, 106 U.S. 432, 436–37 (1882).

18. "American Forestry," *Nation*, 87–88; Powell, *Lands of the Arid Region*, 13, 2nd ed. available online from the U.S. Geological Survey, https://pubs.usgs.gov/unnum bered/70039240/report.pdf; deBuys, *Seeing Things Whole*, 233, 246–49.

19. Wolfe, *Son of the Wilderness*, 139–40, 168–70, 185–86, 191.

20. John Muir, "The American Forests," *Atlantic Monthly*, August 1897.

21. 10 Cong. Rec. 546 (1880); Ise, *United States Forest Policy*, 50, 56, 104.

14. MOVING BEYOND "PAPER PARKS"

1. Bartlett, *Yellowstone*, 327–30.

2. Runte, *National Parks*, 44–45.

3. T. J. Stiles, *Custer's Trials: A Life on the Frontier of a New America* (New York: Knopf, 2015), 312; Chernow, *Grant*, 657–58; Black, *Empire of Shadows*, 424–25.

4. 14 Cong. Rec. 3268, 3488 (1883).

5. Bartlett, *Yellowstone*, 125–41; Nash, *Wilderness and the American Mind*, 113–16; 15 Cong. Rec. 1612 (1884).

6. 22 Stat. 626 (1883) (Interior appropriations bill); Taliaferro, *Grinnell*, 116–19, 121–22, 190–91.

7. Black, *Empire of Shadows*, 424–25.

8. Bartlett, *Yellowstone*, 144–45.

9. Mary S. Culpin, "Yellowstone and Its Borders: A Significant Influence Toward the Creation of the First Forest Reserve," in Steen, *Origins of the National Forests*, 276–83; Bartlett, *Yellowstone*, 226, 312–15; Haines, *Yellowstone Story*, 1:268–69.

10. H. Duane Hampton, *How the U.S. Cavalry Saved Our National Parks* (Bloomington: Indiana University Press, 1971).

11. Bartlett, *Yellowstone*, 226, 257–75, 312–15; Haines, *Yellowstone Story*, 2:3–5.

12. Haines, *Yellowstone Story*, 2:19–21.

13. H.R. Rep. No. 1076, 49th Cong., 1st sess. (March 16, 1886); Cramton, *Early History of Yellowstone*, 9, 62; Blake, *Holmans of Veraestau*, 195–96.

14. Act of April 2, 1866, § 2 (California Legislature, 16th sess.), chap. 86 of the statutes of California.

15. Ise, *Our National Park Policy*, 53–55; 33 Stat. 702–3 (1905).

16. Wolfe, *Son of the Wilderness*, 244–46; Ise, *Our National Park Policy*, 56, 71.

15. WILDLIFE PROTECTION ENTERS THE POLICY UNIVERSE

1. Primary sources for this chapter are Barrow, *Nature's Ghosts*; Bean and Rowland, *Evolution of National Wildlife Law*; Dunlap, *Saving America's Wildlife*; Reed and Drabelle, *Fish and Wildlife Service*; Reiger, *American Sportsmen*; Taliaferro, *Grinnell*; Wilcove, *Condor's Shadow*.

2. Lewis Mumford, "Audubon: Passionate Naturalist," in *Interpretations and Forecasts, 1922–1972* (New York: Harcourt Brace Jovanovich, 1973), 74; Reed and Drabelle, *Fish and Wildlife Service*, 1–4; Dunlap, *Saving America's Wildlife*, xi.

3. Elliott quoted in Reiger, *American Sportsmen*, 28–31, 41.

4. Forester quoted in ibid., 39, 43; Louis S. Warren, *The Hunter's Game: Poachers and Conservationists in Twentieth-Century America* (New Haven, Conn.: Yale University Press, 1997).

5. Lowenthal, *George Perkins Marsh*, 182–85; Thompson et al., *Legal Control of Water Resources*, 762–65.

6. Stegner, *Marking the Sparrow's Fall* (New York: Holt, 1998), 128; Reiger, *American Sportsmen*, 67–104; Dunlap, *Saving America's Wildlife*, 14, 92–93.

7. Barrow, *Nature's Ghosts*, 82–83.

8. 15 Stat. 348 (1869); 16 Stat. 180 (1870); Matthiessen, *Wildlife in America*, 106–7.

9. Reed and Drabelle, *Fish and Wildlife Service*, 1–2; Barrow, *Nature's Ghosts*, 96–100, 124–30; Wilcove, *Condor's Shadow*, 27–30; Price, *Flight Maps*, 1–55.

10. Dan Flores, "Bison Ecology and Bison Diplomacy: The Southern Plains from 1800 to 1850," *Journal of American History* 78, no. 2 (September 1991): 465–85; Walsh, *American West*, 97–98.

11. Andrew Isenberg, *The Destruction of the Bison: An Environmental History, 1750–1920* (Cambridge: Cambridge University Press, 2000), 123–63.

12. 4 Cong. Rec. 1237–41 (1876); Barrow, *Nature's Ghosts*, 83–95; Theodore Roosevelt, *Hunting Trips of a Ranchman: Sketches of Sport on the Northern Cattle Plains* (New York: Putnam's Sons, 1885), 224; Isenberg, *Destruction of the Bison*.

13. Reiger, *American Sportsmen*, 55–56, 80–83.

14. Ibid., 80–87.

15. Taliaferro, *Grinnell*, 96–97.

16. David McCullough, *The Johnstown Flood* (New York: Simon & Schuster, 1968).

17. Taliaferro, *Grinnell*, 210, 234, 337; Reiger, *American Sportsmen*, 135; 18 Cong. Rec. 1145 (1887).

18. Taliaferro, *Grinnell*, 116–19, 121–22, 201–9; John Clayton, "Yellowstone Park, Arnold Hague and the Birth of National Forests," WyoHistory.org, accessed May 26, 2017, www.wyohistory.org/encyclopedia/yellowstone-park-arnold-hague-and-birth-national-forests.

19. Reiger, *American Sportsmen*, 146–74; Taliaferro, *Grinnell*, 137–39.

20. Daniel Cordalis and Amy Cordalis, "Civilizing Public Land Management in the Colorado River Basin," in Robison, McCool, and Minckley, *Vision and Place*, 242, 243; see also William J. Gribb, "John Wesley Powell's Land and Water Policies and Southwestern Native American Agricultural Practices," in ibid., 265, 270–73.

21. Banner, *How the Indians Lost Their Land*, 235; Spence, *Dispossessing the Wilderness*, 38–39, 149n51; Black, *Empire of Shadows*; Russell Thornton, *American Indian Holocaust and Survival: A Population History Since 1492* (Norman: University of Oklahoma Press, 1987).

16. THE CAMPAIGN FOR FOREST RESERVATIONS GAINS MOMENTUM

1. Chester Arthur, Second Annual Presidential Message, December 4, 1882; Third Annual Message, December 4, 1883.

2. Ise, *United States Forest Policy*, 112–13; 15 Cong. Rec. 4743–45 (1884); 16 Cong. Rec. 1930 (1885).

3. Ise, *United States Forest Policy*, 113; *Annual Report of the Secretary of the Interior* (1885), 45.

4. See, for example, *Wolcott v. Des Moines Co.*, 72 U.S. 681, 688–89 (1866); *Bullard v. Des Moines & Ft. Dodge R. Co.*, 122 U.S. 167 (1887).

5. "Mount Whitney Military Reservation," California State Military History and Museums Program, militarymuseum.org/MtWhitney.html.

6. National Park Service, *Administrative History of Crater Lake National Park, Oregon*, 2 vols. (1987, 1991), www.nps.gov/parkhistory/online_books/crla/adhi.

7. Gates, *Public Land Law Development*, 459, 471–79.

8. Hibbard, *Public Lands Policies*, 466–67; *Annual Report of the Commissioner of the General Land Office* (1886), 94–95; Schrepfer, *Fight to Save the Redwoods*, 18–37, 62–64.

9. Fairfax et al., *Buying Nature*, 47–50.

10. Terrie, *Contested Terrain*, 92–96; Nash, *Wilderness and the American Mind*, 116–21.

11. Mary S. Culpin, "Yellowstone and Its Borders: A Significant Influence Toward the Creation of the First Forest Reserve," in Steen, *Origins of the National Forests*, 277–78; Bartlett, *Yellowstone*, 226, 257–75, 312–15; Haines, *Yellowstone Story*, 2:3–5.

12. William Cullen Bryant, ed., *Picturesque America*, rev. ed. (New York: Appleton, 1894), 141.

13. 14 Cong. Rec. 3484 (1883).

14. Martin, *Genius of Place*, 339–49; Pierre Berton, *Niagara: A History of the Falls* (Albany: State University of New York, 1992); Joseph L. Sax, "America's National Parks: Their Principles, Purposes, and Prospects," *Natural History*, October 1976.

15. "An Act for the Establishment of the Waterton-Glacier International Peace Park," 47 Stat. 145 (1932).

16. *Fort Leavenworth Railroad Co. v. Lowe*, 114 U.S. 525 (1885).

17. Ibid. at 530–32, 539 (1885); Coggins et al., *Federal Public Land and Resources Law*, 132–40; Leshy, "Are Public Lands Unconstitutional?," 512–16.

17. CONGRESS CLOSES IN ON MAJOR REFORMS

1. Stegner, *Beyond the Hundredth Meridian*, 299–305; Gates, *Public Land Law Development*, 645–46.

2. 25 Stat. 505, 526 (1888).

3. 19 Cong. Rec. 8504–18 (1888).

4. 19 Cong. Rec. 8535–36, 8626, 8809, 8898 (1888).

5. Grover Cleveland, Fourth Annual Message to Congress, December 3, 1888.

6. Stegner, *Beyond the Hundredth Meridian*, 303–4; Everett Sterling, "The Powell Irrigation Survey: 1888–1893," *Mississippi Valley Historical Review* 27, no. 3 (December 1940): 421–34, at 427; *Annual Report of the Commissioner of the General Land Office* (1889), 50–51.

7. Opinion of Attorney General, May 24, 1890, cited in 21 Cong. Rec. 7727–28 (1890).

8. Ise, *United States Forest Policy*, 99–100; Dana, *Forest and Range Policy*, 100–101; Gates, *Public Land Law Development*, 470.

9. H.R. Exec. Doc. No. 242, 50th Cong., 1st sess. (1888) (Bowers report).

10. Ise, *United States Forest Policy*, 110; Dana, *Forest and Range Policy*, 98, 385.

11. H.R. 7901, 50th Cong., 1st sess. (1888).

12. H.R. Rep. No. 778, 50th Cong., 1st sess. (1888); H.R. 7901, 19 Cong. Rec. 2456–63 (March 27, 1888); 19 Cong. Rec. 5564–73 (June 25, 1888); 19 Cong. Rec. 5627–28 (June 17, 1888); 19 Cong. Rec. 5585–5607 (June 26, 1888).

13. Gates, *Public Land Law Development,* 457–60; 24 Stat. 556 (1887) (land forfeitures by railroads); 24 Stat. 143 (1887) (ICC legislation).
14. Hyde, *American Vision,* 229–30.
15. Lee, *Antiquities Act of 1906,* 81; 25 Stat. 961 (1889) (Casa Grande legislation).

18. CONGRESS GUTS POWELL'S IRRIGATION SURVEY AND ESTABLISHES NEW NATIONAL PARKS

1. Voigt, *Public Grazing Lands,* 6, 327n2.
2. Gates, *Public Land Law Development,* 645–47; Stegner, *Beyond the Hundredth Meridian,* 316–24, 328–43; Pisani, *Water, Land, and Law,* 142–48; Peffer, *Closing of the Public Domain,* 18–22.
3. Everett W. Sterling, "The Powell Irrigation Survey, 1888–1893," *Mississippi Valley Historical Review* 27, no. 3 (December 1940): 421; Stegner, *Beyond the Hundredth Meridian,* 344–46.
4. 21 Cong. Rec. 9184 (1890); Sterling, "Powell Irrigation Survey," 430–31.
5. 26 Stat. 371, 391 (1890) (appropriations bill); 21 Cong. Rec. 9145–57 (1890); deBuys, *Seeing Things Whole,* 20.
6. Pisani, "Forests and Reclamation," 69–70; Powell, "The Non-Irrigable Lands of the Arid Region," *Century,* April 1890, 915, 919–20. This was one of three articles Powell published in that magazine in the early 1890. They are reproduced, with commentary, in deBuys, *Seeing Things Whole,* 245–313. See also Louis S. Warren and Rachel St. John, "Strange Resurrection: The Fall and Rise of John Wesley Powell," in Robison, McCool, and Minckley, *Vision and Place,* 11–27; Robert B. Keiter, "John Wesley Powell and the National Park Idea: Preserving Colorado River Basin Public Lands," in Robison, McCool, and Minckley, *Vision and Place,* 1–5, 106–10; Donald Wurster, *A River Running West: The Life of John Wesley Powell* (New York: Oxford University Press, 2001), 471.
7. R. Orsi, *Sunset Limited,* 362–71; Richard J. Orsi, " 'Wilderness Saint' and 'Robber Baron': The Anomalous Partnership of John Muir and the Southern Pacific Company for Preservation of Yosemite National Park," *Pacific Historian* 29 (Summer/Fall 1985): 135–56; Oscar Berland, "Giant Forest's Reservation: The Legend and the Mystery," *Sierra Club Bulletin* 47 (1962): 68–82; Lary M. Dilsaver and William A. Tweed, *Challenge of the Big Trees: A Resource History of Sequoia and Kings Canyon National Parks* (Three Rivers, Calif.: Sequoia Natural History Association, 1990); Jones, *John Muir and the Sierra Club;* Runte, *National Parks,* 61; Runte, *Trains of Discovery,* 39–40.
8. Robert Underwood Johnson, "The Care of the Yosemite Valley," *Century,* January 1890, 474–75.
9. 21 Cong. Rec. 9072–73 (1890); 21 Cong. Rec. 9829 (1890); 26 Stat. 478 (September 25, 1890); *Annual Report of the Secretary of the Interior* (1889–1890), xx; *Annual Report of the Secretary of the Interior* (1890–91), iii; Berland, "Giant Forest's Reservation."
10. 21 Cong. Rec. 10740, 10751–52 (1890); 26 Stat. 650–52 (1890); John Muir, "The Treasures of the Yosemite," *Century,* August 1890, 483–500; Muir, "Features of the Proposed Yosemite National Park," *Century,* September 1890, 656–67; Wolfe, *Son of the Wilderness,* 249–51.

11. R. Orsi, *Sunset Limited*, 358–64, 370–71; Fox, *John Muir and His Legacy*, 103–7.

12. *Annual Report of the Secretary of the Interior* (1890), cxxiii–cxxvi.

13. Roxanne Dunbar-Ortiz, *An Indigenous Peoples' History of the United States* (Boston: Beacon, 2014), 152–57.

14. John A. Lockwood, "Uncle Sam's Troopers in the National Parks of California," *Overland Monthly*, April 1899, 356–68; "Yosemite: Buffalo Soldiers," National Park Service website, www.nps.gov/yose/learn/historyculture/buffalo-soldiers.htm.

15. Spence, *Dispossessing the Wilderness*, 109.

16. 26 Stat. 333, 336 (1890) (Chickamauga); 28 Stat. 597–99 (1894) (Shiloh); 28 Stat. 651–53 (1895) (Gettysburg); 30 Stat. 841–43 (1899) (Vicksburg); Fairfax et al., *Buying Nature*, 54.

17. Jennifer Errick, "The First Park with a Million Visitors" (blog post), National Parks Conservation Association, October 29, 2019, www.npca.org/articles/2333-the-first -park-with-a-million-visitors.

18. John F. Lacey, "Why Do We Create Battlefield Parks and Erect Monuments Thereon?," in Iowa Conservation Association, ed., *Major John F. Lacey: Memorial Volume*, 248–49 (Cedar Rapids, Iowa: Torch, 1915); Douglass quoted in Faust, *This Republic of Suffering*.

19. C. Vann Woodward, *The Strange Career of Jim Crow* (1955; New York: Oxford University Press, 2001); *Plessy v. Ferguson*, 163 U.S. 537 (1896); 30 Stat. 44 (1897).

20. 26 Stat. 492–95 (1890).

19. CONGRESS GIVES THE PRESIDENT BROAD AUTHORITY
TO RESERVE PUBLIC LANDS

1. Ise, *United States Forest Policy*, 114–15.

2. 21 Cong. Rec. 2349–51 (1890).

3. 21 Cong. Rec. 2351, 2537–38 (1890).

4. 21 Cong. Rec. 2349–53 (1890) (Payson introduced repeal of Timber Culture laws in the House); 21 Cong. Rec. 2537–39 (1890) (passed House); 21 Cong. Rec. 10085–94 (1890) (introduced in the Senate); 21 Cong. Rec. 10454–55 (1890) (passed Senate with amendments); 21 Cong. Rec. 10760 (1890) (Payson asked House not to concur with Senate's amendments and to confer with Senate instead).

5. 26 Stat. 1095, 1103 (1891).

6. Arnold, "Congressman William Holman," 301–13; Clayton, *Natural Rivals*, 126–28, 136–39; Steen, *U.S. Forest Service*, 26–27; A. Dan Tarlock and Sally K. Fairfax, "No Water for the Woods: A Critical Analysis of United States v. New Mexico," *Idaho Law Review* 15, no. 3 (Summer 1979): 509n106, 541–43.

7. Adlai E. Stevenson, *Something of Men I Have Known* (Chicago: McClurg, 1909), 34.

8. 22 Cong. Rec. 3545–47 (Senate), 3611–16 (House) (1891); 22 Cong. Rec. 3893–94 (Senate), 3916 (Senate) (1891); see also *Annual Report of the Secretary of the Interior* (1891), 13–15; *Report of the Commissioner of the General Land Office* (1891), 63–66.

9. The fix bill was 26 Stat. 1093–94 (1891); 21 Cong. Rec. 3801–3 (March 2, 1891) (House); 3893–94, 3916 (March 3, 1891) (Senate).

10. Udall, *Quiet Crisis*, 112–13; Ise, *United States Forest Policy*, 119–20; Wilkinson, *Crossing the Next Meridian*, 122–23; McCarthy, *Hour of Trial*, 16; Alfred Runte, *Public Lands, Public Heritage: The National Forest Idea* (Niwot, Colo.: Roberts Rinehart in

cooperation with the Buffalo Bill Historical Center, 1991), 45; Dana, *Forest and Range Policy*, 99–101; Fox, *John Muir and His Legacy*, 110, 397.

11. 25 Stat. 393 (1888); 26 Stat. 796 (1891) (contemporary examples of Congress giving effect to executive reservations); Blake, *Holmans of Veraestau*, 210.

12. 21 Cong. Rec. 7767 (1890) (Holman); 21 Cong. Rec. 9153 (1890) (Stewart).

20. THE FIRST FOREST RESERVES

1. Principal sources for this chapter are Ise, *United States Forest Policy;* McCarthy, *Hour of Trial;* Muhn, "Forest Reserve Act"; Steen, *U.S. Forest Service;* Wilkinson and Anderson, *Land and Resource Planning.*

2. *Annual Report of the Commissioner of the General Land Office* (1891), 45; General Land Office, "Circular of Instructions Relating to Timber Reservations" (May 15, 1891), in S. V. Proudfit, ed., *Decisions of the Department of the Interior and General Land Office in Cases Relating to the Public Lands,* vol. 12 (Washington, D.C.: Government Printing Office, 1891), 499.

3. "Preservation of Forests," Sen. Rep. No. 1002 to Accompany S. 3235 (1892), 8; "Protection of Forest Reservations," H.R. Rep. No. 52-2437 (1893).

4. Muhn, "Forest Reserve Act," 261–66.

5. Douglas H. Strong, "The Sierra Forest Reserve: The Movement to Preserve the San Joaquin Valley Watershed," *California Historical Society Quarterly* 46, no. 1 (March 1967): 3–17.

6. Proclamation No. 39, 27 Stat. 1052 (1892).

7. McCarthy, *Hour of Trial*, 25–44.

8. "The New Forest Reserves," *New York Times,* February 27, 1893, 4; for a contrasting view, see Fox, *John Muir and His Legacy*, 110 (claiming that Harrison's reserves had no "public support," which showed that conservation "was never more an elitist conspiracy than at its birth").

9. *Annual Report of the Commissioner of the General Land Office* (1893), 79.

10. Gerald W. Williams, "John B. Waldo and William G. Steel: Forest Reserve Advocates for the Cascade Range of Oregon," in Steen, *Origins of the National Forests.*

11. *Report of the Secretary of Agriculture* (1893), 31.

12. Ise, *United States Forest Policy*, 122–28; 25 Cong. Rec. 2430–35 (1893); 27 Cong. Rec. 85, 364–71 (1894); 27 Cong. Rec. 2779–80, 2933 (1895).

13. "Protection of Forest Reservations," H.R. Rep. No. 52-2437 (1893), 2.

14. Steen, *U.S. Forest Service,* 29–30; 25 Cong. Rec. 2435 (1893); Wilkinson and Anderson, *Land and Resource Planning*, 49.

15. 29 Stat. 11 (1896); 27 Stat. 348 (1892); McCarthy, *Hour of Trial*, 48–51.

21. THE GENERAL LAND OFFICE STRUGGLES AND CLEVELAND SPURS CONGRESS INTO ACTION

1. Principal authorities for this chapter are Ise, *United States Forest Policy;* McCarthy, *Hour of Trial;* Muhn, "Forest Reserve Act."

2. *Annual Report of the Commissioner of the General Land Office* (1894), 94–95.

3. Ise, *United States Forest Policy*, 244–45; *United States v. Tygh Valley Land & Live-Stock Co.*, 76 F. 693, 694 (D. Ore. 1896).

4. *Annual Report of the Commissioner of the General Land Office* (1895), 85; *Annual Report of the Secretary of the Interior* (1895), 42.

5. Robert L. McGrath, *Art and the American Conservation Movement* (Boston: National Park Service, 2001), 53, 78 (available on the NPS website).

6. *Annual Reports of General Land Office Commissioner*, 1895, 1896, 1897; Gerald W. Williams and Char Miller, "At the Creation: The National Forest Commission of 1896–97," *Forest History Today*, Spring–Fall 2005, 32–37; Nash, *Wilderness and the American Mind*, 133–40; Pinchot, *Breaking New Ground*, 100–104.

7. Mark Twain, *Roughing It* (1872; New York: Signet Classics, 2008), 42; Robert Underwood Johnson, "Why Not More Forest Reserves?," *Review of Reviews*, December 1894, 651–53.

8. Pinchot, *Breaking New Ground*, 105–9, 130–31; Char Miller, *Gifford Pinchot and the Making of Modern Environmentalism* (Washington, D.C.: Island, 2001), 142–43; "Report of the National Forestry Committee," in *Forest Policy for the Forested Lands of the United States*, S. Doc. No. 55-105 (1897), at 44.

9. 29 Cong. Rec. 2512–17 (1897) (Senate); 29 Cong. Rec. 2677–80 (1897); 29 Cong. Rec. 2930, 2971–74 (1897) (House); McCarthy, *Hour of Trial*, 52–53.

10. 29 Cong. Rec. 2512–13 (1897).

11. 29 Cong. Rec. 2677–80 (1897).

12. Ise, *United States Forest Policy*, 131–32.

13. The modern, strict reading was most prominently advanced by Attorney General Benjamin Civiletti in 1980; see Congressional Research Service, *Shutdown of the Federal Government: Causes, Processes, and Effects* (December 10, 2018), available at https://fas.org/sgp/crs/misc/RL34680.pdf.

14. Ise, *United States Forest Policy*, 130–42; for the history that led to the revision of the bill, see 30 Cong. Rec. 899–902, 908–25, 961–71, 1005–13, 1242–43, 1274–76, 1278–85 (1897).

15. 30 Cong. Rec. 908–23 (1897), Shoup on 910, Carter and White on 917.

16. 30 Cong. Rec. 909–10 (1897).

17. 30 Cong. Rec. 961–71, 1005–13 (1897), Lacey on 963–65, McCrae on 966–68.

18. 30 Cong. Rec. 1280–81 (1897).

19. 30 Stat. 34–36 (1897).

22. AN ORGANIC ACT FOR THE FOREST RESERVES

1. Principal authorities for this chapter are Gates, *Public Land Law Development*; Ise, *United States Forest Policy*; Peffer, *Closing of the Public Domain*; Rowley, *Grazing and Rangelands*; Voigt, *Public Grazing Lands*. The Organic Act is found at 30 Stat. 34–36 (1897).

2. *Annual Report of the Commissioner of the General Land Office* (1899), 116.

3. Ise, *United States Forest Policy*, 139–41, 176–82; Gates, *Public Land Law Development*, 574–76, 586–88.

4. 31 Stat. 614 (1900).

5. *Annual Report of the Commissioner of the General Land Office* (1898), 90; U.S. Bureau of Corporations (predecessor of the Federal Trade Commission), *The Lumber Industry* (Washington, D.C.: Government Printing Office, 1913), 228–30; Robbins, *Our Landed Heritage*, 339–40.

6. Ise, *United States Forest Policy,* 183; Giancarlo Panagia, *Public Policy and Land Exchange: Choice, Law, and Praxis* (New York: Routledge, 2015), 52.

7. 30 Cong. Rec. 965–67 (1897).

8. 30 Stat. 36 (1897).

9. 30 Stat. 35 (1897); Pisani, "Forests and Conservation," 355–56.

10. Peffer, *Closing of the Public Domain,* 27; on the description of Senator Warren, see Rowley, *Grazing and Rangelands,* 82; Pinchot, *Breaking New Ground,* 270 (attributing the remark to Theodore Roosevelt).

11. 30 Stat. 35 (1897).

12. Voigt, *Public Grazing Lands;* R. White, *"It's Your Misfortune,"* 225; Richard White, "Animals and Enterprise," in Milner et al., *Oxford History of the American West,* 267; "Forest Policy for the Forested Lands of the U.S.," S. Doc. No. 55-105 (1897), 20.

13. Knowlton, *Cattle Kingdom;* Smythe quoted in Karen Merrill, *Public Lands and Political Meaning: Ranchers, the Government, and the Property Between Them* (Berkeley: University of California Press, 2002), 1–2, 37–58.

14. *Annual Report of the Commissioner of the General Land Office* (1897), 85.

15. Voigt, *Public Grazing Lands,* 40.

16. Leshy, *Mining Law,* 192–95, 445–47.

23. PARKS, FORESTS, AND PUBLIC LAND POLICY IN THE McKINLEY ADMINISTRATION

1. *Annual Report of the Secretary of the Interior* (1891), xv.

2. Terrie, *Contested Terrain,* 95–97.

3. Fernow, "The Palisades Park," *Forester* 2, no. 3 (May 1896): 26–28; Andrew Denny Rodgers III, *Bernhard Eduard Fernow: A Story of North American Forestry* (Durham, N.C.: Forest History Society, 1991), 232–41; Steen, *U.S. Forest Service,* 37–42.

4. The principal source for the Mount Rainier discussion is Theodore Catton, "Establishment of Mount Rainier National Park," chap. 3 in Catton, *Wonderland: An Administrative History of Mount Rainier National Park* (National Park Service, 1996), available online.

5. 30 Stat. 993, (1899).

6. *Annual Report of the Secretary of the Interior* (1899), 90–91.

7. John Muir, "The American Forests," *Atlantic Monthly,* August 1897, 157; Muir, "Wild Parks and Forest Reservations of the West," *Atlantic Monthly,* January 1898; Wolfe, *Son of the Wilderness* 272–74, 277; 31 Cong. Rec. 56045–46, 56170 (1898).

8. The principal source for the Olympic Forest Reserve is Lien, *Olympic Battleground,* esp. 2, 7–8; see also Ise, *United States Forest Policy,* 165n2; Gates, *Public Land Law Development,* 592.

9. Strong, *Tahoe,* 68–82; Douglas H. Strong, "Preservation Efforts at Lake Tahoe, 1880–1980," *Journal of Forest History* 25 (April 1981): 78–97, esp. 84–89; Donald J. Pisani, "Lost Parkland: Lumbering and Park Proposals in the Tahoe-Truckee Basin," *Forest and Conservation History* 21, no. 1 (January 1977): 4–17.

10. Pinchot, *Breaking New Ground,* 161–67, 244.

11. Ibid., 177–81.

12. *Annual Report of the Commissioner of the General Land Office* (1900), 87, 103, 111, 113–17.

13. *Annual Report of the Secretary of the Interior* (1901), 54–55, 218.
14. Pinchot, *Breaking New Ground*, 192; Ise, *United States Forest Policy*, 179; *Annual Report of the Commissioner of the General Land Office* (1901), 114, 117.

24. NATIONAL AUTHORITY OVER PUBLIC LANDS EXPANDED AND CONFIRMED

1. Bartlett, *Yellowstone;* Bartlett, *Nature's Yellowstone;* Taliaferro, *Grinnell*, 201–8.
2. Bartlett, *Yellowstone.*
3. "An Act to Protect the Birds and Animals in Yellowstone National Park," 28 Stat. 73–75 (1894); Taliaferro, *Grinnell*, 204–8.
4. Examples of court decisions narrowly construing Congress's regulatory power over the economy include *United States v. Dewitt*, 76 U.S. 41 (1871); *The Trade-Mark Cases*, 100 U.S. 82 (1879); *United States v. E.C. Knight Co.*, 156 U.S. 1, 12 (1895).
5. *Shoemaker v. United States*, 147 U.S 282, 297 (1893).
6. *United States v. Gettysburg Electric Railway Co.*, 160 US. 668, 686 (1896).
7. *Camfield v. United States*, 167 U.S. 518, 522, 524, 525, 527 (1897).
8. *United States v. Rio Grande Dam & Irrigation Co.*, 174 U.S. 690 (1899); *Winters v. United States*, 207 U.S. 564 (1908).
9. *Shively v. Bowlby*, 152 U.S. 1, 47–50 (1894); *Stearns v. Minnesota*, 179 U.S. 223 (1900); Leshy, "Are Public Lands Unconstitutional?," 559–63. In its decision in *Ward v. Race Horse*, 163 U.S. 504 (1896), the Court suggested that the "equal footing" idea negated a provision in a U.S.-Indian treaty that preserved tribal hunting rights, but the Court later renounced that suggestion in *Minnesota v. Mille Lacs Band of Chippewa Indians*, 526 U.S. 172, 204–5 (1999), and *Herrera v. Wyoming*, 139 S. Ct. 1686 (2019).
10. *Annual Report of the Commissioner of the General Land Office* (1901), 106–27 (esp. 114), 150–51.

25. THEODORE ROOSEVELT, PUBLIC LANDS, AND THE RECLAMATION ACT

1. Edmund Morris, *Theodore Rex* (New York: Random House, 2001), 3, 6–7; McCarthy, *Hour of Trial*, 75.
2. Edmund Morris, *The Rise of Theodore Roosevelt* (New York: Modern Library, 2001), 15–19, 33–46; Stephen Ponder, " 'Publicity in the Interest of the People': Theodore Roosevelt's Conservation Crusade," *Presidential Studies Quarterly* 20, no. 3 (Summer 1990): 547–55.
3. Brinkley, *Wilderness Warrior*, 356–58.
4. Elmo Richardson, *The Politics of Conservation: Crusades and Controversies, 1897–1913* (Berkeley: University of California Press, 1962), 25; Roosevelt, *Autobiography*, 651.
5. Theodore Roosevelt, First Annual Message to Congress, December 3, 1901; Pinchot, *Breaking New Ground*, 188–91.
6. 28 Stat. 422 (1894); Gates, *Public Land Law Development*, 647–51.
7. Gates, *Public Land Law Development*, 650–51; Reisner, *Cadillac Desert*, 116–17; Pisani, *Water and American Government*, 66–67.
8. Lawrence B. Lee, "William Ellsworth Smythe and the Irrigation Movement: A Reconsideration," *Pacific Historical Review* 41, no. 3 (August 1972): 289–311.

9. Pisani, "Forests and Reclamation," 70–72.

10. Theodore Roosevelt, First Annual Message to Congress.

11. Aida D. Donald, *Lion in the White House: A Life of Theodore Roosevelt* (New York: Basic Books, 2008), 208.

12. 35 Cong. Rec. 6722–78, esp. 6771 (1902).

13. 32 Stat. 388–90 (1902); Reisner, *Cadillac Desert*, 116–18.

14. Peffer, *Closing of Public Domain*, 42.

15. Reisner, *Cadillac Desert*, 118.

16. Gates, *Public Land Law Development*, 658–69; Peffer, *Closing of the Public Domain*, 58–62.

17. 34 Stat. 116–17 (1906).

18. Pisani, "Forests and Reclamation," 72–75; Reisner, *Cadillac Desert*, 54–107; Wilkinson, *Crossing the Next Meridian*, 252–54.

26. FOREST RESERVES EXPAND IN ROOSEVELT'S FIRST TERM

1. Principal authorities for this chapter are Gates, *Public Land Law Development*; Ise, *United States Forest Policy*.

2. Brinkley, *Wilderness Warrior*, 445–49.

3. Lawrence W. Rakestraw, *A History of the United States Forest Service in Alaska* (Anchorage: Alaska Historical Commission, 1981), chap. 2, available online from the Forest History Society, https://foresthistory.org/wp-content/uploads/2017/01/A-History-of-the-US-Forest-Service-in-Alaska.pdf.

4. Brinkley, *Wilderness Warrior*, 509–53.

5. Pinchot, *Breaking New Ground*, 182; Rowley, *Grazing and Rangelands*, 58, 92, 108–9, 130–32, 140, 145.

6. George Stewart, "History of Range Use," in U.S. Department of Agriculture, *The Western Range: A Great but Neglected Resource* (Washington, D.C.: Government Printing Office, 1936), 125; Wilkinson and Anderson, *Land and Resource Planning*, 97–98; *United States v. Blasingame*, 116 F. 654 (S.D. Ca. 1900); *Dastervignes v. United States*, 122 F. 30 (9th Cir. 1903); Clawson, *Western Range Livestock Industry*, 125–29; 27 Stat. 1028 (1892); 33 Stat. 526 (1904).

7. Rowley, *Grazing and Rangelands*.

8. 35 Cong. Rec. 6509–27 (June 9, 1902); 35 Cong. Rec. 6566–74 (June 10, 1902); Catton, *American Indians and National Forests*, 40–44, 301, 310n10.

9. Stephen A. Douglas Puter and Horace Stevens, *Looters of the Public Domain: Embracing a Complete Exposure of the Fraudulent System of Acquiring Titles of the Public Lands of the U.S. (Use and Abuse)* (Portland, Ore.: Portland Printing House, 1908), 59–66; Gates, *Public Land Law Development*, 577–93.

10. Dana, *Forest and Range Policy*, 130; Ise, *United States Forest Policy*, 185–90, 197–98.

11. Gates, *Public Land Law Development*, 591; Ise, *United States Forest Policy*, 187–89; *Annual Report of the Commissioner of the General Land Office* (1904), 50–51.

12. Ise, *United States Forest Policy*, 155–57; Pisani, "Forests and Reclamation," 247.

13. Gates, *Public Land Law Development*, 488–91, 578.

14. Pinchot, *Breaking New Ground*, 246.

15. McCarthy, *Hour of Trial*, 127, 293n107; *United States v. New Mexico*, 438 U.S. 696, 706–8n13 (1978), citing Ise, *United States Forest Policy*, 120–40.

16. 33 Stat. 628 (1905); Gates, *Public Land Law Development,* 579; Pinchot, *Breaking New Ground,* 260.

17. 30 Stat. 908 (1899).

27. THE FOREST SERVICE TAKES CONTROL OF THE FOREST RESERVES

1. James Wilson to Gifford Pinchot, February 1, 1905, transcription available from the Forest History Society, https://foresthistory.org/research-explore/us-forest-service-history/policy-and-law/agency-organization/wilson-letter.

2. 33 Stat. 700, 873 (1905); Pinchot, *Breaking New Ground,* 257.

3. Primary sources for this section are Skowronek, *Building a New American State;* Balogh, *Government Out of Sight,* 277–312.

4. Skowronek, *Building a New American State,* 83.

5. Carl Schurz, *Congress and the Spoils System* (New York: Peck, 1895), 4.

6. 31 Stat. 588, 614 (1900).

7. Greeley, *Forests and Men,* 82. The 1905 *Use Book* (U.S. Department of Agriculture, *The Use of the National Forest Reserves*) is available from the Forest History Society, https://foresthistory.org/wp-content/uploads/2017/10/1905_use_book.pdf.

8. *Annual Report of the Secretary of Agriculture* (1909), 408.

9. Char Miller, *Gifford Pinchot and the Making of Modern Environmentalism* (Washington, D.C.: Island, 2001), 117, 209; Pinchot, *Breaking New Ground,* 147–53.

10. 34 Stat. 684 (1906).

11. 35 Stat. 260 (1908); 37 Stat. 287 (1912); Ise, *United States Forest Policy,* 273–81.

12. Leshy, "Are Public Lands Unconstitutional?," 565–68; Headwaters Economics in Bozeman, Montana, has done numerous studies of these issues, available online.

13. *Annual Report of the Secretary of Agriculture* (1905), 206; Wilkinson, *Crossing the Next Meridian,* 90–91; Flores, *Coyote America,* 95–97.

14. Rowley, *Grazing and Rangelands,* 55–60; Hays, *American People and the National Forests,* 29–30; Voigt, *Public Grazing Lands,* 45–49.

15. 33 Stat. 628 (1905) (Transfer Act); Voigt, *Public Grazing Lands,* 49; Rowley, *Grazing and Rangelands,* 60–64.

16. Rowley, *Grazing and Rangelands,* 60–68, esp. 61n8; Pinchot, *Breaking New Ground,* 270–72; Hays, *Conservation and the Gospel of Efficiency,* 59–60.

17. Rowley, *Grazing and Rangelands,* 67–68; Wilkinson and Anderson, *Land and Resource Planning,* 103.

18. 45 Cong. Rec. 1338–39, 1352 (1910); 46 Cong. Rec. 2291 (1911); Ise, *United States Forest Policy,* 262; Rowley, *Grazing and Rangelands,* 44–45; Pisani, "Forests and Reclamation," 247–51.

19. Wilkinson and Anderson, *Land and Resource Planning,* 133–36.

20. Clary, *Timber and the Forest Service,* 2–15, 29–39, 41–46, 81–93; Wilkinson and Anderson, *Land and Resource Planning,* 135.

21. 33 Stat. 873 (1905) (transfer legislation). For citations to source material regarding the discussion of mining in these paragraphs see, Leshy, *Mining Law,* 61–65, 144–45, 194, 399nn41–43.

22. *Chambers v. Harrington,* 111 U.S. 350, 353 (1884).

23. Leshy, *Mining Law,* 64; *Annual Report of the Chief Forester,* in the *Annual Report of the Department of Agriculture* (1912), 475–80.

24. *U.S. v. Rizzinelli*, 182 F. 675, 682 (1910).

25. *Multnomah Mining, Milling & Development Co. v. United States*, 211 F. 100 (9th Cir. 1914); *United States v. Grand Canyon Cattle Co.*, 247 F. 446 (9th Cir. 1918).

26. Ise, *United States Forest Policy*, 295.

27. Dana, *Forest and Range Policy*, 147–49; 34 Stat. 233 (1906); Gates, *Public Land Law Development*, 512.

28. Gifford Pinchot, *The Use of the National Forests* (Washington, D.C.: Government Printing Office, 1907), i.e., the 1907 *Use Book*, sec. 4, available from the National Park Service, http://npshistory.com/publications/usfs/use-book-1907/sec4.htm; 38 Stat. 1086, 1101 (1915).

28. ROOSEVELT AND CONGRESS USE PUBLIC LANDS TO PROTECT WILDLIFE HABITAT

1. Primary sources for this chapter are Brinkley, *Wilderness Warrior;* Reed and Drabelle, *Fish and Wildlife Service.*

2. *Geer v. Connecticut*, 161 U.S. 519, 522 (1896); 30 Stat. 1074, 1095 (1899).

3. 31 Stat. 187–88 (1900); Dunlap, *Saving America's Wildlife*, 14; Taliaferro, *Grinnell*, 337–38.

4. 35 Cong. Rec. 6509–14, 6517–20, 6566–74 (1902).

5. H.R. Rep. No. 57-3862, at 3 (1902).

6. Henry Clepper, *Professional Forestry in the United States* (Baltimore: Johns Hopkins University Press, 1971), 62; Wilkinson and Anderson, *Land and Resource Planning*, 281–82; Steen, *U.S. Forest Service*, 86–88.

7. Price, *Flight Maps*, 57–58.

8. Merchant, "George Bird Grinnell's Audubon Society."

9. Reed and Drabelle, *Fish and Wildlife Service*, 3–7; Frank Graham, Jr., *Man's Dominion: The Story of Conservation in America* (New York: Evans, 1971), 48.

10. Reed and Drabelle, *Fish and Wildlife Service*, 75.

11. Brinkley, *Wilderness Warrior*, 13–16.

12. Ibid., 13–14, 490–91.

13. Ibid., 9–19.

14. Theodore Roosevelt, Fourth Annual Message to Congress, December 6, 1904.

15. 33 Stat. 614 (1905); Theodore Roosevelt, Proclamation No. 563 (June 2, 1905).

16. Reed and Drabelle, *Fish and Wildlife Service*, 21–22; Lewis Smith, "The Texas Longhorn, Part 2," VisitWimberley.com, http://visitwimberley.com/critters/longhorn2.shtml.

17. 34 Stat. 607 (1906); 34 Stat. 3263 (1906); Brinkley, *Wilderness Warrior*, 756–68.

18. *Pathfinder Mines Corp. v. Hodel*, 811 F.2d 1288, 1291 (9th Cir. 1987).

19. 34 Stat. 536–37 (1906).

20. Reed and Drabelle, *Fish and Wildlife Service*, 8; *Confederated Salish and Kootenai Tribes v. United States*, 437 F.2d 458, 464–65 (1971); Brian Upton, "Returning to a Tribal Self-Governance Partnership at the National Bison Range Complex: Historical, Legal, and Global Perspectives," *Public Land and Resources Law Review* 35 (2014): 114. The Bison Range transfer is in the Montana Water Rights Protection Act, enacted as Division DD of the Consolidated Appropriations Act, 2021, Pub. L. No. 116-260 (December 27, 2020).

21. Fink, "National Wildlife Refuges," 78–82.
22. Brinkley, *Wilderness Warrior*, 792–817.
23. 48 Cong. Rec. 6485 (1912) (Senator Borah); 45 Cong. Rec. 2845 (1910) (Heyburn); Ise, *United States Forest Policy*, 273.
24. Reed and Drabelle, *Fish and Wildlife Service*, 5.

29. PUBLIC LANDS, SCIENCE, AND HISTORY: THE ANTIQUITIES ACT

1. Principal sources for this chapter are Brinkley, *Wilderness Warrior;* Harmon, McManamon, and Pitcaithley, *Antiquities Act;* Ise, *Our National Park Policy*, 143–62; Lee, *Antiquities Act of 1906*, 1–86 (a thorough consideration of the history leading to enactment); Rothman, *Preserving Different Paths;* Sellars, "Very Large Array."
2. Lee, *Antiquities Act of 1906*, 10–12; 13 Cong. Rec. 3777 (1882).
3. 25 Stat. 961 (1889); Lee, *Antiquities Act of 1906*, 81.
4. 31 Stat. 1162 (1901).
5. Lee, *Antiquities Act of 1906*, 39–46.
6. Ibid., 68–76; *Annual Report of the Commissioner of the General Land Office* (1905), 40, and (1906), 48; H.R. Rep. No. 58-3704, 3 (1905).
7. Edgar Lee Hewett, "Government Supervision of Historic and Prehistoric Ruins," H.R. Rep. No. 59-2224 (1906); S. Rep. No. 59-3797 (1906); 34 Stat. 225 (1906) (Antiquities Act).
8. Brinkley, *Wilderness Warrior*, 414, 643–48, 661, 670–72, 689–90.
9. Ibid., 751, 758–59, 762, 776–81, 810–11; Roderick Frazier Nash, "John Muir, William Kent, and the Conservation Schism," *Pacific Historical Review* 36, no. 4 (November 1967): 423–33.
10. Brinkley, *Wilderness Warrior*, 527; "Mr. Roosevelt Sees the Grand Canyon," *New York Times*, May 7, 1903, 2; John Muir, "The Grand Canyon of the Colorado," *Century*, November 1902, 107–16.
11. *Cameron v. United States*, 252 U.S. 450, 455–56 (1920).
12. Leshy, *Mining Law*, 57–60.
13. Lien, *Olympic Battleground*, 16–40.
14. *Annual Report of the Commissioner of the General Land Office* (1909), 19.

30. ROOSEVELT AND NATIONAL PARKS

1. Brinkley, *Wilderness Warrior*, 516–17; Taliaferro, *Grinnell*, 332–33.
2. Lee, *Antiquities Act of 1906*, chap. 6.
3. Theodore Roosevelt, Fourth Annual Message to Congress, December 6, 1904; Fifth Annual Message, December 5, 1905; Brinkley, *Wilderness Warrior*.
4. Ise, *Our National Park Policy*, 156–57.
5. 32 Stat. 202–3 (1902) (Crater Lake National Park).
6. Ise, *Our National Park Policy*, 164–70.
7. Keller and Turek, *American Indians and National Parks*, 32–43; Wilson, *America's Public Lands*, 279n12; D. Smith, *Mesa Verde*, 66–70.
8. Sources for the discussion of the Yosemite Valley are Allin, *Politics of Wilderness Preservation*, 39–40; Brinkley, *Wilderness Warrior;* Ise, *Our National Park Policy*, 71–76; R. Orsi, *Sunset Limited*, 364–70; Runte, *Yosemite*, 67–76; Wolfe, *Son of the Wilderness*, 301–4.

9. Horace Albright, as told to Robert Cahn, *The Birth of the National Park Service: The Founding Years, 1913–1933* (Salt Lake City: Howe Brothers, 1985), 5; Ise, *Our National Park Policy*, 49.

10. Keller and Turek, *American Indians and National Parks*, 27; Ise, *Our National Park Policy*, 139–42; 90 Stat. 235 (1976).

11. Yard, *Our Federal Lands*, 292–93.

31. MAKING NEW FOREST RESERVES: CONGRESS CHALLENGES THE PRESIDENT

1. Principal authorities for this chapter are Gates, *Public Land Law Development*; Ise, *United States Forest Policy*; McCarthy, *Hour of Trial*; Peffer, *Closing of the Public Domain*; Steen, *U.S. Forest Service*.

2. *Annual Report of the Secretary of the Interior* (1903), 18–19; Peffer, *Closing of the Public Domain*, 82.

3. 33 Stat. 547 (1904).

4. "Second Partial Report of the Public Lands Commission" (1905), S. Doc. No. 58-154, 11–12; Peffer, *Closing of the Public Domain*, 45–53, 82–84.

5. *Forest Reserves in Idaho* (Forest Service Bulletin 67, 1905), 40; Ise, *United States Forest Policy*, 194–95.

6. Thomas G. Alexander, *The Rise of Multiple Use Management in the Intermountain West: A History of Region 4 of the Forest Service* (U.S. Forest Service, 1987), available from the Forest History Society, https://foresthistory.org/wp-content/uploads/2017/11/Rise_of_multiple_use.pdf; McCarthy, *Hour of Trial*, 131–54; Pinchot, *Breaking New Ground*, 252; Steen, *U.S. Forest Service*, 74–75; Merchant, "Women of the Conservation Movement"; Unger, *Beyond Nature's Housekeepers*.

7. Theodore Roosevelt, Fifth Annual Message to Congress, December 5, 1905.

8. 34 Stat. 234 (1906).

9. Goodwin, *Bully Pulpit*, 516.

10. Theodore Roosevelt, Special Message to Congress, December 7, 1906.

11. Peffer, *Closing of the Public Domain*, 87–88; Calef, *Private Grazing and Public Lands*, 49–57.

12. 41 Cong. Rec. 4485 (1907).

13. 41 Cong. Rec. 11897–1913, 2957, 3183–3207, 3299, 3520–43, 3604–21 (1907); Peffer, *Closing of the Public Domain*, 90–98.

14. 41 Cong. Rec. 3720 (1907).

15. 41 Cong. Rec. 3721 (1907); Peffer, *Closing of the Public Domain*, 98.

16. Michael P. Malone, "Midas of the West: The Incredible Career of William Andrews Clark," *Montana: The Magazine of Western History* 33, no. 4 (Autumn 1983): 2; D. Smith, *Mining America*, 82.

17. 41 Cong. Rec. 3717, 3720–26, 3869 (1907).

18. Peffer, *Closing of the Public Domain*, 98; Ise, *United States Forest Policy*, 196–201; U.S. Constitution, art. I, § 7, cl. 2.

19. Roosevelt, *Autobiography*, 662.

20. Ibid.; 34 Stat. 1256, 1271 (1907).

21. Roosevelt, *Autobiography*, 662; Ise, *United States Forest Policy*, 188–90, 188n66; Brinkley, *Wilderness Warrior*, 676–78.

22. Theodore Roosevelt, Fourth Annual Message to Congress, December 6, 1904; Theodore Roosevelt, *Outdoor Pastimes of an American Hunter* (New York: Scribner's Sons, 1905), 347.

23. 34 Stat. 1269, 1281 (1907).

24. Steen, *U.S. Forest Service*, 99–100; McCarthy, *Hour of Trial*, 210–35; Dennis L. Lynch and Stephen Larrabee, "Private Lands Within National Forests: Origins, Problems, and Opportunities," in Steen, *Origins of the National Forests*, 198, 213.

32. ROOSEVELT, PUBLIC LANDS, AND ENERGY DEVELOPMENT

1. Principal sources for this chapter are Hays, *Conservation and the Gospel of Efficiency;* Leshy, *Mining Law;* Peffer, *Closing of the Public Domain;* Swenson, "Mineral Resources Exploitation"; Yergin, *Prize,* 78–82; Strand, *Inventing Niagara,* 162; Gordon, *Rise and Fall of American Growth,* which is replete with statistics on the changes in living standards after the Civil War, for example, 113–20; "U.S. Energy Production, Consumption Has Changed Significantly Since 1908," U.S. Energy Information Administration, November 1, 2016, www.eia.gov/todayinenergy/detail. php?id=28592.

2. Theodore Roosevelt, Eighth Annual Message to Congress, December 8, 1908; Richard Hofstadter, *The Progressive Movement, 1900–1915* (New York: Prentice Hall, 1963).

3. Hays, *Conservation and the Gospel of Efficiency,* 73–81; Peffer, *Closing of the Public Domain,* 105–6, 119–25.

4. 35 Stat. 273 (1908) (Rainy River dam project vetoed).

5. Hays, *Conservation and the Gospel of Efficiency,* 82–87; Swenson, "Mineral Resources Exploitation," 726–30; Peffer, *Closing of the Public Domain,* 119.

6. Hays, *Conservation and the Gospel of Efficiency,* 87–90; Peffer, *Closing of the Public Domain,* 125–31; William E. Colby, "The Law of Oil and Gas with Special Reference to the Public Domain and Conservation," *California Law Review* 30, no. 3 (1942): 248, 258–62; *United States v. Southern Pacific Co.,* 251 U.S. 1, 13 (1919).

7. Theodore Roosevelt, Special Message to Congress, December 17, 1906.

8. 41 Cong. Rec. 2614–19 (1907); Swenson, "Mineral Resources Exploitation," 727–28.

9. Theodore Roosevelt, "Message of the President of the United States, Relating to Certain Phases of the Public Land Situation in the United States," February 13, 1907, S. Doc. No. 59-310; Hays, *Conservation and the Gospel of Efficiency,* 84–85; Swenson, "Mineral Resources Exploitation," 728–30.

10. 35 Stat. 844 (1909); 36 Stat. 583 (1910).

11. Swenson, "Mineral Resources Exploitation," 730–40; Leshy, *Mining Law,* 91–92, 103; Hays, *Conservation and the Gospel of Efficiency,* 90.

12. *Chrisman v. Miller,* 197 U.S. 313, 323 (1905); Colby, "Law of Oil and Gas," 252–53; George Otis Smith, *The Classification of the Public Lands,* U.S. Geological Survey Bulletin 537 (Washington, D.C.: Government Printing Office, 1913), 38.

13. Max W. Ball, *Petroleum Withdrawals and Restorations Affecting the Public Domain* (Washington: Government Printing Office, 1917), 21; Smith, *Classification of the Public Lands,* 38.

14. Ball, *Petroleum Withdrawals and Restorations,* 23.

15. Theodore Roosevelt, Sixth Annual Message to Congress, December 3, 1906.

16. Swenson, "Mineral Resources Exploitation," 732; Colby, "Law of Oil and Gas," 254–55; Smith quoted in *United States v. Midwest Oil Co.*, 236 U.S 459, 466–67 (1915).

17. Yergin, *Prize*, 81–82.

18. Hays, *Conservation and the Gospel of Efficiency*, 88–90.

33. PUBLIC LANDS IN THE HANDOFF FROM ROOSEVELT TO TAFT

1. Principal sources for this chapter are Brinkley, *Wilderness Warrior*; Gates, *Public Land Law Development*; Hays, *Conservation and the Gospel of Efficiency*; Ise, *United States Forest Policy*; Steen, *U.S. Forest Service*.

2. Brinkley, *Wilderness Warrior*, 776–95, 806–10.

3. 24 Stat. 388 (1887) (Dawes Act); William deBuys, "Stewart Udall, John Wesley Powell, and the Emergence of a National American Commons," in Robison, McCool, and Minckley, *Vision and Place*, 167, 180.

4. Theodore Roosevelt, *The Winning of the West*, vol. 1, *From the Alleghanies to the Mississippi, 1769–1776* (New York: Putnam's Sons, 1889), 90; Newton, *Federal Indian Law*, § 1.03[6][b], 77–79; § 1603 [2][b], 1041–42; Janet A. McDonnell, *The Dispossession of the American Indian, 1887–1934* (Bloomington: Indiana University Press, 1962), 50.

5. Proclamation No. 859, 35 Stat. 2236 (March 2, 1909); Proclamations Nos. 862–66, 35 Stat. 2239–45 (March 2, 1909); Proclamation No. 871, 35 Stat. 2249 (March 2, 1909); Exec. Order Nos. 1475–85 (Feb. 17, 1912); Catton, *American Indians and National Forests*, 36–37, 49, 309n3, 311n31.

6. Catton, *American Indians and National Forests*, 40, 302.

7. E. White, *Eastern Establishment and Western Experience*, 52–74.

8. E. White, *Eastern Establishment and Western Experience*; William W. Savage, Jr., *The Cowboy Hero: His Image in American History and Culture* (Norman: University of Oklahoma Press, 1979); William W. Savage, *Cowboy Life: Reconstructing an American Myth* (Norman: University of Oklahoma Press, 1975); Evan Thomas, *The War Lovers: Roosevelt, Lodge, Hearst, and the Rush to Empire, 1898* (New York: Little, Brown, 2010), 53; David McCullough, *Mornings on Horseback: The Story of an Extraordinary Family, a Vanished Way of Life, and the Unique Child Who Became Theodore Roosevelt* (New York: Simon & Schuster, 2001), 316.

9. Yard, *Our Federal Lands*, 123; Gates, *Public Land Law Development*, 580.

10. Quoted in Taliaferro, *Grinnell*, 316.

11. 45 Cong. Rec. 6522–29 (May 19, 1910) (Ammons's remarks); Hays, *Conservation and Gospel of Efficiency*, 258–59.

12. William Howard Taft, Special Message to Congress, January 14, 1910; Hays, *Conservation and Gospel of Efficiency*, 258.

13. "National Conservation," *Outlook*, May 14, 1910, 57 (Taft's comments); Ise, *United States Forest Policy*, 373; *Annual Report of the Interior Secretary* (1907), 54.

14. Goodwin, *Bully Pulpit*, 605–27; "Charges Against Ballinger," *Literary Digest*, February 12, 1910, 269.

15. Steen, *U.S. Forest Service*, 69–102.

16. Pinchot, *Breaking New Ground*, 321.

17. Pinchot "The Conservation of Natural Resources," *Farmers' Bulletin* 327 (April 30, 1908), 12, quoted in Ise, *United States Forest Policy*, 377.

34. TAFT'S UNDERVALUED RECORD ON PUBLIC LAND CONSERVATION

1. Hays, *Conservation and the Gospel of Efficiency*, 258.
2. Roosevelt, *Autobiography*, 620.
3. William Howard Taft, Special Message to Congress, January 14, 1910.
4. 45 Cong. Rec. 4644 (1910). The legislative history of the Pickett Act is summarized in Swenson, "Mineral Resources Exploitation," 733–36; Peffer, *Closing of the Public Domain*, 115–16.
5. Peffer, *Closing of the Public Domain*, 115–19; John Ise, *The United States Oil Policy* (New Haven, Conn.: Yale University Press, 1926), 314–19.
6. 36 Stat. 847 (1910); 45 Cong. Rec. 4310, 7474, 7551–55 (1910).
7. *Shaw v. Work*, 9 F.2d 1014 (D.C. Cir. 1925).
8. 37 Stat. 497 (1912).
9. *United States v. Midwest Oil Co.*, 236 U.S. 459, 475 (1915).
10. 37 Stat. 287 (1912); Peffer, *Closing of the Public Domain*, 152–54; Ise, *United States Forest Policy*, 256–58.
11. *Annual Report of the Secretary of the Interior* (1911), 9–10; Peffer, *Closing of the Public Domain*, 153.
12. Voigt, *Public Grazing Lands*, 26; 29 Stat. 484 (1897); James Muhn, "Public Water Reserves: The Metamorphosis of a Public Land Policy," *Journal of Land, Resources, and Environmental Law* 20, no. 1 (2001): 78–79.
13. Taliaferro, *Grinnell*, 218–20, 366–68, 374–75, 377–78.
14. Ibid., 173–79; Keller and Turek, *American Indians and National Parks*, 43–64; Spence, *Dispossessing the Wilderness*, 80–81, 162–63; Proclamation No. 396, 29 Stat. 908 (February 22, 1897).
15. Taliaferro, *Grinnell*, 294; Donald H. Robinson, *Through the Years in Glacier National Park: An Administrative History* (Glacier National History Association, 1960), available from the National Park Service, www.nps.gov/parkhistory/online_books/glac.
16. 36 Stat. 354 (1910).
17. Taliaferro, *Grinnell*, 366–69, 374–78.
18. Ise, *Our National Park Policy*, 157–59, 241–42; Harmon, McManamon, and Pitcaithley, *Antiquities Act*, 75; Hal K. Rothman, *Navajo National Monument: A Place and Its People; An Administrative History* (National Park Service, 1991).
19. Harmon, McManamon, and Pitcaithley, *Antiquities Act*, 289.
20. Christopher E. Johnson, *Nature and History on the Sierra Crest: Devils Postpile and the Mammoth Lakes Sierra* (National Park Service, 2013), 75–82; available at www.nps.gov/depo/learn/historyculture/upload/DEPO_HRS_AdminHist_access.pdf.
21. Exec. Order No. 1732, March 3, 1913.

35. NATIONAL FORESTS BECOME NATIONAL WITH ENACTMENT OF THE WEEKS ACT

1. Principal authorities for this chapter are Bramwell, "1911 Weeks Act"; Bramwell and Lewis, "Law That Nationalized the Forest Service"; Hays, *Conservation and the Gospel of Efficiency*, 47–48; Ise, *United States Forest Policy*, 207–23; Shands and Healy, *Lands Nobody Wanted*; C. Smith, "Appalachian National Park Movement"; C. Smith, "Movement for Eastern National Forests"; Steen, *U.S. Forest Service*, 122–29. Contemporary documents and discussion can be found at "Weeks Act Resources,"

Forest History Society, https://foresthistory.org/research-explore/us-forest-service-history/policy-and-law/the-weeks-act/weeks-act-resources.

2. C. Smith, "Appalachian National Park Movement," 52–53.

3. 31 Stat. 197 (1900); James Wilson, "Report on the Forests and Forest Conditions of the Southern Appalachian Mountain Region," S. Doc. No. 57-84, 166–68 (1901).

4. C. Smith, "Movement for Eastern National Forests," 5–8, 13, 19–20, 27, 44, 49–50, 63, 71–75.

5. Ibid., 104–11, 122–28; Bramwell, "1911 Weeks Act," 328–29.

6. C. Smith, "Movement for Eastern National Forests," 218; Ise, *United States Forest Policy*, 217–18.

7. C. Smith, "Movement for Eastern National Forests," 226–28, 255 (Cannon opposition); 1907 appropriation, 41 Cong. Rec. 3613 (February 22, 1907), 4487–90 (March 2, 1907); 34 Stat. 1281 (1907).

8. James Wilson, *Report of the Secretary of Agriculture on the Southern Appalachian and White Mountains Watersheds* (Washington, D.C., 1908), 7; C. Smith, "Movement for Eastern National Forests," 271; Shands and Healy, *Lands Nobody Wanted*, 13.

9. C. Smith, "Movement for Eastern National Forests," 271; Ise, *United States Forest Policy*, 211–18.

10. *The John Weeks Story: A Chapter in the History of American Forestry* (U.S. Forest Service, 1961), available from the Forest History Society, https://foresthistory.org/wp-content/uploads/2017/02/JohnWeeksStory.pdf; C. Smith, "Movement for Eastern National Forests," 332–35 and appendix 15.

11. C. Smith, "Movement for Eastern National Forests," 277–86 (Weeks; constitutional issue); 42 Cong. Rec. 6328–30, 6385–6401, 6403–9 (May 15–16, 1908); *Kansas v. Colorado*, 206 U.S. 46, 88–94 (1907).

12. C. Smith, "Movement for Eastern National Forests," 295 (governors' testimony).

13. Ibid., 303–6 (discussing the committee report).

14. 43 Cong. Rec. 3245 (Feb. 26, 1909), 3566 (March 1, 1909), 3749–51 (March 3, 1909).

15. 45 Cong. Rec. 4376 (April 7, 1910), 9027 (June 24, 1910) (House vote); C. Smith, "Movement for Eastern National Forests," 276–85, 294–98, 313–15, 321, 335 ("you have my scalp"); Goodwin, *Bully Pulpit*, 626; Ise, *United States Forest Policy*, 219–20.

16. 46 Cong Rec. 2578 (February 15, 1911) (Senate vote; debate on 2577–2602); C. Smith, "Movement for Eastern National Forests," 345–49 (Taft comment, 349), 357–60; *Annual Report of the Secretary of the Interior* (1911), 8.

17. 36 Stat. 961 (1911); James B. Snow, "Implementing the Weeks Act," *Forest History Today*, Spring/Fall 2011, 70, 71, 76n6; Ise, *United States Forest Policy*, 222; Fairfax et al., *Buying Nature*, 68–72.

18. *Kohl v. United States*, 91 U.S. 367, 374 (1875) (state approval not required); Snow, "Implementing the Weeks Act," 72; *U.S. v. Certain Lands*, 208 Fed. 429 (D.N.H. 1913) (upholding state consent); S. Doc. No. 62-137; S. Doc. No. 63-307; H. Doc. No. 65-564.

19. 25 Stat. 357 (1888); *Griffin v. United States*, 58 F.2d 674 (W.D.Va. 1932); *United States v. 16.92 Acres of Land*, 670 F.2d 1369 (7th Cir. 1982); Shands and Healy, *Lands Nobody Wanted*; Fairfax et al., *Buying Nature*, 71.

20. 37 Stat. 828, 855 (1913).
21. *United States v. Polino*, 131 F. Supp. 772 (N.D. W. Va., 1955); *United States v. Belville Mining Co.*, 763 F. Supp. 1411 (S.D. Ohio, 1991), aff'd, 999 F.2d 989 (6th Cir. 1993); *Minard Run Oil Co. v. U.S. Forest Service*, 670 F.3d 236 (3rd Cir. 2011) (conflicts among estate owners).
22. Agriculture Appropriation Act, 38 Stat. 415, 441 (1914).
23. "Editorial: The Appalachian Bill," *American Forestry* 17, no. 3 (March 1911): 168–69.

36. PUBLIC LANDS AT THE END OF THE AGE OF THEODORE ROOSEVELT

1. Coggins et al., *Federal Public Land and Resources Law*, 116–22; Wilkinson, *Crossing the Next Meridian*, 93.
2. Greeley, *Forests and Men*, 79.
3. Rowley, *Grazing and Rangelands*, 66–68.
4. *Grimaud v. United States*, 220 U.S. 506, 509 (1911).
5. Keith E. Whittington and Jason Iuliano, "The Myth of the Nondelegation Doctrine," *Pennsylvania Law Review* 165 (2017): 379, 422–24; Julian Davis Mortenson and Nicholas Bagley, "Delegation at the Founding," *Columbia Law Review* (forthcoming, 2021); *Grimaud*, 220 U.S. at 516.
6. *Grimaud*, 220 U.S. at 522.
7. *Light v. United States*, 220 U.S. 523 (1911).
8. Ibid., 537, 536.
9. Ibid., 535, 538.
10. Greeley, *Forests and Men*, 80–81; Rowley, *Grazing and Rangelands*, 66–68.
11. 42 Cong. Rec. 4475–76 (1908); 43 Cong. Rec. part 4, 3226 (1909); D. Smith, *Henry M. Teller*, 125–26.
12. 36 Stat. 557–79 (1910); John D. Leshy, "The Making of the Arizona Constitution," *Arizona State Law Journal* 20 (1988): 1, 10–31.
13. 48 Cong. Rec. 6478–81 (1912).

37. NATIONAL PARKS TAKE CENTER STAGE

1. Principal sources for this chapter are Albright, *Birth of the National Park Service*; Hays, *Conservation and the Gospel of Efficiency*; Ise, *Our National Park Policy*; Nash, "Muir, Kent, and the Conservation Schism"; Richardson, "Struggle for the Valley"; Righter, *Battle over Hetch Hetchy*; Sellars, *Preserving Nature in the National Parks*; Shankland, *Steve Mather*; Swain, "National Park Service Act"; Wolfe, *Son of the Wilderness*.
2. Muir, "Features of the Proposed Yosemite National Park," *Century*, September 1890, 656–67; 31 Stat. 790–91 (1901) (Right-of-Way Act); Ise, *Our National Park Policy*, 69, 85–96; Runte, *Yosemite*, 81 (citing *Annual Report of the Secretary of the Interior* [1903], 156).
3. Richardson, "Struggle for the Valley," 250.
4. Wolfe, *Son of the Wilderness*, 322–25; Allin, *Politics of Wilderness Preservation*, 46.
5. Dana and Fairfax, *Forest and Range Policy*, 108; Hays, *Conservation and the Gospel of Efficiency*, 192–95; Nash, *Wilderness and the American Mind*, 180–81; Taliaferro, *Grinnell*, 375–77.

6. John Muir, *The Yosemite* (New York: Century, 1912; reprint, Eastford, Conn.: Martino Fine Books, 2017), 262; Fox, *John Muir and His Legacy*, 143–44; Wolfe, *Son of the Wilderness*, 156, 309–17, 322–45.

7. Allin, *Politics of Wilderness Preservation*, 46–48; 38 Stat. 242–51 (1913).

8. Wulf, *Invention of Nature*, 333.

9. Pinchot quoted in Hays, *Conservation and the Gospel of Efficiency*, 196; Sellars, *Preserving Nature in the National Parks*, 29–31.

10. Sellars, *Preserving Nature in the National Parks*, 42, 302n3; Hyde, *American Vision*, 284–85; Swain, "National Park Service Act," 7; Runte, *National Parks*, 99; Shankland, *Steve Mather*, 51–53.

11. Sellars, *Preserving Nature in the National Parks*, 42–43, 60–61, 302n46; Ise, *Our National Park Policy*, 185–90.

12. Albright, *Birth of the National Park Service*, 15–16; Sellars, *Preserving Nature in the National Parks*, 31; Runte, *National Parks*, 99; Shankland, *Steve Mather*, 100–106; Ise, *Our National Park Policy*, 185–93.

13. Journalist quoted in Robert G. Athearn, *The Mythic West in Twentieth-Century America* (Lawrence: University of Kansas Press, 1986), 99.

14. Albright, *Birth of the National Park Service*, 16–18; Shankland, *Steve Mather*, 8.

15. 38 Stat. 798 (1915); Ise, *Our National Park Policy*, 212–13.

16. Shankland, *Steve Mather*, 97–99; Sellars, *Preserving Nature in the National Parks*, 41–43; Swain, "National Park Service Act," 7–9.

17. Sellars, *Preserving Nature in the National Parks*, 28; R. White, "Contested Terrain," 202.

18. "An Act to Establish a National Park Service," 39 Stat. 535 (1916).

19. Keiter, *To Conserve Unimpaired*, 44.

20. Sellars, *Preserving Nature in the National Parks*, 37–41, 301n38; 53 Cong. Rec. 10363–64, 12151, 13005 (1916).

38. THE NATIONAL PARK SYSTEM'S EARLY YEARS

1. The Lane letter is found in Lary M. Dilsaver, ed., *America's National Park System: The Critical Documents* (Lanham, Md.: Rowman and Littlefield, 1994), available from the National Park Service, www.nps.gov/parkhistory/online_books/anps.

2. Principal sources for this chapter are Albright, *Birth of the National Park System;* Ise, *Our National Park Policy;* Keiter, *To Conserve Unimpaired;* Rothman, "Regular Ding-Dong Fight"; Sellars, *Preserving Nature in the National Parks;* Shankland, *Steve Mather;* Yard, *Our Federal Lands.*

3. Yard, *Our Federal Lands*, 230–33; Sellars, *Preserving Nature in the National Parks*, 57–58.

4. James Bryce, "National Parks—The Need of the Future," *Outlook*, December 14, 1912, 811–13.

5. Sutter, *Driven Wild*, 23–30, 106–11.

6. Hyde, *American Vision*, 296–304; Ise, *Our National Park Policy*, 202–3; 43 Stat. 90 (1924); Yard, *Our Federal Lands*, 272–74.

7. Sellars, *Preserving Nature in the National Parks*, 22–30, 47, 75–79, 90, 302n1; Dunlap, "Wildlife, Science, and National Parks," 188–89; Bartlett, *Yellowstone*, 330, 342n11; Keiter, *To Conserve Unimpaired*, 146, 179.

8. Sellars, *Preserving Nature in the National Parks*, 307n76; 39 Stat. 432 (Hawaii), 442 (Lassen), 938 (Mt. McKinley); 40 Stat. 1175 (Grand Canyon); 40 Stat. 1178 (Lafayette-Acadia).

9. 45 Stat. 1553 (1929).

10. 43 Stat. 1914 (1923) (monument); 43 Stat. 593 (national park); 46 Stat. 582 (1930) (renaming); Thomas G. Alexander, "Red Rock and Gray Stone: Senator Reed Smoot, the Establishment of Zion and Bryce Canyon National Parks, and the Rebuilding of Downtown Washington, D.C." *Pacific Historical Review* 72, no. 1 (February 2003): 1–38; Rothman, "Regular Ding-Dong Fight," 105–8; Ise, *Our National Park Policy,* 154–55.

11. Michael G. Schene, "Only the Squeal Is Left: Conflict over Establishing Olympic National Park," *Pacific Historian* 27, no. 3 (Fall 1983): 53–61; Elmo Richardson, "Olympic National Park: Twenty Years of Controversy," *Forest and Conservation History* 12, no. 1 (April 1968): 6–15; Rothman, "Regular Ding-Dong Fight," 99.

12. Ise, *Our National Park Policy,* 331–32; Rothman, "Regular Ding-Dong Fight," 186–210; Barrow, *Nature's Ghosts,* 215; Proclamation No. 1733, 43 Stat. 1933 (1925).

13. 45 Stat. 1314 (1929).

14. 44 Stat. 616 (1926) (Shenandoah and Great Smoky Mountains); 44 Stat. 635 (1926) (Mammoth Cave); 43 Stat. 958 (1925) (land for Shenandoah, Great Smoky Mountains, and Mammoth Cave); 45 Stat. 109 (1928) (size of Shenandoah); 47 Stat. 37 (1932) (leasing of parkland back to donors); 46 Stat. 1514 (1931) (Isle Royale); 52 Stat. 785 (1938) (adding land to Isle Royale); Ise, *Our National Park Policy,* 248–67, 332–33; Sellars, *Preserving Nature in the National Parks,* 135; Zaslowsky and Watkins, *These American Lands,* 27; Rothman, "Regular Ding-Dong Fight," 90, 173; Yard, *Our Federal Lands,* 264–65, 295.

15. Amalia Tholen Baldwin, *Becoming Wilderness: Nature, History, and the Making of Isle Royale National Park* (Houghton, Mich.: Isle Royale and Keweenaw Parks Association, 2011).

16. Justin Reich, "Re-Creating the Wilderness: Shaping Narratives and Landscapes in Shenandoah National Park," *Environmental History* 6, no. 1 (January 2001): 95–117; Fairfax et al. *Buying Nature,* 83–86; Margaret Lynn Brown, *The Wild East: A Biography of the Great Smoky Mountains* (Gainesville: University Press of Florida, 2000); Daniel S. Pierce, *The Great Smokies: From Natural Habitat to National Park* (Knoxville: University of Tennessee Press, 2000).

17. Terence Young, " 'A Contradiction in Democratic Government': W. J. Trent, Jr., and the Struggle to Desegregate National Park Campgrounds," *Environmental History* 14, no. 4 (October 2009): 651–82.

18. Albright, *Birth of the National Park Service,* 158–68.

19. 39 Stat. 938 (1917).

20. 46 Stat. 1043 (1931); Sellars, *Preserving Nature in the National Parks,* 85; Shankland, *Steve Mather,* 201–6.

21. Keiter, *To Conserve Unimpaired,* 241; see also Ise, *Our National Park Policy,* 244, 268; 41 Stat. 1407 (1921).

22. Ise, *Our National Park Policy,* 296–98; Shankland, *Steve Mather,* 221–24; Albright, *Birth of the National Park Service,* 229; Yard, *Our Federal Lands,* 269–70, 295; Sellars, *Preserving Nature in the National Parks,* 69, 308n81.

23. Ise, *Our National Park Policy*, 307–16; Sellars, *Preserving Nature in the National Parks*, 64–65; Shankland, *Steve Mather*, 212–20; Taliaferro, *Grinnell*, 459–65, 468–71.

24. Swain, *Wilderness Defender*, 193; Sellars, *Preserving Nature in the National Parks*, 88, 312n5.

25. Sellars, *Preserving Nature in the National Parks*, 59, 87–88; Ise, *Our National Park Policy*, 321–23; Runte, *Trains of Discovery*, 45–47; Fox, *John Muir and His Legacy*, 146 (Yard quotation).

39. THE NATIONAL FOREST SYSTEM MATURES AND EVOLVES

1. Primary authorities for this chapter are Dana, *Forest and Range Policy*; Dana and Fairfax, *Forest and Range Policy*; Gates, *Public Land Law Development*; Hays, *American People and the National Forests*; Rowley, *Grazing and Rangelands*; Steen, *U.S. Forest Service*; Wilkinson and Anderson, *Land and Resource Planning*.

2. 43 Stat. 653 (1924); 45 Stat. 468 (1928) (McNary-Woodruff). Weeks Act implementation is addressed in Johnson and Govatski, *Forests for the People*; Gates, *Public Land Law Development*, 597; Dana and Fairfax, *Forest and Range Policy*, 128–30; Williams, *Americans and Their Forests*, 465; *Annual Report of the Forest Service* (1933), 12.

3. 45 Stat. 468 (1928); Dana and Fairfax, *Forest and Range Policy*, 130; Steen, *U.S. Forest Service*, 314; Clary, *Timber and the Forest Service*, 83; 43 Stat. 653 (1924); Dana, *Forest and Range Policy*, 223–24.

4. Swain, *Federal Conservation Policy*, 27–28; Ise, *Our National Park Policy*, 256–59; Gates, *Public Land Law Development*, 503, 511.

5. 42 Stat. 465 (1922); 43 Stat. 653–55 (1924); 43 Stat. 1090 (1925); Gates, *Public Land Law Development*, 593; Fairfax et al., *Buying Nature*, 88.

6. Rowley, *Grazing and Rangelands*, 96–103; William deBuys and Craig Allen, "A Historical Chronology of Events and Observations for the Pecos Wilderness in the Territorial Period," *New Mexico Historical Review* 90, no. 4 (2015): 415–87.

7. Rowley, *Grazing and Rangelands*, 112; Voigt, *Public Grazing Lands*, 53–54.

8. Oliver Wendell Holmes, Jr., "The Path of the Law," *Harvard Law Review* 10, no. 8 (1897): 477.

9. Rowley, *Grazing and Rangelands*, 47, 89–91, 117–18, 120; Voigt, *Public Grazing Lands*, 54–57; Wilkinson, *Crossing the Next Meridian*, 106–8; Wilkinson and Anderson, *Land and Resource Planning*, 100–103; Hays, *American People and the National Forests*, 29–30; Clawson, *Western Range Livestock Industry*, 11–13.

10. Hays, *American People and the National Forests*, 79–83; Curt Meine, *Aldo Leopold: His Life and Work* (Madison: University of Wisconsin Press, 2010), 188–89, 204–10, 220; Leopold's "Watershed Handbook" is available online from the Aldo Leopold Archives.

11. 38 Stat. 1101 (1915); Raleigh Barlowe, "Land for Recreation," in Ottoson, *Land Use Policy and Problems*, 255–81.

12. Steen, *U.S. Forest Service*, 159–60; Frank Waugh, *Recreation Uses on the National Forests* (Washington, D.C.: Government Printing Office, 1918), 10, 24, 27, 36–37; Yard, *Our Federal Lands*, 141–44; L. F. Kneipp, "In Supplying Areas for Recreation," in U.S. Department of Agriculture, *The Western Range: A Great but Neglected Resource* (Washington, D.C.: Government Printing Office, 1936), 373–75.

13. 38 Stat. 1101 (1915); Dana, *Forest and Range Policy*, 227–28; Yard, *Our Federal Lands*, 272 (NPS visits); Allin, *Politics of Wilderness Preservation*, 67–68; Wilkinson and

Anderson, *Land and Resource Planning*, 315 (discussing Greeley's 1921 report); Wilkinson, *Crossing the Next Meridian*, 131–35.

14. 39 Stat. 446, 476 (1916); 48 Stat. 400 (1934).

15. Joseph Grinnell, "Wild Animal Life as a Product and as a Necessity of National Forests," *Journal of Forestry* 22, no. 8 (December 1924): 837–45; Alfred Runte, "Joseph Grinnell and Yosemite: Rediscovering the Legacy of a California Conservationist," *California History* 69, no. 2 (Summer 1990): 170–81; Sellars, *Preserving Nature in the National Parks*, 81, 281; Steen, *U.S. Forest Service*, 87.

16. Richard W. Behan, "The Succotash Syndrome, or Multiple Use: A Heartfelt Approach to Forest Land Management," *Natural Resources Journal* 7, no. 4 (Fall 1967): 473 (tracing the emergence of "multiple use").

40. THE FOREST AND PARK SERVICES COMPETE AND COOPERATE

1. Primary authorities for this chapter are Allin, *Politics of Wilderness Preservation;* Dana, *Forest and Range Policy;* Dana and Fairfax, *Forest and Range Policy;* Dunlap, *Saving America's Wildlife;* Leshy, "Legal Wilderness"; Nash, *Wilderness and the American Mind;* Sellars, *Preserving Nature in the National Parks;* Sutter, *Driven Wild;* Van Nuys, *Varmints and Victims.*

2. "National Conference on Outdoor Recreation," S. Doc. No. 68-229 (1924); "National Conference on Outdoor Recreation," S. Doc. No. 70-158 (1928); Yard, *Our Federal Lands*, 327–29.

3. 37 Stat. 287 (1912); 39 Stat. 355, 358 (1916); Dana and Fairfax, *Forest and Range Policy*, 114–15; Sutter, *Driven Wild*, 16, 24, 60–63, 98–99; Leshy, "Legal Wilderness," 554–55.

4. Timothy Egan, *The Big Burn: Teddy Roosevelt and the Fire That Saved America* (New York: Houghton Mifflin Harcourt, 2009).

5. Sellars, *Preserving Nature in the National Parks*, 82–84; 36 Stat. 855, 857 (1910); *United States v. Alford*, 274 U.S. 264 (1927).

6. Van Nuys, *Varmints and Victims*, 40–48; Dunlap, *Saving America's Wildlife*, 37–39; Flores, *Coyote America*, 87–90, 94–96, 100; Rowley, *Grazing and Rangelands*, 77; Matthiessen, *Wildlife in America*, 192–98.

7. 38 Stat. 434 (1914); 38 Stat. 1105 (1915); Van Nuys, *Varmints and Victims*, 53–82.

8. Van Nuys, *Varmints and Victims*, 85–86; Dunlap, *Saving America's Wildlife*, 51; Sellars, *Preserving Nature in the National Parks*, 85–90; Barrow, *Nature's Ghosts*, 221–28; Dunlap, "Wildlife, Science, and National Parks," 192–95; Dunlap, "Values for Varmints," 141–61; Tom Butler, "Refuge System Centennial," *Wild Earth* 13, no. 4 (Winter 2003–4): 8–9.

9. Sellars, *Preserving Nature in the National Parks*, 69–73, 78; Taliaferro, *Grinnell*, 492–93; Fox, *John Muir and His Legacy*, 203; Thomas R. Dunlap, "That Kaibab Myth," *Journal of Forest History* 32, no. 2 (1988): 60, 63–67; Van Nuys, *Varmints and Victims*, 115–18.

10. Dana and Fairfax, *Forest and Range Policy*, 131–32 (citing Donald Cate, "Recreation and the U.S. Forest Service: Organizational Response to Changing Demands," Ph.D. diss., Stanford University, 1963); Rothman, "Regular Ding-Dong Fight," 152; Allin, *Politics of Wilderness Preservation*, 69.

11. 43 Stat. 655 (1924); Dana, *Forest and Range Policy*, 224; Shankland, *Steve Mather*, 217–18.

12. Hal Rothman, "Conflict on the Pajarito: Frank Pinkley, the Forest Service, and the Bandelier Controversy, 1925–32," *Journal of Forest History* 29, no. 2 (April 1985): 68, 72; Harmon, McManamon, and Pitcaithley, *Antiquities Act*, 30–32, 35–38; Herbert Hoover, Proclamation No. 1991, 47 Stat. 2503 (1932).

13. *Annual Report of the Interior Secretary* (1932), 107.

14. Joseph Grinnell and Tracy I. Storer, "Animal Life as an Asset of the National Parks," *Science* 44, no. 1133 (September 15, 1916): 375–80; Leshy, "Legal Wilderness," 553n13; G. Frederick Schwarz, "A Suggestion Regarding National Forest Reserves," *Forestry and Irrigation* 11 (1905): 288–89; Francis B. Sumner, "The Need for a More Serious Effort to Rescue a Few Fragments of Vanishing Nature," *Scientific Monthly* 10, no. 3 (March 1920): 240–41.

15. Nash, *Wilderness and the American Mind*, 185–91; Zaslowsky and Watkins, *These American Lands*, 197–200; Dana and Fairfax, *Forest and Range Policy*, 132–33; Reiger, *American Sportsmen*, 188–95 (sketch of Leopold).

16. William Greeley, "What Shall We Do with Our Mountains?," *Sunset*, December 1927, 14, 85; Allin, *Politics of Wilderness Preservation*, 71–76; Wilkinson and Anderson, *Land and Resource Planning*, 314–21; Zaslovsky and Watkins, *These American Lands*, 200; Yard, *Our Federal Lands*, 147–48.

17. U.S. Department of the Interior, *A Brief History of the National Park Service*, ed. James F. Kieley (Washington, D.C.: Government Printing Office, 1940), www.nps.gov/parkhistory/online_books/kieley/index.htm; Allin, *Politics of Wilderness Preservation*, 75–76; Keiter, *To Conserve Unimpaired*, 16; Miles, *Wilderness in National Parks*, 47–48; Yard, *Our Federal Lands*, 277–80; Sutter, *Driven Wild*, 114–40, 230, 239–41, 250; Sellars, *Preserving Nature in the National Parks*, 102–3, 107, 314n31, 315n45; Fox, *John Muir and His Legacy*, 203–6.

18. Allin, *Politics of Wilderness Preservation*, 73, 97.

19. Leshy, *Mining Law*, 229–31, 458–59.

20. Sellars, *Preserving Nature in the National Parks*, 92, 109–10, 316n53.

21. 46 Stat. 1021 (1930); "History of the BWCAW," Forest Service, www.fs.usda.gov/detail/superior/specialplaces/?cid=stelprdb5127455; Allin, *Politics of Wilderness Preservation*, 76–80; Ise, *Our National Park Policy*, 343, 525; Brinkley, *Rightful Heritage*, 247; 70 Stat. 326 (1956); Dana and Fairfax, *Forest and Range Policy*, 133.

22. Nash, *Wilderness and the American Mind*, 231.

41. RANCHERS, HOMESTEADERS, AND ENERGY DEVELOPERS COMPETE FOR PRIMACY

1. Principal authorities for the SRHA discussion are Gates, *Public Land Law Development*; Hays, *Conservation and the Gospel of Efficiency*; Ise, *United States Forest Policy*; Peffer, *Closing of the Public Domain*; Swenson, "Mineral Resources Exploitation."

2. 35 Stat. 844 (1909) (Coal Lands Act of 1909); 36 Stat. 583 (1910) (Coal Lands Act of 1910); Gates, *Public Land Law Development*, 498–521; Swenson, "Mineral Resources Exploitation," 740–41; Dick, *Lure of the Land*, 305; Walter Prescott Webb, *The Great Plains*, new ed. (1931; Lincoln: University of Nebraska Press, 1981), 387–99, 423; Sara M. Gregg, "Imagining Opportunity: The 1909 Enlarged Homestead Act and

the Promise of the Public Domain," *Western Historical Quarterly* 50, no. 3 (Autumn 2019): 257–79.

3. Gates, *Public Land Law Development,* 513–17; Peffer, *Closing of the Public Domain,* 150–67; Merrill, *Public Lands and Political Meaning,* 55–57.

4. Yard, *Our Federal Lands,* 197 (summary of withdrawals and classifications as of 1927).

5. 46 Cong. Rec. 4016 (1911); 51 Cong. Rec. 13680 (1914); Peffer, *Closing of the Public Domain,* 216.

6. 39 Stat. 862 (1916).

7. Gates, *Public Land Law Development,* 498–501 (Kinkaid Act), 516–19 (SRHA).

8. 39 Stat. 862 (1916).

9. Peffer, *Closing of the Public Domain,* 160–61; Dick, *Lure of the Land,* 306.

10. Donahue, *Western Range Revisited,* 23; Rowley, *Grazing and Rangelands,* 90–91 (effect of the SRHA on the Forest Service's grazing program); Clawson, *Western Range Livestock Industry,* 11, 16; Merrill, *Public Lands and Political Meaning,* 55–61; R. White, "Contested Terrain," 201.

11. Principal authorities for the Mineral Leasing Act are Hays, *Conservation and the Gospel of Efficiency;* Swain, *Federal Conservation Policy;* Swenson, "Mineral Resources Exploitation."

12. 40 Stat. 297–300 (1917) (potassium deposits); Swenson, "Mineral Resources Exploitation," 741; Hays, *Conservation and the Gospel of Efficiency,* 90; Peffer, *Closing of the Public Domain,* 130–32.

13. Swenson, "Mineral Resources Exploitation," 738–45; Hays, *Conservation and the Gospel of Efficiency,* 90 (citing Ise, *U.S. Oil Policy,* 324–55); Gary D. Aho, "History of Utah's Oil Shale Industry," in M.D. Vandenberg, R. Ressetar, and L. P. Birgenheier, eds., *Geology of Utah's Uinta Basin and Uinta Mountains,* Publication 44 (Salt Lake City: Utah Geological Association, 2015), 319–55.

14. 41 Stat. 437, 444–45 (1920); 36 Stat. 847 (1910) (withdrawal of mineral lands).

15. Swenson, "Mineral Resources Exploitation," 742–43.

16. Swain, *Federal Conservation Policy,* 57–59.

17. Swenson, "Mineral Resources Exploitation," 742 (Fall statement); 58 Cong. Rec. 4290 (1919).

18. Principal authorities for the Federal Power Act are Hays, *Conservation and the Gospel of Efficiency;* Jerome G. Kerwin, *Federal Water-Power Legislation* (New York: Columbia University Press, 1926).

19. Ise, *United States Forest Policy,* 271; Hays, *Conservation and the Gospel of Efficiency,* 78–80; Kerwin, *Federal Water-Power Legislation.*

20. *Utah Power & Light Co. v. United States,* 243 U.S. 389 (1917).

21. Knowlton, *Cattle Kingdom,* 286–93; *Best v. Humboldt Placer Mining Co.,* 371 U.S. 334, 336–37 (1963).

22. *Utah Power & Light Co. v. United States,* 243 U.S. at 404–5.

23. Peffer, *Closing of the Public Domain,* 119–32; Robbins, *Our Landed Heritage,* 393–94; Hays, *Conservation and the Gospel of Efficiency,* 80–81; Kerwin, *Federal Water-Power Legislation;* Sam Kalen, "Historical Flow of Hydroelectric Regulation: A Brief History," *Idaho Law Review* 53, no. 1 (2017): 1, 13–20.

24. Wilkinson and Anderson, *Land and Resource Planning*, 215–16 (citing *Annual Reports of the Chief of the U.S. Forest Service*, 1921, 1931, 1936).
25. 41 Stat. 1065–66, 1069, 1072–73 (1920) (§§ 4(d); 10(e); 17).
26. 41 Stat. 1353–54 (1921); Yard, *Our Federal Lands*, 268; Ise, *Our National Park Policy*, 287–89; Shankland, *Steve Mather*, 214–16.

42. THE END OF THE PROGRESSIVE ERA

1. J. Leonard Bates, "Fulfilling American Democracy: The Conservation Movement, 1907 to 1921," *Mississippi Valley Historical Review* 44, no. 1 (June 1957): 53–54; Robbins, *Our Landed Heritage*, 394–97.
2. Leshy, *Mining Law*, 289–92.
3. Ibid., 293–94.
4. Burl Noggle, *Teapot Dome: Oil and Politics in the 1920s* (1962; New York: Norton, 1965), 9–12; David A. Stratton, *Tempest over Teapot Dome: The Story of Albert B. Fall* (Norman: University of Oklahoma Press, 1998), 112–20, 133–34.
5. Stratton, *Tempest over Teapot Dome*, 213–22; Ise, *Our National Park Policy*, 296–314.
6. Stratton, *Tempest over Teapot Dome*, 242–342.
7. Clements, *Hoover, Conservation, and Consumerism*, 162, 278; Swain, *Federal Conservation Policy*, 69; Marion G. Clawson, "Reminisces of the Bureau of Land Management, 1947–48," in Vernon Carstensen, ed., *The Public Lands: Studies in the History of the Public Domain* (Madison: University of Wisconsin Press, 1963), 449, 453.
8. Greeley, *Forests and Men*, 101; Swain, *Federal Conservation Policy*, 160; Warren G. Harding, "Address on the Territory of Alaska . . . July 27" (1923), in *Speeches and Addresses of Warren G. Harding, President of the United States* (1923), available from the Internet Archive, https://archive.org/details/speechesaddresseoohard/page/no.
9. *United States ex rel. McLennan v. Wilbur*, 283 U.S. 414, 419 (1931).
10. Swain, *Federal Conservation Policy*, 62–66; 46 Stat. 1523 (1931); Yergin, *Prize*; William E. Colby, "The Law of Oil and Gas with Special Reference to the Public Domain and Conservation," *California Law Review* 30, no. 3 (1942): 263–64.

43. DEBATING THE FUTURE OF UNRESERVED PUBLIC LANDS

1. Principal sources for this chapter are Clements, *Hoover, Conservation, and Consumerism*; Dana and Fairfax, *Forest and Range Policy*; Gates, *Public Land Law Development* (quotation on 521); Peffer, *Closing of the Public Domain*; Rowley, *Grazing and Rangelands*; Voigt, *Public Grazing Lands*; Yard, *Our Federal Lands*.
2. Peffer, *Closing of the Public Domain*, 175 (quoting Lane's letter to Hayden).
3. 40 Stat. 1316 (1919); "1945 History of the Modoc National Forest," U.S. Forest Service, www.fs.usda.gov/detail/modoc/learning/history-culture/?cid=stelprdb 5310663; Peffer, *Closing of the Public Domain*, 184; Rowley, *Grazing and Rangelands*, 88–95, 112–17; George Stewart, "History of Range Use," in U.S. Department of Agriculture, *The Western Range: A Great but Neglected Resource* (Washington, D.C.: Government Printing Office, 1936), 265; Ise, *Our National Park Policy*, 301–2; Merrill, *Public Lands and Political Meaning*, 67–71.
4. Gates, *Public Land Law Development*, 516–22, 800 (charts showing entries and patents on 520, 800); Peffer, *Closing of the Public Domain*, 127, 139–49, 167; Rowley,

Grazing and Rangelands, 225; *Report of the Committee on the Conservation and Administration of the Public Domain* (Garfield Committee Report), 42–43, tables 2–3 (1931) (disappointing results of the SRHA); Merrill, *Public Lands and Political Meaning*, 44 (chart showing homesteading, reproduced from *The Western Range*, S. Doc. 74-199, 130 [1936]).

5. 59 Cong. Rec. 2724 (1920); *Annual Report of the General Land Commissioner* (1923), 8–9; Peffer, *Closing of the Public Domain*, 181 (Work comment), 200; Rowley, *Grazing and Rangelands*, 90–93, 112–21, 130–33, 148; Voigt, *Public Grazing Lands*, 53, 245–51, 311–15.

6. 39 Stat. 865 (1916); James Muhn, "Public Water Reserves: The Metamorphosis of a Public Land Policy," *Journal of Land, Resources, and Environmental Law* 20, no. 1 (2001): 78–79; Dana and Fairfax, *Forest and Range Policy*, 100; Leigh Raymond and Sally Fairfax, "Fragmentation of Public Domain Law and Policy: An Alternative to the 'Shift-to-Retention' Thesis," *Natural Resources Journal* 39, no. 4 (Fall 1999): 713; Gates, *Public Land Law Development*, 393–99; Peffer, *Closing of the Public Domain*, 167; Kathryn A. Tipple, "Clear as Mud: Recreating Public Water Rights that Already Exist," *Utah Law Review* 2014, no. 5: 1131–60.

7. Peffer, *Closing of the Public Domain*, 181–201; Dana and Fairfax, *Forest and Range Policy*, 122–23, 138; Rowley, *Grazing and Rangelands*, 124, 134–36; Yard, *Our Federal Lands*, 57.

8. *National Forests and the Public Domain: Hearings Before a Subcommittee of the Committee on Public Lands and Surveys*, 69th Cong. 3456 (1925) (statement of Edward T. Taylor, representative of Colorado); 45 Stat. 380 (1928) (Mizpah-Pumpkin Creek Cooperative Grazing Unit); Peffer, *Closing of the Public Domain*, 200–202; Gates, *Public Land Law Development*, 523; Stout, "Cattlemen, Conservationists, and the Taylor Grazing Act," 311, 326.

9. "National Conference on Outdoor Recreation Report" (1928), S. Doc. No. 70-158, 78–79, 88–90.

10. Yard, *Our Federal Lands*, 74–77.

11. Peffer, *Closing of the Public Domain*, 203 (Wilbur comments).

12. Herbert Hoover, Message to the Western Governors Conference on Public Lands Questions, August 27, 1929.

13. 72 Cong. Rec. 408 (1929); Voigt, *Public Grazing Lands*, 248–49; Clements, *Hoover, Conservation, and Consumerism*, 148–68; Dana and Fairfax, *Forest and Range Policy*, 138–40; Gates, *Public Land Law Development*, 524–28; Peffer, *Closing of the Public Domain*, 205–9.

14. Garfield Committee Report, 11–14.

15. Ibid., 4–5, 23.

16. Ibid., 2, 6; Peffer, *Closing of the Public Domain*, 209–10; *Annual Report of Secretary of the Interior* (1931), 13–16.

17. 44 Stat. 1026 (1927) (Jones Act); Leshy, *Mining Law*, 338–39; Garfield Committee Report, 25.

18. Clements, *Hoover, Conservation, and Consumerism*, 153, 160; 46 Stat. 1530, 1548 (1931).

19. Robert W. Wells, Jr., "A Political Biography of George Henry Dern" (MA thesis, Brigham Young University, May 1971), 61–71, 88–96.

20. Leshy, "Unraveling the Sagebrush Rebellion," 321n12, 352n110 (Dern comment); Leonard J. Arrington, "The Sagebrush Resurrection: New Deal Expenditures in the Western States, 1933–1939," *Pacific Historical Review* 53, no. 1 (1983): 1–16.

21. Dana and Fairfax, *Forest and Range Policy,* 140; Garfield Committee Report, 36.

22. Clements, *Hoover, Conservation, and Consumerism,* 164–65; Gates, *Public Land Law Development,* 525–27; Peffer, *Closing of the Public Domain,* 204, 209; Dana and Fairfax, *Forest and Range Policy,* 138–39.

23. 46 Stat. 1468 (1931) (Animal Damage Control Act); Van Nuys, *Varmints and Victims,* 100–101, 107; Flores, *Coyote America,* 109–10.

24. Ward Shepard, "The Handout Magnificent," *Harper's,* October 1931, 594–602.

25. *Annual Report of the Secretary of the Interior* (1932), 17–18; Peffer, *Closing of the Public Domain,* 214; Foss, *Politics and Grass,* 50–52; Clements, *Hoover, Conservation, and Consumerism,* 165–66; Stout, "Cattlemen, Conservationists, and the Taylor Grazing Act," 311–31.

26. Peffer, *Closing of the Public Domain,* 213.

27. Clements, *Hoover, Conservation, and Consumerism,* 163, 168, quoting Hoover, *Addresses upon the American Road* (Stanford, Calif.: Stanford University Press, 1951), 144.

28. Unger, *Beyond Nature's Housekeepers,* 113.

29. 46 Stat. 279 (1930) (Carlsbad Caverns); 46 Stat. 1161 (1931) (Canyon de Chelly); Ise, *Our National Park Policy,* 331; Rothman, *Preserving Different Pasts,* 126.

30. Ise, *Our National Park Policy,* 341–43; Albright, *Birth of the National Park Service,* 275–81.

44. WILDLIFE PROTECTION GAINS PROMINENCE

1. Charles Richard Van Hise, *The Conservation of Natural Resources in the United States* (New York: Macmillan, 1910), quoted in Swain, *Federal Conservation Policy,* 187n2. Besides Swain, principal sources for this chapter are Bean and Rowland, *Evolution of National Wildlife Law;* Fischman, *National Wildlife Refuges;* Reed and Drabelle, *Fish and Wildlife Service;* Taliaferro, *Grinnell.*

2. "Report of the Forester," 27, in *Annual Report of the Secretary of Agriculture* (1921); Wilkinson and Anderson, *Land and Resource Planning,* 282; Swain, *Federal Conservation Policy,* 32–52.

3. 37 Stat. 847–48 (1913); Taliaferro, *Grinnell,* 403–4, 406, 409–12; Charles A. Lofgren, "Missouri v. Holland in Historical Perspective," *Supreme Court Review* 1975, 77–122; Reed quoted in Unger, *Beyond Nature's Housekeepers,* 97.

4. *Geer v. Connecticut,* 161 U.S. 519 (1896); *The Abby Dodge v. United States,* 223 U.S. 166 (1912); *United States v. Shauver,* 214 F. 154 (E.D. Ark. 1914); *United States v. McCullagh,* 221 F. 288 (D. Kansas 1915); Taliaferro, *Grinnell,* 337–40.

5. 37 Stat. 1542 (1911); 39 Stat. 1702 (1916); Bean, *Evolution of National Wildlife Law,* 256; George Reiger, "Song of the Seal," *Audubon,* September 1975.

6. 40 Stat. 755 (1918) (MBTA); Charles G. Curtin, "The Evolution of the U.S. National Wildlife Refuge System and the Doctrine of Compatibility," *Conservation Biology* 7, no. 1 (March 1993): 29, 31.

7. *Pollard v. Hagan,* 44 U.S. 212 (1845); Leshy, "Are Public Lands Unconstitutional?," 531–41; *Missouri v. Holland,* 252 U.S. 416, 433–35 (1920), and pp. 28–29 of

appellant's brief; Linda Greenhouse, "What Got into the Court? What Happens Next?," *Maine Law Review* 57, no. 1 (2005): 1, 7; Brian Richardson, "The Imperial Treaty Power," *University of Pennsylvania Law Review* 168, no. 4 (March 2020): 931, 1003–4; Edward T. Swaine, "Putting Missouri v. Holland on the Map," *Missouri Law Review* 73, no. 4 (2008): 1007–28.

8. Stephen Budiansky, *Oliver Wendell Holmes: A Life in War, Law, and Ideas* (New York: Norton, 2019).

9. J. Orsi, "From Horicon to Hamburgers," 21.

10. Reed and Drabelle, *Fish and Wildlife Service*, 8–9.

11. J. Orsi, "From Horicon to Hamburgers," 20.

12. Fox, *John Muir and His Legacy*, 159–65; J. Orsi, "From Horicon to Hamburgers," 26.

13. 43 Stat. 650 (1924); Reed and Drabelle, *Fish and Wildlife Service*, 45; Fischman, *National Wildlife Refuges*, 83, 171–73, 177; Fox, *John Muir and His Legacy*, 164–77.

14. 45 Stat. 448 (1928); Lynn Greenwalt, interview by Brock Evans, *Wild Earth* 13, no. 4 (Winter 2003–4): 46.

15. *Hunt v. United States*, 278 U.S. 96, 100 (1928).

16. 45 Stat. 1222 (1929); Curtin, "U.S. National Wildlife Refuge System," 31–32; Zaslowsky and Watkins, *These American Lands*, 168–69; Fischman, *National Wildlife Refuges*, 36–37; Bean, *Evolution of National Wildlife Law*, 120; Fairfax et al., *Buying Nature*, 92–94.

17. Fox, *John Muir and His Legacy*, 336 (quoting Hoover); Exec. Order No. 5540 (January 26, 1931).

18. Swain, *Federal Conservation Policy*, 49–52; Dunlap, "Wildlife, Science, and National Parks," 200.

45. PUBLIC LANDS AND MULTIPURPOSE WATER DEVELOPMENT

1. Primary sources for this chapter are Hiltzik, *Colossus*; Pisani, *Water and American Government*, 116–42; Reisner, *Cadillac Desert*, 120–75; Swain, *Federal Conservation Policy*, 73–86.

2. 34 Stat. 259 (1906).

3. Reisner, *Cadillac Desert*, 116; 38 Stat. 686–87 (1914).

4. R. Orsi, *Sunset Limited*, 226–37.

5. 45 Stat. 1057 (1928); Joseph E. Stevens, *Hoover Dam: An American Adventure* (Norman: University of Oklahoma Press, 1988), 18–19.

6. William E. Riebsame, ed., *Atlas of the New West* (New York: Norton, 1997), chap. 3, 80–93; Scott Harrison, "From the Archives: Hoover Dam Electricity Lights Up Los Angeles Party," *Los Angeles Times*, October 19, 2019, quoting Thomas Treanor, *Los Angeles Times*, October 10, 1936; www.latimes.com/california/story/20191-09/from-the-archives-hoover-dam-lights-up-los-angeles-party.

7. Douglas W. Dodd, "Boulder Dam Recreation Area: The Bureau of Reclamation, the National Park Service, and the Origins of the National Recreation Area Concept at Lake Mead, 1929–1936," *Southern California Quarterly* 88, no. 4 (2006): 431–73.

8. Ross B. Talbot, "The Political Forces," in Ottoson, *Land Use Policy and Problems*, 137, 154–55.

46. THE TAYLOR GRAZING ACT

1. Brinkley, *Rightful Heritage*, 53–62.
2. Franklin Delano Roosevelt, Address Accepting the Presidential Nomination at the Democratic National Convention in Chicago, July 2, 1932.
3. John Salmond, *The Civilian Conservation Corps, 1933–1942: A New Deal Case Study* (Durham, N.C.: Duke University Press, 1967), 216, 297n6; Donald Swain, "Harold Ickes, Horace Albright, and the Hundred Days: A Study in Conservation Administration," *Pacific Historical Review* 30, no.4 (November 1965): 463; Swain, "National Park Service and the New Deal," 324–36; Brinkley, *Rightful Heritage*, 338, 380, 583, 523–29; 48 Stat. 195 (1933) (National Industrial Recovery Act, establishing the Public Works Administration).
4. Fox, *John Muir and His Legacy*, 183.
5. Watkins, *Righteous Pilgrim*; Fox, *John Muir and His Legacy*, 201; Ickes, *The Autobiography of a Curmudgeon* (New York: Reynal and Hitchcock, 1943).
6. Principal sources for the enactment of the Taylor Grazing Act are Gates, *Public Land Law Development*, 607–34; Peffer, *Closing of the Public Domain*, 216–35; Stout, "Cattlemen, Conservationists, and the Taylor Grazing Act," 311, 326.
7. Senate Hearings on H.R. 6462, 44, 73rd Cong., 2nd sess. (1934); 86 Cong. Rec. 4198 (appendix) (1940–41); 78 Cong. Rec. 11814–19 (1934); Voigt, *Public Grazing Lands*, 249–50; Peffer, *Closing of the Public Domain*, 216–18.
8. Nixon, *Roosevelt and Conservation*, 1:160; "Ickes Throws Open Vast Grazing Lands," *New York Times*, July 19, 1933, 9; 78 Cong. Rec. 11142–43 (June 12, 1934) (January 1934 opinion on the Pickett Act); Voigt, *Public Grazing Lands*, 251–52 (Ickes's rash claim); "Management of Public Land Resources," *Yale Law Journal* 60, no. 3 (March 1951): 474–75; Gates, *Public Land Law Development*, 610–12.
9. Peffer, *Closing of the Public Domain*, 218–19; Stout, "Cattlemen, Conservationists, and the Taylor Grazing Act," 315.
10. 48 Stat. 1269–75 (1934); 78 Cong. Rec. 11419–20 (1934); 79 Cong Rec. 6013 (1935).
11. Calef, *Private Grazing and Public Lands*; Dana and Fairfax, *Forest and Range Policy*; Donahue, *Western Range Revisited*; Foss, *Politics and Grass*; Voigt, *Public Grazing Lands*.
12. Peffer, *Closing of the Public Domain*, 333; Valerie Weeks Scott, "The Range Cattle Industry: Its Effect on Western Land Law," *Montana Law Review* 28, no. 2 (Spring 1967): 155–83; *Hearings on H.R. 6462 Before the Senate Committee on Public Lands and Surveys*, 73rd Cong. (1934), 53–62 (Forest Service witness Silcox), 63–77 (Interior witness Poole).
13. The most relevant discussion on the Senate floor is found at 78 Cong. Rec. 11148, 11162, 11419–2020 (1934).
14. 78 Cong. Rec. 1145–46 (1934).
15. 79 Stat. 969 (1965).
16. 48 Stat. 1272–74 (1934).
17. Exec. Order No. 6910 (November 26, 1934); Exec. Order No. 6964 (February 5, 1935).
18. Peffer, *Closing of the Public Domain*, 224n.
19. Ibid., 225. Principal sources on TGA implementation, besides Peffer, are Calef, *Private Grazing and Public Lands*; Dana and Fairfax, *Forest and Range Policy*;

Donahue, *Western Range Revisited;* Foss, *Politics and Grass;* Voigt, *Public Grazing Lands.*

20. 49 Stat. 1976 (1936); 68 Stat. 151 (1954).

21. Calef, *Private Grazing and Public Lands,* 57–73.

22. *Annual Report of the Secretary of the Interior* (1938), 15–16, quoted in Foss, *Politics and Grass,* 81–82; Gates, *Public Land Law Development,* 614–15; Dana and Fairfax, *Forest and Range Policy,* 162–64; Peffer, *Closing of the Public Domain,* 225–31; Calef, *Private Grazing and Public Lands,* 64–68; "Management of Public Land Resources," 470n103; Clawson, *Western Range Livestock Industry,* 261.

23. Carpenter quoted in Raymond, *Private Rights in Public Resources,* 216n93.

24. Dana and Fairfax, *Forest and Range Policy,* 162–63. On the Interior-Agriculture turf war in this period, see Peffer, *Closing of the Public Domain,* 232–40. On conflicts with big game, see Rowley, *Grazing and Rangelands,* 165–71; Peffer, *Closing of the Public Domain,* 281–84; Calef, *Private Grazing and Public Lands,* 69.

25. Nixon, *Roosevelt and Conservation,* 1:307–14 (dueling Agriculture and Interior memos on the TGA, and FDR's signing statement); "The Western Range," S. Doc. No. 74-199 (1936); Steen, *U.S. Forest Service,* 204–8; Rowley, *Grazing and Rangelands,* 155–59; Watkins, *Righteous Pilgrim,* 477–83; Gates, *Public Land Law Development,* 615–18; Dana and Fairfax, *Forest and Range Policy,* 162–65; Voigt, *Public Grazing Lands,* 165; Peffer, *Closing of the Public Domain,* 236.

26. Rowley, *Grazing and Rangelands,* 165–71 (Pittman letter). On the O&C Act, see 50 Stat. 874 (1937); Gates, *Public Land Law Development,* 602–5; Dana and Fairfax, *Forest and Range Policy,* 165–67.

27. Voigt, *Public Grazing Lands,* 253–62 (Ickes-Carpenter conflicts); 53 Stat. 1002 (1939); Donahue, "Western Grazing," 751–54 (collecting sources on advisory boards).

28. Watkins, *Righteous Pilgrim,* 479; 53 Stat. 1002 (1939) (amendment to the TGA); Foss, *Politics and Grass,* 79–82, 117–27, 201–4; Calef, *Private Grazing and Public Lands,* 60–63, 73–77, 80–81, 90, 123, 134; Grant McConnell, *Private Power and American Democracy* (New York: Knopf, 1966), 207–11; Voigt, *Public Grazing Lands,* 245–61, esp. 255–59; Peffer, *Closing of the Public Domain,* 230–32, 332–33, quoting S. Rep. No. 78-804 (1943), at 26–27; *Red Canyon Sheep Co. v. Ickes,* 98 F.2d 308, 314 (D.C. Cir. 1938); *McNeil v. Seaton,* 281 F.2d 931 (D.C. Cir. 1960); 56 Stat. 654 (1942); Hugh Kingery, "The Public Grazing Lands," *Denver Law Journal* 43, no. 3 (Summer 1966): 329–48.

29. McConnell, *Private Power and American Democracy,* 206–11.

47. NATIONAL PARKS IN THE NEW DEAL

1. Primary sources for this chapter are Albright, *Birth of the National Park Service;* Brinkley, *Rightful Heritage;* Ise, *Our National Park Policy;* Nixon, *FDR and Conservation;* Sellars, *Preserving Nature in the National Parks;* Swain, "National Park Service and the New Deal"; Watkins, *Righteous Pilgrim;* National Park Service, "Recreational Use of Land in the United States" (part II of the *Report on Land Planning* [1938]).

2. Albright, *Birth of the National Park Service,* 298–302; Brinkley, *Rightful Heritage,* 245, 262–63; Ise, *National Park Policy,* 429; Swain, "National Park Service and the New Deal," 318–20.

3. Brinkley, *Rightful Heritage,* 326.

4. Elmo Richardson, "Olympic National Park: 20 Years of Controversy," *Forest and Conservation History* 12, no. 1 (April 1968): 6, 8–11; Brinkley, *Rightful Heritage*, 408–10, 693n46; Nixon, *FDR and Conservation*, 1:523–35.

5. 52 Stat. 1241; Ise, *National Park Policy*, 382–95; Brinkley, *Rightful Heritage*, 517–40; Brant, *Adventures in Conservation*, 70–144; Ben Twight, *Organizational Values and Political Power: The Forest Service Versus the Olympic National Park* (University Park: University of Pennsylvania Press, 1983).

6. Ise, *National Park Policy*, 251–62, 332–36; 48 Stat. 964 (1934) (Great Smoky Mountains); Nixon, *FDR and Conservation*, 2:471; Brinkley, *Rightful Heritage*, 429, 490–91, 502–3 (Isle Royale).

7. Terence Young, " 'A Contradiction in Democratic Government': W. J. Trent, Jr., and the Struggle to Desegregate National Park Campgrounds," *Environmental History* 14, no. 4 (October 2009): 651–82; Susan Shumaker, *Untold Stories from America's National Parks*, part 1, "Segregation in the National Parks" (2006), 15–36, www.pbs.org/nationalparks/media/pdfs/tnp-abi-untold-stories-pt-01-segregation.pdf; Watkins, *Righteous Pilgrim*, 637–54.

8. 49 Stat. 393 (1935); Ise, *National Park Policy*, 379–82; Brinkley, *Rightful Heritage*, 266–67, 316, 556–58. There are several protected areas across the border from Big Bend. In the Obama administration, the Interior Department signed an agreement with Mexico's Secretariat of the Environment to coordinate management of protected areas on both sides of the border; see Defenders of Wildlife, "In the Shadow of the Wall: Part 2—Borderlands Conservation Hotspots on the Line" (April 2, 2018), https://defenders.org/sites/default/files/migration/docs/defenders-borderreport-partii.pdf .

9. Sellars, *Preserving Nature in the National Parks*, 91–101; Dunlap, "Wildlife, Science, and National Parks," 193–96, 200; Van Nuys, *Varmints and Victims*, 118–27.

10. 45 Stat. 1443 (1929).

11. 48 Stat. 816 (1934); Barrow, *Nature's Ghosts*, 210; Ise, *National Park Policy*, 370–78; Brinkley, *Rightful Heritage*, 201–5, 239–42.

12. 58 Stat. 794 (1944); Ise, *National Park Policy*, 508–11, 521–22; Marjory Stoneman Douglas, *The Everglades: River of Grass* (New York: Rinehart, 1947); Michael Grunwald, *The Swamp: The Everglades, Florida, and the Politics of Paradise* (New York: Simon & Schuster, 2006).

13. 44 Stat. 818 (1926); 54 Stat. 41 (1940); Ise, *National Park Policy*, 396–407; Albright, *Birth of the National Park Service*, 317–18; Fox, *John Muir and His Legacy*, 212–17; Brant, *Adventures in Conservation*, 147–216.

14. Arno Cammerer, "Standards and Policies in National Parks," *American Planning and Civic Annual* (Washington, D.C.: American Planning and Civic Association, 1936), 13–20; Swain, "National Park Service and the New Deal," 324–28; Sellars, *Preserving Nature in the National Parks*, 106, 315n41; Barry Mackintosh, "Harold L. Ickes and the National Park Service," *Journal of Forest History* 29, no. 2 (April 1985): 78, 82; Brinkley, *Rightful Heritage*, 429–32, 451–54 (Kings Canyon).

15. 106 Stat. 2208 (1992); 113 Stat. 13 (2019).

16. 49 Stat. 1894, 1982 (1936).

17. 50 Stat. 669–70 (1937); Brinkley, *Rightful Heritage*, 14–15.

18. Ise, *National Park Policy*, 425–36 (Ickes speech quoted at 426–27); Watkins, *Righteous Pilgrim*, 580–81; Brinkley, *Rightful Heritage*, 375–80.

19. 49 Stat. 666 (1935); Ise, *National Park Policy*, 357–59; Swain, "National Park Service and the New Deal," 326–27; Michael G. Schene, "The National Park Service and Historic Preservation: An Introduction," *Public Historian* 9, no. 2 (Spring 1987): 6–9; Brinkley, *Rightful Heritage*, 188–91, 491–92; Fairfax et al., *Buying Nature*, 117–27.

20. Mackintosh, *National Parks*, 56–57.

21. Brinkley, *Rightful Heritage*, 113–15, 194; Ise, *National Park Policy*, 397–422; 48 Stat. 791 (1934) (Natchez Trace study); 49 Stat. 2041 (1936); 52 Stat. 407 (1938); Fox, *John Muir and His Legacy*, 200 (Ickes quote).

22. Donald T. Sutte, Jr., and Roger A. Cunningham, *Scenic Easements: Legal, Administrative, and Valuation Problems and Procedures*, National Cooperative Highway Research Program Report 56 (Washington, D.C.: Highway Research Board, 1968).

23. Ise, *National Park Policy*, 341, 408–9, 411; Brinkley, *Rightful Heritage*, 194–97, 201–12, 341, 355–56.

24. Ise, *National Park Policy*, 408, 411, 512–13; Brinkley, *Rightful Heritage*, 250, 396, 548.

25. Elmo Richardson, "Federal Park Policy in Utah: The Escalante National Monument Controversy of 1935–1940," *Utah Historical Quarterly* 33, no. 2 (April 1965): 109–33; Robert G. Kaplan, *Earning the Rockies* (New York: Random House, 2017), 117 ("other-worldly" quote).

26. Ise, *National Park Policy*, 341, 411, 476; Brinkley, *Rightful Heritage*, 449–50.

27. Watkins, *Righteous Pilgrim*, 582–83; Brinkley, *Rightful Heritage*, 320.

28. 37 Stat. 293, 847 (1912); Righter, *Crucible for Conservation*, 9, 53, 88.

29. Righter, *Crucible for Conservation*, 103–19; Peffer, *Closing of the Public Domain*, 242–45.

30. Righter, *Crucible for Conservation*, 126–41; 64 Stat. 849 (1950); 90 Cong. Rec. 9086–87, 9183–95 (1944) (debate on the president's powers under the Antiquities Act); *State of Wyoming v. Franke*, 58 F. Supp. 890 (D. Wyo. 1945); Hal Rothman, "The Antiquities Act and the Modern Park System," in *America's National Monuments: The Politics of Preservation* (Lawrence: University Press of Kansas, 1993), chap. 11, www.nps.gov/parkhistory/online_books/rothman/contents.htm; Ise, *National Park Policy*, 490–508; Brinkley, *Rightful Heritage*, 544–58, 562–63; Watkins, *Righteous Pilgrim*, 765–73; Albright, *Birth of the National Park Service*, 320–24; Justin Farrell, *Billionaire Wilderness: The Ultra Wealthy and the Remaking of the American West* (Princeton, N.J.: Princeton University Press, 2020).

31. Watkins, *Righteous Pilgrim*, 773–75.

48. A SYSTEM OF WILDLIFE REFUGES BEGINS TO EMERGE

1. *Annual Report of Secretary of Agriculture, Bureau of Biological Survey* (1932), 224–54; (1933), 236–58; Farley, *Duck Stamps and Wildlife Refuges*, has an appendix showing acreage in refuges from 1903 to 1953. Principal sources for this chapter besides Farley are Barrow, *Nature's Ghosts*; Bean and Rowland, *Evolution of National Wildlife Law*; Brinkley, *Rightful Heritage*; Dunlap, *Saving America's Wildlife*; Fischman, *National Wildlife Refuges*; Gabrielson, "Fish and Wildlife Service"; Reed and Drabelle, *Fish and Wildlife Service*.

2. Fox, *John Muir and His Legacy*, 198; J. Orsi, "From Horicon to Hamburgers."

3. Fox, *John Muir and His Legacy*, 191.

4. Brinkley, *Rightful Heritage*, 228, 268–85.

5. 48 Stat. 401 (1934).

6. 60 Stat. 1080 (1946); 72 Stat. 563 (1958); Bean, *Evolution of National Wildlife Law*, 181–83; Gabrielson, "Fish and Wildlife Service," 181, 189–90; Farley, *Duck Stamps and Wildlife Refuges*, 9–11.

7. Reed and Drabelle, *Fish and Wildlife Service*, 9; Brinkley, *Rightful Heritage*, 268, 280–85; Farley, *Duck Stamps and Wildlife Refuges*.

8. Chase and Madison, "Expanding Ark," 18, 21, 24.

9. Philip Terzian, review of Roger Tory Peterson, *Field Guide to the Birds*, Wall Street Journal, March 1–2, 2008, W8; John Tautin, "Frederick C. Lincoln and the Formation of the North American Bird Banding Program" (U.S. Forest Service General Technical Report, 2005), available online. Lincoln's publications were *The Waterfowl Flyways of North America* (1935) and *The Migration of North American Birds* (1935). Mark V. Barrow, Jr., *A Passion for Birds: American Ornithology After Audubon* (Princeton, N.J.: Princeton University Press, 1998); Bean, *Evolution of National Wildlife Law*, 138–39; Dunlap, *Saving America's Wildlife*, 84–85.

10. Titles III and IV of the 1935 amendments to the Duck Stamp Act, 49 Stat. 378, 381–83; Curtin, "U.S. National Wildlife Refuge System," 29–38; Fairfax et al., *Buying Nature*, 113–14.

11. Gabrielson, "Fish and Wildlife Service," 181, 184.

12. Dunlap, *Saving America's Wildlife*, 92–96; Brinkley, *Rightful Heritage*, 348, 404–7, 471–73; Brant, *Adventures in Conservation*, 15–22.

13. Reed and Drabelle, *Fish and Wildlife Service*, 140–41; Brinkley, *Rightful Heritage*, 513; Curtin, "U.S. National Wildlife Refuge System," 32; Fairfax et al., *Buying Nature*, 114–16.

14. Nancy Langston, *Where Land and Water Meet: A Western Landscape Transformed* (Seattle: University of Washington Press, 2003), 89.

15. Franklin D. Roosevelt, Exec. Order No. 7373, Establishing the Desert Game Range in Nevada (May 20, 1936); Brant, *Adventures in Conservation*, 46–48; Gabrielson, "Fish and Wildlife Service," 181, 184–85; Brinkley, *Rightful Heritage*, 326–29, and appendix B, 600–609, which has a list of FDR's refuges.

16. Reed and Drabelle, *Fish and Wildlife Service*, 19–22; Fischman, *National Wildlife Refuges*, 37, citing Aldo S. Leopold, Clarence Cottam, Ian Cowan, Ira N. Gabrielson, and Thomas L. Kimball, "Report of the Advisory Committee on Wildlife Management" (1968); Franklin Delano Roosevelt, Proclamation No. 2416, 5 Fed. Reg. 2677 (1940).

17. 53 Stat. 561, 813 (1939); 54 Stat. 231 (1940); Brinkley, *Rightful Heritage*, 486–90, 493, 497, 705.

18. Barrow, *Nature's Ghosts*, 234–59.

19. 70 Stat. 1100, 1119, 1123 (1956).

20. 72 Stat. 486 (1958).

21. "Secretary Seaton Establishes New Arctic National Wildlife Range," Department of the Interior Information Service, press release, December 7, 1960, www.fws.gov/news/Historic/NewsReleases/1960/19601207c.pdf; Fischman, *National Wildlife Refuges*, 38 (graph showing growth in the number of refuges by year); Fink, "National Wildlife Refuges," 16–17.

49. OTHER NEW DEAL PUBLIC LAND POLICIES

1. Principal authorities for this chapter are Brinkley, *Rightful Heritage;* Dana, *Forest and Range Policy;* Dana and Fairfax, *Forest and Range Policy;* Gates, *Public Land Law Development;* Hirt, *Conspiracy of Optimism;* Nash, *Wilderness and the American Mind;* Steen, *U.S. Forest Service;* Swain, *Federal Conservation Policy.*

2. Nixon, *Roosevelt and Conservation,* 1:118–19.

3. James B. Snow, "Implementing the Weeks Act: A Lawyer's Perspective," *Forest History Today,* Spring–Fall 2011, 70, 75; Brinkley, *Rightful Heritage,* 219, 281, 363–64, 477, 611–23, 677; Fairfax et al., *Buying Nature,* 108–12; Gates, *Public Land Law Development,* 597–98; "Weeks Act Resources," Forest History Society, https://foreshistory.org/research-explore/us-forest-service-history/policy-and-law/the-weeks-act/weeks-act-resources.

4. *Proceedings of the National Conference on Land Utilization, Chicago, Ill., November 19–21, 1931* (1932), available from the Internet Archive, https://archive.org/details/CAT10505778/page/n5/mode/2u; H. H. Wooten, *The Land Utilization Program, 1934 to 1964: Origin, Development, and Present Status* (U.S. Department of Agriculture, Economic Research Service, 1965); R. Douglas Hurt, "Federal Land Reclamation in the Dust Bowl," *Great Plains Quarterly* 6, no. 2 (Spring 1986): 94–116; Hurt, "The National Grasslands: Origin and Development in the Dust Bowl," *Agricultural History* 59, no. 2 (April 1985): 246–59; James G. Maddox, "The Bankhead-Jones Farm Tenant Act," *Law and Contemporary Problems* 4, no. 4 (1937): 434–55; Elizabeth Howard, "Management of the National Grasslands," *North Dakota Law Review* 78, no. 3 (2002): 409–40.

5. Farley, *Duck Stamps and Wildlife Refuges,* 7–8; Rowley, *Grazing and Rangelands,* 224–30.

6. Hirt, *Conspiracy of Optimism,* 26; Steen, *U.S. Forest Service,* 202–3, 210; Brinkley, *Rightful Heritage,* 159–61; National Park Service, "Recreational Use of Land in the United States," part II of the *Report on Land Planning,* citing Senate Doc. No. 12, 73rd Cong. 465; H. L. Schantz, "Recent Developments in Wildlife Management," *Journal of Forestry* 36, no. 2 (February 1938): 146, 149, 151; Wilkinson and Anderson, *Land and Resource Planning,* 283–84, 321; Barrow, *Nature's Ghosts,* 283–95.

7. 54 Stat. 224 (1940); Hays, *American People and the National Forests,* 79–82; Hirt, *Conspiracy of Optimism,* 38.

8. 14 Stat. 239 (1866) (original grant to the O&C); 39 Stat. 218 (1916); Sean Kammer, "The Railroads Must Have Ties: A Legal History of Forest Conservation and the Oregon & California Railroad Land Grant, 1887–1916." *Western Legal History* 23, no. 1 (Winter–Spring 2010): 1–20.

9. 52 Stat. 874 (1937); Gates, *Public Land Law Development,* 602–3; Dana and Fairfax, *Forest and Range Policy,* 105–8, 165–67; Michael C. Blumm and Tim Wigington, "The Oregon and California Railroad Grant Lands' Sordid Past, Contentious Present, and Uncertain Future: A Century of Conflict," *Boston College Environmental Affairs Law Review* 40, no. 1 (2013).

10. 58 Stat. 132–35 (1944); Steen, *U.S. Forest Service,* 224–26, 250–52, 298–323, 327–28; Dana, *Forest and Range Policy,* 284–85; Dana and Fairfax, *Forest and Range Policy,* 167–68; Hirt, *Conspiracy of Optimism,* 40–41.

11. Benton MacKaye, "An Appalachian Trail: A Project in Regional Planning," *Journal of the American Institute of Architects* 9 (October 1921): 325–30.

12. Donald Dale Jackson, "The Long Way 'Round," *Wilderness Magazine* 51, no. 181 (Summer 1988): 17–24.

13. Sarah Mittlefehldt, *Tangled Roots: The Appalachian Trail and American Environmental Politics* (Seattle: University of Washington Press, 2013).

14. Brinkley, *Rightful Heritage*, 179, 193–94, 265–66, 319; Nash, *Wilderness and the American Mind*, 200–208.

15. National Park Service, "Recreational Use of Land"; Sutter, *Driven Wild*, 67–89.

16. Allin, *Politics of Wilderness Preservation*, 82–85.

17. Leshy, *Mining Law*, 231.

18. Ise, *Our National Park Policy*, 434–35; 50 Stat. 595 (1937).

19. Hiltzik, *Colossus*, 158, 311–12, 374, 381; Watkins, *Righteous Pilgrim*, 382–83; Albright, *Birth of the National Park Service*, 304–5; Dodd, "Boulder Dam Recreation Area."

20. Ise, *Our National Park Policy*, 369, 436, 468.

21. Brinkley, *Rightful Heritage*, 562–64.

22. 49 Stat. 1519, 1521 (1936); 54 Stat. 1059, 1060 (1940).

23. Barrow, *Nature's Ghosts*, 201–33, 275–79, 299–300.

24. U.S. Department of the Interior, *Fading Trails: The Story of Endangered American Wildlife* (New York: Macmillan, 1943), viii.

50. GRAZING AND LOGGING THE PUBLIC LANDS
IN THE POSTWAR ERA

1. McCarran's biography is Michael J. Ybarra, *Washington Gone Crazy: Senator Pat McCarran and the Great American Communist Hunt* (Hanover, N.H.: Steerforth, 2004), 32–33, 378–81. Principal sources for this chapter are Foss, *Politics and Grass*; Gates, *Public Land Law Development*; Hirt, *Conspiracy of Optimism*; Peffer, *Closing of the Public Domain*, 253–56 (tables showing the scale of TGA operations by state), 248 (comment about McCarran); Rowley, *Grazing and Rangelands*; Skillen, *Nation's Largest Landlord*; Steen, *U.S. Forest Service*; Voigt, *Public Grazing Lands*; Wilkinson, *Crossing the Next Meridian*; Wilkinson and Anderson, *Land and Resource Planning*.

2. Voigt, *Public Grazing Lands*, 286, 288; Skillen, *Nation's Largest Landlord*, 17–23; Foss, *Politics and Grass*, 186, 201; Peffer, *Closing of the Public Domain*, 277–78.

3. 59 Stat 613 (1945 Reorganization Act); Skillen, *Nation's Largest Landlord*, 18–23; Peffer, *Closing of the Public Domain*, 267–73.

4. Voigt, *Public Grazing Lands*, 291; George C. Coggins and Margaret Lindberg-Johnson, "The Law of Public Rangeland Management II: The Commons and the Taylor Grazing Act," *Environmental Law* 13, no. 1 (1982): 1–101; Peffer, *Closing of the Public Domain*, 267–78; Clawson and Held, *Federal Lands*, 11–13, 381–82; Gates, *Public Land Law Development*, 615–30; *Annual Reports of the Secretary of the Interior* (1948), 268, and (1949) 236; "Management of Public Land Resources," *Yale Law Journal* 60, no. 3 (March 1951): 455, 474–77.

5. 60 Stat. 237 (1946); George Shepard, "Fierce Compromise: The Administrative Procedure Act Emerges from New Deal Politics," *Northwestern University Law Review* 90, no. 4 (1996): 1562–1683.

6. 60 Stat. at 238 (1946).

7. Peffer, *Closing of the Public Domain*, 279–81, 286; Voigt, *Public Grazing Lands,* 93.

8. Bernard DeVoto, "The West Against Itself," *Harper's,* January 1947, reprinted in *The Western Paradox: A Conservation Reader,* ed. Douglas Brinkley and Patricia Nelson Limerick (New Haven, Conn.: Yale University Press, 2001), 45–73; Gates, *Public Land Law Development,* 628; Richard Neuberger, "Looting the National Forests," *Nation,* April 26, 1947, 471–72. DeVoto's efforts on behalf of conservation are summarized in Fox, *John Muir and His Legacy,* 223–29.

9. Peffer, *Closing of the Public Domain,* 287–90; Voigt, *Public Grazing Lands,* 96–97, 101, 114–17, 206–7.

10. Peffer, *Closing of the Public Domain,* 288; Rowley, *Grazing and Rangelands,* 177–78; Voigt, *Public Grazing Lands,* 74, 93, 110–17, 206–7; 93 Cong. Rec. 2171 (1947).

11. Rowley, *Grazing and Rangelands,* 208; R. A. Baker, *Conservation Politics: The Senate Career of Clinton P. Anderson* (Albuquerque: University of New Mexico Press, 1985), 15.

12. "The Public Domain," *Economist,* February 21, 1948, 304; Peffer, *Closing of the Public Domain,* 279–84.

13. 61 Stat. 681 (1947).

14. Bernard DeVoto, "Sacred Cows and Public Lands," *Harper's,* July 1948, in *Western Paradox,* 74, 98–100.

15. Peffer, *Closing of the Public Domain,* 280–84, 293, 337–38; Clawson, *Western Range Livestock Industry,* 385–86.

16. "Management of Public Land Resources," 474.

17. Voigt, *Public Grazing Lands,* 132–50; Rowley, *Grazing and Rangelands,* 210; 63 Stat. 762 (1949).

18. 64 Stat. 82 (1950).

19. Voigt, *Public Grazing Lands,* 144, 164–65, 205, 215; Steen, *U.S. Forest Service,* 274–75; Rowley, *Grazing and Rangelands,* 112, 158–59, 188–90.

20. Gladwin Hill, "M'Kay Emphasizes U.S. Lands Policy," *New York Times,* November 3, 1953, 25; Hirt, *Conspiracy of Optimism,* 121–25.

21. Rowley, *Grazing and Rangelands,* 222; Voigt, *Public Grazing Lands,* 207–8, 216–29; Richardson, *Dams, Parks, and Politics,* 101–5; Steen, *U.S. Forest Service,* 275–77; Hirt, *Conspiracy of Optimism,* 126.

22. Wilkinson, *Crossing the Next Meridian,* 135–37.

23. Hirt, *Conspiracy of Optimism,* 90–94, xliv; Clawson, *Federal Lands Revisited.*

24. Hirt, *Conspiracy of Optimism,* 90–94, 106–7 (Benson quotation).

25. Ibid., 134–36.

26. Ibid., xxiii, 90–94, 144–49, 197–99, 203–6; 63 Stat. 762 (1949); Wilkinson, *Crossing the Next Meridian,* 136–38.

27. Voigt, *Public Grazing Lands,* 204, citing *Report of the Chief* (1956), 4; Hirt, *Conspiracy of Optimism,* 152–53; Wilkinson, *Crossing the Next Meridian,* 137.

28. Hirt, *Conspiracy of Optimism,* 171–91.

29. Ibid., 176.

30. Ibid., 171–92.

31. 74 Stat. 506 (1960) (Public Land Administration Act); 90 Stat. 2743 (1976) (Federal Land Policy and Management Act).

51. MINERAL POLICY DEVELOPMENTS ONSHORE AND OFFSHORE

1. Principal sources for this chapter are Leshy, "Are Public Lands Unconstitutional?"; Leshy, *Mining Law;* "Conflicting State and Federal Claims," *Yale Law Journal;* Swenson, "Mineral Resources Exploitation."

2. Leshy, *Mining Law,* 55–81, 134–35, 355–56, 287–312, 400–401, 477.

3. Ibid., 76–77.

4. 61 Stat. 681 (1947); 64 Stat. 368 (1955); Leshy, *Mining* Law, 70–71.

5. Leshy, *Mining Law,* 79–82, 405.

6. Elmo Richardson, "The Interior Secretary as Conservation Villain: The Notorious Case of Douglas 'Giveaway' McKay," *Pacific Historical Review* 41, no. 3 (August 1972): 333–45.

7. Swenson, "Mineral Resources Exploitation," 750–56.

8. Raye C. Ringholz, *Uranium Frenzy: Boom and Bust on the Colorado Plateau* (New York: Norton, 1989).

9. Leshy, *Mining Law,* 295–305.

10. Sources cited in *United States v. State of California,* 332 U.S. 19, 33n16 (1947); 1 Stat. 381 (1794).

11. "Conflicting State and Federal Claims," 359n23; Ernest R. Bartley, *The Tidelands Oil Controversy: A Legal and Historical Analysis* (Austin: University of Texas Press, 1953), 66–143.

12. Proclamation No. 2667, Exec. Order No. 9633, 10 Fed. Reg. 12303–5 (1945); "Conflicting State and Federal Claims," 367.

13. Proclamation No. 2667; Watkins, *Righteous Pilgrim,* 827–36; Brinkley, *Rightful Heritage,* 580–81; Bartley, *Tidelands Oil Controversy,* 134–41.

14. H.R. Res. 225, 79th Cong., 2nd sess. (1946); 92 Cong. Rec. 9642, 10316, 10660, 10745 (1946).

15. A thorough discussion of the constitutional issues is found in Leshy, "Are Public Lands Unconstitutional?"

16. *State of California,* 332 U.S. at 30–31, 34–37.

17. *United States v. State of Wyoming,* 331 U.S. 440, 453–54 (1947).

18. Harry S. Truman, Veto of Bill Concerning Title to Offshore Lands, May 29, 1952; Exec. Order No. 10426 (January 16, 1953).

19. 67 Stat. 29 (1953); 99 Cong. Rec. 4488 (Senate vote), 4898 (House vote) (1953).

20. 67 Stat. 29, 32 (1953); *Alabama v. Texas,* 347 U.S. 272 (1954); Wyant, *Westward in Eden,* 220–33.

21. 67 Stat. 462 (1953); Warren M. Christopher, "The Outer Continental Shelf Lands Act: Key to a New Frontier," *Stanford Law Review* 6, no. 1 (1953): 23–68.

22. Christopher, "Outer Continental Shelf Lands Act," 47–48, 56–59.

23. 25 Fed. Reg. 2352 (March 5, 1960); White House, press release announcing the establishment of the Key Largo Coral Reef Reserve, March 16, 1960, U.S. Fish and Wildlife Service, www.fws.gov/news/Historic/NewsReleases/1960/19600316.pdf.

24. The complex rules involving "leagues" versus "miles," and domestic versus international nautical miles, are explained here: "Outer Continental Shelf," Bureau of Ocean Energy Management, www.boem.gov/Outer-Continental-Shelf; see also "Primer on Ocean Jurisdictions: Drawing Lines in the Water," University of North Texas, https://govinfo.library.unt.edu/oceancommission/documents/full_color_rpt/03a_primer.

pdf; "The United States Is an Ocean Nation," National Oceanographic and Atmospheric Administration, Office of General Counsel, www.gc.noaa.gov/docu ments/2011/012711_gcil_maritime_eez_map.pdf.

52. THE WILDERNESS ACT RESHAPES PUBLIC LAND POLICY

1. Hiltzik, *Colossus*, 156–58, 311, 381–82.
2. Principal sources for the Echo Park controversy are Fox, *John Muir and His Legacy;* Harvey, *Symbol of Wilderness;* Leshy, "Legal Wilderness"; Nash, *Wilderness and the American Mind;* Sutter, *Driven Wild;* Turner, *Promise of Wilderness.*
3. 43 U.S.C. 620b; Leshy, "Legal Wilderness," 549, 561–64; Harvey, *Symbol of Wilderness,* 12–13; Nash, *Wilderness and the American Mind,* 209–19; Bill Devall, "David Brower," *Environmental Review: ER* 9, no. 3 (Autumn 1985): 238–53.
4. Harvey, *Symbol of Wilderness,* 174 (Zahniser comment).
5. Principal sources for the Wilderness Act are Allin, *Politics of Wilderness Preservation;* Coggins et al., *Federal Public Land and Resources Law,* 926–80; Graf, *Wilderness Preservation;* Hirt, *Conspiracy of Optimism,* 176, 180, 356–57; Leshy, "Legal Wilderness"; Nash, *Wilderness and the American Mind,* 220–27; Roth, *Wilderness Movement;* Sutter, *Driven Wild;* Turner, *Promise of Wilderness.*
6. 3 Fed. Reg. 1408–9 (Oct. 25, 1937); Nie, "Use of Co-Management," 624–27; Sutter, *Driven Wild,* 228.
7. Allin, *Politics of Wilderness Preservation,* 102–42; Graf, *Wilderness Preservation,* 200–212; Nash, *Wilderness and the American Mind,* 221–26, 248; Sutter, *Driven Wild,* 243; Sarah E. Dant, "Making Wilderness Work: Frank Church and the American Wilderness Movement," *Pacific Historical Review* 77, no. 2 (May 2008): 237–72; Michael McCloskey, "Wilderness Movement at the Crossroads, 1945–1970," *Pacific Historical Review* 41, no. 3 (August 1972): 346, 351n10; 102 Cong. Rec. 12589 (1956) (Saylor); T. Smith, *Green Republican.*
8. Kevin M. Marsh, " 'Save French Pete': Evolution of Wilderness Protests in Oregon," in *Natural Protest: Essays on the History of Environmentalism,* ed. Michael Egan and Jeff Crane (New York: Routledge, 2008), 223, 228.
9. Fox, *John Muir and His Legacy,* 317–20.
10. John F. Kennedy, Special Message to the Congress on Natural Resources, February 23, 1961, 13; T. Smith, *Stewart L. Udall,* 85–86; T. Smith, "Kennedy, Udall, and New Frontier Conservation"; William deBuys, "Stewart Udall, John Wesley Powell, and the Emergence of a National American Commons," in Robison, McCool, and Minckley, *Vision and Place,* 168; Stewart Udall, "To Save the Wonder of the Wilderness," *New York Times Magazine,* May 27, 1962.
11. Hirt, *Conspiracy of Optimism,* 154–59, 193, 202; 72 Stat. 238 (1958) (act establishing the commission); Raleigh Barlowe, "Land for Recreation," in Ottoson, *Land Use Policy and Problems,* 255, 260; Outdoor Recreation Resources Review Commission, *Outdoor Recreation for America* (January 1962); Frank Gregg, "Public Land Policy: Controversial Beginnings for the Third Century," in Lacey, *Government and Environmental Politics,* 152, 179n20.
12. Harvey, *Symbol of Wilderness,* 74 (citing Hays, *Beauty, Health, and Permanence,* 3); "Goldwater's 1964 Acceptance Speech," Republican National Convention, available

from the *Washington Post*, washingtonpost.com/wp-srv/politics/daily/may98 /goldwaterspeech.htm.

13. 78 Stat. 890 (1964).

14. Allin, *Politics of Wilderness Preservation*, 160; Keiter, *To Conserve Unimpaired*, 21–22; Miles, *Wilderness in National Parks*, 110–18, 147–49.

15. 78 Stat. 890 (1964); Bob Marshall, "The Problem of the Wilderness," *Scientific Monthly* 30, no. 2 (February 1930): 141–48; David G. Havlick, *No Place Distant: Roads and Motorized Recreation on America's Public Lands* (Washington, D.C.: Island, 2002).

16. Coggins et al., *Federal Public Land and Resources Law*, 891–912; Allin, *Politics of Wilderness Preservation*, 283–88.

17. Barry Mackintosh, *C&O Canal: The Making of a Park* (National Park Service, 1991), 90–92, available from the National Park Service, www.nps.gov/parkhistory/online_books/choh/making_a_park.pdf; Richard A. Baker, "The Conservation Congress of Anderson and Aspinall, 1963–1964," *Journal of Forest History* 29, no. 3 (1985): 104–19; Michael McCloskey, "The Wilderness Act of 1964: Its Background and Meaning," *Oregon Law Review* 45 (1966): 288–321; McCloskey, "Wilderness Movement at the Crossroads," 349.

18. 16 U.S.C. § 1132(b) (2006); Allin, *Politics of Wilderness Preservation*, 107, 117, 127–31; Dant, "Making Wilderness Work," 242–43; Turner, *Promise of Wilderness*, 32–33.

19. Brock Evans, "The Wilderness Idea as a Moving Force in American Cultural and Political History," *Idaho Law Review* 16 (1980): 389, 401–2; Allin, *Politics of Wilderness Preservation*, 130–31, 173–75, 203; Roth, *Wilderness Movement*, 2–5.

20. 78 Stat. 891–93 (§ 3); National Park Service, *National Parks: Our Treasured Landscapes—America's Wilderness* (June 2009), 2.

21. Turner, *Promise of Wilderness*, 32, 92; Allin, *Politics of Wilderness Preservation*, 144–69.

22. 82 Stat. 883 (1968); 88 Stat. 2096 (1975); Allin, *Politics of Wilderness Preservation*, 157–60, 186; Jeffrey P. Foote, "Wilderness: A Question of Purity," *Environmental Law* 3, no. 2 (Summer 1973): 255–66; McCloskey, "Wilderness Movement at the Crossroads," 357–58.

23. Heritage Foundation, *Mandate for Leadership*, vol. 1 (1981), 373; Leshy, "Natural Resources Policy," 23–26; 96 Stat. 1196 (1982) (blocking oil and gas leasing in wilderness areas).

24. Allin, *Politics of Wilderness Preservation*, 151–58.

25. "Acreages Listed by Year," Wilderness Connect, https://wilderness.net/practitioners/wilderness-areas/summary-reports/acreage-legislated-by-year.php.

26. While the amount of land in the NWPS is easily calculated, the amount of land permanently reserved required the author to make some judgments about permanent versus temporary reservations.

27. "History of Big Cypress," Everglades Online, www.evergladesonline.com/history-big-cypress.htm; Allin, *Politics of Wilderness Preservation*, 184–86.

28. 90 Stat. 2743 (1976); see generally Coggins et al., *Federal Public Land and Resources Law*, 964–80.

29. Allin, *Politics of Wilderness Preservation*, 105–35; Turner, *Promise of Wilderness*, 25–35, 47–54.

30. 88 Stat. 3343 (1975); Klyza and Souza, *American Environmental Policy*, 112–23, 302–3.

31. Coggins et al., *Federal Public Land and Resources Law*, 697–705; Dombeck et al., *From Conquest to Conservation*, 93–95, 110–16; Allin, *Politics of Wilderness Preservation*, 288–92; 85 Fed. Reg. 68888 (October 29, 2020) (repeal of the roadless rule in Tongass).

32. Klyza and Souza, *American Environmental Policy*, 169–74, 299–300, 307; BLM Manual, Part 6320 (2012), www.blm.gov/programs/planning-and-nepa/plan ning-101/special-planning-designations/lands-with-wilderness-characteristics.

33. Confederated Salish and Kootenai Tribes, *Mission Mountains Tribal Wilderness: A Case Study* (Pablo, Mont.: Confederated Salish and Kootenai Tribes, 2005), available online from Wilderness Connect.

53. NEW LABELS AND NEW MEANS OF PROTECTING PUBLIC VALUES IN PUBLIC LANDS

1. 134 Stat. 682 (2020).

2. 78 Stat. 897 (1965); Carol Hardy Vincent, *Land and Water Conservation Fund: Overview, Funding History, and Issues*, RL33531 (Congressional Research Service, 2018), available online from the Federation of American Scientists, https://fas.org/sgp/crs/misc/RL33531.pdf.

3. Dodd, "Boulder Dam Recreation Area," 443–66.

4. "Policy on the Establishment and Administration of Recreation Areas," March 26, 1963, in *America's National Park System: The Critical Documents*, ed. Lary M. Dilsaver (Lanham, Md.: Rowman and Littlefield, 1994), available online from the National Park Service, www.nps.gov/parkhistory/online_books/anps/anps_5g.htm; Coggins et al., *Federal Public Lands and Resources Law*, 875–85.

5. 78 Stat. 1039–41 (1964).

6. *Udall v. Federal Power Commission*, 387 U.S. 428, 450 (1967); 89 Stat. 1117 (1975); Allin, *Politics of Wilderness Preservation*, 182–84; Sara Dant Ewart, "Evolution of an Environmentalist: Senator Frank Church and the Hells Canyon Controversy," *Montana: The Magazine of Western History* 51, no. 1 (Spring 2001): 36–51.

7. 86 Stat. 612 (1972); Sara E. Dant Ewart, "Peak Park Politics: The Struggle over the Sawtooths, from Borah to Church," *Pacific Northwest Quarterly* 91, no. 3 (Summer 2000): 138–49; 129 Stat. 476–84 (2015).

8. "National Recreation Areas Across the U.S.," EmpoweringParks.com, empowering parks.com/recreation-areas.html.

9. See generally Coggins et al., *Federal Public Lands and Resources Law*, 195–200, 981–87; 78 Stat. 608 (1964); Hartzog, *Battling for the National Parks*, 59–70.

10. 82 Stat. 906 (1968); Ewart, "Evolution of an Environmentalist"; Allin, *Politics of Wilderness Preservation*, 172–76.

11. *Del Norte County v. United States*, 732 F.2d 1462 (9th Cir. 1984).

12. 82 Stat. 909–10 (1968).

13. William L. Graf, "Dam Nation: A Geographic Census of American Dams and Their Large-Scale Hydrologic Impacts," *Water Resources Research* 35, no. 4 (April 1999): 1305–11.

14. "About the WSR Act," National Wild and Scenic Rivers System, www.rivers.gov/wsr-act.php; Hartzog, *Battling for the National Parks*, 60–69.

15. Aldo Leopold, A *Sand County Almanac and Sketches Here and There* (New York: Oxford University Press, 1949), 190.

16. Lear, *Rachel Carson*, 454, 578; Rachel Carson, *Silent Spring,* anniversary ed., with an afterword by E. O. Wilson (1962; New York: Houghton Mifflin, 2002); Matthiessen, *Wildlife in America,* 269.

17. Lear, *Rachel Carson,* 233, 260; Stewart Udall, "To Save Wildlife and Aid Us, Too," *New York Times Magazine,* September 15, 1963.

18. 80 Stat. 926–30 (1966); Fischman, *National Wildlife Refuges,* 23–27, 41–53.

19. 83 Stat. 275 (1969); 87 Stat. 884 (1973); Thomas R. Dunlap, "The Federal Government, Wildlife, and Endangered Species," in Lacey, *Government and Environmental Politics,* 214–15; Adam J. Eichenwald, Michael J. Evans, and Jacob W. Malcolm, "U.S. Imperiled Species are Most Vulnerable to Habitat Loss on Private Lands," *Frontiers in Ecology and the Environment* 18, no. 8 (October 2020): 439–46; Wilkinson, *Crossing the Next Meridian,* 150–51, 163–64.

20. 87 Stat. 892 (1973).

21. 87 Stat. 893 (1973); *Babbitt v. Sweet Home,* 515 U.S. 687 (1995).

22. Richard N. L. Andrews, *Managing the Environment, Managing Ourselves: A History of American Environmental Policy* (New Haven, Conn.: Yale University Press, 1999), 202; Turner, *Promise of Wilderness,* 34–35, 95–106, 146–47; Sutter, *Driven Wild,* 73–74; Walter Kuhlmann, "Making the Law More Ecocentric: Responding to Leopold and Conservation Biology," *Duke Environmental Law and Policy Forum* 7, no. 1 (Fall 1996): 133–66.

23. Joseph L. Sax, "Perspectives Lecture: Public Land Law in the 21st Century," *Rocky Mountain Mineral Law Institute Proceedings* 45 (1999): § 1.02.

24. *TVA v. Hill,* 437 U.S. 153 (1978).

25. *Sierra Club v. Morton,* 405 U.S. 727, 734 (1972).

26. 82 Stat. 919 (1968); Bill Bryson, *A Walk in the Woods* (New York: Broadway, 1998), 111; Einberger, *With Distance in His Eyes,* 104, 106; Allin, *Politics of Wilderness Preservation,* 176–78; Sarah Mittlefehldt, *Tangled Roots: The Appalachian Trail and American Environmental Politics* (Seattle: University of Washington Press, 2013).

27. Einberger, *With Distance in His Eyes,* 106.

28. 82 Stat. 919 (1968); 100 Stat. 4302 (1986); 102 Stat. 4571, 4573–75 (1988); Coggins et al., *Federal Public Lands and Resources Law,* 885–86; Allin, *Politics of Wilderness Preservation,* 176–78; Donald Dale Jackson, "The Long Way 'Round," *Wilderness,* Summer 1968, 17–24.

29. Donald T. Sutte, Jr., and Roger A. Cunningham, *Scenic Easements: Legal, Administrative, and Valuation Problems and Procedures,* National Cooperative Highway Research Program Report 56 (Washington, D.C.: Highway Research Board, 1968); Roger A. Cunningham, "Scenic Easements in the Highway Beautification Program," *Denver Law Journal* 45, no. 2 (1968): 181–88; Federico Cheever and Nancy McLaughlin, "An Introduction to Conservation Easements in the United States: A Simple Concept and a Complicated Mosaic of Law," *Journal of Law, Property, and Society* 1, no. 3 (2015): 107, 115–16; Fairfax et al., *Buying Nature,* 121–24; Peter Elkind, "The Billion Dollar Loophole," *ProPublica,* December 20, 2017, www.propublica.org/article/conservation-easements-the-billion-dollar-loophole.

30. 97 Stat. 48 (1983); Peter Harnik, *From Rails to Trails: Pathway to the Re-Greening of America* (Lincoln: University of Nebraska Press, 2021), 62–70; Andrea C. Ferster, "Rails-to-Trails Conversions: A Legal Review," Rails-to-Trails Conservancy, www .railstotrails.org/resource-library/resources/rails-to-trails-conversions-a-legal-review.

31. Martin Nie and Michael Fiebig, "Managing the National Forests Through Place-Based Legislation," *Ecology Law Quarterly* 37, no. 1 (2010): 1, 8; Martin Nie, "Governing the Tongass: National Forest Conflict and Political Decision Making," *Environmental Law* 36, no. 2 (Spring 2006): 385–480; 123 Stat. 991, 1141–47 (2009).

32. John Muir, *My First Summer in the Sierra* (Boston: Houghton Mifflin, 1911), chap. 6; "John Muir Misquoted," Sierra Club, https://vault.sierraclub.org/john_muir_ exhibit/writings/misquotes.aspx.

54. MAKING THE MODERN BUREAU OF LAND MANAGEMENT

1. 78 Stat. 982 (1964). Principal sources for this chapter are Coggins et al., *Federal Public Land and Resources Law;* Leshy, "Natural Resources Policy," "Unraveling the Sagebrush Rebellion," and "Wilderness and Its Discontents"; Dombeck et al., *From Conquest to Conservation;* Einberger, *With Distance in His Eyes;* Muhn and Stuart, *Opportunity and Challenge;* Schulte, *Wayne Aspinall;* Skillen, *Nation's Largest Landlord;* T. Smith, *Stewart L. Udall;* Turner, *Promise of Wilderness;* Wilson, *America's Public Lands.*

2. 78 Stat. 986–88 (1964).

3. 78 Stat. 988–89 (1964).

4. Skillen, *Nation's Largest Landlord,* 44–71; Muhn and Stuart, *Opportunity and Challenge,* chaps. 3, 9–10.

5. John F. Kennedy, Special Message to the Congress on Natural Resources, February 23, 1961, 13; Muhn and Stuart, *Opportunity and Challenge,* chaps. 2–3; Donald B. Stough, "Wonders of the Public Domain," *Our Public Lands* 14, no. 3 (Winter 1965): 4–7; Leshy, "Wilderness and Its Discontents"; Einberger, *With Distance in His Eyes,* 126–39; Bureau of Land Management logo, https://commons.wikimedia.org/wiki/ File:US-DOI-BLM-logo.png.

6. Public Land Law Review Commission, *One Third of the Nation's Land,* 124–33.

7. Ibid., 46–52.

8. 84 Stat. 1067 (1970); 116 Cong. Rec. 32787–91 (1970).

9. Kenneth P. Pitt, "The Wild, Free-Roaming Horses and Burros Act: A Western Melodrama," *Environmental Law* 15, no. 3 (Spring 1985): 503–31; Einberger, *With Distance in His Eyes,* 132; Leisl Carr Childers, *The Size of the Risk: Histories of Multiple Use in the Great Basin* (Norman: University of Oklahoma Press, 2015), 167–205.

10. *Kleppe v. New Mexico,* 426 U.S. 529 (1976).

11. Richard Nixon, Special Message to the Congress Proposing the 1971 Environmental Program; Schulte, *Wayne Aspinall.*

12. 90 Stat. 2744–45 (1976); Coggins et al., *Federal Public Land and Resources Law,* 655–56; *Restoring Quality of the Environment: Report of the Environmental Pollution Panel of the President's Science Advisory Committee* (Washington, D.C.: White House, 1965), 9, 111.

13. 90 Stat. 2751, 2762, 2792 (1976); Coggins et al., *Federal Public Land and Resources Law,* 124, 383–91, 481–86.

14. 90 Stat. 2771–72 (1976); 92 Stat. 1804 (1978).

15. 90 Stat. 2662 (1976).

16. 90 Stat. 303–6 (1976); 94 Stat. 2964–65 (1980).

17. Andrus, speech to National Wildlife Federation, March 26, 1977.

18. Leshy, "Natural Resources Policy," 26–30; Edward Walsh, "Carter Adds 14 Water Projects to 'Hit List,' " *Washington Post*, March 24, 1977.

19. Leshy, "Unraveling the Sagebrush Rebellion"; Frank Gregg, "Public Land Policy: Controversial Beginnings for the New Century," in Lacey, *Government and Environmental Politics*, 154–56.

20. Leshy, "Natural Resources Policy"; *Nevada v. United States*, 699 F. 2d 486 (9th Cir. 1983).

21. R. McGreggor Cawley, *Federal Land, Western Anger: The Sagebrush Rebellion and Environmental Politics* (Lawrence: University Press of Kansas, 1993); on Reagan's ranch, see Lou Cannon, "Reagan's Ranch a Retreat, Tax Shelter, and Security Risk," *Washington Post*, July 7, 1980, www.washingtonpost.com/archive/politics/1980/07/05/reagans-ranch-a-retreat-tax-shelter-and-security-risk/21a64428-60f7-4dac-8603-6b297ab0ad44.

22. Leshy, "Natural Resources Policy," 41–42; Leshy, "Unraveling the Sagebrush Rebellion"; Short, *Reagan and the Public Lands*, 65–78; Lazer, *Open for Business*, 88–92, 101, 111–12, 115; Coggins et al., *Federal Public Land and Resources Law*, 967–68; Turner, *Promise of Wilderness*, 225–62; R. Nelson, *Public Lands and Private Rights*, 167–82.

23. Leshy, "Babbitt Legacy," 208, 221–22; *Public Lands Council v. Babbitt*, 529 U.S. 728 (2000).

24. *Gardner v. United States*, 107 F.3d 1314 (1997).

25. Coggins et al., *Federal Public Land and Resources Law*, 731–32; Bradley J. Gentner and John A. Tanaka, "Classifying Federal Public Land Grazing Permittees," *Journal of Range Management* 55, no. 1 (January 2002): 2–11; *Public Lands Council*, 529 U.S. at 736–37 (statistics on the decline in grazing from 1953 to 1998).

26. Leshy, "Babbitt Legacy," 210–11; Darren Frederick Speece, *Defending Giants: The Redwood Wars and the Transformation of American Environmental Politics* (Seattle: University of Washington Press, 2017); Fairfax et al., *Buying Nature*, 227–28.

27. Bruce Babbitt, "The Heart of the West: BLM's National Landscape Conservation System," in Dombeck et al., *From Conquest to Conservation*, 100–102; "National Landscape Conservation System: National Conservation Areas and Similar Designations," Bureau of Land Management, www.blm.gov/sites/blm.gov/files/uploads/NCAs_and_Sim_Q4_2016.pdf.

55. MAKING THE MODERN FOREST SERVICE

1. Principal authorities for this chapter are Dietrich, *The Final Forest*; Hirt, *Conspiracy of Optimism*; Wilkinson, *Crossing the Next Meridian*; Wilkinson and Anderson, *Land and Resource Planning*; Yaffee, *Wisdom of the Spotted Owl*. For Crowell's proposal, see Hirt, *Conspiracy of Optimism*, 216, 321.

2. Hirt, *Conspiracy of Optimism*, 233–56.

3. Ibid., 113–17.

4. Ibid., 246–47; Wilkinson, *Crossing the Next Meridian*, 140–44.

5. *West Virginia Division of Izaak Walton League of America v. Butz*, 522 F.2d 945 (4th Cir. 1975); *Zieske v. Butz*, 406 F. Supp. 258 (D. Alaska 1975).

6. 88 Stat. 476 (1974).

7. *National Wildlife Federation v. United States*, 626 F.2d 917, 924 (D.C. Cir. 1980).

8. 122 Cong. Rec. 5618–19 (1976).

9. 90 Stat. 2949 (1976); Dennis C. LeMaster, *Decade of Change: The Remaking of Forest Service Statutory Authority During the 1970s* (Westport, Conn.: Greenwood, 1984).

10. 90 Stat. 2957 (1976).

11. Wilkinson and Anderson, *Land and Resource Planning*, 64–90; *Norton v. Southern Utah Wilderness Alliance*, 542 U.S. 55, 71 (2004).

12. Hirt, *Conspiracy of Optimism*, xxxvii; Michael C. Blumm and Tim Wigington, "The Oregon and California Railroad Grant Lands' Sordid Past, Contentious Present, and Uncertain Future: A Century of Conflict," *Boston College Environmental Affairs Law Review* 40 (2013): 1–76.

13. 16 USC 1604(g)(3)(B); 36 CFR 219.19.

14. *Northern Spotted Owl v. Hodel*, 716 F. Supp. 479 (W.D. Wash. 1988); *Seattle Audubon Society v. Evans*, 771 F. Supp. 1081 (W.D. Wash. 1991).

15. Yaffee, *Wisdom of the Spotted Owl*, 137–40, 397–98; Klyza and Souza, *American Environmental Policy*, 66–67; *Robertson v. Seattle Audubon Society*, 502 U.S. 429 (1992).

16. Hirt, *Conspiracy of Optimism*, 266–92; Yaffee, *Wisdom of the Spotted Owl*, 141–43.

17. Lazer, *Open for Business*, 150–53, 233–34; Klyza and Souza, *American Environmental Policy*, 67–76, 165–69.

18. Turner and Isenberg, *Republican Reversal*, 85–89, 91; James R. Skillen, *Federal Ecosystem Management: Its Rise, Fall, and Afterlife* (Lawrence: University Press of Kansas, 2015); 100 Stat. 240–47 (1995).

19. Yaffee, *Wisdom of the Spotted Owl*, 298–377.

20. 117 Stat. 1887 (2003); Robert B. Keiter, "The Law of Fire: Reshaping Public Land Policy in an Era of Ecology and Litigation," *Environmental Law* 36, no. 2 (Spring 2006): 301–84.

21. *Miller v. Mallery*, 410 F. Supp. 1283 (D. Ore. 1976); 91 Stat. 1425 (1977); Donald H. Blanchard, "Clearcutting the Bull Run Watershed: A Standard of Reasonableness in Forest Service Decision-Making," *Environmental Law* 8, no. 2 (Winter 1978): 569, 580–84.

22. 96 Stat. 301 (1982) (Mt. St. Helens National Volcanic Monument); 98 Stat. 1632, 1638 (1984).

23. Samuel P. Hays, *Wars in the Woods: The Rise of Ecological Forestry in America* (Pittsburgh: University of Pittsburgh Press, 2007), 172.

24. As with the graph in chapter 52, the graphs here required the author to exercise some judgment about what is "mostly" protected, either by Congress or by the executive branch.

56. CHARTING THE FUTURE OF PUBLIC LANDS IN ALASKA

1. Principal authorities for this chapter are Allin, *Politics of Wilderness Preservation*, 207–65; Nash, *Wilderness and the American Mind*, 272–315; D. Nelson, *Northern Landscapes*; Turner, *Promise of Wilderness*; Williss, "Do Things Right the First Time." Native population figures are from Weeden, *Alaska*, 4.

2. Williss, *"Do Things Right the First Time"*; McPhee, *Coming into the Country.*

3. 72 Stat. 339 (1958); 85 Stat. 688 (1971); 94 Stat. 2457 (1980).

4. Wolfe, *Son of the Wilderness,* 204–13, 215–21, 222–27, 246–49, 256, 274–75, 279–82; Nash, *Wilderness and the American Mind,* 279–85; Henry Gannett, "The General Geography of Alaska," *National Geographic,* May 1901.

5. Williss, *"Do Things Right the First Time,"* chap. 1B 7.

6. Ibid., chaps. 1B and C 5–13; Robert Marshall, *Arctic Village: A 1930s Portrait of Wiseman, Alaska* (1933; reprint, Fairbanks: University Press of Alaska, 1991); Nash, *Wilderness and the American Mind,* 287–88.

7. D. Nelson, *Northern Landscapes,* 20–21.

8. 23 Stat. 24, 26 (§ 8) (1884); 26 Stat. 1095, 1101 (1891).

9. Kenneth Philp, "The New Deal and Alaskan Natives, 1936–1945," *Pacific Historical Review* 50, no. 3 (August 1981): 309–27; Stephen W. Haycox, "Economic Development and Indian Land Rights in Modern Alaska: The 1947 Tongass Timber Act," *Western Historical Quarterly* 21, no. 1 (February 1990): 20–46.

10. Haycox, "Economic Development and Indian Land Rights," 44; 61 Stat. 920 (1947); Catton, *American Indians and National Forests,* 82–87.

11. D. Nelson, *Northern Landscapes,* 28–29.

12. *Tee-Hit-Ton Indians v. United States,* 348 U.S. 272 (1955); Newton, *Federal Indian Law,* § 1509(1)(d), 1024–25.

13. 72 Stat. 339 (1958).

14. Ibid.; Gates, *Public Land Law Development,* 316.

15. Nash, *Wilderness and the American Mind,* 289–92.

16. Mary Clay Berry, *The Alaska Pipeline: The Politics of Oil and Native Land Claims* (Bloomington: Indiana University Press, 1975); Theodore Catton, *Inhabited Wilderness: Indians, Eskimos, and National Parks in Alaska* (Albuquerque: University of New Mexico Press, 1997); Donald Craig Mitchell, *Take My Land, Take My Life: The Story of Congress's Historic Settlement of Alaska Native Land Claims, 1960–1971* (Fairbanks: University of Alaska Press, 2001).

17. Berry, *Alaska Pipeline*; Wilkinson, *Blood Struggle,* 231–40; Stephen W. Haycox, "Owning It All in Alaska: The Political Poser of a Rhetorical Paradigm," in *Land in the American West: Private Claims and the Common Good,* ed. William G. Robbins and James C. Foster (Seattle: University of Washington Press, 2000), 164, 171–74; Everhart, *National Park Service,* 176–78.

18. D. Nelson, *Northern Landscapes,* 62–65, 73–78.

19. Ibid., 75–77.

20. 85 Stat. 688–716 (1971).

21. 85 Stat. 708–10 (1971); D. Nelson, *Northern Landscapes,* 101–7; Allin, *Politics of Wilderness Preservation,* 215–18.

22. *Wilderness Society v. Morton,* 479 F.2d 842 (D.C. Cir. 1973); D. Nelson, *Northern Landscapes,* 108–18; Peter A. Coates, *The Trans-Alaska Pipeline Controversy: Technology, Conservation, and the Frontier* (Bethlehem, Pa.: Lehigh University Press, 1991).

23. D. Nelson, *Northern Landscapes,* 118–25; Turner, *Promise of Wilderness,* 141–48.

24. D. Nelson, *Northern Landscapes,* 130–48, 160–61.

25. Turner, *Promise of Wilderness,* 143–50.

26. D. Nelson, *Northern Landscapes,* 184.

27. Stuart Eizenstat, *President Carter: The White House Years* (New York: Dunne, 2018), 268–74; Nelson, *Promise of Wilderness*, 198–200.

28. Allin, *Politics of Wilderness Preservation*, 232–36.

29. Klyza and Souza, *American Environmental Policy*, 103–4; D. Nelson, *Passion for the Land*, 140–42; *Anaconda Copper Co. v. Andrus*, 14 Env't. Rep. Cas. (BNA) 1853 (D. Ak. 1980).

30. Williss, "Do Things Right the First Time," 25–27; 125 Cong. Rec. 11457–59 (1979).

31. D. Nelson, *Northern Landscapes*, 237–48; Williss, "Do Things Right the First Time," 28–30.

32. Eizenstat, *President Carter*, 243.

33. 94 Stat. 2371–2551, esp. at 2375–77 (1980); Robert B. Keiter, "Toward a National Conservation Network Act: Transforming Landscape Conservation on the Public Lands into Law," *Harvard Environmental Law Review* 42, no. 1 (2018): 61, 67, 94.

34. Haycox, "Owning It All in Alaska," 177–78.

35. Williss, "Do Things Right the First Time," chap. 3.

57. MAKING THE MODERN U.S. FISH & WILDLIFE SERVICE

1. Principal sources for this chapter are Bean and Rowland, *Evolution of National Wildlife Law*; Fink, "National Wildlife Refuges"; Fischman, *National Wildlife Refuges*; Tredennick, "National Wildlife System Improvement Act." The Refuge Recreation Act is at 76 Stat. 763 (1962).

2. 78 Stat. 701 (1964); M. Lynne Corn, *Fish and Wildlife Service: Compensation to Local Governments*, R42404 (Congressional Research Service, 2014).

3. 80 Stat. 926–30 (1966); Fischman, *National Wildlife Refuges*, 23–27, 45–53.

4. Fischman, *National Wildlife Refuges*, 45–50, 83; Barrow, *Nature's Ghosts*.

5. Einberger, *With Distance in His Eyes*, 114–25.

6. Fischman, *National Wildlife Refuges*, 56–57; Fischman, "Significance of National Wildlife Refuges"; Robert H. MacArthur and Edward O. Wilson, *The Theory of Island Biogeography* (Princeton, N.J.: Princeton University Press, 1967); David Quammen, *The Song of the Dodo: Island Biogeography in an Age of Extinctions* (London: Random House, 1996).

7. Fischman, *National Wildlife Refuges*, 21–22; 90 Stat. 199 (1976); Fink, "National Wildlife Refuges," 25–26.

8. 90 Stat. 199, 2751 (1976); Philip A. DuMont and Henry W. Thomas, *Modification of National Wildlife Refuges* (U.S. Fish & Wildlife Service, 1975).

9. 100 Stat. 3582 (1986); 103 Stat. 1986 (1989); Fink, "National Wildlife Refuges," 19; U.S. Fish & Wildlife Service, "The Canada/Mexico/U.S. Trilateral Committee for Wildlife and Ecosystem Conservation and Management," www.fws.gov/international /pdf/factsheet-trilateral-2013.pdf.

10. Fischman, *National Wildlife Refuges*, 53–56; Fink, "National Wildlife Refuges," 5–6; *Defenders of Wildlife v. Andrus*, 455 F. Supp. 4476 (D.D.C. 1978).

11. Exec. Order No. 12996 (March 25, 1996); 111 Stat. 1252 (1997) (National Wildlife Refuge System Improvement Act); Fischman, *National Wildlife Refuges*, 56–63; Tredennick, "National Wildlife System Improvement Act," 65–76 (tracing the path of the legislation).

12. Wallace Stegner, *Where the Bluebird Sings to the Lemonade Springs: Living and Writing in the West* (1993; reprint, New York: Modern Library, 2002), 126.

13. III Stat. 1252, 1254–55, § 4(a); regarding plants, see Fischman, *National Wildlife Refuges*, 82–84; Robert B. Keiter, "Toward a National Conservation Network: Transforming Landscape Conservation on the Public Lands into Law," *Harvard Environmental Law Review* 42, no. 1 (2018): 61, 71.

14. III Stat. at 1253, § 5(2); Fischman, *National Wildlife Refuges*, 94–98; J. Caudill and E. Carver, *Banking on Nature: The Economic Contributions of National Wildlife Refuge Recreational Visitation to Local Communities* (U.S. Fish & Wildlife Service, 2017; revised 2019); U.S. Fish & Wildlife Service, press release, November 29, 2017; *Wingtips*, December 22, 2017, publication of Friends of the Migratory Bird / Duck Stamp, www.friendsofthestamp.org/wp-content/uploads/2017/12/Wingtips-22-December-2017.pdf; Andy McGlashen, "Duck Stamp Artists Turn to Spent Shotgun Shells to Meet New Pro-Hunting Mandate," *Audubon*, October 6, 2020, www.audubon.org/news/duck-stamp-artists-turn-spent-shotgun-shells-meet-new-pro-hunting-mandate.

15. III Stat. 1256–57, § 6; Fischman, *National Wildlife Refuges*, 116–21; Tredennick, "National Wildlife System Improvement Act," 84–87.

16. Fischman, *National Wildlife Refuges*, 112–25, 193–99; Tredennick, "National Wildlife System Improvement Act," 103n303; 88 Stat. 2121 (1975) (Canaveral National Seashore); Fink, "National Wildlife Refuges," 1, 21, 75; U.S. Fish & Wildlife Service, *National Wildlife Refuge System Land Protection Projects: An Assessment of Land Protection Projects; A Plan for Strategic Growth* (2013).

17. III Stat. 1252, 1254–55, § 5; Robert Fischman and Vicky J. Meretsky, "Managing Biological Integrity, Diversity, and Environmental Health in the National Wildlife Refuges: An Introduction to the Symposium," *Natural Resources Journal* 44, no. 4 (2004): 931, 941; Fischman, *National Wildlife Refuges*, 100–108 (comprehensive planning).

18. See, for example, Tredennick, "National Wildlife System Improvement Act," 64n110, 66, 81–83, 199.

19. Flores, *Coyote America*, 165–72; Donald W. Hawthorne, "The History of Federal and Cooperative Animal Damage Control," *Sheep and Goat Research Journal* 6 (October 2004): 12–15.

20. "Oppose Attacks on the Alaska National Wildlife Refuge Rule," Defenders of Wildlife, https://defenders.org/sites/default/files/publications/oppose-attacks-on-the-alaska-national-wildlife-refuge-rule-defenders.pdf; "2016 National Survey of Fishing, Hunting, and Wildlife-Associated Recreation," U.S. Fish & Wildlife Service, April 2018, www.fws.gov/wsfrprograms/subpages/nationalsurvey/nat_survey2016.pdf.

21. *Cappaert v. United States*, 426 U.S. 128 (1976); see also *Hunt v. United States*, 278 U.S. 96 (1928); Chase and Madison, "Expanding Ark," 18–24.

22. 43 C.F.R. § 24 (Interior Department state-federal relations); Fischman, *National Wildlife Refuges*, 87–88.

23. Jeffrey Mervis, "Why NOAA Is in the Commerce Department," *Science*, January 13, 2012, www.sciencemag.org/news/2012/01/why-noaa-commerce-department.

24. 86 Stat. 1027 (1972) (Marine Mammal Protection Act); 86 Stat. 1052, 1061 (1972); William J. Chandler and Hannah Gillelan, *The Makings of the National Marine Sanctuaries Act: A Legislative History and Analysis* (Washington, D.C.: Marine

Conservation Biology Institute, 2005) (the 1966 report was called *Effective Use of the Sea*); Dave Owen, "The Disappointing History of the National Marine Sanctuaries Act," *New York University Environmental Law Journal* 11, no. 3 (2003): 711–57.

25. Carol Hardy Vincent, *National Monuments and the Antiquities Act*, R41330 (Congressional Research Service, 2018), https://fas.org/sgp/crs/misc/R41330.pdf.

26. Darryl Fears and Juliet Eilperin, "Trump Lifts Limits on Commercial Fishing at Ocean Sanctuary off New England," *Washington Post*, June 5, 2020, www.washing tonpost.com/climate-environment/2020/06/05/trump-fishing-seamounts-marine- national-monument; Wil S. Hylton, "History's Largest Mining Operation Is About to Begin," *Atlantic*, January–February 2020.

27. Fischman, *National Wildlife Refuges*, 24–31; Fink, "National Wildlife Refuges," 23; U.S. Fish & Wildlife Service, *National Wildlife Refuge System Land Protection Projects: An Assessment of Land Protection Projects; A Plan for Strategic Growth* (2013); Russell D. Butcher, *America's National Wildlife Refuges: A Complete Guide*, 2nd ed. (Lanham, Md.: Taylor Trade, 2008); Matthiessen, *Wildlife in America*, 269.

58. MAKING THE MODERN NATIONAL PARK SERVICE

1. Principal sources for this chapter are Einberger, *With Distance in His Eyes*; Foresta, *America's National Parks*; Gonzales, "Park Service Goes to the Beach"; Hartzog, *Battling for the National Parks*; Keiter, *To Conserve Unimpaired*; Mackintosh, *National Parks*; D. Nelson, *Passion for the Land*; Runte, *National Parks*; T. Smith, *Stewart L. Udall*. On Cape Hatteras, see Ise, *Our National Park Policy*, 425–26, 516.

2. 75 Stat. 284 (1961) (Cape Cod National Seashore).

3. 80 Stat. 1309 (1966); 133 Stat. 232–33 (2019), www.nps.gov/indu/learn/historycul ture/index.htm.

4. 75 Stat. 780 (1961) (Mount Vernon viewshed); Ise, *Our National Park Policy*, 518–19; Fairfax et al., *Buying Nature*, 145–50, 158–60.

5. Keiter, *To Conserve Unimpaired*, 148–52.

6. Einberger, *With Distance in His Eyes*, 109–10.

7. Ibid., 71–89.

8. Hartzog, *Battling for the National Parks*; John McPhee, "Profiles: Ranger," *New Yorker*, September 11, 1971.

9. 114 Stat. 598 (2000); 119 Stat. 2570 (2005); 128 Stat. 3792–98 (2014); Ray H. Mattison, "The Tangled Web: The Controversy over the Tumacacori and Baca Land Grants," *Journal of Arizona History* 8, no. 2 (Summer 1967): 71–90; Melinda Harm Benson, "Shifting Public Land Paradigms: Lessons from the Valle Caldera National Preserve," *Virginia Environmental Law Journal* 34, no. 1 (2016): 1–51.

10. Schrepfer, *Fight to Save the Redwoods*, 52, 63, 156–58.

11. 82 Stat. 931 (1968) (Redwood National Park); Susan R. Schrepfer, "Conflict in Preservation: The Sierra Club, Save-the-Redwoods League, and Redwood National Park," *Journal of Forest History* 24, no. 2 (April 1980): 60–77; Schrepfer, *Fight to Save the Redwoods*, 226; Fairfax et al., *Buying Nature*, 163–67; Lyndon B. Johnson, Remarks on Signing Four Bills Relating to Conservation and Outdoor Recreation, October 2, 1968.

12. Darren Frederick Speece, *Defending Giants: The Redwood Wars and the Transformation of American Environmental Politics* (Seattle: University of Washington Press, 2017), 34.

13. 82 Stat. 933 (1968) (cooperative agreements); 92 Stat. 166 (1978); Schrepfer, *Fight to Save the Redwoods*, 213–28.

14. *Sierra Club v. Morton*, 405 U.S. 727 (1972); 16 U.S.C. 45h (1978); Tom Turner, *Wild by Law: The Sierra Club Legal Defense Fund and the Places It Has Saved* (New York: Random House, 1990).

15. 40 Stat. 1175, 1178 (1919); Byron E. Pearson, "Salvation for Grand Canyon: Congress, the Sierra Club, and the Dam Controversy of 1966–1968," *Journal of the Southwest* 36, no. 2 (Summer 1994): 159–75.

16. 82 Stat. 886 (1968) (Colorado River Basin Project Act); Reisner, *Cadillac Desert*, 283–307; Nash, *Wilderness and the American Mind*, 227–38; Allin, *Politics of Wilderness Preservation*, 178–81.

17. Keiter, *To Conserve Unimpaired*, 238–40; Jacobs, *Rage for Justice*, 361–79; 92 Stat. 3518–19 (1978); D. Nelson, *Passion for the Land*, 144–45; Allin, *Politics of Wilderness Preservation*, 196–97.

18. 102 Stat. 4571, 4573, 4575, 4599 (1988).

19. 108 Stat. 4471 (1994); Frank Wheat, *California Desert Miracle* (San Diego: Sunbelt, 1999).

20. 84 Stat. 826 (1970), building on 67 Stat. 496 (1953).

21. 90 Stat. 1939, 1942–43, § 12(b) (1976); 92 Stat. 3467, 3518–19 (1978).

22. 90 Stat. 1342 (1976); 36 C.F.R. Part 9; Coggins et al., *Federal Public Land and Resources Law*, 539; D. Nelson, *Passion for the Land*, 107–8.

23. Exec. Order No. 10092 (December 17, 1949); *United States v. Perko*, 108 F.Supp. 315 (D. Minn. 1952), aff'd 204 F.2d 446 (8th Cir. 1953); 88 Stat. 2089, 2091 (1975).

24. 101 Stat. 674 (1987).

25. Allin, *Politics of Wilderness Preservation*, 88–89; Keiter, *To Conserve Unimpaired*, 34–35; 114 Stat. 185–97 (2000).

26. 112 Stat. 3497–523 (1998); Sellars, *Preserving Nature in the National Parks*.

27. 79 Stat. 969–72 (1965); Keiter, *To Conserve Unimpaired*, 149–54.

28. 112 Stat. 3497 at 3503–18 (1998); Coggins et al., *Federal Public Land and Resources Law*, 888–91; Nancy Bouchard, "Yosemite National Park Gets Its Names Back," *Outside Magazine*, July 17, 2019.

29. "About Us," National Park Service, www.nps.gov/aboutus/visitation-numbers .htm.

59. MINERAL AND ENERGY DEVELOPMENT IN THE MODERN ERA

1. Principal sources for the Mining Law discussion are Leshy, *Mining Law*; Leshy "Mining Law Reform Redux."

2. Leshy, *Mining Law*, 81–82, 222–23.

3. Leshy, "Mining Law Reform Redux," 462–64; John Cushman, "Forced, U.S. Sells Gold Land for Trifle," *New York Times*, May 17, 1994; Timothy Egan, "Billions at Stake in Debate on a Gold Rush," *New York Times*, August 14, 1994.

4. McPhee, *Encounters with the Archdruid*, 1–76; Adam M. Sowards, *An Open Pit Visible from the Moon: The Wilderness Act and the Fight to Protect Miners Ridge and the Public Interest* (Norman: University of Oklahoma Press, 2020).

5. Principal sources for the remainder of the chapter are Coggins et al., *Federal Public Land and Resources Law*; Turner and Isenberg, *Republican Reversal*.

6. 91 Stat. 524 (1977); 30 U.S.C. § 1304(c); 90 Stat. 1083, 1085 (1976) (Federal Coal Leasing Amendments Act).

7. Coggins et al., *Federal Public Land and Resources Law,* 553–60; Turner and Isenberg, *Republican Reversal,* 66–72.

8. Coggins et al., *Federal Public Land and Resources Law,* 504–5; U.S. Office of Technology Assessment, *An Assessment of Oil Shale Technologies,* vol. 2, *A History and Analysis of the Prototype Federal Oil Shale Leasing Program* (Washington, D.C.: Government Printing Office, 1980), https://ota.fas.org/reports/8024.pdf; Peter M. Crawford, Christopher Dean, Jeffrey Stone, and James C. Killen, "Assessment of Plans and Progress on U.S. Bureau of Land Management Oil Shale RD&D Leases" (U.S. Department of Energy, 2013), www.energy.gov/sites/prod/files/2013/04/fo/BLM_Final.pdf; Patty Limerick, Jason L. Hanson, and Ryan Rebhan, *What Every American Should Know About Oil Shale* (Boulder, Colo.: Center of the American West, 2008).

9. Proclamation 5030, March 10, 1983, 97 Stat. 1557–58; 92 Stat. 932 (1978) (definition of "minerals" in the OCS Lands Act Amendments).

10. 104 Stat. 555 (1990) (Outer Banks Protection Act); *Mobil Oil Exploration and Producing Southeast, Inc. v. United States,* 530 U.S. 604 (2000); Turner and Isenberg, *Republican Reversal,* 70–72; Mark Kurlansky, *Cod: A Biography of the Fish that Changed the World* (New York: Penguin, 1998).

11. *Secretary of the Interior v. California,* 464 U.S. 312 (1984); 104 Stat. 1388-307, 308 (1990).

12. 109 Stat. 557, 563–66 (1995); Turner and Isenberg, *Republican Reversal,* 71; 120 Stat. 3000, 3004–6 (2006).

13. Coggins et al., *Federal Public Land and Resources Law,* 594; National Commission on the BP Deepwater Horizon Oil Spill and Offshore Drilling, *Deep Water: The Gulf Oil Disaster and the Future of Offshore Drilling* (Washington, D.C.: Government Printing Office, 2011); Claire B. Paris-Limouzy et al., "Invisible Oil Beyond the *Deepwater Horizon* Satellite Footprint," *Science Advances* 6, no. 7 (February 12, 2020).

14. *Thor-Westcliffe Development v. Udall,* 314 F.2d 257, 260 (D.C. Cir. 1963) (upholding Interior's lottery); 96 Stat. 1196 (1982) (blocking oil and gas leasing in wilderness areas).

15. 101 Stat. 1330, 1330-256–63 (1987); Coggins et al., *Federal Public Land and Resources Law,* 553–55; Patricia J. Beneke, "The Federal Oil and Gas Leasing Reform Act of 1987: A Legislative History and Analysis," *Journal of Mineral Law and Policy* 4, no. 1 (1988): 11–47.

16. Zellmer, "Mitigating Malheur's Misfortunes," 509, 529–37.

17. Turner and Isenberg, *Republican Reversal,* 176; 119 Stat. 594, 694 (2005); Coggins et al., *Federal Public Land and Resources Law,* 504–5, 589–91.

18. Thompson et al., *Legal Control of Water Resources,* 762–68; Leshy, "Babbitt Legacy."

19. *Escondido Mutual Water Co. v. La Jolla Band of Mission Indians,* 466 U.S. 765 (1984).

20. 119 Stat. 594, 660 (2005).

21. 119 Stat. 594, 744–47 (2005); 78 Fed. Reg. 33898 (2013).

22. Marc Humphries, *U.S. Crude Oil and Natural Gas Production in Federal and Nonfederal Areas,* R42432 (Congressional Research Service, October 23, 2018); leasing statistics are available on the BLM website.

60. PUBLIC LANDS AND NATIVE AMERICANS IN THE MODERN ERA

1. Principal authorities for this chapter are Catton, *American Indians and National Forests;* Coggins et al., *Federal Public Land and Resources Law;* Keiter, *To Conserve Unimpaired;* Keller and Turk, *American Indians and National Parks;* Nie, "Use of Co-Management."

2. 45 Stat. 62 (1928); Jessica Shoemaker, "An Introduction to American Indian Land Tenure: Mapping the Legal Landscape," *Journal of Law, Property, and Society* 5 (2019).

3. Watkins, *Righteous Pilgrim,* 199–201, 275, 328–29, 737–53; *United States v. Santa Fe Pacific Railroad Co.,* 314 U.S. 339 (1941); Sarah Krakoff, "Not Yet America's Best Idea: Law, Inequality, and Grand Canyon National Park," *University of Colorado Law Review* 91, no. 2 (2020): 559, 584–95; Fox, *John Muir and His Legacy,* 239–44 (William O. Douglas).

4. 60 Stat. 1049 (1946); Cohen, "Original Indian Title," 28, 34–43; Harry S. Truman, Statement upon Signing Bill Creating the Indian Claims Commission, August 13, 1946.

5. 46 Stat. 1161 (1931); Catton, *American Indians and National Forests,* 74–80; 48 Stat. 816 (1934); *Miccosukee Tribe of Indians v. United States,* 980 F. Supp. 448 (S.D. Fla. 1997) (construing the language as prioritizing park management); 72 Stat. 1751 (1958); Brian Upton, "Returning to a Tribal Self-Governance Partnership at the National Bison Range Complex: Historical, Legal, and Global Perspectives," *Public Land and Resources Law Review* 35 (2014): 53, 105–12; "Stewardship at Grand Portage National Monument," National Park Service, www.nps.gov/articles/grand-portage-national-monument-ojibwe-management.htm.

6. 84 Stat. 1437 (1970); William Deverell, "The Return of Blue Lake to the Taos Pueblo," *Princeton University Library Chronicle* 49, no. 1 (Autumn 1987): 57–73.

7. Exec. Order No. 11670, May 20, 1972, 37 Fed. Reg. 10431 (1972); Andrew H. Fisher, "The 1932 Handshake Agreement: Yakama Indian Treaty Rights and Forest Service Policy in the Pacific Northwest," *Western Historical Quarterly* 28, no. 2 (Summer 1997): 186–217.

8. 86 Stat. 719–21 (1972); "The McQuinn Strip Boundary Dispute," Confederated Tribes of Warm Springs, https://warmsprings-nsn.gov/treaty-documents/the-mcquinn-strip-boundary-dispute.

9. 40 Stat. 1175, 1177 (1919); Stephen Hirst, *I Am the Grand Canyon: The Story of the Havasupai People* (Grand Canyon, Ariz.: Grand Canyon Association, 2006).

10. 88 Stat. 2089 (1975); Keller and Turk, *American Indians and National Parks,* 170.

11. 92 Stat. 244 (1978); 98 Stat. 1533 (1984).

12. Coggins et al., *Federal Public Land and Resources Law,* 1010–16; 93 Stat. 721 (1979).

13. 104 Stat. 3048 (1990) (Native American Graves Protection and Repatriation Act); Coggins et al., *Federal Public Land and Resources Law,* 1032.

14. 80 Stat. 915 (1966).

15. 107 Stat 4653, 4657, § 4006(a)(6)(A) (1992); Kathryn Sears Ore, "Form and Substance: The National Historic Preservation Act, Badger–Two Medicine, and Meaningful Consultation," *Public Land and Resources Law Review* 38 (2017): 206–43; Catton, *American Indians and National Forests,* 168–70, 129, 223–25.

16. Exec. Order No. 13,007, 61 Fed. Reg. 26771–72 (1996); Zellmer, "Sustaining Geographies of Hope"; Erik B. Bluemel, "Accommodating Native American

Cultural Activities on Federal Public Lands," *Idaho Law Review* 41, no. 3 (2005): 475–563; Marren Sanders, "Implementing the Federal Endangered Species Act in Indian Country: The Promise and Reality of Secretarial Order 3206," Joint Occasional Papers on Native Affairs no. 2007-01 (Tucson, Ariz.: Native Nations Institute and the Harvard Project, 2007).

17. Secretarial Order #3342 (October 21, 2016).

18. 98 Stat. 1632, 1638 (1984); 101 Stat. 1539 (1987); Kathryn Mutz and Doug Cannon, *El Malpais Area: National Monument, National Conservation Area and the West Malpais and Cebolla Wilderness Areas* (Boulder: University of Colorado School of Law, 2005).

19. 102 Stat. 3327–30 (1988).

20. *Lyng v. Northwest Indian Cemetery Protective Association,* 485 U.S. 439 (1988); 104 Stat. 3209 (1990).

21. 114 Stat. 1875 (2000); Burnham, *Indian Country, God's Country;* Theodore Catton, *To Make a Better Nation: An Administrative History of the Timbisha Shoshone Homeland Act* (Missoula: University of Montana, 2009); Keiter, *To Conserve Unimpaired,* 132–34.

22. 114 Stat. 1362 (2000); 114 Stat. 1655, 1658, 1659 (2000).

23. 112 Stat. 2964–73 (1998).

24. 117 Stat. 279–93 (2003); Nie, "Use of Co-Management," 617, 629–30.

25. 116 Stat. 1994 (2002); 118 Stat. 2403 (2004); 120 Stat. 3028, 3042–43 (2006); 119 Stat. 2106 (2005) (Ojito); Nie, "Use of Co-Management," 614–17, 627–29, 631–35.

26. Barack Obama, Proclamation No. 9558 and No. 9559 (December 28, 2016); Donald J. Trump, Revision of Proclamation No. 9558 (December 4, 2017).

27. 35 Stat. 251, 267–68 (1908); 35 Stat. 1039, 1051 (1909) (authorizing expansion to 20,000 acres); *CSKT v. United States,* 437 F.2d 458, 465 (Ct. Cl. 1971) (finding an illegal taking of property under the Fifth Amendment); 108 Stat. 4250, 4270 (1994); Upton, "Tribal Self-Governance Partnership"; Nie, "Use of Co-Management."

28. *United States v. Sioux Nation,* 448 U.S. 371 (1980); Lazarus, *Black Hills/White Justice: The Sioux Nation Versus the United States, 1775 to the Present* (Lincoln: University of Nebraska Press, 1999); 118 Stat. 805 (2004) (Western Shoshone Claim Distribution Act).

29. Keiter, *To Conserve Unimpaired,* 141–42, 164–65; 106 Stat. 3173 (1992); Philip M. Bender, "Restoring the Elwha, White Salmon, and Rogue Rivers: A Comparison of Dam Removal Proposals in the Pacific Northwest," *Journal of Land, Resources, and Environmental Law* 17, no. 2 (1997): 189–246.

30. Michael C. Blumm and Andrew B. Erickson, "Dam Removal in the Pacific Northwest: Lessons for the Nation," *Environmental Law* 42, no. 4 (Fall 2012): 1043–1100.

31. 29 Stat. 353 (1895); 36 Stat. 354 (1910); 120 Stat. 3050 (2006); Ore, "Form and Substance;" Solenex, LLC v. Bernhardt, __ F.2d. __ (D.C. Cir. 2020).

32. 45 Stat. 1553 (1929); 49 Stat. 1979 (1936); 53 Stat. 2521 (1939); 94 Stat. 3467, 3521 (1978) (Badlands National Park); Keiter, *To Conserve Unimpaired,* 134–38.

33. Marc Heller, "Trump's Tongass Rule Deepens Alaska Tribal Divides," *E&E News,* December 11, 2019, www.eenews.net/stories/1061783693.

61. THE POLITICS OF PUBLIC LANDS IN THE MODERN ERA

1. Principal sources for this chapter are Leshy, "Lands Policy After the Trump Administration," "Still Made for You and Me?," "Natural Resources Policy," "Natural Resources Policy in Bush (II)"; MacLean, *Democracy in Chains;* Turner and Eisenberg, *Republican Reversal.*

2. Stewart L. Udall, "The West and Its Public Lands: Aid or Obstacle to Progress," *Natural Resources Journal* 4, no. 1 (1964): 2–4.

3. MacLean, *Democracy in Chains,* xix, 29–96, 125–26; Milton Friedman, *Capitalism and Freedom* (Chicago: University of Chicago Press, 1962); Daniel R. Barney, *The Last Stand: The Nader Study Group Report on the U.S. Forest Service* (Washington, D.C.: Center for Responsive Law, 1972).

4. Turner and Eisenberg, *Republican Reversal,* 52–53; MacLean, *Democracy in Chains,* 120–21, 174–77; Richard W. Behan, *Plundered Promise: Capitalism, Politics, and the Fate of the Federal Lands* (Washington, D.C.: Island, 2001).

5. Brian Allen Drake, "The Skeptical Environmentalist: Senator Barry Goldwater and the Environmental Management State," *Environmental History* 15, no. 4 (October 2010): 587–611.

6. Phillips-Fein, *Invisible Hands,* 162–72; Heritage Foundation, *Mandate for Leadership* (1980), 373; Lou Cannon, *President Reagan: The Role of a Lifetime* (New York: Simon & Schuster, 1991), 469; Leshy, "Natural Resources Policy," 23–26; 96 Stat. 1196 (1982) (blocking oil and gas leasing in wilderness areas); Short, *Reagan and the Public Lands,* 65–78.

7. Klyza, *Who Controls Public Lands?,* 93–107.

8. Babbitt quoted in Frank Gregg, "Public Land Policy: Controversial Beginnings for the Third Century," in Lacey, *Government and Environmental Politics,* 171, 176–77; Charles Wilkinson, "The End of Multiple Use," *High Country News,* March 30, 1987, 15–16.

9. Gregg, "Public Land Policy," 177.

10. Turner and Eisenberg, *Republican Reversal,* 78–79; H. Doc. No. 104-141 (December 6, 1995) (message vetoing H.R. 2491).

11. 110 Stat. 4093–4281 (1996); 111 Stat. 1252 (1997); 112 Stat. 3497–3523 (1998).

12. *Bush v. Gore,* 531 U.S. 98 (2000); Erik Baard, "George Bush Ain't No Cowboy," *Village Voice,* September 21, 2004; 115 Stat. 413, 471 (2001) (prohibiting oil and gas leases on national monuments); Christine A. Klein, "Preserving Monumental Landscapes Under the Antiquities Act," *Cornell Law Review* 87, no. 6 (September 2002): 1333, 1385–89.

13. Frank Luntz, Memorandum to Bush White House, "The Environment: A Cleaner, Safer, Healthier America" (2002), available at *A Sibilant Intake of Breath* (blog), www.sindark.com/NonBlog/Articles/LuntzResearch_environment.pdf; Leshy, "Natural Resources Policy in Bush (II)," 352–53, 357–58. Clarke's remarks came in a speech to the Society of Rangeland Management, quoted in "The Ungreening of America: Behind the Curtain," *Mother Jones,* September–October 2003, www.moth erjones.com/politics/2003/09/ungreening-america-behind-curtain; Turner and Eisenberg, *Republican Reversal,* 196–99.

14. 116 Stat. 2012 (2002); 118 Stat. 2403–19 (2004); 120 Stat. 2922, 3028–30 (2006); 117 Stat. 1887–1215 (2003) (Healthy Forests).

15. Turner and Eisenberg, *Republican Reversal*, 73.

16. 123 Stat. 991 (2009).

17. 128 Stat. 3292, 3833 (2014); 129 Stat. 484 (2015); Robert B. Semple, Jr., "President Obama's Eleventh-Hour Conservation Efforts," *New York Times*, August 14, 2015; 130 Stat. 999 (2016).

18. Republican Platform 2016, 21; "Q&A: Donald Trump on Guns, Hunting, and Conservation," *Field and Stream*, January 22, 2016, www.fieldandstream.com /articles/hunting/2016/01/qa-donald-trump-on-guns-hunting-and-conservation.

19. Turner and Eisenberg, *Republican Reversal*, 209–16.

20. John McCain, "Nature Is Not a Liberal Plot," *New York Times*, November 22, 1996.

21. David J. Sousa and Christopher McGrory Klyza, " 'Whither We are Tending': Interrogating the Retrenchment Narrative in U.S. Environmental Policy," *Political Science Quarterly* 132, no. 3 (2017): 467–94; 131 Stat. 2054, § 20001 (2017).

22. 133 Stat. 580–844 (2019).

23. 78 Stat. 897–904 (1964) (LWCF authorization); 133 Stat. 754, § 3001 (2019) (reauthorization); Carol Hardy Vincent, R. Eliot Crafton, Anne A. Riddle, and Laura A. Hanson, *Land and Water Conservation Fund: Processes and Criteria for Allocating Funds*, R46563 (Congressional Research Service, October 6, 2020); "State of the Rockies," Colorado College, www.coloradocollege.edu/stateoftherockies/ conservationinthewest.

24. 134 Stat. 686–87 (2020); Vincent et al, *Land and Water Conservation Fund*.

62. PUBLIC LANDS TODAY

1. See, for example, 114 Stat. 1655 (2000) (establishing the Steens Mountain, Oregon, "cooperative management and protection area"); 133 Stat. 668–84 (2019) (establishing the "San Rafael Swell Recreation Area," without the adjective "national," in Emery County, Utah).

2. See, for example, Jan G. Laitos and Thomas A. Carr, "The New Dominant Use Reality on Multiple Use Lands," *Proceedings of the Rocky Mountain Mineral Law Institute* 44 (1998): 1.

3. Leshy, "Federal Lands in the Twenty-First Century," 133; Dana and Fairfax, *Forest and Range Policy*, 155–56.

4. 123 Stat. 991 (2009); Courtney A. Schultz, Theresa Jedd, and Ryan D. Beam, "The Collaborative Forest Landscape Restoration Program: A History and Overview of the First Projects," *Journal of Forestry* 110, no. 7 (October–November 2012): 381–91.

5. Cronon, *Uncommon Ground*, 27–28, 57–66.

6. Keiter, *To Conserve Unimpaired*, 221–26; Grunwald, *Swamp*.

7. Leshy, "Public Land Policy After the Trump Administration," 481–84.

8. Coggins et al., *Federal Public Land and Resources Law*, 195–205; Keiter, *Keeping Faith with Nature*; Robert B. Keiter, "Public Lands and Law Reform: Putting Theory, Policy, and Practice in Perspective," *Utah Law Review* 2005, no. 4: 1127–1227; Martin Nie and Michael Fiebig, "Managing the National Forests Through Place-Based Legislation," *Ecology Law Quarterly* 37, no. 1 (2010): 1–52.

9. U.S. Departments of the Interior and Agriculture, *National Land Acquisition Plan* (2005), 10 (statistics on public land exchanges); James R. Rasband, "Buying Back

the West," *Journal of Land, Resources, and Environmental Law* 24, no. 2 (2004): 179–86; James R. Rasband and Megan E. Garrett, "A New Era in Public Land Policy? The Shift Toward Reacquisition of Land and Natural Resources," *Rocky Mountain Mineral Law Institute Proceedings* 53 (2007): 11-1–11-63.

10. A comprehensive overview of this area, including statistics by agency and program, and a comparison of the advantages and disadvantages of tools like easements and exchanges, can be found in U.S. Departments of the Interior and Agriculture, *National Land Acquisition Plan* (February 2005); see also *National Wildlife Refuge System Land Protection Projects* (U.S. Fish & Wildlife Service, March 2013); Ryan Richards and Matt Lee-Ashley, *The Race for Nature* (Center for American Progress, 2020), 7–8 (summary of federal conservation easement acquisition programs).

11. *Leo Sheep v. United States*, 440 U.S 668 (1980); "Inaccessible Public Lands," Theodore Roosevelt Conservations Partnership, www.trcp.org/unlocking-public-lands; 133 Stat. 759–62, § 4105 (2019); Carol Hardy Vincent, R. Eliot Crafton, Anne A. Riddle, and Laura A. Hanson, *Land and Water Conservation Fund: Processes and Criteria for Allocating Funds*, R46563 (Congressional Research Service, October 6, 2020), 2.

12. Strong, *Tahoe*, 82–84.

13. Ibid., 85–94, 137–44; 94 Stat. 3380 (1980); Jacobs, *Rage for Justice*, 391–94.

14. 112 Stat. 2343 (1998); Fairfax et al., *Buying Nature*, 211–15. The BLM maintains an informative website on the SNPLMA, and statistics on lands sold and acquired are reported in the BLM's *Public Land Statistics* (2019), table 5-10, 215–18.

15. 114 Stat. 613 (2000); reauthorized in §§ 301–2 of the Omnibus Appropriations Act for Fiscal Year 2018, Pub. L. No. 115-141, 1828–33 (2018).

16. Gates, *Public Land Law Development*, 310–11; 21 Stat. 287–88 (1880); Amelia Pak-Harvey, "Opportunity Lost," *Las Vegas Review-Journal*, December 21, 2019.

17. 102 Stat. 4571–73 (1988).

18. R. Nelson, *Public Lands and Private Rights*, 178–79; 107 Stat. 995 (1993); 110 Stat. 4093 (1996).

19. 112 Stat. 3139 (1998); 114 Stat. 1059 (2000); 123 Stat. 1982 (2009); Leshy, "Babbitt Legacy," 220–21. Two works examine how states have managed lands granted them at statehood for public education: Jon A. Souder and Sally K. Fairfax, *State Trust Lands: History, Management, and Sustainable Use* (Lawrence: University Press of Kansas, 1996), and Peter W. Culp, Andy Laurenzi, Cynthia C. Tuell, Alison Berry, *State Trust Lands in the West: Fiduciary Duty in a Changing Landscape*, rev. ed. (New York: Columbia University Press, 2015).

20. 122 Stat. 1651 at 2267–74, § 15316 (2008).

21. 102 Stat. 4571 (1988).

22. David G. Havlick, "Disarming Nature: Converting Military Lands to Wildlife Refuges," *Geographical Review* 101, no. 2 (April 2011): 183–200; Catherine Cortez Masto, press release, October 23, 2020, www.cortezmasto.senate.gov/news/press-releases/cortez-masto-highlights-what-nevadans-are-saying-about-her-northern-nevada-rural-land-management-conservation-and-military-readiness-act.

63. PUBLIC LANDS AND THE FUTURE

1. Much of this chapter is drawn from and elaborated on in Leshy, "Land Policy After the Trump Administration," and Leshy, *Debunking Creation Myths*.
2. Karin Kir, "Fact Check: No, the Glaciers Are Not Growing in Glacier National Park," *Yale Climate Connections*, September 13, 2019, https://yaleclimateconnections. org/2019/09/fact-check-no-the-glaciers-are-not-growing-in-glacier-national-park; Marguerite Holloway, "Your Children's Yellowstone Will Be Radically Different," *New York Times*, November 15, 2018, www.nytimes.com/interactive/2018/11/15/ climate/yellowstone-global-warming.html.
3. Alejandro E. Camacho and Robert L. Glicksman, "Legal Adaptive Capacity: How Program Goals and Processes Shape Federal Land Adaptation to Climate Change," *University of Colorado Law Review* 87, no. 3 (2016): 711–826.
4. Wilderness Society, "The Climate Report 2020: Greenhouse Gas Emissions from Public Lands," www.wilderness.org/sites/default/files/media/file/TWS_The%20 Climate%20Report%202020_Greenhouse%20Gas%20Emissions%20from%20 Public%20Lands.pdf.
5. Elizabeth Kolbert, *The Sixth Extinction: An Unnatural History* (New York: Picador, 2014); Kenneth V. Rosenberg et al., "Decline of the North American Avifauna," *Science* 366, no. 6461 (October 4, 2019): 120–24, https://science.sciencemag.org/ content/366/6461/120; Intergovernmental Science-Policy Platform on Biodiversity and Ecosystems, *The Assessment Report on Land Degradation and Restoration* (March 2018), https://ipbes.net/assessment-reports/ldr; Matt Lee-Ashley, "How Much Nature Should America Keep," Center for American Progress, August 6, 2019, www.americanprogress.org/issues/green/reports/2019/08/06/473242/much-nature-america-keep; Ed Yang, "Wait, Have We Really Wiped Out 60 Percent of Animals?," *Atlantic*, October 31, 2018.
6. Edward O. Wilson, *Nature Revealed: Selected Writings, 1949–2006* (Baltimore: Johns Hopkins University Press, 2006), 617; Wilson, *Half Earth: Our Planet's Fight for Life* (New York: Liveright, 2016); Lindsay Rosa, Jacob Malcom, *Getting to 30x30: Guidelines for Decision-Makers* (Washington, D.C.: Defenders of Wildlife, 2020).
7. "Ecological Sciences for Sustainable Development," UNESCO, December 2013, unesco.org/new/en/natural-sciences/environment/ecological-sciences/biosphere-reserves/br-wh-sites-ramsar-sites/.
8. Nash, *Wilderness and the American Mind*, 331.
9. Roderick Nash, "River Recreation: History and Future," in *Proceedings: River Recreation Management and Research Symposium* (St. Paul, Minn.: U.S. Forest Service, 1977); David N. Cole, "The Grand Canyon of the Colorado: A Challenge to Float, a Challenge to Manage," *Western Wildlands*, Fall 1989, 2–7; Leshy, *Debunking Creation Myths*, 41; Keiter, *To Conserve Unimpaired*, 57–58; Laitos and Carr, "Transformation on Public Lands"; Power, *Lost Landscapes and Failed Economies*; numerous reports from Headwaters Economics, Bozeman, Mont., https://headwatersceconomics.org; Nash, *Wilderness and the American Mind*, 316–41.
10. Cassidy Randall, "A Rewilding Triumph," *Guardian*, January 25, 2020.
11. Power, *Lost Landscapes and Failed Economies*, 182–85; Donahue, "Federal Rangeland Policy," 318, 345.

12. Leshy and McUsic, "Where's the Beef?," 368–97; Leshy, "A Trump Plan Breaks a Great Deal for Ranchers and Park Lovers," *New York Times*, March 3, 2020, www.nytimes.com/2020/03/03/opinion/environment-ranchers-trump.html; 123 Stat. 991 (2009) (Owyhee); 129 Stat. 484 (2015) (Boulder–White Clouds).

13. Leshy, *Debunking Creation Myths*, 30–31.

14. "Federal Firefighting Costs (Suppression Only)," National Interagency Fire Center, March 11, 2020, www.nifc.gov/fireInfo/fireInfo_documents/SuppCosts.pdf; Robert B. Keiter, "The Law of Fire: Reshaping Public Land Policy in an Era of Ecology and Litigation," *Environmental Law* 36, no. 2 (Spring 2006): 301–84.

15. Richard Nixon, Special Message to the Congress Proposing the 1971 Environmental Program, February 8, 1971.

16. Outdoor Foundation, "2019 Outdoor Participation Report," January 29, 2020, https://outdoorindustry.org/resource/2019-outdoor-participation-report.

17. Edward O. Wilson, afterword to the anniversary edition of Rachel Carson, *Silent Spring* (New York: Houghton Mifflin, 2012).

18. Adam Smith, *An Inquiry into the Nature and Causes of the Wealth of Nations*, vol. 2 (1776; Chicago: University of Chicago Press, 1976) 349; *Proceedings of a Conference of Governors in the White House, Washington, D.C., May 13–15, 1908* (Washington, D.C.: Government Printing Office, 1909), 153–57; available online from the Hathi Trust, https://babel.hathitrust.org/cgi/pt?id=nnc1.cu09109439&view=2up&seq=202.

BIBLIOGRAPHY

BIBLIOGRAPHIC NOTE

Material such as congressional records, presidential actions, governmental reports, statutes at large, and judicial decisions are readily available online. The text or endnotes provide enough information to locate such sources, and for the most part they are not listed here.

For example, much presidential material is available at the site of the American Presidency Project, hosted by University of California at Santa Barbara, www.presidency.ucsb.edu. Statutes at large are available from the Library of Congress, www.loc.gov/law/help/statutes-at-large. Congressional materials are available from the online edition of the *Congressional Record*, www.govinfo.gov/app/collection/crecb/_crecb. Annual reports of the secretaries of the Interior and Agriculture, subcabinet agencies such as the General Land Office and the U.S. Forest Service, and special governmental bodies such as the Outdoor Resources Review Commission are available online from the Hathi Trust, https://catalog.hathitrust.org. Election results, political party platforms, and brief biographies are readily available on *Wikipedia* and elsewhere.

Useful additional information about particular units of public land may be found in administrative histories or other documents available through the websites of the four major land management agencies. The National Park Service and the U.S. Forest Service make available online extensive collections of administrative histories of national park and national forest system units. The U.S. Fish & Wildlife Service and the Bureau of Land Management have less comprehensive but still useful collections.

Wikipedia has pages, including maps, on practically all public lands that carry some sort of designation such as "national conservation area," "national park," "national forest," "national monument," or "national recreation area."

SELECTED BIBLIOGRAPHY

Ablavsky, Gregory. "The Rise of Federal Title." *California Law Review* 106, no. 3 (2018): 631–95.

Albright, Horace. *The Birth of the National Park Service: The Founding Years, 1913–1933.* As told to Robert Cahn. Salt Lake City: Howe Brothers, 1986.

Allin, Craig. *The Politics of Wilderness Preservation.* Westport, Conn.: Greenwood, 1982; reprint, with epilogue, Fairbanks: University of Alaska Press, 2008.

Amar, Akhil Reed. *America's Constitution: A Biography.* New York: Random House, 2006.

Arnold, Ron. "Congressman William Holman of Indiana: Unknown Founder of the National Forests." In Steen, ed., *Origins of the National Forests,* 301–13.

Balogh, Brian. *A Government Out of Sight: The Mystery of National Authority of Nineteenth Century America.* New York: Cambridge University Press, 2009.

Banner, Stuart. *How the Indians Lost Their Land: Law and Power on the Frontier.* Cambridge, Mass.: Belknap, 2007.

Barrow, Mark V., Jr. *Nature's Ghosts: Confronting Extinction from the Age of Jefferson to the Age of Ecology.* Chicago: University of Chicago Press, 2009.

Bartlett, Richard A. *Nature's Yellowstone.* Tucson: University of Arizona Press, 1974.

———. *Yellowstone: A Wilderness Besieged.* Tucson: University of Arizona Press, 1989.

Bean, Michael J., and Melanie J. Rowland. *The Evolution of National Wildlife Law.* 3rd ed. Westport, Conn. Praeger, 1997.

Black, George. *Empire of Shadows: The Epic Story of Yellowstone.* New York: St. Martin's Griffin, 2013.

Blake, Israel George. *The Holmans of Veraestau.* Oxford, Ohio: Mississippi Valley, 1943.

Blumm, Michael C., and Kara Tebeau. "Antimonopoly in American Public Land Law." *Georgetown Environmental Law Review* 28, no. 2 (2016): 155–217.

Bramwell, Lincoln. "1911 Weeks Act: The Legislation that Nationalised the US Forest Service." *Journal of Energy and Natural Resources Law* 30 (2012): 325–36.

Bramwell, Lincoln, and James G. Lewis, "The Law That Nationalized the U.S. Forest Service." *Forest History Today,* Spring/Fall 2011, 8–16.

Brant, Irving. *Adventures in Conservation with Franklin D. Roosevelt.* Flagstaff, Ariz.: Northland, 1988.

Brinkley, Douglas. *Rightful Heritage: Franklin D. Roosevelt and the Land of America.* New York: HarperCollins, 2016.

———. *The Wilderness Warrior: Theodore Roosevelt and the Crusade for America.* New York: HarperCollins, 2009.

Burnham, Philip. *Indian Country, God's Country: Native Americans and the National Parks.* Washington, D.C.: Island, 2000.

Calef, Wesley. *Private Grazing and Public Lands: Studies of the Local Management of the Taylor Grazing Act.* Chicago: University of Chicago Press, 1960.

Cameron, Jenks. *The Development of Governmental Forest Control in the United States.* Baltimore: Johns Hopkins University Press, 1928.

Catton, Theodore. *American Indians and National Forests.* Tucson: University of Arizona Press, 2016.

Chase, Steve, and Mark Madison. "The Expanding Ark: 100 Years of Wildlife Refuges." *Wild Earth* 13, no. 4 (Winter 2003–4): 18–27.

Chernow, Ron. *Grant.* New York: Penguin, 2017.

Clary, David A. *Timber and the Forest Service.* Lawrence: University Press of Kansas, 1986.

Clawson, Marion. *The Federal Lands Revisited.* Washington, D.C.: Resources for the Future, 1983.

———. *The Western Range Livestock Industry.* New York: McGraw-Hill, 1950.

Clawson, Marion, and Burnell Held. *The Federal Lands: Their Use and Management.* Baltimore: Johns Hopkins University Press, 1957.

Clayton, John. *Natural Rivals: John Muir, Gifford Pinchot, and the Creation of America's Public Lands.* New York: Pegasus, 2019.

Clements, Kendrick A. *Hoover, Conservation, and Consumerism: Engineering the Good Life.* Lawrence: University Press of Kansas, 2000.

Coggins, George C., Charles F. Wilkinson, John D. Leshy, and Robert L. Fischman. *Federal Public Land and Resources Law.* 7th ed. St. Paul, Minn.: Foundation, 2014.

Cohen, Felix S. "Original Indian Title." *Minnesota Law Review* 32, no. 1 (1947): 28–59.

Cramton, Louis C. *Early History of Yellowstone National Park and Its Relation to National Park Policies.* National Park Service, 1932.

Cronon, William. *Changes in the Land: Indians, Colonists, and the Ecology of New England.* Rev. ed. New York: Hill and Wang, 2003.

———, ed. *Uncommon Ground: Rethinking the Human Place in Nature.* New York: Norton, 1996.

Curtin, Charles G. "The Evolution of the U.S. National Wildlife Refuge System and the Doctrine of Compatibility." *Conservation Biology* 7, no. 1 (March 1993): 29–38.

Dana, Samuel Trask. *Forest and Range Policy: Its Development in the United States.* New York: McGraw-Hill, 1956.

Dana, Samuel Trask, and Sally Fairfax. *Forest and Range Policy: Its Development in the United States.* 2nd ed. New York: McGraw-Hill, 1980.

deBuys, William, ed. *Seeing Things Whole: The Essential John Wesley Powell.* Washington, D.C.: Island, 2001.

Dick, Everett. *The Lure of the Land: A Social History of the Public Lands from the Articles of Confederation to the New Deal.* Lincoln: University of Nebraska Press, 1971.

Dietrich, William. *The Final Forest: Big Trees, Forks, and the Pacific Northwest.* Seattle: University of Washington Press, 2010.

Dodd, Douglas W. "Boulder Dam Recreation Area: The Bureau of Reclamation, the National Park Service, and the Origins of the National Recreation Area Concept at Lake Mead, 1929–1936." *Southern California Quarterly* 88, no. 4 (Winter 2006–7): 431–73.

Dombeck, Michael P., Christopher A. Wood, and Jack E. Williams. *From Conquest to Conservation: Our Public Lands Legacy.* Washington, D.C.: Island, 2003.

Donahue, Debra L. "Federal Rangeland Policy: Perverting Law and Jeopardizing Ecosystem Services." *Journal of Land Use and Environmental Law* 22, no. 2 (Spring 2007): 299–354.

———. "Western Grazing: The Capture of Grass, Ground, and Government." *Environmental Law* 35, no. 4 (Fall 2005): 721–806.

———. *The Western Range Revisited: Removing Livestock from Public Lands to Conserve Native Biodiversity.* Norman: University of Oklahoma Press, 1999.

Dunlap, Thomas R. *Saving America's Wildlife: Ecology and the American Mind, 1850–1990*. Princeton, N.J.: Princeton University Press, 1988.

———. "Values for Varmints: Predator Control and Environmental Ideas, 1920–1939." *Pacific Historical Review* 53, no. 2 (May 1984): 141–61.

———. "Wildlife, Science, and the National Parks, 1920–1940." *Pacific Historical Review* 59, no. 2 (May 1990): 187–202.

Einberger, Scott Raymond. *With Distance in His Eyes: The Environmental Life and Legacy of Stewart Udall*. Reno: University of Nevada Press, 2018.

Ellis, Joseph J. *The Quartet: Orchestrating the Second American Revolution, 1783–1789*. New York: Vintage, 2016.

Everhart, William. *The National Park Service*. Boulder, Colo.: Westview, 1983.

Fairfax, Sally K., Lauren Gwin, Mary Ann King, Leigh Raymond, and Laura A. Watt. *Buying Nature: The Limits of Land Acquisition as a Conservation Strategy, 1780–2004*. Cambridge, Mass.: MIT Press, 2005.

Farley, John L. *Duck Stamps and Wildlife Refuges*. Fish and Wildlife Service Circular 37. Washington, D.C.: Government Printing Office, 1955.

Farrand, Max. *The Framing of the Constitution of the United States*. 1913. Reprint, New Haven, Conn.: Yale University Press, 1962.

———. ed. *The Records of the Federal Convention of 1787*. 3 vols. New Haven, Conn.: Yale University Press, 1911.

Faust, Drew Gilpin. *This Republic of Suffering: Death and the American Civil War*. New York: Knopf, 2008.

Fehrenbacher, Don E. *The Dred Scott Case*. New York: Oxford University Press, 2001.

Feller, Daniel. *The Public Lands in Jacksonian Politics*. Madison: University of Wisconsin Press, 1984.

Fink, Richard J. "The National Wildlife Refuges: Theory, Practice and Prospect." *Harvard Environmental Law Review* 18, no. 1 (1994): 1–135.

Fischman, Robert L. *The National Wildlife Refuges: Coordinating a Conservation System Through Law*. Washington, D.C.: Island, 2003.

———. "The Significance of National Wildlife Refuges in the Development of U.S. Conservation Policy." *Journal of Land Use and Environmental Law* 21, no. 1 (2005): 1–22.

Flores, Dan L. *Coyote America: A Natural and Supernatural History*. New York: Basic Books, 2016.

Foresta, Ronald. *America's National Parks and Their Keepers*. Washington, D.C.: Resource for the Future, 1984.

Foss, Phillip. *Politics and Grass: The Administration of Grazing on the Public Domain*. Seattle: University of Washington Press, 1960.

Fox, Stephen, *John Muir and His Legacy: The American Conservation Movement*. Boston: Little, Brown, 1981.

Gabrielson, Ira N. "The Fish and Wildlife Service." *Scientific Monthly* 65, no. 3 (September 1947): 181–98.

Gates, Paul W. *History of Public Land Law Development*. Washington, D.C.: Zenger, 1968.

Goetzmann, William H. *Exploration and Empire: The Explorer and the Scientist in the Winning of the American West*. 1966. Reprint, Austin: Texas State Historical Association, 2000.

Gonzales, Jackie M. M. "The National Park Service Goes to the Beach." *Forest History Today*, Spring 2017, 19–27.

Goodwin, Doris Kearns. *The Bully Pulpit: Theodore Roosevelt, William Howard Taft, and the Golden Age of Journalism.* New York: Simon & Schuster, 2013.

Gordon, Robert J. *The Rise and Fall of American Growth.* Princeton, N.J.: Princeton University Press, 2016.

Graf, William L. *Wilderness Preservation and the Sagebrush Rebellions.* Savage, Md.: Rowman and Littlefield, 1990.

Greeley, William. *Forests and Men.* Garden City, N.Y.: Doubleday, 1951.

Greever, William S. "A Comparison of Railroad Land Grant Policies." *Agricultural History* 25, no. 2 (April 1951): 83–90.

Grunwald, Michael. *The Swamp: The Everglades, Florida, and the Politics of Paradise.* New York: Simon & Schuster, 2006.

Haines, Aubrey L. *The Yellowstone Story: A History of Our First National Park.* Rev. ed. 2 vols. Niwot: University Press of Colorado, 1977.

Hamilton, Alexander, James Madison, and John Jay. *The Federalist Papers.* With an introduction, table of contents, and index of ideas by Clinton Rossiter. New York: Mentor, 1964.

Harmon, David, Francis P. McManamon, and Dwight T. Pitcaithley, eds. *The Antiquities Act: A Century of American Archaeology, Historic Preservation, and Nature Conservation.* Tucson: University of Arizona Press, 2006.

Hartzog, George B., Jr., *Battling for the National Parks.* Mt. Kisco, N.Y.: Moyer Bell, 1988.

Harvey, Mark W. T. *A Symbol of Wilderness: Echo Park and the American Conservation Movement.* Albuquerque: University of New Mexico Press, 1994.

Hays, Samuel P. *The American People and the National Forests: The First Century of the U.S. Forest Service.* Pittsburgh: University of Pittsburgh Press, 2009.

———. *Beauty, Health, and Permanence: Environmental Politics in the United States, 1955–1985.* Cambridge: Cambridge University Press, 1987.

———. *Conservation and the Gospel of Efficiency: The Progressive Conservation Movement.* New York: Atheneum, 1975.

Hibbard, Benjamin Horace. *A History of the Public Lands Policies.* 1924. Reprint, New York: Macmillan, 1939.

Hiltzik, Michael. *Colossus: Hoover Dam and the Making of the American Century.* New York: Free Press, 2010.

Hirt, Paul W. *A Conspiracy of Optimism: Management of the National Forests Since World War Two.* Lincoln: University of Nebraska Press, 1994.

Hyde, Ann Farrar. *An American Vision: Far Western Landscape and National Culture, 1820–1920.* New York: New York University Press, 1990.

Ise, John. *Our National Park Policy: A Critical History.* Baltimore: Johns Hopkins University Press, 1961.

———. *The United States Forest Policy.* New Haven, Conn.: Yale University Press, 1920. Reprint, Charleston, S.C.: Bibliolife, 2010.

Jacobs, John. *A Rage for Justice: The Passion and Politics of Phillip Burton.* Berkeley: University of California Press, 1995.

Jensen, Merrill. *The Articles of Confederation: An Interpretation of the Social-Constitutional History of the American Revolution, 1774–1781.* Madison: University of Wisconsin Press, 1970.

Johnson, Christopher, and David Govatski. *Forests for the People: The Story of America's Eastern National Forests.* Washington, D.C.: Island, 2013.

Jones, Holway R. *John Muir and the Sierra Club: The Battle for Yosemite.* San Francisco: Sierra Club, 1965.

Keiter, Robert B. *Keeping Faith with Nature: Ecosystems, Democracy, and America's Public Lands.* New Haven, Conn.: Yale University Press, 2003.

———. *To Conserve Unimpaired: The Evolution of the National Park Idea.* Washington, D.C.: Island, 2013.

Keller, Robert H., and Michael F. Turek. *American Indians and National Parks.* Tucson: University of Arizona Press, 1998.

Kluger, Richard. *Seizing Destiny: The Relentless Expansion of American Territory.* New York: Vintage, 2007.

Klyza, Christopher McGrory. *Who Controls the Public Lands? Mining, Forestry, and Grazing Policies, 1870–1990.* 2nd ed. Chapel Hill: University of North Carolina Press, 1996.

Klyza, Christopher McGrory, and David J. Sousa. *American Environmental Policy: Beyond Gridlock.* Cambridge, Mass.: MIT Press, 2013.

Knowlton, Christopher. *Cattle Kingdom: The Hidden History of the Cowboy West.* New York: Houghton Mifflin Harcourt, 2017.

Lacey, Michael J., ed. *Government and Environmental Politics: Essays on Historical Developments Since World War Two.* Washington, D.C.: Woodrow Wilson Center Press, 1989.

Laitos, Jan G., and Thomas A. Carr. "The Transformation on Public Lands." *Ecology Law Quarterly* 26, no. 2 (1999): 140–242.

Lazer, Judith A. *Open for Business: Conservatives' Opposition to Environmental Regulation.* Cambridge, Mass.: MIT Press, 2012.

Lear, Linda. *Rachel Carson: Witness for Nature.* New York: Holt, 1997.

LeDuc, Thomas. "History and Appraisal of U.S. Land Policy to 1862." In *Land Use Policy and Problems in the United States,* edited by Howard W. Ottoson, 3–17. Lincoln: University of Nebraska Press, 1963.

Lee, Ronald F. *The Antiquities Act of 1906.* Washington, D.C.: National Park Service, 1970.

Leshy, John D. "Are U.S. Public Lands Unconstitutional?" *Hastings Law Journal* 69, no. 2 (February 2018): 499–582.

———. "The Babbitt Legacy at the Department of the Interior: A Preliminary View." *Environmental Law* 31, no. 2 (Spring 2001): 199–228.

———. *Debunking Creation Myths About America's Public Lands.* Salt Lake City: University of Utah Press, 2018.

———. "Federal Lands in the Twenty-First Century." *Natural Resources Journal* 50, no. 1 (2010): 111–37.

———. "Legal Wilderness: Its Past and Some Speculations on Its Future." *Environmental Law* 44, no. 2 (Spring 2014): 549–622.

————. *The Mining Law: A Study in Perpetual Motion.* Baltimore, Md.: Resources for the Future, 1987.

————. "Mining Law Reform Redux, Once More." *Natural Resources Journal* 42, no. 3 (2002): 461–90.

————. "Natural Resources Policy." In *Natural Resources and the Environment: The Reagan Approach,* edited by Paul Portney, 13–46. Washington, D.C.: Urban Institute Press, 1984.

————. "Natural Resources Policy in the Bush (II) Administration: An Outsider's Somewhat Jaundiced Assessment." *Duke Environmental Law and Policy Forum* 14, no. 2 (Spring 2004): 347–62.

————. "Public Land Policy After the Trump Administration: Is This a Turning Point?" *Colorado Natural Resources, Energy, and Environmental Law Review* 31, no. 3 (Spring 2020): 471–507.

————. "Still Made for You and Me?" *American Scholar,* Autumn 2020, 34–47.

————. "Unraveling the Sagebrush Rebellion: Law, Politics and Federal Lands." *U.C. Davis Law Review* 14, no. 2 (Winter 1980): 317–55.

————. "Wilderness and Its Discontents—Wilderness Review Comes to Public Lands." *Arizona State Law Journal* 1981, no. 2 (1981): 361–446.

Leshy, John D., and Molly S. McUsic. "Where's the Beef? Facilitating Voluntary Retirement of Federal Lands from Livestock Grazing." *New York University Environmental Law Journal* 17, no. 1 (2008): 368–97.

Lien, Carsten. *Olympic Battleground: The Power Politics of Timber Preservation.* 2nd ed. Seattle: Mountaineers Books, 2000.

Lowenthal, David. *George Perkins Marsh: Prophet of Conservation.* Seattle: University of Washington Press, 2000.

Mackintosh, Barry. *The National Parks: Shaping the System.* Rev. ed. Washington, D.C.: National Park Service, Harpers Ferry Center, 2005.

MacLean, Nancy. *Democracy in Chains: The Deep History of the Radical Right's Stealth Plan for America.* New York: Viking, 2017.

Madley, Benjamin. *An American Genocide: The United States and the California Indian Catastrophe, 1846–1873.* New Haven, Conn.: Yale University Press, 2016.

Martin, Justin. *Genius of Place: The Life of Frederick Law Olmsted.* Cambridge, Mass.: Da Capo Press, 2011.

Matthiessen, Peter. *Wildlife in America.* Rev. ed. New York: Viking Penguin, 1987.

McCarthy, G. Michael. *Hour of Trial: The Conservation Conflict in Colorado and the West, 1891–1907.* Norman: University of Oklahoma Press, 1977.

McPhee, John. *Assembling California.* New York: Noonday, 1994.

————. *Coming into the Country.* New York: Farrar, Straus and Giroux, 1977.

————. *Encounters with the Archdruid: Narratives About a Conservationist and Three of His Natural Enemies.* New York: Farrar, Straus and Giroux, 1971.

Merchant, Carolyn. "George Bird Grinnell's Audubon Society: Bridging the Gender Divide in Conservation." *Environmental History* 15, no. 1 (January 2010): 3–30.

————. "Women of the Progressive Conservation Movement: 1900–1916." *Environmental Review* 8, no. 1 (Spring 1984): 57–85.

Merrill, Karen R. *Public Lands and Political Meaning: Ranchers, the Government, and the Property Between Them.* Berkeley: University of California Press, 2002.

Miles, John C. *Wilderness in National Parks: Playground or Preserve.* Seattle: University of Washington Press, 2009.

Milner, Clyde A., II, Carol A. O'Connor, and Martha A. Sandweiss, eds. *The Oxford History of the American West.* New York: Oxford University Press, 1994.

Muhn, James. "Early Administration of the Forest Reserve Act." In Steen, *Origins of the National Forests,* 259–75.

Muhn, James, and Hanson R. Stuart. *Opportunity and Challenge: The Story of BLM.* Washington, D.C.: Government Printing Office, 1988.

Mumford, Lewis. *The Brown Decades: A Study of Arts in America, 1865–1895.* 1931. Reprint, New York: Dover, 1971.

Nash, Roderick Frazier. "John Muir, William Kent, and the Conservation Schism." *Pacific Historical Review* 36, no. 4 (November 1967): 423–33.

———. *Wilderness and the American Mind.* 5th ed. New Haven, Conn.: Yale University Press, 2014.

Nelson, Daniel. *Northern Landscapes: The Struggle for Wilderness Alaska.* Washington, D.C.: Resources for the Future, 2004.

———. *A Passion for the Land: John Seiberling and the Environmental Movement.* Kent, Ohio: Kent State University Press, 2009.

Nelson, Robert H. *Public Lands and Private Rights.* Lanham, Md.: Rowman and Littlefield, 1995.

Newton, Nell, ed. *Cohen's Handbook of Federal Indian Law.* Newark, N.J.: LexisNexis, 2012.

Nie, Martin. "The Use of Co-Management and Protected Land-Use Designations to Protect Tribal Cultural Resources and Reserved Treaty Rights on Federal Lands." *Natural Resources Journal* 48, no. 3 (Summer 2008): 585–648.

Nixon, Edgar B. *Franklin D. Roosevelt and Conservation, 1911–1945.* 2 vols. Hyde Park, N.Y.: Franklin D. Roosevelt Library, 1957.

Onuf, Peter S. *Statehood and Union: A History of the Northwest Ordinance.* Bloomington: Indiana University Press, 1987.

Orsi, Jared. "From Horicon to Hamburgers and Back Again: Ecology, Ideology, and Wildfowl Management, 1917–1935." *Environmental History Review* 18, no. 4 (Winter 1994): 19–40.

Orsi, Richard J. *Sunset Limited: The Southern Pacific Railroad and the Development of the American West, 1850–1930.* Berkeley: University of California Press, 2005.

Osgood, Ernest Staples. *The Day of the Cattleman.* Chicago: University of Chicago Press, 1968.

Ottoson, Howard, ed. *Land Use Policy and Problems in the United States.* Lincoln: University of Nebraska Press, 1963.

Peffer, E. Louise. *The Closing of the Public Domain: Disposal and Reservation Policies, 1900–1950.* Stanford, Calif.: Stanford University Press, 1951.

Phillips-Fein, Kim. *Invisible Hands: The Businessmen's Crusade Against the New Deal.* New York: Norton, 2009.

Pinchot, Gifford. *Breaking New Ground.* 1947. Reprint, Washington, D.C.: Island, 1998.

Pisani, Donald J. "Forests and Conservation, 1865–1890." *Journal of American History* 72, no. 2 (September 1985): 340–59.

———. "Forests and Reclamation, 1891–1911," in Steen, *Origins of the National Forests*, 237–59.

———. *Water and American Government: The Reclamation Bureau, National Water Policy, and the West, 1902–1935*. Berkeley: University of California Press, 2002.

———. *Water, Land, and Law in the West: The Limits of Public Policy*. Lawrence: University Press of Kansas, 1996.

Powell, John Wesley. *Report on the Lands of Arid Region of the United States, with a More Detailed Account of the Lands of Utah*. 1879. Facsimile of the 2nd ed., with an introduction by T. H. Watkins. Harvard, Mass.: Harvard Common Press, 1983.

Power, Thomas Michael. *Lost Landscapes and Failed Economies: The Search for a Value of Place*. Washington, D.C.: Island, 1996.

Price, Jennifer. *Flight Maps: Adventures with Nature in Modern America*. New York: Basic Books, 1999.

Public Land Law Review Commission. *One Third of the Nation's Land: A Report to the President and to the Congress*. Washington, D.C.: Government Printing Office, 1970.

Rae, John Bell. *The Development of Railway Land Subsidy Policy in the United States*. New York: Arno, 1979.

Rakove, Jack. *The Beginnings of National Politics: An Interpretative History of the Continental Congress*. New York: Random House, 1979.

Raymond, Leigh. *Private Rights in Public Resources: Equity and Property Allocation in Market-Based Environmental Policy*. Washington, D.C.: Resources for the Future, 2003.

Reed, Nathaniel P., and Dennis Drabelle. *The United States Fish & Wildlife Service*. Boulder, Colo.: Westview, 1984.

Reiger, John F. *American Sportsmen and the Origins of Conservation*. 3rd ed. Corvallis: Oregon State University Press, 2001.

Reisner, Marc. *Cadillac Desert: The American West and Its Disappearing Water*. New York: Viking, 1986.

Richardson, Elmo. *Dams, Parks, and Politics: Resource Development and Preservation in the Truman-Eisenhower Era*. Lexington: University Press of Kentucky, 1973.

———. "The Struggle for the Valley: California's Hetch Hetchy Controversy, 1905–1913." *California Historical Society Quarterly* 38, no. 3 (September 1959): 249–58.

Righter, Robert. *The Battle over Hetch Hetchy*. New York: Oxford University Press, 2005.

———. *Crucible for Conservation: The Struggle for Grand Teton National Park*. 1982. Reprint, Moose, Wyo.: Grand Teton Natural History Association, 2000.

Robbins, Roy. *Our Landed Heritage: The Public Domain, 1776–1936*. 1941. Reprint, Lincoln, Neb.: Bison, 1962.

Roberts, Darwin P. "The Legal History of Federally Granted Railroad Rights-of-Way and the Myth of Congress's '1871 Shift.' " *University of Colorado Law Review* 82, no. 1 (2011): 85–166.

Robison, Jason, Daniel McCool, and Thomas Minckley, eds. *Vision and Place: John Wesley Powell and Reimagining the Colorado River Basin*. Berkeley: University of California Press, 2020.

Roosevelt, Theodore. *An Autobiography*. 1913. Reprint, New York: Literary Classics of the United States, 2004.

Roth, Dennis. *The Wilderness Movement and the National Forests, 1964–1980.* Washington, D.C.: U.S. Forest Service, 1984.

Rothman, Hal. *Preserving Different Pasts: The American National Monuments.* Champaign: University of Illinois Press, 1989.

———. " 'A Regular Ding-Dong Fight': Agency Culture and Evolution in the NPS-USFS Dispute, 1916–1937." *Western Historical Quarterly* 20, no. 2 (May 1989): 141–61.

Rowley, William D. *U.S. Forest Service Grazing and Rangelands: A History.* College Station: Texas A&M University Press, 1985.

Runte, Alfred. *National Parks: The American Experience.* Lincoln, Neb.: Bison, 1984.

———. *Trains of Discovery: Western Railroads and the National Parks.* 4th ed. Boulder, Colo.: Roberts Rinehart, 1998.

———. *Yosemite: The Embattled Wilderness.* Lincoln: University of Nebraska Press, 1990.

Rybczynski, Witold. *A Clearing in the Distance: Frederick Law Olmstead and America in the 19th Century.* New York: Touchstone, 1999.

Schrepfer, Susan R. *The Fight to Save the Redwoods: A History of the Environmental Reform, 1917–1978.* Madison: University of Wisconsin Press, 1983.

Schulte, Steven C. *Wayne Aspinall and the Shaping of the American West.* Boulder: University Press of Colorado, 2002.

Sears, John F. *Sacred Places: American Tourist Attractions in the Nineteenth Century.* Amherst: University of Massachusetts Press, 1998.

Sellars, Richard West. *Preserving Nature in the National Parks: A History.* New Haven, Conn.: Yale University Press, 1997.

———. "A Very Large Array: Early Federal Historic Preservation—The Antiquities Act, Mesa Verde, and the National Park Service Act." *Natural Resources Journal* 47, no. 2 (Spring 2007): 267–328.

Shands, William E., and Robert G. Healy. *The Lands Nobody Wanted: Policy for National Forests in the Eastern United States; A Conservation Foundation Report.* Washington, D.C.: Conservation Foundation, 1977.

Shankland, Robert. *Steve Mather of the National Parks.* 3rd ed. New York: Borzoi, 1970.

Short, C. Brant. *Ronald Reagan and the Public Lands.* College Station: Texas A&M University Press, 1989.

Skillen, James R. *The Nation's Largest Landlord: The Bureau of Land Management in the American West.* Lawrence: University Press of Kansas, 2009.

Skowronek, Stephen. *Building a New American State: The Expansion of National Administrative Capacities, 1877–1920.* Cambridge: Cambridge University Press, 1982.

Smith, Charles D. "The Appalachian National Park Movement, 1885–1901." *North Carolina Historical Review* 37 (1960): 38–65.

———. "The Movement for Eastern National Forests, 1899–1911." PhD. diss., Harvard University, 1956.

Smith, Duane A. *Henry M. Teller: Colorado's Grand Old Man.* Boulder: University Press of Colorado, 2002.

———. *Mesa Verde National Park: Shadows of the Centuries.* Rev. ed. Boulder: University Press of Colorado, 2002.

————. *Mining America: The Industry and the Environment, 1800–1980*. Lawrence: University Press of Kansas, 1987.

Smith, Henry Nash. *Virgin Land: The American West as Symbol and Myth*. Cambridge, Mass.: Harvard University Press, 1970.

Smith, Thomas G. *Green Republican: John Saylor and the Preservation of America's Wilderness*. Pittsburgh: University of Pittsburgh Press, 2006.

————. "John Kennedy, Stewart Udall, and New Frontier Conservation." *Pacific Historical Review* 64, no. 3 (August 1995): 329–62.

————. *Stewart L. Udall: Steward of the Land*. Albuquerque: University of New Mexico Press, 2017.

Spence, Mark David. *Dispossessing the Wilderness: Indian Removal and the Making of National Parks*. New York: Oxford University Press, 1999.

Steen, Harold, ed. *The Origins of the National Forests*. Durham, N.C.: Forest History Society, 1992.

————. *The U.S. Forest Service: A History*. Seattle: University of Washington Press, 2004.

Stegner, Wallace. *Beyond the Hundredth Meridian: John Wesley Powell and the Second Opening of the West*. 1953. Reprint, New York: Penguin, 1992.

Story, Joseph. *Commentaries on the Constitution*. 3 vols. Boston: Hilliard, Gray, 1833.

Stout, Joe A., Jr. "Cattlemen, Conservationists, and the Taylor Grazing Act." *New Mexico Historical Review* 45, no. 4 (Oct. 1, 1970): 311–31.

Strand, Ginger. *Inventing Niagara: Beauty, Power, Lies*. New York: Simon and Schuster, 2009.

Strong, Douglas H. *Tahoe: An Environmental History*. Lincoln: University of Nebraska Press, 1984.

Sutter, Paul S. *Driven Wild: How the Fight Against Automobiles Launched the Modern Wilderness Movement*. Seattle: University of Washington Press, 2002.

Swain, Donald. *Federal Conservation Policy, 1921–1933*. Berkeley: University of California Press, 1963.

————. "The National Park Service and the New Deal, 1933–1940." *Pacific Historical Review* 41, no. 3 (August 1972): 312–32.

————. "The Passage of the National Park Service Act of 1916." *Wisconsin Magazine of History* 50, no. 1 (Autumn 1966): 4–17.

————. *Wilderness Defender: Horace M. Albright and Conservation*. Chicago: University of Chicago Press, 1970.

Swenson, Robert. "Legal Aspects of Mineral Resources Exploitation." In Gates, *History of Public Land Law Development*, 699–764.

Taliaferro, John. *Grinnell: America's Environmental Pioneer and His Restless Drive to Save the West*. New York: Liveright, 2019.

Terrie, Philip G. *Contested Terrain: A New History of Nature and People in the Adirondacks*. 2nd ed. Syracuse, N.Y.: Syracuse University Press, 2008.

Thompson, Barton, Jr., John D. Leshy, Robert Abrams, and Sandra Zellmer. *Legal Control of Water Resources: Cases and Materials*. 6th ed. St. Paul, Minn.: West, 2018.

Tocqueville, Alexis de. *Democracy in America*. 1835, 1840. Translated, edited, and with an introduction by Harvey C. Mansfield and Delba Winthrop. Chicago: University of Chicago Press, 2001.

Treat, Payson Jackson. *The National Land System, 1785–1820.* 1910. Reprint, Buffalo, N.Y.: Hein, 2003.

Tredennick, Cam. "The National Wildlife System Improvement Act of 1997: Defining the National Wildlife Refuge System for the Twenty-First Century." *Fordham Environmental Law Review* 12, no. 1 (Fall 2000): 41–110.

Turner, James Morton. *The Promise of Wilderness: American Environmental Politics Since 1964.* Seattle: University of Washington Press, 2012.

Turner, James Morton, and Andrew C. Isenberg. *The Republican Reversal: Conservatives and the Environment from Nixon to Trump.* Cambridge, Mass.: Harvard University Press, 2018.

Udall, Stewart. *The Quiet Crisis.* New York: Avon, 1970.

Unger, Nancy C. *Beyond Nature's Housekeepers: American Women in Environmental History.* New York: Oxford University Press, 2012.

Utley, Robert M., and Barry Mackintosh. *The Department of Everything Else: Highlights of Interior History.* Washington, D.C.: U.S. Department of the Interior, 1988.

Van Nuys, Frank. *Varmints and Victims: Predator Control in the American West.* Lawrence: University Press of Kansas, 2015.

Voigt, William, Jr. *Public Grazing Lands: Use and Misuse by Industry and Government.* New Brunswick, N.J.: Rutgers University Press, 1976.

Walsh, Margaret. *The American West: Visions and Revisions.* Cambridge: Cambridge University Press, 2005.

Walters, Raymond, Jr. *Albert Gallatin: Jeffersonian Financier and Diplomat.* 1957. Reprint, Pittsburgh: University of Pittsburgh Press, 1969.

Watkins, T. H. *Righteous Pilgrim: The Life and Times of Harold L. Ickes, 1874–1952.* New York: Holt, 1990.

Weeden, Robert B. *Alaska: Promises to Keep.* Boston: Houghton Mifflin, 1978.

White, G. Edward. *The Eastern Establishment and the Western Experience: The West of Frederic Remington, Theodore Roosevelt, and Owen Wister.* Austin: University of Texas Press, 1989.

White, Richard. "Contested Terrain: The Business of Land in the American West." In *Land in the American West: Private Claims and the Common Good,* edited by William G. Robbins and James C. Foster, 190–205. Seattle: University of Washington Press, 2000.

———. *"It's Your Misfortune and None of My Own": A New History of the American West.* Norman: University of Oklahoma Press, 1991.

———. *Railroaded: The Transcontinentals and the Making of Modern America.* New York: Norton, 2011.

Wilcove, David S. *The Condor's Shadow: The Loss and Recovery of Wildlife in America.* New York: Freeman, 1999.

Wilkinson, Charles F. *Blood Struggle: The Rise of Modern Indian Nations.* New York: Norton, 2006.

———. *Crossing the Next Meridian: Land, Water, and the Future of the West.* Washington, D.C.: Island, 1992.

Wilkinson, Charles F., and H. Michael Anderson. *Land and Resource Planning in the National Forests.* Washington, D.C.: Island, 1987.

Williams, Michael. *Americans and Their Forests: A Historical Geography*. Cambridge: Cambridge University Press, 1989.

Williss, G. Frank. *"Do Things Right the First Time": Administrative History; The National Park Service and the Alaska National Interest Lands Conservation Act of 1980*. Washington, D.C.: National Park Service, 1985.

Wills, Garry. *A Necessary Evil: A History of American Distrust of Government*. New York: Simon & Schuster, 1999.

Wilson, Randall K. *America's Public Lands: From Yellowstone to Smokey Bear and Beyond*. Lanham, Md.: Rowman and Littlefield, 2014.

Wolfe, Linnie Marsh. *Son of the Wilderness: The Life of John Muir*. Madison: University of Wisconsin Press, 1945.

Worster, Donald. *A Passion for Nature: The Life of John Muir*. New York: Oxford University Press, 2008.

———. *Under Western Skies: Nature and History in the American West*. New York: Norton, 1992.

Wulf, Andrea. *Founding Gardeners: The Revolutionary Generation, Nature, and the Shaping of the American Nation*. New York: Vintage, 2011.

———. *The Invention of Nature: Alexander von Humboldt's New World*. New York: Knopf, 2015.

Wyant, William. *Westward in Eden: The Public Lands and the Conservation Movement*. Berkeley: University of California Press, 1982.

Yaffee, Steven Lewis. *The Wisdom of the Spotted Owl: Policy Lessons of a New Century*. Washington, D.C.: Island, 1994.

Yale Law Journal. "Conflicting State and Federal Claims of Title in Submerged Lands of the Continental Shelf." Vol. 56, no. 2 (January 1947): 356–70.

Yard, Robert Sterling. *Our Federal Lands: A Romance of American Development*. New York: Scribner's Sons, 1928.

Yergin, Daniel. *The Prize: The Epic Quest for Oil, Money, and Power*. New York: Touchstone, 1992.

Zaslowsky, Dyan, and T. H. Watkins. *These American Lands: Parks, Wilderness, and the Public Lands*. Washington, D.C.: Island, 1994.

Zellmer, Sandra B. "Mitigating Malheur's Misfortunes: The Public Interest in the Public's Public Lands." *Georgetown Environmental Law Journal* 31, no. 3 (Spring 2019): 509–61.

———. "Sustaining Geographies of Hope: Cultural Resources on Public Lands." *University of Colorado Law Review* 73, no. 2 (2002): 413–520.

Michigan, 59, 63; Isle Royale National Park, 337, 411; Mackinac Island National Park, 266
Michigan Territory, 63
Migratory Bird Conservation Act (1929), 387, 421, 423
Migratory Bird Conservation Commission, 530
Migratory Birds, Convention for the Protection of (1916), 383–84, 427
Migratory Bird Treaty Act (MBTA, 1918), 384–85, 387, 421, 424, 582
Miller, George, 532, 553
Miller, John F., 129
Mills, Enos A., 328
Mineral Leasing Act (MLA, 1920): Alaska pipeline and, 520; coal leasing, 555; conflicts over claims, 452; consideration and enactment, 219, 280, 359–61; discretion under, 369; oil shale and, 556; Progressives and, 365; provisions of, 356, 361–62, 450; royalties, 374, 377, 390; unreserved public land and, 376
mining and mineral policy, 17; auctioning rights, 92; coal policy, 282–84; coastal zone, 453–54; environmental impact of, 553–54; federal government and, 69–71; Hot Springs reserve, 66; hydraulic mining and mercury, 120–21; Isle Royale National Park, 337; lead leasing program, 69–72; mineral leasing, 358, 361, 452–53; national parks and, 338; ouster legislation and, 70, 74; public lands revenue, 75–77; Spanish land grant claims and, 70–71; split-estate policy, 284–85; uranium, 452; western discoveries, 75, 120; Yellowstone and, 131
Mining Law (1866), oil shale management, 556–57
Mining Law (1872), 447, 548, 554, 556–57, 566; abuses of, 242–43; in Congress, 92, 94–95, 365–66, 450–52, 493, 496, 552–54; difficulties posed by, 359; energy development and, 280; national parks and, 203, 260; oil and gas claims, 360; oil and gas policy, 286–88;

privatization of public land, 96, 185, 343; protections under, 120–22; public lands and, 183; state control, 378; withdrawals under, 297. See also Mineral Leasing Act; Pickett Act
Mining in the Parks Act (1976), 548
Minnesota, 59, 549; Boundary Waters Treaty (1910), 463; Grand Portage National Monument, 565; Indian lands and, 229–30, 291; Mississippi National River and Recreation Area, 547; statehood, 212; Superior National Forest, 301, 354; Voyageurs National Park, 542
Minnesota Territory, 35
Mississippi, 10, 57, 59; forest land reserved, 65; Natchez Trace Parkway, 416, 487; OCS petroleum revenue, 558
Missouri, 59, 70–71
Mondell, Frank, 231, 241, 246, 258, 284–85, 298, 309, 318, 371
Monongahela decision, 504–5, 521
Monroe, James, 70
Montana: Badger–Two Medicine area, 560, 573; Big Hole National Monument, 304; bison protection, 250, 291; Bitterroot National Forest, 187, 504; Charles M. Russell NWR, 534; Confederated Salish and Kootenai Tribes (CSKT) land purchase, 250; Conservation Management Area, 581; Glacier National Park, 143, 302–4, 334, 349–50, 560; Indian lands and, 475, 573; Lewis and Clark Cavern National Monument, 267; Mizpah-Pumpkin Creek Cooperative Grazing Unit, 372; National Bison Range, 571; predator control, 349, 350; statehood, 163
Montana Legacy Project, 595
Montana Territory, 87
Moran, Thomas, 109–10, 380
Morrill, Justin, 86
Morrill Land-Grant College Act (1862), 85–86, 224
Morris, Gouverneur, 22, 24
Morse, Wayne, 464
Morton, J. Sterling, 181
Morton, Rogers, 494, 513, 521, 530, 541–42